PERFORMING THE US LATINA AND LATINO BORDERLANDS

PERFORMING THE US LATINA & LATINO BORDERLANDS

EDITED BY

Arturo J. Aldama, Chela Sandoval, & Peter J. García

Indiana University Press
Bloomington & Indianapolis

This book is a publication of

Indiana University Press
601 North Morton Street
Bloomington, IN 47404-3797 USA

www.iupress.indiana.edu

Telephone orders 800-842-6796
Fax orders 812-855-7931

⊜ The paper used in this publication meets the minimum requirements of the American National Standard for Information Sciences—Permanence of Paper for Printed Library Materials, ANSI Z39.48-1992.

Manufactured in the
United States of America

Library of Congress
Cataloging-in-Publication Data

Performing the US Latina and Latino borderlands / edited by Arturo J. Aldama, Chela Sandoval, and Peter J. García.
p. cm.
Includes bibliographical references and index.
ISBN 978-0-253-00295-2 (cloth : alk. paper) — ISBN 978-0-253-00574-8 (pbk. : alk. paper) — ISBN 978-0-253-00877-0 (electronic book) 1. Hispanic Americans in the performing arts. 2. Hispanic Americans—Ethnic identity. I. Aldama, Arturo J., [date] II. Sandoval, Chela, [date] III. García, Peter J.
PN1590.H57P47 2012
790.20868—dc23

2012013047

1 2 3 4 5 17 16 15 14 13 12

For Gloria Anzaldúa.

Her work, and her life, have given us the courage
to embrace our borderland identities
and to seek out a
de-colonizing global justice.

We can transform our world by imagining it differently, dreaming it passionately via all our senses, and willing it into creation. As we think inspiring, positive, life-generating thoughts and embody these thoughts in every act we perform, we can gradually change the mood of our days, the habits of years, and the beliefs of a lifetime. . . .

Let's use art and imagination to discover how we feel and think and help us respond to the world. It is in nepantla that we write and make art, bearing witness to the attempt to achieve resolution and balance where there may be none in real life.

GLORIA ANZALDÚA

CONTENTS

THE DAWNING OF THE AGE OF ALTER-NATIVE* LIBERATION: A FOREWORD

ALICIA GASPAR DE ALBA

Today I'm performing some new identities: photographer, videographer, art assistant. I'm helping the artist Alma Lopez (one of whose other identities is legally wedded wife of yours truly) with the biographical video that she's submitting to Season 2 of the Bravo Channel's *Work of Art* show, a reality contest like *Top Chef* or *American Idol*. She's already reached the third level, which requires that she produce a five-minute video about herself and her artistic process as well as a self-portrait that captures her "essence," both due in a week. I snap dozens of pictures of her standing in the pose she has chosen for the portrait, a pose she calls "guilty as charged," even though she doesn't *do* guilt and is twisting the term around to mean "if you accuse me of loving women, I stand accused." In the studio, I document her every move as she selects the photo that will be the basis of her self-portrait and then Photoshops the image into a digital sketch that approximates her idea for this painting. Now she transfers the design onto a 3'×4' canvas in phthalocyanine blue. As I stand behind her recording the first blue strokes of the brush, I see three Almas: the original, the Photoshop version, and the acrylic one emerging onto the white canvas. I am reminded of Aristotle's *Poetics*. Art is but an imitation of the original creation (or nature), which itself is but a simulation of the image in the mind of God. I am watching mimesis in action. God/Alma is creating the image/painting that is a representation of the idea/design in her mind.

If I analyze Alma's creative process utilizing the language of "decolonizing performatics" or "performantics" as delineated by the editors of *Performing the US Latina and Latino Borderlands,* I realize that what I am witnessing, what I am participant observing, is the enactment of creation "at the margins of a marginalized community," as described in the introduction to this volume. But I am also watching, witnessing, and assisting in a methodology of the oppressed: artistic interventionism. Although painting isn't typically considered a performance art, Alma is engaging the technology of two-dimensional art-making specifically to intervene as a queer Chicana visual artist in an aesthetic/cultural space in which she has never seen herself reflected or represented. Thus, art-making can be considered one of the many "*designed interventionist actions* that are designated to intercede on behalf of egalitarianism within any larger (cultural or aesthetic) performance," and function as a "decolonizing performatic" process meant to decolonize the *Work of Art* show for Chicana lesbians.

Writing this Foreword *mano a mano* while video-recording Alma's process extends this methodology even further. Not only is Alma enacting the process of artistic interventionism but also, together, we are engaged in a collaborative antic or adventure of performing creativity and chronicling our performativity. We're creating the story even as we watch the representation of the story unravel before our eyes, much as the image of the Virgen de Guadalupe unraveled before the skeptical eyes of her first witnesses. "The need for creating, performing, and actively witnessing the de-colonizing perform-antics that energize the heart of Latina and Latino Borderland stories has never been more urgent," write the editors in their introduction. The very simultaneity of Alma's and my perform-antics mirrors the urgency of the stories encapsulated in this volume, which collectively seek to "mediate colonial wounds" in a transnational age. Stories about the music, dance, and theater of the Borderlands are interlaced with stories about other cultural performances of Latinidad that include sexuality and the erotic, binationality and bilingualism, queer indigeneity and cholo aesthetics, the continued criminalization of the brown body, and the perpetual "nepantla state" of the border dweller that more and more encompasses the Latino/a community from sea to shining sea.

Materially, this collection is a crash course in a new field that the editors call Borderlands Performance Studies. Chicana/o and Latina/o cultural practitioners and scholars, many of us border-born, -bred, and

-trained during what the editors see as "the great de-colonial era of the twentieth century," have been tilling this field for several decades, and the book joins the ranks of other collections (Chabram-Dernersesian's *Chicana/o Cultural Studies Reader,* Habell-Pallan's *Latina/o Popular Culture,* and my own *Velvet Barrios* come quickly to mind) that have a similar interventionist agenda in the broader field of Cultural Studies. What is especially valuable here, other than the breadth of research contained between these covers, is the methodology that bridges radical Chicana feminist theory à la Chela Sandoval with border epistemology à la Gloria Anzaldúa and connects all of these performance studies or decolonizing performatics across genre, gender, sexuality, and ethnicity into one vibrating manifestation of alter-Native liberation, which is our own "age of Aquarius."

Whether or not Alma gets selected for *Work of Art,* her work lives in the "Heaven" of our border memories. By documenting her artistic interventionism here as an example of decolonizing perform-antics, I am performing a work of heart.

NOTES

* In *Chicano Art Inside/Outside the Master's House: Cultural Politics and the [1998] CARA Exhibition,* I define the alter-Native as a person or a culture that is "both indigenous and alien to the United States . . . whose identity has been carved out of a history of colonization and struggle" (18). By indigenous, I mean native to a landbase by virtue of ancestral longevity, using time, place, and family to track nativity rather than post-conquest racial constructions or the nation-state. In the conceptual motherland of Aztlán, this includes native Americans as much as Mexicans and Chicanas/os whose ancestry and occupancy in the American West and the Southwest dates back to before the Mayflower. This definition circumscribes the colonizing blood quantum criterion by which indigenous people are measured as authentic or inauthentic. Like the mestizo or mestiza, the alter-Native both contains and "differs from, is changed by, and changes the dominant culture" (17). In academic praxis, the alter-Native "eye/I does not assume only one correct, authentic interpretation (if that even exists), but allows for an interpretive stance framed by the politics of self-representation" (27). All of the work collected in *Performing the US Latina and Latino Borderlands,* then, is alter-Native.

PERFORMING THE US LATINA AND LATINO BORDERLANDS

INTRODUCTION

Toward a De-Colonial Performatics of the US Latina and Latino Borderlands

CHELA SANDOVAL, ARTURO J. ALDAMA, AND PETER J. GARCÍA

Latinas and Latinos represent the largest and fastest-growing ethnic community in the United States after "non-Hispanic" Whites (14 percent of the US population, approximately 55 million people in 2010).[1] Yet the cultural impact of US Latina and Latino aesthetic production has yet to be fully recognized within the US nation-state and beyond. This book moves beyond the by now de-politicized and all-too-familiar cultural theory of the twentieth century and beyond so-called "radicalized" examples of aesthetic production to unravel how *culture is performance.* Moreover, the following chapters travel beyond the linguistic surfaces and aesthetic limitations of "Latina and Latino" cultural production to reveal the less familiar and unexplored performance terrains of the "Borderlands." Indeed, *Performing the US Latina and Latino Borderlands* is a book that challenges readers to engage those profound intercultural, psychic, social, and transnational effects that are being generated through US Latina and Latino *testimonio,* theater, ceremony, ritual, storytelling, music, dance, improvisation, play, *nagualisma-o,* call-and-response, spoken-word, visual, body, digital, and sculptural enactments. Each contributing author introduces readers to performance topics, performing artists, and performative enactments that comprise the field of Borderlands Performance Studies. This field is identifiable through its commitment to an alter-Native cultural engineering, the technologies of which we editors identify as "de-colonizing performatics," and the mestizaje, the hybridity, the bricolage, the rasquache interventions organized around de-colonization that we call "perform-antics." Join us then as we set the academic stage where complex scholarly engagements are linked with the entertaining, enlightening, and emancipatory aesthetics of Borderlands Performance Studies.[2]

BORDERLANDS PERFORMANCE STUDIES

Each chapter develops a method that explores and reveals a borderlands approach to the still-emergent field of Performance Studies. Borderlands Performance Studies rises from an insistent intercultural methodology that appears in many modes across theoretical terrains, artistic disciplines, aesthetic philosophies, and geographic hemispheres.[3] This method codes and re-codes performance activities by utilizing diverse "performatic" techniques from a multiplicity of Latina and Latino sources including 1) what linguistic scholars call "code switching," a toggling between world languages and their mixtures; 2) *rasquachismo,* the development of parodic-pastiche, hybrid, bricolage aesthetics for generating myriad possibilities for expression; 3) "theater of the oppressed" enactments designed to connect the body/mind/affect matrix in order to liberate the colonized personality through "games," "exercises," and "performances" of a particular kind; and 4) "*haciendo caras,*" "*la conciencia de la mestiza,*" and "*conocimiento,*" activities for remaking the self through negotiating and shifting identities in situational and culturally specific ways. However diverse, these techniques are drawn together under the rubric of this method we alternatively call "de-colonizing performatics" or, in their specificity as action, "de-colonizing perform-antics."[4]

We contend that the diverse performatics developed across the fields of Indigenous, Chican@,[5] Asian, Latin@, African, Feminist, and Cultural Studies contribute to a particular approach that expands the developing field of Performance Studies and that is a specific intercultural performance methodology. In brief, this performance methodology understands and deploys "acts" in order to intervene in and arbitrate among sign systems with the aim of inviting difference to the realm of egalitarianism. Within the purview of what we identify as Borderlands Performance Studies, then, such acts work as de-colonizing, interventionary deployments that become systematically linked and raised to the level of method through practitioners' shared understanding of performance as an effective means of individual and collective liberation. De-colonizing performatics generate a pause in the activity of coloniality; their activity discontinues its ethos. Before clarifying their function further, we now break for a brief intermission.[6]

INTRODUCING THE CHARACTERS

The impetus for this volume was an academic panel called "*No Somos Criminales:* Latina/o Musics as Decolonizing Practices" in the 2008 Enjoy Music Pop (EMP) conference in Seattle, Washington, where scholars from ethnomusicology and performance, film, visual, religious, and cultural studies came together to discuss how Latina and Latino identity is performed.[7] Even though these fields have unique genealogies, methodologies, and theoretical foundations, we found that today they overlap in terms of shared critical vocabularies, research applications, and concerns about how identity, memory, and culture are internalized and enacted in formal public, social, ritual, and private settings. This volume challenges Performance Studies scholars to consider what performance means in alternate cultural genealogies grounded within US Indigenous, mestiz@, African@, and Spanish-language traditions and epistemologies of dance, food, music, clothing, language, religions, styles, and identities.[8] More fundamentally, this book is informed by the materiality of those cultures that remain misunderstood and criminalized and that live on lands literally colonized and dispossessed by Anglo-driven westward colonization and the imposition of Euro- and white American–centric cultural norms. There is a methodology of the oppressed that emerges from this materiality that opens the field of Performance Studies to the de-colonizing Borderlands approach to theory and action.[9]

United States Latin@, Chican@, African@, Asian mestiz@, and Indigenous communities have dynamic histories of performance activism that are steeped in similar political aims and border crossings, such as those generated by *Teatro Campesino,* the *Nueva Cancíon* movement, the pedagogy and theaters of the oppressed, and spoken word performances as enacted by radical performance artists and ensembles including ASCO, Culture Clash, Monica Palacios, TENAZ (*El Teatro Nacional de Aztlán*), *Teatro Luna,* Guillermo Gomez-Peña, Luis Alfaro, Marga Gomez, Coco Fusco, El Vez, Xela, Alma Lopez, Mujeres de Maíz, and

Carmelita Tropicana, among many others. These performers, performance works, and performance strategies are similarly motivated by a de-colonizing effort that pushes their works beyond the boundaries and limits of colonial meanings. The scholarship in this book recognizes this shared de-coloniality of meaning as it affects the topics of indigeneity; place; cultural citizenship; immigration; equity; de-colonization; mestizaje; the construction of the self; and race, class, spirituality, sex, and gender compositions.

A note regarding terminologies: In engaging the de-colonial promise of this book, the editors realize that the terms "Latina" and "Latino" must be interrogated. When the US government asks Latinas or Latinos about their ethnic identity, they might refer to themselves as Mayan, Afro-Latina/o, Chilean, Chicana/o, Xican, Mexican, Boricua, Puertorican, Cuban American, Tejana/o, Hispana/o, Dominicana/o, Asian Latin@, Nuevo Mexicana/o, Caribbean, Guatemalan, Indigenous, Tewa, Pueblo, and so on, depending on their specific ethnic origins. In this book, we use the term "Latin@" as an umbrella term for linking a diversity of cultures, ethnicities, and genders across this hemisphere. This naming seeks connection among people who differ in nation, ethnicity, gender (thus the technological @ ending), race, and class but who nevertheless share a similar de-colonial relationship to western European imperial histories—that is, to the current global *neo*-colonial cultural and economic forces of the twentieth and twenty-first centuries.[10]

In part, imperializing powers work through the denigration and replacement of indigenous languages with European languages (including English, Spanish, French, and Portuguese) and through the cultural and economic relocation of all "Latin@" bodies, perceptions, and presences to a subservient status in relation to the colonizing Eurocentric gaze and apparatus. This book thus historically, philosophically, and culturally interrogates the terms "Latino" and "Latina" for their at once liberating and confining applications. What emerges through this interrogation is the conflation of another global, and dissident, constituency the editors of this volume describe as an Indigenous/Chican@/Latin@/African@ mestizaje: This is a radical "Latinidad" that is unique to the Américas. This de-colonizing and conflated presence is what generates the relative *interculturality* of Borderlands Performance Studies.[11]

Each chapter in this volume speaks to complex politics of discourse, representation, and the body. Yet what makes this volume unique is that each chapter aims to analyze not just the most valorized, famous, commercial, or popular aesthetic productions but the psychic and communal practices that arise *at the margins of a marginalized community.* This means, for instance, that contributing scholars analyze peoples and practices that represent spaces contesting the homophobic, sexist, racist, classist, and culturalist practices in dominant US culture as well as in the cultural spaces of Latinidad. It is from an outsider location, from the margins of the margins, that the version of Borderlands Performance Studies that we identify here rises. Each chapter thus features a politics of performance that emerges out of specific border spaces that are made subaltern by race, class, sex, culture, and gender oppressions. As such, it is necessary to identify, re-define, and extend terms within the arsenal of the current field of Performance Studies to account for the de-colonizing contributions rising from these other, subaltern, bordered locations.

On a fundamental level, such redefinitions depend upon the recognition of an additional requisite for human survival, one that exceeds the usually cited list of "food, water, and shelter." This additional requisite is the human need "to be seen and heard." This book addresses the contents, forms, and qualities of this last fundamental human need insofar as it has been lifted to an insistent demand for democratic egalitarianism by peoples throughout the US Indigenous, Chican@, African@, feminist, and Latin@ Borderlands. Another important distinction: since the term "colonization" points to the imposition of hierarchical powers through the cannibalization of meaning by imperialistic meaning, the volume editors understand *de*-colonization as an affirmative process of reversing, releasing, and altering an established coloniality of power. This reversal occurs through liberating power from normative shackles of hierarchy through the avowal of aesthetic possibility. The commitments to liberation pointed to throughout this book rely upon our focus on the healing powers of storytelling, our aim toward egalitarianism, and our insistence on the creation and recognition of the de-colonizing performatics and antics that arise from the borders of the Borderlands.

RECOGNIZING DE-COLONIZING PERFORMATICS / THE ANTICS OF THE OPPRESSED

The research collected here emerges out of discoveries made during the great de-colonial era of the twentieth century.[12] This era was as transformative to human consciousness on a planetary level as were the twentieth-century world wars, the invention of the atomic bomb, and the economic globalization of capital. Yet the profound de-colonizing cultural and aesthetic consequences of this era have yet to be fully comprehended. The following chapters make such incomprehension impossible by providing in-depth analyses that draw from an *other* order.

Contemporary Performance Studies is deeply influenced by (another result of) the de-colonial era: twentieth-century Cultural Theory. Both of these theoretical domains recognize that everything can be analyzed as a "performance" (even if it is not meant to be one). Moreover, theorists of "performativity" understand how specific modes of performance are capable of creating reality through the very process of their enactment.[13] The method we describe as "de-colonizing Performatics" or "antics" names a micro/macro apparatus that allows scholars to self-consciously identify performance practices when these are deployed specifically to intervene in cruel social and psychic realities. Beyond "performance" as generally understood, then, or "performativity" recognized as a magically transitive enactment, de-colonizing performatics names another kind of logical technology self-consciously utilized in the activation of liberatory political and ethical enactments. De-colonizing performatics and antics are *designed interventionist actions* that intercede on behalf of egalitarianism within any larger (cultural or aesthetic) performance.[14]

The term "de-colonizing performatics" has a technological ring. It refers to the techniques, tools, and practical knowledges necessary for transforming psychic and material cultures. But the term has a playful side as well, since it signifies the one or more *antics* necessary for making the transformation occur. Antics are ephemeral or permanent exploits, liminal adventures, and serious or humorous incidents that become, under the rationality of de-colonizing performatics, processes of catharsis or recovery. Thus, whether appearing inside cosmically crazy enactments or sober roles, de-colonizing perform-antics always serve the possibilities of personhood, egalitarianism, and happiness. Whether understood as technology, then, or as what the technology permits, de-colonizing performatics/antics are aimed toward generating egalitarian exchanges. Put another way, de-colonizing performatics/antics are the specific manufactured components, no matter how small or large, of a greater mind-body-affect and social circuit that is aimed toward the de-colonization of meaning. Understood as a methodological approach, these antics can be recognized as the components of an aesthetics of liberation, part of a larger methodology of emancipation meant to transform the world.[15]

The following chapters reveal sets of activating de-colonizing performatics. Norma Cantú's chapter reveals the submerged de-colonizing performatics of indigeneity as they lend potent meanings to a community-based Catholic religious dance. In this process, Cantú's chapter leads habituated modes of seeing toward de-colonizing perceptual freedom. Emma Pérez's chapter compiles historical examples that effectively open hearts and minds to the possibility that colonial powers have been organized to debase the erotic and sexual expressions of Latin@ citizen-subjects living on the US/México border—and that these same forces imbricate us all. Pérez's analysis, however, also points to the ways in which Latin@ subjects are constructing and enacting specific de-colonizing emancipatory performatics that contradict and intervene in these very forces. So too, throughout this volume, authors document diverse modes of de-colonizing performatics—the antics of the oppressed—through exhibiting, researching, and analyzing powerful modes of intervention, rage, love, democratics, and oppositional consciousness.

OPENING CREDITS: RESEARCH AS AN ALCHEMY OF REDEMPTION

Performing the US Latina and Latino Borderlands connects authors, subjects, readers, performers, and witnesses with similar players across this continent whose labors are transforming the Américas. Throughout and across each chapter, readers can follow creative threads of de-colonizing scholarship in a weaving that supports transdisciplinary matrices. Inside these matrices, knowledges chimerically meet and merge in a performance of the undeniable interculturality and transculturality of the Borderlands. This book presents the scholarship of researchers, writers, and performers who track de-colonizing performatics in an effort to reconcile power through Borderland alchemies of redemption. Their analyses work to challenge normative degrees of understanding around performance and to go beyond them.

The chapters in this volume are classified into four primary sections, or ACTOs. These ACTOs influence and build upon the others in an alchemy that lies at the foundation of de-colonizing Borderlands

Performance Studies. Human consciousness—its diseases and utopian expansions—is vitally linked to the experiences we have within our families, communities, and cultures, to our economic worlds, to the conditioned knowledges of our peoples, and especially to the ways we become visible by telling, performing, and witnessing our stories. The need for creating, performing, and actively witnessing the de-colonizing perform-antics that energize the heart of Latina and Latino Borderland stories has never been more urgent.

The stories in ACTO 1 "perform emancipation" insofar as each research project differently demonstrates how liberation occurs through a profound, committed, and transformative relationship between "inner work" and "public acts."[16] Thus the chapters in ACTO 1, "Performing Emancipation: Inner Work, Public Acts," as in all three of the ACTOs to follow, document the kinds of de-colonizing performatics that can make psychic and social liberation possible. ACTO 2 presents "Ethnographies of Performance," with each chapter a topography that maps the visual theater and audio soundtrack of the Borderlands: readers are invited to witness, view, and listen along "the Río Grande and Beyond." ACTO 3 documents "Nepantla Aesthetics in the Trans/Nacional" with chapters that analyze the relationship between inner work, public acts, or with ethnographic studies that reveal third-space meanings across continental divides. What connects each different project-chapter in ACTO 3, however, is their similar reach toward definitions of liberation. Finally, the chapters in ACTO 4, "(De)Criminalizing Bodies: Ironies of Performance," bring readers face-to-face with outlaw performances that destroy, wound, or traumatize or that propose and enable healing possibilities for the emancipation and de-colonization of psyche and community.

ACTO 1: PERFORMING EMANCIPATION: INNER WORK, PUBLIC ACTS

The opening scene of this book reveals the "Body as Codex-ized Word." Performance scholar Micaela Díaz-Sánchez's Borderlands performance scholarship teaches readers to de-code what she calls "Chicana/Indígena and Mexican Performative Indigeneities." Readers are taught to witness performative Indigeneities as these are enacted through pan-indigenous rites and rituals, visual aesthetics, and storytelling inventions. Díaz-Sánchez shows how these pan-indigenous rites, rituals, aesthetics, and inventions comprise a revolutionary re-making, a de-colonizing performatics enacted in the performance artworks of Jesusa Rodríguez and Celia Herrera-Rodríguez. Their messages are made material through their bodies, a theory in the flesh that works to remap the Américas and re-generate the world, politics, and being. Audiences are allowed to witness their inner dialogue made public to the point where a *post*-border consciousness becomes visible, an alter-Native and dissident mode of planetary consciousness that thinkers and activists from Gloria Anzaldúa to Fredric Jameson are seeking.

Philosopher Maria Lugones's scholarship enacts a "Performative Testimonio" as she dances "The Tango, Torta Style." This is a performance of *lesbian*-style tango that engenders what Lugones calls "Macha Homoerotics." The reader can hear the music and feel the dance through an ethnographic engagement directed toward teaching readers to rise out of dualistic active/submissive connections to masculinity/femininity. Indeed, Lugones insists that readers step free from the commodified erotics of male/female or butch/femme and shift to a different kind of erotics to utilize de-colonizing race-gender-sex performatics in a dance of and toward liberation.

Cultural critic Angie Chabram-Dernersesian's study of de-colonizing performatics tunes us in to a TV commercial inserted inside a popular telenovela. The camera zooms in on a fast-moving train. The train suddenly swerves, enlarges, and heads toward the spectator as if to burst through the screen while a masculinized voice-over calmly queries, "Do you suffer from panic disorder?" Viewers are offered relief in the form of an anti-depressant anxiety medication. Chabram-Dernersesian points out that this commercial works by generating in viewers an "unwelcome participatory spectatorship." She argues that this is the very mode of traumatized spectatorship forced on children who "unwillingly witness brutality between their parents." Moreover, this is the very mode of perception Latina diasporic/migrant subjects are taught to experience and that is encouraged in *all* colonized subjects who become trapped inside a nationally conditioned prison house of perception.

Indeed, it may be that this is the very mode of spectatorship from which we must *all* be released. How? For performance theorists including Agusto Boal, Alicia Arrizón, Jose Esteban Muñoz, Gloria Anzaldúa, Michelle Habell Pallán, and indeed, for all contributors to this volume and especially for author Tiffany Ana López, "critical witnessing," being seen and heard (or as Sandoval puts it, witnessing and being witnessed), is the primary human need. Once this need is met, trauma, terror, anxiety, and agoraphobia can be released. Indeed, it is this human need expressed that becomes "performance" and the basis for challenging the colonial construction of self through a heroic re-construction of being.[17]

Cultural anthropologist Karen Mary Davalos's chapter reveals how visual art contains radical de-colonizing performatics. Davalos's provocative analyses of the paintings and installations of iconic artist Diane Gamboa open up new terrains for understanding how perceptual transformation occurs. Davalos's deep reading of a Gamboan exhibition shows us how the artist Gamboa 1) teaches spectators to view a "male" from a "female" point of view and vice versa, 2) transforms inner work into public acts, and 3) converts imagined spaces into performative spaces. Finally, Davalos argues that Gamboa's artwork challenges the conventional theoretical and methodological approaches of Chican@ art historians who remain as yet unable to witness and comprehend the transformative contributions of Gamboa's artwork to Chican@ liberation.

Literary theorist Carl Gutiérrez-Jones's "Human Rights, Conditioned Choices, and Performance in Ana Castillo's *Mixquihuala Letters*" considers how the dialogues and inner lives of characters in Castillo's travelogue and epistolary novel serve as contributions to global human rights literature. Castillo's book expands US-based human rights discourse (which commends itself on enforcing human rights internationally) and asks dominant-citizen-subjects to look within their own national borders for examples of how to produce freedom. In this process, Gutiérrez-Jones forces the question of how human rights issues are ignored for communities of color in the United States and especially for working-class women of color.

ACTO 1 concludes with Daphne V. Taylor-García's reminder that emancipation depends on ending colonial relationships. Taylor-García's research de-colonizes gender performativity while at the same time boldly identifying a "thesis for emancipation" which she finds in the early Chicana feminist thought produced between 1969 and 1979. Taylor-

García's research carefully reveals how the race and gender demands that were placed on sixteenth-century indigenous and other colonized women during the colonization of the Américas were very different from the race and gender demands placed on Anglo-Christian women during that same period. But colonial differences, she demonstrates, continue today! Taylor-García then goes on to reveal the emancipatory insights of 1969–1979 Chicana/Latina/Indigenous feminist writers. These allow readers to "take a de-colonial turn" away from historically produced relations of power and instead enact the de-colonizing performatics found in everyday life—the inner work and public acts of emancipation.

ACTO 2: ETHNOGRAPHIES OF PERFORMANCE: THE RÍO GRANDE AND BEYOND

The chapters in ACTO 2 examine the de-colonizing performatics of transcendence that occur through ritual, music, dance, spoken word, theater, and visual art performances or, alternately, through the innovative methods of ethnographic analysis that these performances perform, which further push the reader/spectator/witness/listener/dancer over, through, and out of the coloniality of power. Cultural theorist Norma Cantú's ethnographic investigation identifies the performance of "Indigeneity in a South Texas Community" through her analysis of "Los Matachines de la Santa Cruz." Her analysis of a sacred dance that is devoted to the feast of the Holy Cross and celebrated in a Tejano barrio in Laredo, Texas, unravels an Indo-Hispano-Tejano complex of de-colonizing performatics. The mysteries revealed by Cantú are the de-colonizing performatics of indigenized expression that are hidden in the dance but now revealed through an analytic display that challenges previous academic modes of Eurocentric historical interpretation and ethnographic knowledge.[18]

Yolanda Broyles-González's enlivening study of popular Brownsville-born bolero singer Chelo Silva (1922–1988) adds to the growing body of interdisciplinary work informed by critical theory from Chicana and Indigenous cultural studies and from third-world feminism that excavates and honors the agency of female Borderland performers. During the 1950s, Chelo Silva was one of the best-selling Tejana recording artists on both sides of the border. Broyles-González presents and analyzes

Chelo Silva's original interpretations, performances, and recordings of boleros and demonstrates Silva's powerful influence upon iconic Mexican singer Juan Gabriel as well as many other Tejana/o popular singers. Broyles-González's chapter on Chelo Silva expands our understanding and analysis of two of the Southwest's most influential musicians: Chelo Silva and Lydia Mendoza, two of the "Grandes de Texas."[19]

In a chapter structured like a corrido or music video, theorist William Nericcio experiments with a Barthesian mode of radical semiotics as a method for re-viewing the US/Mexican borderland territories. His chapter is about how the twin cities split by the US/México border of Laredo, Texas, and Nuevo Laredo, México, are performed within a symbolic economy that locates border towns and border spaces as Dionysian places of lust, addiction, excess, and liberation from puritanical taboos, all before a backdrop of institutionalized poverty, marginalization, and Baudrillardian hyper-reality. In doing so, Nericcio teaches readers how to transform perception and comprehension by taking us on a magical tour of "Bordertown Laredo." Nericcio's own de-colonizing performatics are contained in a writing modality that provides readers the opportunity to witness an over-the-top performance by a Chicano border intellectual of the jumbled poetics of the border.

De-colonial feminist theorist Emma Pérez examines how Mexican@ and Chican@ "queers of color" negotiate their survival and perform their identities on the El Paso, Texas, and Juárez, México, border. Peréz examines ethnographic interviews that show a variety of struggles and strategies that queers of color use to live as "out" within homophobic and patriarchal family structures, the overarching homophobia in Mexican cultures, and racism and homophobia in US cultures inflected by the material space of the border. Pérez provides an analysis of how racialized sexualities on the border are intersected by a coloniality of power that punishes and even kills people for their sexuality, poverty, skin color, and racialized positions, as pointed out in her discussion of Arlene Diaz, a transgendered Chican@ murdered in 2002.

Ethnomusicologist Peter J. García's chapter examines the de-colonial performatics of Latin pop singer / song writer Lorenzo Antonio and his celebrity sister onda grupera (women's vocal quartet), Sparx. These New Mexico native performers have become household names in México, Latin America, Spain, and the Latina/o Borderlands thanks to their vocal virtuosity and original arrangements of Latin pop songs. Most admirable about Sparx is their organic connection to their local Nuevomexicano social fan base and their political activism, which brings attention to the serious drug epidemic plaguing the "Land of Enchantment," the failing school system, the dreaded water crisis endemic to the Río Grande / Río Bravo, and the emerging drought facing the Southwest Borderlands as a result of changing climates and global warming.

The "Sonic Geographies" chapter by Roberto D. Hernández continues the analysis of US/México Borderlands musics as a material enunciative site of musical productions. These musics combine and redefine such genres as punk, *Rock en Español,* and hip-hop corridos to critique the legitimacy of the nation-state that seeks to erase the indigenous identities of Mexicans crossed by the US/Mexican border. Hernández charts how the well-known saying "[w]e did not cross the border, the border crossed us!" is articulated in several musical texts that critique the materiality of racism, nativism, manifest destiny, and the sense of racial entitlement of Anglo colonial modes of power and discourse on the US/México border.

This issue of multiraciality and the reclamation of indigenous and mestiza identities also drives another contemporary mestiza singer and performer, Lila Downs, who is of Mexican Mixteca and Zapotec heritage and Minnesota Swede background. Brenda M. Romero's chapter "Lila Downs's Borderless Performance: Transculturation and Musical Communication" examines how Lila Downs represents a dynamic experimental approach to new musical performance imbued with an understanding of the sacredness, indigeneity, and power of this "nueva mestiza" performing artist. Lila Downs's music is filled with Afro-Latin percussion, West African *kora,* Veracruz harp traditions, and jazzy brass sounds, and her bands include virtuoso musicians. Romero's chapter positions Lila Downs's artistry as an important contribution to the recovery of voices and soundscapes subjugated by colonial, neocolonial, and patriarchal violence toward indigenous cultural knowledges.[20]

Each chapter in ACTO 2 contains an ethnographic analysis that mediates colonial wounds, de-colonizes Latin@ bodies, and sustains communities of color. Through their analyses, each author identifies compelling modes of de-colonizing performatics that are aimed toward re-humanizing our communities.[21]

ACTO 3: AESTHETICS IN THE TRANS/NACIONAL

The chapters in ACTO 3 reach across and through differences, across continents from the United States to Spain, and across and through genders and sexualities as well as racial and ethnic categories in order to identify new planetary routes for Borderland Performance Studies—and for the de-coloniality of being.[22]

Such novel radical effects are evident in the chapter by performance critics Paloma Martínez-Cruz and Liza Ann Acosta, who describe how female performers who are Indígena, Chicana, and Latina members of the theater group *Teatro Luna* "become men in their performances." Their analysis of "El Macho" and transformative gendering extends far beyond similarly evoked themes in analyses of Shakespeare's cross-gendering interventions, for example, insofar as the enactments by *Teatro Luna* are grounded in the 1970s race, sex, gender, and class transformations that were demanded by US, third world, and Chicana feminisms. *Teatro Luna*'s de-colonizing performatics thus are self-consciously organized to (at least temporarily) transform both performers and spectators by inviting all to enter into a field of race, gender, and sex undecidability. Like the lesbian erotics described in ACTO 1 by philosopher Maria Lugones, their aim is to escape any binary understanding of gender and to instead enter into a differential realm, or rather, as the authors put it, into a pulsating "continuum of gender" that reaches beyond all previously conceived divisions of gender.

In considering the transnational effects of Latina-centered performance, performance theorist Tiffany Ana López allows readers to experience how two different productions of the same play, *Real Women Have Curves,* generate profoundly different political meanings when produced in two different countries. A version enacted on one continent generates effective de-colonizing performatics, but the radical work of these performatics evaporates when the play is produced in another country under differing cultural conditions. López's analysis binds East LA to Barcelona, Spain, through her own performed action that is aimed toward healing violence and trauma. This "suturing" work allows the author to identify and define important perceptual and methodological apparati including "critical witnessing," "borderlands violence," and "Chingona feminism."

Marivel Danielson's "Loving Revolution: Same-Sex Marriage and Queer Resistance in Monica Palacios's *Amor y Revolución*" illustrates the de-colonizing performatics that emerge during the solo performances of this radical Chicana lesbian playwright and actress. Danielson focuses on one performance in particular. On May 15, 2008, California's supreme court declared that same-sex couples could enter into legal marriages. In November 2008, even though there was the historic US presidential election of Barack Obama, a landmark in US civil rights, California passed Proposition 8 to annul same-sex marriages by declaring "marriage" as legal only if between a "male" and a "female." In the face of Prop 8's passage, performance artist Monica Palacios courageously staged a dissenting voice in the form of a performed-protest-action that confronts the lack of lesbian, gay, bisexual, transgender, and queer civil rights. Danielson recounts the de-colonizing performatics of Palacios's theater, pointing out the techniques that can mobilize an oppressed queer community of color, help visualize a more egalitarian future, and enable audiences to rehearse the actions necessary for creating change.

Jennifer Esposito's "Is Ugly Betty a Real Woman?" continues the discussion of racialized constructions of gender in the case of a highly visible representation of a Latina body in mainstream commercial television. The protagonist of *Ugly Betty*, the ABC-aired popular crossover series, is a US adaptation of a popular sitcom from Colombia. Esposito's discussion of the contradictory discourses that represent the social body of Betty shows how gender is performed in a racialized symbolic economy that labels Latin@s as outsiders, exotic, or punishable by Eurocentric norms of beauty and femininity, and how marginalized subjects subvert these racialized and patriarchal practices.

Issues of mixed racial legacies in the United States and among Latin@s and Native Americans are complex.[23] Such is the case with Felipe Rose, a queer Native American rock star from a 1970s disco music group. Gabriel S. Estrada's chapter, "Indian Icon, Gay Macho: Felipe Rose of Village People," traces the struggles the performer has undertaken in reclaiming and developing a Native American consciousness. As an indigenous Lakota Sioux mixed blood (Indo-Jibaro) gay man with Puerto Rican roots (including indigenous Taino and Afro-American origins), Estrada explains that over the course of three decades, Felipe Rose transformed his image from an ambiguously ethnic disco singer playing an Indian role to an urban Indian-identified performer who sings both contemporary Native American and classic disco music.

The chapters in ACTO 3 speak to, from, and across spaces of sex, gender, race, and culture and across and through nations, classes, and ethnicities. As the authors cross spaces, geographies, nations, borders, and boundaries of social and representational orders, each identifies creatively differential spaces of subjectivity to identify new versions of egalitarianism. The authors in ACTO 3 talk back to binary systems of sex, gender, and race formations to suggest performing from a space of the in-between, the space of nepantla. Anzaldúa writes, "[I] use the word nepantla to . . . talk about those who facilitate passages between worlds, whom I've called nepantleras. I associate nepantla with states of mind that question old ideas and beliefs, acquire new perspectives, change worldviews, and shift from one world to another" (248). The Nahuatl cosmological concept *nepantla,* "living in between worlds," describes the space from which the de-colonizing performatics of the ACTOs arise. Like Anzaldúa, the authors of the chapters argue for shape-shifting genders/sexualities/ethnicities and nations to create kinder worlds.

ACTO 4: (DE)CRIMINALIZING BODIES: IRONIES OF PERFORMANCE

Throughout this book, the activities of the de-colonizing perform-antics identified arc toward justice. Still, the painful irony is that US Latin@s, like all communities of color, must negotiate such perform-antics within oppressive rubrics of race, class, gender, and sexual intersectionalities—not only in historic and institutionalized terms but also in everyday contexts. De-colonizing performatics such as those seen during the 1940s zoot suit phenomenon have been criminalized in absolute terms so that destroying the actual zoot dress style became the goal of sailor violence toward youth.[24] It is also common to see Latin@ culture appropriated, deracinated from its complex origins and practices, Anglicized, and reconstructed to fit within mainstream symbolic economies such as Taco Bell, Cinco de Mayo, margaritas, mojitos, rum, and corporate-driven Fiesta (party) cultures and consumption practices. Other examples include shows such as *Dancing with the Stars* or mainstream dance-related shows, where the rich traditions of Cha-Cha-Cha, Tango, or Rumba become Cha-Cha and contain just a few stereotypical moves without the musical complexity and structures that drive all Chican@/Latin@/Indigenous/African@ and mestizaje music and dance cultures. This is also mirrored in the professional and competitive dance circuits, where Latin@-origin dances are practiced by non-Latin@s who tan and pose in a colonial simulacrum of Latin@s. The patterns of appropriation, redefinition, and minstrelsy are similar to those we witness in the African American community from the Jazz Age through to modern-day hip-hop.

Several chapters in ACTO 4 speak directly to how Borderlands Performance Studies becomes a space of cultural affirmation and resistance to the criminalization and invisibilization of Latin@ subjects and their social and cultural spaces. Arturo J. Aldama's "*No Somos Criminales:* Crossing Borders in Contemporary Latina and Latino Music" examines several contemporary songs, performances, and music videos that challenge the unbridled nativist racism, criminalization, and abjection of those perceived as "illegal" in the "necropolitics" of the US/México border zone. In considering a variety of the musicians Molotov, Ricardo Arjona, and Lila Downs, Aldama queries the intersected complexities of anti-racist and anti-sexist music discourses within songs about the US/México border zone.

Sociologist Victor Rios and Patrick Lopez-Aguado's chapter "Chicano Cholos Perform for a Punitive Audience" looks at how contemporary Chicano youth dress styles, like 1940s zoot suits, continue to be essentialized as evidence of criminal activity. The authors argue that through an uncritical semiotic link, male youths' ways of dressing and their modes of self-expression, including hairstyle, jewelry, tattoos, and non-white skin color, are seen as signifiers of violence and social deviance. They examine how such modes of de-colonizing performatics are criminalized by the dominant culture and predetermine a violent police response to male youth. They also consider how males in these youth cultures, though policed by the dominant culture, also reproduce the same oppressive schema of policing, displacing their own imposed hostilities by acting out scripts of sexual hostility toward their female peers.

Cultural analyst Pancho McFarland's chapter, "Mexica Hip Hop: Male Expressive Culture," looks at the construction of the male and racialized masculinities in his overview of how (male) Chicano hip-hop groups recover indigenous identities while at the same time reproducing hetero-normative male gender privilege, as if all these acts can be considered de-colonizing. Such acts proceed, however, by ignoring the fact that most indigenous communities in this hemisphere have been and are matrilineal. Moreover, these communities do not criminalize their members for being "two spirit" (or for being what are seen in the western context as members of the GLBT community).[25] McFarland's chapter allows for the radical appearance and possibilities of de-colonial antics and performatics in these groups while at the same time addressing the need to de-colonize the intertwined sexist and heterosexist binaries of raced male domination as well.

Daniel Enrique Pérez brings a de-colonial and queering modality to examine how stereotypes of the Latin Lover are performed in US popular culture. He considers three case studies of Ramón Novarro, Desi Arnaz, and Mario López, familiar and successful Hollywood stars from different epochs whose sexualities have always been called into question. Pérez argues that the "Latin lover," the icon of the hetero male lover, is "queer" because his identity and sexuality are constantly fluctuating along a gender and sexual continuum.

Jennifer Alvarez Dickinson's chapter, "The Latino Comedy Project and Border Humor in Performance," examines the humor of a group called The Latino Comedy Project insofar as it propagates racially offensive stereotypes toward Mexican immigrants. Her research questions the potential for parody as a counter-hegemonic strategy for disrupting the logics of a racial nativism that criminalizes all Latin@s as dirty, primitive, illegal, and morally bankrupt. Alvarez Dickinson's scholarship highlights the contradictory spaces in which US citizens of Mexican, Indigenous, mestiz@, and Latin@ descent reinforce their own US belonging by joining the anti-immigrant political mainstream and denigrating those without papers.

ACTO 4 concludes with a chapter that considers how de-colonizing, community-creating antics and performatics are criminalized, policed, punished, and removed from public spectacle. Specifically, Berta Jottar-Palenzuela's chapter, "Rumba's Democratic Circle in the Age of Legal Simulacra," considers how Latin@ public spaces are performed in New York City's Central Park through her discussion of the Cuban-origin Rumba circle that started there in the 1970s. The chapter looks at the genealogy and the de-colonizing antics and performatics of this community in order to examine the ways in which people as well as civic cultural space itself are literally policed and disciplined—in particular by former Mayor Giuliani's effort to "clean up" New York City and enact the localized state violence of cultural intolerance.

The struggle to perform Latinidad is literally a struggle of bodies, minds, emotions, space, and being. Conga circles call forth a *ritmo* (rhythm) of being, the transcendent force of *Orishas*, the respect for ancestors, and a communal jouissance of diasporic and resistant *vida*/life. Indeed, de-colonizing performatics and antics carry legacies of cultural vibrancies that drive Latin@/African@/Indigenous/mestiz@ historical and contemporary expressions through the aesthetics of dance, movement, speech, thought, emotion, and spirituality. The de-colonizing performatics and antics of the Borderlands represent the aesthetic processes of de-criminalization.

EPILOGUE

Our argument is for the recognition of another field—Borderlands Performance Studies—and for the recognition of its primary method, which we call de-colonizing performatics. De-colonizing performatics are composed of the "antics" of the oppressed—their effects are designed to exceed all oppressive and criminalizing social orders. In recounting the de-colonizing antics necessary to performatics, the chapters of ACTOs 1–4 singly and together overrun traditional academic, disciplinary, and popular compartmentalizing.

Some scholars in this book focus on gender, sex, or race. Others allow readers to better recognize and imagine the radical de-colonizing performatics of a mestizaje/Indigenous/Chican@/Latin@/African@ enactment. United States Latin@ Borderland Performance Studies is grounded in indigeneity. This field challenges the coloniality of power that artificially disconnects and pulls apart race from gender and from sexuality. Some chapters point out the psychic diseases linked to subjugation and insist that we face these head-on in order to heal. Every chapter deals with representation, aesthetics, performance, and power. And every author and performer included in this volume is adamant in claiming that de-colonial liberation means believing in and recovering one's body—its voice, its sensations, its perceptions, its connections to mind and feeling. From these recognitions, readers are encouraged to enact their own unique modes of artistry, witnessing, performance, spect-acting, and being.

The book insists upon demonstrating and performing a Borderlands consciousness—a type of vital insurgency that inscribes alter-Native cultural vocabularies, musical times, and communal emotionalities. This book bears witness to a great lineage of de-colonizing performatics and their antics. From this lineage we editors too are *Performing the US Latina and Latino Borderlands*. Our aim, shared with Luis Valdez, Gloria Anzaldúa, Augusto Boal, Paula Gunn Allen, and, indeed, with every author named in this text, is to disrupt and end the colonization of psychic life—to undo the conditioned mind-body-affect matrix—to utilize performance as a portal to liberation.

NOTES

The image on the cover of this book serves as our Mistress of Ceremonies. Her/his performance opens the way for all that follows. Beamed from a "Mayan Ballroom," our MC was created by the great Chicana feminist artist Maya Gonzalez, whose work can also be found on the book covers of *Living Chicana Theory* and *Contemporary Chicana and Chicano Art.*

1. See the 2010 US Census count for the Hispanic population http://www.census.gov/prod/cen2010/briefs/c2010br-02.pdf (accessed July 13, 2011).

The 2010 census attempted to put into practice strategies to overcome the undercount. See http://www.gao.gov/products/GAO-08-1167T (accessed Sept. 13, 2011). However the state of Texas filed a lawsuit in 2011 to challenge the undercount of the Hispanic population of Texas. See http://www.reuters.com/article/2011/05/09/us-census-texas-idUSTRE74863W20110509 (accessed Jan. 13, 2012).

2. The field of Borderlands Performance Studies here introduced is organized around nine more or less formalized schools of thought that, however they may overlap, can be summarized as 1) the East Coast school typified by scholars such as Richard Schechner and, in our view, the de-colonizing performatic works of scholar Diana Taylor and the *Hemispheric Institute of Performance and Politics,* "a consortium of institutions, scholars, artists, and activists in the Americas"; 2) the vibrant school of *Teatro Campesino* associated with Luis Valdez; 3) the transnational school of the Theatre and Pedagogy of the Oppressed associated with Augusto Boal; 4) the Native Indian de-colonizing school of storytelling performance whose contributors include Paula Gunn Allen, Joy Harjo, Craig Womack, Julie Pearson-Little Thunder, Arnold Krupat, and Gordon Henry; 5) the transnational and intensely prolific feminist, queer Borderland school (à la Gloria Anzaldúa) associated

with scholars such as Yvonne Yarbro-Bejarano, David Román, Daystar/Rosalie Jones, Alicia Arrizón, José Esteban Muñoz, Alicia Gaspar de Alba, Yolanda Broyles Gonzales, Michele Habell Pallán, Coco Fusco, María Herrera-Sobek, Emily Hicks, Deborah Vargas, Luz Calvo, and many of the contributors to this book; 6) a school we typify as "West Coast" whose contributors include Gronk, Hector Aritzabal, the *Mujeres de Maiz* performance collective, Chicano Secret Service, and associates of the *Aztlán Journal* directed by UCLA film theorist Chon Noriega; 7) the Afro-Latino performance school whose contributors include Gay Johnson, Juan Flores, and George Lipsitz; 8) the Zapatista school of performance for freedom enabled through the "word as weapon," a feminist and native emphasis that is also typified by many of the scholars on this list; and 9) the anthropological lineage begun by Américo Paredes and taken up by the University of Texas with participants including Richard Bauman, Gerard Behágue, Manuel Peña, Richard Flores, José Limón, Olga Najera-Ramirez, Candida Jaquez, and Peter J. García. Each of these schools utilizes to a greater or lesser degree what we describe in the following pages as a method of de-colonizing performatics. Their shared utilization of this approach permits their unification in this introduction under the broad classificatory label we identify as—following Gloria Anzaldúa—Borderlands Performance Studies. Alicia Gaspar de Alba states that "[a]ll of the work collected in *Performing the US Latina and Latino Borderlands,* then, is alter-Native." See her foreword to this book.

3. Scholar and performance activist Diana Taylor provides a related argument for and definition of "hemispheric performance studies" in her influential book *The Archive and the Repertoire: Performing Cultural Memory in the Americas* (Durham, NC: Duke University Press, 2003). See especially chapter 1, "Acts of Transfer," 1–52.

4. For definitions of *haciendo caras* (making face) and *conocimiento* (inner knowledge), see Gloria Anzaldúa's *Making Face / Making Soul: Haciendo Caras Creative and Critical Perspectives by Feminists of Color* (San Francisco, CA: Aunt Lute Books, 1995) and *This Bridge We Call Home,* eds. Gloria Anzaldúa and AnaLouise Keating.

5. Our use of the technological ending @ for labels such as Chican@ and Latin@ is a way of 1) challenging the binary of gender constructions (endings with "o" as masculine and endings with "a" as feminine) present in the Spanish language, 2) honoring the fluidity of gender identity, and 3) reclaiming indigenous-centered gender identities that are not defined by these either/or linguistic rigidities.

6. For now, suffice it to say that this approach can be understood as the performance aspect of Chela Sandoval's theory of oppositional consciousness enacted differentially as described in "US Third World Feminism: The Theory and Method of Oppositional Consciousness in the Postmodern World," *Genders* X (1990).

7. For conference and panel details, see the 2008 *Enjoy Music Pop* conference archive at http://www.empsfm.org/index.asp. As the ideas for this book began to germinate, Arturo Aldama and Peter García organized a related panel for the 2008 American Studies Association annual meeting in Albuquerque, New México, that included Chela Sandoval and her upcoming work on shaman-witnessing, SWAPA (Story-Wor(l)d-Art-Performance-Activism), and de-colonial performatics. Because of the success of these panels and the reception from the audience members, our group decided to work on this book project.

8. On food, language, dance, musics, clothing, language, religions, styles, and identities, the phenomenology-influenced anthropological work of Richard Baumann and Charles Briggs is formative. Their work on de-contextualizing the epistemics of performativity from a Eurocentric analytic frame and re-contextualizing performativity to non-western generative spaces was useful in thinking of the philosophical stakes of de-colonial performatics. See Richard Baumann and Charles Briggs, "Poetics and Performance as Critical Perspectives on Language and Social Life," *Annual Review of Anthropology,* Vol. 19 (1990), 59–88.

9. The theory and method of Borderlands Performance Studies and the method of de-colonizing performatics and -antics identified and described here are closely linked to the differential US third-world feminist, womanist, and Xican theory and method of oppositional consciousness, politics, and performance that can be tracked throughout the writings of Gloria Anzaldúa. Practitioners of this oppositional performance mode must learn to enact five interlinking skills: 1) reading signs in order to cooperatively determine when and how to intervene in oppressive power relations; 2) learning when and how to de-construct an oppressive sign-system; 3) learning when and how to re-decorate an already present sign-system; 4) learning to move signs and meanings through perception and consciousness differentially; and 5) engaging in each and every skill for the sole purpose of bringing about egalitarian exchanges. Activation of these five skills creates an emancipatory "methodology of the oppressed." Practitioners learn these skills through the practice of "Story-Wor(l)d-Art-Performance-Activism" (SWAPA). SWAPA is the political technique developed within 1970s U.S third-world feminist "Nahuatl-witness" ceremonies. See the published interview that outlines the basic tenets of SWAPA by Chela Sandoval in "Critical Moments: A Dialogue Toward Survival and Transformation," *Caribbean Review of Gender Studies,* issue 1 (April 2007). See also "Interview," *Spectator: Journal of Film and Television Criticism*, vol. 26, no. 1 (Spring 2006) and "Feminist Forms of Agency" in *Provoking Agents,* ed. Judith Kegan Gardiner (Urbana: University of Illinois Press, 1995).

10. There are many recent discussions of the aesthetics linking "Latina" and "Latino" performance and cultural practices. These include contributions by Alicia Arrizón, *Latina Performance: Traversing the Stage* (Bloomington, IN: Indiana University Press, 1999); Coco Fusco, *English is Broken Here: Notes on Cultural Fusion in the Americas* (New York: New Press, 1995) and *The Bodies that Were Not Ours: And Other Writings* (New York: Routledge, 2002); Michelle Habel Pallán's *Loca Motion: The Travels of Chicana and Latina Popular Culture* (New York: NYU Press, 2005); Jose Esteban Muñoz's *Disidentifications: Queers of Color and the Performance of Politics* (Minneapolis, MN: University of Minnesota Press, 1999); Gloria Anzaldúa, *Borderlands / La Frontera: The New Mestiza* (San Francisco, CA: Spinsters / Aunt Lute, 1987); the collection by Diana Taylor and Roselyn Costantino titled *Latin American Women Perform: Holy Terrors* (Durham, NC: Duke University Press, 2003); and Diana Taylor's *The Archive and the Repertoire: Performing Cultural Memory in the Americas* (Durham, NC: Duke University Press, 2003), among many others.

11. Here it is important to recognize how often Borderlands Performance theorists grapple with the labels that signify our identities. Some examples: performance studies theorist David Román discusses the promises of "pan-Latino" identity practices in *Performance in America* (Durham, NC: Duke University Press,

2005, 110–135). So too, the website for organizing "Afro-Latin@ Studies" advocates for the use of a technological @ ending to signify the inclusion of *all* genders. See their definition described in "Who Are Afro-Latin@s?" at http://afrolatinoproject.org. Gloria Anzaldúa provides a radically transformative epistemic under the rubric of "mestizaje," which she re-defines to mean a US mixture of "African, Indigenous, Spanish, Asian, and Anglo" identities. Her work on language recognizes the myriad languages spoken by "Latin@s," with a list that includes the languages of the working classes, the upper classes, Castilian Spanish, other forms of Spanish, English, and/or Caló, African-inflected languages, and the myriad languages of all indigenous communities and civilizations (Mexica, Maya, Yoeme, Diné, and Nahuatl are examples). Sandoval argues for a unifying use of the label "Xican" to signify the *indigeneity* of US mestizaje in "On the State of Chican@ Studies" in *Aztlán: A Journal of Chicano Studies,* vol. 27, no. 2 (Fall 2002).

12. Many economic, cultural, and Marxist histories track historical epochs and argue that they have or will evolve in the following manner: Primitive Communism–Slavery–Feudalism–Market Capitalism–Monopoly Capitalism–Global Capitalism–Socialism. Here, we editors insist on one more addition and recognition: that of the *de*-colonial era that arose within and in spite of the imperatives of monopoly capital and its imperialist colonial drives. The influences of this de-colonial era and its unique politics, once named "third world liberation," continue today, from the politics of Sojourner Truth to those of Fanon, Anzaldúa, and the rebellions of the Middle East. In this introduction we situate de-colonial third-world liberation movements of the 1950s in their manifestations as Chican@/Latin@/Indigenous movements, indeed, to all US liberation activities and to the concomitant international liberation movements in Cuba, Vietnam, India, Latin America, and South Africa.

For example, in New York's Spanish Harlem and in Chicago, a Puerto Rican nationalist group called the Young Lord's Party became activist around independence for Puerto Rico and democratic rights for Neo-Ricans, which helped to empower Latina/o barrios within the United States. The Young Lords, who began as a street gang, were soon involved in a global human rights struggle. This book, *Performing the US Latina and Latino Borderlands,* once understood as itself an interventionist action—as a de-colonizing perform-antic—can be recognized as emerging out of the continuing legacy of the de-colonial era. Let us list a few of the other many manifestations of humanity's decolonial era: the Black Power and Asian American movements, the anti–Vietnam War movement, the free speech movement, the women's movement, the poor people's movement, the American Indian movement, the Matachín Society and (post-Stonewall) Radical Fairies, Gay Liberation, the *Nueva Cancíon* performatics heard throughout Latin America, Cuba, and New Mexico along with the folk music revivals of the mid-1960s, the red diaper babies, and the hippie counterculture, encounter group, T-group, and humanistic psychology movements in the United Kingdom and across the United States—the list goes on! And these phenomena name only a handful of the emergent tendencies that made real the de-colonial era we wish to name and identify here, and out of which rises our naming of the performance politics that are "decolonizing performatics."

13. To find out more about the theories connected to Performance Studies, see Richard Schechner's book *Performance Studies: An Introduction* (New York: Rout-

ledge, 2007), which tracks his own thinking on the matter as well as the thinking of many other major theorists of performance. Indeed, Schechner stands in relation to the field of Performance Studies in the same way as Christian Metz is positioned in relation to the field of Film Studies. Usual definitions of "performativity" cite J. L. Austin's *How to Do Things with Words* (1962) and Judith Butler's *Bodies That Matter: On the Discursive Limits of "Sex"* (New York: Routledge, 1993) and *Gender Trouble: Feminism and the Subversion of Identity* (New York: Routledge, 1999). It is important to note, however, that neither Schechner nor Butler cites Anzaldúa or other similarly located thinkers of de-colonial performance and performativity. A 1987 quote from Anzaldúa drives home the importance of this lacuna in relation to this volume. This quote is only one arbitrarily selected from Anzaldúa's many meditations on performance. This one is from *Borderlands / La Frontera:* "My 'stories' are encapsulated in time, 'enacted' every time they are spoken out or read silently. I like to think of them as performances and not inert 'dead' objects (as western culture thinks of art works)."

Instead, Anzaldúa writes, "each work" has its own "identity" that is (in its own unique way) aimed toward freedom. Such living identities represent an unquenchable desire for de-colonizing liberation. Our identification with, relation to, and creation of such identities encourages the construction of de-colonizing performatics/antics and is the basis for Borderlands Performance Studies.

14. *Note on conceptual terminologies:* The terms "performatics" and/or "antics" function similarly to the term "semiotics." All these terms refer to technological processes for decoding or encoding performance events. "Performatics/antics," however, refers to the construction of acts that create *de-colonizing* effects, where "semiotics" does not necessarily do so. It is useful to think of de-colonizing performatics functioning as the "parole" to the "langue" of Borderlands Performance Studies. So too, for us, the term "performology" signifies in the same way as does the term "semiology." We define performology as the general study of the nature of outlaw performance and performers, actors and what is enacted, spectators and their responses.

15. The Indigenous/Chican@/and Latin@ texts that define and engage de-colonizing performatics include the following: *Methodology of the Oppressed* by Chela Sandoval (Minneapolis, MN: University of Minnesota Press, 2000), which shows how de-colonial performatics utilize radical semiotics, de-construction, meta-ideologizing, differential perception, and democratics as tools for creation; *The Decolonial Imaginary* by Emma Perez (Bloomington, IN: Indiana University Press, 1999); *Disrupting Savagism* (Durham, NC: Duke University Press, 2001) by Arturo J. Aldama; *Borderlands, La Frontera* by Gloria Anzaldúa (1987, 1992); *Off the Reservation* by Paula Gunn Allen (Boston, MA: Beacon Press, 1999); and the forthcoming *Decolonizing Enchantment: Lyricism, Ritual, and Echoes of Nuevo Mexicano Popular Music* by Peter J. García (Albuquerque, NM: University of New Mexico Press, 2012). Other theories that engage de-colonizing performatics can be tracked in the re-energizing second wave of de-colonial theory and method movement. The "coloniality of power" models proposed by Latin American / US scholars including Nelson Maldonado Torres, Laura Peréz, Ramon Grosfuguel, María Lugones, Walter Mignolo, and Daphne Taylor-García are making important contributions to human thought.

16. This title comes from Anzaldúa's discussion of the necessary relation between one's "inner work" and the transformation to social egalitarianism made possible through our "public acts" in her manifesto titled "now let us shift . . . the path of conocimiento . . . inner work, public acts" in Anzaldúa and Keating, eds., *This Bridge We Call Home: Radical Visions for Transformation* (New York, Routledge, 2002, 540–579).

17. Thanks go to activist/scholars Helene Shulman, Mady Schutzman, Brant Blair, and the Pedagogy and Theatre of the Oppressed organization for their work on how trauma is healed and a sense of personhood recovered through performance and witnessing. See their collected work in "Therapy: Social Healing and Liberatory Politics: A Round-Table Discussion" by Mady Schutzman with Brent Blair, Lori Katz, Helene Lorenz, and Marc Rich in *The Boal Companion: Dialogues on Theatre and Cultural Politics,* eds. Mady Schutzman and Jan Cohen-Cruz (New York: Routledge, 2006) and Mary Watkins and Helene Shulman, *Toward Psychologies of Liberation* (New York: Palgrave Macmillan, 2008).

18. Our consideration of Río Grande performance studies here is deeply influenced by the University of Texas Austin school of border ethnographies. Texas Mexican folklorist Americo Paredes's early critique of ethnographers in his own ethnographic investigations of folklore performance takes into account the role of the fieldworker and the informant illustrating the performative dimensions of the ethnographic encounter in "The Décima on the Texas-Mexican Border: Folksong as an Adjunct to Legend," *Journal of the Folklore Institute,* vol. 3 (1968): 154–167 and in "Folk Medicine and the Intercultural Jest," in *Spanish Speaking People in the United States,* ed. J. Helm (Seattle, WA: University of Washington Press, 1977), 104–119. Additional works such as Gerard Behágue, *Performance Practice: Ethnomusicological Perspectives* (Westport, CT: Greenwood Press, 1984); Richard Bauman, *Verbal Art as Performance* (New York: Newbury House, 1997); and Charles Briggs, *Competence in Performance: The Creativity of Tradition in Mexicano Verbal Art* (Philadelphia: University of Pennsylvania Press, 1988) further de-construct dominant western conceptions of language, music, and social life as a vital, ongoing facet of a larger project.

19. Broyles-Gonzalez's contributions to studies of Chicana/Latina and Indigenous ethnomusicology dance and performance are key to those fields. Other key references include John Storm Roberts, *The Latin Tinge: The Impact of Latin American Music on the United States* (Oxford University Press, 1979); Steven Loza, *Barrio Rhythm: Mexican American Music in Los Angeles* (Urbana: University of Illinois Press, 1993); Frances R. Aparicio and Cándida Frances Jáquez, *Musical Migrations: Transnationalism and Cultural Hybridity in Latin/o America* (New York: Palgrave Macmillan, 2003); and three books by Manuel Peña, *The Texas-Mexican Conjunto: History of a Working-Class Music* (Austin: University of Texas Press, 1985); *The Mexican American Orquesta: Music, Culture and the Dialectic of Conflict* (Austin: University of Texas Press, 1999); and *Música Tejana: The Cultural Economy of Artistic Transformation* (College Station: Texas A&M University Press, 1999). The most recent, *Dancing Across the Borders,* ed. Olga Nájera-Ramirez, Norma E. Cantú, and Brenda Romero (Urbana: University of Illinois Press, 2009), expands the understanding of how dance culture, like music, is not a separate and elevated spectacle but a core factor in Latin@ cultural lives.

20. For discussions of how indigenous epistemic systems are impacted by colonial violence in the Américas, see Antonia Castañeda's "Sexual Violence in the Politics and Policies of Conquest: Amerindian Women and the Spanish Conquest of Alta California," in *Building With Our Hands: New Directions in Chicana Studies,* ed. Adela de la Torre and Beatríz M. Pesquera (Berkeley: University of California Press, 1993, 15–33); Walter Mignolo, *The Darker Side of the Renaissance: Literacy, Territoriality, and Colonization,* 2nd ed. (Ann Arbor: University of Michigan Press, 2003); Andrea Smith, *Conquest: Sexual Violence and American Indian Genocide* (New York: South End Press, 2005); and Jack Forbes, *Columbus and Other Cannibals,* rev. ed. (New York: Seven Stories Press, 2008) .

21. The Mayan prophecies observing the completion of the Great Cycle of thirteen Baktuns indicate a much-needed shift in consciousness to a higher and more compassionate form of being and social tolerance. Native American scholar Ines Hernandez-Avila writes, "According to the Aztec oral tradition (which yes, is very much alive), we are moving into the next sun, Coatonatiuh, the Sixth Sun of Consciousness and Wisdom. We are presently in the tumultuous transition period between the old sun and the new" (2006, 200). Chicana historian Emma Pérez reminds us that a subjectivity introduced by some Chicanas/os and Native Americans of the Southwest is a subjectivity that has challenged histories of the region. She explains that while many Chicana/o academicians . . . have resisted with knee-jerk reactions any mention of coloniality . . . others are eager to cross over to postcoloniality. The time lag between the colonial and postcolonial can be conceptualized as the de-colonial imaginary. [Homi] Bhabha names that interstitial gap between the modern and postmodern, the colonial and the postcolonial, a time lag. This is precisely where Chicana/o history finds itself today, in a time lag between the colonial and the postcolonial. (1999, 6)

It is this "in-between" state and its de-colonial possibilities in which we are most interested. The Nahuatl word *nepantla* signifies an in-between world of possibility. But this world of possibility can also be a world of what Chicana art historian Laura Perez calls a "postconquest condition of cultural fragmentation and social indeterminancy." Third-world feminist Alicia Gaspar de Alba also describes a "state of cognitive disorientation—a psychological side effect of 150 years of Anglo colonization"—the dark side of nepantla. The Hopis in northern Arizona and New Mexico's Tiwa Pueblos understand the worlds of nepantla. Our ancestors' lives were forced out of balance, our villages destroyed following the initial contact and colonization by our Spanish ancestors. Indeed, the Tiwa Pueblos came to live among the Hopi after 1680 for a time in the immediate fall-out from the San Lorenzo rebellion or the Pueblo Indian Revolt. What certain Pueblos call "*Koyannisqatsi,*" meaning life out of balance, is very similar to what Chicana writer Gaspar de Alba describes as cultural schizophrenia, the presence of "mutually contradictory or antagonistic beliefs, social forms, and material traits in any group whose racial, religious, or social components" have become a "hybrid of two or more cultures (also known by its colonial label as mestizaje)" (2003, 199). Numerous indigenous terms contribute to the theorization of border consciousness, including the Hopi "*Koyannisqatsi,*" the Nahuatl "*Nepantla*" or "*Coatonatiuh,*" and the Mayan "*In Lak' Ech,*" "*Hunab Ku,*" and "*Panche Be.*" These ancient philosophical and mystical concepts already are being used in U.S. ethnic studies curricula.

22. There is exciting new scholarship on the coloniality of being. The authors of this introduction, however, are especially interested in the *de*-coloniality of being. On the coloniality of being, see Nelson Maldonado-Torres's "On the Coloniality of Being: Contributions to the Development of a Concept," in *Cultural Studies,* vol. 21, issue 2 (March 2007), 240–270. Also see Anibal Quijano's foundational discussion of the coloniality of power, the hegemonic matrix of colonial race and gender power that informs the Eurocentricity that drives global power relations: "Coloniality of Power, Eurocentrism and Latin America," *Nepantla: Views from South,* vol. 1, no. 3 (2000), 533–580. For an overview of these matters, see also *Latino/as in the World System: Decolonization Struggles in the 21st Century U.S. Empire,* ed. Ramon Grosfoguel, Nelson Maldonado Torres, and José Saldívar (Herndon, VA: Paradigm Publishers, 2005); Laura Peréz, "Enrique Dussel's Etica de la liberación, U.S. Women of Color Decolonizing Practices, and Coalitionary Politics amidst Difference" in *Qui Parle,* number 2, Spring 2010, 121–146; and Maria Lugones, "Heterosexualism and the Colonial/Modern Gender System," *Hypatia*, vol. 22, no. 1 (Winter 2007), 196.

23. Society struggles to move beyond conceptions of phenotype based on skin color, hair, and other stereotypical ethnic markers in order to comprehend the complexity of mixed-race identity and the struggles of multiracial people. President Barack Obama's biracial status allows us a glimpse of mixed-race complexities. Raised by his white maternal grandparents, married to an African American woman, and a longtime member of a black church, Obama identifies himself and is identified by media as African American despite mixed racial origins. After Obama's election, openly lesbian black comedian Wanda Sykes performed at the White House correspondents' dinner, where she brought attention to the matter in jest. Sykes explained that the nation would remember Obama as "the first Black president" but cautioned Obama, "That's unless you screw up. . . . Then it's going to be, what-up with the half white guy?" This example illustrates the complexities surrounding multiracial "mestiz@" identities.

24. For critical discussions of how the zoot suit style was criminalized and how it provoked widespread vigilante violence during the 1940s leading up to the zoot suit riots, consider Mauricio Mazón, *The Zoot-Suit Riots: The Psychology of Symbolic Annihilation* (Austin: University of Texas Press, 1984) and the more recent comparative study by Luis Alvarez, *The Power of the Zoot: Youth Culture and Resistance during World War II* (Berkeley: University of California Press, 2008). For the specific ways that the criminalization of youth culture affected young women, see Catherine S. Ramirez's discussion of Pachuca identities in *The Woman in the Zoot Suit: Gender, Nationalism, and the Cultural Politics of Memory* (Durham, NC: Duke University Press, 2009).

25. For a discussion of two-spirit identity formations in indigenous communities, see Will Roscoe's *Changing Ones: Third and Fourth Genders in Native North America* (New York: Palgrave Macmillan, 2000); *Two Spirit People: Native American Gender, Sexuality, and Spirituality* (Urbana: University of Illinois Press, 1997); Paula Gunn Allen, "Some Like Indians Endure," from *Common Lives, Lesbian Lives* (1982), republished in *Living the Spirit: A Gay American Indian Anthology,* ed. Will Roscoe (New York: St. Martin Press, 1988); and William Walters, *Spirit and the Flesh: Sexual Diversity in American Indian Culture* (Boston, MA: Beacon Press, 1992).

ACTO ONE

Performing Emancipation: Inner Work, Public Acts

ONE

Body as Codex-ized Word / *Cuerpo Como Palabra (en-)Códice-ado:* Chicana/Indígena and Mexican Transnational Performative Indigeneities

MICAELA DÍAZ-SÁNCHEZ

In the performance work of Mexican actress, writer, and director Jesusa Rodríguez and Chicana/Tepehuana[1] painter / installation artist / performance artist Celia Herrera-Rodríguez, the body functions as the critical site for the (de)construction of national and Indigenous identities. The corporeal operates as the primary signifier in the reclamation of denied histories. Through the self-consciously performative style of cabaret and *espectáculo* (spectacle), Jesusa Rodríguez monumentalizes México's Indigenous histories as she employs discourse central to Mexican national identity and cultural citizenship. Celia Herrera-Rodríguez enacts Indigeneity as intimate ritual and positions her work as personal historical recovery and pedagogy aimed at creating dialogue among Indigenous communities on a global level. Their aesthetic methodologies are mediated by multifarious contradictions, colonial epistemologies, and discursive strategies for survival. In the critical recognition and negotiation of these refractory mediations, performance functions as an embodied attempt at reclamation of Indigenous narratives, in and out of the "nation."

How can one body traverse historical moments in performance, specifically between elements of contemporary Chicana and Mexican cultural production and pre-Columbian Indigenous practices? How are mythologies mapped and weighted onto specific bodies? What if that body is Indigenous? And what marks it as Indigenous? What if that body is queer? How do nation and citizenship function in the performative monumentalizing?

Influential Latin American historians and performance scholars Jean Franco, Diana Taylor, and Roselyn Costantino have most prominently examined Jesusa Rodríguez's body of work spanning the past two decades. Central to many of their analyses are the stylistic methodologies with which Rodríguez so incisively critiques repressive institutional figures and ideologies central to popular Mexican historical narratives that systematically exclude Indigenous communities and feminist figures. Costantino asserts that as a performer, Rodríguez "chooses forms that permit her to render corporeal and, thus, visible, the tensions among the ideological, religious, social, political, and economic discourse operating on and through the individual and collective human body."[2] Rodríguez deploys her body as an expedient for the critique of colonial legacies in the Mexican national imaginary and contemporary governmental regimes. Jean Franco writes,

> The remarkable thing about these performances is not only their polymorphous nature, their infinite and baroque metamorphoses, not even the gusto with which Jesusa dances, moves, sings, speaks, mimes, but how she uses her body. She is not so much nude as naked, and it is a nakedness that gives the body a power of expression that we normally associate with the face alone.[3]

Rodríguez utilizes this explicit corporeality in her performances, and through this "nakedness" she exposes multiple contradictions in the political histories of the Americas. Embodying images of multiple historical figures, contemporary Mexican performance artists, like Rodríguez, draw from what Diana Taylor identifies as "the repertoire to add historical depth to their political and aesthetic claims."[4] While Franco, Taylor, and Costantino discuss how Rodríguez's performances function in these critiques of the Mexican nation-state, I am invested in a transnational analysis that interrogates how class and sexuality function in the work of this highly controversial Mexico City–based artist.

In Celia Herrera-Rodríguez's performance work, she offers generative mandates for this transnational framework, expanding its focus to a hemispheric exploration of Indigeneity while negotiating her subject position as a Chicana/Tepehuana living and teaching visual art practices in Oakland, California. She is predominately recognized for her painting and installation art; there remains little discussion of Herrera-

Rodríguez's body of performance work.[5] One of the most critical moments in the trajectory of Herrera-Rodríguez's work is the moment at which she stepped out of her canvases and began to perform as part of her installation pieces in order to re-claim her Indigenous identity. Herrera-Rodríguez inserts herself in the installations, creating landscapes—often in the form of altars—on which to interrogate multiple iterations of Chicana and Indigenous subjectivities.

Despite their distinct artistic processes and contrasting audiences on both sides of the Mexican/United States border, Jesusa Rodríguez and Celia Herrera-Rodríguez inscribe multiple colonial histories on their bodies. Their staged cultural practices function in terms of what Diana Taylor identifies as an embodied "process, a praxis, an episteme, a mode of transmission."[6] Unsettling aesthetic disciplines, these artists create spaces in which to challenge transnational representations of Indigenous identities.

PERFORMING NATIONAL INDIGENEITY: JESUSA RODRÍGUEZ'S *COATLICUE*

Since the 1990s, Rodríguez has employed the figure of Mexica[7] mother goddess Coatlicue at a number of public protests and formal theatrical presentations.[8] She most famously performs as this deity in "La Gira Mamal de la Coatlicue,"[9] in which she scrutinizes the media coverage and national resources expended for the Pope's 1996 visit to México. Performing as Coatlicue, Rodríguez embodies an articulation of what Taylor conceptualizes as the "repertoire."[10] Taylor cites a critical distinction not between the written and spoken word "but between the archive of supposedly enduring materials (i.e., documents, buildings, bones) and the so-called ephemeral repertoire of embodied practice/knowledge (i.e., spoken language, dance, sports, ritual)."[11] Belonging to the "archive" by virtue of its archaeological excavation and framing in Mexico City's *Museo Nacional de Antropología,*[12] the image of Coatlicue sustains the power of having survived the destruction of the conquest.

In her critique of the Pope's visit, Rodríguez utilizes the "repertoire" of the mother goddess to attack the relegation of the Indigenous past to the museum and the 1996 quincentenary celebrations of the "discovery" of the Americas by Christopher Columbus. From inside a mammoth foam puppet of Coatlicue, she publicly exclaims to the Mexican public in the nation's capital,

> Listen to me carefully, Mexicans, Mexarians, Mexers, Mexants, and resident aliens! I am the origin of origins. But nobody has ever met me at the airport. Unlike the other idol, I can't get them to print 500,000 posters to advertise me. They haven't built my mammarydome; they have yet to come up with a machine that will allow me to kiss the floor of the airport. Nobody's organized an official visit to Chapultepec or Tlatelolco, let alone Chalco. I've never been able to realize my beautiful dream of a mammary tour—for the purpose of carrying on my evangelical mission, of course. And yet the time is ripe for an ecological religion. Listen, ungrateful offspring! Unlike these other idols I still love you. Even though you rub the Buddha's belly button, even though you spend your money on medals and rosaries and even though you'll search for Mecca from here to eternity, you'll always be my children.[13]

Rodríguez positions the Indigenous female deity as speaking subject and juxtaposes herself as the mother of all modern-day Mexican citizens. Addressing her offspring with farcical monikers, Coatlicue scolds the citizens of México for their ingratitude, their *falta de respeto,* or lack of respect. Analogizing herself with the Pope, she sardonically refers to the "Holy Father" as the "other idol." Mocking the Pope's diplomatic reverence while visiting *his* "children," (the extensive touring of local Catholic churches and other sacred sites in which he performs acts of worship), Coatlicue alludes to the fact that she cannot even properly revere her homeland upon returning by kissing the airport floor. Instead, the mother goddess must navigate her tour without technological assistance despite the hindrance of her colossal stone frame. Critiquing her children's contemporary veneration of non-Mexican/non-Indigenous deities in the place of her Mexica pantheon, she scathingly accuses her children of a new-age/de-contextualized appropriation of the ancient global spirit practices of Islam and Buddhism. But in the end, she affirms that, despite their utter lack of respect, she still loves her "ungrateful offspring."

In this performance, Rodríguez situates herself as the powerful Mexica matriarch testifying against the early-twentieth-century celebration of pre-Columbian artifacts in the name of nation-building by federally funded Mexican archeologists.[14] The Mexican government invested in the excavation and preservation of México's Indigenous past while simultaneously enacting policies leading to the genocide of the descendants of the very deities erected in museums. The unearthing and public presentation of Mesoamerican artifacts and monuments overseen by the Mexican government became a lucrative business and continues to make many regions in México attractive tourist destinations. As Bolivian cultural theorist Javier Sanjinés writes, "Indigenous exteriority calls into question the dialectics and philosophies of history that the discourses of national construction lean on for support, as do the discourses of power."[15] In this case, the Mexican government remains dependent on the signifying power of the ancient for contemporary nation-building and violently restructures communities of those who remember and practice "the ancient" into the Mexican nationalist rhetoric of *mestizaje*.

In México, *mestizaje* was central to modernist ideologies of nation-building and the consolidation of ethnic and religious identities within a sovereign state, specifically in the years following the Mexican Revolution. María Josefina Saldaña-Portillo writes, "The discourse of mestizaje was deployed as a strategy of national identification and unification in the aftermath of a divisive revolutionary war against the oligarchic class of the *porfiriato*."[16] Despite the violently embedded discrimination against Indigenous communities and privileging of Europe's legacy in México, political leaders purported a rhetoric of México as a nation of *mestizos* and *mestizas*. Influential Mexican anthropologist Manuel Gamio (often referred to as the "father of Mexican anthropology") served as general inspector of archeology in México and later became the director of the International School of Archaeology and Ethnohistory. In *Handbook to Life in the Aztec World*, Manuel Aguilar-Moreno states, "Gamio left the field of archaeology to devote himself to working to solve the social problems of the Indians of Mexico."[17] Gamio's vehement commitment to the "social problems" of México's Indians was deeply rooted in the nationalist project of *mestizaje* that he explicated in his treatises. Among the most famous of these treatises is *Consideraciones sobre el problema del indigenismo* (Considerations on the Problem of Indigenismo) (1948). In this seminal text, Gamio focuses on the cultural assimilation of Indigenous communities into the racially mixed society of México. Sheila Contreras writes,

> Public policies designed to acculturate Indians—most especially through the institutions of schooling, anthropological projects, such as Gamio's world-renowned stratospheric excavations at Teotihuacan . . . contrived to make past greatness visible and cement public acceptance of the desirable characteristics of Indigenous cultures.[18]

Through the enactment of these policies, the state could increase the number of Mexicans classified as *mestizo* and decrease the number of citizens classified as Indigenous. Principles of Mexican citizenship were predicated on the abandonment of Indigenous identities and practices, which were professed as "residual" and cast as hindrances to modernist notions of progress. These systemic campaigns of assimilation relegated the Indian to a historical past, one that was well preserved in the *Museo Nacional de Antropología* and other museums around the country. As Contreras affirms, "These approaches, however, belie the basic premise of Mexican state indigenism: the only good Indian is the mythic Indian."[19]

However, Mexican historian and anthropologist Guillermo Bonfil Batalla reminds us that the survivors of the project of *mestizaje,* those who embody epistemological practices that are transferred onto pre-Columbian monuments, constitute the very nation. Performing the monolithic figure of Coatlicue, Rodríguez asserts herself as Mexica matriarch. In this allegorical move, Rodríguez as Coatlicue spectacularizes this legacy as she indicts the Mexican government for its institutional exaltation of an Indigenous past and simultaneous repression of contemporary Indigenous communities.

In Jesusa Rodríguez's 2004 "Cabaret Pre-Hispanico," the massive foam Coatlicue puppet returns, erupting as a centerpiece with pulsating heart, fluttering mouth, and rotating serpent heads, kicking up her heels to amplified *banda* music.[20] The "repertoire" literally cites the "archive," as Coatlicue on stage mirrors the one that stands erect in the gallery named "La Sala Mexica" in the Mexico City museum.

Visually, it is astounding when Rodríguez's petite frame is born from the pulsating foam labia of Coatlicue: you realize that she was the only one moving the puppet's various body parts, enacting multiple elements of the mythology. We hear grunts as she struggles to emerge from Coatlicue in the shiny regalia of a modern-day *danzante Azteca* or "Aztec dancer," shaking *sonajas* proclaiming, "Ay, traditions are heavy."[21] A Viennese ambassador, played by her wife and collaborator of over twenty-five years, Argentine composer/pianist Liliana Felipe, delivers her headdress. Rodríguez secures the feathered artifact returned from the museum on her head, fixes her long braids, straps on her high heels, and, with a staunchly serious facial expression, attempts to re-enact a "traditional" *danza Azteca.* Except she fails miserably. She doesn't know how to do "it," the dance that she is supposed to know how to dance; there is a failure of what she relies on as embodied memory. Instead, employing the repertoire of a contemporary "Aztec dancer" born of the mother goddess, she prances around the stage with radiating conviction, attempting to execute modern dance phrases and falling while the crowd howls with laughter. As the "Aztec dancer" character, she centers Indigenous exteriority, but there is slippage in the embodied spiritual practice of the Indigenous subject. While reifying the signifying power of "Aztec dancer's" regalia and instruments, Rodríguez humorously rejects the specifics of the ritualized dance. The frivolity of the cabaret style allows Rodriguez to critique popular media images and tourist consumption of contemporary Indigenous performances.

Jesusa Rodríguez is often cited as a "chameleon," famous for her transformation from one iconographic embodiment to another (Sor Juana Inés de la Cruz, Hitler, Frida, Jesus, Salinas de Gortari, Malinche, "the Devil," Coatlicue, etc.). As performer, she executes the transference of these bodies from both the "archive" and the "repertoire." These stark conversions are presented beyond the functions of makeup, costume, and intricate physical portraiture. On one body, she renders and inscribes intersections of religious, economic, sexual, political, and ideological discourses. She maps trajectories among tensions pulsating from hundreds of years ago alongside headlines from this morning's newspaper, employing the topical approach of cabaret performers.[22] Through her infamous sardonic wit, she dissects the layered signifiers with the accuracy of a surgeon's scalpel. In the midst of the dissection, I am always conscious of her body as lesbian, as woman, as fair-skinned. Costantino comments, "By continually circulating her body as text, she brings to each site that history, a manifestation of what James C. Scott refers to as 'hidden transcripts'—instances of ideological resistance to and critique of power by subordinate groups. A consideration of hidden transcripts provides 'a different study of power that uncovers contradictions, tensions, and immanent possibilities . . . short of actual rebellion'."[23] Scott positions these "hidden transcripts" in tension with what he identifies as "public transcripts," discourse of the dominant. In his conceptualization, the practices that constitute "hidden transcripts" take place "'offstage,' beyond direct observation by powerholders."[24] I would argue that when one recognizes the signifying power and historical legacies of the artist's body as female and queer in the Mexican public sphere, the transcripts are not hidden; instead, the ideological resistance is marked because of the visibility of that very body.

PERFORMING PERSONAL INDIGENEITY: CELIA HERRERA-RODRIGUEZ'S *ALTAR AS PERFORMANCE*

I transpose Jesusa Rodríguez's Coatlicue with an image from the performance work of Celia Herrera-Rodríguez. In her 2004 piece "Altar as Performance," Herrera-Rodríguez begins by making sacred the silent rite of ironing. After several moments of silence, she finally speaks, detailing memories of how her grandmother taught her the intimate ceremony as she conjures up the familial/historical significance of each piece of fabric she pulls from a basket. Laura Pérez comments that Herrera-Rodriguez's work is testament to the fact that the "sacred and the Indigenous have survived by exploiting the colonialist blindness to the non-Eurocentric, by being hidden, ironically, in the daily activities seemingly dissociated from the indigenous in Mexican nationalist discourses of *mestizo* identity received Chicana/os."[25] Whereas Jesusa Rodríguez's performances operate as widely circulated satirical condemnations of Mexico's relegation of Indigenous communities as archival, Herrera-Rodríguez focuses on the ritualized reclamations of effaced personal Indigenous histories.

At one point during the performance, Herrera-Rodriguez cannot immediately recall the Spanish translation of one word. She looks up and smiles, saying, "it's hard to remember and pronounce at the same time."[26] We experience the loss of the word with her as she masters the moment with humor. It is heavy to remember back and forth over lands and languages. She navigates the route of remembrance of her own Indigeneity, enacting the critical practice of "viscerality," a term presented by Sanjinés that functions as "a metaphor that helps explain how Indigenous subalternity has resisted giving up its identity to rationalist Western discourse."[27] In Herrera-Rodríguez's performance work, she situates her body and the colonial legacies of that corporeality as the primary signifier.

Dressed simply in black pants and a black long-sleeved shirt, Herrera-Rodríguez walks to the center of the stage. We watch as she takes the time to carefully dress herself in a long, cream-colored *huipil.*[28] She asks, "Does anyone remember how to sit on a blanket?" This query activates a myriad of interpretations, from the rhetorically abstract to the unmistakably literal. Simple in its utterance, the question invokes both tentative utterances and enthusiastic lamentations. This question echoes a previous performance cited by Irma Mayorga in which Herrera-Rodríguez asked the audience, "None of you remember how to open up a blanket?" followed by *"No tenga miedo"* or "Don't be afraid."[29] There is no definitive answer to the question posed during "Altar as Performance," and my own mournful response to the query as an audience member summoned a sense of deficiency resonating with what Mayorga identifies as Herrera-Rodríguez's "aesthetics of loss."[30]

One by one, volunteers from the audience join Herrera-Rodríguez on a blanket as she continues detailing stories of her family and—ultimately—her journey to that specific place and time. On stage, she functions as teacher/storyteller, detailing narratives of when she learned how certain things "are done": how to build a fire, how to make an altar, how to put the brush to the canvas, how to feed the spirits. In citing her lifelong journey through those lessons, I am reminded of what Bonfil Batalla writes about "Mexico Profundo," a term he utilizes to refer to the Indigenous legacies of México: "There is no special time or place for learning what needs to be known. One observes, practices, asks questions, and listens, at whatever time and wherever one may be."[31] Herrera-Rodríguez affirms that when those practices silence who you are as queer or female, then you create new epistemic approaches and new ceremonies. Her performances function as reformulations of ancient rituals, and the creations of these new ceremonies respond to contemporary exigencies. Claiming agency as queer Chicana/Indigenous, Herrera-Rodríguez creates her own repertoire, her own way of knowing. Taylor writes, "The repertoire allows for alternative perspectives on historical processes of transnational contact and invites a remapping of the Americas."[32] Herrera-Rodríguez requires the presence of her community as an audience that participates in the (re)production and transmission of bodies of knowledge from North and South. Pérez asserts that Herrera-Rodríguez's work is "perhaps less about dispelling romantic and otherwise unreal cultural and visual images of Indianness than it is about countering the myth, widespread among Chicana/os, other US Latina/os, and Latin Americans, and about claiming for Chicana/o culture a literal, not just ideological, identification with the Native American."[33] Herrera-Rodríguez discusses her early engagement with Chicana/o nationalism, but her point of entry into Indigenous historical narratives is not rooted in the widely cited iconography of Mexica cosmologies central to Chicana/o movement representations. Instead, she situates her personal Indigenous history within the lineage of her mother's family from the Sandias Tepehuanes in Durango, México.

Citing the work of contemporary Chicana performance artists, Laura Gutíerrez argues that Chicana cultural workers are, in fact, "involved in a project that includes direct or indirect references to—and more importantly, scrutinizes—the nation-state of México as well as mythical, historical, and contemporary Mexican culture, including the manner in which it has been constructed in the so-called diasporic imagination."[34] However, in Herrera-Rodríguez's "remapping," as she interrogates routes and epistemologies of "home," she does not identify or desire the "imagined community" of the nation-state of México. Instead, she calls for the land of the Tepehuanes, the hills of Durango on which, according to her grandmother, her people have lived, "since the sun began to shine."[35]

On stage, Herrera-Rodríguez does not cite widely circulated emblematic Mexica or Mayan images; instead, she performs a remembrance of the rocks that her mother and grandmother kept in specific places in the house, recognizing this practice as critical in Tepehuan communities and thus integral in her personal historical recovery. In "Altar as Performance," she declares the inquiry that drives her work: "I look for faces that will lead me home."[36] There is no monumental foam puppet; instead, Herrera-Rodríguez moves to the center of the stage and carefully places a small pre-Columbian icon made of stone on her outstretched tongue. Standing still for a few moments, she performs a Chicana/Indigenous glyph, locating herself as the museum artifact and codex that has broken out of the glass enclosure as speaking subject to tell us of her own journey as maker of art and maker of generations to come. She revises

FIG. 1.1. Celia Herrera-Rodríguez in "Altar as Performance." Nitery Theater, Stanford University, 2004. *Permission granted by the artist.*

historiographies as she performs the material recovery of hemispheric spirit practices and celebrates our mothers and grandmothers who have kept them alive. Her revisions operate in terms of what Emma Pérez conceptualizes as "the decolonial imaginary," a category that makes Chicana agency transformative. Emma Pérez clarifies that the decolonial imaginary "is that time lag between the colonial and postcolonial, that interstitial space where differential politics and social dilemmas are negotiated."[37] It is in this ruptured space that Herrera-Rodríguez makes her performative intervention, employing her body as the site of the "decolonial(-izing)" project. Conjuring the multiple and dissident subjectivities of this contemporary imaginary, Herrera-Rodríguez generates dialogue among hemispheric Indigenous communities and urges Chicana/os to critically reclaim their own Indigeneity, to search for sacred images and practices with and through their bodies.

Herrera-Rodríguez's performances function as embodied responses to her work as a visual and installation artist. She steps out of her canvas and into her installation art to perform in and out of multiple mediums and arranges the stage as altar, creating a de-colonial topography on which we will bear witness to ritual (re)membering. Each object carries with it multiple representational powers defined not by convention but by their relationship to performer and community. In "Altar as Performance," she runs her fingers through a bowl of corn and mourns the corporate genetic modification of a foundational element for Indigenous peoples in the Americas. Then she reminds us how to grind corn ourselves with a *metate*.[38] This pedagogical exercise refuses notions of domesticity in Chicana/Mexicana/Indigena communities. Instead, it functions as a corporeal attempt at activating memory, both literally and metaphorically. She embodies the negotiation between the performance of an individual autobiographic self with a collective recuperation of Indigenous practices in Chicana/o communities. As modern-day Chicana/Indígena *tlamatinime,* or scribe, she creates glyphs on stage that re-imagine popular mythologies and de-center colonial narratives. She repositions female subjectivities and ceremonies that circulated before the institution of the border that separates the United States and México. Herrera-Rodriguez's commitment to creating a pan-Indigenous dialogue is central to the transformative agency of her work.

"THIS IS WHAT'S LEFT OF MY LAND":[39] TRANSNATIONAL IMPLICATIONS

The decision to write about Rodríguez and Herrera-Rodríguez in the same context requires a transnational framework. Does Jesusa Rodríguez's citizenship as a Mexican national allow her to clearly position her attacks against a specific nation-state hegemony? In her comparative study of Chicana and Mexican feminist literature, Anna Sandoval echoes the role of national citizenship in the formation of subjectivity, "while Mexicanas have the privilege of writing against a national discourse that at least includes them, Chicanas write against a national discourse that does not recognize them."[40] However, in problematizing that binary, it is imperative to discuss the history of Mexican feminisms. In her foundational work on gender and representation in México, Jean Franco traces the positionalities of women in the imposed narrative of México's history from colonial times through the Church and official nationalism and through modernization that has situated Mexican women in seemingly contradictory but in the end very logical poles. The first pole makes Mexican women an absence by erasing their presence or nullifying their potential power in public spheres (as intellectuals and artists), by denying them the right to authorship; the second pole appropriates woman as a sign to be used strategically, if not cynically, in a male-authored project (1988). Jesusa Rodríguez ruptures this narrative through an expansive deployment of strategies. Together with her wife, Liliana Felipe, Rodríguez founded a famous cabaret in Mexico City, El Hábito, which became famous for featuring Rodríguez's and Felipe's biting social critiques of the Mexican government while federal authorities shouted back at them from the audience. Rodríguez is highly visible as an advocate for Indigenous rights; she leads national marches and offers her performance space as a site for grassroots organizing. She threatened outspoken religious and Mexican homophobic activists by "mock-marrying" her longtime partner Felipe in a 2001 nationally televised ceremony.

In one of the final images of "Cabaret Pre-Hispanico," Liliana Felipe lies on the ground at center stage, legs wide open, while Jesusa Rodríguez holds a small sparkler as if she might attempt penetration with the firework.[41] They sing the Mexican national anthem against a backdrop of the famous volcanoes outside Mexico City in an obvious reference to *la leyenda de los volcanes*. In this legend, the present-day volcanoes are said to be the remains of a forlorn Aztec princess, Iztaccihuatl, and her deceased lover, Popocatepetl.[42] They compulsively repeat both Nahuatl names, switching the phonetic emphases several times until "Iztaccihuatl" becomes *"Estás igual."*[43] As Felipe's outstretched body mirrors the image of Iztaccihuatl, Rodríguez seems to declare the legacy of popular mythologies and national imaginaries that violently play out on the bodies of Indigenous women. Or the moment can be read, as Yvonne Yarbro-Bejarano interpreted it, as one of the many moments of queer desire in "Cabaret Pre-Hispanico": Rodríguez standing above her wife chanting, *"Estás igualita"* as the male Popocatepetl disappears from the conversation all together. As Rodríguez lifts Felipe from the floor, we are reminded that women continue to retrieve each other from volcanic depths that attempt to silence them. Rodríguez's queerness imbues her work and facilitates a critique of nationalist rhetoric. However, her subject-position as the daughter of a surgeon, as upper-middle-class, as educated, as fair-skinned, allows her mobility and enables her to traverse public spheres in ways that an Indigenous woman in contemporary México cannot travel as fluidly.

This discussion of class, race, and Indigenous identities operates as a critical contention in the transnational discourse among Chicana and Mexican feminist cultural producers. Most scholarship on this topic consists of published accounts of gatherings of Chicana and Mexican feminist writers.[44] Referencing one such conference in Tijuana, Baja California, Norma Alarcón examines the assumptions about Chicana identities by Mexican and European participants, "The fact that one needs 'signs of identity' should tip us off to the requirements of subordination to the nation-state that (non)citizens must comply with and the fact that inside/outside/inside occupied by Chicanas is not just symbolic but sociopolitical as well . . . Racism (or the particular historical constructions of mexicanness) makes her subject to a constant demand for the production (proof) of 'ethnic' identity and citizenship in both Mexico and the United States."[45] However, it cannot be denied that United States citizenship is a privilege that carries with it inextricable cultural capital. In her critique of upper-middle-class Mexican feminist writers, Alarcón continues, "Few upperclass Latin American women would admit to being a colleague to someone who could have been the household maid but for the grace of a minoritizing education in the United States."[46] These concerns are primarily introduced by Chicana intellectuals, like Alarcón, who situate the history of Chicana cultural production in working-class communities. In October of 2001, a colloquium entitled "Miradas Cruzadas" in Oaxaca brought together Chicana and Mexican visual and performance artists, Jesusa Rodríguez and Celia Herrera-Rodríguez among them. Echoing Alarcón's class critique, Moraga's response to the gathering was quoted in Mexican newspaper *La Jornada: "Una de las primeras ponentes fue Cherrie Moraga, quien nos recibió diciendo que ellas, las chicanas, eran las hijas de nuestras sirvientas."*[47]

To whom would a queer Chicana Coatlicue rattle off in the United States, as Jesusa Rodríguez did in Mexico City? Except that in the United States, Chicanas *have* often written against Chicana/o nationalist discourse, making critical interventions and altering the very trajectory of that discourse. In her foundational essay "Queer Aztlán," Cherríe Moraga challenges the heterosexist and monolithic legacies of Chicano nationalism and re-envisions the discourse of the nation: "The nationalism I seek is one that decolonizes the brown and female earth as it decolonizes the brown and female body. It is a new nationalism in which la Chicana Indígena stands at the center, and heterosexism and homophobia are no longer the cultural order of the day. I cling to the word 'nation' because without the specific naming of the nation, the nation will be lost."[48] The nation-state of México is not the site for this critical (re)imagining by Chicana cultural producers like Moraga and Herrera-Rodríguez. Herrera-Rodríguez's identification as a queer Chicana/Tepehuana artist operates both within and against ideological discrepancies of the national discourse that excludes her power as speaking subject on both sides of the border. My discussion of the class critique by Chicanas in transnational contexts is not intended to posit an oppositional framework; the accounts of these *encuentros* also acknowledge the feminist solidarity of Chicana and Mexican feminist writers, or what Norma Alarcón identifies as "an alternative discursive site."[49]

The aesthetic approaches of both artists and their respective points of entry position them as distinct in their identities as Mexican and Chicana/Indígena. Jesusa Rodríguez performs Indigenous iconography as political satire, positioning her critique within the rhetoric and legacy of Mexican national identity and against the symbolics of the state. Celia Herrera-Rodríguez performatively reclaims specific Indigenous practices as personal legacy rooted in transformative political power within Chicana/o communities. By positioning their bodies as canvases on which to contest elements of sexist, racist, homophobic, and colonial legacies that expose the trajectory of the conquest to contemporary neoliberalism, Jesusa Rodríguez and Celia Herrera-Rodríguez interrogate and deconstruct the power of those collective cultural inheritances.

EPILOGUE

The Wednesday after George W. Bush won re-election, I was up before sunrise working on a presentation about the Huarochirí Manuscript, an ancient Andean story of the *huacas* and how the land got made. The two-hundred-page document has extensive footnotes detailing the monumental task of translation, from the struggles of interpreting Quechua semantics to the task of exposing words that the Spanish simply refused to use from the original Quechua document (usually references to the human body that transcend stable biological explanations). One of the words that translators consistently stumbled on is "*huaca,*" which simply fails to be translated as "deity," as it could function as a child or an aqueduct or a llama or a mountain. With Father Francisco de Avila standing over their shoulders, the Andean scribes documented the intricate sacred practices and stories of their land—the energized matter to whom they offered their labor and prayers—so that Avila would know *exactly* what to destroy in the Indigenous communities. As I sat there shivering in a corner of the twenty-four-hour section of the library, the text quickly and viscerally humbled me. I reflected on how the collections of sacred images and spirit-practices survived ravaging fires and multiple trips across expansive bodies of water, how they functioned as toys to the children of various European royal families. The obvious was (re)affirmed in every part of my body: in documenting our struggles to remember our own *huacas*—whether embodied or inscribed or inscribed on our bodies—we are creating new *códices*.[50] As Cherríe Moraga affirms, "A codex is a history told and foretold."[51] And some of the palimpsests will transcend translation except to those who need to hunger to remember, those who are looking for answers and those who interrogate the very posing of the questions.

In creating our post-conquest *códices,* we write, dance, paint, sing, drum, or weave knots into rope because we remember in our bodies and with our bodies. These performative interventions operate as ways of knowing. Our rites take multiple forms on our journeys toward home, or our sometimes painful affirmation of the authority to remember our own Indigeneity or diasporic subjectivities.

NOTES

1. Tepehuanes are an Indigenous group from northwestern México along the Sierra Madre Occidental.

2. Roselyn Costantino, "Jesusa Rodríguez: An Inconvenient Woman," *Women and Performance: A Journal of Feminist Theory* 11.2 (2000), 186.

3. Jean Franco, "A Touch of Evil: Jesusa Rodríguez's Subversive Church," in *Negotiating Performance: Gender, Sexuality, and Theatricality in Latin/o America,* Ed. Diana Taylor and Juan Villegas (Durham, NC: Duke University Press, 1994), 163.

4. Diana Taylor, *The Archive and the Repertoire: Performing Cultural Memory in the Americas.* (Durham, NC: Duke University Press, 2003), 50.

5. See Laura Pérez's *Chicana Art: The Politics of Spiritual and Aesthetic Altarities* (2007), Irma Mayorga's Stanford University dissertation, "Constructing Stages of Hope: Performance and Theatricality in the Aesthetic Logics of Chicana Expressive Culture" (2005), and Constance Cortez's "History/Whose-History? Postcoloniality and Contemporary Chicana Art" in *Chicana/Latina Studies* 6.2 (2007).

6. Taylor, *The Archive and the Repertoire,* 15.

7. I employ the word "Mexica" as opposed to "Aztec" because the latter term was introduced in the "nineteenth century by European and Anglo-American anthropologists and archaeologists; 'Mexica' probably more closely resembles the name by which the 'Aztecs' referred to themselves." Sheila Marie Contreras, *Blood Lines: Myth, Indigenism, and Chicana/o Literature* (Austin: University of Texas Press, 2008), 168, n.5.

8. Coatlicue is the Aztec Mexica "mother" goddess of Aztec deities of the moon and the sun, Coyolxauhqui and Huitzilopochtli. She is often represented as a female figure wearing a necklace made of human hands, skulls, and hearts as well as a skirt of serpents. The monolithic statue in the National Museum of Anthropology was discovered in 1790.

9. "The Mammary Tour of Coatlicue."

10. Taylor, *The Archive and the Repertoire,* 50.

11. Taylor, *The Archive and the Repertoire,* 19.

12. National Museum of Anthropology.

13. Franco, "A Touch of Evil," 174–175. Franco translates the first line from "Óiganme bien, mexicanos, mexiquenses, mejicones, mejidatarios y extranjenses!"

14. In 1938, the first government-supported organization, Instituto Naçional de Antropologia e Historia (INAH), was founded under the Ministry of Education. In 1964, the Museo Nacional de Antropología was opened in Mexico City's Parque Chapultepec. In 1972, legislation was passed decreeing that all archaeological artifacts found in México are part of a national heritage and that any lands containing archaeological remains become national property.

15. Javier Sanjinés, *Mestizaje Upside-Down: Aesthetic Politics in Modern Bolivia* (Pittsburgh, PA: University of Pittsburgh, 2004), 9.

16. María Josefina Saldaña-Portillo, "In the Shadow of NAFTA: Y tu mama tambien Revisits the National Allegory of Mexican Sovereignty," *American Quarterly* 57.3, September 2005, 762.

17. Manuel Aguilar-Moreno, *Handbook to Life in the Aztec World* (New York: Facts on File, 2006), 21.

18. Contreras, *Blood Lines: Myth, Indigenism, and Chicana/o Literature,* 25.

19. Ibid.

20. A popular brass-based musical genre originally from the northern Mexican state of Sinaloa famous for its high-energy syncopation and dancing.

21. Jesusa Rodríguez and Liliana Felipe, "Cabaret Pre-Hispanico," Brava for Women in the Arts Center, San Francisco, California, November 19, 2004.

22. In November of 2004, I participated in a cabaret workshop with Rodriguez and Felipe, and we literally referred to the *San Francisco Chronicle* as a source for performance material.

23. Costantino, "Jesusa Rodríguez: An Inconvenient Woman," 192.

24. James C. Scott, *Domination and the Arts of Resistance* (New Haven, CT: Yale University Press, 1990), 4.

25. Pérez, *Chicana Art*, 157.

26. Celia Herrera-Rodríguez, "Altar as Performance," Nitery Theater, Stanford University, Stanford, California, November 22, 2004.

27. Sanjinés, *Mestizaje Upside-Down: Aesthetic Politics in Modern Bolivia*, 5.

28. Indigenous textile/tunic or blouse worn traditionally in Southern México and Northern Central America.

29. Mayorga, "Constructing Stages of Hope," 108.

30. Mayorga, "Constructing Stages of Hope," 36.

31. Guillermo Bonfil Batalla, *México Profundo: Reclaiming a Civilization*, Trans. Philip A. Dennis (Austin: University of Texas Press, 1996), 29.

32. Taylor, *The Archive and the Repertoire*, 20.

33. Pérez, *Chicana Art*, 159.

34. Laura Gutiérrez, "Deconstructing the Mythical Homeland: Mexico in Contemporary Chicana Performance," in *Velvet Barrios: Popular Culture and Chicano/a Sexualities*, Ed. Alicia Gaspar de Alba (New York: Palgrave Macmillan, 2003), 63.

35. Herrera-Rodríguez, "Altar as Performance," 2004.

36. Ibid.

37. Emma Pérez, *The Decolonial Imaginary: Writing Chicanas into History* (Bloomington: Indiana University Press, 1999), 6.

38. Ancient Mesoamerican instrument made of volcanic rock used to grind corn.

39. From Herrera-Rodríguez's performance at the 2001 "Miradas Cruzadas" colloquium in Oaxaca.

40. Anna Sandoval, "Unir los Lazos: Braiding Chicana and Mexicana Subjectivities," in *Decolonial Voices: Chicana and Chicano Cultural Studies in the 21st Century* (Bloomington: Indiana University Press, 2002), 45.

41. At this moment in the performance, Rodríguez and Felipe have just mourned the increase in transgenic corn products, echoing the lament in Herrera-Rodríguez's performance.

42. Iztaccihuatl was the daughter of an Aztec emperor in the Valley of México. After falling in love with one of her father's warriors, he sent her lover away to a war in Oaxaca. He told the young man that if he survived and returned, he would give him Iztaccihuatl as his wife. The emperor never intended for the young warrior to return, as he planned to marry Iztaccihuatl to another man. While her lover was away, Iztaccihuatl was told he was dead, and she died of grief. Upon the young warrior's return, he took Iztaccihuatl's body in his arms and carried her to the mountains. He placed her down on the ground and knelt beside her, himself dying of grief. The gods took pity on them, covering them with a blanket of snow and transforming them into mountains. Iztaccihuatl today is known as the "Sleeping Woman," as the mountain looks like a woman lying on her side. He became Popocatepetl, or "Smoking Mountain," the volcano that still rains down his revenge for the death of his lover.

43. "You are the same. You are the same as me."

44. Among them are "Literatura Escrita Por Mujeres Chicanas" from June 24–25 at UNAM in Mexico City as well as *coloquios* in Tijuana, Baja California, in 1987, 1988, and 1989 at El Colegio de México y El Colegio de la Frontera Norte.

45. Norma Alarcón, "Interlocutions: An Afterword to the Coloquio," in *Las Formas de Nuestras Voces: Chicana and MeChicana Writers in Mexico,* Ed. Claire Joysmith (México: Universidad Nacional Autónoma de México, Centro de Investigaciones sobre América del Norte, 1995), 71.

46. Alarcón, "Interlocutions," 71.

47. "One of the first presenters was Cherríe Moraga who said that Chicanas were the daughters of our servants," by Mónica Monica, in "Pobreza, racismo, y machismo: triple discrimanación contra artistas indígenas," http://www.jornada.unam.mx/2002/dic02/021202/articulos/52_arts_indias.htm, March 13, 2005.

48. Cherríe Moraga, *The Last Generation: Prose and Poetry* (Boston: South End Press, 1993), 150.

49. Alarcón, "Interlocutions," 277.

50. Or in the case of ancient Andean communities, *qhipus,* collections of knotted ropes that served as textual archives.

51. Cherríe Moraga, "A Xicanadyke Codex of Changing Consciousness," in *Sing Whisper Shout Pray: Feminist Visions for a Just World,* Ed. M. Jacqui Alexander, Lisa Albrecht, Sharon Day, and Mab Segrest (New York: Edge World Press, 2003), 202.

REFERENCES

Aguilar-Moreno, Manuel. *Handbook to Life in the Aztec World.* New York: Facts on File, 2006.

Alarcón, Norma. "Interlocutions: An Afterword to the Coloquio," in *Las Formas de Nuestras Voces: Chicana and MeChicana Writers in Mexico.* Ed. Claire Joysmith. México: Universidad Nacional Autónoma de México, Centro de Investigaciones sobre América del Norte, 1995.

Bonfil Batalla, Guillermo. *México Profundo: Reclaiming a Civilization.* Trans. Philip A. Dennis. Austin: University of Texas Press, 1996.

Contreras, Sheila Marie. *Blood Lines: Myth, Indigenism, and Chicana/o Literature.* Austin: University of Texas Press, 2008

Costantino, Roselyn. "Jesusa Rodríguez: An Inconvenient Woman." *Women and Performance: A Journal of Feminist Theory* 11.2 (2000): 183–212.

———. "Uncovering and Displaying Our Universes: Jesusa Rodríguez in/on Mexico," in *The Color of Theater: Race, Culture, and Contemporary Performance.* Ed. Roberta Uno and Lucy Mae San Pablo Burns. London: Athlone Press, 2002.

Franco, Jean. "A Touch of Evil: Jesusa Rodríguez's Subversive Church," in *Negotiating Performance: Gender, Sexuality, and Theatricality in Latin/o America.* Ed. Diana Taylor and Juan Villegas. Durham, NC: Duke University Press, 1994.

Gutiérrez, Laura. "Deconstructing the Mythical Homeland: Mexico in Contemporary Chicana Performance," in *Velvet Barrios: Popular Culture and Chicano/a*

Sexualities. Ed. Alicia Gaspar de Alba. New York: Palgrave Macmillan, 2003.

Mayorga, Irma. "Constructing Stages of Hope: Performance and Theatricality in the Aesthetic Logics of Chicana Expressive Culture" Ph.D Dissertation, Stanford University, 2005.

Moraga, Cherríe. *The Last Generation: Prose and Poetry*. Boston: South End Press, 1993.

———. "A Xicanadyke Codex of Changing Consciousness," in *Sing Whisper Shout Pray: Feminist Visions for a Just World*. Ed. M. Jacqui Alexander, Lisa Albrecht, Sharon Day, and Mab Segrest. New York: Edge World Press, 2003.

Pérez, Emma. *The Decolonial Imaginary: Writing Chicanas into History*. Bloomington: Indiana University Press, 1999.

Pérez, Laura. *Chicana Art: The Politics of Spiritual and Aesthetic Altarities*. Durham, NC: Duke University Press, 2007.

Rodríguez, Celia Herrera. "Altar as Performance," Nitery Theater, Stanford University, Stanford, California, November 22, 2004.

Rodríguez, Jesusa, and Liliana Felipe. "Cabaret Pre-Hispanico," Brava for Women in the Arts Center, San Francisco, California, November 19, 2004.

Saldaña-Portillo, María Josefina. "In the Shadow of NAFTA: Y tu mama tambien Revisits the National Allegory of Mexican Sovereignty." *American Quarterly* 57.3 (September 2005): 751–777.

Sandoval, Anna. "Unir los Lazos: Braiding Chicana and Mexicana Subjectivities," in *Decolonial Voices: Chicana and Chicano Cultural Studies in the 21st Century*. Bloomington: Indiana University Press, 2002.

Sanjinés, Javier. *Mestizaje Upside-Down: Aesthetic Politics in Modern Bolivia*. Pittsburgh, PA: University of Pittsburgh, 2004.

Scott, James C. *Domination and the Arts of Resistance*. New Haven, CT: Yale University Press, 1990.

Taylor, Diana. *The Archive and the Repertoire: Performing Cultural Memory in the Americas*. Durham, NC: Duke University Press, 2003.

TWO

Milongueando Macha Homoerotics: Dancing the Tango, Torta Style (a Performative Testimonio)

MARIA LUGONES

I have spent most of my life thinking up close to and in the middle of people, people to people. Recently I have been looking at the need to rethink gender in a historical and global manner so that one could no longer separate gender, class, sexuality, and race but could not think of them as intersecting, either. The relation of intersection still requires conceptually separable entities, categories. Today I said to myself, "Let's think about the tango with these things in mind and see what I can make of it without losing a sense of the erotic."

I am someone with an intimate connection with tango style, music, dance, lyrics, its lived geography, both from within circles of affection and from within the moving anonymous encounters of the street, the milongas, tango bars like chapels where one listens to someone sing, getting in touch with the sacred within pain. I am also a witness to the development of tango tourism.

Robert Duval, an american tango aficionado and a self-proclaimed authority on the tango, confuses it with a dance and finds its attraction in the impression that "here is a people that know that men are men and women are women and are not all embarrassed about it," a claim he makes with a great sense of pride of having found a people so close to his own sensibilities. By this he means that men lead—on the floor of life as it were—and women follow, in a debased sense of the word. The tango for him is a dance understood to be a quintessentially heterosexual performance of the active/submissive understanding of masculinity/femininity. No sexual ambiguities, thus no ambiguities about agency. I want to think about the logic of tango here as a more complex phenomenon than the one tango tourism sells.

But first let me make a detour through Jorge Luis Borges's affinity with Robert Duval. Though Borges is not really into women. The women disappear from his tango lyrics, as the tango is an affair of men, where women—despised, abject, passive, absurdly mindless beings—disappear altogether from the picture.

Here is Borges:

Tango que he visto bailar contra un ocaso Amarillo,

Por quienes eran capaces de otro baile, el del cuchillo . . . (Alguien le dice al tango)

I have seen tango danced against the shadow producing background of yellow sunsets by those capable of another dance, that of the knife [my translation]

Me acuerdo, fue en Balvanera, en una noche lejana, que alguien dejo caer el nombre de un tal jacinto Chiclana. Algo se dijo tambien de una esquina y de un cuchillo. Los anos no dejan ver el entrevero y el brillo. (Jacinto Chiclana)

I remember: it was in Balvanera, a night, long ago, when someone dropped the name of a Jacinto Chicana. The years obscure the embrace of the fight and the shine of the blade. [my translation]

A un compadrito le canto . . .

Como luz para el manejo, le marcaba un garabato en la cara al mas garifo, de un solo brinco, a lo gato. (El titere)

I sing to a compadrito . . .

He was like lightning handling the knife, with one jump, cat-like, he would cut a crude drawing on the face of the most garifo. [my translation]

Borges imagines the spatiality of tango as a explosive mimicry of male-on-male violence. Before the immigration wave at the turn of the twentieth century, the tango had a storyline of masculine prowess. Borges was enthralled by this inhabitation of masculinity, which he saw as emblematic of the salvajismo he celebrated in his adoption of Sarmiento's dichotomy between civilization y barbarism: knife duels among men, the shine of the blade, blood, love expressed as honor and revenge, a willingness to kill. His own tangos consistently take up this theme. This is nostalgic in two ways. First, there is nostalgia for the hegemony of a view of marginalized men as barbaric, intrinsically violent, whose dexterity with the knife is their essence. And second, nostalgia for a time in the history of the tango, before the immigration wave of the end of the nineteenth century, when tango lyrics celebrated marginal men's negotiation of the bajo fondo, the limits of the city of Buenos Aires, where deep poverty dictated a violent negotiation for survival. Borges did not see these conditions as what called for violence; violence, rather, is for him the essence of autochthonous masculinity. Now the violence has escalated, but in the tango and in the society, the time for individual male heroes killing each other to exercise their essence has passed. Yet this is what tango tourism sells. But it sells it as a stereotypically heterosexual dance.

If the tango is a choreography of male-on-male violence, it would make sense when two men dance that the woman be thought of as irrelevant or as passive, the occasion for male activity, for initiative. Men dancing in the prostibules waiting for putas is part of that image. The puta, as I see her, is a woman who lets herself be fucked for money without putting out anything but the smallest amount of energy. So, if sex is a wasteful outburst of energy, la puta puts out in a survival mode, while the men are fighting out in an explosive homoerotic choreography. Male-on-male initiative fits the logic of spatial initiative required by tango as a dance, but that male heroism no longer fits the cityscapes that lived tango takes up.

The male/male/puta irrelevant trio was never in the dance. Because as so described, la puta can't dance, move, occupy space in the way that constitutes the dance. It is too intelligent a dance. Estela Arcos, a tango choreographer, said to me, "El tango as a dance is a problem que se resuelve entre dos." She also says that one dances it from within extreme emotional attention to the music. I want to add some descriptive reflections of what I learned from dancing the tango. Then I want to add some of the elements that constitute the mere focus on movement without geography and geography without meaning as misguided and as fitting rather the idealized tourist fuck out of time and space. If tango tourism sells the stereotyping of gender that I describe here, and that stereotyping constitutes the dances as a rehearsing of sex, and the dance takes the ones who "follow" to be quasi-inanimate, passive, then the tourist can only be "satisfied" if he is satisfied with very little, or if his desire is a necrophiliac's desire. But notice that it's all in his head.

TANGO EROTICS: DE A DOS

I learn that tango is always spoken as if "he" is the only one responsible, but I learned to dance the falsehood of that. As we dance, we do mirror each other. I indicate my intentions in movement with my chest, not with my eyes, or with the forcefulness of the embrace. A firm, open suggestion for you to mirror what I will design on the floor. I ask, intimate, propose; you respond. There is no reason why this should be a closed circle. There is no reason why the intentionality and the activity of the one who responds needs to be interpreted as passivity, nor why the logic of the relation is one of "following." The logic of indicating intention is not restricted to following. But following itself is intelligent, embodied reading and response. The sense that the logic of the relation only calls for following presupposes that the one who responds cannot also suggest movement. But since the intimation requires response rather passive movement, it requires keen attention to the embodied intentionality of the other, and thus the attention can be mutual.

To follow in dance, as in living with others, can mean to come after with one's own thing, to understand the embodied thought and respond, or to thoughtlessly do whatever one is asked to do. Even the last one requires bodily intelligence. I studied this logic as a torta, a lesbian woman who attempts to reject the exercise of the tyrannies of learned male forcefulness on another through the dancing of the tango. I just see men pushing women around on the dance floor as bad dancers. I think of dancing the tango as an erotic pastime, a coming into a knowledge of each other's bodies, of each other's bodily intelligence.

I go to the milongas, and I know that many men believe the tango is danced by forcing the woman to move like a marionette. Even further, many men believe that when you dance and you feel no resistance, then you are leading a passive creature. Such a man has no sense of the bodily intelligence that it takes for a woman to respond so precisely that there is almost no time in between his intimating his intention and her response.

He is aroused by her abandonment, her loss of will, the sense that she is not quite alive. He moves her body.

I think that there is something interesting, rather, in being aroused by the response, by the willful being-with-you in the moving, often anonymously, in a brief encounter. It is more complicated than moving alone, than moving with a solipsistic understanding of the dance. It is interesting that the logic of the dance does not allow for the solipsistic possibility. Yet as men show off before each other on the floor, they make up the dance as a performance of domination. The masculine arrogance in heterosexual eroticism makes a man believe himself to be someone who moves a non-willing being masterfully, dominates her completely, and makes her do whatever he wants. He moves her body. This is what tango tourism sells. But all he gets for his money is to fuck a woman who is intelligently conserving her energies for better things.

TORTA STYLE TANGO

[Dance performance here: smooth, symmetrical, mirrored, role reversal call and response]

My sister came to class for the first time. She was trying out the steps with me. At some point, several couples were asked to demonstrate, and we did. Not an easy combination. Then we went back to dancing. A guy asks her to dance and pushes her around and tells her: You looked as if you knew how to dance just now. What happened?

A spatial problem to be resolved between two people. It is to the style of posing the problem and figuring out its resolution that I address myself now. In doing so, I want to blend this problem with the spatiality of the emotions in tango lyrics, paying very close attention to the relation between pain and space.

The dance encounter can certainly be anonymous. It is most of the time. It is also intelligent. The knowing is fleetingly and excruciatingly embodied—it requires all of one's embodied attention. The exchange of gestures is complex, not particularly filled with meaning, self-contained in an open way. The anonymity is really important in highlighting the logic. There is a complex reading of movement, or there is a reductive one. The logic of reduction is doll making, *titereteando la relación*. The complex reading follows the fleeting, highly embodied movement that is not as focused on meaning as on the syncopated 4/4 that marks the encounter of the tango. Thus the communicative reading of each other amounts not to getting into each other's heads but into each other's moving bodies. The complex reading follows the partners' moving bodies, resolving the problems with which a particular tango circumscribes their movements. The problem is posed by a number of elements:

*The background place remembered by the words of the song. The space is an aspect of the space in which you move during the dance. It is a space you come to partially inhabit: the urban space of loneliness, of poverty tied to place, of the longing for belonging, of the harsh processes of falling into many forms of self-destruction, of the many forms of pain that make up loving, all spatialized in forceful sketches of quotidian spaces. A familiar yet despairing geography. You move within your everyday spatiality into this heightened spatiality of social pain.

GARUA (CADÍCAMO) *Garúa . . . /Solo y triste por la acera/Va este corazón transido/Con tristeza de tapera . . .*

Its raining a fine mist and there is this heart, alone and sad, moving on the sidewalk/ cut through and through with pain for home

Qué noche llena de hastío . . . y de frio . . . /No se ve a nadie cruzar por la esquina . . . /Sobre la calle, la hilera de focos,/lustra el asfalto con luz mortecina

A cold night, filled with chilled boredom, no one around, the line of lights hovering over the street, polishing the asphalt with a mournful light

*There is also your own understanding of who you are with respect to the man/woman binary in doing what you do, dancing in the circle of suggesting, initiating, taking in, and responding. In the milongas, we all watch people dance to learn this and to ponder whether we want an encounter with the styling of gender or of gender defiance they represent.

*And there is your own living and an exploration of how you can spatialize that living in movement. How well you can express intentions in an embodied way, conversationally or solipsistically.

*And there is also each person's ability, intelligence, in understanding proposals of movement and intelligence in understanding the moving, moving with and in response. As you think about this element of the problem, watch it in slow motion and see the proposal and the response; catch the nuances of intelligence (or its absence).

Tango dancing in the torta style is good cruising practice: it hones your intelligence in movement, in gestural communication within a spatiality that remakes/rejects the suffocating, closed, bound, dumb, normed spatiality of oppressions. One gets practice in bodily comportment as one cruises, moving from hangout to hangout, throwing out (life)lines, taking some things out of the mix and reading in others.

Pero en la milonga, a pesar de esta riqueza en mis pasos, por el miedo a la transgresión erótica te da miedo o asco bailar conmigo. But in the milonga, in spite of this richness in my step, because of your fear of erotic transgression, you are afraid of or repulsed by my embodied solicitation.

REFERENCES

Jorge Luis Borges, "Alguien le dice al tango," with music by Astor Piazzola. In *4 Canciones Porteñas,* Editorial Pigal.

———, "Jacinto Chicana," with music by Astor Piazzola. In *4 Canciones Porteñas,* Editorial Pigal.

———, "El Titere," with music by Astor Piazzola. In *4 Canciones Porteñas,* Editorial Pigal.

Enrique Cadicamo, "Garúa," with music by Anibal Troilo, Editorial Musical Korn-Intersong S.A.I.C.

Sarmiento, Domingo Faustino (2003). *Facundo: Civilization and Barbarism,* trans. Kathleen Ross, Berkeley: University of California Press (published first in 1845).

THREE

The Other Train That Derails Us: Performing Latina Anxiety Disorder in "The Night before Christmas"

ANGIE CHABRAM-DERNERSESIAN

> Anxiety is an activation of our senses and our physical readiness so we can assess our surroundings or look for dangers—and so we can be more ready to run or fight. Like the flashing red lights and crossing guards that come down over a railroad track when the train—still miles away—goes over a switch.
>
> DR. J., "ANXIETY, PRACTICALLY SPEAKING"

After a hard day's work, Doña Elena sits down to watch her favorite *telenovela,* armed with a piping hot cup of *café con leche* (coffee with milk) and her favorite *pan dulce* (pastry). She has much company in this much-awaited daily ritual, according to transnational studies of Spanish media culture (see, e.g., LaPastina n.d.).[1] Across Latina/o America, viewers of Spanish-language television—men, women, and children alike—join her in savoring yet another installment of this hugely popular televisual genre.

In this particular instance, not long after a reprise of the previous day's melodramatic plot line, Doña Elena's television ritual is rudely interrupted by a program change. In a programmed announcement, Doña Elena and her fellow viewers are met head-on with the image of a larger-than-life train that threatens to barrel out of control, lunging out of the small screen and engulfing their bodies, spirits, and home spaces. The burning light of the train offers no escape from televisual darkness or human entrapment. Viewers are thus caught unawares, somehow right in front of the path of the monumental, horrific train, provoking a primal urge to flee or seek protection—what therapists call the "flight syndrome."[2]

Confronted with this instance of unwelcome participatory spectatorship, viewers of Spanish-language television, who are also longtime connoisseurs of Mexican art, sense that this is not the "familiar" train that accompanies heroic Mexican figures in restaurants, books, and films. In the menacing image that penetrates this particular domestic realm, Latina/o viewers are confronted with an antagonist (the train) that has the upper hand and occupies an extensive social, ideological, and symbolic panorama. Here, viewers of Spanish-language television are incorporated into a televisual spectacle where the traditional narrative of machismo and valor is supplanted by one of fear and possible victimization—emotions that have no place in the fiercely nationalistic Latina/o landscape of archetypal political struggles and icons. To the viewers' relief, however, this troubling and unfamiliar scenario vanishes almost as quickly as it appears. A question appears in small print at the bottom of the TV screen: "¿Padece Ud. del trastorno de pánico?" (Do you suffer from panic disorder?)

Viewers like Doña Elena relax: what they are watching is a public service announcement informing the Spanish-language public of this ailment and offering a hotline number for those who need help. The advertisement has simply made TV viewers *feel as if* they have experienced a panic/anxiety attack in the intimacy of their own homes. The train is a metaphor for anxiety illness, an ailment that can plague its sufferers and their families for life if not treated.

In the Spanish-language virtual culture of the Internet, people coping with this ailment offer testimonials that describe anxiety disorder in equally frightening terms: "Todo ocurre de repente, siento una tremenda ola de miedo sin ningún tipo de razón. Mi corazón comienza a agitarse, me duele el pecho, y me cuesta respirar. Todo lo que pienso es que voy a morir." ("It happens all of a sudden, I feel a huge wave of fear without any rhyme or reason. My heart starts pounding, my chest hurts, and I have difficulty breathing. All I can think of is that I'm going to die." [Hendrix n.d.]).

Recent literature on the topic suggests that we live in an "age of anxiety" and that "chronic anxiety is the most ubiquitous yet least recognized psychiatric condition in America today" (Davidson and Dreher 2003, 3–4). In addition, "At least 19 million Americans suffer from anxiety disorders—even more than those who suffer from depression" (3). Not surprisingly, English-language media now pay substantial attention to anxiety disorders within commercials or print advertisements sponsored by pharmaceutical companies that supply testimonials from people who couldn't do various activities out of fear, social anxiety, or generalized anxiety—but now can, thanks to the companies' medications!

Delving into the multiethnic social contexts of this disorder through commercials and popular self-help literature is challenging. Both genres are notorious for their limited discussions of the social contexts of communities whose members have anxiety/panic disorders. What abounds are general discussions of symptoms and anxiety triggers such as stress, workaholism, illness, perfectionism, familial disposition toward anxiety, chemical imbalances, intake of caffeine, poor eating and sleeping habits, and so on.

Clearly, alternative forms of health literacy are required that can expand the zones of engagement available for public discussion of this widespread ailment. Toward this end, my essay recuperates a narrative performance of Latina anxiety disorder though an analysis of a story that revolves around an impoverished Latina whose family supplements seasonal farm labor with work in the service and domestic sectors. The story in question, "The Night before Christmas," is an important part of Tomás Rivera's classic text . . . *Y no se lo tragó la tierra/ . . . And the Earth Did Not Devour Him* (1971).

For years, critics have described . . . *Y no se lo tragó la tierra* as a work that sets into motion the dynamics of contemporary Chicana/o literature. What is understated in the scholarship base is that Rivera provides another important legacy—an early representation of Latina anxiety disorder that is valuable for contemporary readers who seek to view and understand anxiety within particular gendered ethnic and class contexts. This representation incorporates an important journey to a Kress department store that highlights not only Latina anxiety disorders but also instances of Latina self-determination. However, it does not provide a sustained challenge to patriarchal, capitalist kinship arrangements and their discourses about women's places in society.

In this essay, I am as much interested in illustrating how anxiety disorder can be read through gender(ed) social relations and places of habitation as I am in confirming the idea that (Chicana/o) literature is a signifying (meaning-producing) performative textual practice that transcends academic and popular compartmentalization. Indeed, literature incorporates vital links to culture, the economy, society, health, storytelling, experiential knowledge, and family.

MEETING THE TRAIN HEAD-ON IN LITERATURE: DOÑA MARÍA'S *FRIGHTENING JOURNEY TO KRESS*

. . . *Y no se lo tragó la tierra* is a book with strong testimonial overtones that "records many things that are seen as well as heard" in an effort to make sense of the campesina/o experience within a transnational US Latina/o agricultural and familial context. This book records the downside of Christmas in the United States for the working poor and the anxiety driven through the story of Doña María's frightening journey to Kress.

Like many of her compatriots, Doña María suffers from panic disorder as well as agoraphobia, which is often described as "fear of the market place" or fear of being "stuck in situations you cannot easily escape" or control, such as "crowded spaces," open spaces, or the "outside world" (Davidson and Dreher 2003, 51). Doña María is increasingly confined to her home because she avoids public places such as downtown Wilmar, Minnesota, and situations such as streets where her anxiety has soared in the past. Following the insights of Lisa Capps and Elinor Ochs in *Constructing Panic,* it is clear that Doña María's ailment is most appropriately described as a fear of being anyplace where she "might feel alone and vulnerable to fear and panic" (1996, 3). Yet Doña María's "frightening" ailment—which is notably omitted from Paul Espinosa's widely celebrated film version of Rivera's novel—deviates from popular clinical and ethnographic portraits of people with agoraphobia in a number of ways. For example, as a campesina, Doña María lives in a highly mobile and unpredictable agricultural context where workers must move continuously from place to place—this is a fact of life and survival. For people like her, who must follow the crops, there is no such thing as a "stable phobic nest" like the ones described in the Western, Eurocentric psychological literature on agoraphobia. This literature—including self-help books—often describes a comfortable "retreat"—a room or house of one's own—where the anxious human subject can seek refuge when fear and discomfort mount to intolerable levels. For the Latina protagonist of this story, however, the conditions of life and work in the fields, the inability to really get to know a place, and the lack of resources all aggravate her condition until she remains field- and homebound in a notoriously mobile transitional space that offers little stability or protection from the outside world.[3] Her condition is summed up by the idea expressed in the latter part of . . . *Y no se lo tragó la tierra.* Here, the campesinos lament that they move and move, and they dream of moving, yet they are still stuck: they never quite arrive at their destination. Poverty, illness, poor working conditions, exploitation, discrimination, and the demand for cheap seasonal labor offer these farmworkers few opportunities for social mobility or a "house of their own." In the case of Doña María, this is tantamount to being stuck and fearful in a place that is neither safe nor private and is marked by social, institutional, economic, and gender constraints.

"The Night before Christmas" also challenges in other meaningful ways the strict divisions between the public and the private that are fundamental to current understandings of agoraphobia.[4] From the very beginning, readers are informed that the borders of the Latina/o family and of Latinas with agoraphobia are indeed permeable—that the family is susceptible to what goes on in the outside world. To elaborate, in the first sentence of the story there is an allusion to circuits of culture (the radio and the honking of a truck that announces movie commercials for the Teatro Ideal) that seem to "push" Doña María to the marketplace with "song, *business* and blessings."[5] The children of the family are also privy to the far-reaching effects of a consumer-driven media culture that awakens unrealistic expectations in them around Christmastime.

Saturated with this culture, the children want gifts instead of a sack of oranges and nuts for Christmas; they want to celebrate Christmas rather than the Mexican holiday Los Reyes;[6] and they want a visit from the gift-giving Santa, not the food-giving Don Chon—their father. In effect, these children serve as emissaries of commercial circuits of culture to the immigrant farmworker family. Not only do they formulate rhetorical arguments (another cultural circuit) in favor of a Christmas experience that includes gift giving and shopping, but they refute the annual parental discourse that urges patience and directs them to Los Reyes. The children also echo an idea from "'Twas the Night before Christmas": that good children (like them) should get gifts.

In this story, it is up to Doña María to negotiate different transnational cultural rituals, an economic situation that has made it impossible to buy gifts previously, a cultural economy that demands not only cultural but also capitalist assimilation, and an anxiety disorder that has rendered her housebound in a highly public, media-saturated transitional migrant space. If in the past Doña María has ignored her children's pleas and placed economic necessity over their desires and US Christmas rituals, in the present she is no longer able to do so. Painfully aware that her children have come of age and have been affected by the American way, she lets go of her rationalization that they don't need anything for Christmas, and in an effort to do good and achieve the impossible for her children, she makes up her mind to buy them something even "though they don't have money for toys" (Rivera 1987, 130). The strain generated by the children's demands, her desire to please them at all costs, and the economic requirements of labor and cultural consumerism are played up for the reader, who is told that eighteen hours of work cooking and washing dishes won't pay for the toys but rather for a much-needed, life-sustaining trip to Iowa for more seasonal work. Nonetheless, Doña María insists on buying toys for her adored children in order to appease them and enable them to partake in an annual cultural ritual along with other children of their ages.

But in order to do so, she must win the consent of her husband, who "arrives tired after work," doesn't believe the children need anything, and made his own toys as a child in México. As in many traditional Latino households, where the father is emotionally distant from or inaccessible to the children because he is either feared or has a socially privileged position in the family, the mother intercedes on behalf of the children, who do not speak for themselves and must rely on indirect female discourse. And intercede she does. Like her children, Doña María responds to his arguments by articulating a counter-discourse that focuses on the importance of "desire" over "need." Yet her arguments differ from theirs in a substantial way: *she* insists that children need presents (their desire) because "*here* things are different from there" (México) and because here "the children *see* many things." In this way, not only does she play up the shaping influence of social environment (i.e., the US cultural and national space) on the family but she herself becomes a cultural emissary and circulates dominant societal conceptualizations about Christmas and cultural practice to the immigrant father in an effort to convince him. Finally, she prevails in her rhetorical arguments and, despite leading a circumscribed and agoraphobic life, declares, "I'll go to Kress *myself*."

With this declaration of her intent to exit the fluid domestic-private space, it would appear that Doña María acquiesces to dominant ideology and US media messages around the commodification of culture and Christmas. But her will to purchase the presents does not guarantee that her plans will actually be realized and that she'll close a circuit of consumption with a journey to Kress. Nonetheless, Doña María's decision to leave the home space is important on other counts: this journey into what is, arguably, a dangerous public space signals a break with mainstream representations of agoraphobia that portray people with this ailment as closeted forever unless forced out of the house by someone else. In addition, Doña María's journey to Kress can also be read as a rebellion against her husband's authoritarian and hegemonic discourses on a woman's place in family and society.

Significantly, she is not dissuaded by his initial disapproval of her prospective journey or by his substantive efforts to play the role of the phobic's overprotective "safe person" (in this case, the seemingly benevolent Latino patriarch and husband who keeps the agoraphobic Latina in check, maintains traditional gender roles, and supposedly guards her sanity). Viewed within this context, her declaration of her intention to venture outside of her circumscribed life is a monumental step in her recovery and the remaking of her identity and traditional marriage, for she asserts her desire to venture out even without the sustained support of her husband, who typically perpetuates her problem by guiding her forays into the public sphere.

As the narrator explains, "The fact was that Doña María very rarely left the home. . . . And she only went to church when someone died and, occasionally, when there was a wedding. But she went with her husband, so she never took notice of where she was going. And her husband always bought her everything" (131).

Rather than encouraging her to do these things for herself and supporting her necessary forays into the field/outside world—what is called "exposure therapy"—her husband discourages her from leaving the house. His lack of real support is made evident in this dialogue, where he voices his disbelief that she would even go to Kress alone:

"You?"

"Yes, me."

"Aren't you afraid to go downtown? You remember that time in Wilmar, out in Minnesota, how you got lost downtown? Are you sure you're not afraid?" (131)

Through his disbelief, questioning, and disapproval, her husband replays the negative script about fear that is sharply criticized as counterproductive in self-help books such as *How to Help Your Loved One Recover from Agoraphobia*. In this book, Karen Williams suggests that family members, particularly overprotective spouses, often infantilize the person with agoraphobia, further eroding his or her self-confidence and opportunities to recover (Williams 1993, 93). In "The Night before Christmas," however, the husband's catastrophizing[7] and discourses on a woman's place are not enough to deter Doña María who, without psychological counsel or medication, boldly embarks on her course of action without companionship.

In a near-Herculean effort, she remembers her fear but does not let it paralyze her. She retorts, "Yes, yes, I remember, but I'll just have to get my courage up. I won't get lost here" (131). Using a strategy of visualization, she imagines a positive outcome and challenges her husband's catastrophizing with her own positive vision and self-talk. Without the advice of a doctor or psychologist, she devises this clever plan of mapping out her journey in stages: "Look, I go out to the street. From here you can see the ice house. It's only four blocks away." Doña María also enlists the help of friends such as Doña Regina—thereby following advice given in popular self-help books on anxiety that were published decades after . . . *Y no se lo tragó la tierra*. Although her husband reluctantly agrees with her plan ("he guesses it really shouldn't be difficult to go Kress"), he also raises the specter of the dreaded and unfamiliar crowded spaces that so terrify Doña María with his assertion, "But be careful *vieja,* there's a lot of people downtown these days" (131).

Armed with a new sense of self-confidence, Doña María sees past his fearful scenarios and endeavors, venturing out to Kress the very next day. Yet anxiety-producing thoughts are present at every turn, and Doña María must constantly counter a laundry list of "what ifs" with self-talk and strategies, as can be seen in this mapping of her journey:

> My God, I don't know why I'm so fearful. Why, downtown is only six blocks from here. I just go straight and then after I cross the tracks turn right. Then go two blocks and there's Kress. On the way back, I walk two blocks and then I turn to the left and keep walking until I'm home again. God willing there won't be any dogs on the way. And I just pray that the train doesn't come while I'm crossing the tracks and catches me right in the middle. . . . I just hope there's no dogs. . . . I hope there's no train coming down the tracks. (132)

Although Doña María does not understand that hers is a widespread social ailment,[8] prayer, hope, and a strategy—together with an acknowledgment of her fear—eventually propel her forward and onward. She walks "the distance from the house to the railroad tracks rapidly" (132), and though she fears that "she might get bitten by a dog or someone will grab her" (132), she does not confront any of these dreaded mishaps along the way. In addition, her fears are downplayed by the narrator, who elaborates to the reader that "in actuality there was only one dog along the entire stretch and most of the people didn't even notice her walking downtown, and not a single car passed by" (132). Yet her precarious position is made clear with a phrase that echoes her husband's catastrophizing: "otherwise she wouldn't have known what to do" (132). Later, her highly tenuous position is graphically illustrated when she finally arrives at the railroad crossing and is suddenly struck by a more intense and debilitating fear than previously.

In this scene, which captures both the metaphorical rendition of the train seen in the Spanish-language public service announcement and the material presence of a train that might derail her progress and personhood, Doña María faces a real and present danger. Here, her journey toward wellness and Kress is temporarily interrupted by the sound of moving trains and their blowing whistles. We know that these are "unnerving her" and she is "too scared to cross" the tracks (132). It is at this juncture that Rivera masterfully constructs the ongoing struggles against anxiety, the absence of linear progress, and the trial and error that are so central to recovery. Doña María attempts to overcome her fear, but whenever "she musters up enough courage to cross the tracks," she hears the train whistle and, frightened, she retreats and winds up in the same place later. Winding up in the same place, however, does not mean retreating from her journey altogether. It means composing herself in order to proceed onward. Ultimately, Doña María overcomes her fear and crosses the tracks, eyes shut. Notwithstanding this symbolic blindfold, she meets the specter of the menacing steel horse—and does so with her own brand of courage.

But there is no one to applaud her, and her trials and tribulations are only beginning. This encounter with anxiety is soon followed by another and another, and Doña María is tested to the point of total exhaustion by circumstances and her condition. She is flanked by people on a crowded sidewalk, her anxiety soars, and her ears start "to fill up with a ringing sound" that just won't stop (132). Disoriented by the crowd, she becomes more and more frightened. She wants to turn back but is "caught in the flow of the crowd," which shoves her onward "toward downtown." The "ringing sound in her ears becomes more pronounced," and she is "unable to remember why she was there amidst the crowd of people" in the first place (131–132). Once again, she pauses in her journey, stopping "in an alley way between two stores" in order to regain her composure a bit. But her anxious dialogues mount again and seem to confirm to her the tragic destiny laid out for her by her overprotective husband. She sighs, "Oh my God, what is happening to me? I'm starting to feel the same as in Wilmar."

As is common among people with anxiety disorder, Doña María is fearful of another panic attack, of loss of control, or of a worse condition, such as death. Though confused and panicked to the point of wondering whether she should have stayed home, she nonetheless tries to draw on her own resources and revisits her "directions" to Kress. When she is unable to make sense of them, she adopts a proactive approach and asks someone for directions (133). But at this point, her fear and anxiety have already escalated beyond her ability to control them, and her "exposure" to the field is now overwhelming. The exposure doesn't occur in the incremental, manageable steps favored by therapists and medical practitioners, who are all too aware of the dangerous consequences of overstimulation and going too fast. And Doña María does not have the energy to implement the big four: LEAVE, RETREAT, RELAX, RECOVER, and TRY AGAIN (Liebgold 2004, 44) Not surprisingly, then, upon her arrival at Kress, things really fall apart for Doña María. The "noise and pushing of the crowd" is worse inside than outside (Rivera 1987, 133), and she is entering a new and more disturbing phase of her journey. Her anxiety soars, and a "flight syndrome" is activated. All she wants to do is leave the store, but she can't find the doors anywhere. What she encounters are "stacks and stacks of merchandise and people crowded against one another" (133). At this point, Doña María begins to experience the classic symptoms of a full-scale and unbridled panic attack—that is, an intense, debilitating fear, "a sense of detachment or unreality, fears of losing sanity or losing control, or fears of dying" (Davidson and Dreher 2003, 51), and a "compulsion to escape" (Bourne 2005, 185).

These dreadful emotions play out in a crowded store, full of unfamiliar people who appear to be swarming all around her and pushing up against her. Here, the reader bears full witness to the intense fear, terror, alienation, and exhaustion that often accompany panic disorder—and to the changes in perception and the sense of unreality that can accompany activities of daily life. But this is not the sole cause of Doña María's terrifying experience and panic at Kress. This experience can also be read as a part of her alienation (i.e., the alienation of immigrant women farmworkers) from products (i.e., commodities) that appear to be divorced from human labor and relations of production. In Doña María's case, not only do commodities exist outside of her (see Marx 1867, chap. 1, sec. 4, para. 2) but they also deliver fearful and distorted human representations that mystify and confound her senses. Not surprisingly, when the narrator suggests that Doña María begins to hear voices coming from the merchandise (Rivera 1987, 133), the human voices (discourse) are separated from the body and united with commodities in an unnatural and menacing way.

Confronted with the combined terror of a crowded space and commodities that have lost use value and acquired fantastic and unfamiliar forms, Doña María "gazes blankly" and "forgets the names of things" (i.e., merchandise; 133). Yet she is conscious of people staring at her and feels them pushing her aside, and she is able to discern some objects (some toys and a wallet, which she stuffs in her bag). Even so, her senses are not functioning well, and "suddenly she no longer" hears "the voice of the crowd" (133). Now that the crowd is silent, all she sees are people moving about, people whom she visualizes as disembodied. She sees their "legs, arms, their mouths" (133).

Dona María's terrifying and alienating experience does not, however, render her helpless. She asks where the exit is and "starts in that direction." Finally, she presses "through the crowd, pushing her way" until she pushes the door open and exits the store (133). But this is not the end of this Latina anxiety story, for the doting mother with anxiety disease who miraculously makes her way to the street and endeavors once again to figure out her location is confronted by someone who "grabs her arm, grabs it so tightly that she lets out a cry" (133). Her assailant, who informs her he has been watching her, is neither named nor described by the narrator. What matters is the physical apprehension and assault, the wounding words, the class biases, the stereotypical views of the racial profiler and surveillance team member who accuses her, a woman, of stealing just like her "people": Here *she* is . . . these damn people, always stealing something, stealing." (133).

This scene is followed by a moment of riveting silence then another bodily injury, which Rivera personalizes and describes through sight and physical sensations: "All she saw was the pavement moving swiftly toward her face and a small pebble that bounced into her eye and was hurting a lot. She felt someone pulling her arms and when they turned her face up, all she saw were faces far away" (133).

Confronted by the reality of surveillance, the tight grip of the store personnel, the gun of a security guard, and a desperate and fearful emotional state, she finally cries, loses consciousness, and feels as if she's drifting in a sea of people whose arms "bruise against her like waves" (132). The very disturbing symptoms of her anxiety disorder combined with the unexpected assault of the surveillance team cause her to feel as if she is going mad or losing her mind. Her trip to Kress seems to confirm her husband's foreboding words and her own fear that things will get worse, not better, if she ventures out of her home space alone. And to a certain extent, they have gotten worse, for not only has she experienced an escalation of anxiety, not only is she exhausted by her multiple efforts and the ever-present challenges of agoraphobia and panic, but the surveillance team at Kress has apprehended and emotionally abused her and turned her over to the authorities for shoplifting. Her efforts to be independent have been thwarted, and she ultimately has to resort to the patriarchal protection of her husband and the traditional gender roles and discourses on women's place that regulate their behavior at home.

By infusing Doña María's anxiety-ridden journey with an equally horrific social scenario that leads to her social and ideological confinement and literal incarceration, Rivera allows readers to see that Doña María's fear is neither unfounded nor the product of an irrational impulse or delusion. Instead, her fear has a rational basis; it is the product of particular social and economic arrangements, practices, and systems that feed off the racialization, exploitation, gender oppression, and displacement of female migrants and their social dis-ease. The social root of Doña María's ailment becomes painfully clear when she, an impoverished Latina immigrant and woman, comes up against the store's surveillance team and becomes the victim of racial profiling, class bias, and a social context that did not appear in the worst of her imagined scenarios. In this sense, once at Kress she meets the earth that threatens to devour her, the train that derails her progress, and the social context that is missing in most descriptions of anxiety disorders and recovery. The combined effect of social and health diseases produces a tragic outcome that is far worse than being sent to jail temporarily for shoplifting.

As consumers of this Latina story, we can take a step back to look beyond the tragic spectacle that Tomás Rivera portrayed. We can revisit the debilitating scenarios that prevent recovery and openly dignify the struggles of the Doña Marías of the world who lack community and professional support for their exhausting health work and labor in the fields and at home. We can counter the message in the popular self-help literature that the bark of anxiety is always worse than its bite. We can reject framings of anxiety disorder that focus on individuals and individual volition, thus failing to attend to the social relationships and triggers that contextualize this disorder in everyday life. We can encourage a frank and open dialogue about an ailment that goes hand in hand with life and work in the contemporary era. We can reflect on the fact the world in which we live, the people we are, the work we do, the transnational communities we inhabit, and the health status that we possess all ffect whether we succumb to anxiety disease or face it head-on and heal. Only by addressing both the situational and social dynamics of anxiety illness can we identify and mitigate those triggers that appear to provide a breeding ground for anxiety illness among specific populations who have yet to be fully seen or heard. People within these populations find it hard to get out of limiting situations that are by their very nature frightening. These are people who have much to gain from challenging the clinical descriptions that fail to consider the dangerous worlds in which they live. These are the courageous Latinas among us who venture out into a dangerous world armed with a purpose and a strategy, notwithstanding anxiety, disapproving family members, racial profilers, and any number of "trains" that threaten to derail them.

NOTES

The title of this chapter is taken from an English translation of Tomás Rivera's . . . *Y no se lo tragó la tierra,* pp. 130–34.

1. According to Anthony LaPastina, the *telenovela* is a form of melodramatic serialized fiction produced and aired in most Latin American countries.

2. Many self-help books, including Reneau Z. Peurifoy's *Anxiety, Phobias and Panic,* describe the flight response in relation to the sympathetic nervous system "which suspends any non-essential activity in the body and increases activity in any system necessary to fight or flee from an external physical threat."

3. Joseph Hovey (2001) identifies a number of common stressors among Mexican migrant workers that include the unpredictable nature of finding work or housing, the feeling of instability due to constant uprooting, and the necessity of acculturating to a new environment with a lack of familiar roots and Spanish media.

4. For more on the division between public and private in the agoraphobia literature, see Siegal (2001).

5. I am translating from the Spanish-language version of "La Nochebuena" (Rivera 1987, 54) because the English translation is inadequate in this case.

6. "On January 6, most of the Hispanic world celebrates El Día de Reyes, the Epiphany, remembering the day when the Three Wise Men following the star to Bethlehem, arrived bearing their treasured gifts of gold, frankincense and myrrh for the Baby Jesus" ("¡Ya vinieron los Reyes Magos!" 1999–2006, para. 1).

7. According to Edmund J. Bourne (2005, 168) "catastrophizing is a distorted mode of thinking in which you inaccurately view a situation as terrible, insufferable, or catastrophic."

8. Although many people with agoraphobia consider themselves unique in their ailment, this is not the case. As Edmund J. Bourne (2005, 6) states, "Of all the anxiety orders, agoraphobia is the most prevalent. It is estimated that one in twenty, or about 5 percent of the general population, suffers from agoraphobia."

BIBLIOGRAPHY

Bourne, Edmund J. 2005. *The anxiety and phobia workbook.* 4th ed. Oakland, CA: New Harbinger Publications.

Capps, Lisa, and Elinor Ochs. 1996. *Constructing panic: The discourse of agoraphobia.* Cambridge, MA: Harvard University Press.

Davidson, Jonathan, and Henry Dreher. 2003. *The anxiety book: Developing strength in the face of fear.* New York: Riverhead Books.

de la Fuente, Patricia. 1985. Invisible women in the narrative of Tomás Rivera. In *International studies in honor of Tomás Rivera.* Ed. Julián Olivares, 81–89. Houston: Arte Público Press.

Hendrix, Mary Lynn. n.d. Desórdenes de pánico. http://panico.itgo.com/panfly.html (accessed Oct. 2006).

LaPastina, Anthony. n.d. Telenovela. www.museum.tv/archives/etv/T/htmlT/telenovela/telenovela.htm (accessed Oct. 2006).

Liebgold, Howard. 2004. *Freedom from fear: Overcoming anxiety, phobias, and panic.* New York: Citadel Press.

Marx, Karl. 1867. *Capital.* www.marxists.org/archive/marx/works/1867-c1/ch01.htm.

Peurifoy, Reneau Z. 1998. *Anxiety, phobias and panic.* Toronto: Life Skills.

Rivera, Tomás. 1987. . . . *Y no se lo tragó la tierra.* Trans. Evangelina Vigil-Piñon. Houston: Arte Público Press.

Siegal, Suzie. 2001. *Safe at home: Agoraphobia and the discourse on women's place.* Master's thesis, University of South Florida, Department of Women's Studies.

Williams, Karen P. 1993. *How to help your loved one recover from agoraphobia.* Far Hills, NJ: New Horizon Press.

FOUR

The Art of Place: The Work of Diane Gamboa

KAREN MARY DAVALOS

In 2008, Southern California witnessed its first major "post-ethnic" art exhibition in *Phantom Sightings: Art After the Chicano Movement.*[1] Building on the performances and visual arts of Asco, the Los Angeles–based collective originally composed of Harry Gamboa, Jr., Gronk, Willie Herrón, and Patssi Valdez, the exhibition at the Los Angeles County Museum of Art (LACMA) intended to challenge conventional parameters of Chicana/o art and offer one strategy for interpreting conceptual art produced by artists who came of age after the Chicano Movement. Co-curators Rita Gonzalez, Howard Fox, and Chon Noriega posit that the temporal curatorial model of art produced *after something* allowed them "the freedom to follow an idea, rather than represent a constituency."[2] Interestingly, the show was simultaneously a complete success and a dramatic failure. Ticket sales evidence that it was overwhelmingly popular, breaking LACMA attendance records. Yet local artists and critics found the exhibition lacking. They hosted several public discussions, generated hundreds of blog posts, and published articles in regional and national media to address the show's historical, aesthetic, and positional errors. Some critics responded by producing their own exhibitions performed as errata that offered a corrective vision of Chicana/o art in Los Angeles.[3]

Certainly, *Phantom Sightings* captured the inaccuracy of scholarly notions of Chicana/o art by unwittingly masking the range of visual arts *during* the Chicano Movement. As noted by Nizan Shaked, the co-curators' "apologetic tone" and "unease with the term *identity pol-*

itics" created "an unwillingness to engage . . . why it is that identity politics have been subject to so much criticism and backlash."[4] Their "excuse-me-tongue" curatorial style—to use poet Lorna Dee Cervantes's characterization of cultural embarrassment—supported the inaccurate interpretation that art *of* the Chicano Movement expressed a "cultural essence" or represented a "coherent Chicano culture and history," a "constituency," and that art *after* this historical moment produced something else, something implicitly more advanced in its vision of culture, identity, and art.[5]

Although the co-curators insightfully avoided a retrospective exhibition of all Chicana/o art production over the past "two decades," they sidestepped the questions on everyone's mind and implied in the subtitle: What is Chicana/o art? Is the Chicano Movement its only benchmark?[6] The real phantom in Los Angeles was curatorial attention to the subject and an analysis of identity-based art and it related exclusion from LA's publicly supported museum. The co-curators' characterization of Chicana/o art also eliminated decades of Chicana feminist analysis of multiple subject positions and the interrogation of essentialism.[7] In this context, *Phantom Sightings* reinforces a liberal color-blind perspective that imagines only racialized people as participants in identity politics and leaves whiteness and its privileges unmarked. Thus, without the benefit of recurrent surveys, biennials, and juried exhibitions—and, I add, significant scholarship on Chicana/o art—this major exhibition could not satisfy its critics, who craved complex answers and read the co-curators' apologetic tone as a condemnation and an oversimplification of Chicana/o art.

This chapter argues that Chicana artist Diane Gamboa's sense of place represents a distinguishing feature of Chicana/o visual arts and offers critical response to *Phantom Sightings* as a show that helped to bring the problem of Chicana/o art history to public attention.[8] My reading explores Gamboa's visual work of the 1990s to illustrate the centrality of place and its generative ability to empower. Gamboa's placeness is a territorial or land-based notion of belonging that is grounded in three pivotal components: history, cultural memory, and Chicana subjectivity. From these three critical elements emerge her representations of actual places and fictive social spaces, and these sites force viewers to reconsider convenient and narrow notions of Chicana/o visual art. Her imaginary places function as anti-sexist, anti-racist, and anti-heteronormative interrogations of the social injustices within actual Chicana, working-class, urban spaces. Her work makes critical commentary on social and ideological violence and thus performs critical consciousness. Gamboa's proclamation "Los Angeles *is* Chicano-*landia;* Los Angeles *was* Mexico," illustrates a historiography of Los Angeles informed by cultural and temporal-spatial meaning, a childhood immersed within the Chicano civil rights movement, a decade of experience in black and white documentary photography of the 1980s punk scene, and working-class style and economies.[9]

In the early 1970s, while still attending Garfield High School, Diane Gamboa first heard the charge that her work was "not Chicano enough" when a teacher rationalized his whitewashing of her quilt-motif mural.[10] This accusation was leveled against many Chicana artists during the Chicano Movement.[11] As Shifra M. Goldman notes, Chicana artists were concerned with personal matters that were often determined to be superfluous to Movement campaigns.[12] For Gamboa, the indictment of insufficiency has become a source of critical consciousness. Defiantly, she agrees, and she re-affirms a gendered location: "I am a Chican*a* artist."[13]

The grammatical premise of Gamboa's subjectivity may confuse the uninitiated. In Spanish, the word "Chicanos" refers to a group of Mexican American males and females or a group of males, but heritage speakers and feminists in the United States are more sensitive to the authority of patriarchy that imagines a group of men or boys. In addition, Spanish and English code-switching—that is the linguistic and political moments in which "Chicano" becomes a word in English—allowed "Chicano" to silence women when employed as an adjective, as in phrase "the Chicano Movement" or "Chicano art." The norm for feminists is to use both the feminine and masculine endings: "Chicana/o."[14] As Angie Chabram Dernersesian illustrates in her argument about Chicana cultural production, the double-code affirms women's presence and creates a sign that "could better accommodate multiple subjects" *and* "combat exclusion."[15] Gamboa's positionality as a Chicana artist participates in and supports the discourse of multiplicity and inclusion; it is a performative moment of gendered and raced presence.

As suggested by Judith Butler, Gamboa is not, therefore, merely naming her female presence; she is performing a socio-spatial critique.[16] She enacts a feminist consciousness against Chican*o* cultural nationalism and the imperialist erasure of Mexican-origin people that began in 1848 with the Treaty of Guadalupe Hidalgo, which annexed nearly half of México's northern frontier and with a stroke of the pen made Mexican residents into foreigners on their own land. Her visual practice constructs a Chicana consciousness against normative heteropatriarchy, the privileging of whiteness, and cultural annihilation and assimilation.

Gamboa's body of work produced during the 1990s consists largely of figurative images of women and men as well as androgynous people, shallow-space interiors, and bold canvas tableaux. The pieces from this period are paradigmatic of the intersection of performance, cultural production, and the borderlands. Her work from this decade includes the widely collected serigraphs *Little Gold Man* and *Malathion Baby* (both from 1990); the unfinished series *Pin Up*, which consumed her artistic expression for over a decade; and her response to that series, *In the Name of Love*. The prints, drawings, and paintings I describe in this essay are characteristic of Gamboa's style, in which "every available centimeter of canvas [or paper is filled] with something," an aesthetic approach of profusion and abandon.[17] An excess of visibility through ornamentation is precisely the site and strategy of place-making and critical utopia. As Krista Thompson notes about bling in hip-hop visual culture, "it's a state of hypervisibility"—and although not blinding in Gamboa's case, the "overdetermined surface" is a critical reflection on the previously unseen and the social forces that had made Gamboa's figures hidden subjects.[18]

INTRODUCING AND INTERPRETING DIANE GAMBOA

Born and raised in Los Angeles, Diane Gamboa produces visual works that require viewers to expand how they think about gender and sexuality, beauty and pleasure, power and authority, history and culture. Gamboa's versatility in multiple media—painting, drawing, ephemera paper costume, silkscreen, props, and tattoos—mixes high and low forms of art that often upset the calculations of art historians, curators, and Chicano cultural nationalists. Her unapologetic use of unconventional forms and subjects has been the source of her success. She worked as art director of *Chismearte*, a California-based literary journal; an instructor for the Barrio Mobile Art Studio, the first education program of Self-Help Graphics and Arts (SHG); and a curator of the SHG's Maestra Atelier III:

Uprising of the Urban Goddess in 2001–2002. Her work has been shown nationally and internationally. Although she briefly attended Otis/Parsons School of Design, she identifies as a self-taught artist.

Drawing on intimate familiarity with and keen observations of urban youth and multi-racial, but predominantly Mexican American, neighborhoods, her artwork invokes both actual places in Los Angeles and fictive spaces that conjure up utopian moments in which gender/sex equity and self-respect are the norm. Her drawings, paintings, and prints are powerful and elaborately adorned renderings of the human figure, from full bodies to facial portraits, and many works explore social relations. Explaining the original source of her aesthetic approach, Gamboa notes,

> I was always interested in fashion from the time my aunt used to sell things at the swap meets and I played with the stuff. In the early 1960s, I went to elementary school in short white go-go boots and fishnet stockings. Later I became interested in hippie fashions and bought vintage clothes at thrift shops in East Los Angeles. I have always collected accessories, jewelry and hats. I admired the pachuca and chola looks, but I wanted to dress unusually.[19]

Her style emerges from working-class aesthetics and markets and rejects the readily available representations of the pachuca, the chola, the virgin, and the Latin spitfire. Her characters are glamorous, androgynous, and typically clothed only in tattoos, body piecing, jewelry, headdress, and chains. Her renderings of the human figure tend to emphasize nudity, but her characters' ornate style makes it difficult to consider them unclothed. When figures appear in a setting, the foreground is also richly textured, and the patterns echo her characters' style. Notably, an enduring tension charges these elegantly adorned places and figures as Gamboa asks who and what determines beauty and power.

Invested in alternative representations and aesthetics, Gamboa's characters are urban dwellers from the "unpopular culture," a term she coined to acknowledge the "dirty secrets" of the Los Angeles sex trade and the muffled cultural experiences of Chicanas and Chicanos who are not cholos, low riders, or *vatos locos*.[20] The visualization of the unpopular antagonizes and disturbs the popular perceptions of Chicanos and Chicanas. In the spaces of ostracism, Gamboa drives against social conventions with a new sensibility. In these sites, punk styles are joined by patterns and designs reminiscent of Mesoamerican motifs, but for Gamboa these aesthetics are not cultural contact zones of hybridity. In Gamboa's renderings, scenes of Chicano-*landia* are not a mestizaje of cultural and social phenomena but whole and genuine Chicana experiences.

At times, she consciously draws on codes more recognizable to art dealers and critics looking for traces of pre-Columbian civilizations and Mexican culture. For example, *Bloody Coffee* (1990) records a woman's *remedios* for healing—in this case, for maintaining a man's monogamy and protecting against the trauma of his infidelity.[21] As the title indicates, the remedy is one drop of menstrual blood in his morning coffee. But even when Mesoamerica icons appear, Gamboa is never merely representing identity or cultural essence. Gamboa's references are female-centered; *la curandera,* the Mexican spiritual healer, and her medicine for survival and belonging emerge from a critical consciousness. Most of her work, however, refers to a Los Angeles underground of unrecognized but legitimate residents in Chicano-*landia*. Thus, where the Chicano cultural nationalist eye or critic sees Mayan headdress or Aztec iconography, Gamboa sees "the drag queen" from the nightclub.[22] Where the eager folklorist sees obsidian, turquoise, or a rich Latin American pallet, she visualizes "the color of a '57 Chevy," low and cruising the boulevard, or the current hair color of urban punks.[23]

Feminist scholars and critics pay particular attention to Gamboa's use of the body.[24] Although I agree that her figurative style requires interpretative analysis, I want to think more spatially about her use of the body. Laura E. Pérez's important analysis of Chicana art argues that Gamboa's attention to ornamentation is a "double metaphor of the social body as text."[25] Finding mimicry and satire within the lavish and fantastic paper dresses of Gamboa, Pérez argues that the artist appropriates the design language of the fashion industry in order to challenge its gender, race, and material biases. Using inexpensive and everyday items, she creates paper fashions for those who do not typically have access to the symbols of social status. The decoration of the body is, therefore, a social commentary on how working-class Chicanas, transgender people of color, and other invisible bodies construct their own empowerment and dignity and challenge restrictive social and material hierarchies. But for Perez, the ornamented flesh is the social skin on which desire

FIG. 4.1. "Tight Rope." *Permission granted by Diane Gamboa.*

and pain are written. The body visually records the ambivalence of the Gamboa's characters.

This ambivalent subjectivity is evident in *Tight Rope* (Figure 4.1), a lithograph that textually and visually makes a pun about contemporary relationships, awkward moments between men and women, or bondage. The rope is taut, binding two red-haired lovers at the arms as they turn away from each other. They depict the proverbial balancing act that holds in counterweight self-interest and commitment. The strain and tension is made palpable by the intense, bold coloration and the composition of the rope that cuts across the mid-section of each bejeweled figure. This is a complicated heterosexual relationship. Alternatively, Gamboa teasingly captures sexual bondage. Their awkward comportment and gaze-avoidance indicates they simply did not achieve pleasure. In this reading, the cause of unfulfilled sexual satisfaction is explained by the excessively tight rope. Either reading confronts Victorian sex norms by placing the encounter in front of a curtain, which is more than just an embellished backdrop, as it calls attention to Gamboa's act of exposure. The curtains—as well as the recurring image of a straight-backed chair that appears in several works in the 1990s—are metonymic referents for the "unpopular culture" of Chicano-*landia*. Gamboa stages this scene to conjure within the viewer's mind the causes of our social binding.

However, while forceful critiques of the body reveal ambivalent subjectivities, the emphasis on the body short-circuits analysis of place in Gamboa's visual production. "Gamboa's characteristic love of ornamentation" enacts desire, as Perez points out, but I argue it enacts a desire for a new social space, a site of belonging, or place.[26] Just as Henri Lefebvre argues that social space is "not a thing but rather a set of relations between [objects and products]," Gamboa visually renders the production of space.[27] The artist creates richly elaborate human forms, but it is their social world that generates their empowerment as it allows for their performance of alternative genders, sexualities, and cultural memories.

THE PLACENESS OF DIANE GAMBOA

Recording a specific geography around the downtown area and radiating northwest and east, Gamboa creates the neighborhoods of "Boyle Heights, East LA, Echo Park, Silver Lake, West Feliz, [and] Chinatown."[28] These communities of her childhood were graphically clarified during a school field trip to city hall, which at the time was the tallest building in Los Angeles. Looking out from the tower's viewing station, Gamboa mapped her world while standing at her "reference point."[29] Although the east side communities were important destinations for Russian, Jewish, and Japanese immigrants at the beginning of the twentieth century, at the time of Gamboa's birth in 1957, Mexican Americans had carved out significant social space. By the time she reached high school, the east side communities were fully developed sites of creative, political, and collective Chicano and Chicana action.

Coming of age during the late 1960s, Gamboa understood space as the nexus through which power flows. She states, "I grew up you know . . . basically walking, literally walking the streets of the [Chicano] moratorium; getting tear-gassed and . . . so [I was] growing up in this cloud of pepper spray."[30] At thirteen years old, Gamboa participated in one of the largest anti-war mass protests, the Chicano Moratorium. Between 1968 and 1970, Chicana/o activists called for the end of the Vietnam War and brought attention to the disproportionate numbers of Mexican Americans that had been drafted, wounded, or killed. Though Chicanos formed only ten percent of the population in the United States, they accounted for nearly twenty percent of those killed in Vietnam. On August 29, 1970, twenty thousand people attended the rally to support the moratorium. The peaceful demonstration ended at Laguna Park, where the participants relaxed for an afternoon of music and speeches, but a massive police response created a riot. It was a chaotic and ugly scene of police brutality. Their excessive force, as Gamboa recalls, involved batons, pepper spray, and tear gas, the latter responsible for the death of Ruben Salazar, a reporter who became a symbol for the cost of waging battle against institutionalized inequalities. The mapping of her geographic territory from her "reference point" coincided with collective struggle in Chicano-*landia*.

Gamboa learned at a young age that Los Angeles was a fragmented city segregated by race, class, and power. As Raul H. Villa notes about east side communities, subsidized private urban development dislocated Chicano residents. Freeways, industrial zones, and public spaces re-classified into private development zones split neighborhoods into isolated areas.[31] Gamboa responded to her social isolation by turning to punk music because it provided a discourse of non-conformity and an unapologetic and anti-establishment attitude.[32] Gamboa translated the directness of the punk scene into a visual frankness about society and a wholesale rejection of social norms.

However, Gamboa never turned the punk culture of non-conformity into cynicism and withdrawal. "My perspective is that of a voyeur *and* a participant," she claims.[33] The blunt statement charges the visual places she creates, her relationship to them, and her aesthetic approach. Her visual project is a form of "critical witnessing" on the streets of LA, making her imaginary spaces into utopias that resolve such cruelties. Each painting, drawing, and print of the unpopular culture of Chicano-*landia* is "more than a focused act of looking or bearing witness," as Tiffany Ana López argues about the act of critical witnessing in her analysis of Latino cultural production engaged with issues of violence and trauma. López demonstrates that such narratives entail a position or means of spotlighting the very conditions, inequalities, or violence that brought the story or visual narrative into being.[34] Critical witnessing extends observation and visuality. It is an analysis of violent social realities that provokes critical consciousness in the retelling—Gamboa's actual places—or in the visual restaging of reality—Gamboa's fictive spaces. The artist's representations of space serve as critical witnesses to actual sites of violence and racial inequality, material production and excess, and sexism in Chicano-*landia*.

POWER AND ITS REVERSAL: NEW SPACES OF CRITICAL CONSCIOUSNESS

Gamboa is interested in the reversal of social hierarchies as a method of interrogating current norms and inequalities. The widely circulated and published serigraph *Malathion Baby* (1990) depicts Gamboa's reversal of power.[35] The print is a testament to the urban powerless of the east side communities that could not see the Mediterranean fruit flies that threatened to endanger agribusiness of California. In 1981 and 1988, helicopters administered industrial pesticide over people's heads, cars, and homes throughout southern California but especially on the working-class communities of Los Angeles. Yet the dangerous fly and its capability to harm agribusiness were unclear and unseen to those neighborhoods. Ill health and asthma were the visible effects of the pesticide that transformed their lives. The single fly that Gamboa states appears in the serigraph represents an imbalanced society in which residents were not given the same consideration as the capitalist market. With deformed human figures who parade as if nothing is out of the ordinary,

FIG. 4.2. "Boy Toy." *Permission granted by Diane Gamboa.*

Gamboa documents the over eleven thousand people who were adversely affected by the Malathion spraying.

As critical witness to the unpopular culture, Gamboa's provocative images also make no attempt to obscure the trappings of unchecked power. *Boy Toy* (Figure 4.2) illustrates a domestic scene of a glamorous Chicana with a hat fetish who collects lovers as well as Catholic sacred hearts and Mexican masks. The painting reproduces several of Gamboa's personal possessions. Thus, the work functions as a self-portrait and a reframing of the construction of space and identity. *Boy Toy* includes two copies of Gamboa's figurative paintings, one behind the male figure who is holding a doll, his toy, and another on top of the suitcase in the upper register; a collection of millinery; and her signature chair, the metonymic piece of furniture from her studio. This place, however, is not a catalog of her ethnic heritage. It is her site of experience and her space of belonging and power. The male is her toy and she the puppeteer behind the curtain. The self-portrait is revealing but also deliberately critical of visual and cultural production. This place is cluttered, weighted down by the accumulation of things, and the social self is clearly encased by her belongings. Gamboa visually achieves this critical view of capitalist accumulation, commodity fetishism, and sexual domination by foreshortening the perspective of the chair, table, and screen and by altering the perspective of several items. The technique allows her to stuff more things into the painting, and it visually tightens the distance between capitalism accumulation and sexual domination, calling into question all forms of inequity and the intersection of such inequalities.

The *Pin Up* series is a bold interrogation of patriarchy, heteronormativity, and sex/gender roles, and its quantity indicates her compulsion to trouble social expectations. Gamboa draws beautiful men in positions more commonly associated with women. The series also demonstrates her wit and sense of humor, as each work operates with double meanings: the drawings at once appear to be sadomasochistic scenes *and* relaxing portrayals of glamorous men. In 1990, Gamboa began *Pin Up* (alternatively known as *Pin Up / Pin Down*) with twelve ink drawings on vellum for a calendar that satirized the objectification of the female body.[36] Reversing the gaze of the pin-up calendar made popular in the 1950s, Gamboa's in-depth study of "the male from the female point of view" rapidly expanded from twelve into 366 drawings, one image for each day of the year, and she re-envisioned the series as a book. This work-in-progress is approximately three-fourths complete, performing alternative masculinities and femininities through repetition and redundancy, although the latter subjectivity is conceptualized through the reiteration of the female gaze. Each male image conjures up a new female subjectivity; meek, passive, and sexually available Chicanas simply could not gaze at or control the men Gamboa has created.

At several moments during the creation of the series, Gamboa grew tired of rendering male figures, and her feminist positionality inspired her to return to the female form. *Old Fashioned Romance* (1992), from the *In the Name of Love* series, is one such drawing that provided Gamboa with a break. Similar to the book project, this work maintains her wry social critique of heterosexual relations and her imaginary social world of female power. In this case, "old" refers to the woman. The wrinkles on her face, her arthritic hands, and her sagging breasts indicate her age. But in opposition to social codes that discard and devalue women over twenty-nine years old, this elderly woman is the dominatrix who controls two younger men; both are smitten with her love, as indicated by the duplicated heart necklace that hangs around each man's neck. The old-fashioned romance of heterosexual convention has been "converted," and the old woman controls her two lovers even to the timing of orgasmic pleasure, as indicated by a cock ring.[37] Not only is patriarchy is dead, but notions of beauty have been expanded in her imaginary social space. It is a place of female human agency.

Even when the visual narrative is not directly feminist or about female power, Gamboa makes use of the gaze to empower her characters. In her imaginary landscapes, witnessing produces power; the act of visual recognition generates authority. The serigraph *Little Gold Man* illustrates the grace and dignity of men, women, transgender people, and monsters that return the gaze of the viewer.[38] In this meticulously detailed scene, the glamorous partygoers are regal in their postures. They do not avoid eye contact with each other because, as some art critics suggest, they have difficulty communicating and forming meaningful relationships. On the contrary, Gamboa has them looking directly at the viewer because they are resilient and powerful individuals whose sense of authority emerges from their production of their social space. They stare down the viewer, a compositional strategy located in their unflinching ability to look at and perceive their world.

This site enacts Foucault's theory of the panopticon.[39] Gamboa's fictive space is entirely a place to see and to be seen, and power is derived from the visual experience. Contrary to Foucault's notion that "the unequal gaze" reinforces social hierarchies and control, the exquisitely adorned crowd is empowered by the gaze. If we hold our breath, we can almost hear Gamboa's favorite pun, "They are dressed to kill," a phrase which suggests the potential violence of this fictive world but also implies the power of visuality. Looking and being seen are not simply visual actions confined to sight; here, perception and the gaze of the viewer generate consciousness, the cognitive and socio-spatial moment of being.

In this imaginary place, they are visually witnessed and thus validated. While lethal style can assault the mind and eye, the fictive site that Gamboa crafts is less about brutality and more about the newfound source of power or new spatial locations of power. Gamboa gives palpable form to the performative action of constructing a new critical consciousness. The serigraph could serve as an allegory of Gamboa's Chicano-*landia;* although invisible, unpopular, or ignored by the media, Hollywood, and the art-market, Chicanas and Chicanos urban punk youth are present in this environment, and their gaze endows their authority.

CRITICAL *FRONTERA*

Although Chicana and Chicano visual arts production has multiplied and expanded over the past forty years, Chicana/o scholarship has not kept pace with its subject.[40] Therefore, scholars, curators, critics, and artists continue to hold narrow and uninformed views of Chicana/o art, particularly because the earliest period of Chicana/o art production has not been fully documented and analyzed in order to identify important benchmarks against which more current work is assessed. By way of conclusion, I posit that Gamboa's work teases out the errors of Chicano art historiography and its emphasis on the temporal moment of art production: either *of* or art *after* the Chicano Movement. While clearly historic, the Chicano Movement may not be the only handle by which scholars can assess and classify the visual cultural production attributed to Mexican-origin artists. Even if it could serve as a major register for analyzing Chicana/o visual art, scholars have yet to agree on the Movement's duration, political style, and orientation, as regional variation and gender has complicated the picture.

The premise for *Phantom Sightings* is a fundamentally flawed view of Chicana/o art as bisected by the Movement. Although not specifically referenced by the co-curators, the exhibition relied on Shifra M. Goldman and Tomás Ybarra-Frausto's classificatory scheme for Chicana/o art, which was announced in their historic reference index, *Arte Chicano.*[41] Goldman and Ybarra-Frausto distinguish between two phases of Chicano cultural production, 1968–1975 and 1975–1981.[42] Aligned with the then current view of the beginning and ending of the Chicano Movement, 1968–1975, the first period is celebrated and considered the benchmark. The latter moment is typically described as less political or confrontational than a prior period. Indeed, this classificatory scheme erupted in a debate between Goldman and Malaquías Montoya and Lezlie Salkowitz Montoya, who argued for an art of politics, as both tried to persuade artists to critically consider their actions and aesthetic styles.[43] *Phantom Sightings* tacitly construed the earlier period as "cultural essence" or "constituency" art concerned with a "coherent Chicano culture and history." This description certainly fits some work, but it is unsubstantiated whether the overwhelming majority of Chicana/o visual art can be organized around such a definition.[44]

More importantly, the period after the Chicano Movement includes works that directly confront the viewer, and Gamboa's 1990s visual record is one example with its aggressive and provocative graphic format. Although Chicana visual artists such as Gamboa, along with creative writers and performers, eloquently challenged the image of the singular Chicano subject and successfully interrogated the false image of coherence, Chicana/o art history has not modified its classificatory system, which assesses cultural production against masculinist political activism of the 1970s. Gamboa's feminist resistance and positionality is one example of multiple subjectivities that upset the coherent, masculine, singular (Chicano) subject. Granted, the analysis of one artist is not sufficient to unhinge the underlying assumption that Chicano art assumes a particular style, strategy, or approach, but Gamboa's feminist visual narrative of place suggests that the categories are in need of revision.

Her sense of place can perhaps suggest that cultural production in the borderlands is relational: subjectivity emerges at the nexus of space, history, and cultural memory. Gamboa's placeness is anchored in critical witnessing of Chicano-*landia*. Gamboa's visual production begins with the lived reality of space and critically explores the processes of spatial practice, namely racialization, capitalist accumulation, and patriarchy, and violence against women. Her identity is a position for her aesthetic engagement—the visual arts—but the cultural, political, and gender consciousness that her work performs is sometimes out of this world, unknown, or unimagined That is the point. Her imaginary places do not depend on notions of the Chicano community or culture, as they take the unpopular culture of Chicano-*landia* as their reference. This signification of the unpopular inhabitants of the city could not articulate the cultural essence of Chicanos because they have not been admitted membership. It is this documentation of "unpopular culture" for which art historians, critics, and collectors cannot account because it is outside of expectations and rejected from the Chicano and dominant constituencies. In Gamboa's visual imaginary from the 1990s, we have a place of belonging and a social location, or consciousness, from within that space. These are whole social landscapes in which Chicana power and beauty are real, in places all their own.

NOTES

1. Ruben R. Mendoza, "Deciphering the Decoy: Phantom Transformations and the Decolonial Imaginary of Chicana/o Art (*Review:* LACMA's Phantom Sightings: Art after the Chicano Movement)," LatinArt.com. Accessed on Dec. 12, 2008.

2. Rita Gonzalez, Howard N. Fox, and Chon A. Noriega. "Introduction," *Phantom Sightings: Art after the Chicano Movement* (Berkeley: University of California Press and Los Angeles County Museum of Art, 2008), 13.

3. *Vaguely Chicana,* the solo exhibition of Linda Arreola, at Tropico de Nopal Gallery/Art Space in Los Angeles, was one corrective to *Phantom Sightings.* Arreola's work is abstract, conceptual, and devoid of the human figure. I do not wish to imply that all visual art exhibitions function as performance; it is the discursive engagement between *Phantom Sightings* and *Vaguely Chicana* that transforms the visual arts into an utterance of the performative.

4. The first quotes are from Nizan Shaked, "Event Review: Phantom Sightings: Art after the Chicano Movement," *American Quarterly* 60, No. 4 (Dec. 2008): 1068; the quote following the ellipse is from page 1058.

5. Gonzalez et al., "Introduction," 13.

6. Ibid.

7. Norma Alarcón, "The Theoretical Subject(s) of *This Bridge Called My Back* and Anglo-American Feminism," *Making Face, Making Soul: Haciendo caras,* ed. G. Anzaldúa (San Francisco, CA: Aunt Lute Foundation Book, 1990); Norma Alarcón, "Chicana Feminism: In the Tracks of 'the' Native Woman," *Living Chicana Theory,* ed. Carla Trujillo (Berkeley, CA: Third Woman Press, 1998), 371–382; Gloria Anzaldúa, *Borderlands/La Frontera* (San Francisco, CA: Aunt Lute Books, 1987); Cherrie Moraga and Gloria Anzaldúa, eds. *This Bridge Called My Back: Writings by Radical Women of Color* (Watertown, MA: Persephone Press, 1981).

8. In 2004. Diana Gamboa granted me an interview that occurred over several days. Interviews on September 1, 2004, and January 9, 2005, in Los Angeles support this article. As co-participants, we collaborated on the questions and direction of the conversation, and we both recorded the interview. I had the interview transcribed, and she received a copy of the transcription and a copy of the original tapes. She generously provided me with access to her slide collection and copies of announcements and art criticism of her work.

9. Diane Gamboa interview conducted by Karen Mary Davalos, January 9, 2005, in Los Angeles (hereafter, Gamboa Interview, Jan. 9, 2005).

10. Pat Villeneuve, "Diane Gamboa," *Contemporary Chicana and Chicano Art,* ed. Gary Keller (Tempe, AZ: Bilingual Press / Editorial Bilingüe, 2002), 256.

11. Chicana artists Linda Arreola, Barbara Carrasco, Yreina D. Cervántez, Carolina Flores, Carmen Lomas Garza, and Yolanda M. López and the members of Mujeres Muralistas, Patricia Rodriguez, Consuelo Mendez Castillo, Irene Perez, and Graciela Carrillo, were among those accused of not being Chicano enough or sufficiently political in their work. See Sybil Venegas, *Image and Identity: Recent Chicana Art From "La Reina Del Pueblo De Los Angeles De La Porcincula,"* Vol. 2, No. 1, *Art of Greater Los Angeles in the 1990s* (Los Angeles, CA: Loyola Marymount University, 1990); Kathy Vargas, "Carolina Flores: Artist and Mother," *Tonantzin,* Vol. 3, No. 2 (Jan. 1989): 3; and Maria Ochoa, *Creative Collectives: Chicana Painters Working in Community* (Albuquerque: University of New Mexico Press, 2003).

12. Shifra M. Goldman, "'Portraying Ourselves': Contemporary Chicana Artists," *Feminist Art Criticism,* ed. Arlene Raven, Cassandra L. Langer, and Joanna Frueh (Ann Arbor, MI: UMI Research Press, 1988), 193–195.

13. The quotation is a paraphrase. Critics have consistently posed the rhetorical question, "Is your work Chicano art?" See "Big Wheel Artist Profile: Diane Gamboa," *Big Wheel: California's Premier Preview Magazine,* Vol. 12 (August 2006): 52–54.

14. Chela Sandoval further analyzes multiplicity in her examination of the ampersand. See Karen Mary Davalos, Eric R. Avila, Rafael Pérez-Torres, and Chela Sandoval, "Roundtable on the State of Chicana/o Studies," *Aztlán,* Vol, 27, No. 2 (Fall 2002): 150.

15. The first quote comes from Angie Chabram-Dernersesian, "And, Yes . . . The Earth Did Part: On the Splitting of Chicana/O Subjectivity." *Building with Our Hands: New Directions in Chicana Studies,* eds. Adela de la Torre and Beatríz M. Pesquera (Berkeley: University of California Press, 1993), 42; the second comes from page 40 of the same volume.

16. Judith Butler, *Gender Trouble: Feminism and the Subversion of Identity* (New York: Routledge, 1990).

17. Kinney Littlefield, "Savage, Menacing Insights: Grimacing vision of LA Contempo-Hip," *Press-Telegram,* Nov. 24, 1991.

18. Krista Thompson, "The Sound of Light: Reflections on Art History in the Visual Culture of Hip-Hop," *Art Bulletin* Vol. XCI, No. 4 (Dec. 2009): 481–505.

19. Shifra M. Goldman, *Dimensions of the Americas: Art and Social Change in Latin America and the United States* (Chicago: The University of Chicago Press, 1994), 207.

20. Diane Gamboa interview conducted by Karen Mary Davalos, September 1, 2004, in Los Angeles (hereafter, Gamboa Interview, Sept. 1, 2004).

21. *Bloody Coffee* (1990), acrylic on canvas, is published on the cover of *Chicana/Latina Studies* Vol. 4, No. 2 (2005).

22. The quote is from Gamboa Interview, Jan. 9, 2005. For critics who typically read Mexican and Mesoamerican symbols, see Dinah Berland, "A 'Point Blank' Vision of Pain, Pleasure," *Press Telegram,* July 29, 1990, section 1; Littlefield, "Savage,

Menacing Insights," 1991; Leah Ollman, "Providing A Potion for What Ails You," *Los Angeles Times,* June 25, 2004, E34; and Villeneuve, "Diane Gamboa," 256.

23. Gamboa Interview Jan. 9, 2005.

24. Laura E. Pérez, "Writing on the Social Body: Dresses and Body Ornamentation in Contemporary Chicana Art," *Decolonial Voices: Chicana and Chicano Cultural Studies in the 21st Century,* ed. Arturo J. Aldama and Naomi H. Quiñonez (Bloomington: Indiana University Press, 2002), 30–63; Pérez, *Chicana Art: The Politics of Spiritual and Aesthetic Altarities* (Durham, NC: Duke University Press, 2007); Sybil Venegas, *Image and Identity*; Villeneuve, "Diane Gamboa."

25. Pérez, *Chicana Art,* 51.

26. Pérez, *Chicana Art,* 69.

27. Henri Lefebvre, *The Production of Space,* trans. Donald Nicholson-Smith (Cambridge, MA.: Blackwell, 1991), 83.

28. Gamboa Interview Sept. 1, 2004.

29. Gamboa Interview Sept. 1, 2004.

30. Gamboa Interview Sept. 1, 2004.

31. Raúl Homero Villa, *Barrio-Logos: Space and Place in Urban Chicano Literature and Culture* (Austin: University of Texas Press, 2000).

32. In the early 1980s, Gamboa did not have a studio but identified the East Los Angeles and Hollywood punk world as her workspace, photographing the performances of The Plugz, the Brat, Black Flag, the Germs, and Los Illegals. She frequented Club Vex, the East Los Angeles venue within Self-Help Graphics and Art. See Carolina González, "Punk Pioneers Dez Cadena of Black Flag, Willie Herrón of Los Illegals and Tito Larriva of the Plugz Flip Through the Lost Pages of Music History," *Frontera* (Los Angeles), Spring Issue (1997): 43; and "Big Wheel Artist Profile: Diane Gamboa," 52–54.

33. *Puro Latino* (Los Angeles), "Diane Gamboa: Art from an Untamed Soul," Sept. 6, 1996, n.p., emphasis in the original.

34. Tiffany Ana López, "Critical Witnessing in Latina/o and African American Prison Narratives," *Prose and Cons: Essays on Prison Literature in the United States,* ed. D. Quentin Miller (Jefferson, NC: McFarland and Company, 2005), 64.

35. *Malathion Baby* (1990), serigraph, is published in *Across the Street: Self-Help Graphics and Chicano Art in Los Angeles,* Bolton T. Colburn and Margarita Nieto (Laguna Art Museum, 1995), 46.

36. For examples of *Pin Up*, see Pérez, *Chicana Art,* 77; Latino Art Community http://mati.eas.asu.edu/community/ChicArt/ArtistDir/DiaGam.html. Accessed on March 15, 2010.

37. Alejandra Rosas, "Diane Gamboa expone en el nombre del amor," *La Opinion* (Los Angeles), Mayo 1992, 1E+. Translation by author.

38. *Little Gold Man* (1990), serigraph, is published in Pérez, *Chicana Art,* 76.

39. Michel Foucault, *Discipline and Punish: The Birth of the Prison* (New York: Random House, 1975).

40. This lacuna in art history is a structural problem of higher education. Shifra M. Goldman and Sybil Venegas, the first to focus their careers on Chicana/o art history, received mixed support from the discipline. Because of this bias, art historians of Chicana/o art used their doctoral studies to investigate adjacent fields, such as pre-Columbian or Mexican art. The publication venues of art history rarely

publish articles or reviews on Chicana/o art. See Rita Gonzalez, "Undocumented History: A Survey of Index Citations for Latino and Latina Artists," *CSRC Research Report* 2 (August 2003): 1–8. Research centers have undertaken efforts to correct this problem. The UCLA Chicano Studies Research Center has launched the book series *A Ver: Revisioning Art History*, dedicated to US Latina/o artists; the Museum of Fine Arts Houston initiated *Documents of 20th Century Latin American and Latino Art, A Digital Archive and Publications Project*; and the Museum of Modern Art launched *METRO MoMA Survey of Archives of Latino and Latin American Art*.

41. Shifra M. Goldman and Tomás Ybarra-Frausto, introduction to *Arte Chicano: A Comprehensive Annotated Bibliography of Chicano Art, 1965–1981*, ed. Shifra M. Goldman and Tomás Ybarra-Frausto (Berkeley: Chicano Studies Library Publication Unit, University of California, 1985).

42. The latter period is truncated because it aligns with the tenure of their research in the 1980s. Elsewhere, Ybarra-Frausto elongates the period into the late 1980s and early 1990s. See Tomás Ybarra-Frausto, "The Chicano Movement/the Movement of Chicano Art," *Exhibiting Cultures: The Poetics and Politics of Museum Display*, eds. Ivan Karp and Steven D. Lavine (Washington and London: Smithsonian Institution Press, 1991), 128–150.

43. Shifra M. Goldman, "Response: Another Opinion on the State of Chicano Art," *Dimensions of the Americas* (Chicago: University of Chicago Press, 1994) 383–393. Originally published in *Metamórfosis* Vol. 3, No. 2 & 4, No. 1 (1980–1981): 2–7; Malaquías Montoya and Lezlie Salkowitz-Montoya, "A Critical Perspective on the State of Chicano Art," *Metamórfosis* Vol. 3, No. 1 (1980): 3–7. In *Exhibiting Mestizaje* (Albuquerque: University of New Mexico Press, 2001), I incorrectly assess the dialogue between the Montoyas and Goldman as a debate, as if they stood at opposite shores. Here I recant that claim. Although Goldman assumes a stance of opposition against the Montoyas, her argument depends upon the culture of resistance for which the Montoyas call.

44. Gonzalez et al., "Introduction," *Phantom Sightings*, 13; Fox, "Theater of the Inauthentic," 78.

WORKS CITED

Alarcón, Norma. "The Theoretical Subject(s) of *This Bridge Called My Back* and Anglo-American Feminism." In *Making Face, Making Soul: Haciendo Caras*, edited by Gloria Anzaldúa, 365–369. San Francisco, CA: Aunt Lute Foundation Book, 1990.

———. "Chicana Feminism: In the Tracks of 'the' Native Woman." In *Living Chicana Theory*, edited by Carla Trujillo, 371–382. Berkeley, CA: Third Woman Press, 1998.

Anzaldúa, Gloria. *Borderlands/La Frontera: The New Mestiza*. San Francisco, CA: Spinsters/Aunt Lute, 1987.

Berland, Dinah. "A 'Point Blank' Vision of Pain, Pleasure." *Press Telegram*, July 29, 1990, S1.

"Big Wheel Artist Profile: Diane Gamboa." *Big Wheel: California's Premier Preview Magazine*, August 2006, 52–54.

Butler, Judith. *Gender Trouble: Feminism and the Subversion of Identity.* New York: Routledge, 1990.

Chabram-Dernersesian, Angie. "And, Yes . . . The Earth Did Part: On the Splitting of Chicana/O Subjectivity." In *Building with Our Hands: New Directions in Chicana Studies,* edited by Adela de la Torre and Beatríz M. Pesquera, 34–56. Berkeley: University of California Press, 1993.

Davalos, Karen Mary, Eric R. Avila, Rafael Pérez-Torres, and Chela Sandoval. "Roundtable on the State of Chicana/o Studies." *Aztlán* Vol. 27, No. 2 (Fall 2002): 143–154.

"Diane Gamboa: Art from an Untamed Soul." *Puro Latino,* Sept. 6, 1996, n.p.

Foucault, Michel. *Discipline and Punish: The Birth of the Prison.* New York: Random House, 1975.

Goldman, Shifra M. "'Portraying Ourselves': Contemporary Chicana Artists." In *Feminist Art Criticism: An Anthology,* edited by Arlene Raven, Cassandra L. Langer, and Joanna Frueh, 187–205. Ann Arbor, MI: UMI Research Press, 1988.

———. *Dimensions of the Americas: Art and Social Change in Latin America and the United States.* Chicago: The University of Chicago Press, 1994.

Goldman, Shifra M., and Tómas Ybarra-Frausto, eds. *Arte Chicano: A Comprehensive Annotated Bibliography of Chicano Art, 1965–1981.* Berkeley: Chicano Studies Library Publications Unit, University of California, 1985.

González, Carolina. "Punk Pioneers Dez Cadena of Black Flag, Willie Herrón of Los Illegals and Tito Larriva of the Plugz Flip through the Lost Pages of Music History." *Frontera* 1997, 41–43.

Gonzalez, Rita. "Undocumented History: A Survey of Index Citations for Latino and Latina Artists." *CSRC Research Report* No. 2 (August 2003): 1–8.

Gonzalez, Rita, Howard N. Fox, and Chon A. Noriega. *Phantom Sightings: Art after the Chicano Movement.* Los Angeles and Berkeley: University of California Press and Los Angeles County Museum of Art, 2008.

Lefebvre, Henri. *The Production of Space,* translated by Donald Nicholson-Smith. Cambridge, MA: Blackwell, 1991.

Littlefield, Kinney. "Savage, Menacing Insights: Grimacing Vision of LA. Contempo-Hip." *Press-Telegram* (Long Beach, CA), November 24, 1991, S1.

López, Tiffany Ana. "Critical Witnessing in Latina/O and African American Prison Narratives." In *Prose and Cons: Essays on Prison Literature in the United States,* edited by D. Quentin Miller, 62–80. Jefferson, NC: McFarland and Company, 2005.

Mendoza, Ruben R. "Deciphering the Decoy: Phantom Transformations and the Decolonial Imaginary of Chicana/o Art (Review: LACMA's *Phantom Sightings: Art after the Chicano Movement*)." LatinArt.com. Accessed on Dec. 12, 2008.

Montoya, Malaquías, and Lezlie Salkowitz-Montoya. "A Critical Perspective on the State of Chicano Art." *Metamórfosis* Vol. 3, No. 1 (1980): 3–7.

Moraga, Cherríe, and Gloria Anzaldúa, eds. *This Bridge Called My Back: Writings by Radical Women of Color.* Watertown, MA: Persephone Press, 1981.

Ochoa, María. *Creative Collectives: Chicana Painters Working in Community.* Albuquerque: University of New Mexico Press, 2003.

Ollman, Leah. "Providing a Potion for What Ails You." *Los Angeles Times,* June 25, 2004, E34.

Pérez, Laura E. "Writing on the Social Body: Dresses and Body Ornamentation in Contemptorary Chicana Art." In *Decolonial Voices: Chicana and Chicano Cultural Studies in the 21st Century,* edited by Arturo J. Aldama and Naomi H. Quiñonez, 30–63. Bloomington: Indiana University Press, 2002.

———. *Chicana Art: The Politics of Spiritual and Aesthetic Altarities.* Durham, NC: Duke University Press, 2007.

Rosas, Alejandro. "Diane Gamboa Expone En El Nombre Del Amor." *La Opinion,* Mayo 1992, 1E+.

Shaked, Nizan. "Event Review: Phantom Sightings: Art after the Chicano Movement." *American Quarterly* Vol. 60, No. 4 (2008): 1057–1072.

Thompson, Krista. "The Sound of Light: Reflections on Art History in the Visual Culture of Hip-Hop." *Art Bulletin* Vol. XCI, No. 4 (2009): 481–505.

Vargas, Kathy. "Carolina Flores: Artist and Mother," *Tonantzin* Vol. 3, No. 2 (Jan. 1989): 3.

Venegas, Sybil. *Image and Identity: Recent Chicana Art From "La Reina Del Pueblo De Los Angeles De La Porcincula."* Vol. 2, Art of Greater Los Angeles in the 1990s. Los Angeles, CA: Loyola Marymount University, 1990.

Villa, Raúl Homero. *Barrio-Logos: Space and Place in Urban Chicano Literature and Culture.* Austin: University of Texas Press, 2000.

Villeneuve, Pat. "Diane Gamboa." In *Contemporary Chicana and Chicano Art,* edited by Gary Keller, 256–257. Tempe, AZ: Bilingual Press/Editorial Bilingüe, 2002.

Ybarra-Frausto, Tomas. "The Chicano Movement/the Movement of Chicano Art." In *Exhibiting Cultures: The Poetics and Politics of Museum Display,* edited by Ivan Karp and Steven D. Lavine, 128–150. Washington and London: Smithsonian Institution Press, 1991.

FIVE

Human Rights, Conditioned Choices, and Performance in Ana Castillo's *Mixquihuala Letters*

CARL GUTIÉRREZ-JONES

An acclaimed poet known for combining protest themes and formal experiment, Ana Castillo became part of a new wave of Chicana fiction writing with the publication of her 1986 novel *Mixquiahuala Letters.* Like her poetry, the novel is particularly striking for its formal play and especially its attention to narrative structure. Mimicking Julio Cortazar's novel *Rayuela* (1963), Castillo presents her reader with various choices regarding how to participate in the text's construction, soliciting a self-conscious performance that resonates with inquiries regarding the nature of choice—how choices are recognized and conditioned—by characters in the novel. Specifically, Castillo divides *Mixquiahula Letters* into numbered chapters, then invites readers to restructure the order of the original presentation along certain suggested paths (paths that reorder the letters, sometimes omitting certain letters). For Cortazar, the announced goal was to distinguish active from passive reading, a distinction that he infamously coded in explicitly sexist terms—male reading equated with active interpretation, female reading equated with passive capitulation. (To his credit, Cortazar offered an apology for this formulation later in his career.) Castillo playfully appropriates this narrative territory in order to flip Cortazar's initial sexual politics on its head: in *Mixquiahuala Letters,* responsible, engaged reading and the construction of understanding itself inevitably partake of a Chicana feminist critical analysis informed by the human rights movement.

Focusing on the performance invited by the novel, this essay explores Castillo's play with the idea of choice—a play that shapes both the themes and style of the novel—to situate *Mixquiahuala Letters* and Chicana feminist activism in debates that are central to the modern human rights movement. Though the *Declaration of Human Rights* (1948) signified a crucial step toward building international agreement regarding universal rights, the document's non-binding status speaks volumes about the Cold War–era ideological tensions that deeply troubled this and subsequent efforts to define these rights in a manner that carried legal weight. Put crudely, the Soviet Union and its eastern bloc allies strongly preferred recognition of economic and social rights (to education, to economic equity, to health care, to unionize), whereas the United States and its allies endorsed instead civil and political rights (to freedom of speech, to liberty, to equality before the law). In literature, one finds a host of authors who engage these ideological debates in order to rethink and constructively critique the human rights movement; prominent examples include Aleksandr Solzhenitsyn, the Russian novelist and historian who interrogates the horrors of the Soviet gulag (prison system), and Elie Wiesel, the Jewish Holocaust survivor who documents his life before, during, and after his internment in the Nazi death camps. This essay argues that Ana Castillo engages the central human rights debate described but also that Castillo's contribution extends beyond the parameters of the debate as described. Specifically, *Mixquiahuala Letters* offers a human rights–oriented intervention that is shaped strongly by developments in Chicana feminism, as this movement undertakes dialogues with Third World feminism and "mainstream" US feminism. Castillo's groundbreaking contribution, then, involves rethinking, and creating a bridge between, two debates that were both being defined by ideas regarding people's choices and how they are, or how they should be, conditioned.

As noted, the human rights movement was enthralled in a conflict that pitted the individual's liberty against the equitable distribution of resources among social groups. Each option suggested that certain kinds of choices (e.g., to express oneself freely, or to unionize) were more important and deserved greater legal recognition and protection than those emphasized by the opposing camp. At the same time, since the 1970s, many Chicana and women of color feminists had been critical of "pro-choice" arguments as articulated by the US feminist movement. In a nutshell, these women of color found the "choice" of this pro-choice movement too simple because it ignored the intersection of race, class, and gender that made the life experiences and political goals of women of color seemingly invisible to the mainstream feminist movement. For these activists, the right to an abortion had inappropriately and selectively eclipsed other rights and choices that also merited committed political action. (Such action, for example, has since become the basis for the Reproductive Justice movement, where it is just as important to ask what kind of life a mother and child must negotiate as it is to ask whether abortion should be an option.) In sum, *Mixquiahuala Letters* offers a valuable bridge between these debates by staging a powerful inquiry regarding the performance of life choices and the complex ways that they are conditioned by the language of rights. Crucially, Castillo invites the reader to participate in a self-conscious performance of choice; in the process, the reader may become more aware of how choices are constructed. The liberatory implications are significant, especially if the conditions impacting choices can be reconstructed in order to free readers from problematic habits of thought and self-imposed constraints.

In undertaking this work, Castillo is participating in a long history of Chicano political activism that has engaged human rights thinkers from throughout the world. Such work was especially crucial as the Chicano Movement was getting off the ground and as Chicana literary and scholarly contributions significantly reworked and critiqued the project. In this vein, Mahatma Ghandi, the great human rights thinker and activist, had a tremendous influence on Cesar Chavez, the leader of the United Farm Workers. This relationship is perhaps the best-known example of exchange involving the Chicano Movement, but such exchange in fact permeated many of the most celebrated Chicano political actions, from the Tierra Amarilla Courthouse Raid (1967) to the LA Unified Blowouts (1968) and the Chicano Moratorium (1970). Chicano lawyers, including Oscar Zeta Acosta, used this same human rights discourse to gain legal recognition of Chicanos as a group that is subject to discrimination and therefore capable of making claims for remedy. Yet despite these efforts to build on diverse human rights thinking, some prominent Chicano historians have construed the story of protest and activism as largely self-contained and auto-referential. Perhaps the most prominent example of this tendency is Rodolfo Acuña's *Occupied America: A History of Chicanos,* a work that has been reissued numerous times and that remains one of the most cited texts treating the topic. The failure of such texts to engage adequately the role of human rights dialogue in Chicano history is perhaps not so much evidence of pointed exclusions as it is an expression of a certain insularity that one might expect at the moment a new social identity is coming into being after an extended period of discrimination and violent subjection.

This largely male-dominated insularity regarding the role of human rights was effectively challenged, and to a significant degree surpassed, by the insights of the Chicana wave of the eighties and beyond, including contributions by Helena Maria Viramontes, Sandra Cisneros, Cherríe Moraga, Gloria Anzaldúa, Maria Herrera Sobek, Chela Sandoval, Rosa Linda Fregoso, Norma Alarcón, Emma Pérez, and a host of scholars and creative writers invested in complicating and enriching the politics animating Chicano activism by rethinking the intersections of race, class, gender, and sexuality. In situating Ana Castillo's addition to this powerful rethinking of the Chicano Movement, this essay invites readers to approach *Mixquiahuala Letters* as something of a corrective regarding the stories that the Chicano Movement told about itself. This is an effort not simply to recognize what has been left out—the key interactions with human rights and feminist thinking and activism—but also an effort to understand how the story telling itself changed to facilitate this re-newed vision. Castillo deserves credit for telling a more accurate, compelling, and inclusive story and also recognition for her novel's contribution to the evolution of human rights literature and its experiments with performativity and ideas of choice specifically.

* * *

Mixquiahuala Letters is a combination of travelogue and epistolary novel that contains forty numbered "letter-chapters." Two things are immediately striking about the letters. First, all of them are authored by the same character, Teresa, and addressed to the same recipient, Alicia, whose epistolary responses are not represented in the novel. Given that much of the work explores the forces that divide the women, especially those that have been internalized by Teresa and Alicia, the lack of responses from Alicia accentuates a theme noted by Castillo in a 1991 interview: the novel tracks various failures of communication between the two women.

Second, the letters read less like letters and more like diary entries. Since much of the action described in the letters was experienced by both of the women as they undertook travels through México, the point of the letter writing seems to fall on gaining—through after-the-fact communication—a better understanding of events. In some cases, the focus is devoted to the men whom the travelers encountered, men whose actions seemed to flip all too easily between the roles of fairytale suitor and lying manipulator, or much worse. But although Castillo very effectively conveys the seemingly ubiquitous menace waiting for the women as they break convention by traveling on their own, greater attention is devoted to the interactions between the two women. From Teresa's perspective, the various betrayals between the women kept their relationship from becoming the sort that could help them better negotiate the sexism and discrimination perpetually impacting their lives.

These two facets—the focus on failed communication and the diary-like meditation—combine to imply that the book is in part a record of self-examination and therapy through writing. To read it as such, one need not assume that Alicia is imagined by Teresa, nor is it necessary to assume that the letters have no responses because they were never sent. Indeed, we might view the incomplete and ultimately unexplained one-sided communication as indicative of the principal problem that Teresa is trying to work through with her writing. Letter Thirty-Two announces just this sort of commitment to a talking cure as Teresa describes a nadir in her life after an especially grim breakup and an abortion. The climax of this letter involves a return to a particularly powerful scene of pain in the novel, one that Castillo repeats in various letters. Teresa is haunted by this scene because in this defining moment, she witnessed Alicia's pain in the wake of a failed romance and refused to acknowledge what was clear to her then and is all the more obvious in retrospect: despite their feminist rhetoric, Alicia's and Teresa's lives were ruled and may continue to be ruled by their own desire for male approval and their adherence to patriarchal notions of legitimacy. Teresa is especially angry with herself because she lied to Alicia in the original scene, telling Alicia that she did not understand her investment in the suitor nor the self-hatred that followed the rejection. Teresa's self-destructive actions throughout the novel act as foil to her denial in this scene, making the lie all the more glaring. Both women reinvest in the patriarchal fantasy again and again, with the same disappointments predictably repeated. As such, the novel asks how these women might construct/condition and perform choices enabling a break of the cycle.

In fact, the narrative is both more and less dire than this description suggests, and this is possible because Castillo invites the reader to reconstruct the text along three different paths that she describes at the opening of the work, as though one were being supplied with three alternative tables of contents. Designated "For the Conformist," "For the Cynic," and "For the Quixotic," each of these paths disrupt the order of the numbered "letter-chapters." None of the paths instructs the reader to begin with Letter One. In fact, only one version (the quixotic) includes this letter at all, and here the reader is instructed to take it up last. Most of the paths include most of the letters, but key letters are omitted in the different versions; for example, only the path labeled "For the Cynic" includes Letter Thirty-Six, in which Teresa announces that she and Alicia have never been lovers. This path also leaves out Letter Thirteen, which includes a crucial moment of honest communication as Teresa examines her own racial attitudes toward Alicia. Seemingly small adjustments to these paths thus carry great cumulative impacts. The overall structure demands a type of reading that attends to non-linear connections and that demonstrates a sensitivity to patterns of meaning arising from association. Most importantly, Castillo insists from the outset on a degree of readerly self-reflection regarding the desires brought to the scene of interpretation.

In terms of outcomes, the three paths are distinguished by varying prospects for caring, self-aware communication. The conformist reading concludes with the women thoroughly detached as Teresa, now comfortably married, has only begun to let go of the blame that she has directed at Alicia for their attempts to challenge gender roles. The cynical reading ends with both women in hetero-normative relationships that are emotionally lacking, if not outright self-destructive. As noted, this version eliminates key letters that suggest self-reflection regarding the forces undermining the relationship between the two as well as any suggestion that their relationship might have been more than platonic. Only the quixotic path offers a future for the women, as it ends with the two planning yet another trip to México, a venture that seems especially promising given that the penultimate letter in this series is the most compelling call for authentic communication and self-examination to be found in the novel.

The prospects for gaining a critical consciousness while traveling are strong in this text when the women are operating in the quixotic mode. Teresa and Alicia are not entirely devoid of the kinds of problematic fantasies and projections that shape other travel narratives in which US tourists visit México, but the women see and hear with the eyes and ears of the other.[1] In addition, they undertake the work of reconciling, or at least critically examining, the conflicts between their pre-conceived visions of México and the "realities" of what they encounter. The presentation of these realities is informed by Castillo's long-standing investments in human rights activism and translates into characters who recognize what other tourists do not, including political oppression, revolutionary actions, racism, sexism, and class struggle.

At crucial moments in the novel, romantic love is reconfigured in terms of human rights awareness. These moments mark an important alternative to the dead-end patriarchal fantasies that so often win the women's obedience. Consider, for example, Teresa's inspired debate with a would-be suitor in Letter Twenty-Two.

> Ponce, the engineer who had thought that we were from South America took the seat next to me. . . . I had the idea that this man was no fool and that we were about to enter a battle of wits. He began, "I think you are a liberal woman. Am I correct?" His expression meant to persuade me that it didn't matter what I replied. In the end, he would win. . . . In that country, the term "liberated woman" meant something other than what we strived for back in the United States. In this case it simply meant a woman who would sleep nondiscriminately with any man that came along.
>
> "What you perceive as 'liberal' is my independence to choose what I do, with whom, and when. Moreover, it also means that I may choose *not* to do it, with anyone, ever." (*Mixquiahuala Letters*, 78–79)

Teresa closes this letter by proclaiming "checkmate." The battle of wits might be read as a question of whether or not Ponce's seduction will succeed, but Castillo invites something more as she uses the occasion to interrogate the term "liberal." Here she is inviting readers to think about the deeper political and philosophical roots of the term where it describes the notion of the individual's fundamental freedom and liberty. Interpreted in this fashion, Letter Twenty-Two presents a struggle over the basic nature of an individual's ability to choose. Teresa responds not simply by rebutting the seduction but also by questioning the assumptions of the seduction plot itself. She refuses the notion that her choices are beside the point, and she bluntly dismisses the idea that she must necessarily be written into the seduction plot at all.

Similarly, Letter Twenty-Seven offers a dream of love and resistance, a dream that presents an activist-author taking up arms to defend the poor, the young, and the principle of freedom of expression.

> I swung around to a confrontation with the intellectuals who criticized my intentions. In a rage, I tore open the worn shirt to reveal flesh. "i am a woman," i shouted, "but i am first human. . . ." Hurrying to a shelf piled with rags and feeling underneath, it was there. My weapon. . . . The hour had come. (*Mixquiahuala Letters*, 103)

With its artist-lover standing alone against marching troops (the intellectuals nowhere in sight), Letter Twenty-Seven appears to portend a "massacre of the dreamers," a scenario that anticipates Castillo's 1995 essay collection by the same title. Combining what we find in the novel with the arguments presented in Castillo's essay collection, we may surmise that Castillo is committed to exploring the power of filial and loving bonds (the ostensible focus of the epistolary genre) because these have powerful human rights implications. The human rights movement itself may be thought of, at least in part, as an effort to (re)create feelings and ideas of empathy and responsibility that we might extend to people far different from ourselves (understanding that, in many circumstances, an obsessive focus on romance within one's immediate context might block the development of cross-cultural human rights bonds). Taken together, Castillo's essay collection and novel argue for redirecting the desires and energies that may be contained by the socially insulating properties of the hetero-normative romance scenario. Through this reform, the desires and energies may feed new notions of social relations, or that modified sense of cosmopolitanism that the noted philosopher, cultural theorist, and novelist Kwame Anthony Appiah has tried to describe in his recent work. For Castillo, such reform involves rethinking how choices are conditioned and how politics is performed throughout a broad spectrum of public and private actions. This rethinking may, as is the case in *Mixquiahuala Letters*, involve characters who are, to a significant degree, caught in cycles of betrayal and missed opportunities for communication. The associative patterns that arise out of the text both mirror and set in critical relief thought processes that condition the self-defeating choices.

In this vein, Castillo's novel holds a strong resemblance to a variety of "existential" inquiries to be found in human rights literature. Here existentialism signifies a focus on the human subject—not merely the thinking subject, but the acting, feeling, living human individual and his or her conditions of existence (that is, the factors that shape a person's choices in life and the significance people ascribe to those choices). Elie Wiesel, of course, studied with the famous existentialist philosopher Jean-Paul Sartre at the Sorbonne in Paris after his emancipation from the Nazi death camps. Focusing on Sartre's impact, numerous reviewers have emphasized those aspects of Wiesel's first and perhaps most famous narrative, *Night,* that fit popular conceptions of existentialism. In this context, existentialism underscores the importance of choices undertaken by an individual who is faced with an irrational world. As such, existentialism is also an attempt to think beyond what the renowned American novelist Joseph Heller termed the "chains of inherited habit" leading to war and beyond the submission of the individual to fascism and to bureaucracy. While aspects of *Night* and Wiesel's Nobel Prize speech reinforce this sense of a commitment to existentialism (consider, for example, the conclusion of the speech, and Wiesel's admonition, "There may be times when we are powerless to prevent injustice, but there must never be a time when we fail to protest"), *Night* also carefully documents the Nazi program of destroying social connections and group values among those imprisoned in the death camps. Further, the text subtly underscores the possibilities of keeping these connections and values alive, even under the harshest of conditions. In other words, Weisel pays close attention to the ways that choices are conditioned by social forces.

Alexander Solzhenitsyn's 1962 novel *One Day in the Life of Ivan Denisovitch,* another canonical text in human rights literature, develops a similarly complicated engagement of existentialist ideas. The first text to convey the horrors of the Gulag system to an international, as well as to a Soviet, audience, this novel has been taken to foreground the existentialist work ethic of the protagonist. This work ethic does indeed serve as a survival strategy, but it is also an indicator of the moral and physical strength of the Russian folk. A scathing critique of the legal system under Stalin and of the Gulag bureaucracy, the novel poses the main character's relation to certain forms of work as a means of fulfillment; in this vein, Ivan Denisovich literally makes it through a physically and emotionally torturous day in sub-zero weather by finding self-worth and meaning in his vocation as a bricklayer. However, both the survival ethic and the satisfaction gained from the work are inherently related to the alternative family structure described in the novel: the work gang. Ivan chooses to invest himself in the work (a strategy that makes him recognizable as an existentialist), but without the connection to his work crew, and without his deep reverence for the social values instilled in the crew's structure, this investment would be difficult to imagine.

These "canonical" human rights texts implicitly negotiate the deep ideological split that profoundly shaped, and at times threatened, the modern human rights movement. Much post-WWII human rights literature wrestles with this tension as it tries to accommodate very different narrative demands—and we may specify narrative demands, because the two most prominent sides of this debate told very different stories regarding what constitutes the human and the rights indelibly associated with the human. With the horrors of WWII as a prompt and the ongoing threat of mutually assured nuclear destruction, all participants in the human rights movement had compelling reasons to invest in change. Their stories not only embodied their particular priorities but also served a rhetorical function. In this vein, certain types of characterizations and narrative tensions may serve particularly well for communicating the civil and political rights that the United States and its allies held in highest esteem. Struggles among individual characters who must overcome social obstacles in order to distinguish themselves as autonomous and free actors reinforce such values. Likewise, particular narrative techniques may foreground the social, economic, and cultural values that emerged as the human rights priorities of the Soviet bloc. Narratives that experiment with collective voices representing social groups may conjure ideas of social relationships and communal responsibility that are especially crucial in this vein. Ultimately, the novels most closely aligned with one side or the other of the human rights debate might use both their content and style to persuade readers toward the authors' preferences. In this sense, such literary works are shaped, implicitly or explicitly, by rhetorical goals. One might also claim that the most compelling, most resonant human rights literature creates a productive dialogue within these tensions by carefully modulating the ideologically-loaded themes and techniques indicative of the two sides of the debate.

Many of the most celebrated human rights narratives in the west (e.g., *Night, One Day in the Life of Ivan Denisovich, Catch-22, Waiting for the Barbarians, Widows, Beloved*) foreground existential issues in order to set up these compelling dialogues, and in this manner, it may be said that these texts are oriented for a reader at least partially indoctrinated in western priorities (including a prioritizing of civil liberties above social and economic mechanisms keyed toward achieving societal/group equity). In such cases, the authors draw the readers into the debate by building on familiar ground, since existential narratives are conventionally associated with crises involving an individual's exercise, or deferral, of self-defining choice, a territory of conventional interest for western liberal audiences. That said, we might recall noted literary critic Lucio Ruotolo's assertion that the narrative journey through individual existential crisis may in certain cases lead to renewed engagement with socio-historical processes where authors hold such reincorporation as a value. According to Ruotolo, this renewed engagement could cultivate conceptions of existential agency more in keeping with the side of the human rights debate favoring social, economic, and cultural concerns. Such agency might take the form of a collective/communal voice, but it might also entail the representation of individual characters who embrace the radical contingency of their identities, the ways that they are literally made up by the people around them. It is certainly possible for human rights authors to emphasize the individual as an autonomous actor in an absurd environment. But as I have suggested, texts like *Night, One Day in the Life of Ivan Denisovich,* and *Mixquiahuala Letters* are far more attentive to the seemingly inescapable ways that choices are conditioned than can be accommodated by the conventional understandings of existentialism that dominate much of the criticism devoted to the literature.

Ana Castillo is keenly aware of the human rights debates that I have been describing. We know this from examining her creative and scholarly writings and from tracking her participation in human rights activities. She is also well read in the canon of human rights literature. These points should be taken into account as we consider her decision to rework Cortazar's famously existential novel. Specifically, she has engaged the epistolary form—a genre that foregrounds social bonds—and framed it with a highly self-conscious existentialist twist in order to rethink the limits of hetero-normative romance. She thereby invites readers to better understand how choices are conditioned by social, economic, and cultural factors. In this manner, her work contributes to a tradition of narrative experimentation that has evolved, in part, as a response to the debates at the core of the human rights movement. Her central character, Teresa, is in a sense fundamentally isolated (no letters from Alicia are reproduced in the text), and yet her writing records a wish for alliance and a recognition of her social contingency. Castillo invites readers to value this contingency, in part because it sustains a political and social awareness on Teresa's part. This capacity, in turn, allows Teresa to think about life choices in complicated ways that engage the intersections of class, race, gender, and sexuality. When Teresa chooses to undertake an abortion, the decision is strongly shaped by considerations regarding the social context that the mother and child would inherit. The novel, in fact, carries many reminders that reproductive politics need to be rethought in light of the intersections noted. We learn, for example, that Alicia was subject to forced sterilization while using a Puerto Rican friend's identification in order to receive medical services.

Castillo focuses on the right to reproductive choice, a central theme of the mainstream feminist movement, but she carefully explicates the specific concerns that were leading Chicana feminists to articulate an alternative project, one that has been subsequently formalized in the Reproductive Justice movement. In this regard, Castillo has generated a powerful merging of debates. She has combined the rethinking of existentialism that is so prominent in human rights literature with a significant intervention in feminist reproductive politics. Crucially, she has built this exploration of conditioned choices so as to compel the reader to participate in the continuous making of the text. Each suggested reading path throws new light not only on the choices ascribed to the characters but also on the decisions credited to the reader. In the process, we self-consciously participate in the construction of different forms of knowledge. We literally and figuratively perform the choices put in motion in the novel, and from this encounter readers may find that they, like the Teresa of the novel's quixotic version, end by beginning the journey again, this time with the prospect of realizing empathy and alliances that have proved precarious in the past.

NOTE

1. Consider, for example, Jack Keroauc's *On the Road* and the epiphany that the narrator associates with a visit to a Mexican brothel.

REFERENCES

Acuña, Rodolfo. *Occupied America: A History of Chicanos.* New York: Longman, 2006.

Appiah, Kwame Anthony. *Cosmopolitanism: Ethics in a World of Strangers.* New York: Norton, 2007.

Castillo, Ana. *Massacre of the Dreamers: Essays on Xicanisma.* New York: Plume, 1995.

Cortazar, Julio. *Rayuela.* Madrid: Catedra, 2008.

———. *Mixquiahuala Letters.* Tempe, AZ: Bilingual Review Press, 1986.

Solzhenitsyn, Alexandr. *One Day in the Life of Ivan Denisovitch.* New York: Farrar, Straus and Giroux, 1991.

———. *Nobel Lecture.* New York: Farrar, Straus and Giroux, 1972.

Wiesel, Elie. *Night.* New York: Hill and Wang, 2006.

SIX

Decolonizing Gender Performativity: A Thesis for Emancipation in Early Chicana Feminist Thought (1969–1979)

DAPHNE V. TAYLOR-GARCÍA

In the early twenty-first century, our visual field is still gendered by colonial/racial dynamics. Many of the first Chicana feminist writers foregrounded an analysis of colonization in their evaluation of the struggles of contemporary US women of color, directly connecting the 1960s uprisings in the United States to those in the Caribbean, South America, Africa, China, and more. Pathbreaking documents written by Chicana feminists in the 1970s that grappled with intersectional injustices and the challenge of exposing the stifling role of racialized gender dynamics illuminated a consistent connection between colonialism and contemporary struggles.[1]

Bernice Rincón's 1971 piece titled "La Chicana: Her Role in the Past and Her Search for a New Role in the Future" encapsulated the sentiment of a generation caught between revolutionary action, on the one hand, and culturally sedimented expectations of being "women," on the other. Rincón wrote,

> Sisters are working to develop a strategy that will enable us to be women people, rather than chattels or pets . . . Women are [considered by traditional Mexican culture] inferior beings . . . Their inferiority is constitutional and resides in their sex, their submissiveness, which is a wound that never heals . . . He does not attribute evil instincts to her; he even pretends she does not have any . . . [I]t is impossible for her to have a personal, private life, for if she were to be herself, if she were to be mistress of her own wishes, passions or whims, she would be unfaithful to herself.[2]

This 1971 article clearly articulated the suffocating demands of stereotyped women's roles. By defining the stereotype, Rincón opened up the possibility for a critical evaluation of the confluences of race, sex, gender, and agency. Chicana feminists like Rincón were a crucial part of a burst of discussions happening around the world and created the conditions in which Judith Butler's highly influential theory on the performativity of gender—that gender is a heterogeneous social construct—was articulated.[3] Women of color feminists voiced the contentious nature of organizing a unified feminist movement across gender, race, and class difference and highlighted the discursive and scopic dimensions of gender in normative power relations, exposing the need for a genealogy of the very category "women."[4] Latina feminist philosopher Maria Lugones traced this genealogy and found that the lived experience of "women" under colonization looked very different than it did in Western Europe. She has proposed that gender itself, as defined by patriarchy and heteronormativity, is a colonial construct.[5] It is at this radical juncture that Lugones proposes—that colonialism introduced a unique modality of relations called "gender"—that we can look more closely at the contributions of early Chicana feminist thought in the articulation of decolonization as a thesis for emancipation.

* * *

The 1960s Chicano Movement rose in resistance to the persistent social injustices prevalent within the United States, but it was also part of a broader global uprising that expressed disenchantment with the narrative of European superiority constructed over the last five hundred years.[6] In the decades leading up to the 1970s, events like the rise of the Third Reich in Germany and their attempt to exterminate other *Europeans* (including not only German Jews but also Polish, Czechoslovakian, Hungarian, Yugoslavian, and French peoples, among others) instilled a profound sense of shock around the world. The popular rhetoric espoused by countries like the United States and Britain to inspire opposition to Hitler was implicitly anti-racist and democratic, which exposed a contradiction (many would say this is deeper than a contradiction): the United States' opposition to fascism and the *herrenvolk* state on the one hand, but the continued practice of Jim Crow and the *Bracero* Program on the other. This new insight imbued many oppressed people with a fresh determination to uproot racist ideologies and institutions at home.[7] Within the United States, people in the Chicano Movement pointed out there was a contradiction between the rhetoric of "life, liberty and the pursuit of happiness" and the lived reality of racialized communities, both multi-generational and *bracero* in the Chicana/o context, who worked hard but still found themselves *barrio*ized in American social and economic life.[8] For colonized/racialized peoples, the aftermath of World War II facilitated a reevaluation of non-Western histories and ways of being and, in many ways, vindicated the populations' epistemic and political worth in a context where they had been thoroughly devalued by the legacy of a colonial education.[9]

The period of renewed dedication to usurping racism in the United States during the 1960s and 1970s faced a number of challenges.[10] The claims to a new consciousness, the turn to Indigenous pride, and the resistance to Anglo-American hegemony in the Chicano Movement did not necessarily spur a consistent critique of sexist gender relations, and for many of the women in the movement this contradiction was another challenge in realizing decolonization.[11] Clearly, the world had changed dramatically between the early colonial period and the post–World War II decades, yet these scholar-activists pointed to a particular dynamic that persisted over the centuries. The 1970s works by Chicana feminists are thus early contributions in the study of the relationship between colonial expansion and its constitutive role in our contemporary world. What they argue, as we will see, is that the colonization of the Américas and the entrenchment of the Atlantic slave trade were not incidental, isolated historical events, but rather constitutive elements of the material and intersubjective parameters of the modern world.[12]

* * *

For the purposes of this article, "the de-colonial turn" is defined in the following two ways.[13] First, one of the defining characteristics is, as we discussed in the beginning of the article, the expression of disenchantment with Eurocentric narratives of progress and Western superiority. A second defining characteristic is the foregrounding of ethics and the self-Other relationship in social and intersubjective analyses.[14] This dialogical ethics involves being willing and committed to take seriously many different perspectives and, in particular, pay special attention to those perspectives that are seen as dispensable, irrelevant, and/or insignificant. An important aspect of the social movements of the 1960s, the Chicano Movement included, was the demand that the perspectives of minoritized communities be listened to, addressed, and taught in academic institutions.[15] However, certain peoples were marginalized *within* these movements; for example, Chicanas often found themselves excluded from decision-making processes and realized there was a specific need to address race, class *and* gender if a decolonized world was indeed going to be realized. As one illustration for the need to specifically address gendered dynamics within colonized communities in revolt, Mariana Marin and Yolanda García recounted at the Fortieth Anniversary Encuentro of the 1969 *El Plan de Santa Barbara* the highly problematic gender relations that occurred during its writing. During this time at UC Santa Barbara, Chicanas were essentially invisiblized as thinkers and agents of change within the movement and relegated to the task of typing up men's plans.[16] This kind of experience was widespread and the response decisive; Francisca Flores, editor of the Los Angeles feminist publication *Regeneración,* wrote in 1971,

> [Chicanas] can no longer remain in a subservient role or as auxiliary forces in the [Chicano] movement. They must be included in the frontline of communication, leadership and organizational responsibility . . . The issue of equality, freedom and self-determination of the Chicana—like the right of self-determination, equality, and liberation of the Mexican [Chicano] community—is not negotiable.[17]

Chicana de-colonial feminisms emerged as resistance to racialized sexist oppression, with some feminists maintaining a militant nationalist consciousness and others emphasizing a transnational relationship with Third World struggles.[18] The inability of some people within a racialized group, such as the Chicana/o Movement, to accept the intellectual contributions from those differentiated only by a presumed (and desired—as the current sign of being fully human) dimorphism was explained by early feminists such as Adelaida Del Castillo, Enriqueta Longeaux Vasquez, Elizabeth "Betita" Martinez, Anna Nieto Gómez, and Mirta Vidal as a manifestation of an unexamined colonial Eurocentrism.[19]

De-colonization is a multidimensional political project that seeks change on many levels, including the epistemic.[20] On the epistemic level, de-colonization entails taking seriously the intellectual production of colonized/racialized peoples. This is a key point because a defining aspect of colonial subjugation is to deny the intellectual potential and contributions of those being subjugated.[21] However, the situation facing Chicanas was not only a case of colonizer-colonized relations but also a particular form of coloniz*ed*-colonized relations. It is in this context that gender as a theoretical concept takes on significance in fully realizing decolonization. Maria Lugones argues the persistent disavowal of women of color / US Third World feminist critique by people who have themselves been victimized by racist oppression stems from a fatally flawed understanding of gender as the universal socialization of biological differences and the limitation of their analyses to heterosexual understandings of disputes over the control of sex and its resources and products.[22] However, if we look at early accounts of the colonial encounter, as some early Chicana feminists suggest, we see a more multidimensional narrative of gender and sexuality that does not follow these biological or material prescriptions.[23] A performance installation by artists Coco Fusco and Guillermo Gomez-Peña, *The Couple in the Cage: A Guatinaui Odyssey,* reenacts a popular representation from an early print of people in the Américas. In one scene, a voice-over lists the prices for seeing "the Guatinaui" dance and/or tell a story, and then announces that five dollars is the price to see the "male specimen's genitalia." The voice continues, "They tend to be a rather demonstrative people, if not, shall we say, highly erotic. Public exposure doesn't bother them one bit," at which point the man unclips his elaborately decorated loincloth in one swift motion to expose what could be a woman's genitalia—or, more specifically, that he doesn't have a penis.

This performance reminds us of the actual woodcuts of men in the Américas in books such as Hans Stadens's 1557 *A True History and Description of a Land Belonging to the Wild, Naked, Savage, Man-Munching People, Situated in the New World, America,* and other texts and images from early colonial print such as Amerigo Vespucci's 1504 letter, *Mundus Novus:* "For their women, being very lustful, cause the private parts of their husbands to swell up to such a huge size that they appear deformed and disgusting; and this is accomplished by a certain device of theirs, the biting of certain poisonous animals. And in consequence of this many lose their organs which break through lack of attention, and they remain eunuchs."

Gomez-Peña's character performs the latter condition of a man who, due to the supposed lasciviousness of Amerindian women, has lost his genitalia and turned into a eunuch. Examining colonial discourse reveals that referencing a universal, homogeneous, biologically based patriarchy and/or a universal male/female difference to understand the history of gender in racialized communities does not suffice. Rather we need to examine the unique way that masculinity and femininity are specifically constituted in colonized-colonizer relations and performed in colonized-colonized relations. Mirta Vidal, in 1969, provides context and a direction for future research:

> The inferior role of women in society does not date back to the beginning of time. In fact, before the European came to this part of the world women enjoyed a high position of equality with men. The submission of women, along with institutions such as the church and the patriarchy, was imported by the European colonizers.[24]

This is an important intervention to ahistorical understandings of gender that claim "women" have been the victims of a universal misogyny from time immemorial.[25] Rather, early Chicana feminists situate gender as a context-specific construct, the particularities of which can be traced in part to the modalities of relations entrenched during the period of colonization in the Américas.[26] Enriqueta Longeaux Vasquez wrote in 1969 that rather than the ubiquitous socialization of "natural" biological differences, women held and in many cases still hold, an honored position in Indigenous civilizations and that the current dilemma faced by Chicanas is a result of being subjected to Spanish social norms.[27] Although recent scholarship elucidates that gender and sexuality norms were undergoing radical shifts in Western Europe also, and that it was not a gendered totality that was imposed on the Américas but rather a gender system being *invented* vis-à-vis the colonization of the Américas, Vasquez clearly makes the point that our current gender system is a colonial construct.[28] Furthermore, the crucial works of early Chicana feminists elucidate that contemporary gender systems cannot be separated from race and economic status but rather must be understood as mutually intersecting to produce the poor woman of color's circumstance and experience.[29]

Elizabeth "Betita" Martinez, author of the recently published *500 Years of Chicana History*, recognized the early colonial period as having a special, if unwritten, importance in the configuration of our contemporary conditions. She too spelled out a research agenda back in 1972 that called for an analysis of the relationship between colonial expansion and the entangled dynamics of gender, race, and class in the configuration of our current conditions. Martinez specifically and clearly stated that we must do the work to understand the *links between* race, gender, sexuality, and class to undo the wrongs historically wrought by the Euro-Christian, capitalist, colonial project.[30] It is this research agenda that many future Chicana/Latina feminists would carry out, expanding our understanding of the epistemic, social, psychological, spiritual, and material impacts of colonization.[31]

RACIAL AND DIMORPHIC *AFFECT*: A DEFINING CONDITION OF MODERN/COLONIAL GENDER

In a 1975 article titled "La Chicana—Legacy of Suffering and Self-Denial," Anna Nieto Gómez outlined a key, defining feature of colonization: racial and gendered affect. She begins, "The roots of the psyche of la Chicana lies deep within the colonial period . . ."[32] Nieto Gómez's diagnosis connects the psychic internalization and anxious normalization of sexual, social, and economic violence against Chicanas to relations entrenched in the colonial period and goes on to explain the contemporary manifestation of the Chicana situation through a historical (albeit very brief) account of the legacy of Spanish anti-Muslim sentiment during the Inquisition and the simultaneous events resulting in the entrenchment of a new colonial order in México: namely, a human hierarchy closely linked to appraisals of phenotype that had negative implications for the social, psychological, and economic well-being of Indigenous women.[33] It is this insight that pierces the multidimensional character of the colonial condition: the impact of colonization is not only (however importantly) material and cultural but also located in our everyday cognitions of face-to-face relations. Nieto Gómez's analysis highlights that it is not only the abstract ideas or uninformed representations that colonists had of the Américas that enslaved and murdered Indigenous people and attacked their social, psychological, and material well-being; it was also that a scopic regime was forged wherein the appearance of people in the Américas gained a meaning it previously did not have—the basis of actively defining and later determining everyone's location in a human hierarchy emergent in the Américas.[34] This new meaning given to the appearance of the body would transform face-to-face interactions and social dynamics.

The scopic regime that emerged vis-à-vis the colonization of the Américas was gendered as well as racialized.[35] The visual dynamic required for determining "masculine" and "feminine" categories emerged as a defining feature of colonial relations in tandem with "epidermalization." An often-overlooked aspect of physiognomy is the dimorphic dimension. Normative Euro-Christian feminine and masculine categories were not attributed to Indigenous peoples of the Américas and Africa in sixteenth-century colonial narratives, as can be seen in, for example, the "discovery" narratives of Christopher Columbus, Pedro Álvares Cabral, Dr. Diego Álvarez Chanca, Pedro de Sintra, and Amerigo Vespucci. Lugones rightly points out that "natural sexual difference"—heterosexualism and patriarchy—were juridically definitive only of the colonizer's side of gender.[36] In contrast, gender as discursively constructed about the colonized in the early modern period is defined by the *absence* of a clear-cut dimorphism, heterosexual alliance, and/or patriarchal law.[37] To account for this colonial/racial aspect of gender within the definition of *de-colonial reason* as dialogical and intersubjective (rather than monological, monotopical and internal like Cartesian reason), it will serve us well to specify and critique the production of the "man-woman" binary within colonial/racial communities, alongside colonized-colonizer relations.[38]

COLONIALISM AND THE GENDER BINARY

Anna Nieto Gómez, perhaps the most consistent out of the 1970s feminist writers to cite the colonization of the Américas as central to understanding the Chicana struggle, critiqued the *mujer buena / mujer mala* binary that emerged in the early colonial period and defined Christian European women as chaste and non-Christian Amerindian women as unchaste. Noting that this *buena/mala* binary was being reinterpreted and reproduced in our contemporary world, Nieto Gómez asserted that this limited option of possible roles for Chicanas was insufficient. To break out of the binary's constraint, Nieto Gómez invoked Indigenous women's active business, religious, and artistic leadership roles in their community and world. She is careful to assert that the social location of Indigenous women was not inherently or necessarily egalitarian but that they were "different" and "comparatively freer."[39] To accept the *buena/mala* dichotomy only reinscribes a social requirement that maintains the colonial status quo. Moreover, on the part of those who struggle to subvert racism but continue to try to perform the demands of the colonizer's side of the gender system, it is an attempt to achieve recognition as human, but in the terms defined by those who instituted the modern/colonial system. In other words, it falls short of fulfilling the de-colonial turn. Anna Nieto Gómez astutely summarizes the situation in a 1976 article,

> Racism-Sexism. Both the Chicano and Chicana experience is affected by these two ideologies. In fact, both the Chicano and Chicana experience racist-sexism. Colonized men of color are considered as inferior as women since colonized men do not have the power or authority to rule, provide economically and protect the family. Thus racist-sexism considers Mexican males as either effeminate, or a "Macho," overcompensating because of his powerless position in his society.[40]

To fully embrace a de-colonial project, one must go beyond examining the relationship between discourse and power during the colonial expansion and consequently accept the colonized analyses of our social context,[41] which includes those deemed to be women or women-like.[42] What Nieto Gómez is doing in this article is slightly different than, for example, what Aimé Césaire accomplishes in *Discourse on Colonialism,* wherein he demonstrates a connection between the logic of Nazi fascism and the logic of colonialism so as to enlighten the beneficiaries of the colonizer's side of life about the centuries-long plight of the colonized. Nieto Gómez introduces another dynamic. She, too, is absolutely clear on the problem of colonial subjugation along racial lines, but here she is again raising the issue of dimorphism in the colonized experience. If we understand the effeminization of humans in this instance as an ideological ruse to subordinate certain groups to those defined as masculine, then Nieto Gómez successfully demonstrates gender to be a concern of not only those defined as women in the colonial/racial group but also of the men. She points out the way that gender roles can be blurred in poor communities of color (for example, financial heads of household), and argues that machismo is no more than a performance to overcompensate in the face of effeminization. To maintain a commitment to enacting this ruse is to fail to come to terms with the history of colonization and the de-colonial project.

* * *

There is an explicit epistemic dimension to the de-colonial turn that goes beyond the current Eurocentric limits of most critical theory.[43] As discussed earlier, there is the need to further examine the Renaissance period as constituted *in relation* to the colonization of the Américas and the establishment of the Atlantic slave trade. One of the earliest examples of this focus in a Chicana feminist vein was written in 1974 by Adelaida R. Del Castillo and aptly titled "Malintzin Tenepal: A Preliminary Look into a New Perspective." Castillo refused to subordinate gender to race in her analysis of the sixteenth-century Spanish usurpation of the Mexica, and she approaches the inherited nationalist narrative of *La Malinche* with a healthy dose of skepticism. She notes several deficiencies in the narrative: it does not take into account Mexica religion or political structures or the relationship of other Indigenous peoples to Mexica rule, nor does it consider Doña Marina's own life or perspective on the issues.[44] Castillo traces Marina's life as a noble child sold into slavery by her own mother so as to pass on her inheritance to their second-born child, a son. Castillo does not soften her analysis of the gendered social relations that allowed this to happen to Marina, nor of Mexica imperialism that, she argues, laid much of the groundwork for their own downfall. Castillo's research reveals a serious flaw in the nationalist narrative of *La Malinche*, namely,

> when Doña Marina is accused of being "una traidora a la patria," one wrongly assumes that there was a "patria" (similar to the patrias of today). The fact is, there were many Indian nations within the Aztec Empire and these nations were always attempting, through one rebellion or another,

> to regain their former independence . . . It is willful to forget that the concept of Mexican nationalism (la patria) was introduced only long after the conquest of Mexico and *not* before.[45]

A reexamination of the history of México and asking questions about gender and hierarchy expose dynamics that have otherwise gone misinterpreted in social movements. Furthermore, she makes a critical connection:

> Woman is perceived as being one whose innately negative nature only serves to stagnate man, if not corrupt him entirely. So just as Eve was chosen long ago by misogynistic men to represent the embodiment of "the root of all evil" for western man, Mexico's first and most exceptional heroine, Doña Marina "La Malinche" now embodies female negativity (traición) for our Mexican culture.[46]

Castillo identifies what is basically a twentieth-century recasting of the most negative interpretations of the biblical creation story on to the colonization of México. It is narratives such as these that Castillo rightly critiques as a colonial legacy, inscribing our current "unconscious, if not intentional, misogynistic attitude towards women in general," especially women who are assertive or otherwise exhibit behaviors deemed the purview of "men."

What Nieto Gómez and Castillo accomplished here was a beginning point for conducting a much-needed broader investigation into colonial relations, genealogies of "women," the scopic regimes that limit our possibilities, and performances of gender norms. This research project has been pursued by later generations of writers, visual and performance artists such as Cherríe Moraga, Monica Palacios, and Cihuatl-Ce, to name a few, and it established Malintzin Tenepal as a paradigmatic figure in contemporary Chicana/Latina feminist thought.[47]

CONCLUSION

One of the defining features of Chicana feminist thought was a turn to the early colonial period (pre-1848) as crucial for understanding the historical construction of our contemporary condition, including gender relations. They situate the colonization of the Américas as constitutive events of our contemporary world and foreground the power dynamics established between the European Renaissance and the subjugation of Amerindian, underscoring the dimorphic dimension of physiognomy. Emergent from these atrocities was a gender system that discursively constructed the colonized very differently from the colonizers. Therefore if we are to fulfill the de-colonial turn that in many ways was initiated by these early Chicana feminist writers, then a specific acknowledgment and critique of gender dynamics within colonized communities must be accounted for. Drawing from Anna Nieto Gómez in particular and other early Chicana feminists generally, I have also highlighted a method of analysis that is helpful for coming to terms with the colonial scopic regime, an approach that facilitates taking into account not only the "epidermalization"[48] of human relations but also the complex *dimorphic dimension* that emerges under colonization.

Early Chicana feminists exposed gender roles as something socially constructed and therefore changeable. They suggested we examine the colonization of the Américas as a crucial period in the formation of contemporary gender relations; these studies have revealed that the gendered demands placed on colonized women were very different than those for Euro-Christian women. It is these differences that continue to define our lived experiences today and call us to interrupt the uncritical performance of racial and dimorphic categories and take the de-colonial turn.

NOTES

1. See Alma M. García, ed., *Chicana Feminist Thought: The Basic Historical Writings* (New York: Routledge, 1997).

2. Bernice Rincón, "La Chicana: Her Role in the Past and Her Search for a New Role in the Future," *Regeneración* vol. 1 no. 10 (1971): 15–18.

3. *Gender Trouble* was published in 1990, in the decade directly following the radical challenges made by women of color feminists in books such as *This Bridge Called My Back: Writings by Radical Women of Color* and *All the Women Are White, All the Blacks Are Men, But Some of Us Are Brave.* See *Gender Trouble* footnotes, Chap. 1; 24, 34, 53 and Chap. 2; 23.

4. Judith Butler, *Gender Trouble* (New York: Routledge, 1999), 5.

5. Maria Lugones, "Heterosexualism and the Colonial/Modern Gender System," *Hypatia* vol. 22 no. 1 (Winter 2007): 186.

6. The disenchantment with Eurocentrism characteristic of the late twentieth century is highlighted in the 1969 *El Plan de Santa Barbara.* For further discussion

of "disenchantment," see Sylvia Wynter, "On Disenchanting Discourse: 'Minority' Literary Criticism and Beyond," *The Nature and Context of Minority Discourse* (New York: Oxford University Press, 1991) and Nelson Maldonado-Torres, "Cesaire's Gift and the Decolonial Turn," *Radical Philosophy Review* vol. 9 no. 2 (2006): 111–138.

7. Manning Marable, *Race, Reform, Rebellion: The Second Reconstruction in Black America, 1945–1982* (New York: Palgrave Macmillan, 1984), 14. See also Maggie Rivas-Rodriguez, ed., *Mexican Americans and World War II* (Austin: University of Texas Press, 2005).

8. See Albert Camarillo, *Chicanos In A Changing Society: From Mexican Pueblos To American Barrios In Santa Barbara And Southern California, 1848–1930* (Cambridge, MA: Harvard University Press, 1979).

9. See Rita Sanchez, "Chicana Writer Breaking Out of Silence," *De Colores* vol. 3 no. 3 (1977): 31–37, for an example of this renewed sense of the vindication of indigenous societies.

10. For example, making race a central category of analysis in materialist analyses was one such struggle.

11. For texts that explore and/or problematize Chicana/o claims to Indigenous identities in the Américas, see, for example, Sylvia Wynter, "1492: A New World View," *Race, Discourse, and the Origin of the Americas: A New World View*, ed. Vera Lawrence Hyatt and Rex Nettleford (Washington, DC: Smithsonian Institution Press, 1995); María Josefina Saldaña-Portillo, "Wavering on the Horizon of Being: The Treaty of Guadalupe-Hidalgo and the Legacy of Its Racial Character in Américo Paredes' George Washington Gómez," *Radical History Review*, issue 89 (Spring 2004): 135–164; Norma Alarcon, "Chicana Feminism: In the Tracks of 'The' Native Woman," in *Living Chicana Theory*, ed. Carla Trujillo (Berkeley: Third Woman Press, 1998); Sheila Marie Contreras, *Blood Lines: Myth, Indigenism and Chicana/o Literature* (Austin: University of Texas Press, 2008); Guisela LaTorre, *Walls of Empowerment: Chicana/o Indigenist Murals of California* (Austin: University of Texas Press, 2008); or Laura E. Pérez, *Chicana Art: The Politics of Spiritual and Aesthetic Altarities* (Durham, NC: Duke University Press, 2007).

12. See Walter Mignolo, *The Darker Side of the Renaissance: Literacy, Territoriality, & Colonization* (Ann Arbor: University of Michigan Press, 2003).

13. See Nelson Maldonado-Torres, *Against War: Views from the Underside of Modernity* (Durham, NC: Duke University Press, 2008), 8.

14. The self-Other relationship is presented with a unique set of challenges in a colonial anti-black context. See Lewis Gordon, *Bad Faith and Anti-Black Racism* (Atlantic Highlands, NJ: Humanities Press, 1995).

15. The Third World Liberation Front struggles successfully forced academic institutions to open Ethnic Studies programs that taught the humanities and social sciences from a colonial/racial perspective. This had an important impact on the very production of books and knowledge. See "Ethnic Studies at 40," *Oakland Tribune*, March 20, 2009. See also the film *On Strike! Ethnic Studies 1969–1999*, directed by Irum Shiekh, 1999.

16. Mariana Marin and Yolanda García, "Memories of the 1969 Plan de Santa Barbara Conference" (paper presented at the Conference on the Fortieth Anniver-

sary of *El Plan de Santa Barbara*, Santa Barbara, CA, November 21, 2008). See also Mary Pardo, "A Selective Evaluation of El Plan de Santa Barbara," *La Gente de Aztlan* (March/April 1984): 14–15.

17. Francisca Flores, "Comisión Feminil Mexicana," *Regeneración* vol. 2 (1971): 6.

18. See Alma M. Garcia, ed., *Chicana Feminist Thought: The Basic Historical Writings* (New York: Routledge, 1997), 1–16. Also, personal communication with Chela Sandoval, April 19, 2009.

19. See Maldonado-Torres, "Cesaire's Gift," 131.

20. Ibid., 132–133.

21. See for example Pilar Gonzalbo Aizpuru, *Historia de la Educación en la Época Colonial: El Mundo Indígena* (México D.F.: El Colegio de México, 1990). Also, Judith A. Carney, *Black Rice: The African Origins of Rice Cultivation in the Americas* (Cambridge, MA: Harvard University Press, 2002) and John Milloy, *A National Crime: The Canadian Government and the Residential School System—1879 to 1986* (Winnipeg: University of Manitoba Press, 1999).

22. See Maria Lugones, "Heterosexualism and the Colonial/Modern Gender System," *Hypatia* vol. 22 no. 1 (Winter 2007): 186–209.

23. See Anne Fausto-Sterling, *Sexing the Body: Gender Politics and the Construction of Sexuality* (New York: Basic Books, 2000) for a compelling critique that demonstrates that even physical sex is socially constructed through scientific discourse.

24. Mirta Vidal, "New Voice of La Raza: Chicanas Speak Out," *International Socialist Review* (October 1971): 7–9, 31–33.

25. An example of scholarship that posits a universal, timeless patriarchy as endemic to some non-Western civilizations even prior to capitalist expansion is Rosemary Joyce and Lynn Meskell, *Embodied Lives: Figuring Ancient Egypt and the Classic Maya* (New York: Routledge, 2003).

26. For further reading, see Sheila Pelizzon, "Writing on Gender in World Systems Perspective," *The Modern/Colonial/Capitalist World-System in the Twentieth Century: Global Processes, Antisystemic Movements, and the Geopolitics of Knowledge* (Westport, CT: Praeger Publishers, 2002). Also, Laura Stoler, *Race and the Education of Desire: Foucault's History of Sexuality and the Colonial Order of Things* (Durham, NC: Duke University Press, 1995).

27. Enriqueta Longeaux Vasquez, "¡Despierten Hermanas! The Women of La Raza—Part II," *El Grito del Norte* vol. 2 no. 10 (July 26, 1969): 3.

28. See for example Silvia Federici, *Caliban and the Witch: Women, The Body, and Primitive Accumulation* (Brooklyn, NY: Autonomedia, 2004).

29. See also Gerda Lerner, ed., *Black Women in White America: A Documentary History* (New York: Vintage Books, 1972).

30. Elizabeth "Betita" Martinez, "La Chicana," *Ideal* (September 5–20 1972): 34.

31. The publications of later scholars Gloria Anzaldúa, Cherríe Moraga, Norma Alarcon, Chela Sandoval, Laura Pérez, Emma Perez, Teresa Cordova, and Irene Lara, to name a few, all engage the struggle of de-colonization.

32. Anna Nieto Gómez, "La Chicana: Legacy of Suffering and Self-Denial," *Scene* vol. 8 no. 1 (1975): 22–24.

33. Ibid., 49.

34. The casta system of eighteenth-century México, in which a taxonomy of miscegenation was elaborated, is one of the clearest examples of this phenomenon. See Ilona Katzew, *Casta Painting: Images of Race in Eighteenth-Century Mexico* (New Haven, CT: Yale University Press, 2005).

35. See Stuart Hall, "The Spectacle of the 'Other,'" *Representation: Cultural Representations and Signifying Practices* (Thousand Oaks, CA: SAGE Publications, 2003).

36. Lugones, "Heterosexualism," 6.

37. See Daphne Taylor-García, *The Emergence of Racial Schemas in the Americas: Sexuality, Sociogeny and Print Capital in the Sixteenth-Century Atlantic* Ph.D. dissertation, 2008. See also Kimberlé Crenshaw, "Demarginalizing the Intersection of Race and Sex: A Black Feminist Critique of Antidiscrimination Doctrine, Feminist Theory and Antiracist Politics," in *The Black Feminist Reader* (Malden, MA: Blackwell Publishers, 2000).

38. For more on "de-colonial reason" see Maldonado-Torres, "Cesaire's Gift," 131.

39. Nieto Gómez, *Chicana Feminism*, 57. Gender norms differ substantially among different Indigenous societies.

40. Anna Nieto Gómez, "Sexism in the Movimiento," *La Gente de Aztlan* vol. 6 no. 4 (1976): 10.

41. Maldonado-Torres, "Cesaire's Gift," 111–138.

42. See Irene Lara, "Beyond Caliban's Curses: The Decolonial Feminist Literacy of Sycorax," *Journal of International Women's Studies* vol. 9 no. 1 (November 2007): 80–98.

43. See Chela Sandoval, *Methodology of the Oppressed* (Minneapolis: University of Minnesota Press, 2000) for another example of demonstrating the liberatory possibilities of continental theorists but also their limits for a de-colonial project.

44. Adelaida R. Del Castillo, "Malintzín Tenepal: A Preliminary Look into a New Perspective," *Encuentro Feminil* vol. 1 no. 2 (1974): 58–78.

45. Ibid.

46. Ibid.

47. See Norma Alarcón, "Traddutora, Traiditora: A Paradigmatic Figure of Chicana Feminism," *Dangerous Liaisons: Gender, Nation and Postcolonial Perspectives* (Minneapolis: University of Minnesota Press, 1997).

48. Ibid.

WORKS CITED

Alarcón, Norma. "Traddutora, Traiditora: A Paradigmatic Figure of Chicana Feminism," in *Dangerous Liaisons: Gender, Nation and Postcolonial Perspectives*. Eds. Anne McClintock, Aamir Mufti, and Ella Shohat. Minneapolis: University of Minnesota Press, 1997. 278–297.

———. "Chicana Feminism: In the Tracks of 'The' Native Woman," in *Living Chicana Theory*. Ed. Carla Trujillo. Berkeley, CA: Third Woman Press, 1998. 371–382.

Alcoff, Linda. "Mignolo's Epistemology of Coloniality," *CR: The New Centennial Review* vol. 7 no. 3 (2007): 79–101.

Blake Tyrrell, William. *Amazons: A Study in Athenian Mythmaking.* Baltimore, MD: John Hopkins University Press, 1989.

Butler, Judith. *Gender Trouble.* New York: Routledge, 1999.

Camarillo, Albert. *Chicanos In A Changing Society: From Mexican Pueblos To American Barrios In Santa Barbara And Southern California, 1848–1930.* Cambridge, MA: Harvard University Press, 1979.

Carney, Judith A. *Black Rice: The African Origins of Rice Cultivation in the Americas.* Cambridge, MA: Harvard University Press, 2002.

Columbus, Christopher. "First Voyage of Columbus," in *Select Documents Illustrating the Four Voyages of Columbus: Volume 1.* Germany: Hakluyt Society, 1930.

Contreras, Sheila Marie. *Blood Lines: Myth, Indigenism and Chicana/o Literature.* Austin: University of Texas Press, 2008.

Crenshaw, Kimberlé. "Demarginalizing the Intersection of Race and Sex: A Black Feminist Critique of Antidiscrimination Doctrine, Feminist Theory and Antiracist Politics," in *The Black Feminist Reader.* Eds. Joy James and T. Denean Sharpley-Whiting. Malden, MA: Blackwell Publishers, 2000. 208–237.

Del Castillo, Adelaida R. "Malintzín Tenepal: A Preliminary Look into a New Perspective," *Encuentro Femenil* vol. 1 no. 2 (1974): 58–78.

Fausto-Sterling, Anne. *Sexing the Body: Gender Politics and the Construction of Sexuality.* New York: Basic Books, 2000.

Federici, Silvia. *Caliban and the Witch: Women, The Body, and Primitive Accumulation.* Brooklyn, NY: Autonomedia, 2004.

Flores, Francisca. "Comisión Femenil Mexicana," *Regeneración* vol. 2 (1971), 6.

Fusco, Coco, and Guillermo Gomez-Peña. *The Couple in the Cage: A Guatinaui Odyssey.* New York: Third World Newsreel, 1993.

García, Alma M., Ed. *Chicana Feminist Thought: The Basic Historical Writings.* New York: Routledge, 1997.

Gonzalbo Aizpuru, Pilar. *Historia de la Educación en la Época Colonial: El Mundo Indígena.* Mexico, D.F.: El Colegio de México, 1990.

Gordon, Lewis. *Bad Faith and Anti-Black Racism.* Atlantic Highlands, NJ: Humanities Press. 1995.

Hall, Stuart. "The Spectacle of the 'Other,'" in *Representation: Cultural Representations and Signifying Practices.* Thousand Oaks, CA: SAGE Publications Inc., 2003.

hooks, bell. *Ain't I a Woman?* Boston, MA: South End Press, 1981.

Hull, Gloria T., Patricia Bell Scott, and Barbara Smith, Eds. *All the Women Are White, All the Blacks Are Men, But Some of Us Are Brave: Black Women's Studies.* New York: The Feminist Press at The City University of New York, 1982.

Joyce, Rosemary, and Lynn Meskell. *Embodied Lives: Figuring Ancient Egypt and the Classic Maya.* New York: Routledge, 2003.

Katzew, Ilona. *Casta Painting: Images of Race in Eighteenth-Century Mexico.* New Haven, CT: Yale University Press, 2005.

LaTorre, Guisela. *Walls of Empowerment: Chicana/o Indigenist Murals of California.* Austin: University of Texas Press, 2008.

Lerner, Gerda, Ed. *Black Women in White America: A Documentary History.* New York: Vintage Books, 1972.
Lugones, Maria. "Heterosexualism and the Colonial/Modern Gender System," *Hypatia* vol. 22 no. 1 (Winter 2007): 186–209.
Maldonado-Torres, Nelson. "Cesaire's Gift and the Decolonial Turn," *Radical Philosophy Review* vol. 9 no. 2 (2006): 111–138.
———. *Against War: Views from the Underside of Modernity.* Durham, NC: Duke University Press, 2008.
Marable, Manning. *Race, Reform, Rebellion: The Second Reconstruction in Black America, 1945–1982.* New York: Palgrave Macmillan, 1984.
Marin, Mariana, and Yolanda García. "Memories of the 1969 *Plan de Santa Barbara Conference.*" Paper presented at the Conference on the Fortieth Anniversary of *El Plan de Santa Barbara*, Santa Barbara, CA, November 21, 2008.
Martinez, Elizabeth 'Betita.' "La Chicana," *Ideal* (September 5–20, 1972): 34.
Mignolo, Walter. *The Darker Side of the Renaissance: Literacy, Territoriality, & Colonization.* Ann Arbor: University of Michigan Press, 2003.
Moraga, Cherríe, and Gloria Anzaldúa, eds. *This Bridge Called My Back: Writings by Radical Women of Color.* Latham, NY: Kitchen Table, Women of Color Press, 1983.
Mudimbe, V. Y. *The Idea of Africa.* Bloomington: Indiana University Press, 1994.
Nieto Gómez, Anna. "La Chicana: Legacy of Suffering and Self-Denial," *Scene* vol. 8 no. 1 (1975): 22–24.
———. "Sexism in the Movimiento," *La Gente de Aztlán* vol. 6 no. 4 (1976): 10.
On Strike! Ethnic Studies 1969–1999, directed by Irum Shiekh, 1999.
Pelizzon, Sheila. "Writing on Gender in World Systems Perspective," in *The Modern/Colonial/Capitalist World-System in the Twentieth Century: Global Processes, Antisystemic Movements, and the Geopolitics of Knowledge.* Eds. Ramón Grosfoguel and Ana Margarita Cervantes-Rodríguez. Westport, CT: Praeger Publishers, 2002. 199–211.
Pérez, Laura E. *Chicana Art: The Politics of Spiritual and Aesthetic Altarities.* Durham, NC: Duke University Press, 2007.
Rayburn, Kelly, and Kristin Bender. "Ethnic Studies at 40," *Oakland Tribune* (March 20, 2009).
Rincón, Bernice. "La Chicana: Her Role in the Past and Her Search for a New Role in the Future," *Regeneración* vol. 1 no. 10 (1971): 15–18.
Rivas-Rodriguez, Maggie, ed. *Mexican Americans and World War II.* Austin: University of Texas Press, 2005.
Saldaña-Portillo, María Josefina. "Wavering on the Horizon of Being: The Treaty of Guadalupe-Hidalgo and the Legacy of Its Racial Character in Ámerico Paredes' George Washington Gómez," *Radical History Review* Issue 89 (Spring 2004): 135–164.
Sanchez, Rita. "Chicana Writer Breaking Out of Silence," *De Colores* vol. 3 no. 3 (1977): 31–37.
Sandoval, Chela. *Methodology of the Oppressed.* Minneapolis: University of Minnesota Press, 2000.
Stoler, Laura. *Race and the Education of Desire: Foucault's History of Sexuality and the Colonial Order of Things.* Durham, NC: Duke University Press, 1995.

Taylor-García, Daphne. *The Emergence of Racial Schemas in the Americas: Sexuality, Sociogeny and Print Capital in the Sixteenth-Century Atlantic*. Ph.D. Dissertation. University of California, Berkeley, 2008.

———. "The Discursive Construction of Women in Las Americas," *Worlds and Knowledges Otherwise Web-Dossier*. http://www.duke.edu/~wmignolo/links-of-interest/WKODTG/WKO-DTGindex.html

Vidal, Mirta. "New Voice of La Raza: Chicanas Speak Out," *International Socialist Review* (October 1971): 7–9, 31–33.

Wynter, Sylvia. "On Disenchanting Discourse: 'Minority' Literary Criticism and Beyond," in *The Nature and Context of Minority Discourse*. Eds. Abdul R. JanMohamed and David Lloyd. Oxford: Oxford University Press, 1991. 432–469.

———. "1492: A New World View," in *Race, Discourse, and the Origin of the Americas: A New World View*. Eds. Vera Lawrence Hyatt and Rex Nettleford. Washington, DC: Smithsonian Institution Press, 1995. 5–57.

ACTO TWO

Ethnographies of Performance: The Río Grande and Beyond

SEVEN

Performing Indigeneity in a South Texas Community: Los Matachines de la Santa Cruz

NORMA E. CANTÚ

It's a brisk morning in early March 2009 in San Antonio, Texas, and the annual women's march celebrating International Women's Day is about to begin. We will march past the Alamo, past San Fernando Cathedral, past the hotels and businesses with early morning tourists and local patrons. The march will go from Travis Park to Milam Park—Anglo names for spaces that in the old days were called "plazas." A young girl no older than twelve, dressed in a long brown cotton skirt and a red blouse with a red headband across her forehead, holds an eagle feather. She will do a water blessing before the march begins. Her father, who also has a red headband and is wearing a white cotton shirt and pants, beats a flat drum solemnly. The crowd of a couple of hundred people hushes solemnly and listens to her soft song. She dips the feather in water and sprinkles the ground. Some of us face the four directions as she sings her blessing prayer in a language we don't understand. Could it be Coahuiltecan? That was how Fabiola, one of the organizers, introduced her—as a member of the Coahuiltecan nation. But pretty much all vestiges of the many dialects of that language that were spoken in South Texas for centuries are gone. Erased. Only scraps survive, mostly in old prayer books; the Christian prayers used to indoctrinate the native people paradoxically remain as testaments of the old language. As a child, I went to "la doctrina" to learn the Catholic prayers—in Spanish, of course. But I also went to see the *matachines* dance to the beat of the drum. In this chapter, I focus on the latter, the folk religious dance tradition of *los matachines,* as I interrogate the indigenous identity we as

Chican@s identify and disidentify with in the particular area of South Texas.

In a number of other writings, I have described the fiesta de *Matachines* (1993) and analyzed the traditional ceremonial dress (1995) and aspects of the celebration (2009). Here, I look at the performance as a ritual of recovery of what has been all but erased, our indigenous identity answering key questions about our Xicana/o selves as a way of inserting the indigenous into the Chicana/o identity.[1] I ask, how does this clearly indigenous celebration, the *matachines*, reconcile with the Christian elements of our identity? And why do the dancers, who don't necessarily define themselves as Indigenous, continue to dance dressed as Indians? How can we reconcile the obvious identification of this sector of Laredo with "lo indio" and the ostentatious and clearly constructed and imagined "Indianness" of the Pocahontas celebration that occurs as part of Laredo's celebration of George Washington's birthday?

I begin with a few anecdotes and *recuerdos* to situate my discussion along a theoretical continuum. Then I offer a brief historical overview and finally analyze the elements that hearken back to that indigenous existence, markers of a certain indigenous origin, because I believe it will be useful to understand the fiesta and how it figures so prominently as an indigenous act within a hegemonic narrative that seeks to invalidate it.

ARE WE INDIANS OR NOT?

One of my former students, a Chicana Comanche, went to graduate school in the Midwest, where she thought she would at long last be welcomed by the indigenous groups; her experiences in Laredo had forced her to hide her Comanche origins, only cautiously claiming a mexicana identity while hiding her father's indigenous teachings. Instead, she found that indigenous groups in the Midwest questioned her authenticity, and she was discouraged from identifying as Indigenous. As a "detribalized Comanche," as she says it, she is not enrolled in any government list, mostly because, as her father explained to her and her siblings, he was not going to have a piece of paper tell him who he was.[2] Many others in Texas have done the same; they grew up as Mexicans but were really Kickapoo or Lipan Apache. No doubt such subterfuge was an act of survival.

Browsing through the children's books section recently, I found an attractive publication that claimed that "There are no Indians in Texas."[3] I was disheartened to see such a claim in a book intended to teach children about Texas. Scholars like Ines Hernández Ávila, Ines Talamantez, and Patrisia Gonzalez remind us that there have been Indians in Texas for many generations. As Gloria Anzaldúa claims, "this land was Mexican once, / was Indian always / and is. / And will be again" (25). Other Chicana scholars who are both Indigenous and Chicana or who seek to identify with their indigenous past have written about this nepantla state that my student experienced. In the 1990s, I participated in various gatherings of the Indigenous Women's Network at Alma de Mujer, a retreat center in Austin, Texas. The groups included a mixture of Chicanas and Indigenous women, and everyone recognized that in the Chicana mestizaje lay vestiges of an indigenous past. Not all the Chicanas identified with that indigeneity, but for others it was reclamation of an indigenous past that had been denied them and virtually erased from their consciousness. Yes, we are Indian, we Chicanas. I ask that you keep this in mind as I now turn to a discussion of the origins of the *matachin* group in Laredo and situate their existence within the mestizo world that is Laredo.

A HISTORY AND DEFINITIONS

The generic term "*los matachines*" refers to a religious dance tradition that dates back to the conquest of México and that can be found throughout the Américas (Romero). The tradition, a blend of European and Indigenous dance elements, made its way into the US Southwest and the South as the Spanish brought indigenous groups to the area from México as part of their colonizing project. Scholars such as Sylvia Rodríguez, Peter García, Claude Stephenson, and Brenda Romero have studied the tradition in New Mexico. Romero has researched the tradition as it appears throughout the Américas; other scholars have sought a root origin to the tradition (See Harris, Stephenson, and Treviño and Gilles); in my mind, the evidence is inconclusive, and the search for the origin is ultimately only an attempt to privilege either the Indigenous (Treviño and Gilles) or the European (Harris).

Three main types of *matachin* dance traditions exist: *de la pluma* (of the feather), *de la flecha* (of the arrow), and *de la palma* (of the palm, or trident). *De la flecha* is the one danced by the group in Laredo that is the focus of this paper; the Coahuiltecan tribes of the area were the likely first dancers. In general, the *matachin* dance consists of music, dance steps, particular dress, and instrumentation. It also includes a deep religious or spiritual devotion to a particular saint, such as San Lorenzo in Bernalillo, New Mexico, or the Virgen of Guadalupe in many of the groups in the South and elsewhere where Mexican-origin Latinos from Texas or northern México live, such as in North Carolina, Georgia, and Texas.

In the Coahuiltecan *matachines* tradition, the dancers generally wear red nagüillas, skirts made of two flaps of red velvet fabric, adorned with *carrizo,* reed cane, and vests displaying sequin-embroidered images of the Virgen, the Holy Cross, or other religious items as well as the dancer's last name or the group's church affiliation. Many of the December fiestas honor the Virgen de Guadalupe, whose feast day is celebrated on December 12; the dancers wear long pants under their nagüillas, especially in areas where the temperatures are colder than what they are used to in México or South Texas. While red and yellow predominate, some groups choose blue or other colors associated with the devotion of their particular saint. In Guadalupe, Arizona (a suburb of Phoenix), for example, they wear blue in honor of the Virgen de San Juan. In the past, huaraches, leather sandals, were the required footwear, but nowadays dancers can wear boots or even tennis shoes to perform the intricate and strenuous foot-stomping dance steps. Headdresses called *cupiles* or *coronas* are common; some dancers still don a hat with a long fringe covering the face to lend a semblance of anonymity. The *cupiles,* adorned with bits of broken mirror or colorful beadwork, are sometimes only worn by the *capitanes* or the *monarcas,* the dance captains or monarchs, the leaders.

In northern México, groups dance to one or more drummers; in New Mexico, the violin is essential, for the music is more European; in South Texas, the accordion appears to be the most important musical instrument. There are over fifty *sones* (tunes) recorded, but not all groups dance to the same tunes. Most groups have a repertoire of no more than five or eight tunes; these include specific ones for dancing a greeting and a farewell as well as a tune to be played and danced to when the group goes in procession.

PERFORMING IDENTITY

While the tradition exists in Greater México,[4] recent immigrants from Texas and México have brought the *matachines* dance tradition to places where it had been heretofore unknown, such as the Raleigh/Durham area. But in New Mexico and in south Texas, the tradition has been passed down from one generation to the next for over a century.

Barrio de la Santa Cruz

Every year, on certain weekday evenings in early April, in a working-class *barrio* of Laredo, Texas, known as *La Ladrillera* (the brick factory) along the banks of the Rio Grande, a group of children and a few adults gather to rehearse the dances, or *sones,* that they will perform for the fiesta of the Holy Cross on May 3. Throughout this discussion on the fiesta—both as performed in early May for the Day of the Holy Cross and in mid-December in honor of the Virgen de Guadalupe—I emphasize the significance of the survival of this folk religious celebration. José Limón's (1994: 178–179) observations of other events are useful here, as the prevailing *matachines* tradition can be classified as the expression of "postmodernity, the cultural logic of late capitalism." The same can be said about the Pocahontas celebration that forms part of the community's larger and much more ostentatious community celebration around George Washington's birthday (Barrera 2009). While I acknowledge this other presentation of indigeneity in the community, my focus is on the *matachines*, because the questions of identity and the connection to the indigenous past of the community appear more clearly manifested here. Because the fiesta adheres closely to what it has always been—a religious folk tradition firmly rooted in what I consider a private world, and not the public world of the community like the Pocahontas celebration—an analysis of its "cultural logic" must include the many threads that weave its rich tapestry.

I begin with a cursory discussion of the Holy Cross celebration, presenting the elements found in the fiesta as they appear in chronological order. I follow with a description of the *matachin* dress—the construction and the materials used in the *naguilla* (skirt) and *chaleco* (vest). Equally significant are the accoutrements carried by the dancers—the *flecha* and *sonaja*. My discussion further looks at the changes in construction and preparation of the once-essential elements of the *traje*—the *huaraches* and the *corona*. I explore some of the practices that are concomitant with the tradition, including the preparation period as well as the annual "dressing" of the cross. The private world of the *matachines* exists within a small segment of the community, but it is in constant contact with and affected by outside, often Anglo, hegemonic forces. Yet the fiesta remains true to its religious, social, and cultural values and worldview. The Santa Cruz and Virgen de Guadalupe fiestas do not occur in a vacuum; I contextualize them within the frame of the church (and the community) and the cycle of liturgical and secular celebrations. In doing so, we can also infer that it fulfills a need at some level for an easily identifiable indigenous tradition.

The *fiesta de los matachines* in Laredo, as in a number of other venues, includes elements as varied as a procession, special meals, distinctive dress, and the *sones, juegos* (music and dance steps), and prayers that form the core of the festival. Structurally, the *fiesta* adheres to a model established by the medieval churches of Spain where the practice of honoring a patron saint proliferated during the sixteenth century (Christian 1981). Yet the unitary elements are sometimes rooted in indigenous practice. The Huichol *matachines* who dance in Real de Catorce in central México and the Jemez Pueblo *matachines* in New Mexico, for example, are equally rooted in their communities.

After an extended period of preparation, an initial ritual sets the fiesta in motion. Once the activities have passed, a closing event—the *despedida*—brings closure to the year's celebration and prefaces the next year.

The Preparations

The community begins its preparations for the celebration during the preceding fall, gradually building in intensity up to the rehearsals. During the fall, some of the members of the community of *matachines* begin by cutting reeds from the riverbank; the reeds are then sized and strung to the *nagüilla*. This practice of using the reed cane from the river may soon disappear, as Homeland Security measures have all but destroyed the vegetation along the river. In some cases, the dancers have been driven to use plastic straws to adorn the nagüilla. During the time of preparation, the women are engaged in embroidering the *traje,* or dress, while others, mostly the men, construct and decorate *guajes* (gourds) and *flechas* (literally "arrows," but in this case stylized bow and arrow noisemakers, or clackers). Also in the fall, Claudina Liendo, the official "dresser" of the cross, identifies a theme for the "dress" that will embellish the cross and begins to gather the necessary materials—silk or plastic flowers, greenery, fabric, and a white sheet.

The *prácticas* are held in the community-owned *terreno* (plot of land) in the afternoon or evening to accommodate after-school activities and the workday. Not every dancer wears the *nagüilla* during the practices, but everyone carries a *guaje* or *sonaja* and a *flecha.* Novice dancers usually borrow the required accessories for the practices, and even sometimes for the *fiesta* dancing, until they get their own *nagüilla.* Usually there are more children than adults participating in the dancing, and predictably most of them live nearby in the *barrio* that was once known as *La Ladrillera* and is now mostly referred to as Santa Cruz. During the course of the practices, Florencio Ortiz always took time to instruct the dancers on the seriousness of the occasion and the origin and history of the tradition. After his passing in 1993, his sons Reynaldo and Javier Ortiz assumed the charge of the dance rehearsals and the new dancers' orientation to the tradition.

While the dancers practice their *sones,* community members attend to the final details of the preparations. The men and women apply their finishing touches to the *nagüillas, guajes,* and *flechas.* Doña Francisca (Panchita) Ortiz, Florencio Ortiz's widow, and Teresita, Ortiz's niece, purchase the groceries for the festive meals; Reynaldo and Javier Ortiz ensure that the *andamia* (the stand that supports the Cross) is sound. They and others from the community repair and paint the *capillita* (the little chapel), its nearby benches, and the tall posts from which lights are strung.

While the *Fiesta de la Santa Cruz* requires months of steady, ongoing preparation, a whirlwind of activity kicks into gear come the last two weeks of April. An air of anticipation reigns in the community during these final weeks. The children get new clothes and shoes. Since Easter has just passed, many wear their Easter outfits. Some of the dancers may wear a newly embroidered *nagüilla,* new tennis shoes, or, at the very least, a new T-shirt, a unique article of clothing being a significant addition to their costume. I have noted that to *estrenar* (that is, to wear a piece of clothing never before worn) is as critical to *fiesta* attire as it is for other seasonal celebrations, such as Easter and the first day of school. A new *nagüilla* is particularly special, eliciting admiring comments on the handiwork and beauty of the embroidery.

El Mero Día

The fiesta can last anywhere from four to six days, depending on which day of the week the third of May falls. In 1974, for instance, when Alfonso Peña attended, the *fiesta* began with a formal rehearsal on May 2 and concluded on May 5 with the *Despedida.* The *fiesta* date is always set around the weekend closest to May 3, often beginning on the Thursday preceding the weekend. Word of the exact dates is made public about a month in advance so that all can make their plans to attend.

At long last, the day arrives. A crowd of people gathers at the *terreno;* they mill about, greeting each other and talking among themselves. In the *terreno* by the *capillita,* the Ortiz brothers and others have erected the Holy Cross on its *andamia* in front of the chapel. At about five o'clock in the afternoon, the drumbeat calls the gathered dancers to formation, and the fiesta begins. The dancers don their *nagüillas* and hold *guajes* in their right hands and *flechas* in their left. They form two long lines in front of the cross. The *fiesta* begins with the first *son,* a greeting to the cross. After dancing in line, the *capitanes* escort the dancers in groups of four from the rear of the lines forward to greet the cross, dancing all the while. The dancers step forward between the rows, accompanied by the *capitanes,* until they are at the foot of the Cross, where they genuflect and offer a personal prayer or greeting. The length of the *son* depends on the number of dancers. While it can last up to two hours, generally it runs thirty to sixty minutes. As Florencio Ortiz explained,

> (En) algunas ocasiones hemos durado hasta una hora sin parar porque hacemos lo mismo, pero cuando son muchos (*matachines*)

> lo haces con cada pareja; te tardas mucho porque son muchas parejas . . . A veces mis hijos lo recortan cuando está muy grande nomás lo hacen de aquí para allá y dura media hora, ya no lo hacen de allá para acá porque ya duraron media hora y como está muy fuerte el sol.
>
> (On some occasions this dance lasts up to an hour without stopping because we do the same, but when there are many dancers, and you do it with each couple, you take long because there are many couples. . . . Sometimes my sons cut it short when it is too long then they only dance from here to there and it lasts a half hour or so and they won't go back because they have already been dancing for an hour and the sun is too hot.)

During this initial dance, the drummer keeps the beat as the accordionist plays the rhythm. The *capitanes*—two located at the head and two at the rear—lead the two rows of dancers through the *son,* calling out to correct dancers who are not in line.[5] They raise their left hands and signal with their *flechas,* maintaining the beat with their footwork and with the *guajes* in their right hands. Some *sones* require special footwork; if it is a *corridita,* for example, the dancers must move very quickly.[6]

While the footwork cannot be attributed directly to an indigenous tradition, it appears to be most akin to traditional dances among particular groups in central México. In addition to special footwork, the *juegos* sometimes require intricate line weaving or complex formations that make the shape of the cross, an "X," a circle, or, as in an earlier dance, the words "la Santa Cruz." When asked, Ortiz dismissed this more elaborate form of dancing, saying it would be like a school band marching in formation and claiming, with something like false modesty, that the dancers were not smart enough to execute such steps:

> Ahora si fueramos nosotros otra clase de gente que bailaban otras cosas como las bandas de música que forman letras . . . no somos no somos tanto smart para hacer tantas cosas.
>
> (Now, if we were another kind of people. Those who would dance other things, like marching bands that shape letters . . . no we are not as smart as to do such things.)

Yet Scarff and Alfonso Peña (1972) describe exactly this kind of *juego,* where the dancers' movements form letters or designs.

In procession, the dancers take the cross to the nearby church on Saturday. On Sunday morning, they return it to the neighborhood site, where the dancing continues until noon, at which time the dancers are treated to a festive meal. Florencio Ortiz insisted that the dancers be well fed and nourished. Although for some of the dinners, they eat sandwiches or fried chicken, for the major Sunday meal, they feast on traditional *fiesta* dishes such as chicken *mole* or brisket and rice, beans, and potato salad. A red punch (usually a blend of pineapple juice and Hawaiian Punch or Kool-Aid), previously prepared and given to the dancers between dances and along the procession, is served at the lunch, too.

The Sunday meal is served on long wooden picnic tables, flanked by the same benches used by the dancers' family members during the *fiesta.* The dancers are fed first, followed by the members of the various families, many of whom have helped with the preparation and execution of the *fiesta.* Special guests, such as the priest or visiting ex-dancers, are also invited. They often sit down to eat with the last *tanda,* the last group, which usually includes the women who have cooked and served the meal. After a break of about two hours, the dancing resumes at four o'clock in the afternoon, and the *matachines* continue to dance into the night, as they did on Saturday, until about eleven PM. Alfonso Peña also notes that the dancing continues late into the night.

Monday is the final day of the fiesta, with the *despedida,* but Sunday is without question the principal day. When the group was still dancing the intricate *sones* of *La Trenza* and *La Malinche y el Viejo,* they always danced them on Sunday afternoon. *El Son del Viejo* is also performed on Sunday, either in the afternoon, after the group has returned from church, or in the evening.

The performance of the *Despedida* takes place on the last day of the fiesta. Again, the dancers gather at five PM and dance until the scheduled procession back to the chapel on the *terreno.* After dancing a few final *sones* in the *terreno,* the group performs the last dance of the *fiesta, la Despedida,* with its distinctive music and dance maneuvers. As in the opening *son,* the dancers are brought forth in groups of four to genuflect before the cross; this time, they say their goodbyes and offer their final prayers. At this point, the elders of the community usually pray before the Holy Cross and leave an offering. Many lit candles and flowers accumulate at the base on the *andamia* during the course of the *fiesta*. The dancers cross themselves as they finish their prayers and dance in place in their rows until everyone has come forth. They conclude the *Despedida* with the same ending used in all the dances—namely, each pair of dancers makes a clockwise turn before kneeling, starting from the front row to the back, until all are kneeling. Then the *capitanes* signal the end.

Following the final dance and in between the prayers, Teresita González leads the members of the community in a prayer. Dancers and others add their prayers: some lament the sickness of a loved one and ask publicly for the prayers of all present; others pray silently, in their hearts, for someone who may be absent or in jail or for some special request, such as a problem pregnancy, help getting employed, or any of life's trials needing divine intervention. Many also voice their gratitude and offer their vows for special favors granted over the past year. One year, Teresita shared her thanks to the Holy Cross because her grandmother, who suffers from diabetes, did not require a foot amputation. Juanita Vega offered a moving prayer of thanksgiving a few years ago after her daughter was healed from an incurable illness. With the conclusion of this very emotional ritual, the *fiesta* comes to an end. Some members gather one last time to drink punch and eat sandwiches or cake, but most of the group disperses, for it is, by now, close to midnight, and tomorrow is a workday.

The *Matachines de la Santa Cruz* continues to dance for the Santa Cruz *fiesta* annually. Most of them will return in December to dance for the Virgen de Guadalupe festival, for many have vowed to dance in both *fiestas*.

LOS JUEGOS

The various *sones* have corresponding dance steps (*juegos*) and choreography. The *juegos* bear names that are usually descriptive of the choreography used in the dance—*La Cruz, El Escaleriado, Matachin Tocale al Guaje, Entreverado, Estrella, Flecha, Terciado, Las Letras* or *Letrado, El Cuadro, Unos Adentro Otros Afuera, La Trenza, El Viejo* or *La Muerte Del Viejo, La Malinche y el Viejo*. When talking about the individual dances, Florencio Ortiz referred to the dancing as the *juego* and to the music as the *son,* indicating a subtle distinction between the two that can take some time to appreciate. Although many of the *sones* have been lost, the core of ten or so that still remain, and their accompanying *juegos,* keep the tradition alive. The elders could recall up to fifty *sones* and as many *juegos* in the mining communities of Las Minas, including other forms of *matachin* dancing, such as the traditions of *La Palma, La Pluma,* and of course, *La Flecha.* It is the latter tradition that this group still follows. While *La Palma* or *La Pluma* seems to have survived in New Mexico, the Northern México tradition seems to have generalized to *La Flecha.* This fact sustains my argument that the dancers and this particular group is identifying with an indigenous past as Indigenous people. Peña (1972) writes that Benito Castro mentions over seventy *sones.*[7] There were also *la Danza del Caballito* and many others that are no longer performed by the group.[8] Obviously, the surviving *sones* and *juegos* are those that speak to the dancers and that they identify with; it is no coincidence, I submit, that they are the more "Indian" of the *sones,* in that they use the *flecha* and the *guaje.*

In fact, Alfonso Peña (1972: 3) postulates that the *fiesta* dates back to the earliest existence of the coal mines in the area in 1897. Ortiz offers a likely explanation for why many of the *juegos* are no longer performed: "Sabe que cuando ya pasa el tiempo alguien se encarga y entonces ya va cortando ciertas cositas diferentes . . . Y entonces probablemente ya no está tan completa como 90 años atrás." (You know, how when time passes and someone is in charge and then he or she is cutting certain things, differently, and then probably it is not as complete as ninety years before.) But, true to his word, in the late 1980s, Florencio Ortiz reached his goal of incorporating some of the early *juegos;* he taught the group *La Trenza* and *El Son de la Malinche y el Viejo.* I discuss *el son de la Malinche* below as part of what I am calling the dramatic *juegos. La Trenza,* reminiscent of the spring Maypole dances of Europe, requires a group of twenty practiced and focused dancers and four seasoned *capitanes.* It is considered a much harder dance to perform.[9] But I submit that the similarity is such that it could well be influenced by Tlaxcaltecan indigenous tradition. Florencio Ortiz reintroduced and taught the dance to the group in 1988, and it was performed annually until his death in 1993; now, it is only sporadically performed.

Some of the juegos clearly point to an indigenous tradition. Only experienced and practiced dancers try the *Escaleriado,* for example. Its intricate footwork includes hops that increase in number as the *juego* progresses from one to two, three, or even four hops. The rhythmic clicking of the bow and arrow continues throughout, escalating the difficulty of the dance.

THE DRAMATIC DANCES

The *Son de la Malinche y El Viejo* belongs to a group of *sones* that I call the dramatic dances because they act out complete scenarios, replete with symbolic action and plot. They often point to a clash between Spanish and indigenous traditions, as occurs in the Moros y Cristianos celebrations. *La Malinche* plays a clear dramatic role in the New Mexico tradition. In the Laredo tradition, the part is subtler, yet may have played as significant a role in years past.[10] The dramatic moves of *la malinche* as she dances between the *capitanes,* weaving in and out of the dancers' lines and advancing forward to honor the cross, place her in a position similar to that of *la malinche* of New Mexico; namely, she is intermediary and intercessor, an obvious reference to the indigenous woman, Malinche, who served as Cortez's translator. Dressed in white and obviously functioning as a link between the cross and the dancers, she is the only dancer throughout the *fiesta* who performs a solo. Ortiz explains at length the phenomenon of the *Danza de la Malinche,* harkening back to the history of the conquest and her role in it. But in describing *la malinche* in the *danza,* conflicting details arise as he recounts the tale of a Spanish woman who is pursued by an Indian. He says,

> Como es parte de la historia de los indios, lo hacen pero actuando con una Malinche y los indios . . . pero esto es al reves los indios quieren conquistarse a una española, me entiendes, y entonces anda un indio de tras de ella queriendo bailar y ay viene otro indio y se la quiere quitar, y ay anda *y asina le debíamos de hacer nosotros, mas antes lo hacíamos* . . . Sí pos al indio ya le habían ganado con la (mujer) de él entonces un indio trata de y lo hacen como un juego en la danza nomas que nosotros tenemos tiempo que no lo hacemos pero ese lo hacíamos tambien. . . . (emphasis mine) (SI 3).
>
> (Since it is part of the history of the Indians, they do it, but acting with a Malinche and the Indians . . . but here it is reversed. The Indians want to conquer the Spanish, you understand, and then

> there is an Indian after her wanting to dance and then another Indian comes as if to take her away and there he is persisting. That is how we are supposed to do it, and back then we did it . . . Yes, well, the Indian they had taken this woman and then he, the Indian, tries and they do it like a dance except we have not performed it in a while but we did do it also).

It is very possible that this *malinche* is not the one allied with Cortez but the one that was either daughter or wife of Montezuma, as Harris's analysis explains (2000). If that is the case, the confusion as to the role of the "indio" is even more significantto my argument that the dancers are indeed performing an indigenous identity.

Although the *Son de la Malinche* has been reintroduced, thanks to Ortiz's insistence, its survival in the repertoire is not guaranteed. For instance, in 1960, Scarff notes that several dances are graced with *la malinche,* but in 1974, Peña notes that only two dances including *la malinche* survive. In both observations, it is clear that women did not participate in the dance, except for the *malinche* dancer. Peña notes that women began dancing in 1968. Also, the choreographed drama, *danza de la Malinche,* that Ortiz taught the group did not include a Spanish woman. In another *juego, La Malinche y El Viejo,* the *malinche* is present and dances; that is, the action centers around the engagement of *El Viejo* and *La Malinche*. In 2010, none of the dances included a *malinche,* and the *Danza del Viejo,* a particular *son* whereby a dancer dressed as an old man and carrying a doll is ritualistically killed, was performed on Saturday and Sunday nights.

The significance of *la Malinche* can be seen as the embodiment of the community's Indian soul, outside the conqueror's tradition, yet mediating between the two worlds and honoring the Holy Cross as a unifying spirit. The dance *El Juego del Viejo y la Malinche* contains the same disruptive force as that found in *El Juego del Viejo,* but here, through his harassment of *la malinche, el viejo* clearly represents the forces of evil. These two dances or *juegos—El Juego de la Malinche y El Viejo* and *El Viejo*—are perhaps the most dramatic in content, for they act out a stirring plot through dance. One of the most popular *juegos, El Viejo,* still survives in the group's repertoire. In the dance, *el viejo* is ousted from the group, yet continues to disrupt the dancing until he is ritualistically killed.[11]

The dancers in both *juegos* represent the community that continues to honor the cross despite the disruptive forces in their lives, which may, as dramatized by the attempts made by *el Viejo,* thwart their prayers. On a semiotic level, the cross assumes the values of the idea, the good, that which the *matachines* strive for and defend, a unifying symbol of their own best self as community and as individuals. *El viejo* assumes the oppositional values of evil, disruption, chaos, the worse self of a community and individuals. *La malinche* is the spirit, mediator, between the community and the cross. The dancers defeat themselves (the disruptive influences) as they honor the cross and overcome all obstacles.

The *juegos* remain an integral part of the *fiesta.* Above all, however, we should remember that the *fiesta* exists for a particular cultural logic and that the *sones* and *juegos* have a specific function within the *fiesta.* The *fiesta,* as religious and ritual dance, includes other key elements besides the *juegos.* For instance, in order to dance, a *matachin* must wear special clothes that signal the activity she or he is engaged in. A *matachin completo,* attired in the traditional *traje de matachin,* is also a testament to the indigenous influence. The red of the vest and the nagüilla, the reed cane decorations that are painstakingly added, the insistence on the right sound of the jingle bell, and the footwear all lead to a conclusion that the dress is an integral part of the celebration that also signifies indigeneity. Of course, the very act of dressing as a *matachin* constitutes performing a role as a *matachin,* as an indigenous person.

PRINCESS POCAHONTAS IN LAREDO?

This discussion naturally leads to another celebration that occurs in the community where young people dress in an imagined Native American fashion: The George Washington's Birthday Celebration (GWBC). But here it is young people of a different class who don obscenely expensive dress for a created and constructed narrative that includes Pocahontas, who, at the end of an imagined reenactment, receives the keys to the city. Just like the *matachines* celebration of La Santa Cruz, the annual celebration has been taking place for over a hundred years and takes a whole year of preparation; just like the *matachines*, there are prescribed elements that must be included in the celebration. But here the similarity ends, for the two *fiestas* could not be any more dissimilar. While the *matachines* celebration is grassroots and wholly and totally religious in nature as well as inclusive, the secular Pocahontas section of the GWBC is public and exclusive; only the eighteen-year-old daughters of the Pocahontas Council members and representatives from the local high schools are allowed to participate in the celebration, which is akin to a presentation into society.

In earlier celebrations, the dress was not as elaborate, and the recreation of an imagined event was mostly told and not acted out. But since the 1980s founding of the Council, the celebration has taken on grander dimensions, complete with a pageant and a recreation of a non-event with a script that details the happenings and attempts to make meaning of the event. But I did not set out to analyze this other event, which obviously is also reclaiming an indigenous past but is rooted in the imagined and often stereotypical portrayal of the Indian. I will conclude by merely affirming that the community at all levels of social strata is at once still colonized enough to deny its Indianness, or at least to romanticize and relegate it to an imperialist nostalgic past, to use Rosaldo's term, where the Indian maiden is given the keys to the city. Whether it is the GWBC Pocahontas Council and the presentation pageant or the *matachines* dance, a sense of Indianness still persists. Even when disavowed or disidentified, this sense remains in the subconscious desire and in the performance of a Chicana/o Indian identity.

CONCLUSIONS

The *danza de matachines* as it exists today in Laredo, Texas, and in a number of venues in Greater México stands as a living testament to the identity of Mejican@s and Chican@s as Indians. Focusing on the community of Laredo, Texas, we can see that the tradition extends back over a hundred years and that it survives as a folk Catholic tradition replete with signifiers that beg to be read as indigenous. These thoughts on the construction of an Indian identity may be seen as contestatory insofar as it has been the custom to disidentify with all things Indian. As a child,

I remember being chided for not wearing shoes or for not combing my hair because I would be "una india" barefoot and uncombed. Stereotypes, no doubt, but also strong didactic messages that would inculcate a desire to be non-Indian. Yet, the Indian in us is there, as Gloria Anzaldúa reminds us. We must reclaim it and celebrate it. Only then will we be totally whole—European and Indigenous, mestiz@s.

NOTES

1. The use of "X" in spelling the term "Chicano" instead of the more common "Ch" references the indigenous roots of the mestizaje that this ethnic group embraces. I use "Indigenous" to refer to the Indian population in the United States and in México; I do not capitalize it when it is an adjective. For a discussion of the indigenous origins and claims in Chican@ studies, see Roberto Rodríguez's book *The X in La Raza* and Ana Castillo's *Massacre of the Dreamers: Essays on Xicanisma.*

2. Although he was eligible to be registered, he resisted. Rose Rodríguez Rabin, Plenary address, MELUS, 2005.

3. Eric Bruun, *State Shapes: Texas.* New York: Black Dog & Lowenthal Publishers, 2005.

4. The term "greater México" was coined by folklorist Américo Paredes for the general area of the United States where Mexican Americans reside.

5. Alfonso Peña calls these dancers *guías;* perhaps the term has changed over time (1974, 36).

6. There are several sources of videos that show the footwork of the Corridita and the other steps of the *sones* at the Texas Folklife Resources in Austin, Texas, and at the Smithsonian Institution in Washington, DC. The video *Matachines* produced by KLRN, the public broadcasting station in San Antonio, also has excellent footage of the dancing.

7. Alfonso Peña notes that many of the seventy *sones* are no longer danced in 1972; I find that even fewer are currently danced.

8. González, interview.

9. A similar *danza de las cintas* exists in Tlaxcala, México, although the authors of *Danzas y bailes tradicionales del estado de tlaxcala,* when discussing the few instances of *matachines,* indicate that "*esta danza no tiene nada que ver con las danzas de matachines de otros sitios de la República*" (212). (This dance has nothing to do with other *matachin* dances in other areas of the Republic [of México].)

10. The *malinche* character in the New Mexico tradition has been researched and written about by various scholars, including Romero, Hawley 1948, Rodríguez, Harris, and Treviño and Gilles.

11. Hawley (1948: 39) describes a "grandfather" ritualistically killing and quartering a bull in a Jemez Pueblo *matachin* dance in the 1940s, and various other scholars corroborate that this event is found in a number of traditions.

REFERENCES

Alamo Public Telecommunications Council. 1996. *Los Matachines.* San Antonio, TX: KLRN.

Anzaldúa, Gloria. 1987. *Borderlands/La Frontera: The New Mestiza.* San Francisco, CA: Aunt Lute Press.

Barrera, Cordelia. 2009. *Border Places, Frontier Spaces: Deconstructing Ideologies of the Southwest.* PhD dissertation, University of Texas, San Antonio.

Berlandier, Jean Louis. 1965. *The Indians of Texas in 1830.* Ed. John C. Evers. Trans. Patricia R. Leclercq. Washington, DC: Smithsonian Institution, 51.

Cantú, Norma E. 1995. "Los Matachines de la Santa Cruz de la Ladrillera, Notes toward a Socio-Literary Theory." *Feasts and Celebrations in North American Ethnic Communities.* Ed. Ramón A. Gutierrez and Geneviève Fabre. Albuquerque: University of New Mexico Press.

———. 2009. "The Semiotics of Land and Place: Matachines Dancing in Laredo, Texas." In *Dancing Across Borders: Danzas y Bailes Mexicanos.* Champagne-Urbana: University of Illinois Press, 97–115.

Castillo, Ana. 1994. *Massacre of the Dreamers: Essays on Xicanisma.* Albequerque: University of New Mexico Press.

Ceballos, Manuel. 1992. "La epopeya de la fundación de Nuevo Laredo: El nexo entre la tradición y la historia." In *Entre la magia y la historia: Tradiciones, mitos y leyendas de la frontera.* Compilador Manuel Valenzuela. Tijuana, BC, México: COLEF Programa Cultural de las Fronteras, 99–107.

Christian, William. 1981. *Local Religion in Sixteenth Century Spain.* Princeton, NJ: Princeton University Press.

Cohen, Jeffrey H. 1993. "*Danza de la Pluma:* Symbols of Submission and Separation in a Mexican Fiesta." *Anthropological Quarterly* 66:149–158.

Harris, Max. 1994. "The Arrival of the Europeans: Folk Dramatizations of the Conquest and Conversion in New Mexico." *Comparative Drama* 28:141–165.

———. 1996. "Moctezuma's Daughter: The Role of La Malinche in Mesoamerican Dance." *Journal of American Folklore* 109:149–177.

———. 2000. *Aztecs, Moors, and Christians in Mexico and Spain, Festivals of Reconquest.* Austin: University of Texas Press.

Hawley, Florence Ellis. 1948. "Dance of the Devil Chasers." *New Mexico Magazine* 26.9:16. Ed. George Fitzpatrick.

Jáuregui, Jesús, and Carlo Bonfiglioli, Eds. 1992. *Las danzas de Conquista en el México Contemporáneo.* México: Consejo Nacional papa la Cultura y las Artes-Fondo de Cultura Económica

"Matachines." 2002. *Diccionario de autoridades.* Madrid: Editorial Gredos.

Newcomb, W. W. Jr. 1961. *The Indians of Texas: From Prehistoric to Modern Times.* Austin: University of Texas Press.

Peña, Alfonso Felix. 1972. Unpublished paper. University of Texas, Austin.

Peña, Felix. 1977. Folklore as a Means to Educate the Chicano Community. Austin, TX: Rare Books.

Richardson, Marlene, Director. 1995. *Los Matachines de la Santa Cruz,* video production.

Rodríguez, Sylvia. 1991."The Taos Pueblo Matachines: Ritual Symbolism and Interethnic Relations." *American Ethnologist* 18.2: 234–256.

———. 1996. *The Matachines Dance: Ritual Symbolism and Interethnic Relations in the Rio Grande Valley.* Albuquerque: University of New Mexico Press.

Romero, Brenda M. 1993. "The Matachines Music and Dance in San Juan Pueblo and Alcalde, New Mexico: Contexts and Meanings." Ph.D. dissertation, University of California, Los Angeles.

———. 1997. "Cultural Interaction in New Mexico as Illustrated in the Matachines Dance." In *Musics of Multicultural America.* New York: Schirmer, 155–185.

———. 1999. "Old World Origins of the Matachines Dance of New Mexico." In *Vistas of American Music, Essays and Compositions in Honor of William K. Kearns.* Detroit Monographs in Musicology / Studies in Music, No. 25. Sterling Heights, MI: Harmonie Park Press, 339–56.

———. 2002. "The New Mexico, Texas, and Mexico Borderlands and the Concept of *Indio* in the Matachines Dance." Proceedings of "Musical Cultures of Latin America: Global Effects, Past and Present," an interdisciplinary conference held at UCLA, May 28–30, 1999. Los Angeles: The Regents of the University of California and the Department of Ethnomusicology.

Scarff. 1960. MA thesis, University of Texas, Austin.

Sevilla, Amparo, Hilda Rodríguez, and Elizabeth Camara. *Danzas y bailes tradicionales del estado de Tlaxcala.* 2ª edición. Tlahuapan, Puebla, MX: Premiá Editora de libros.

Sklar, Deidre. 2001. *Dancing with the Virgin.* Berkeley: University of California Press.

Stephenson, Claude. 2001. *A Comparative Analysis of Matachines Music and its History and Dispersion in the American Southwest.* Albuquerque: University of New Mexico Press.

Tijerina, Andres. 1977. *Tejanos and Texas: The Native Mexicans of Texas, 1820–1850.* Austin: University of Texas Press.

Treviño, Adrian, and Barbara Gilles. 1991. *The Dance of Montezuma: Some Remarks and History of the Danza de los Matachines in Northern New Mexico.*

EIGHT

Re-Membering Chelo Silva: The Bolero in Chicana Perspective (Women's Bodies and Voices in Postrevolutionary Urbanization: The Bohemian, Urban, and Transnational)

YOLANDA BROYLES-GONZÁLEZ

RE-MEMBERING CHELO SILVA

Chelo Silva, the prominent borderlands singer whose fame extended from the United States to México and all of Latin America and the Caribbean, was born Consuelo Silva on August 22, 1922, in the small border town of Brownsville, Texas, across from the neighboring Mexican town of Matamoros. Silva came from a working-class family, and she showed an early inclination toward song performance. While working as a sales clerk in Brownsville in her early teens, she began to earn local notoriety by virtue of her beautiful singing voice. By the 1950s, she had earned immortality across the Américas as a beloved interpreter of the musical song type known as the "bolero." In fact, her recordings circulate today more than those of Agustín Lara.

Given the urbanite and internationalist nature of her song repertoire, her millions of fans outside of Texas do not generally associate her with the Texas borderlands that are her homeland. Not surprisingly, music—in its ability to migrate—resembles the flight of birds and the movement of wind and water; it cannot always be tied to physical geographies. Thus we might ask, Did Chelo Silva arise from an existing Tejana musical tradition? And do Chelo Silva and Lydia Mendoza serve as a foundation to other Tejana musicians? In another paper, I refer to Silva and Mendoza as the yin and yang of what can very loosely be called "Tejana music." They rose to prominence by very different trajectories of borderlands song performance. Lydia Mendoza's musical repertoire had deep borderlands roots carried by popular oral tradition. Her mother and grandmother introduced her to the old 1880s canción, to música de antaño, and to the corrido trajectory. She evolved those musical vocabularies through her voice and aesthetics. *Lo ranchero,* in the form of the land base–inspired canción ranchera and also the corrido, ultimately became Mendoza's chief staples. She performed in brightly sequined dresses that exhibited indigenous Mexican symbols. By contrast, Silva did not draw from those established norteño Tejana musical vocabularies. Her ambiance was the nightclub; her attire was slick, sexy, and markedly internationalist and cosmopolitan. Silva adopted the newly evolved urbanite Mexican bolero music, which reached the Tejano borderlands (and the entire hemisphere) in the 1930s through the recently established mass medium of radio. She can be credited with being in the forefront of promulgating the bolero, and with introducing a new song repertoire into the ever-changing Tejana/o norteño sphere, after establishing herself outside of Texas. Silva performed, for example, in Mexico City's mega-radio station XEW, the continent's most powerful broadcaster. Mendoza, by contrast, made a conscious choice to remain with her touring family on the US side of the border. One of Mendoza's greatest accomplishments arises from the extraordinary length (six decades) of her musical career.[1] Mendoza's musical repertoire, ensemble, instruments, and interpretation of norteño song style from the oral tradition withstood the test of time more than Silva's musical style and instrumentation. Yet both women carry the great distinction of having inspired and opened the performance world for many other women, in Texas and beyond; they both navigated within a business world controlled primarily by men.

In spite of Silva's illustrious singing career and her popularity across the Américas, the written record has not preserved her memory. Scholars have not yet recognized the contributions of one the most widely heard and known Chicana voices of the twentieth century. Not a single academic article exists on Silva, who died on April 2, 1988. This article marks an attempt to remember Chicana singer Chelo Silva's life and contributions to American and Chicana music and women's history.[2] Unfortunately, many of the basic facts about her life are unavailable. I endeavor to piece her together from disparate parts that include old press clippings, photos, oral histories with her fans and her social adversaries, my own reception of her music, and elusive references to her by notables such as culture critic Carlos Monsiváis and singers Juan Gabriel, Paquita la del Barrio, and Lydia Mendoza. My richest source of material concerning her career is, of course, Silva's extensive musical repertoire.

Chelo Silva was but one of dozens of young women who used their voices to rise from poverty to stardom, from minimum-wage work to the night work of the entertainer. Any woman who embarked upon that path became a businesswoman and artist who had to maneuver within a male-controlled music industry. Like many other Texas women singers of her generation—such as Lydia Mendoza, Rita Vidaurri, and Eva Garza—Silva's radius of influence grew along with the new radio and recording sound media, which had come of age in the 1930s. In fact, Silva's first move from visual live performance to that of disembodied sound began at a local radio program. In the late 1930s, she sang at a radio program hosted by one of her future husbands, Américo Paredes. Silva and Paredes had a son together and divorced not too long thereafter. Silva then continued her performance career singing at the Corpus Christi Texas Continental Club. In the 1940s, she recorded with small Texas labels such as the pioneering Texas-Mexican record company Discos Falcon. By the late fifties, she had recorded with the transnational label Columbia Records and become one of the best-selling women singers in all of México and Latin America. What are her contributions? What were the particulars of this US-Mexican's rise to fame? What musical meanings, gendered meanings, class meanings, and sexual meanings did her voice and person express? What did it mean to be a woman nightclub performer in the 1940s and beyond? How did she perform gender and sexual politics in working-class communities, which were her prime constituents?

As a cultural citizen of the Borderlands, Chelo Silva must be seen in light of both Mexican and US American histories. The Golden Era of Mexican song from 1935 to the 1950s saw the transnational emergence of the Cuban-Mexican bolero. It embraced many countries—both México and the United States, for example—because the radio waves of the 1930s blurred the supposed separation of nations and created new imagined communities. Chelo Silva grew up on the Texas/Matamoros borderlands with radio-transmitted boleros, tangos, ranchera music, canciones, and corridos. She came to find her voice in the bolero genre, the new voice of urban working-class modernity. Initially the bolero had enjoyed a strong middle-class following, particularly in its more masculine and less sexually aggressive forms as performed by the suave male guitar trios such as Trio Los Panchos, Los Tres Ases, Los Dandys, or Los Tres Reyes.[3] Those suave trios tended to perform a rather sweet, romantic intimacy rooted in the expressive, romantic lyric poetry of a bygone era. As I will show, Chelo Silva unmasked that romanticism..

The rise and spread of the new bolero song genre in the thirties, forties, and fifties is related to many factors. Powerful new media technologies could transmit musics across national geographies, creating a multi-national following for formerly regional musics. The new bolero aesthetic found favor in part because it captured and resonated with changing social desires, needs, and historical experiences. Song and dance traditions, as memory arts, articulate socio-cultural engagements of both producers and consumers. Musics are aesthetic social interactions and social workings differentiated by categories such as age, economic class, local culture, global cultural flows, sexualities, gender, nation, and race identities. The memory arts of the oral tradition construct and reconstitute experiences we wish to remember while also enabling us to selectively forget. The need to forget was great in post-revolutionary México and post–World War II United States. México was devastated by the death of over one million men and women, both combatants and non-combatants; the populace was furthermore devastated by the displacements of millions into new cities and urban life as well as by migration northward into the United States. The impoverished masses of Mexicans were disillusioned by the broken promises of politicians and by continued corporate greed and exploitation on both sides of the border. It was these impoverished masses that relished the bolero's inwardly directed expressivity. The bolero provided a release from the turmoil of displacement and poverty by providing a refuge within innermost emotional life. It could also be said that the bolero helped give shape to new modes of gender/sex/class consciousness in the spaces opened up by the Mexican Revolution, on the one hand, and by World War II on the other.

At the same time the bolero—through its performance—provided a new tool with which to mark oneself as an urbanite eager to disassociate from the class- and-race-stigmatized rural experience. The urbanist effort to set oneself at arm's distance from one's rural roots even involves the contradictory working-class appropriation of city clothes imitative of the elite class and a supposed cosmopolitan sophistication.

WOMEN'S PERFORMATIVITY: BOLERO POETICS AND GENDER/CLASS/SEXUAL RELATIONS

The nightclub became the setting most closely associated with the new bolero music and with working-class urban modernity in all of its mixed and contradictory modes. Nightclub culture evolved in the 1930s as a transnational urban movement. The common ground of transnationalism is fashion and the musical instrumentation of the nightclub such as the piano, the cornet and trumpet, some string instruments, and percussion. Yet the expressivity of the songs within nightclub culture tended to be more localized and culture-specific. The nightclub songs of Chelo Silva, Billie Holliday, and Edith Piaf are very different, even as they share a common ground: an urbanite nightclub culture, their attire, and musical instruments. In the case of México, the nightclub became synonymous with the bolero and with the voices and personas of the bolero singers.

The bolero came onto the musical scene as an import from Cuba in the 1920s. It subsequently became Mexicanized by Mexican composers, by the guitar trios, and also by an earlier generation of women solo singers such as Chicana singer Evelina Garcia, who in 1938 (at age fifteen) signed her first recording contract on the Columbia label and then went on to attain international recognition. Mark Pedelty, in "The Bolero: the Birth, Life, and Decline of Mexican Modernity" identifies what he feels is an urban "sense of loss and longing" in the bolero and situates its emergence in the context of post-revolutionary urbanity and modernism.[4] His focus is exclusively on bolero composer/performer Agustin Lara, with no attention given to women bolero performers or composers—such as Agustín's sister María Teresa Lara, who composed many of Agustín's hit boleros. Although I would agree that the bolero thrived in the context of urban uprootedness, the moral challenges of city life can also be said to have initiated new dialogues about love, sex, romance, courtship, and morality in general. The urbanization process, quite beyond triggering a sense of loss, required collective and individual adjustments, and it was connected to working-class discourse about and practical shaping of a new reality.

The bolero, in fact, encodes noticeable shifts and explorations of sexual and gender politics. It is through the voices of performers such as Chelo Silva that intimacy becomes a sustained public movement and discourse. Publicly performed and recorded explicit love songs transform women's private, intimate spheres into public ones. Through publicly performed song, one's most intimate feelings and sexual experiences become publicly manifest discourse; the experience is made available to the collective for commentary, evaluation, analysis, and renewed action in the context of treacherous and unaccustomed urban environments. Post-revolutionary Mexican cities as well as postwar US cities attracted record numbers of migrants and created new contexts, challenges, and possibilities (both positive and negative) for newly urbanized women. The bolero becomes the new music for a new society and an important expressive medium in constructing and circulating dimensions of a new womanhood.

Significantly, the new music abruptly shifts part of the focus of Mexican music away from the accustomed rural imaginary domain (where the longstanding canción ranchera finds inspiration) and away from themes of social historical cataclysm (portrayed in so many corridos). It could be said that the bolero wants to forget the social turmoil of the last thirty years as it turns its focus to inward geographies and sexual turmoil. Outward references to social environments are avoided. The love scenarios played out in boleros appear closely related to nightlife, reflect an urbanite alienation from the land, and manifest a recourse to the confines of the nightclub. The picture on the cover of one of Chelo Silva's famed long-play records tells a part of the story: a man lighting her cigarette, cognac snifters filled, candlelight, urban attire. It is a heterosexual romantic scene centering sex, drugs, and the nightlife. It was the imagery of an imagined urban sophistication.

Chelo Silva can be credited with having usurped the sweet velvet bolero so esteemed by the elite classes. Her deep, sultry solo voice is a marked departure from the smooth, three-part voice harmonies of the bolero guitar trios and their constructions of love. Emotive openness, explicitness, and excess are at the heart of Chelo Silva's bolero song repertoire. Chelo Silva's boleros foreground extreme forms of affect and sexuality, oftentimes disastrous and tied to experiences of obsession, anguish, abandonment, casual sex, violence, betrayal, fleeting ecstasy, and of course also unhappy, unrequited love. Love relationships are portrayed as inherently disastrous. Most of her songs bespeak painful aftermaths filled with lingering recrimination. Silva's songs tend to highlight and play out many extremes. Hers is a marked departure from the grip of dominant elite rosy love ideologies. Within upper-middle-class establishment culture, love was a many-splendored thing involving permanency, stability, marriage, women's sexual passivity and purity, procreation, domesticity, and clearly drawn lines of inheritance. Chelo Silva's bolero repertoire, by contrast, only very rarely featured harmonious love. More often than not, she gave voice to love's multiple disharmonious possibilities. Significantly, her love situations are unattached to domesticity and child rearing. As such, her representations of love and sexuality contradict and challenge mainstream elite ideological ideals concerning the sanctity (domestication) of women and of state-sanctioned domestic love. Silva's repertoire thus defies male dominance and provides a sounding board and model for the emergent community of working-class urban women. She models sexual independence, free experimentation with life, and self-assertiveness outside of domestic orthodoxy. Silva's deep, rich, and highly nuanced voice is well-suited to the expressivity of gut-wrenching, torrid love affairs and stories of impossible loves that end in heartbreak or, conversely, in eviction of an undesirable partner. She performs all extremes of love relations, at times describing an autonomous woman's power and at times woman's weakness and downfall. Hence perdition also emerges as a frequent theme: the woman who gives all and loses all due to betrayal and/or abandonment.

Silva's songs can be construed positively as signposts and warnings to women listeners. They bespeak the consequences of blind faith in urban love relationships within a patriarchal urban environment. Although there is an occasional happy love song, more often than not love is the source of anguish. Silva's very song titles mark, encapsulate, and symbolize the entire songs: "Mal Camino" ("Down a Bad Road"), "Amor Burlado" ("A Betrayed Love"), "Judas" ("Judas"), "Por equivocación" ("By mistake"), and the lonely "Estoy sin ti" ("I am without you"). The era's urban fascination with nightlife includes the theme of the "cabaretera" (bar and worker) and/or sex worker. Yet those female figures are drawn with great compassion in Silva's songs such as "Besos callejeros" ("Street Kisses") and "Amor de la Calle" ("Street Love"). It is not only the nightclub but also the street that proclaim the presence of the public woman outside of domesticity, bourgeois morality, and even established sex laws. Yet the topos of the streetwalker is only one means of proclaiming the public presence of women in the 1950s.

One should not underestimate the power of female sentimental expression emanating from these songs and from women performers who sang them from the 1930s to the 1950s. These singers greatly expanded the range and nature of women's sexual agency in ways that contradicted the attempted moral power grip of national elites over women's bodies. Audiences were and are able to find themselves in (and constitute themselves through) song narratives of desire, courtship, seduction, bliss, abandonment, and all other possibilities of the love relationship. Chelo Silva's performative discourse maps a new geography of woman's sexual desire, sexual politics, and gender identity. Silva rehearses and voices women's newfound urban freedom and social/sexual struggles and independence. Chelo Silva's bolero songs serve as witness and accomplice to the audience's longings or passions. Simon Frith tells us that love songs are important, for example, "because people need them to give shape and voice to emotions that otherwise cannot be expressed without embarrassment or incoherence" (Frith 1987, 141). Thus Silva's songs map out a relational system of heart/body/soul experiences.

It is not difficult to imagine how Chelo Silva earned one of her popular epithets: Angel de la Guarda de las Mujeres, "Guardian Angel of Women." Chelo Silva, in singing bluntly about women's love tragedies, about sexual relations, about abusive relationships, and about love's ecstasies, was far ahead of her time. Sexuality discourse had not entered into song with the language of the streets prior to her. And it was virtually unheard of for any woman to sing a public denunciation of a sexual partner. Silva's widespread appeal speaks to her audience's hunger for and reception of this discourse. We can also recall that Lydia Mendoza's first major hit was precisely such a denunciatory song: "Mal hombre" ("Wicked Man") in 1934. Part of the great importance of Silva's voice has to do with the discursive space she opened for the public display of gender and sexual relations and for the exploration and transformation of sexual identities. Many of her boleros feature a new performative freedom regarding social morals. In many of her songs, she transgresses sexual boundaries and restrictive sexual expectations put forth by elite middle-class morality, national powerholders, and church institutions. This is manifest, for example, in her song line "Que murmuren, no me importa que murmuren" ("Let them whisper, I don't care; let them talk"). She defies elite nationalist social conventions and advocates following one's heart. At the same time, she is ready to speak of a bad partner in boldly explicit vernacular terms such as "Te voy a arrancar los ojos, para dejarte en tinieblas" ("I'm going to tear out your eyes and leave you in the shadows"). In the bolero *Vete* ("Leave!") she assumes an autonomous womanist stance by showing her lover the door, indicating she can no longer tolerate the lover's insanity and lies. She thus performs for urban and rural women (and men) the act of liberating oneself from a bad love situation. The innovative nature of her sexualized and in-your-face song repertoire of course meant controversy, and what she faced was not unlike what Agustín Lara experienced when he sang poetically about the innate goodness of sex workers. Silva's very presence as a heavily drinking and smoking public woman who freely used explicit sexual language during performances defied the normative patriarchal performance of womanhood. According to eyewitnesses, men would often boo and heckle Silva at her concerts in the 1950s and 1960s. Yet this did not bother or deter her.

Silva pushed the bolero to new denunciatory extremes which male boleristas—such as Trio Los Panchos—never dared to sing. In the song "Ponzoña," for example, she calls the love experience "the black virus of betrayal," and she likens that love to a deadly "poisonous stinger" and to a "curse." She relates that she healed from a rattlesnake bite but that the lover's betrayal was a far greater poison. Silva and other women bolero singers also draw heterosexual identities into question. By virtue of her performativity, any singer could fashion a song as a heterosexual or homosexual one by virtue of her choice of pronouns and vocabulary. In one of her great hits, "Pasatiempo" (Pastime), Silva is singing about love with a woman. Or in the song "Fracaso," she sings, "You are the woman I have adored the most." ["Tu has sido la mujer que yo mas he adorado. A ti mi amor he consagrado."] I would disagree with Lupe San Miguel's view that songs written from a so-called male point of view and sung by women create what he calls "absurd situations" of women singing to women.[5] That heteronormative view disregards the power of women's performative presence, which imbues such songs with new meanings. Far from being "absurd," such performances can, for example, easily disrupt the heterosexual regime. They also create a gender dissonance when a woman sings explicitly male-voiced and thus defies the sexist division of emotions.

At times Chelo Silva's songs feature a schizophrenic dualism, which includes both a denunciation and unflinching affection in the same song. Such is the case in one of her most famous hits, "Hipócrita" ("Hypocrite"), which berates the disloyal lover, calling him/her "perverse," poisonous, and even deadly. Yet by the end of the song, there is a sudden injection of masochism: "Y como no me quieres, me voy a morir" ("And since you don't love me, I'm going to die").

Another dimension of this love without boundaries is the fantasy of total submission ("entrega total") to the loved one. This act of total submission and self-abnegation—carried to a masochistic extreme—is best expressed in another of her hits, "Como un Perro" ("Like a Dog"), "Por tener la miel amarga de tus besos, he tenido que arrastrar mi dignidad" ["Just to enjoy the bitter honey of your kisses, I've had to trash my own dignity"]. This song ultimately expresses a desire to love "like a dog," that is, silently and at the feet of the beloved. Of course, dogs can also bite.

Lyrics such as these may be difficult to grasp in the post-feminist era. They could, however, function as a coded representation of violence or masochistic submission within love relationships. Or, depending on how much irony is in the performance, this song could also become a parody and mockery of obedient love. In other songs, Silva rehearses the opposite: the subject voice kicking out the bad lover. Happy love is rather rare in her repertoire. Among the rare exceptions is her hit "Espérame en el cielo," which exhorts the lover to wait for her in heaven if the love partner dies first. In contradistinction to Hollywood romance, love is not romanticized without inclusion of its downsides, its ambiguities, and conflicts. The power of those anguished moments in the bolero is magnified by the absence of any narrative context (a feature more common in the ranchera song).

Silva's strong following perhaps also has to due with her dramatic and provocative presence offstage and onstage. Offstage, she frequently gave provocative press comments to the leading daily in Mexico City, *Excelsior,* challenging the conditions under which she worked. The newspaper record reveals the struggles she faced in finding acceptance in México's capital city. In 1955, she publicly protested and even announced a strike in order to gain entry into the continent's mega-station XEW which broadcasted throughout Latin America, México, and the United States. In an interview with the daily *Excelsior,* she proclaims: "No trabajaré en teatro y cabaret alguno, de esta capital, hasta que logre mi sueño dorado: cantar por la XEW. Lástima que debido a tanta política no haya podido lograrlo!"[6] ["I will not work in any theater or night club of this capital city until I achieve my golden dream: to sing on XEW. It's a shame that I have not achieved that dream due to so much politics."] My sense is that the music industry kept her at arm's distance because of her powerful iconoclastic personality and sexually free musical vocabulary, and because she was from the other side of the border, a Chicana.

Chelo Silva furthermore stood firm, for example, in demanding a just wage and the right conditions for her artistic work. In September 1955, she explains her boycott of various radio and television media who refuse to meet her price. She tells *Excelsior,* "Durante mi estancia en esta ciudad, no he querido aceptar ninguna de las proposiciones que me han hecho para actuar en radio y televisión, porque además de no pagarme lo que pido, los programas son muy cortos."[7] While waiting to receive an invitation from XEW she boasts to *Excelsior* of earning US $60,000 per year just on royalties.[8]

Her strike was effective, and she became one of the few Chicanas to perform at XEW. *Excelsior* announced Chelo Silva's XEW debut performance in understated terms as "Chelo Silva, la cancionera del nuevo estilo"[9] ["Chelo Silva, the songstress of the new style"]. Clearly, Chelo Silva handled her musical and monetary matters with great aplomb.[10]

THE URBAN GENDERED BODY POLITIC: ON BEING A PUBLIC WOMAN AND LA VIDA NOCTURNA

Viewed in its entirety, Silva's repertoire gives voice to the open expression of female desire and agency. No wonder that the bolero was regarded as scandalous by elite moralists. Song lyrics and the nightclub culture in which women displayed their bodies were in fact targeted by the state and its agents of public morality. In this regard, Silva's bodily presence as a nightclub performer demands further analysis. Women bolero singers were necessarily public women, and their domain was the nightclub. Women such as Chelo Silva played an important role in affirming a new imaginary of the public woman whose body—or parts of whose body—was on public display. The nightclub is no doubt a contradictory space. What meanings does the nightclub hold for gender and sexual relations? The fact of erotic display or even non-erotic body presence holds many historical meanings. Are scantily clad women in public (or private) seductresses? Temptresses? Or are they perfectly natural? To what extent does someone like Silva control her nightclub self? Her art and her body? Why do nation-states target nakedness? We should not forget that nakedness has a much longer history in the Américas than manufactured clothing. A woman's exposed body can be viewed as a continuation of Indigenous presence. Indigenous women of the Mexican countryside in the 1960s walked village streets bare-breasted (and still do in some places) while their urban counterparts submitted much earlier to covering their bodies and internalizing a new morality centered on the body and body-shame concepts such as "Honestia." Honestia is an elite summons to young women's bodies. It denotes submission to a wide spectrum of body controls. Hiding women's bodies was one of the most salient features first of European colonialism and later of capitalist nation-states. Indigenous communities, by contrast, have a long history of affirming both the private and public presence of women and their bodies. Even in many contemporary Native American societies, women are not confined to a narrowly circumscribed domesticity. By upper-middle-class and colonial standards, however, a public woman and an unclothed woman were anathema.

Nation-state control has always extended to women's bodies. As the post-revolutionary patriarchal Mexican nation (and the Catholic Church) moved to consolidate their power, women's bodies became prime targets of renewed neo-colonial subjugation. The state's body control mechanisms include, for example, marriage licensing, so-called decency laws, inheritance laws, sex work laws, labor laws, and curfew laws, which include today's two-AM closure of nightclubs. In their early days, nightclubs catered to customers all night and even 24/7. The nightclub performativity was a resistive one in the context of tense power relations between men/women/elites/and the indigenous-based masses. The nightclub was a space that featured women's bodies on display and a discourse of sexuality. Both bolero lyrics and the bodies of women bolero performers articulated and even flaunted a new display of individual emotional needs, body experiences, and desire. In some cases, women's bodies spoke without words; such was the case with the immortal and immensely popular dancer Yolanda Montes, known as "Tongolele." In spite of her star status (on both sides of the border), her expressive seminude dancing and celebration of body movement were more than the Mexican state and the Church could stand. They asserted their control over her body by deporting her.

Public dancing in a nightclub—let alone unchaperoned—was considered scandalous and synonymous with indecency by upper-middle-class national tastes and by many of the working class who aspired to the middle class. Nightclubs were viewed by elite morality as dens of iniquity. Alberto Dallal in his book *El "Dancing" Mexicano* refers to nightclub dancing as one of the first acts of women liberating themselves from traditional (that is, middle-class and elite) social roles for women.[11] Publicly dancing women were thought—by some—to submit their bodies to the male gaze and to provoke aggressive male attentions. But what economic classes subscribed to and enforced such views? Whose traditions sought to confine women to the private and away from public domains? Clearly, the nightclub in many ways challenged (and in other ways also reproduced) sexual ideologies and practices, body repression, and heterosexist dominion.

Mexican intellectual Carlos Monsiváis provides some insight in his book, which is named in fact after one of the best-known bolero songs, "Amor perdido."[12] He sketches the Mexican post-revolutionary era as one in which women's rights are constitutionally denied, in spite of women's co-equal participation in the armed struggle of the Mexican Revolution. Monsiváis traces a corresponding patriarchal power grab by the classist national bourgeoisie. My own sense is that a good portion of the power and determination of the soldaderas and of Rosita the Riveter—the soldier women of the Mexican Revolution and the women who had participated in industrial occupations in the United States during WWII—was reincarnated in the nightclub and nightlife after the Revolution's fighting stopped and after the soldaderas were banished from urban civic and governmental processes.

With regard to moral standards, Monsiváis describes an ascendant post-revolutionary Mexican middle class that tries to restrict women's powers by resurrecting elite practices and "appearances" of morality propagated under the Porfirian dictatorship. Elite circles regard and designate themselves as Buenas Familias whose moral slogans include being "cautious, timid, prudent . . . respectful of domesticity, a legitimate daughter . . . and nothing that might offend Mr. Government" ["recatada, tímida, prudente . . . respetuosa del hogar, hija de familia . . . sin que haya ofensa para el Señor Gobierno"].[13] Nightclub culture and the bolero posed a major challenge to those patriarchal governing bodies who espoused the morality of "Las Buenas Familias" and "El Señor Gobierno" [Good Families and Mr. Government]. The bolero constructed its own resistive regimen of gendered morality and body politicking. It was a mujerista (womanist) regimen.

Even famed bolero composer Agustin Lara—who was buried with state honors when he died in 1970—was targeted for eradication by the Mexican government in the early stages of his career. In the 1940s and 1950s, Agustin Lara became the target of a hostile nation-state that sought to prohibit and banish his boleros, calling his music "inmoral y degenerada" ["immoral and degenerate"].[14] Middle-class morality also spoke through the Congreso de Mujeres Intelectuales contra la Prostitución [Congress of Intellectual Women against Prostitution], who proposed a boycott of Lara. Indeed, La Secretaria de Educación Pública declared the banishment of Lara's music from music schools because it allegedly perverted children.

But Monsiváis points out that for the masses, the bolero served an important compensatory function. He regards the excesses of love found in the bolero as the impoverished urban working masses' only means of compensating for social marginalization: "la enorme credulidad de los sectores mayoritarios de las ciudades que ven en el desboradamieto amoroso su gran y única compensación ante la pérdida de la juventud y el estrago del tiempo y el abatimiento económico y la marginación social."[15] He also sees the bolero and night life as a symbolic means of fleeing from oppressive domesticity and into a sense of contemporary urban uncertainty.

THE LEGACY OF CHELO SILVA

Chelo Silva died in Corpus Christi, Texas, of cancer and the hard life at the age of sixty-five (April 1988). Yet her legacy lives on. She is widely remembered among the Mexican working class (on both sides of the border) for her distinctive style and the unique power of her musical expression, even though the ranchero aesthetic ultimately both absorbed and eclipsed the "cosmopolitan" bolero. Musically, the gulf between the urban-associated bolero and the more rural-identified canción ranchera was, on the one hand, bridged by the new composite bolero-ranchero (whose first exponents were Juan Mendoza and Trio Tariácuri). On the other hand, various rural-origin ranchero musical ensembles—such as the button-accordion-based Tejano conjunto music—adopted some bolero songs into the older repertoire of corridos, ranchero polkas, redovas, shotis, and other dance songs. In Texas, it was conjunto pioneer Valerio Longoria who played the first boleros on his button-accordion, whereas the urbanite expression of the bolero and its instrumentations went largely dormant.

It would be no exaggeration to say that in her prime, Chelo Silva figured among the most prominent of all torch singers. She enjoyed a far-flung transnational fame exceeding that of any male Chicano musician. Her fame and popularity even exceeded those of the many other well-known Mexican-born bolero performers such as Elvira Rios, Amparo Montes, or Toña La Negra. Her fame as a bolerista is comparable to that of Tejana Eva Garza and Arizona native Adelina García. Silva left behind a vast number of recordings, including almost a hundred long-play albums. In her lifetime, she recorded with both regional and international recording companies. Tejana/o grassroots audiences never forgot Chelo Silva, perhaps because she frequently went home. Her transnational pendulum movements in fact reconfigured the Tejano musical "home." Within academic print culture, however, the strong masculinist ideologies of varied Tejano music historians have lamentably obscured the contributions of a number of Tejanas, including Chelo Silva.[16] Deborah Vargas' recent study of Tejana musical performers reveals that "Texas Mexican culture studies have consistently centered male subjects *particularly* within the cultural site of music and folklore."[17] Vargas cites Americo Paredes, Manuel Peña, Jose Limón, and Guadalupe San Miguel among those who have consistently centered male subjects. By contrast, Vargas examines how Chelo Silva's performance "generated alternative knowledges and subjectivities, enacting women's sexual agency and reminding us that passion [. . .] is as much a historical modality as an emotional one."[18] Various canonical texts continue to marginalize Silva. For example, Jaime Rico Salazar omits Chelo Silva in all five editions of his massive bolero anthology, *Cien Años de Boleros.*[19]

It is not only the transnational, working-class Tejanos and Tejanas that remember and love Chelo Silva. She influenced the next generation of performers and intellectuals in México as well. As the twentieth century drew to an end, Mexican culture critic Carlos Monsiváis, for example, was asked to name the people he considered most memorable in that waning century. Chelo Silva figures among the very few women and the only Chicana he names. Singers are among the most powerful erasers of the national and of recently imposed national borders. It is my sense that many who love Chelo Silva—outside of Texas—simply assume she was from México and not from Brownsville, Texas. Contemporary singing idol and composer Juan Gabriel refers to Chelo Silva as a major influence in his musical career. He mistakenly (yet understandably) names Chelo Silva as an influence "de acá" (from México).

Chelo Silva's legacy continues today and is also closely reincarnated in the hugely successful singer "Paquita la del Barrio" from Mexico City (who performs those boleros in ranchera style). In all of her interviews, Paquita credits Chelo Silva with the inspiration for her singing career. Paquita recounts how she suffered betrayal at the hands of her husband and one night ended up in her car in a state of despair. She turned on the radio and heard Chelo Silva's famous interpretation of "Cheque en blanco" ("Blank Check"), a composition by Emma Elena Valdelamar. In that classic song, which confidently denounces a bad lover's behavior, Paquita found not only solace and companionship but also the courage and determination to begin her own singing career at mid life. She has found a very strong following across national borders. Paquita la del Barrio sets forth the legacy of Chelo Silva, singing the songs that expose, condemn, celebrate, or even deride bad love partners. In the middle of her songs, she always calls out, "¿Me estás oyendo inútil?" ("Are you listening, you good-for-nothing?").

Chelo Silva also has enjoyed iconic status within various gay/lesbian/bi-sexual/trans-sexual communities, such as in 1980s California. Into the twenty-first century, she remains iconic throughout México. She is a standard among drag performers. In this world of compulsory patriarchal heterosexuality, Chelo Silva also figures as a lightning rod and vector of the spectrum between gay liberation and homophobia. Virtually all conversations about Chelo Silva sooner or later turn into debates as to whether or not she was lesbian or straight, or both. Many stories are told. Epithets are hurled. Whispers turn to raised voices and interminable rumor-mongering. The myth of Chelo Silva continues to grow long after her burial in Corpus Christi, Texas.

ACKNOWLEDGMENTS

I deeply appreciate the enthusiastic reading of colleagues Chela Sandoval, Arturo Aldama, and Peter García. My research and writing on Chelo Silva began in 1981 and evolved through invited lectures at places I would like to thank: UTEP (2003), the University of Arizona (2003), and The University of Illinois, Urbana Champaign (2006).

NOTES

1. I refer you to Yolanda Broyles-González, *Lydia Mendoza's Life in Music/La Historia de Lydia Mendoza. Norteño Tejano Legacies,* New York: Oxford University Press, 2001.

2. I must take issue with Frances Aparicio's fine book *Listening to Salsa. Gender, Popular Music and Puerto Rican Culture,* as she repeatedly claims that boleros feature a "predominance of male singing subjects" and that "the overt articulation of power differentials during sexual interaction reveals the dominance of the male over the female in songs" (1998, 133). In fact, the borderlands and México provide us with dozens of examples of female singing subjects of boleros. What is more, boleros cannot be reduced to words separated from their living performative and historical contexts. When a woman interprets (sings) a male-composed bolero,

many of its meanings are subverted. Olga Nájera-Ramírez has written about how women's performative within the ranchera tradition can expose and subvert male privilege, even when women sing a "male song." See her article "Unruly Passions: Poetics, Performance, and Gender in the Ranchera Song," *Chicana Feminisms,* ed. Gabriela Arredondo et al., Durham, NC: Duke University Press, 2003, 184–210. Similarly, Iris Zavala in "De heroes y heroinas en lo imaginario social: El discurso amoroso del bolero" (published in *Revista Casa de las Américas* 179 (1990): 123–128) stresses the bolero's "yo" and "tu" which—depending on the singer's and the listener's sexual identities—become interchangeable in their gendered and sexual meanings.

3. For a testimonio from one of these groups, see Celina Fernandez, *Los Panchos: La Historia de los Embajadores de La Canción Romántica Contada Por Su Voz Rafael Basurto,* Martinez Roca, 2005. For a general oversight into the bolero in México, see Rodrigo Bazan Bonfil, *Y Si Vivo Cien Años, Antologia de Bolero,* Fondo de Cultura Económica USA, 2005.

4. Published in *Latin American Music Review* 20.1 (Spring/Summer 1999): 30–58. Pedelty does not even mention Chelo Silva or, for example, Agustín's sister, María Teresa Lara, who composed many of Agustín's hit boleros.

5. Guadalupe San Miguel, Jr., *Tejano Proud. Tex-Mex Music in the Twentieth Century,* College Station: Texas A&M Press, 2002, 41.

6. Aug. 24, 1955.

7. Sept. 18, 1955, page 3D.

8. Oct. 20, 1955.

9. Oct. 28, 1955.

10. On November 19, 1955 (page 23a), *Excelsior* reports on Chelo Silva's steady rise to fame: "Chelo empieza a subir." Two days later, Silva shows herself in touch with her working-class constituents: "Mi voz no tiene nada de particular—subrayó—simplemente se acopla al tipo de canciones que gustan a las masas" ["There is nothing special about my voice—she underscored—it simply matches the kinds of songs that the masses like"]. *Excelsior,* Nov. 21, 1955, p. 18A.

11. México, D.F.: Editorial Oasis, 1982.

12. *Amor perdido,* México: Ediciones Era, 1977.

13. *Amor perdido,* p. 69.

14. *Amor perdido,* p. 79.

15. *Amor perdido,* p. 80.

16. See her dissertation, "Las Tracaleras: Texas-Mexican Women, Music, and Place," UC Santa Cruz, 2003.

17. P. 9

18. Deborah R. Vargas, "Borderland Bolerista: The Licentious Lyricism of Chelo Silva," *Feminist Studies* 34.1–2 (2008): 173–197. Here, p. 175.

19. Bogotá: Panamericana, 5th edition, 1999. George Torres's brief overview of the bolero's development from Cuba to México is largely male-centered, focusing on the trio romántico bolero genre and ignoring women bolero interpreters. See his "The Bolero Romántico. From Cuban Dance to International Popular Song," *From Tejano to Tango. Latin American Popular Music,* ed. Walter Aaron Clark, New York: Routledge, 2002, 151–171.

WORKS CITED

Aparicio, Frances. *Listening to Salsa.* Hanover, NH: University Press of New England, 1988. Print.

Bazán Bonfil, Rodrigo. *Y Si Vivo Cien años, Antologia de Bolero.* México: Fondo de Cultura Económica, 2001. Print.

Broyles-González, Yolanda. *Lydia Mendoza's Life in Music/La Historia de Lydia Mendoza. Norteño Tejano Legacies.* New York: Oxford University Press, 2001. Print.

"Chelo habla." (N.A.) *Excelsior* 21 November 1955. 18a. Print.

"Chelo empieza a subir." (N.A.) *Excelsior* 19 November 1955. 23a. Print.

George Torres George. "The Bolero Romántico. From Cuban Dance to International Popular Song." *From Tejano to Tango. Latin American Popular Music.* Ed. Walter Aaron Clark. New York: Routledge, 2002: 151–171. Print.

Fernandez, Celina. *Los Panchos: La Historia de los Embajadores de La Canción Romántica Contada Por Su Voz Rafael Basurto.* México: Martinez Roca, 2005. Print.

Dallal, Alberto. *El "dancing" Mexicano.* México, DF: Editorial Oasis, 1982. Print.

Frith, Simon. *Taking Popular Music Seriously.* Aldershot: Ashgate, 2007, 1987. Print.

Monsiváis, Carlos. *Amor perdido.* México: Ediciones Era, 1977. Print.

Nájera-Ramírez, Olga. "Unruly Passions: Poetics, Performance, and Gender in the Ranchera Song." *Chicana Feminisms.* Ed. Gabriela Arredondo et al. Durham, NC: Duke University Press, 2003: 184–210. Print.

Pedelty, Mark. "The Bolero: the Birth, Life, and Decline of Mexican Modernity." *Latin American Music Review* 20.1 (Spring/Summer 1999): 30–58. Print.

Rico Salazar, Jaime. *Cien Años de Boleros.* Bogota: Panamericana, 5th edition, 1999. Print.

San Miguel Jr., Guadalupe. *Tejano Proud. Tex-Mex Music in the Twentieth Century.* College Station: Texas A&M Press, 2002. Print.

Vargas, Deborah R. "Borderland Bolerista: The Licentious Lyricism of Chelo Silva." *Feminist Studies* 34.1–2 (2008): 173–197. Print.

Vargas, Deborah R. "Las Tracaleras: Texas-Mexican Women, Music, and Place." Diss. UC Santa Cruz, 2003. Print.

Zavala, Iris. "De heroes y heroinas en lo imaginario social: El discurso amoroso del bolero." *Revista Casa de las Américas* 179 (1990): 123–128. Print.

NINE

Roland Barthes, *Mojado,* in Brownface: *Chisme*-laced Snapshots Documenting the Preposterous and Fact-laced Claim That the Postmodern Was Born along the Borders of the Río Grande River

WILLIAM ANTHONY NERICCIO

THE FIRST FRAME: PREFACE/PRE-FACE/BROWN-FACE

The editors have asked that I add a prolegomena to the forehead or face of this essay, and I am happy to do so. Way back in the day (old *skool* grad school days, when this son of *la frontera* was kidnapped by the Ivy League and whisked away to freeze his *nalgas* off in Ithaca, New York), I was a big fan of Roland Barthes—I thrilled to the *jouissance* of the pleasures of the text, read and reread the dispatches in *Mythologies,* etc. etc. Long story short, I escaped the wicked pirates of Cornell, got a job at the University of Connecticut, jumped ship to Califas and SDSU and, my first year there (1991, shh shh!) I wrote an in-house grant proposal and was awarded five hundred smackeroos to purchase my first 35 mm camera. The rest, as they say, is history. What follows are the theory-laced meditations of a Chicano on crack Kodak, a Mexi*cameran*-American (that's me in the center there to the right of Edward James Olmos; Barthes's there to the right of *me,* or at least his photoshopped ghost is); I am utterly responsible for the contents of this *rasquache* semiotic whatsit and beg you reward the editors of this collection for allowing it to appear in these pages.

THE SECOND FRAME: POSTMODERNITY IN A POST-COLONIAL WORLD

Let us begin with a cosmopolitan barbershop quartet of sorts. Brilliant, each individually, they forge collectively a kind of man-heavy Greek chorus, auguring much of what herein follows.

TABLE 9.1

Modernity, coloniality, the post, and the multiple combinatorial possibilities of these terms have held much of our academic discourse in thrall for some time now . . . Ultimately, however, our explorations of the issues implied by these terms must countenance the ambiguous question I posit here at a moment we identify as postmodern, in this era we designate as postcolonial: what are we after?[1] DJELAL KADIR	What remains, however, beside the essential enemy (the bourgeois norm), is the necessary conjunction of these two enterprises: no denunciation without an appropriate method of detailed analysis, no semiology which cannot, in the last analysis, be acknowledged as semioclasm.[3] ROLAND BARTHES, 1970
Now if there is anything that radically distinguishes the imagination of anti-imperialism, it is the primacy of the geographical in it. Imperialism, after all, is an act of geographical violence through which virtually every space in the world is explored, charted, [catalogued], and finally brought under control.[2] EDWARD SAID, 1988	The crisis of the grand narrative and the rise of micro-narratives are ultimately the crisis of the "grand" as well as the "little," the advent of disinformation in which disproportion and incommensurability are to postmodernity what the philosophic resolution of problems and the resolution of the image (pictorial, architectural) were to the birth of the Enlightenment.[4] PAUL VIRILIO, 1984

NOTES TO TABLE 9.1

1. Djelal Kadir, "Postmodernism/Postcolonialism: What Are We After," *World Literature Today* 69:1 (1995): 17.

2. Edward Said, "Yeats and Decolonization," in *Remaking History: DIA Art Foundation Discussions in Contemporary Culture IV*, ed. Barbara Kruger and Phil Mariani (Seattle, WA: The Bay Press, 1989), pp. 3–29.

3. Roland Barthes, *Mythologies*, trans. Annette Lavers (New York: Hill and Wang, 1972), p. 9.

4. Paul Virilio, "The Overexposed City," *Zone* 1:1–2 (1986): 28–29. The translation by Astrid Hustvedt is based on a selection from Virilio's *L'espace critique* (Paris: Christian Bourgois, 1984). This initial issue of *Zone* has been of no little use for individuals and institutions seeking to speak to the dynamics of contemporary urban spaces.

THE THIRD FRAME: LAREDO, FRAMED, OR, LIGHTS, CAMERA, LA FRONTERA

Contemporary critics of postmodern architecture and city planning have focused their attention on trendy centers of cutting-edge design—New York, Toronto, Milan, San Francisco, Hong Kong, Miami, Tokyo, Berlin—without ever considering the provocative landscape of domestic US bordertowns.[1] Urban enigmas developing on the fringes of national geography, bordertowns represent sites of cultural identity and cultural non-identity, the margin that contains mutating versions of both the self and the other. Perched as they are on the boundaries between cultures, bordertowns represent fractured biospheres where rivaling essences of contrasting national myths come into direct conflict.[2] In the humble view of your somewhat biased guide, if you want to survey the epitome of the postmodern city, then Laredo, Texas, USA and Nuevo Laredo, Tamaulipas, EUM are the place to be. As one drives dirt roads on the way to concrete interstate highways, *petit bourgeois,* Mexican American–piloted imported British Jaguars revving their way past *vaquero* Mexican American–piloted imported horses (*bourgeois, vaquero,* and horse alike tracing at least part of their ancestry back to Spain), one encounters the bizarre reality of urban/rural entropy on the margins, on the very border, of national, existential, and economic legitimacy. What happens to the architecture and the financial and semiotic economy of the urban landscape, what happens to the social relations and cultures of the borderzone's urbanaut inhabitants, when they are divided by and formed through the geographical reality (the Río Grande / Bravo river) and historically manufactured reality (the peripatetic line separating the United States from México) of this site? In order to capture some of this alleged chaos—without totally domesticating it—we will be using pictures to focus on the cultural architecture that has developed amid two distinct nations and two distinct, if symbiotically determined, border cities.

Literary critics and would-be cultural studies *aficionados* lacking credentials to speak to the complexities of photographs would do well to return to the underrated findings of Susan Sontag to underwrite their course of action. Opening *On Photography,* Sontag asks what is "the most grandiose result of the photographic enterprise[?]" Her response: it "give[s] us the sense that we can hold the whole world in our heads—as an anthology of images."[3] Sontag's words here act as picturesque talismans, warding away the totalizing hubris that might allow us to momentarily imagine that the pictures in this essay hold the truth, giving the lie to the prose that cozily surrounds them. For the span of this essay, neither word nor image shall reign sovereign: each reveals what is lacking in the other.

Let us now turn to some jottings by Paul Virilio on the ubiquity of the photographic. Virilio writes specifically of war, cinema, and culture, but more wide-ranging applications are not without some use here: "The problem is . . . no longer so much one of masks and screens, of camouflage designed to hinder long-range targeting; rather, it is a problem of ubiquitousness, of handling simultaneous data in a global but unstable environment where the image (photographic or cinematic) is the most concentrated, but also the most stable, form of information."[4] An opportunistic reading of Virilio's statement allows us to imagine an encounter with images within the context of an essay where they function as a means to knowing, not as supplements begging for captions but as legitimate, if visual, *paragraphs* in the strict sense, "lines drawn in the margin," no less players in the masque of syntax than the commas, periods, and quotations marks that wend their ways through this narrative. The assertions of Kadir, Barthes, Said, and Virilio positioned as section epigraphs above emerge as uncanny amulets for our journey and as keys to this collection of picture-laced *chisme* (Spanish for gossip, an order of discourse with a sublime power); in the pages that follow, a collection of words and images as a proxy for what might have been called in the past a *cogent* understanding.

The other thing Virilio's words remind us of is something that has become ever more true since they were first published in 1991[5] some eighteen years ago: the *photomilitarization* of the US-México borderlands—even now, as I revise these words, works continue on walls and fences as predator drones hum overhead.[6] Even now, as you read, the geographic southlands of Tejas, once rigid save for the occasional meandering of the Río Grande River, are being transformed by the panopticonic logic of Homeland Security and by the "War on Drugs," Inc., and its partner in crime, narco-gangland eruptions. These are remaking the culture of the American Southwest and Northern México.

The photos in this piece are of another time and place—almost as nostalgic as the cunning reminiscences to be found in Norma Cantu's *Canicula*—another Roland Barthes–kissed writing.[7]

THE FOURTH FRAME: WHEREIN THE SEMIOTIC INEPTITUDE OF A YOUNG VOYEUR LEADS TO MISREADING THE BULL

It begins with this bull, the Bordertown Drive-In bull. It hit me like a revelation, like a vision, like a lightning bolt, one morning after I had turned nineteen in a small South Texas bordertown—Laredo, Texas, USA, to be exact. Throughout my childhood, I thought that the mural featured on the Bordertown Drive-In was of a giant mutant bull terrorizing the countryside and being attacked by US Air Force jets as a giant cowboy heatedly pursued from behind.

I was wrong, of course.

That is, I had *read* it wrong.

The giant bull was merely a personal, idiosyncratic creation, a misreading, owing to a mistake in perspective. Without the tools to understand the concept of perspective in an illustration, I had taken the mural at face value: giant drawing of bull = giant monster, mutant bull. That the animal was merely foregrounded and thus larger than its surroundings was, at the time, a concept as abstract as quantum mechanics or multilateral arms-control negotiations.

The painting was misread. The mural in question faced out on the main strip leading out of and into Laredo and adorned the back side of a projection wall for the local drive-in, called the Bordertown Twin Drive-In Theater. Some fifteen years ago, the Bordertown had been a booming two-screen haven of movies, alcohol, and sexual abandon for auto aficionados, raucous families, and young adults on both sides of the Río Grande River. But in 1988, that monument was slowly falling apart. No longer a haven for moviegoers, it was home to a flea market, open on the weekends, where one could find various used articles, recycled furniture, and a huge assortment of deserted, dated consumer artifacts that could have passed as trash in any dumpster. In the half-decade before the current period, when the North American Free Trade Agreement and individuals associated with its passage were heralding the arrival of the New World Order, the Bordertown Drive-In was an icon for Laredo itself—a depressed market selling trash in various disguises as merchandise. But then again, even *trash* is not trash in and of itself; *trash* is not a generic designation (trash for one may be treasure to another). Given the depleted economic resources of the city, even trash might be repackaged in some way so as to serve a purpose or garnish a profit. Even the Drive-In had been repackaged as a *pulga*, as a flea market.

But let us not allow the caress of nostalgia to blind us from the present, for I must report that the Bordertown Drive-In/*pulga* is no more. The Godzilla-esque bull has been erased from the space of Laredo—my photograph must serve as a proxy for the structure, as a kind of ersatz visual relic. The structure was torn down and sold to the Wal-Mart corporation. On the site of the giant cow[8] arose the specter of what is known as Sam's Warehouse—a discount marketer of groceries and other assorted sundries. Gross sales of Laredo's Sam's Warehouse and Wal-Mart were so huge that just before his death in 1992, Sam Walton flew to Laredo to celebrate his profits. Walton was visibly weak and ailing as he greeted cheering workers and shoppers like some latter-day vision of Cortez.[9] I would have included a picture of the store if I didn't miss the cow so much.

A Disclaimer, as the Author Mourns the Loss of a Precious Bovine

This section, as one will have noticed already, represents less a cohesive analysis than a leisurely tour—a pictorial travelogue or post-colonial safari. Some will view such an approach as critical eclecticism.[10] So be it. As Stuart Durant concludes, "eclectics have never been strong on theory. Eclecticism seems essentially the mode of practitioners."[11] Though Durant speaks here of collectors of furniture and their tastes, he may have struck upon something useful to would-be theorists of Postmodernity: one may have to focus, like it or not, on either theory or practice in order to accomplish anything with one or the other—one must select a fetish and stay with it lest the fetish devolve into a dalliance, a whim. If this travelogue adds nothing to the current debate in Postmodern theory, it would at the very least like to be considered a bastard example of Postmodern critical practice—bastard in that it feigns no interest in and makes no claim to legitimacy in any way, shape, form, or species.

This approach asks much of its readers/spectators/tourists: that they suspend common, even enlightened, understandings of Postmodern design and architecture; that they consider how intriguing architectural fracture and cultural production go on outside the metropoles, those cities that represent the headliners, the core, the cream of the crop, the advance guards of capital, production, and consumer innovation.[12] But what of the backroads? What of the border? If one isolates a core, one must also have a periphery to isolate that otherwise abstract center. Enter Laredo, as bizarre a periphery as any one is to find in the global safari one calls urban criticism, architectural inquiry, or textual analysis. Laredo is eccentric; it is, to signal this author's debt to Canadian theorist Linda Hutcheon, "ex/centric": both outside and inside, in short, deliciously and uniquely marginal.[13]

THE FIFTH FRAME: THE HUNT IS ON FOR MORE JOBS IN LAREDO

As we passed into the next century, Laredo is beginning to emerge from one of its periodic crises of economic turmoil—the upturn in the Mexican economy spurred by the policies of then president Carlos Salinas de Gortari (most often cited then as the "Harvard-educated President of Mexico," now a criminal of international proportions), which had a favorable impact on the prosperity (at least for parts of select classes) of both Laredo and Nuevo Laredo.

The economies of these sister cities are bound intimately to each other. When currency values plunge, so goes the fate of the two cities. So while United States tourists reap the rewards of cheap Corona beers and ridiculously underpriced Mexican leather goods, in Laredo, Texas, USA, downtown merchants shake their collective heads and wonder where the business went. Recall here that the eighties was the decade when oil-price futures went bust in Texas and that South Texas, Laredo included, is one of the richest oil and gas regions in the fifty states. Now one begins really to understand why "the hunt is on for more jobs" in Laredo. These savage and elusive beasts are just too scarce for the standard safari, so Laredo's largest financial institution, The Laredo National Bank, has come in on the project as sponsor of this semiotically disturbing series of billboards and TV commercials (television spots featured footage of ferocious lions roaming green, dangerous jungles and grass-strewn plains).

The lion, incidentally(?), is the trademarked icon of the Laredo National Bank. Do you hunt the lion? Or does the lion hunt you? Laredo National Bank's latest semiotic enterprise, their online banking service, illustrates that when it comes to transnational capital, banks on the border must speak at least two languages: dollars and pesos, English and Spanish, Washington and Juarez.

THE SIXTH FRAME, WHEREIN IT IS SHOWN THAT EVEN APPLIANCES HAVE CAGES ON THIS SAFARI

The theoretical/rhetorical level of this essay has yet to ascend to the ethereal heights of the bona fide analytical, and there is good reason. Before one can analyze "los dos Laredos / the two Laredos," one must first get a taste of its dusty unpaved avenues and blazing relentless heat. Those who look down upon such travelogue narratives or safaris may graze elsewhere till we return to further critical analysis. The rest of us are on a "safari," but the hunt, here, is not on for jobs, as in the advertising campaign just cited, but for commentary on the legitimacy or illegitimacy of Laredo as Postmodern city.

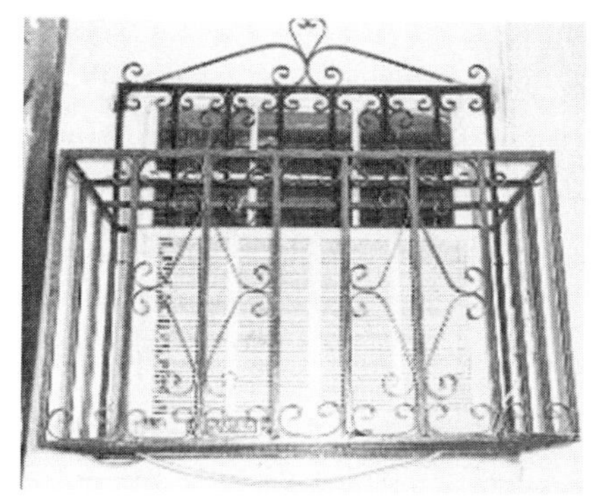

And what beast do we have here?

While the photo in question might be a representative offering from a MOMA exhibition in New York or MOCA exhibit in Los Angeles, that it comes from a backyard in Laredo, Texas, is entirely significant. The result of the scarcity of jobs in Laredo, Texas, is a numbing increase in the crime rate in the city, particularly burglary and armed robbery. In times of economic despair and growing unemployment, one either sucks up one's gut, tightens one's belt, and joins a job safari or else deals drugs and steals. Hence, the air conditioner in the photograph has been placed in a cage of black wrought iron to help guarantee it will stay in place—without benefit of its protective wrapper, it might have ended up at the old Bordertown *pulga*.

Even at the height of the economic bust of the mid-eighties in Texas, Laredo had a larger number of prospering banking and saving institutions than many other cities in the Lone Star state. Then again, perhaps this is not as surprising as one might think at first. The US Drug Enforcement Administration (DEA) has shut down much of the Miami cocaine connection, but Latin American drug barons continue to move with relative freedom through México. With one avenue of distribution cut off, the drug mules have turned more and more to South Texas and Southern California to export these tasty narcotic goodies. The profits from these transactions don't usually end up in the proverbial grimy bus-station locker. In fact, with growing frequency, drug captains are turning to legitimate financial institutions to shelter their wealth. One has a better idea now of exactly whose money finances part of the Laredo National Bank's "hunt for new jobs" in Laredo.

For the rest of Laredo, though, belt-tightening is the only recourse. With 117°F temperatures during Laredo's summers, air conditioners are as valuable as water in the desert, and the best one can do is encage the house and hope for the best. The air conditioner in a cage may well serve as an icon of Laredo's periodic economic crises, trapped as it is behind the bars of economic inertia. On this safari we've reached what may well be a point of despair—Laredo's two icons are a flea market recycling yesterday's refuse and an appliance ensconced in a black iron cage.[14]

THE SEVENTH FRAME, WHEREIN GEORGE WASHINGTON MEETS POCAHONTAS AND HAS A PECULIAR FIESTA IN LAREDO

A total of seven flags have flown at one time or another over the lands presently designated Laredo, Texas, USA.[15] This has led, as one might imagine, to a bit of schizophrenia, loosely speaking, in the cultural identity of the community and in its celebrations—which are, after all, the best reflection of the complexion of a community. If one is what one eats, then it might just as easily be said that a city is what it celebrates.

How decidedly strange and "Postmodernesque," then, that Laredo's largest celebration each year is The George Washington Birthday celebration. Apparently started by a group of nostalgic Anglos and outsiders living in Laredo after the turn of the last century, the celebration continues to prosper in Laredo's largely Mexican American community.[16] Each year, the haves and the have-nots line the famous streets of Laredo for a week-long celebration that includes a colonial ball(!), debutantes, parades, cook-outs, and a carnival; also, said extravaganza includes Pocahontas.

It taxes the imagination to wonder how a celebration of the United States of America's first president and noted slave owner, George Washington, ever got caught up in a beauty/popularity contest for the role of Pocahontas in the annual George Washington's Birthday Parade—an award whose chief distinction is parading on horseback for the better part of a morning. One imagines the founding fathers (of the yearly celebration, not of the country) thought that since both Pocahontas and George Washington could be found within a certain range of pages in a high-school history book, why not link the two together—or something like that. In any event, every year during the celebration, one lucky (read: popular and politically well-placed) young woman gets to don a leather outfit and become Pocahontas, riding her decorated horse up and down Laredo's avenues with marching bands in front and festive floats and street sweepers bringing up the rear.

Let us move to the snapshot in question. Pocahontas, horse, mountains, sky and all, adorns the front wall—a mural commemorating the yearly ritual—beside a money-exchange house where tourists may, à la McDonalds, drive up and exchange their dollars for pesos at the latest going rate before driving across the Juarez-Lincoln International Bridge. The conflation of murals, Pocahontas, money exchange, George Washington, and debutantes provides a succinct example of the narrative/festival pastiche rituals informing the matrices of Laredo.

THE EIGHTH FRAME, WHEREIN IT IS ANNOUNCED, AND NOT FOR THE FIRST TIME IN HERMENEUTIC HISTORY, THAT CELEBRITIES ARE COMMODITIES

In a town as predominantly Mexican-American as Laredo, Texas, one might imagine that the idea of bilingual or wholly Spanish advertisements would have been a fixture of the community for quite some time. The fact is, however, that these campaigns have gained in popularity only recently in this border city. That said, one can move now to an analysis of the picture. Here, Rozenda Bernal, a *cantadora* (singer) popular both in northern México and the Southwest United States, hawks pre-measured tortilla mixes. Bernal's star status and signature sombrero assure us that "The White Wings Flour Company" knows its way around a Mexican tortilla while her celebrity status reassures her audience that the product is of value. The logic here is familiar, both utterly banal and powerful: go with the product that celebrities use, and you will a) look like them; b) act like them; or c) at the very least, trust them not to steer you wrong. As celebrities go, so goes the market. John Berger has described it as a "process of manufacturing glamour,"—and glamor, of course, sells.[17]

There are some nasty side effects, however. Advertising contributes to the process of alienation and the "progress" of assimilation, and it may even contribute, in Berger's view, to political alienation and disenfranchisement because it "turns consumption into a substitute for Democracy"(149). Alienation of the citizenry occurs simultaneously as dissemination of products prospers in the by-now overdetermined marketplace. In short, beware of Rozenda Bernal.

Why dally here with a billboard? Functioning as both ideological citations and changeable urban tattoos, billboards reflect like giant mirrors the taste of the urb they decorate. Like mirrors, they also affect the tastes, appearance, and actions of the individuals and communities who gaze at their reflections. As top-bill performers that share the stage with buildings, monuments, murals, and historical sites, billboards are beasts central to this safari.

THE NINTH FRAME, WHICH TREATS OF THE BIZARRE CASE OF THE DISPLACED BORDERED SENTINEL LOST SOMEWHERE AMIDST AFRICA, MÉXICO, AND THE PLANTATION-ERA DEEP SOUTH

The place? Laredo, Texas. *The object captured by the photographer?* An African American groomsman statuette / hitching post stands behind a standard cyclone fence. A provocative common piece of Americana and an outdoor-furniture design peculiarity as well as a pertinent historical artifact that speaks to a particularly "American" form of racism, here the mute servant marks the modest domestic habitat of a lower-middle-class Mexican American family—unlikely to have slaves or grooms, let alone horses, milling about their 1½-car outdoor garage. Demographically as well as geographically, the statuette is out of place here in the borderlands of the South Texas / Mexican border. Not that one could not imagine a context where said statuette might be appropriate. Surely Supreme Court Justice Clarence Thomas's foyer cries out for such a monument?

THE TENTH FRAME, WHICH FINDS US PAUSING ASTRIDE THE BORDERLINE DIVIDING THE UNITED STATES AND MÉXICO SO AS TO MALINGER AND WITNESS AN INTERNATIONAL CRIME

On the left of this picture is Los Estados Unidos de México. On the right rests the United States of America. In the middle (see speck) floats a Mexican national in an inner tube, rafting his way down the middle of the Río Grande river, which, incidentally, is called El Río Bravo by Mexicans who reside on the left side of this picture.

This image renders the split that produces the heterogeneous peoples found on both sides of the river. This is where it all happens, in history (border clashes and raids by armies and bandits from both sides of the river) and in the present (drug smuggling, illegal immigration, illegal sewage and radioactive toxic waste dumping on both sides of the river). The explosion of maquiladoras—multinational-owned and -operated factories producing goods for export on Mexican soil—has accelerated this dumpage.

A few minutes after this picture was taken, the subject in question, dressed only in underwear with a bundle of clothing in his lap, floated under and past the bridge I was standing on, shouting obscenities and choice epithets to friends and spectators along the railing of the bridge. The last I saw of him, he was docking his craft and scurrying intently up the banks on the US side of the river. Never before had the self-importance of an international boundary line seemed so insignificant; never before had the autonomy of two nations seemed so arbitrary and capricious. Never before, that is, until one minute later, when horse-riding, gun-toting officials from the US Border Patrol came up and apprehended our aquatic boundary challenger.

What began as a significant displacement of the now-not-so-abstract borderline became an everyday, legally determined, and quite common international incident. One expects that the boundary crosser will return at some point to the United States, probably sooner rather than later as standard procedure in these cases is simple deportation—a handcuffed two-minute walk across the International Bridge back to México, freedom, and, perhaps, more inner tubes.

THE ELEVENTH FRAME, WHERE A PHOTOGRAPH LEADS YOUR GUIDE TO A DREAM OF A NEW BERLIN

The cropped portion of the boundary marker reads "one for all and all for one" like a line out of a Three Musketeers movie—and given the cinematically determined reality of the United States during the Reagan administration (movie star / president, *Star Wars* the movie and Star Wars the Pentagon weapons initiative, etc.), such a coincidence is not altogether surprising.

Below this slogan are the important words: "Boundary of the United States" and "Límite de la República Mexicana," established in 1848 and "re-established by the treaties of 1884–1889." This *really* is the borderline, the margin, the end of the frame, the inside/outside boundary, the point where self and other differentiate their particular identities—*this is no metaphor.* Just ask the floating speck in the last frame.

Alternatively, one can see the border as the site that licenses all metaphorics—the border as autochthonous agent for all concepts communicating difference, metaphors included. In any event, this boundary marks one of the many spaces where the United States of America and Los Estados Unidos de México both begin and end. But in an age of Postmodern sensitivities, we should be in tune with the fact that such an absolute binary must be taken with a healthy dose of skepticism. It is interesting to note that as one looks in either direction, on either side of that boundary marker, an ongoing process of salacious willed and unconscious intercontamination prospers on both sides of the line.

THE TWELFTH FRAME, WHEREIN OUR VOYEUR HOLDS FORTH WITH EARNEST GUILT AS HE WRESTLES WITH PUBLIC SPECTACLES, A CAMERA, AND PANHANDLING

Some are more innovative than others. All of us have met them in one form or another—some of us have *been* them. They range in name from street performer to panhandling bum. What they have in common are the streets, passing strangers, and fear of the authorities, whoever they might be. Here, in this photograph taken in Nuevo Laredo, the dancer wears vestments akin to those sported by Mexica warriors at the height of their imperial reign some five hundred years ago. He has, however, exited the frame of that period (traditional vestments become

mere costumes once outside their particular ideological contexts) and entered a very different cultural enclosure.

The street performer's dancing and chanting patterns derive from the theocratic, polytheistic ritual of one of the indigenous peoples of México. Here, the ritual has been translated from one of political and theological (theocratic) significance into one of mainly economic significance—he's dancing for money. One moves from the interpretive economy of theocultural rite to the interpretive economy of the soliciting spectacle, the economy of the unique, individual act. In addition, the dancer enters here, also, the very literal camera frame of the safarist/analyst photographer and the critical frame of our ontology/anthology.

He has been translated once again—and unwillingly (the dancer in question turned to avoid the camera several times, forcing me to slip inconspicuously across the street to seize [t]his image away from him). He is now more than just a performer earning his keep; he now becomes an interpretable image/text, an alienated object. When Sontag notes that the "photographer is not simply the person who records the past but the one who invents it" (67), she reveals the determining and objectifying logic of photography. The dancer has become a suspended iconic signifier begging for description in the antiseptic pages of an academically sanctioned intellectual safari.[18]

THE THIRTEENTH FRAME, WHICH DOCUMENTS THE CHANCE RENDEZVOUS OF SPAIN'S DON QUIXOTE, AZTLÁN'S QUETZALCÓATL, AND ENGLAND'S OZZY OSBOURNE

Walking down Nuevo Laredo's main street, La Guerrero, down a few blocks from the International Bridge, one finds a beautiful plaza—a park with trees, swing sets, shoeshine stands, and running children.[19] In the center of this park stands a small library with a beautifully detailed mural gracing its front entrance wall.

The mural depicts Don Quixote atop his steed charging toward Quetzalcóatl, a Mexica deity. The mural in question does not depict a scene from the text of Miguel de Cervantes's *Don Quijote de la Mancha*. Rather, the unsigned mural renders the complex fusion of European Spanish literature and culture and indigenous Mexican literature and culture. In it, the eyes of spectators witness the condensation of elements

from two sixteenth-century avatars, one Spanish and one Aztec, into the medium of the public mural. Epic figures from mythology and literature are given to our eyes as pictures. In the middle of Nuevo Laredo, a story from Spain meets a story from México. Both find translation in an instant upon the wall of a public library—note how the mural shows both figures rising out of the pages of texts, the European printed and bound book and the Aztec printed codices.[20] Textual denizens here become agents in the domain of pictures, and the photograph of this image immediately becomes analytic property—a semiotic artifact.

But there is more here than initially meets the eye. Our tenth frame illustrates a troublesome semiotic development as a Postmodern anomaly interrupts our analytical progress. Someone has intercepted this mural.[21] Someone has re-signed this mural and displaced further the already complicated semiotic overdetermination of the original mural, which combines the literary and cultural peculiarities of two disparate tribes, Euro-Spanish and Pre-Columbian Mexican.

Look again at the picture.

Down toward the bottom of the mural, across the pages of the Aztec codices and Cervantes's book, lurks the following readable autograph: "ozzys Boys."

Just who are these "ozzys Boys?" Ozzy Osbourne, late of "Black Sabbath" and currently a solo rock performer, is a somewhat popular English "heavy metal" rock star. Aside from a few scattered hits and appearances on MTV, he is known mainly for biting the heads off live bats in concert to the delight of his adoring fans, one of whom, it is apparent, scrawled his graffiti autograph upon the scene of this mural.

Interception. Ozzy meets Quixote meets Quetzalcóatl. That the already complex depiction of a meeting between México and Spain, with all its imperialistic and exploitative history, has been further complicated by a British autograph from a Mexican American hand leaves one with little if anything to add. More words would only distract from the already eloquent testimony of the photograph.

Sometimes, the caption must shut up.

THE FOURTEENTH FRAME, WHERE WE WITNESS AS THE GEOGRAPHIC CONTOURS OF A NATION PROXY A SPOKESMODEL WITH A BEER PHALLUS

Walking down the Guerrero, just past the intriguing signature of "ozzys Boys," we find a monument worthy of México's rich history: a lighted, extravagant billboard extolling one of the champions of México's export economy. "*Corona, La Cerveza de Mexico* / Mexico's beer," the sign bellows out for all to see. While the message will be familiar to Unitedstatesians, who are daily bombarded with beer advertisements, it is the image itself that is most striking in this instance—a detailed and geographically accurate rendition of Los Estados Unidos de México with a huge bottle of Corona Beer splashed across and jutting out from it at a provocative angle.

One might, if one wished, dissolve the descriptive frame at this point and begin a Derridean, Lacanian, Freudian, or Bergerian analysis of this lovely montage and document the overdetermined iteration potential of this image. Or one could, à la Barthes, wittily pinpoint the connections between the image and the culture of the natives daily who whiz past it only unconsciously conscious of the display's influence. One might also assume a Marxist bent and read this giant ad as an allegory chronicling the incredible growth of Corona beer sales in North America. Rather than explore these trails, this safari's listless docent would, instead, enjoy asking the following question: is nationalism (the prehistoric grandfather of what marketers called branding) becoming implicitly the most marketable means of expanding market share in the current period?

THE FIFTEENTH FRAME, WHICH CHRONICLES THE UNLIKELY MARRIAGE OF A TREE AND A FUNERAL HOME

Still on the Guerrero, one comes across Sánchez Funeral Home, a necessary if depressing commercial enterprise situated on the main business strip. It is a sad, drab outlet situated beneath a small apartment complex.

The striking feature here is the live palm tree growing up through the first floor and out the ceiling of the second floor balcony. From the first time I saw it, I did not doubt what I

saw. There are some places where one never doubts what one sees—Las Vegas is one, the South Bronx another, and Nuevo Laredo yet another.

This was more than just another visual oddity, though. The mating of human and natural architecture was charming—as if the two architectures, not wanting to offend each other and yet strapped for space, had decided "what the hell" and taken up residence on the same plot of land. Here again, travelogue spectators and ideational safari enthusiasts are presented with much in the way of semantic/semiotic conjecture—life meets death, tree meets mortuary. In a symbiosis almost too rich for the inhabitants of an increasingly homogenized reality to comprehend, one is immediately confronted with the seductive contradiction of life breaking boundaries (the palm tree) versus the mundane bureaucratic reality of death (local funeral laws in México mandate the interment of bodies within a twenty-four-hour period). Postmodernity cannot claim the rights to such a sight—it was there and growing before Derrida ever sent a postcard. It would be all right to contend, though, that a dutiful worship of this semiotic tableau embodies a signature ritual within the canon of Postmodern practice.

THE TRAGIC SIXTEENTH FRAME FROM 1998, AKA THE END OF THE POSTMODERN MOMENT IN FIRST WORLD HISTORY

So I go back to Nuevo Laredo some ten years almost to the day after I took my first photographic safari, and I see it. I see it in all its allegorical potential—the tree for me that symbolized the domain of the ironic, the Sánchez Funeral Home that for me embodied all I understood about the unsettled and turbulent, not to mention comedic, dynamics of the México/US borderlands had been altered. Some clumsy, unlicensed, would-be tree surgeon had, in the effort of trimming this public, natural "sign," killed the damned thing. Uncanny how things change, how the years fly by. Still uncannier, a van with a roof ladder figures prominently in the right margin of two photographs divided by a decade of life and chaos.

THE SEVENTEENTH FRAME, WHEREIN A LAREDOAN'S MEMORIES OF THE CADILLAC BAR DRENCH AN INDULGING READER READY TO COME UP FOR AIR

No other site on either side of the river gathers more tourists than the Cadillac Bar and Restaurant pictured here in Nuevo Laredo, México. "The Cadillac," as it is affectionately nicknamed, serves also as a haven for alcohol-starved teenagers from Laredo and Nuevo Laredo (the drinking age in Nuevo Laredo, Tamaulipas, varies in ways that recall the logic of roulette wheels). Thirsty tourists out for a good time or a rest (Nuevo Laredo is well known for its treacherous streets and sidewalks), Mexican nationals stopping in for a quick lunch or dinner, and businessmen and women from both sides of the river talking finances over a Ramos Gin Fizz® all make their way through this tavern's history-rich double doors.

Waiters bustle about in their prim white jackets, tight black slacks, and audacious ties serving tough steaks and warm nachos to their boisterous audience. At night and on weekends, diners and drinkers find themselves treated to the piano-accompanied singing of Mexican and United States musical standards by strong-throated Mexican crooners.

The Cadillac favorite is "New York, New York," a song guaranteed to lift the spirits and delight the senses of tourists from all over the fifty states. This watering hole certainly enhances the cultural topography of the sister cities, Laredo and Nuevo Laredo. When aging tourists from the American Midwest make their way through here with their circa-WWII song requests, it is as if Glenn Miller never died, Hope and Crosby were still a team, and Ronald Reagan were a harmless affable, if insufferable, B-movie actor.

Sitting around, downing a Dos Equis *cerveza* and surveying the local and visiting wildlife one night, I was struck by the youth and abandon of the mingling throngs. Young Laredo Catholic-school girls, some barely fourteen, sauntered and swayed about in fashions out of *Elle* or *Vogue*, cigarette and drink dangling from each hand. Young boys, dark or blond, moussed and arrayed in the latest fashions by Ralph Lauren, Perry Ellis, or Giorgio Armani, accompanied the young ladies, all partying gloriously to the strains of "New York, New York" while patient waiters assisted them with their every wish and need.

In Laredo, Texas (on "the other side" of the river), meanwhile, the have-nots or the unlucky were cruising up and down Malinche Avenue trying to buy beer at some convenience store down the way (that is, if they were lucky or had an older sibling). As a result of the vagaries of alcohol procurement, Laredo high-school students, college-goers and other assorted fun-seekers spend most of their hours on the Mexican side of the border, where the favorable dollar/peso exchange rate and unpredictable law enforcement create an urban nightlife as alive, innovative, and dangerous as any in Toronto, New York City, or Milan. For 25 cents, one crosses a turnstile and enters a heterogeneous oasis where all things good and bad are possible. Crossing that line, Laredoans enter another world.[22]

CONCLUSION: A BORDER CULTURE PRIMER

Laredo has a little bit of everything. More international goods pass over its bridges than at any other inland port in the nation. As such, many nationalities find themselves represented here. For the most part, though, the community is Mexican-American. This being a semiotic enterprise, the term "Mexican-American" is as good a place as any to bring this safari to a close.

You will remember the International Bridge referred to earlier. It would not be far from the truth in suggesting that Mexican-Americans carry a graphic signifier of that bridge wherever they write their collective autograph, wherever the word "Mexican-American" or "Mexican American" is written, spoken, or acknowledged.

Mexican [-] American

Estados Unidos de México [-] United States of America

How much imagination does one need to see that hyphen as a bridge? The fracture of subjectivity (the alienation) thus depicted, one might think that a further exploration of alienation, anomie, or cultural schizophrenia might be in order. Unfortunately, the demands of this almost denouement do not allow for it.

One could propose, in contrast to that view, that the hyphenated interaction of these two rich cultures across that bridge creates the generative space from which the semiotically rich contradictions of bordertown culture are born. Determined by their proximity to each other, Laredo, Texas, USA and Nuevo Laredo, Tamaulipas, EUM continue to manufacture their own brand of Postmodern urban reality. Although many would perhaps rest content to catalog the depressing alienation of such an economically malaised and culturally marginal pair of communities, it seems just as valid to view them otherwise: as representative, contiguous constellations enacting subversive metastrophic exchanges that produce continually new versions of their contradicting and derivative identities. In the end, Laredo and Nuevo Laredo are not representative of the Postmodern moment. They are its birthplace.

NOTES

1. I swear I did the archival spelunking expected of a trained scholar—scout's honor! All I found was Paul Mann's peculiar, if riveting "Stupid Undergrounds" (*Postmodern Culture* 5.3 http://muse.jhu.edu/journals/postmodern_culture/v005/5.3mann.html); Lawrence Herzog's *From Aztec to High Tech: Architecture and Landscape across the Mexico-United States Border—Creating the North American Landscape* (Baltimore, MD: The Johns Hopkins University Press, 1999); and Claire Fox's *The Fence and the River: Culture and Politics at the US-Mexico Border* (Minneapolis: The University of Minnesota Press, 1999). All quite good, all quite certainly *not* contending that the mommies and daddies of Baudrillard, Virilio, Barthes, et al. hailed from Laredo, Texas!

2. Works of interest on the singular dynamics to be found at the border, domestic and international, literal and figural, include *Criticism in the Borderlands: Studies in Chicano Literature, Culture, and Ideology,* eds. Héctor Calderón and

José David Saldivar (Durham, NC, and London: Duke University Press, 1991); *Out There: Marginalization and Contemporary Cultures,* eds. Russell Ferguson et al. (Cambridge, MA, and London: MIT Press, 1990); and *Frontiers* (London: BBC Books, 1990). Lastly, one ought not to miss the graphically and theoretically striking tome edited by Sunil Gupta, *Disrupted Borders: An Intervention in Definitions of Boundaries* (London: Rivers Oram Press, 1993). Not for nothing has the border become an issue here as we approach the third millennium (our third millennium, in any event). The "collapse" of the Soviet Union, the re-balkanization of the Balkan republics, and the rise of what can only be called neo-Nationalisms across the globe bring the issue of borders to the forefront of political, economic, and, necessarily, intellectual discussion.

3. Susan Sontag, *On Photography* (New York: Farrar, Straus and Giroux, 1977), p. 3.

4. Paul Virilio, *War and Cinema,* trans. Patrick Camiller (Verso: New York, 1990), p. 71.

5. Paul Virilio, *Guerre et Cinema* (Paris: Cahiers du Cinema, 1991).

6. Anne Broache, "'Virtual' Fence Along US/Mexico Border Delayed," http://news.cnet.com/8301-10784_3-9881621-7.html (accessed May 1, 2009).

7. Norma Cantú, *Canicula: Snapshots of a Girlhood en la frontera* (Albuquerque: University of New Mexico Press, 1997). For a cool piece on Cantú's work, see Timothy Dow Adams's "'Heightened By Life' Vs. 'Paralyzed By Fact': Photography and Autobiography In Norma Cantú's *Canícula,*" *Biography* 24.1 (2001): 57–71.

8. Here's another mistake I have asked to be left in place for the published version of this piece: in everyday conversation, I always refer to the "bull" as a "cow." As well as issues with optical perspective, I also seem to have problems when it comes to bovine gender.

9. The allusion to Hernán Cortez is introduced more on the grounds of economic precision than rhetorical artistry—Wal-Mart's expansion continues to dis-order and alienate the delicate balance of economic exchange along the border. Local merchants were less than thrilled with the patriarch's appearance, though the Hearst-owned and operated *Laredo Times* covered the festivity with the sycophantic glee it usually demonstrates for big business.

10. Were I to write an extensive and nuanced reflection on the inappropriate nature of "safari" as a metaphor for guiding much of this essay, I would have begun with a close reading of J. Amy Staples, "Safari Adventures: Forgotten Cinematic Journeys in Africa" (*Film History* 18:4 (2006): 392–411) and then returned to the well-thumbed pages of Edward Said's *Orientalism* for more "ammunition." But, truth be told, it was an empirical experiment that stayed my hand and spared you my deathless prose. I brought a camera into my Sex in Film and Literature class and raised it to take a picture. You should have seen the grimaces and sounds that ensued. Cameras are uncanny, and they *do* poach—aggressively and cleverly, they touch the space of the self and steal something away. Read the term "safari" with a grain of salt as you peruse this piece. It is there for a reason!

11. Stuart Durant, "Proto Post Modernism," *Art & Design* 3:3–4 (1987): 77.

12. Bias in Postmodern criticism may be found in the most surprising of places. In *Metropolis,* an architecture and design magazine that makes the Postmodern, the Post-structural, and the Post-industrial its point of departure, one sees a ten-

dency toward a reborn imperialistic ethnocentrism that, having left the realm of international relations and Western European sociology, now enters the vocabulary of design criticism. Romanticizing the present state of consumer products, Karrie Jacobs writes, "living the Post Industrial life we work with our heads, our eyes, our fingertips. We don't callus. We don't sweat. The big dirty machines have gone elsewhere—Korea, Malaysia, Timbuktu[, Laredo]—or else they've been reduced to the size of a dust mote and embedded in silicon." Though Jacobs's statement appears in a throw-away, glossy intro to a generally interesting essay on the shrinking size of consumer technology, it is reprehensible nonetheless that such an attitude toward the margins, here the so-called Third World, should be resurrected in a magazine that imagines itself progressive. For the full article, see "Making Work" in *Metropolis* 7:4 (1987): 58.

13. Linda Hutcheon, *A Poetics Of Postmodernism: History, Theory, Fiction* (New York: Routledge, 1988).

14. Postscript circa 1998: The growing economic prosperity associated with the South Texas border region has had no impact on elements of this inertia, and while it is true that corporate America has discovered Laredo in recent years (a new airport, a huge new Target outlet, etc.), many of the troubling circumstances documented in this essay continue.

15. Since the colonial era, the following nations' and republics' flags have flown over Laredo: Spain, France, México, The Republic of the Río Grande, The Republic of Texas, The Confederate States of America, and The United States of America.

16. "Outsiders" is a term used regularly by prominent Laredoans when referring to threats of contamination from outside its city limits. It is most often used as a rallying cry around election time. The largest influx of "outsiders" (read: Anglo Americans) to enter Laredo after the turn of the century was during and after WWI, when Fort Macintosh prospered on the banks of the Río Grande.

17. John Berger, *Ways of Seeing* (London: Penguin, 1986), p.131.

18. It goes without saying, but I'll state it anyway, that it would be impossible to imagine a context where the term "safari" would be anything but suspect.

19. "La Calle Guerrero" is Guerrero Street, the central esplanade leading to the International Bridge in Nuevo Laredo, Tamaulipas, México. It is called "La Guerrero" or "the Guerrero" or "the strip" by inhabitants on both sides of the Río Grande / Río Bravo. In the narco-war days of the present (and I am copyediting this footnote in June of 2010), the Guerrero is a ghost town, but this is fodder for a future essay.

20. The displacement is not so great for the Aztec figure as for Quixote. As the surviving historical codices of the Aztecs show, their recordings of history, theology, and astrology made liberal use of pictograms and illustrated figures and events.

21. Here "interception" is used as in United States football. An image easily readable in terms of one hermeneutic tradition has been violently dislocated and replaced by another semiotic context. Perhaps the closest approximation to this would be framing a Rembrandt with hundred-dollar bills—or, depending on intent of the message, human excrement. For more on this and related issues, see Arthur Kroker's *The Post Modern Scene: Excremental Culture and Hyperaesthetics* (New York: St. Martin's Press, 1986).

22. I am sad to report the demise of the Cadillac Bar. After a family feud between Nuevo Laredo oligarchs by the name of Longoria and Salido over ownership

of the name of the Cadillac, the landmark has had to change its moniker. It is now called the El Dorado Club and is painted in a sickly orange with an even more hideous trim. Though tourists still frequent its largely unchanged interior, the catastrophe of its metastrophe has changed the place forever.

WORKS CITED

Adams, Timothy Dow. "'Heightened By Life' Vs. 'Paralyzed By Fact': Photography and Autobiography In Norma Cantú's *Canícula.*" *Biography* 24.1 (2001): 57–71.

Barthes, Roland. *Mythologies.* Translated by Annette Lavers. New York: Hill and Wang, 1972.

Berger, John. *Ways of Seeing.* London: Penguin, 1986.

Broache, Anne. "'Virtual' Fence Along US/Mexico Border Delayed," accessed May 1, 2009, http://news.cnet.com/8301-10784_3-9881621-7.html.

Calderón, Hector, and Saldívar, José David, editors. *Criticism in the Borderlands: Studies in Chicano Literature, Culture, and Ideology.* Durham, NC, and London: Duke University Press, 1991.

Cantú, Norma. *Canícula: Snapshots of a Girlhood en la frontera.* Albuquerque: University of New Mexico Press, 1995.

Durant, Stuart. "Proto Post Modernism." *Art & Design* 3.3–4 (1987): 77.

Ferguson, Russell, editor. *Out There: Marginalization and Contemporary Cultures.* Cambridge and London, MIT Press, 1990.

Fox, Claire. *The Fence and the River: Culture and Politics at the US-Mexico Border.* Minneapolis: The University of Minnesota Press, 1999.

Gupta, Sunil. *Disrupted Borders: An Intervention in Definitions of Boundaries.* London: Rivers Oram Press, 1993.

Herzog, Lawrence. *From Aztec to High Tech: Architecture and Landscape across the Mexico-United States Border—Creating the North American Landscape.* Baltimore, MD: The Johns Hopkins University Press, 1999.

Hutcheon, Linda. *A Poetics Of Postmodernism: History, Theory, Fiction.* New York: Routledge, 1988.

Jacobs, Karrie. "Making Work." *Metropolis* 7.4 (1987): 58.

Kadir, Djelal. "Postmodernism/Postcolonialism: What Are We After." *World Literature Today* 69:1 (1995).

Kroker, Arthur. *The Post Modern Scene: Excremental Culture and Hyperaesthetics.* New York: St. Martin's Press, 1986.

Mann, Paul. "Stupid Undergrounds." *Postmodern Culture* 5.3 (1995) http://muse.jhu.edu/journals/postmodern_culture/v005/5.3mann.html.

Nericcio, William. *Tex[t]-Mex: Seductive Hallucination of the "Mexican" in America.* Austin: University of Texas Press, 2007.

Pollan, Michael. *The Omnivore's Dilemma: A Natural History of Four Meals.* New York: Penguin, 2006.

Said, Edward. "Yeats and Decolonization." In *Remaking History: DIA Art Foundation Discussions in Contemporary Culture IV,* edited by Barbara Kruger and Phil Mariani, 3–29. Seattle, WA: The Bay Press, 1989.

Sontag, Susan. *On Photography.* New York: Farrar, Straus and Giroux, 1977.

Staples, J. Amy. "Safari Adventures: Forgotten Cinematic Journeys in Africa." *Film History* 18.4 (2006): 392–411.

Swartz, Mimi. "Once Upon a Time in Laredo." *National Geographic,* November 2006, http://ngm.nationalgeographic.com/2006/11/laredo/swartz-text.

Virilio, Paul. *Guerre et Cinema.* Cahiers du cinema: Paris, 1991.

Virilio, Paul. "The Overexposed City." Translated by Astrid Husvedt. *Zone* 1.1–2 (1986).

Virilio, Paul. *War and Cinema.* Translated by Patrick Camiller. Verso: New York, 1990.

Weinstein, Joshua I. "The Market in Plato's *Republic.*" *Classical Philology* 104 (2009): 439–458.

TEN

Decolonial Border Queers: Case Studies of Chicana/o Lesbians, Gay Men, and Transgender Folks in El Paso / Juárez

EMMA PÉREZ

> . . . but I don't consider myself gay, not because I think, that "ugh!" you know, it's because I see me and I see a gay male right here, and then I see [a] heterosexual male on the other side, you know what I mean, and I'm like, in the middle . . .
>
> ORAL INTERVIEW WITH TRANSGENDER COCA SAPIEN (2001)

How do queers in the US-México cities of El Paso and Juárez "recognize themselves as subjects of a sexuality," and what "fields of knowledge" and types of normativity have led Chicana/o lesbians, gay men, and transgender folks to experience a particular subjectivity?[1] I want to consider this specific, historical, political border to argue that for these border queers of color, the particular fields of knowledge that make up their sexuality constitute an epistemology of coloniality. More importantly, queers in El Paso and Juárez must engage and perform decolonial practices to survive the colonial landscape.

When I began my study of queer Chicanas/os and Mexicanas/os in a region that was my home for fourteen years, I realized that questions outnumbered answers and that the twenty-four transcripts of oral interviews in my possession would only provide cursory insights into the lives of a few lesbians, gay men, bisexuals, and transgender folks in these geographic borderlands.[2] My friend and former colleague at the University of Texas in El Paso, Gregory Ramos, conducted the oral interviews from 2000 to 2002 and subsequently wrote a poignant performance piece,

"Border Voices," inspired by the LGBTQ folks he interviewed. Of the twenty-five interviewees, seven were women, seventeen were men, and one was a transgender woman. Six of the seven women identified as Chicana, fronteriza, or Hispanic. One was white. Of the men, twelve identified as Chicano, Hispanic, or Mexicano; one was African American, one was Latino with parents from El Salvador, and three were white men.[3] Overall, the majority of interviewees identified as Chicana/o, Mexican, or Hispanic. Those interviewed probably represent a cross-section of the predominantly Chicana/o and Mexican communities of El Paso, where seventy-eight percent of the population is of Mexican origin. Although some of the Chicano/a interviewees may have been born in Juárez or have family in Juárez, only one of the twenty-five said he was a Mexicano from Juárez. Although he lived in El Paso, his dual citizenship allowed his allegiance to México.[4]

Making sense of the wide-ranging circumstances of Chicana/o queers on the United States–México border in the twenty-first century is not an easy task. I can only offer preliminary thoughts on a population of queers whose experiences are often neglected in more dominant discourses about queers in the United States. I have constructed this introductory groundwork of border queers by borrowing from their words. Of the twenty-five interviewed, thirteen were Chicano or Mexican men who identified as gay or bisexual. Five were Chicanas who identified as lesbians; however, one of the women opted not to call herself a lesbian and declared more than once that she was not gay despite having lived with her female partner for over fifteen years. Only one transgender Chicana/Mexicana told her story to Ramos, and hers was a powerful, evocative story. I'll not have an opportunity to quote from all of the interviews, but I have attempted to offer a glimpse of life on the border as a queer of color, whether visibly out or not. From this cursory assessment, I argue that border queers are always already negotiating between a colonial burden and their decolonial practices.[5]

Before I discuss the interviews, a concise historical background may clarify why I call the region a colonial space to be negotiated by those who live in these borderlands. To begin, the US-México War of 1846–1848 solidified a political border between two countries that could not agree where their geographic boundaries would divide their citizens. The Nueces River in Texas was the border between "Anglo" Texas and

México's state of Tejas y Chihuahua in 1836, but United States President Polk pushed the boundary farther south to instigate war with México when he sent US troops to cross the Nueces River into Mexican territory. Shots were fired, a war was started, and subsequently el Río Bravo, known on the US side as el Río Grande, became the recognized border.[6] But rivers shift and change, as do people. The boundary may have been recognized politically, but for those who had families on both sides of the Río Grande, crossing remained a daily occurrence. Not until the immigration laws of the late nineteenth and early twentieth centuries did the crossing back and forth become a predicament for Mexican nationals living south of the border. Eithne Luibhéid claims that the Immigration Act of 1891 began the process of excluding immigrants "guilty of moral turpitude, that is, charges of adultery, bigamy, rape, sodomy," as well as anyone who exhibited "sexually abnormal behavior or appetites."[7] In her thought-provoking study, *Entry Denied,* Luibhéid introduces a case study of a Mexican lesbian in 1960 who was stopped at the border in Juárez for "looking like a lesbian," hence permitting the immigration officials to employ the Act of 1891.[8] The repercussions of this act and other immigration laws continue to affect the border communities, suggesting that even today, border queers decide cautiously whether they will reveal their sexual identities.[9]

At least half of those interviewed expressed that although they may not live closeted lives, they remain discreet from fear of being ostracized. Immigration laws, when examined through a Foucauldian lens as a system of rules and constraints, reinforce racist and homophobic practices along the border. These practices, I argue, serve to silence queers of color who would ordinarily be far more open in a city not on the US-México border. It is tricky for queers of color on the border to resist inequitable moral codes—which are not only imposed through laws and religion but also by way of hate crimes.

In other words, I'm stating that the policing and closing of the border meant securing a white, colonial, heteronormative way of seeing and knowing, hence fusing race with sexuality. As the Mexican Revolution of 1910 impelled many to flee north to the United States, the "Nativist" movement grew stronger and succeeded in passing quota acts in the early twentieth century favoring "Nativist" ancestors—white, Northern European immigrants. At the same time, eugenicists and sexologists worked hand in hand. As many looked south to México, they imagined the impurities of a brown race threatening once again to overwhelm the white, pure race, perhaps even leading to miscegenation.[10] Sexual unions between brown and white had been dreaded since the US-México War of 1846–1848, and "Nativists" inherited that alarm.[11] Closing the border was the method of evading the raced, sexed body from México.

Queers of color on the borderlands have inherited this thorny colonial history. I have argued elsewhere that to decolonize history, a deconstructive method that I call the decolonial imaginary may be taken up. It is an interstitial space in which political and social dilemmas are negotiated and deconstructed. In that space one is neither oppressed or victimized nor oppressor or victimizer. Rather, one navigates between and among one's identities to favor the identity that is most viable for that political, historical moment. The ongoing process of the negotiation itself must be understood as that—a process. In other words, the decolonial is a dynamic space in which subjects are actively decolonizing their lives. Unlike the colonial imaginary, which is a narrow, binary, "us" versus "them" standpoint, the decolonial imaginary instead is a liberatory, mobile frame of mind. The decolonial is a deconstructive tool. It seeks out and disputes that which is written in history to write an alternative story. The decolonial imaginary unravels colonial, binary relations that we have inherited from historical circumstances such as wars and invasions.[12]

These oral histories are alternative stories even if the stories do not seem so unlike emblematic coming-out stories. Border queers are not vastly dissimilar from queers throughout the United States who navigate daily struggles and contradictions. Lesbians, gay men, bisexuals, and transgender folks continue to challenge discriminatory laws and social conventions globally, but some geographic spaces are safer than others. In the United States, for example, LGBTQ populations flock to urban areas like New York City, San Francisco, Los Angeles, and Chicago, where many can live in clusters. Urban queers, nonetheless, face hate crimes and bigotry in these cosmopolitan cities, but often, a large population of queers may draw together to combat discriminatory practices. On the border, where many queers of color prefer to be discreet, confronting homophobia is complex. Border queers face a delicate existence given the political, historical, and socioeconomic challenges on the US-México border. The interviews described here show how LGBTQ Chicanas/os are creative, forgiving, and eager for social change even though the changes are for "liberal" gay rights.

Chicana lesbian feminist and border theorist Gloria Anzaldúa reminded us that when living on the border, one is both scapegoat and forerunner of a new race; one is both man and women but also neither. In the borderlands, whether physical or metaphoric, queer experience is somewhere in the middle, somewhere in that interstitial space that I call the decolonial imaginary between the colonial and the postcolonial. And somewhere "in the middle," to quote transgender Chicana/Mexicana Coca Sapien, are the many genders that we have yet to recognize or name.[13] Perhaps an investigation into these geographic borderlands, in which dualities of knowledge are common, can help us further understand global and transnational queer experiences.

I also claim that queers on the border realize their sexuality through a political economy founded on a colonial history and, as a result, must navigate decolonial ways of being and knowing. The laws and discourses emerging from this colonial history pose specific contradictions for queers of color. Foucault has shown us the consequence of scrutinizing the *production* of sexuality rather than its *origins,* and embedded in that style of investigation was his concern for other kinds of oppressive conditioning. Like racism. If one turns to his lectures presented at the College of France from 1975 to 1976, published posthumously in 1997 in France and 2003 in the United States, one sees Foucault not only pursuing the production of history but also considering that which he has been accused of ignoring: race and discourse of racism. When he argued that history produces processes, whether the process is the language of sex and how sex is "put into language" or whether the process is war and how racism became the discourse of war, he questioned power, the power that creates that knowledge, and the relations of power and knowledge that have come to be in the present.[14] As I read his lectures, I realized that those of us who turn to Foucault's methodology have not been wrong to link race to sexuality. The persistent production of race, as it is linked to sex, is crucial. When we explore racialized sexualities, then we must also peer closely at the persistent production of colonial relations to decide how colonial relations are often raced and sexed. When Foucault pointed out that "history is an operation of power, an intensifier of power," he acknowledged that the manner in which history is remembered or erased creates those who will be considered the lasting ideologues of an era.[15] He is, in fact, referring to the hegemonic, colonial stories that will be imparted through the decades and then through the centuries to construct a common understanding of our past.[16]

This study, then, is an initial look at the production of racialized sexualities and the manner in which queers of color have survived and negotiated their identities on the US-México border, where the nation-state is as dubious as it is rigidly patriotic.

NEGOTIATING COLONIAL AND DECOLONIAL SPACES

On the first of May, 2002, I sat in my kitchen in El Paso, Texas, drinking my morning cup of coffee. As I perused the *El Paso Times,* a headline seized my attention: "Victim of Hate Crime Led 2 Lives, Friends Say." A photograph of a transgender Chicana accompanied the story. Hector Arturo "Arlene" Diaz had been shot in the back and left to die on Anapra Road, not far from a convenience store. The story read, "At home in Sunland Park, he was the baby boy of a hard-working mother, the sibling of nine brothers and sisters. At night, the 28 year old man dressed in women's clothing and became 'Arlene,' a fixture of the gay scene in Downtown El Paso."[17] The murder had occurred on April 10, a few weeks before I read the story about Arlene. In fact, the newspaper on April 11 only reported that a man had been found dead in Sunland Park. There was no mention of a possible hate crime until further into the article. It's no wonder I hadn't read it. But the report of May 1 stunned me. By the time the police arrested the alleged killer on April 22, they had classified Diaz's murder as a hate crime quite possibly motivated by "Diaz's sexual orientation."

The murder of Arlene, a transgender Chicana, shook the LGBTQ communities in El Paso. But queers on the border were not unfamiliar with hate crimes and gay bashing. In 1998, LAMBDA Community Service Center reported a 53-percent increase in assaults against queers while the police department claimed that there were almost no hate crimes in El Paso. The LAMBDA Center, which opened its doors in El Paso in 1991, pointed out that victims of anti-gay hate crimes do not report to the police but do report to LAMBDA. "In 1997, the police documented only two incidents out of a total of eleven crimes motivated by prejudice. And 42 percent of the people reporting crimes to LAMBDA never called the police."[18]

Unfortunately, Arlene Diaz's murder did not garner national attention, not in the same way Brandon Teena's or Mathew Shepherd's brutal murders alerted us to the severity of anti-queer hate crimes in the United States. But the "historical emergencies" that occur on the border of the United States and México often do not receive much notice.[19] Since 1993, hundreds—perhaps closer to a thousand—of women in Juárez have been murdered or have been reported missing. The murders and disappearances occasionally receive media attention beyond the region, but those who live on the border cannot ignore the crisis. When I read about one more murder, one more hate crime, I was distraught. I also recognized that even if the murderer were found guilty, social and moral codes on the border would continue to attempt to frighten queers of color into silence and hence into a colonial regime.

I do not want to characterize border queers as victims; they are anything but passive sufferers. Queers of color survive, resist, and create defiant measures to transform attitudes, rules, and social codes on the border. For many, the border is a zone of tolerance, *una zona de tolerancia,* that serves to contain illicit, unwanted behaviors within specific spaces.[20] I argue that coming out on the border is a negotiation of a colonial space, compelling those who live out loud to become decolonial in their actions. Conceptually, a term like "tolerance" conveys a colonial perspective. Tolerance, after all, affirms the hierarchical ideology imposed from above by those who judge themselves as the only real, worthy citizens and those being tolerated as less than worthy. But what happens when we question how decolonial agency plays out for each queer of color who chooses to come out on the border, especially as queers become more and more direct, outspoken, and active. Realistically, when queers break out and away from the safe zones of colonial tolerance in which they are contained to protect a heteronormative society, they face harsh criticism, hostility, and hate crimes. It is outside of the zones of colonized tolerance that queers practice their decolonial political activity. But I seem to be making value judgments. I do not assume that within those colonial zones, border queers do not also practice subtle resistances. Anybody who lives in the margins knows that daily life is a decolonial practice in which one must negotiate various power structures to survive. I'm merely pointing out that when border lesbians, gay men, and transgender women and men break out of the spaces in which they are contained, whether those spaces are designated as bars or homes, so that they do not contaminate a pure, heteronormative society, that the breaking out itself is an act of defiance that surpasses any imposed notions of tolerance. In this way, queers of color on the border become decolonial performers.

"I'm Here, a Brown Queer!"

An archetypal progress narrative surfaced as queers of color from El Paso and Juárez told their stories, eager to share openly their identities as queer Chicanas/os and Mexicans. The older gay men and lesbians, who came out as early as the 1950s, had harsh stories to tell about their lives on the border while a younger generation expressed a rebelliousness made possible by the LGBTQ rights fought for after the 1970s.

One of the oldest of the gay men interviewed, Manuel Madrid, was seventy years old at the time of his interview in 2002. Manny was born in San Elizario, Texas, a small town outside of El Paso, and his parents moved to the city when he was nine years old. Although he could not speak English when they moved, he learned the language swiftly in a grade school with a majority of English-speaking non-Mexicans. When his parents separated, he was left with his grandmother, who raised him.[21] By the time Manny reached high school, probably as early as 1948, he identified his sexual feelings for boys and decided to confess his yearning to a priest. When the priest told him he was committing a sin, Manny decided resolutely never to speak again to a Catholic cleric about his same-sex desire. Unlike other devout Catholics who were interviewed, Manny escaped guilt and did not brand himself a sinner. Instead, he and his best friend in high school would single out boys to each other, commonly referring to them as "joto," and concluding "I think he's with us."[22] He asserted that he did not come out in El Paso because in the 1950s most queers were closeted and as far as he knew there was only one bar in town that accepted a gay clientele. He would, however, pick up Fort Bliss soldiers and have sex with them in the desert. Manny said he finally came out in 1966 when he moved to Los Angeles, where he lived with his partner, Marshall, of twenty-two years. But after Marshall died of colon cancer, Manny returned to El Paso.[23] "I could kick my butt for moving back to El Paso," he said.[24] Grieving for his partner, those first few years were difficult, but after eight years back on the border, Manny said, "El Paso is beautiful and a healthier place to live than LA."[25]

The only family member that Manny came out to was his niece, a lesbian. Although his aunt lived in the same house with Manny and his partner, Manny did not tell her he was gay. "I think our sexuality is nobody's business but our own," he concluded.[26]

Similarly, Armando, a self-identified bisexual, was forty-seven at the time of his interview. He asserted, "The gay community is very much, I guess, reflective of me, of how I am . . . pretty much everybody's in hiding."[27] Unlike Manny, Armando stayed in El Paso and fell in love with an older married man with children. The married man, who claimed to be "Christian," left Armando broken-hearted. The experience, however, gave Armando the courage to face his sexuality despite choosing a closeted life.[28]

By contrast, Yolanda Leyva, forty-five in 2002, came out at the age of eighteen when she began to go to queer bars in El Paso. A Chicana lesbian who is currently a professor of history at the University of Texas in El Paso, Yolanda was born in Juárez and grew up in El Paso. Going to bars "made me really aware of how dangerous it was to be a gay person in El Paso" in the 1970s, she said.[29] In other words, harassment was common. Queers had to cope with the police, who would enter the bars, order the lights turned on, and then file the clientele into the parking lot to check their identification. To add to that harassment, patrons of the bar endured persecution from drunk, seemingly heterosexual men who lingered in the parking lot with the sole purpose of bullying regulars.[30]

The harassment did not stop Yolanda from patronizing bars or other queer spaces. She even cross-dressed sometimes, and her mother would help her dress in men's suits, declaring, "Mija, you look so handsome, the women are really gonna love you."[31] However, when her sixty-year-old mother realized that Yolanda was actually dating women, they had an argument, and her mother called her a "jota."[32]

Shortly after their argument, Yolanda moved to Austin, where she became active with lesbian groups. After living in Austin, Tucson, and San Antonio, she returned to her home in El Paso. Although she had other job opportunities, she chose El Paso because for her, the border is a unique space where its inhabitants can explore multiple identities created by the many cultures in the region.

For Yolanda, growing up gay in a Chicano family is different from "mainstream" America: "I think a lot of people have this stereotype that it's harder to be gay in a Chicano family and part of that is because of Catholicism and because Chicanos are seen as more conservative socially. But what I've seen . . . is that because Chicanos put such emphasis on family, that I've seen a lot of gay men and lesbians really accepted by their families, even though the families don't like that their children are queer, I've seen a lot of acceptance."[33]

It's an interesting double-turn of colonial imposition and decolonial practice for those coming out on the border. While on the one hand, Armando and Manny were for the most part closeted, there were family members, as in Manny's case, who more or less accepted the queer in the family so long as the secret was not discussed or flaunted. In other words, Chicana/o lesbians and gay men are expected to keep silent and remain loyal to the patriarchal familial oppression that is convenient for their/our families. Even while practicing the decolonial, radical politics of "I'm here, a brown queer," Chicanas/os are asked to abide by "don't ask, don't tell" homophobic diplomacy that erases our very existence.[34] However, many still defy homophobic colonial tolerance, choosing to speak out and perform their decolonial agency. Hence, many queers renegotiate their place in the family. As Leyva pointed out, Chicana/o families may not like that they have a queer daughter or son, but the acceptance occurs more often than not. At the same time, however, the acceptance still transpires within a patriarchal familial structure that queers are obligated to mediate.

Jorge Garcia, also known as Sasha, felt compelled to leave his home in El Paso before he could come out. At nineteen years old, he lived in San Angelo, Texas, where he was attending technical school in 1988. He walked into a gay bar in San Angelo and experienced a gratifying homosexual encounter, the second of his life. The first had occurred when he was a thirteen-year-old high school student. Jorge said he was sexually assaulted by a "jock" who had persistently hassled him. In the urinal one day, Jorge realized the jock had always wanted to have sex with him and asked him to "suck" his dick. Frightened and excited, the young men walked to the desert where they could be alone, and the "jock" proceeded to assault Jorge.[35] "I kept telling him to stop and he wouldn't

... I was on the floor, on the ground, the dirt, on my stomach and he was on top of me. And he wouldn't stop."[36] The "jock" finally released Jorge, who got up, put on his pants, and walked home silently.

When he was older, Jorge moved to Dallas and was content with the queer communities he encountered. But after a breakup with a lover, Jorge returned to El Paso in 1993 to attend the University of Texas in El Paso. Because he felt stifled, he spent summers in California, where he was "taken aback" by Gay Pride in San Francisco.[37] Having performed "drag" in his early twenties in San Angelo and in Dallas, Jorge decided to perform again when he impersonated Lorena Bobbit in a Halloween skit. Around 1998, he told his mother and sister about his drag performances, and they encouraged him. At the gay bar the Old Plantation (OP), he would impersonate Linda Ronstadt and sing from her album,*Canciones de mi Padre,* or mimic Eartha Kitt. Pageants became important to Jorge, who by now was known more by his drag name, Sasha.[38] Sasha, who came out at nineteen, claimed that life for queers in El Paso had improved so much since his high school experience that in 2001 he could sit in a Denny's coffee shop with his queer friends, each of them dressed in drag, and not be harassed.

Pepe Porras, a gay Mexicano born in El Paso but raised in México, grew up with the privilege of country clubs and boarding schools. He was kicked out of the house in Juárez where he lived with his family when his father discovered Pepe naked in bed with a man. His father, while screaming *maricón,* ordered him to leave. Humiliated, yet relieved that his family finally knew he was gay, Pepe left his home. He returned the next day for his clothes and other personal items. His parents had already burned his possessions and painted his bedroom. The thirty-six-year-old left Juárez, took his first job, and found an apartment in El Paso. Pepe said that his father grieved for months that his son was gay. He only acknowledged him by offering Pepe a monthly allowance under the condition that he would never have to see his son again.[39]

Pepe, along with other gay men and lesbians interviewed, discussed machismo in Mexican culture, which served to reinforce roles among some queers. For example, Pepe confessed that when he was sixteen and initially experimenting with other men, he "was afraid to engage in penetration for fear he'd wake up feeling like a woman."[40] Now that he's older, he claims that he has no problem being gay because he's not identified as a gay man, whether in Mexico City, San Francisco, or New

York City. He prefers not to flaunt his lifestyle and states that queers who are too open are the cause of violence against them. He concluded: "I don't see color, I don't see sexuality, I'm just me."[41]

Although Pepe and Armando are from different generations, they seem to share similar judgments that reinforce sexual hierarchy among gay men. "In Mexico, if you're the top, then you're the male, hence not gay. But if you're on the receiving end, then you're the gay one. In Juárez, lots of married men have sex with other men."[42]

Myrna Avalos, a Chicana lesbian, also commented on machismo. She believes that the border city breeds machista attitudes toward women, which take the form of drunkenness, womanizing, and battering. She was exceedingly critical of this "cultural thing."[43] Myrna observed that butch women in lesbian bars exhibit territorial behavior that she does not like. She said she used to go to You Got It, a lesbian bar that closed down around 1996 because the police had to break up fights between lesbians too often. "I mean these women would literally fight. Throw bottles at each other. I mean, territorial. . . . with their women. 'This is my woman, you leave her alone, Bop!' "[44] She named their territorial behavior a "butch pussy-stance" and refused to engage in the type of restrictive role-playing that was anti-feminist. Identifying as a butch lesbian for Myrna meant negotiating role-playing within a patriarchal structure that already condemned women. She adamantly reclaimed her butch identity as a role beyond "machista" behavior that was confining to women, particularly lesbians.[45]

Myrna came out in El Paso at the age of seventeen. Before then, she endured six brothers and their homophobic remarks as well as an extended family who persistently asked her when she planned to marry.[46] After coming out, she worked at The Old Plantation (a problematic colonial name), one of the longest standing gay bars in El Paso, having opened in the early 1970s. Myrna noted that it was once taboo to mention the OP, but that around the mid-1990s, heterosexuals began to go to the club.[47] In fact, almost all of the queers interviewed mention that the OP has become increasingly "straight" and that queers do not attend on Saturday nights when heterosexuals swarm the space. Myrna declared that in 2002 she saw police officers and lawyers, both gay and straight, at the bar. In and around 1994–1995, it was customary for homophobic straight clientele to go to the queer bar expressly to beat up gays and lesbians. Subsequently, a sign has been placed on the wall that announces, "This business is gay owned and gay operated," and Myrna also claims that gays no longer put up with the bashing in their own queer space. Most accept that queers will be the majority on Friday nights. She claims that gay men and lesbians have stopped going on Saturdays when so many heterosexuals overrun the bar. What Myrna also noted was the stigma about being an out gay person. When she saw clients in the other spaces of the city, they ignored her for fear that she would recognize them as customers of the OP.[48] In a sense, Myrna attributes the less-than-open queer community to the fact that there is no authentic lesbian group or organization in El Paso to meet her needs. She also blames what she has coined "pussy-stance mentality" for hindering lesbians from activism that would confront homophobia. Instead, lesbians are too busy fighting over "their women." She also accuses a conservative population in Texas of severe homophobia that impedes successful organizing in El Paso.[49]

Twenty-one-year-old David Andrew Rubalcava identifies as a Hispanic American gay male. He was born and raised in El Paso and was a student at UTEP during the time of the interview. His queer play *A Piece of Mind* was staged in El Paso at the LAMBDA Center to a supportive El Paso audience. David has supportive, loving parents, siblings, and friends.[50] He believes that people in the border region have closed-minded attitudes toward gays. David enjoys dispelling stereotypes by coming out to as many people as he can. He believes that education will transform the border into a more egalitarian place, compelling the population to eradicate homophobia. David expressed that coming out and living an openly gay life gives him the opportunity to educate heterosexuals who hold stereotypes about queers. As a young man, he is unyielding about his rights as a gay man. When asked about Catholicism, he remarked, "Fuck that, I'm not gonna listen to this bullshit because who are they to say who I can fall in love with, who I can have sex with, what kind of sex I can have, if I can use birth control or not, if I can make decisions about my own body."[51]

Decolonial Performers

After reviewing the voices in these interviews, I infer that by living their lives in what could be considered a decolonial critical stance, queers of color assert a negotiable posture that must navigate between what has been inherited—a history of racism, homophobia, coloniality—what is being contested and decolonized—racism, homophobia, coloniality—and what is hoped for—an end to racism, homophobia, coloniality. Hence there is a subtle move toward the postcolonial ideal, which remains an impossible dream for US Chicanas/os. What is possible, however, is a decolonial way of being and knowing on the US-México border, where Chicana/o and Mexican lesbians, transgender folks and gay men negotiate their lives as "out" citizens with third class rights.[52]

Queer theorist José Muñoz argues that "the politicized agent must have the ability to adapt and shift as quickly as power does within discourse."[53] We must assume the agent is politicized in ways that will permit a decolonial queer method. But even if not politicized, border queers of color are creative daily as they bargain for their dignity and survival. Having lived in El Paso for ten years and in Juárez for one year in the 1990s, I witnessed and experienced the manner in which homophobia pressed down against the queer of color population, but I also saw Chicana/o queers constructing full lives while being cognizant that living on the border is its own political challenge. Queers on the border do not and cannot forget the poverty and racism that infects their region. Myrna speaks as a politicized agent who is eager to decolonize the border while realizing that change is imperative if one is to survive. She states,

> We need to fight . . . we've lost our humanity. I'm not just speaking about El Paso . . . we have the border right here, we see cardboard boxes, homes. That's their home. . . . We talk about "world poverty" and "world hunger" when I can just turn around and see, see the reality. And people just read it in books . . . here especially too, they read, "oh, there's world hunger?" Just look across the border, just look. . . . I think we should fight for humanity a little more, especially here in El Paso.[54]

David, one of the youngest of those interviewed, embraces his gay life. By doing so, he defies the homophobia still present in the borderlands. Sasha, also of a younger generation, prevailed over the assaults he had experienced as a younger man in El Paso by choosing to be out as a queer performer. Yolanda, an out Chicana lesbian and scholar-activist born in the 1950s, consistently contests the status quo and promotes social justice in El Paso. The older generation, like Manny and Armando, live gratifying queer lives despite the severity of the homophobia they encountered.

El Paso and Juárez queers negotiate a severely racist and heteronormative colonial space that attempts to negate their lived experiences. Anyone living in the borderlands knows that, but to be a queer of color *en la frontera* also makes the task that much trickier. Arlene Díaz, the transgender Chicana who was murdered by an enraged homophobic man, represents the overarching sense of despair in a region that continues to harbor violence inherited from a history of coloniality. Queers who live in El Paso and Juárez must perform decolonial practices to survive the colonial landscape in a space where "people walk through you, the wind steals your voice, you're a burra, buey, scapegoat, forerunner of a new race, half and half—both woman and man, neither—a new gender . . ."[55]

NOTES

1. Michel Foucault, *The Use of Pleasure: Volume 2 of the History of Sexuality*, trans. Robert Hurley (New York: Vintage Books, 1985), 4. The full quote: "In short, it was a matter of seeing how an 'experience' came to be constituted in modern Western societies, an experience that caused individuals to recognize themselves as subjects of a 'sexuality,' which was accessible to very diverse fields of knowledge and linked to a system of rules and constraints. What I planned, therefore, was a history of the experience of sexuality, where experience is understood as the correlation between fields of knowledge, types of normativity, and forms of subjectivity in a particular culture." I find this passage particularly vital because Foucault claims to have abandoned the task of writing a history of sexuality that spoke to the experience of sexualities and how they were constructed by laws, religion, medical tracts, etc. Instead, he offered an analysis of ideologies and discourses that shaped sexualities, and yet by doing so, he also put forth a valuable paradigm for writing the history of racialized sexualities.

2. I am employing "queer" as a term that includes lesbians, gays, transgender folks, and bisexuals while acknowledging that many of those interviewed did not refer to themselves as queer but instead chose to be specific about their identities, whether racial, national or about their sexuality. None of these terms of self-identity are static and each transforms throughout history. "Queer" can also apply to heterosexuals who practice non-heteronormative sexualities. "Transgender" is more current and perhaps the least understood. For an insightful look at "transgender," see Judith Halberstam, *In a Queer Time and Place: Transgender Bodies, Subcultural Lives* (New York: New York University Press, 2005). On page 53, she points out, "Transgender is for the most part a vernacular term developed within gender communities to account for the cross-identification experiences of people who may not

accept all of the protocols and strictures of transsexuality. Such people understand cross-identification as a crucial part of their gendered self, but they may pick and choose among the options of body modification, social presentation, and legal recognition available to them." For an inspired discussion of the Chican@ transbody, see the exceptional dissertation by J. Frances Galarte *El sabor del amor y del dolor: Violence, Affect and the (Trans)Body in the Chican@ Historical Imaginary* (PhD dissertation, University of Illinois at Urbana-Champaign, 2011).

3. Gregory Ramos interviewed twenty-five queers in El Paso; however, there are twenty-four transcripts and/or tapes of the interviews. All are housed at the Institute of Oral History, University of Texas, El Paso, and were conducted between 2000 and 2002. (Record of the human subjects' permission to publish the data, now necessary even for cultural studies, are also on file at UTEP.) He initially titled his performance piece *Border Voices* but has since revised the piece and calls it *Border Stories*. In a powerful one-man performance, Ramos melds the voices of the interviewees to show a complex life for queers on the border, some of whom are HIV-positive. Professor Ramos currently teaches in the theater department at the University of Vermont, where he is expanding his research to include Canadian queers. He is contrasting the lives of queers on two transnational borders.

4. Let me say a word about racial and national self-identity. The term "Chicana/o" came into being as part of a political project that emerged from the Chicana/o movements of the 1960s and 1970s. Chicanas/os are of Mexican descent and live in the United States. Although those who call themselves Chicana/o do not embrace the term "Hispanic," it is important to note that "Hispanic," while riddled with problems, is a term of self-identity used by Mexican Americans and other Latinos who live in the United States. "Latina/o" has become an umbrella term of self-identity for all people of Latin American, Central American, and Mexican descent who live in the United States. I have opted to use "Chicana/o" or "Mexican" because all but one of the interviewees identify as Chicana/o or Mexican. I make note of the one interviewee who identifies as "Hispanic."

5. I am not assessing the oral interviews through a social science lens, although that kind of assessment is undeniably significant. I am interested in writing the narrative that speaks to the colonial bind for Chicana/o queers on the US-México border, particularly in El Paso, Texas, who find themselves engaged in decolonization through mere participation in their daily queer lives.

6. There are hundreds of historical texts addressing Manifest Destiny and the battles of the Alamo and San Jacinto (1836) in which Coahuila y Tejas became the Texas Republic, followed by the US-México War in 1846 when Texas and the southwestern states of New Mexico, Arizona, and California specifically became occupied by the United States. For examples, see Rodolfo Acuña, *Occupied America: A History of Chicanos*, 3rd Edition (New York: Harper and Row, 1988) and Juan Gómez-Quiñones, *The Roots of Chicano Politics* (Albuquerque: University of New Mexico Press, 1994).

7. Eithne Luibhéid, *Entry Denied: Controlling Sexuality at the Border* (Minneapolis: University of Minnesota, 2002), 4.

8. Luibhéid, *Entry Denied*. See Chapter 4, "Looking Like a Lesbian."

9. The anti-immigration law SB1070 in Arizona permits yet another round of vicious hatred against Mexicans as we move into the twenty-first century.

10. See Siobhan B. Somerville, *Queering the Color Line: Race and the Intervention of Homosexuality in American Culture* (Durham: Duke University Press, 2000) for an excellent argument regarding the 1986 Supreme Court case *Plessy v. Ferguson*, which established a "separate but equal" clause legalizing the segregation of blacks from whites. At that same moment, the United States also established distinctions between heterosexual and homosexual. For an incisive discussion of eugenics on the US-México Border, see Alexandra Stern, "Buildings, Boundaries, and Blood: Medicalization and Nation-Building on the US-Mexico Border, 1910–1930," *Hispanic American Historical Review* 79:1 (Feb. 1999), 41–81.

11. Senator John C. Calhoun of South Carolina, in his speech before Congress in January 1847, argued against annexing all of México because Mexicans were mestizos and Indians, both of whom were inferior to the pure, white race of Americans. See David Weber, *Foreigners in Their Native Land* (Albuquerque: University of New Mexico, 1977). In 1924, Samuel Holmes, a professor of zoology at the University of Berkeley, was a Nativist who did not want more Mexicans entering the United States. He said, "You cannot let a foreign group into a country without its having the effect of keeping a great many thousand, perhaps millions, of our own native population from being born. Are you going to sacrifice our children for the sake of assimilating the Mexican?" In Mark Reisler, *By the Sweat of their Brow* (Berkeley: University of California Press, 1979).

12. Recently that same thing has been identified as nothing more than liberal civil rights under a capitalist socio-economy that allows queers to consume and live daily lives comfortably without much thought to "racial, gendered and sexual hierarchies of the nation-state" that must be understood as endemic to "the problems of the political economy." See David Eng, Judith Halberstam, and José Munoz, "What's Queer About Queer Studies Now?" *Social Text* 84–85: 3–4 (2005), 1.

13. What I mean by my use of "imaginary" is that it is much like the unconscious—that which exists but is difficult to trace since it has been accepted for so long as "normal."

14. Michel Foucault, *"Society Must be Defended": Lectures at the Collège De France, 1975–1976*, trans. David Macey (New York: Picador Press, 2003), 65.

15. Foucault, *"Society Must be Defended,"* 70.

16. As I became more of a Foucauldian, I began to see how I could use his methods to unravel colonialist ideology. I came up with my notion of decolonizing history and a theoretical construct that I name the decolonial imaginary. To decolonize our history and our historical imaginations, we must listen to voices from the margins instead of falling prey to that which is easy: allowing the white, colonial, heteronormative gaze to reconstruct and interpret the lives of queers on the border. However, as of late, the white, patriarchal, homonormative gaze must be interpreted as a colonial gaze. On homonormativity, see Lisa Duggan, *The Twilight of Equality? Neoliberalism, Cultural Politics, and the Attack on Democracy* (Boston, MA: Beacon, 2003). Also refer to Linda Heidenreich, "Reflections on Euro-Homo Normativity: Gay and Lesbian Studies and the Creation of a Universal Homosexual," *Critica* (Spring 1999): 41–49. For an influential study that braves an innovative critique of homonormativity and submits "homonationalism" as a crucial concept, see Jasbir K. Puar, *Terrorist Assemblages: Homonationalism in Queer Times* (Durham, NC: Duke University Press, 2007).

17. *El Paso Times,* May 1, 2002. Louie Gilot reported the story.

18. *El Paso Times,* March 4, 1998. By Laura Smitherman. The story also shows that in 1997, one third of the anti-gay hate crimes occurred on a school or college campus, a 22-percent rise over the previous year, which was attributed to crimes reported to LAMBDA.

19. I am referring to Walter Benjamin's "historical emergencies of national and global consequence" that Eng, Halberstam, and Muñoz refer to in "What's Queer About Queer Studies Now?" 1.

20. Lionel Cantú Jr., "De Ambiente: Queer Tourism and the Shifting Boundaries of Mexican Male Sexualities, " *GLQ* 8:1–2 (2002), 144–145. Cantú cites the study by James R. Curtis and Daniel D. Arreola to point out how these zones of tolerance were created in Mexican border towns in the early twentieth century so that deviance could be controlled. "Male homosexual and transvestite bars" on the Mexican side of the border became the *zonas*, the "legitimized spaces for 'immoral' activity that attracted sexual tourism from north of the border." James R. Curtis and Daniel D. Arreola, "Zonas de Tolerancia on the Northern Mexico Border," *Geographical Review* 81 (1991): 333–347. Also refer to Cantú's recent publication, *The Sexuality of Migration: Border Crossings and Mexican Immigrant Men* (New York: New York University Press, 2009) for a more detailed analysis. The anthology edited by Eithne Luibheid and Lionel Cantu Jr., *Queer Migrations: Sexuality, US Citizenship and Border Crossings* (Minneapolis: University of Minnesota, 2005), is also a good collection of essays.

21. Manuel Madrid, February 23, 2002, 1.

22. Madrid, 7.

23. Madrid, 13, 18–19.

24. Madrid, 24.

25. Madrid, 44.

26. Madrid, 34.

27. Armando, July 4, 2002, 11. He did not give a last name.

28. Armando, 8.

29. Yolanda Leyva, August 31, 2001.

30. Leyva, 7.

31. Leyva, 8.

32. Ibid.

33. Leyva, 11.

34. Refer to Sarah Schulman, *Ties that Bind: Familial Homophobia and Its Consequences* (New York: New Press, 2009). Schulman introduces a razor-sharp critique of familial homophobia while offering excellent examples of how lesbians use patriarchal laws against each other, particularly in child custody battles.

35. Jorge Garcia, September 19, 2001, 1–5.

36. Garcia, 6.

37. Garcia, 13–15.

38. Garcia, 17–18, 20, 25–26.

39. Pepe Porras, August 22, 2001, 1, 20, 23.

40. Porras, 4. For an early discussion of "passive" versus "active" sex for gay men, see Tomás Almaguer, "Chicano Men: A Cartography of Homosexual Identity

and Behavior," *The Lesbian and Gay Studies Reader,* ed. Henry Abelove, Michèle Aina Barale, and David M. Halperin (New York: Routledge, 1993), 255–273.

41. Porras, 8.
42. Armando, 11.
43. Myrna Avalos, December 5, 2001, 10.
44. Avalos, 1.
45. Avalos, 24.
46. Avalos, 4, 11.
47. Avalos, 14–15.
48. Avalos, 17–18, 21.
49. Avalos, 26.
50. David Andrew Rubalcava, November 29, 2000, 1, 5, 8–15.
51. Rubalcava, 28.
52. I say "third-class" rather than "second-class" because Chicanos/as and Mexicans were relegated to second-class status after the US-México War in 1846–1848. Chicana/o and Mexican queers find themselves further down the political and socioeconomic hierarchy of liberal civil rights.
53. José Muñoz, *Disidentifications: Queers of Color and the Performance of Politics* (Minneapolis: University of Minnesota, 1999). I am drawn to Muñoz's critique of prominent queer theorists and how he notes what Chela Sandoval refers to as the apartheid of theoretical domains. In other words, for too long, theorists have operated in separate but unequal academic discussions. Hegemonic or first-world theorists read each other's work, cite each other's work, and are transformed by each other's work while US third-world theorists read hegemonic first-world theorists and cite first-world theorists at the same time that we read, keep up with, and are transformed by US third-world theorists. Unfortunately, there is not enough exchange between and among cultural critics and theorists, and the same dynamic has begun among queer theorists. If, indeed, as queer theorists we are all, for the most part, concerned with what Foucault refers to in the *History of Sexuality* as power and its relation to the constructions of knowledge, then perhaps as queer theorists it's time we listened to each other more. Hiram Pérez, in his essay "You Can Have My Brown Body and Eat it, Too!" *Social Text* 84–85: 3–4 (2005), 188, addresses the manner in which queer theory has become invested in protecting "white, patriarchal structures of knowledge."
54. Avalos, 30–31.
55. Gloria Anzaldúa, *Borderlands/La Frontera: The New Mestiza* (San Francisco, CA: Aunt Lute Books, 1987), 216. From the poem "To Live in the Borderlands Means You."

WORKS CITED

Acuña, Rodolfo. *Occupied America: A History of Chicanos.* 3rd Edition. New York: Harper and Row, 1988.

Almaguer, Tomás. "Chicano Men: A Cartography of Homosexual Identity and Behavior." In *The Lesbian and Gay Studies Reader.* Editors Henry Abelove, Michèle Aina Barale, and David M. Halperin. New York: Routledge, 1993.

Anzaldúa, Gloria. *Borderlands/La Frontera: The New Mestiza.* San Francisco, CA: Aunt Lute Books, 1987.

Cantú, Lionel, Jr. "De Ambiente: Queer Tourism and the Shifting Boundaries of Mexican Male Sexualities." *GLQ* 8, nos. 1–2 (2002): 139–166.

Curtis, James R., and Daniel D. Arreola. "Zonas de Tolerancia on the Northern Mexico Border," *Geographical Review* 81 (1991): 333–347.

Duggan, Lisa. *The Twilight of Equality? Neoliberalism, Cultural Politics, and the Attack on Democracy.* Boston, MA: Beacon, 2003.

Eng, David, with Judith Halberstam and José Muñoz. "What's Queer About Queer Studies Now?" *Social Text* 84–84, nos. 3–4 (2005): 5–18.

Foucault, Michel. *"Society Must be Defended": Lectures at the Collège De France, 1975–1976.* Translated by David Macey. New York: Picador Press, 2003.

———. *The Use of Pleasure: Volume 2 of the History of Sexuality.* Translated by Robert Hurley. New York: Vintage Books, 1985.

Galarte, J. Frances. *El sabor del amor y del dolor: Violence, Affect and the (Trans) Body in the Chican@ Historical Imaginary.* PhD dissertation, University of Illinois at Urbana-Champaign, 2011.

Gómez-Quiñones, Juan. *The Roots of Chicano Politics.* Albuquerque: University of New Mexico Press, 1994.

Halberstam, Judith. *In a Queer Time and Place: Transgender Bodies, Subcultural Lives.* New York: New York University Press, 2005.

Heidenreich, Linda. "Reflections on Euro-Homo Normativity: Gay and Lesbian Studies and the Creation of a Universal Homosexual," *Critica* (Spring 1999): 41–49.

Luibhéid, Eithne. *Entry Denied: Controlling Sexuality at the Border.* Minneapolis: University of Minnesota, 2002.

Luibhéid, Eithne, and Lionel Cantú, Jr. Editors. *Queer Migrations: Sexuality, US Citizenship and Border Crossings.* Minneapolis: University of Minnesota, 2005.

Muñoz, José. *Disidentifications: Queers of Color and the Performance of Politics.* Minneapolis: University of Minnesota, 1999.

Oral History Collection, University of Texas, El Paso.

Pérez, Hiram. "You Can Have My Brown Body and Eat it, Too!" *Social Text* 84–85, nos. 3–4 (2005): 171–192.

Puar, Jasbir K. *Terrorist Assemblages: Homonationalism in Queer Times.* Durham, NC: Duke University Press, 2007.

Reisler, Mark. *By the Sweat of their Brow.* Berkeley: University of California Press, 1979.

Schulman, Sarah. *Ties that Bind: Familial Homophobia and Its Consequences.* New York: New Press, 2009.

Somerville, Siobhan B. *Queering the Color Line: Race and the Intervention of Homosexuality in American Culture.* Durham, NC: Duke University Press, 2000.

Stern, Alexandra. "Buildings, Boundaries, and Blood: Medicalization and Nation-Building on the US-Mexico Border, 1910–1930." *Hispanic American Historical Review* 79, no. 1 (Feb. 1999): 41–81.

Weber, David. *Foreigners in Their Native Land.* Albuquerque: University of New Mexico, 1977.

ELEVEN

"Te Amo, Te Amo, Te Amo": Lorenzo Antonio and Sparx Performing Nuevo México Music

PETER J. GARCÍA

It's a hot summer afternoon and I am driving with my mother and my tío or her oldest brother heading west on Interstate 40 entering Albuquerque's city limits following an intense extended family reunion held over the Fourth of July weekend held in my maternal ancestral village of *el Torreon* near Manzano, Abó, Chilili, Tajique, Estancia, and Mountainair in Torrance County. These picturesque New Mexican village communities remain hidden byways and represent some of the last bastions of the former Spanish pastoral rancheritos and former Mexican land grants from throughout the Río Abajo. Older Nuevomexicano residents remain rooted here and to the former ways of life that have survived now for centuries in a place twice colonized but which remains home to a unique raza heritage and a rooted, what Alicia Gaspar de Alba calls "alter-Native" Chicana/o culture with a unique New Mexican style in culinary and visual arts, architecture, music, language, and expressive culture. Throughout the entire Río Abajo, Mexicano settlements continue the older way of rural living with milpas, and similar to northern New Mexico and southern Colorado, further picturesque chains of village hamlets situated throughout the Sandía, Sangre de Cristo, Jemez, and Manzano mountain communities are located north, northeast, and directly east of Albuquerque. Many of my maternal family members and close relatives now live in *Alburquerque* but return often to the maternal village and my grandparents' *terreno* for various family gatherings, solemn occasions, and fiestas.

Heading west on what was once the old Route 66 into what is now called the "Duke City," my uncle observes "ya llegamos a *Alburquerque*" pronouncing the city name correctly with the initial "bur" in his 1940s generation of Chicano Spanish—a Nuevo Mexicano mixture of the native Mexican language that Chicanos across the Southwest call "Mexicano"—a regional language that exhibits specific translocal dialects and also expresses generational linguistic codes very similar to urban Caló from the West Coast. As part of the state's local colorful heritage, my uncle also recognizes the familiar young faces of *Nuevo México's* international Latina pop music celebrities—Veronica, Rosamaria, Carolina, and Kristina. Better known as "Sparx," these women represent New Mexico's successful *onda grupera* (multi-vocal quartet) and are New Mexican celebrity royalty, especially in their role as international popular entertainers. For my mother and my uncle, "son las hijas de Tiny Morrie y Gloria Pohl"—whose parents and extended family are New Mexican popular bilingual singers from the Chicano generation who rose to fame during Nuevo México's violent and turbulent civil rights era and throughout the Cold War era. Sparx provides an important cultural and linguistic connection to the greater Spanish-speaking world, which tragically in the United States continues to be marginalized by chronic violence, racism, and an overdetermined self-assured cultural arrogance on the part of Anglo-American citizens regarding their disappearing entitlement and sense of superiority that motivates the failing English-only movement. As an intellectual hyperbole, "English only" reminds us of Jim Crow "separate but equal" mandated de jure racial segregation that is now undermining so-called US exceptionalism through its legalization and promotion of monolingualism in a multicultural and polylingual globalizing society. Linguist Ofelia García explains how from "its earliest contacts with the conquered inhabitants of the Southwest to its dealings with the colonized people of Puerto Rico, the US government has maintained a policy of eradicating Spanish by encouraging a shift to English. It has done so by adopting a policy of debasing and racializing Spanish, linking it to subjugated populations, immigration, poverty, and lack of education."[1] These genocidal policies and racist legal practices have had devastating consequences for Nuevo Mexicano citizens, who became US citizens following 1848 and who remain mostly bilingual.

Maintaining the Spanish Mexicano language while resisting forced structural and linguistic assimilation into the United States has driven the Nuevomexicano population into what Alicia Gaspar de Alba calls "cultural schizophrenia." Today, following eight long years that subjected the world to an incompetent political leadership during the George W. Bush presidency, the United States finds itself economically bankrupt and bereft of moral authority. Sparx has a large fan base throughout México, Latin America, Spain, and the US Latina/o borderlands, and its members are celebrated as local, native, "organic" celebrities at home in New Mexico. Passing giant postmodern Pueblo pottery simulacra, exotic-looking Anasazi Indian casinos and resorts, Route 66 gas stations and motels, and the Coronado shopping mall, the large billboard photo image of New Mexico's superstar Latina celebrities is every bit as glamorous as if Sparx had just posed for the pages of *Latina* magazine.

The larger-than-life Hollywood photo image and highway billboard sign features Sparx and their brother—singer/songwriter Lorenzo Antonio's—upcoming benefit concert scheduled annually for late August at the Sandía resort and casino outdoor amphitheater. On the car radio, KANW 89.1 FM (New Mexico public radio) is playing indigenous local Spanish language tunes or what the station deejays call "New Mexico music" when Lorenzo Antonio's hit cover of Ramon Ayala's "*Cruz de Madera*" begins and we in the car all sing along. Contemplating "*Cruz de Madera*" makes me reconsider New Mexico's neocolonial status as a fragmented cultural system, as there is no question that today *Nuevo México* remains an important musical and Chicana/o subcultural art center in the aesthetic heart of Aztlán, Greater México, and/or the US Latina/o borderlands. According to Guillermo Gómez-Peña,

> "Americans" (or rather USians) arrived in the twenty-first century with acute vertigo, our sense of worth and prosperity as a nation blown out of proportion by the "success" of the new virtual economy, paired with the absence of formidable enemies abroad. The old Soviet menace had been replaced first by mythical enemies, including immigrants and drug lords from south of the border, and later on (after 9/11) by real enemies as the "terrorists" from the Middle East.[2]

This acute vertigo is symptomatic of the region's neocolonization on the part of the United States and is another manifestation of the acute "cultural schizophrenia" that characterizes the urgency of the current era. New Mexico's local indigenous Native American heritage includes nineteen Pueblo village-centered reservations representing three language groups: Tanoan (six Tewa, four Tiwa, one Towa), seven Keresan, and one Zuñi, plus two Athabascan languages in three reservations, Diné (one Navajo) and Indé (two Apache). Yet another term for this acute vertico among the Puebo Indians is "*Koyannisqatsi,*" which is the Hopi term for "life out of balance." Another distinct ethnic group with a differential consciousness rooted in Nuevo México's neocolonialism is the "Indo-Hispano" or mestizo communities, which have mixed among eastern Plains Kiowa tribes including two Shoshonean groups, Ute and Comanche, who resisted US imperial aggression and at the same time were assimilated into Mexicano society during the nineteenth century. Despite captivity, slavery, and later cultural adoption (symbiosis), strong mixed indigenous consciousness persists today among many Nuevomexicana/os who represent the older Indo-Hispano or *mestizo* population that settled the region in 1598 and intermarried with the local indigenous populations.

Nuevo México survived an especially violent, unstable, and dangerous colonial past and equally turbulent Mexican (1821–1848) and US territorial (1848–1912) eras until statehood was granted in 1912. The varied list of ethnonyms used by New Mexicans to refer to themselves reflects the intense dynamics of ethnicity negotiated in a social context of subordination, racism, and white supremacy. The labels includes Nuevomexicanos, Mexicanos, Indo-Hispanos, Spanish-Americans, Mexican Americans, Chicanos, and Latinos, sometimes used in different combinations within the same family. For Guillermo Gómez-Peña,

> What ten years ago was considered "subculture" is now mere pop. The satiable mass of the so-called "mainstream" (remember the film, *The Blob*?) has finally devoured all "margins" and the more dangerous, thorny, and exotic these "margins," the better. In fact, *stricto sensu,* we can say that there are no "margins" left, at least no recognizable ones. "Alternative" thought, "fringe" subcultures, and "radical" behavior, as we knew them, have actually become the mainstream. Nowadays, spectacle replaces content; form gets heightened; "meaning" (remember meaning?) evaporates, or rather, fades out; boredom sinks in and everybody searches for the next "extreme" image or experience. Ethical and political implications are fading memories of the past century.[3]

ETHNIC INTERACTIONS IN A TWICE-CONQUERED LAND

Amid today's fringe subcultures, represented by postmodern faux Anasazi Indian casinos, chic Anglo-owned Santa Fe style restaurants, boutiques, and spas, garish Indian trading posts and highway stops, and other Southwest-themed tourist attractions located throughout many of the former old town plazas of Alburquerque, Santa Fe, and Taos, contemporary *Nuevomexicanos* are keenly aware of their second-class citizenship within this complex third-world area and of the racial hierarchy that continues to privilege white skin and the English language in the United States despite the prevalence of Spanish and other dominant languages spoken throughout the Southwest. Nuevo México's past geographic borders were very different in colonial times, stretching across the blazing hot Sonora desert or what is now the neighboring state of Arizona and including the San Luis Valley and Pueblo, Colorado, and places as far south as El Paso, Texas.

Nuevomexicana/os represent the oldest indigenous Spanish-Mexican, Indo-Hispano, or Chicano neocolonized populations in North America, settling the frontier of New Spain in 1598, mixing with the indigenous Native American populations, and being brought into the United States following the 1846 war, invasion, and ongoing occupation of northern México. Like neighboring *California* and *Tejas,* most of *Nuevo México* was soon relegated to third-world status, and its indigenous Hispanic and Native American residents became second-class citizens within the US imperial social hierarchy throughout the twentieth century. The intense emotional and psychological trauma experienced by the Spanish-speaking survivors following the US invasion, occupation, land theft, and political interference has led to the development of a distinct although often misunderstood Indo-Hispano[4] (*mestizo*) music, culture, language, cuisine, architecture, and spirituality that remain resilient against hypercapitalism and the symbolic extermination of the people through the simulation and mass-produced culture that is replacing in most of North American what was once called "vernacular" culture or regional flavor. One cultural trait that stands out among Nuevomexicanos is our retention of ancient Mexican forms of music making, which is another powerful form of resistance against the hegemonic Anglo-American mass culture, suburbanization, and fast food that drives the national hyper-capitalist economy today. This emphasis on language as civil rights is especially important, as Ofelia García explains: "No longer viewed as the language of original settlers, or even of the conquered and colonized who might be entitled to language and civil rights, but characterized as the language of foreign immigrants, often undocumented, and blamed for the poverty and the low level of education of US Latinos, Spanish is held in contempt in political and educational circles."[5]

Alicia Gaspar de Alba explains how "cultural schizophrenia is the presence of mutually contradictory or antagonistic beliefs, social forms, and material traits in any group whose racial, religious, or social components are a hybrid of two or more cultures (also known as *mestizaje*)."[6] However, providing a definition for the symptom hardly provides an adequate diagnosis of just how dire the current situation in New Mexico is today. Pulitzer-winning Latino journalist Héctor Tobar points out several important historical facts that inform my understanding of the ongoing interethnic meltdown in *Nuevo México*. Tobar's writing is based on his own journalistic observations while reporting on the contemporary situation in the northern village of Córdova, New Mexico. He writes:

> The church that looms over the plaza was built in 1832, sixteen years before the town officially became part of the United States after what's known in American history books as "the Mexican War." As in other conquered places, the locals in Córdova and the rest of New Mexico lost the right to be educated in their own language and in general became second-class citizens . . . In American New Mexico, a new social construction was born that would dominate the next 150 years of Latino history in all the territories that had once been part of the Republic of Mexico: the barrio.[7]

Tobar's grim portrait of Córdova accurately describes barrios as "insular places, born of de facto and de jure segregation." Tobar also explains how barrios produce proud community leaders and a sense of identity and defiance vis-à-vis the outside world but also a variety of self-destructive behaviors ranging from the usual urban gang banging to paint sniffing. However, Tobar concludes, "before heroin arrived in northern New Mexico in the late 1990s . . . self-destruction would have taken a decade or decades to complete, because alcohol would have been their weapon of choice."[8]

This neocolonial situation has led to the highly unusual rates of drug addiction, chronic alcoholism, and suicide among New Mexico's Hispanic and/or "Indo-Hispano" and Native American residents today. The resilient cultural heritage has helped *Nuevomexicana/os* cope with the crushing blows of capitalist democracy and the failing United States empire, as the homogenizing effects of what Guillermo Gomez-Peña calls "corporate multiculturalism" produce a seriously toxic popular culture and mass media which is now imagined and marketed as the "American dream." While regional identity survives alongside the commercial, popular "English-only" culture, the older Spanish-language organic folk culture has proven itself resilient in resisting Anglo gentrification. But the destruction of the language and culture illustrates the compromises necessary for survival within a political economy that is primarily based on working-class wage labor, a dysfunctional and inadequate public education system, and the darker side of modern cultural tourism industries. Within this hyper-capitalist context, it is important to define "popular" culture as an analytic concept that accurately explains New Mexico music culture and local performers.

Cultural critic Stuart Hall defines "popular" as "those forms and activities which have their roots in the social and material conditions of particular classes; which have been embodied in popular traditions and practices" and in what the editors of this volume call "de-colonial performatics." What is essential to Hall's definition are the relations which "define 'popular culture' in a continuing tension (relationship, influence, and antagonism) to the dominant culture,"[9] whereas seen as a category of performance analysis, popular culture performance here satisfies the additional requisite for human survival beyond those usually cited needs of "food, water, and shelter." This last requirement is the need "to be seen and heard."

According to Omayra Zaragoza Cruz and Raiford Guins, "this important notion of popular, in particular, has heralded heated debate because . . . it is not always necessarily clear what we're looking at when we look to popular culture. Its definitions are historically contingent and therefore frequently incongruous."[10] The popular also often draws from the connotations of "folk culture" especially in Latin America and throughout the US Latina/o borderlands. *Folklórico* or *música popular* are often evoked to conceptualize the cultural practices and forms—for instance, the folksongs of an oral tradition, a popular dance, and material culture circulating in pre-industrial and pre-urban (third-world US) societies and very much alive in New Mexico today. However, the popular is notoriously irreverent of the boundaries meant to distinguish mass-produced culture from more "organic" or ostensibly "rooted" culture, such as those musical performances of Sparx and Lorenzo Antonio. As more familiar Mexican and international Latino genres emerged throughout the southwest borderlands after the introduction of early radio in the 1940s, more ancient ways of music making have undergone an aesthetic transformation, developing into dynamic popular forms of musical resistance and differential consciousness[11] that mimic, simulate, and imitate the same popular forms heard and seen throughout the greater Spanish-speaking world and especially music from Greater México. The ideology[12] behind Indo-Hispano popular or folk or popular music—the arguments about what records, singing artists, or live performance means, what the music is for—has always been articulated more clearly by fans, journalists, and music critics than by performing musicians or businessmen. Through their musical recordings, videos, and live performances, New Mexico's celebrity Latin pop artists further illustrate Jacques Attali's radical definition of music as "prophecy," which he explains as:

> its styles and economic organization are ahead of the rest of society because it explores, much faster than material reality can, the entire range of possibilities in a given code. It makes audible the new world that will gradually become visible, that will impose itself and regulate the order of things; it is not only the image of things, but the transcending of the everyday, the herald of the future. For this reason musicians, even when officially recognized, are dangerous, disturbing, and subversive; for this reason it is impossible to separate their history from that of repression and surveillance.[13]

Here we hear the process of de-colonization as understood in a more affirmative sense as a fiesta of egalitarianism, as power released from the shackles of hierarchy in a tumult of aesthetic possibility including forms recently introduced, cannibalized, and/or imitated, appropriated, and fashioned into "our own." In this process of de-colonization, Nuevomexicana/os actively resist the consequences of political, territorial, aesthetic, intellectual, cultural, religious, and linguistic colonization.

REFIGURING LATINA/O POP *ESTRELLAS* AS NEW MEXICO ORGANIC INTELLECTUALS

Lorenzo Antonio is best recognized by most Latina/os in the United States and México as a talented and famous Latino "pop" music sensation with long-standing generational, musical, and familial ties (*querencia*) to *Nuevo México* as a greater homeland. His four physically attractive and equally talented sisters—Veronica, Rosamaria, Carolina, and Kristina—are known as Sparx, a popular Latina vocal ensemble. As *Nuevomexicana* Latin pop artists, the members of Sparx create familiar sounds and gendered images similar to those seen and heard throughout Latin America and Greater México through what performance theorists call "performativity."[14] By performing and promoting those internationally familiar Latino/a musical sounds, body movements, and popular fashion styles within and outside of the neocolonial Land of Enchantment, Lorenzo Antonio's and Sparx's performance on the international stage reverses the neocolonial order based on white racism while at the same time mediating imperial fatigue among Nuevomexicana/os today. According to Guillermo Gómez-Peña,

> Under the new corporate logic, it was fine for Blacks to advertise Nikes, and Latinos were definitely OK when we were shaking our butts to "La Vida Loca." . . . It was no coincidence that the last Latino "boom"—1998/2001—was a dim parade of forgettable pop singers, low-calorie entertainers who could barely speak at all (much less speak Spanish) . . . The most obvious feature of that finisecular Latinocracy was that, unlike prior booms, it did not include one intellectual—not one social critic, articulate spokesperson, or civil-rights activist.[15]

Returning to the barrio villages and urban Alburquerque and the social margins of Nuevo México: at the musical and linguistic levels, Lorenzo Antonio and Sparx are regarded as organic performing artists, singers, and celebrity entertainers and at the same time are recognized as culturally connected to local community through their leadership and social activism. As younger artists and entertainers, they have earned and maintained a large transnational fan base throughout the Southwest and abroad, bridging *Nuevo México* and the greater Spanish-speaking worlds. Likewise, the singers use their success and fame to assist less fortunate *Nuevomexicana/os* through the scholarships and financial assistance they offer from their earnings from live performances, concert tours, public appearances, and commercial recordings. Their musical performance may be seen as an important de-colonial intervention resisting capitalist ideology—a survival tactic developed by oppressed people of color as a consequence of over 150 years of Anglo prejudice and dominance. Simon Frith explains how "Stardom" describes a curious relationship between performer and audience, and in rock this relationship can take on a cultural life of its own. Frith describes how rock's youthful setting gives the fans' identification with the stars a material edge, and, partly for this reason, the most important rock event is the *live* performance, where performers and audiences genuinely react to each other in the way film stars and their fans in the Hollywood star system never did.[16]

LATIN POP PERFORMANCE: FROM *TECHNOCUMBIA* TO *MARIACHI, RANCHERA*, AND *CORRIDOS*

The first signs of stardom for Lorenzo Antonio appeared as he performed alongside his sisters, who later attained equally impressive celebrity status as popular musical entertainers throughout Latin America, México, Spain, and the US Latina/o borderlands. Like the late *Tejano* singer Selena, these artists rose to fame first in México and Latin America and are now attaining further stardom in the United States. As children, the younger-generation performers first competed in a 1982 Mexico City talent show called *Juguemos a Cantar.* In addition to singing, Lorenzo and his sisters Veronica and Rosamaria played violin while Carolina and Kristina played harmonica, winning first prize in the talent show. Lorenzo Antonio was twelve, and the sisters were a few years younger. With that performance, the singers earned themselves a strong fan base in México that continues today. Likewise, what is astounding is how the members of the family, like many Nuevomexicana/os, have maintained the alter-Native Mexicano language despite the linguistic terrorism and cultural war waged on Spanish-speaking citizens of the United States. In 1991, Sparx produced a new album and returned to the concert scene in a series of anti-drug performances aimed at Hispanic youth, and they continue sponsoring local events throughout New Mexico and around the world, earning money for the Sparx / Lorenzo Antonio Foundation. According to Ofelia García,

> Almost 13 percent of all US schoolchildren speak Spanish at home, and Spanish represents almost 70 percent of all languages other than English spoken by US students aged five to seventeen. In California and Texas, one in three children—and in Arizona and New Mexico, one in four children—speaks Spanish at home . . . Ignoring the Spanish that these children speak at home robs educators of the ability to build on the children's strengths and use an important pedagogical tool—the language spoken at home.[17]

What I find most remarkable is that the celebrity musicians have always found value in the Spanish language and the native New Mexican music culture, providing their fans with original musical material that at the same time is used as a tool of de-colonial performatics. The Sparx / Lorenzo Antonio Foundation's official mission[18] is "to provide and encourage higher education for New Mexico high school seniors, by helping to lessen the financial burden of going to college."[19] Sparx and Lorenzo Antonio's celebrity status has further enabled other downtrodden, marginal, and alter-Native singers to become organically grounded community leaders, political activists, and local performing entertainers. As influential performing artists and advocates for *la raza* within and outside of New Mexico, through their charity work and benefit concerts, they use their de-colonial performatics to bring attention to the failing local public school system, the replacement of the Mexicano language with an unfamiliar and racist English language and commercial culture, and the unusually high drug addiction and overdose rates among *Nuevomexicana/os* today.

Throughout his youth, Lorenzo Antonio developed his musical performance, sound, and image as a Latino pop singer and original songwriter, performing regularly on the Mexican and Latin American musical circuits and amassing several music television appearances and popular videos. Despite his attempts to remain out of the Spanish-language tabloid gossip columns, there have been rumors questioning Lorenzo Antonio's sexuality, mostly stemming from his close friendship and professional association with Mexican composer and popular singer Juan Gabriel. Despite the tabloid *chisme,* Lorenzo Antonio, like many attractive Latino male celebrities and stars, enjoys iconic status within various gay/lesbian/bisexual/transsexual communities who celebrate his music regardless of his sexual identities or tabloid gossip. Despite rumors regarding Mexican celebrity singer/songwriter Juan Gabriel,[20] Lorenzo Antonio remains a loyal friend of and enjoys a close *amistad* with "Juanga,"[21] whom he first met in 1989 while shopping at a Toys 'R' Us in Albuquerque. Juan Gabriel also lives in New Mexico, and a close friendship soon ensued, with Lorenzo Antonio recording two popular tribute albums to Juanga. According to Lorenzo Antonio's website, the up-tempo album *Mi Tributo a Juan Gabriel,* recorded in 1992 and released in 1993, spanned chart-topping hits such as "*Como, Cuando y Porque,*" a popular Juan Gabriel original composition, and "*Cuando Me Vaya de tu Lado.*" Lorenzo Antonio expresses his genuine affection and admiration for Juan Gabriel as follows: "Juan Gabriel is not only one of the most talented persons of the 20th and 21st centuries, he is also one of the most generous and nicest people I've ever met. I will always cherish his friendship."[22]

ONDA GRUPERA: SPARX

Throughout Lorenzo Antonio's musical career, his arrangements for and concerts with Sparx have built upon and defined the re-emergent female vocal genre of *onda grupera* (multipart vocal group) that has a long history in the US Latina borderlands. Lorenzo Antonio and Sparx reached another important collaborative zenith with their two albums of *corridos* re-introducing older heroic ballads like "*El Corrido de Gregorio Cortez,*" "*El Hijo Desobediente,*" and "Rosita Alvirez" to a more contemporary and younger audience throughout Greater México and Latin America and among US Latina/os and Chicana/os.

These recordings feature original and complex harmonic arrangements skillfully re-composed with dramatic poetic setting and feminine sounds, highlighting seldom-heard higher and perfectly blended female vocal virtuosity accompanied by *mariachi.* Many of the traditionally male solo heroic ballads that are popular throughout the US Latina borderlands are transformed in this creative process in yet another act of de-colonial performatics. Tejana critic Deborah Vargas's analytical concept *cruzando frontejas* marks the complications and contradictions of Chicana/o, Mexicana/o, and Tejana/o transnational movement into new Latino and Latin American music markets as well as *raza* performers like the late Selena's impact on the "place" of Tejano and Latina/o music.[23] Lorenzo Antonio and Sparx's recorded performance represents a bold and creative place where musical innovations are realized and gender, linguistic, class, and racialized borders cross and intersect with the usual south-to-north binary aesthetic axis and discursive terrain.

"TE AMO, TE AMO, TE AMO": CRUZANDO IDIOMAS Y FRONTERAS

Ethnomusicologist Manuel Peña reminds us that "while the cultural economy of late capitalism was transforming the post-Chicano generation into a fragmented, heterogeneous mass with a 'decentered' sense of ideological purpose,"[24] Sparx recorded two successful volumes of popular *corridos* with Lorenzo Antonio that were released in 1996 and 1998. Several eclectic Latin pop *cumbia* hits experimenting with steady mechanical beats and synthesized accompaniments complemented by abstract melody lines, smooth choreography, and sexy fashion statements prepared the performers for two challenging *mariachi* CDs, which further solidified the artists as bona fide pop artists in Central America and the greater Spanish-speaking regions of the US Latina/o borderlands. However, according to journalist Jeff Commings, "the 1994 album by the same name as the single "*Te Amo, Te Amo, Te Amo*" made Sparx household names and celebrity superstars south of the border."[25]

The 1994 hit recording was Sparx's first gold and platinum album, selling more than one million copies. "*Te Amo, Te Amo, Te Amo*" was written by Lorenzo Antonio,[26] and at least two other selections on this album also did well, including "*Zapatos Nuevos*" and "*Los Hijos de Pantaleon*"—an international *technocumbia* hit popularized throughout the 1990s and recorded by several groups in styles as diverse as *banda, Tejano,* and *electrónica.* Many of the notable female Chicana vocal duets from the Southwest borderlands include Margarita and Maria, Las Hermanas Padilla[27] who "performed on Spanish-language radio in Los Angeles in the mid-1930s singing an extensive repertory including *corridos*—then somewhat rare for women singers—and almost all the other popular song types of their day."[28] Likewise, another important duo was Juanita and Maria, who were known as Las Hermanas Mendoza[29] and were sisters of the legendary Tejana *cancionera de los pobres* Lydia Mendoza.[30] At times, the three Mendoza singers performed together at nightclubs and theaters, and they toured for a brief period. Las Hermanas Mendoza produced an extensive series of recordings, principally for Discos Azteca in Los Angeles and Discos Ideal in Alice, Texas. Another popular Tejana duo was Carmen and Laura Hernandez, who recorded with many important Tejano musicians, including accordionists Narcisso Martínez and Paulino Bernal and *orquesta* leader Beto Villa. Likewise, the 1960s East LA Chicana trio known as the Sisters included Rosella, Ersi, and Mary Arvizu, who, like Sparx, were also raised in a musical family. Their father was also a popular singer, and their mother was a familiar local singer and composer. Ersi Arvizu later became lead female singer for El Chicano.

LORENZO: NUEVO MÉXICO'S *HIJO DEL PUEBLO*

The summer of 2004 was another high point for Lorenzo Antonio and Sparx. Juan Gabriel invited them on his México tour, and they made special guest appearances in Aguascalientes, La Paz, Morelia, Monterrey, Mexicali, Tijuana, and Hermosillo. In 2009, Lorenzo Antonio released his own calendar. On his official website, he writes,

> I really enjoy writing songs and making records, but nothing compares with performing live. I love being on stage and it's always a great feeling when I see all my fans in the audience. I'm very lucky to be doing what I love and I hope to be doing it for many years to come.[31]

Based on linguistic realities and recent demographic transformations in California and Texas, I hear Chicano or Mexicano Spanish becoming the dominant language of the US Latina/o borderlands. As US society finds itself falling victim to the empty promises and high-carb diets eroding the quality of life across the nation, Nuevomexicana/os continue to question the fading American dreams of twenty-first-century capitalism. It seems clear that materialistic values, unsustainable individualism, and sedentary unhealthy lifestyles are having an adverse effect on the larger population and on the fragile environment. Throughout the late eighties,[32] Lorenzo Antonio's recording "*Doce Rosas*" was one of the top Latin pop songs of 1987, not only in México but also throughout Latin America. Lorenzo Antonio has toured México,

Ecuador, Colombia, Venezuela, Perú, the Dominican Republic, and the United States. "*Doce Rosas*" received several awards in different countries for record sales and has become Lorenzo's own personal "hymn." Although Lorenzo Antonio has enjoyed popularity throughout Latin America since the 1980s, today he is listed among the newest generation of best-selling Latin pop solo artists along with Luis Miguel, Shakira, Enrique Iglesias, Ricky Martin, Christina Aguilera, Thalía, Paulina Rubío, and others.

Of Lorenzo Antonio's numerous recorded solo albums and compact disc recordings, it is his three most recent solo volumes of *rancheras* (2008, 2007, and 2005) and the two earlier *corrido* albums recorded with Sparx that suggest a musical maturation shifting away from the earlier commercial "pop" toward more challenging timeless Mexican *canciones*[33] and classic epic ballads from the Greater *Mexicano* past. Lorenzo Antonio's recording *Canta Rancheras y Mas* represents the singer's attempt to adapt older musical styles and popular genres for new audiences while coming to terms with a rapidly transforming capitalist music industry and digital recording technology.[34] For ethnomusicologist Candida Jáquez, "aspiring Spanish-language popular singers in *mexicano* traditional musics are expected to have command over the vocal inflections, vibrato, and extreme timbre shifts associated with a good *ranchera* singing style. Indeed, in some circles the measure of a good singer of *mexicano* traditional musics is how well a singer can sing a *ranchera*. It becomes a litmus test against which all other abilities are measured."[35] Despite Lorenzo Antonio's commercial musical success, it is his interesting recording of "La Delgadina" that resounds with Nuevo México historically and responds directly to the environmental crisis and disaster at hand. According to Texas-Mexican folklorist and Chicano performance theorist Américo Paredes,

> "DELGADINA" is a Spanish *romance* about a cruel king who falls in love with his beautiful and virtuous daughter. Incest is a favorite subject for ballad singers, just as it has been for tragic dramatists and for novelists . . . If any Spanish-speaking group in any part of the world is given to the singing of old ballads, the chances are that "Delgadina" will be in their repertory. We could find no better example of the unity within diversity that characterizes the Spanish-speaking world. The Border "Delgadina" belongs to a general Mexican variant of the Spanish *romance*, one that is known throughout the Greater Mexican area. The text is somewhat Mexicanized: the king and his daughter go to church in Morelia, Michoacán.[36]

"La Delgadina" is included on Lorenzo Antonio and Sparx's 2003 *"Grandes éxitos" con mariachi.* Chicana historian and de-colonial theorist Emma Pérez explains that Delgadina is the "object of desire in a popular corrido that forecasts bleak consequences for women if they do not embrace patriarchy and femininity."[37] Pérez explains,

> The corrido, or ballad, of Delgadina is an evocative representation of the seduction scene in which the daughter thwarts her father's incestuous advances. The father's desire leads to tragedy for both father and daughter. The lesson, however, is for Delgadina, who had no choice but to guard her womanhood. Entering sexuality is her burden. Her sexual, enticing body tempted her father—she becomes the evil Eve, the temptress who caused her father's ruin. Delgadina, like any other young woman, was supposed to have hidden her sex. She is to blame for having a sexed, female body that a man will desire. Yet as a sexed woman, she enters a double bind. There is no way she can guard her sex enough from male seducers. By becoming a woman, she has already failed; despite the fact that she refused her father, opted for imprisonment, and finally dies, she is still blamed, however. It is left intact. The father is pitied and the daughter is jailed.[38]

According to critical theorist Maria Lugones, "colonialism did not impose precolonial, European gender arrangements on the colonized. It imposed a new gender system that created very different arrangements for colonized males and females than for white bourgeois colonizers. Thus, it introduced many genders and gender itself as a colonial concept and mode of organization of relations of production, property relations, of cosmologies, of ways of knowing."[39] Like Delgadina, *Nuevo México* has too often been blamed for our refusal to assimilate or Americanize into a lethal, toxic, and racist USA, and Nuevomexicana/os have been regarded as failures, resulting in the unusually high drug addiction, unfathomable incarceration and high school dropout rates, land and language loss, and high suicide rampant throughout the state. The following verse suggests an important metaphor for this contemporary analysis.

Papacito de mi vida	Father of my life
un favor te estoy pidiendo;	one favor I ask of you;
que me des un vaso de agua	that you give me one glass of water
que de sed me estoy muriendo.	because I am dying of thirst.

I believe the corrido serves as an important neocolonial metaphor raising important issues regarding contemporary water rights and environmental justice in the drought-stricken Southwest borderlands. Today, the mighty *Río Grande* watershed is listed among the top ten endangered rivers. Within the ballad, Delgadina does request water from her father and is granted her request; however, the water arrives too late. When it is finally delivered to the jail cell, Delgadina is found with her mouth open, having unfortunately died of thirst—or, as I regard it, of a dire neocolonial consequence of the American dream. Anthropologist Sylvia Rodríguez believes that the most important ecological, political, and economic conditions in New Mexico include limited water, urban growth, state (mostly federal) control of roughly half of the land, and tourism. Rodríguez explains,

> The water crisis in the North American desert borderlands is just one of many in the world. Scarcity and the preservation of clean freshwater supplies are global and transnational issues because borders affect water rights, access, and liability. Moreover, water has become an international commodity, and a limited one, for sale to those who can pay. The New Mexico water rights adjudication is a manifestation of the world-wide conflict over who owns what water, how it should be used, and whether it should be treated as a human right or a commodity. In this context and in similar situations, local moral economies struggle against the hegemonic zero-sum, winner-take-all ethic of global capitalism.[40]

The 1960s Chicano Movement emerged in resistance to the chronic racism, persistent violence, and social injustice prevalent within the United States. In New Mexico, the political issue was primarily land grant activism and water rights. Returning once again to our drive from the mountain villages east of Albuquerque as Lorenzo Antonio's cover of "Cruz de Madera" fades into a KANW public announcement, I ponder just how far these homegrown musicians have come. Having matured musically, some of the sisters are married and raising children, but they continue performing as a family. Following the success of *Canta Rancheras y Mas,* Lorenzo Antonio once again recorded another album, *Rancheras Volume 2,* released by Universal and Viva Records in April of 2007. In describing his original sound, Lorenzo Antonio explains,

> My sound on this album is a blend of some of my musical influences, which include my father, Tiny Morrie, Mariachi music, Regional Music, Rock, as well as Blues. And of course, I can't leave out my classical background. That's really the foundation of my guitar playing, and you can hear that classical influence throughout this album.[41]

In the same newspaper interview with Albuquerque journalist Jeff Commings, the reporter asked "whether or not Sparx has any intention of recording an English-language album [some of Lorenzo Antonio's albums feature bilingual songs]?" Sparx replied that "a crossover project is not likely. I don't think we need to do it," says Veronica. "We like the music that we sing."[42]

Lorenzo Antonio and Sparx's recent album "Fiesta" does include a few English-language covers of past female vocal groups like the Andrews Sisters' "Boogie Woogie Bugle Boy," "Baby I Love You," and "Sincerely" by the McGuire Sisters, but it also features the Latin Grammy Award–winning hit "*La Negra Tiene Tumba'o.*" I don't think this recording was intended as an official crossover. According to Ofelia García, "US policy has racialized US Latinos, specifically by assigning negative characteristics to their variety of Spanish and bilingualism. Even more important . . . education—even when Spanish is used in teaching—has been instrumental in that racialization, inasmuch as it perpetuates the stereotype that the language practices of Latinos reflect their supposed intellectual deficits and inferiority as a people and race."[43] In conclusion, Lorenzo Antonio and Sparx's artistic leadership, financial generosity, and political activism make up for those pseudo-intellectual deficits, providing a beacon of hope for Nuevomexicana/os in an otherwise tragic postmodern and uncertain globalizing world.

NOTES

1. Ofelia García, 2009, "Racializing the Language Practices of US Latinos: Impact on Their Education" in *How the United States Racializes Latinos: White Hegemony & Its Consequences,* edited by José A. Cobas, Jorge Duany, Joe R. Feagin, Paradigm Publishers, 111.

2. Guillermo Gómez-Peña, 2005, *Ethno-techno: Writings on Performance, Activism, and Pedagogy,* Routledge, 48.

3. Gómez-Peña, *Ethno-techno,* 51.

4. Land grant activist Reies Lopes Tijerina used and popularized the term "Indo-Hispano" with the *Alianza Federales de Pueblos Libres* during the 1960s land grant struggles in northern New Mexico. "Chicano" was also applied to the land grant struggle from the Greater Civil Rights Movement activists and political leaders.

5. García, "Racializing the Language Practices of US Latinos," 109.

6. Alicia Gaspar de Alba, 2003, "Rights of Passage: From Cultural Schizophrenia to Border Consciousness in Cheech Marin's *Born in East L.A.*" in *Velvet Barrios: Popular Culture and Chicana/o Sexualities,* Palgrave Macmillan, 199.

7. Hector Tobar, 2005, *Translation Nation: Defining a New American Identity in the Spanish-Speaking United States,* New York: Riverhead Books, 169.

8. Tobar, *Translation Nation,* 170.

9. Stuart Hall, 2005, "Notes on Deconstructing 'The Popular'" in *People's History and Socialist Theory,* edited by Raphael Samuel, London: Routledge, 1981.

10. Raiford Guins and Omayra Cruz, 2005, *Popular Culture: A Reader,* London: Sage Publications, 4.

11. What Chela Sandoval has called "differential consciousness" is an oppositional consciousness of self, citizenship, and nation that actively refutes and re-orders oppressive hierarchies of power and control. According to Sandoval, all social orders hierarchically organized into relations of domination and subordination create particular subject positions that, once self-consciously recognized by their inhabitants, can be transfigured into effective sites of resistance to an oppressive ordering of power relations (Chela Sandoval, 2000, *Methodology of the Opressed,* Minneapolis: University of Minnesota Press, 61).

12. See Simon Frith, 1981, *Sound Effects: Youth, Leisure, and the Politics of Rock 'n' Roll,* New York: Pantheon Books, 165.

13. Jacques Attali, 2006 [1985,1977], *Noise: The Political Economy of Music,* translated by Brian Massumi, *Theory and History of Literature,* Vol. 16, Minneapolis: University of Minnesota Press, 11.

14. For Ramón García, performativity describes this relation of being implicated in that which one opposes, this turning of power against itself to produce alternative modalities of power, to establish a kind of political contestation that is not a "pure" opposition, a "transcendence" of contemporary relations of power, but a difficult labor of forging a future from resources inevitably impure (Ramón García, 2006, "Against Rasquache: Chicano Camp and the Politics of Identity in Los Angeles" in the *Chicana/o Cultural Studies Reader,* edited by Angie Chabram-Dernersesian, New York: Routledge, 2006, 220).

15. Gómez-Peña, *Ethno-techno,* 49.

16. Simon Frith, 1981, *Sound Effects: Youth, Leisure, and the Politics of Rock 'n' Roll,* New York: Pantheon Books.

17. García, "Racializing the Language Practices of US Latinos," 106.

18. Established in 2001, the Sparx and Lorenzo Antonio scholarship has been awarded to various underprivileged, academically promising, and economically challenged Chicana/o, Mexicana/o, Hispana/o, and Native American youth who might not otherwise be able to afford higher education. They have awarded numerous scholarships to students attending the University of New Mexico, New Mexico State University, ITT Technical Institute, the Albuquerque public schools, and to Albuquerque ENLACE high school students.

19. http://www.slafoundation.org/english/our_mission.asp.

20. Juan Gabriel admittedly has four children and has stated in numerous newspaper reports and interviews that they are not adopted, revealing that he had them with "mi mejor amiga para toda la vida" (my best friend for all of my life). Juan Gabriel, as he was interrogated about his being gay, once replied to a journalist, "Lo que se ve no se pregunta m'ijo . . . Yo no tengo por qué decirle cosas que a usted, como a muchas otras personas, no les interesa, yo pienso que soy un artista . . . que he dado mucho con mis canciones" (What you see ought not be asked, son

. . . I don't have to answer to you, or other people, you are not interested, I believe that I am an artist. . . that has given much with my songs" (translation mine).

21. Music and literary analysis of certain selections from Juan Gabriel's many recordings and original romantic compositions has been published by literary critic Gustavo Geirola, who writes, "Claro está que tanto Monsiváis como Lumsden parten del supuesto de la homosexualidad del ídolo ("la personalidad obviamente gay—dice Lumsden—de Juan Gabriel" [1991: 77 nota]). Sea como fuera la intimidad de Alberto Aguilera, queda claro que Juan Gabriel no tiene intenciones del salir del clóset, porque toda la estrategia de su figura consiste otra vez en el doble juego paradojal propuesto por él y al que, propuesto por los otros, se somete: propuesto, porque la ambigüedad de su figura, de sus gestos y de su vestimenta, hacen perder consistencia a la fuerte oposición macho y hembra de la cultura mexicana; sometimiento, por cuanto Juan Gabriel no quiere hacer jugar la sexualidad en el peligroso cauce de una reivindicación (ni revolucionaria ni de otro tipo). Juan Gabriel es esa misma pulsíon discriminatoria ejercida por el poder y que ahora regresa desde los márgenes al seno de uno clase que tiene que redefinir sus estrategias y consagrar algo de lo marginado, entre otras concesiones necesarias después de Tlatelolco" (Gustavo Geirola, 1993, "Juan Gabriel: Cultura Popular y Sexo de Los Angeles" in *Latin American Music Review,* Vol. 14, No. 2 (Fall/Winter): 237).

22. http://www.lorenzoantonio.com.

23. Deborah Vargas, 2002, "*Cruzando Frontejas:* Remapping Selena's Tejano Music 'Crossover,'" in Norma Cantú and Nájera-Ramírez, *Chicana Traditions: Continuity and Change,* Urbana: The University of Illinois Press, 224–236.

24. Manuel Peña, 1999, *Música Tejana: The Cultural Economy of Artistic Transformation,* College Station: Texas A&M University Press, 189.

25. Jeff Commings, "Family of Flair: Latin Pop Sensations (and Siblings) Sparx and Lorenzo Antonio Balance Fame and a Love for Their Hometown," *Albuquerque Tribune Online.* (http://www.abqtrib.com), accessed June 2, 2007.

26. The music video for "*Te Amo, Te Amo, Te Amo*" depicts the four attractive girls driving in a top-down jeep, pulling into a gas station where the handsome, male, working-class attendant's attractive physique and face earn the curiosity of Kristina. The video is somewhat reminiscent of similar "puppy love" sentiments expressed in much Latino pop music from this era; however, this time, a feminist agency affirms a cultural sexuality with a new perspective on historical roots. The video also engages important gender issues based on class, playing on the middle-class girl / working-class boy dichotomy and a differential dynamics of power. The girl drives the jeep and has the money to pay for the gas, but the physically attractive attendant has her attention.

27. The duo was also regarded as the Mexican version of the Andrews Sisters and were the first popular vocal duo to sing in harmony on both sides of the border.

28. John Koegel, 2002, "Crossing Borders: Mexicana, Tejana, and Chicana Musicians in the United States and Mexico" in *From Tejano to Tango: Latin American Popular Music,* edited by Walter Aaron Clark, New York and London: Routledge, 105.

29. According to Koegel, the Mendozas ultimately became one of the most important female duets (without Lydia) and were known throughout the Southwest and México, rivaling for a time Las Hermanas Padilla (Koegel, "Crossing Borders," 114).

30. Yolanda Broyles-González, 2002, "Ranchera Music(s) and Lydia Mendoza: Performing Social Location and Relations" in *Chicana Traditions: Change and Continuity,* edited by Olga Najera-Ramirez and Norma Cantú, Chicago: University of Illinois Press.

31. http://www.lorenzoantonio.com.

32. From 1988 and 1990, Lorenzo Antonio studied music theory and ear training, astronomy, psychology, and philosophy, immersing himself in conservatory music studies.

33. According to Lorenzo Antonio's website, this period was when he decided to record *ranchera* music. His father, Tiny Morrie, was well known for singing and performing this style of music, and since his father had always been a major musical influence on Lorenzo, his transition to this style seemed very natural. Lorenzo would soon find out that this would be easier said than done. As Lorenzo was in the studio recording, there was something that was missing from the songs; the magic just wasn't happening. He was on the verge of giving up and trying something else when he picked up his guitar. Although at the time no one realized it, this proved to be a turning point, not only for the recording, but also for Lorenzo's career. http://www.lorenzoantonio.com.

34. In 2002, Lorenzo Antonio restarted his own record company as a reaction against the drastically changing record business.

35. F. Cándida Jáquez, 2002, "La Cantante in Verse, Song, and Performance" in *Chicana Traditions: Change and Continuity,* edited by Olga Najera-Ramirez and Norma Cantú, Chicago: University of Illinois Press, 172.

36. Américo Paredes, 1995 [1976], *A Texas-Mexican Cancionero: Folksongs of the Lower Border,* Austin: University of Texas Press, 7.

37. Emma Pérez, 1999, *The Decolonial Imaginary: Writing Chicanas into History,* Bloomington: Indiana University Press, 101.

38. Pérez, *The Decolonial Imaginary,* 115.

39. Maria Lugones, 2007, "Heterosexualism and the Modern Colonial Gender System" in *Intimate Interdependencies: Theorizing Collectivism Anew* in *Hypatia,* Vol. 22, No. 1: 186.

40. Sylvia Rodriguez, 2006, *Acequia: Water Sharing, Sanctity, and Place,* Santa Fe, NM: A School for Advanced Research Resident Scholar Book, 128.

41. http://www.lorenzoantonio.com.

42. Commings, "Family of Flair."

43. García, "Racializing the Language Practices of US Latinos," 111.

REFERENCES

Antonio, Lorenzo. http://www.lorenzoantonio.com/

Anzaldúa, Gloria. 1987. *Borderlands / La Frontera: The New Mestiza.* San Francisco, CA: Aunt Lute.

Attali, Jacques. 2006 [1985, 1977]. *Noise: The Political Economy of Music.* Translated by Brian Massumi. *Theory and History of Literature,* Vol. 16. Minneapolis: University of Minnesota Press.

Baudrillard, Jean, and Sheila Faria Glaser. 2010 [1994]. *Simulacra and Simulation.* Translated by Sheila Faria Glaser. Ann Arbor: University of Michigan Press.

Broyles-González, Yolanda. 2002. "Ranchera Music(s) and Lydia Mendoza: Performing Social Location and Relations." In *Chicana Traditions: Change and Continuity.* Edited by Olga Najera-Ramirez and Norma Cantú. Chicago: University of Illinois Press.

Butler, Judith. 1993. "Imitation and Gender Insubordination." In *The Lesbian and Gay Studies Reader.* New York: Routledge.

Commings, Jeff. "Family of Flair: Latin Pop Sensations (and Siblings) Sparx and Lorenzo Antonio Balance Fame and a Love for Their Hometown." In *Albuquerque Tribune Online,* http://www.abqtrib.com/, accessed June 2, 2007.

Frith, Simon. 1981. *Sound Effects: Youth, Leisure, and the Politics of Rock 'n' Roll.* New York: Pantheon Books.

García, Ofelia. 2009. "Racializing the Language Practices of US Latinos: Impact on Their Education." In *How the United States Racializes Latinos: White Hegemony & Its Consequences.* Edited by José A. Cobas, Jorge Duany, and Joe R. Feagin. Paradigm Publishers.

García, Peter J. 2010. *Decolonizing Enchantment: Echoes of Nuevo Mexico Popular Musics.* Albuquerque: University of New Mexico Press.

García, Ramón. 2006. "Against Rasquache: Chicano Camp and the Politics of Identity in Los Angeles." In *The Chicana/o Cultural Studies Reader.* Edited by Angie Chabram-Dernersesian. New York: Routledge.

Gaspar de Alba, Alicia. 2003. "Introduction, or Welcome to the Closet of Barrio Popular Culture." In *Velvet Barrios: Popular Culture and Chicana/o Sexualities.* Palgrave Macmillan, xviiii–xxviii.

———. "Rights of Passage: From Cultural Schizophrenia to Border Consciousness in Cheech Marin's Born in East L.A." In *Velvet Barrios: Popular Culture and Chicana/o Sexualities.* Palgrave Macmillan.

Geirola, Gustavo. 1993. "Juan Gabriel: Cultura Popular y Sexo de Los Angeles." In *Latin American Music Review,* Vol. 14, No. 2 (Fall/Winter): 232–237.

Guins, Raiford, and Omayra Cruz. 2005. *Popular Culture: A Reader.* London: Sage Publications.

Gómez-Peña, Guillermo. 2005. *Ethno-techno: Writings on Performance, Activism, and Pedagogy.* London: Routledge.

Hall, Stuart. 2005. "Notes on Deconstructing 'The Popular.'" In *People's History and Socialist Theory.* Edited by Raphael Samuel. London: Routledge.

Jáquez, Cándida F. 2002. "La Cantante in Verse, Song, and Performance." In *Chicana Traditions: Change and Continuity.* Edited by Olga Najera-Ramirez and Norma Cantú. Chicago: University of Illinois Press.

Koegel, John. 2002. "Crossing Borders: Mexicana, Tejana, and Chicana Musicians in the United States and Mexico." In *From Tejano to Tango: Latin American Popular Music.* Edited by Walter Aaron Clark. New York and London: Routledge.

Lugones, Maria. 2007. "Heterosexualism and the Modern Colonial Gender System." In *Intimate Interdependencies: Theorizing Collectivism Anew. Hypatia,* Vol. 22, No. 1: 186–209.

Paredes, Américo. 1995 [1976]. *A Texas-Mexican Cancionero: Folksongs of the Lower Border.* Austin: University of Texas Press, 1995.

Peña, Manuel. 1985. *The Texas-Mexican Conjunto: History of a Working Class Music.* Austin: University of Texas Press.

———. 1999. *Musica Tejana: The Cultural Economy of Artistic Transformation.* College Station: Texas A&M University Press.

Pérez, Emma. 1999. *The Decolonial Imaginary: Writing Chicanas into History.* Bloomington: Indiana University Press.

Rodriguez, Sylvia. 2006. *Acequia: Water Sharing, Sanctity, and Place.* Santa Fe, NM: A School for Advanced Research Resident Scholar Book.

Sandoval, Chela. 2000. *Methodology of the Oppressed.* Minneapolis: University of Minnesota Press.

Tobar, Hector. 2005. *Translation Nation: Defining a New American Identity in the Spanish-Speaking United States.* New York: Riverhead Books.

Vargas, Deborah. 2002. "*Cruzando Frontejas:* Remapping Selena's Tejano Music 'Crossover.'" In *Chicana Traditions: Continuity and Change.* Edited by Norma E. Cantú and Olga Nájera-Ramírez. Urbana: The University of Illinois Press, 224–236.

TWELVE

Sonic Geographies and Anti-Border Musics: "We Didn't Cross the Border, the Borders Crossed Us"

ROBERTO D. HERNÁNDEZ

> What must be done is to restore this dream to its proper time . . . and to its proper place . . .
>
> FRANTZ FANON (1967)

Strong whirling sounds grow louder and louder. The surrounding brush sways violently and is nearly uprooted. A helicopter hovering overhead nears, and you hear the desperate words, "Levántate compadre / ¿Que pasa? / ¿Oyes ese zumbido? / Si, compadre . . . es el helicóptero . . . / Métete debajo de esos matorrales . . . de volada, apúrate. / Híjole, se me hace que ya me agarraron / Eso es lo de menos compadre, se me hace que ya nos llevo, la que nos trajo compadre."

(Get up compadre / What's happening? / Do you hear that noise? / Yes, compadre . . . it's the helicopter . . . / Get under those bushes . . . quickly, hurry up. / Oh shit, I think they got me . . . / that is the least of it, compadre . . . I think the one that's taking us . . . is the one that brought us here, compadre.)[1]

The above exchange opens Tijuana NO's 1998 hit song "La Migra," whose land and soundscape bears an eerie resemblance to the terrain near my childhood home, where corrugated steel extends into the Pacific Ocean, creating a rhythmic rumbling sound as wave after wave crashes up against the U-S///México border[2] wall in the area once known as Friendship Park.[3]

Elsewhere, the swooshing sounds of strong currents gushing through trenches and valleys of the Río Grande basin, increasing in strength as they empty into the Gulf of México. In early June of 2000, to the fleeting sound of "¡agarra la cuerda!" ("grab the rope!") the rapid waters swallow two migrants attempting to cross the border near Brownsville, Texas. One could hear a drowning victim's last gulp of air and the accompanying screams and gasps of worried onlookers attempting rescue.[4] Such are the sonic geographies etched on landscapes of the U-S///México border through long histories of state-sanctioned and extralegal violence. In this essay, we will travel across stories made audible by the materiality of the U-S///México border to understand the contested nature not only of the region itself but also of various narratives that have sought to make sense of the Borderlands. In doing so, we will better understand the implications and stakes of the salient debates around the spatial and temporal frameworks used in the study of the U-S///México border and border music. Specifically, through a close reading of three songs—Tijuana NO's "Stolen at Gunpoint" featuring Kid Frost (1998), Los Tigres del Norte's "Somos Mas Americanos" (2001), and Aztlán Underground's "Decolonize" (1998)—I will argue that a spatiotemporal frame distinct from the dominant focus on 1848 is crucial for Chicana/o Studies.

If we are to fully appreciate the soundscapes outlined above, we must consider how border theory has been approached given the geopolitics of knowledge, or where one is "thinking from" in relationship to power. In *Borderlands / La Frontera,* Gloria Anzaldúa (1987) characterized the border region as an open wound, "una herida abierta where the Third World grates against the first and bleeds. And before a scab forms it hemorrhages again, the lifeblood of two worlds merging to form a third country—a border culture" (3). Forged in blood, Anzaldúa's border is grounded in the historical and material realities of the two-thousand-mile geopolitical divide, but it extends to include many borders—racial, sexual, linguistic, psychological, among others—that define and divide places and populations that at once form "a vague and undetermined place created by the emotional residue of an unnatural boundary" (ibid). Thinking, feeling, and speaking from "this thin edge of barbwire" she calls home, Anzaldúa points to the Borderlands' many inhabitants as those whom borders fail to easily define: the squinted-eyed, the perverse, the queer, the mulatto, the mongrel, the mestiza, etc. Following

Anzaldúa, a broad array of scholars have deployed the trope and metaphor of "the border" in the service of highlighting multiple crossings, hybridities, and transgressions in their respective objects of study and disciplines.[5] Often missing from such scholars' work, however, are the material histories and legacies of violence constitutive of Anzaldúa's articulation of the border/lands, itself a critique of modernity's juridical partitioning of the globe into geopolitical units (nation-states) reflected in the "staking [of] fence rods in [her] flesh" as a way of visualizing both the territorial and embodied experience of colonization. How, then, does mapping the geographies of theory, of sound, of the planet itself in terms that recognize the effects of colonization enable us to see, hear, become differently?

THE BORDERLANDS ACADEMIC COMPLEX AND CULTURAL PRODUCTION

Although the metaphor of the border has generated several insightful analyses, some applications of it instead obfuscate the workings of power and violence formative in the work of Anzaldúa. An example of the often-problematic uses I refer to as the *Borderlands academic complex* can be found when Josh Kun writes of "the aural border" as one of mixing, hybridity, and fluidity of languages, genres, and sounds.[6] By Borderlands academic complex, I mean politically safe and institutionally supported adaptations of Anzaldúa's border that, even if inadvertently, conceal power. Institutional support is received through acclaim and circulation, a hegemonic counterinsurgency strategy whose function is to dislodge its counterpart, an emerging discourse on violence and the militarization of the border that began gaining currency in the mid-1990s.[7] To be clear, my argument is not reducible to a humanities / social science divide. José David Saldívar's "transfrontera contact zone," for example, draws on Mary Louise Pratt to make colonization visible and is thus cultural studies work in the tradition of Anzaldúa.

Examining *Pocha Nostra Productions*, for Kun "the border is mobile and fluctuating, no longer bound to one specific geographic configuration; it belongs to a continental map of communities in motion and cultures in contact" (15). The "musical and technological mergers" embodied in the performances of Guillermo Gomez-Peña, and the "hybridized and recycled" sounds of Rock en Español at the heart of his work, stand in contradistinction to the sonic geographies along the U-S/// México border in response to state-sanctioned violence and policing of movements of people across man-made geopolitical boundaries. Void in much of the work of the "Borderlands academic complex" and its many practitioners are the embodied understandings and intersections of violence and colonization central to Anzaldúa's theorizations.

Among border music, corridos have long narrated or made the border audible to listeners, and they have received much attention from scholars on both sides of the U-S///México border.[8] Some distinguish between Mexican and Chicano corridos; others uphold continuity between the two. Here, I am concerned with how sonic geographies written *about, from,* and *on* both sides of la frontera are reflected in other musical genres. While some have deemed corridos critical counterhegemonic narratives,[9] Yolanda Broyles-Gonzalez critiques the broad attention given to them and the privileging of the lyrical text as historical fact at the expense of the study of other genres and the consideration of music as holistic experience and living social practice.[10] Others note that corridos are predominantly male-oriented and heterosexualist (to borrow from Maria Lugones) narratives that often reproduce impingements upon Mexicana/Chicana subjects.[11] My study of music across genres and as contextual experience concurs with their assessments and further finds that masculinist cultural productions often mirror Mexicano/ Chicano political and scholarly emphasis on a presupposed universal subject, assumed to be male, able to enter into "contract among equals" (other males); this emphasis is reflected in the scholarly focus on 1848 and The Treaty of Guadalupe Hidalgo as constituting the birth of the Chicano as historical subject. Foregrounding 1848 as a moment of origin stands in contrast to embodied understandings of colonization etched on the female body, as noted by Anzaldúa and other Chicana feminist scholars. Kun only briefly considers corridos, but to his credit, this might be to expand the scope of border music. Nonetheless, his frame of Rock en Español as "transborder performance" reveals his view of "the border" vis-à-vis the Borderlands academic complex.

Josh Kun's widely read article "The Aural Border" (2000) tracks the hybrid sounds of Rock en Español and the audio bites accompanying the performances of Guillermo Gomez-Peña and *La Pocha Nostra* collective to identify a future in which the border is erased through mixing of peoples, cultures, and sounds. Kun argues, "in terms of musical geography and sonic migration, the 'borderless future' that Gómez-Peña performs and theorizes has already been realized by the music of rock en español itself, which has been a key point of cultural contact—a sort of musical hyperspace—between Latino/a communities on both sides of the border" (21). While Rock en Español and other musical forms such as Control Machete or Maldita Vecindad are indeed "transnational," I trace a different genealogy made audible not by *mobility* across borders or hybridity at borders as posited by the Borderlands academic complex but by their rooted-ness and insistence on *another cartography and calendar of knowledge* altogether.[12] By this, I ask, how do anti-border musics reconceptualize the inherited spatiotemporal frames of the modern/colonial nation-state through a focus on embodied experience? What does a different cartography and calendar of knowledge sound and look like?

As noted by Broyles-Gonzalez, most scholars focus on one or another of the musical genres that collectively constitute Chicana/o cultural production; other transnational sounds that have shaped Mexicana/o and Chicana/o experiences receive less attention than corridos (197).[13] I cross genres to analyze symbolic resonances of sonic geographies across musical divides. As such, the 1990s are central to my understanding of shifts in Chicana/o cultural production; during this period, a burgeoning recession gave rise to a wave of anti-immigrant sentiment that corresponded with the three songs that form the subject of this essay. The U-S///México border and its militarization—both processes constituted in violence—are the sociopolitical and historical context marking the Borderlands as a contested terrain and site of oppositional cultural production as knowledge production.[14] California's Proposition 187 in particular is often held as the prime catalyst for a renewed wave of Chicana/o cultural production. Instead, I argue that a distinct spatial-temporal frame foregrounding 1992 and the protests of quincentennial celebrations of Columbus's voyage provide a crucial lens for understanding cultural production in the Borderlands.

According to feminist theorist Norma Alarcón, "the juridical text is generated by the ruling elite, who have access to the state apparatus through which the political economy is shaped and jurisprudence is engendered, whereas representations in the cultural text may include representations generated by herself [raced/sexed woman]" (2003, 357). In other words, cultural texts are openings for explaining how we come to experience and know our social world, thus providing alternative epistemic counterdiscourses that simultaneously articulate and disrupt raced/gendered violence constitutive of Anzaldúa's frontera. The centrality Chicano male scholars give to 1848 (or even 1994), in this regard, reproduces logics complicit with "the juridical text" and colonization as lived through the raced/sexed body.

In this essay, I am interested in how the border is figured in sonic geographies of various "transnational" groups that cater to Mexican and Chicana/o audiences alike. My analysis of the above songs points to the limits and implications of the Borderlands academic complex. It delineates what I call an anti-border politic and the possibility of cultural texts produced by "males" to articulate a feminist sensibility and analysis in line with Lugones's "decolonial feminism" that recognizes "male" feminist positionings through her critique of a rigid male/female binary in the colonial/modern gender system.[15] I focus on three tracks that not only "cross" the border or make it audible but also take a firm political and intellectual stand against both the U-S///México border and the modern/colonial juridical concept of nation-states more broadly. The critique of the European modern/colonial interstate system, what I call an anti-border politic, stands in opposition to a focus on 1848 and the relocating of said border to its previous location, a view prevalent in Chicano Studies that maintains the nation-state and its violence intact.

CHICANO STUDIES AND THE SONIC GEOGRAPHIES OF THE U-S///MÉXICO BORDER

Héctor Calderón, focusing on Maldita Vecindad, notes, "Chicana and Chicano studies as practiced in the United States has become, especially in literary scholarship, almost exclusively an English-language study of the US Southwest" (97).[16] For Calderón, "US scholars engaged in 'border studies' more often than not stop at the border. The same is true of Mexican scholars engaged in the Mexican version of border studies." For many on both sides, "a clear political and disciplinary borderline divides the greater Mexican cultural diaspora that has existed in North America since the sixteenth century" (ibid). Calderón provides an expansive genealogy of cross-border music, noting that Maldita Vecindad was influenced by "the music of Pérez Prado, Tin Tan, Lalo Guerrero, and Don Tosti fused . . . with rock, punk, ska, Algerian, and Moroccan rhythms" resulting in "un funky mambo, o la cumbia punk o el chacha reggae" (114). His genealogy charts a distinct cartography and calendar than a crossing of the post-1848 U-S///México border in much of Chicano Studies. However, his reference to a "greater Mexican cultural diaspora . . . since the sixteenth century" reinscribes a national (and colonial) narrative with an expanded temporal frame.

Discussing corridos primarily written and sung in Spanish, José David Saldívar says of Los Tigres del Norte, "[their] border music is simultaneously national and transnational in that it affects everyday life in the local (Silicon Valley) region and thematizes the limits of the national perspective in American Studies" (1997, 3). Los Tigres, a Grammy award–winning Norteño band from Sinaloa, now based in San Jose, California, and popularly known as defenders of immigrants, debuted their hit song "El Corrido" (1989) as a tribute to the genre that made them famous. The opening verses illustrate characteristics and qualities of the corrido as a vehicle for social and political protest while making references to the Río Grande that forms part of the border proper and is often hailed as the birthplace of the musical form.

Como la corriente	Like the current
de un río crecido	of a grown river
que baja en torrente	that flows in torrent
impetuoso y bravío.	impetuous and fierce.
Voz de nuestra gente	Voice of our people
un grito reprimido	a repressed scream
un canto valiente	a valiant song
eso es el corrido	that is the corrido

For Los Tigres, the corrido is a valiant song that carries with it the story of a people. Here, it is useful to recall the essay's opening vignettes: the helicopter's whirling blades and the rushing river, each a sonic geography that tells us of many lives lost in its currents, under its spotlights. In other words, both speak of the subjugated knowledges of border crossings and other tribulations.

It is from this description of the corrido and its influence mirrored in distinct border music genres that I consider the three songs' epistemic potential for critiquing and countering hegemonic discourses and colonial realities by mapping and chronicling a different cartography and calendar of knowledge and an inherently anti-border politics. The songs in this study voice their lyrics in Spanish, English, Spanglish, and a few indigenous languages. As such, rather than a "translation" of the lyrical texts, I show "an other thinking/logic" that underpins border music speaking to the violence of la frontera and, in turn, navigates the texts across musical, geopolitical, and disciplinary borders alike. These songs stand as examples of anti-border musics with critical approaches to violence that contest the logics of nation-state borders altogether.

BORDER AND ANTI-BORDER MUSICS

Let us now turn to the cultural production of the three distinct performers, across musical styles, located in different urban spaces, and each with distinct experiences with relation to the U-S///México Border, who nonetheless speak to similar concerns. Although we are accustomed to calling corridos—and increasingly Rock en Español—border music, I am concerned that through such designation we run the risk of reinscribing musics into a national narrative premised upon borders many of the songs are eager to abandon. To illustrate my point, it is useful to consider Linda Bosniak's discussion of the conundrum in which immigrant rights activists find themselves:

> "Progressives" acquiescence to national border enforcement works at cross-purposes with their commitment to defending the interests of the undocumented. For to the extent they retain the attachment, or acquiescence, to borders, they ensure that the immigrants will continue to be marginalized; but conversely, to the extent they effectively attack the marginalization the immigrants suffer, they necessarily must challenge the enforcement of borders as well. The two commitments (against marginalization of persons and for borders around the community) are mutually incompatible (593).[17]

In other words, the naming of "*immigrant* advocacy" as such, limits political discourse into a framework consisting of competing national bodies from which migrants cannot be divorced, for they are bound to the body politic of one modern nation state or another (sending or receiving country). The border is thus normalized in the very act of taking a stand in the favor of those on whom it impinges. In a similar vein, Bosniak points out much transnational activism has pursued justice *within* individual states whose very legitimacy is reinforced in the act of challenging the excesses of global capital. In this context, we can argue that in crossing musical borders, the border is itself naturalized. Bosniak thus clarifies my definition of Los Tigres del Norte, Tijuana NO with Frost, and Aztlán Underground's songs as anti-border music given their aim of shifting the cartography and calendar of knowledge about the U-S///México border.

So why focus on these particular groups? Why *walk* and *think* through sonic geographies carved out by the anti-border songs "Stolen at Gunpoint" by Tijuana NO with Frost, Los Tigres del Norte's "Somos Mas Americanos," and Aztlán Underground's "Decolonize"? How do their lyrics constitute a shift in knowledge of the U-S///México border? These examples—the three group, each drawing from distinct musical traditions and locations on both sides of the border—share in their lyrics the line, "We didn't Cross the Borders, the Borders Crossed Us." This shared lyrical phrase forces us to think about the nature of the border beyond physical, discursive, and/or musical crossings of the U-S///México national boundary and to consider the role of borders in structuring and compartmentalizing the globe along presumably stable nation-state lines.[18]

What does it mean when three groups speak to the same problem from the significantly different traditions of Ska/Punk, Rap/Hip-Hop, and Norteñas/Corridos? From San Jose via Sinaloa, Los Angeles via Manifest Destiny, and Tijuana via Mexico City? How do the conceptual similarities point to fundamental concerns of Chicana/o and Mexicana/o cultural production and the ever-present, seemingly timeless, yet post-1848 U-S///México border? Although each of the three genres has attendant linguistic and regional audiences, my analysis points to shared concerns across different sets of cultural formations. What are the politics that underlie the distinct yet shared sonic geographies of "Stolen at Gunpoint," "Somos Mas Americanos," and "Decolonize"? What are the implications of the connections among the musical ofrendas and the collective sensibilities I argue they point to? What is the future of Chicana/o cultural production, and what future does Chicana/o cultural production imagine into being?

To outline briefly, I ground my reading of these sonic texts in the material conditions that have popularized the shared line. By this, I mean the slogan's popular usage beyond Chicana/o communities. To trace the phrase's popular history some have pointed to the recent immigrant marches. I consider this and other scholarly and popular explanations of the slogan's origins. I then analyze the lyrics themselves and conclude by elucidating what I argue are the politics, poetics, and implications of the shared sonic geographies, which point to a collective memory with a long historical, indigenous, feminist, and anti-border sensibility that forces us to think beyond the U-S///México border and Chicana/o Studies as currently conceptualized.

SO, WHEN DID WE *NOT* CROSS THE BORDER?

As a political slogan, many in print and electronic media and academe alike highlight the recent immigrant rights marches as the moment when "We didn't cross the borders, the borders crossed us" gained broad currency. Many seasoned observers—including Ruben Martinez in his article "Prop 187: Birth of a Movement?"—point to 1994 mobilizations against California's Proposition 187 as the moment when the saying emerged as a widely circulating narrative to disrupt criminalization and illegalization of a Mexicana/o (and Latina/o) presence in the United States. In a related vein, others have suggested a direct lineage to Chicano Movement politics of the 1960s and 1970s and the slogan "somos un pueblo sin fronteras" of the Chicano organization CASA (Centro de Acción Social Autónoma), which published a newspaper *Sin Fronteras.* In Chicago, for example, one of the organizational bases for recent immigrant rights marches was Centro Sin Fronteras, which has a distinct yet shared history with CASA in California.[19]

Vicki Ruiz and Virginia Sanchez Korrol take us further and point to turn-of-the-century women writers (Leonor Villegas de Magnon, Sara Estela Ramirez, and sisters Andrea and Teresa Villareal) as the first to express the sentiment after being separated from their families after 1848.[20] Whether we have in mind 2006 or 1994, the 1960s and 1970s, or the late 1800s, one thing is clear: the reference point is the changing physical location of one geopolitical border, the pre-1848 U-S///México border, from one place to another, and the historical moment resulting in the "transfer of land" from a presupposed and unquestioned nation-state to a second vis-à-vis the Treaty of Guadalupe Hidalgo. In other words, most place its origin as hinging on (not) being crossed by one political-juridical border (in singular form) in 1848 in particular. While this view is reflected to varying degrees in the three songs, I contend we also see different sonic geographies mapped aurally in said tracks.

In *Perspectives on Las Américas* (2003), an edited collection bridging a divide between Latina/o Studies and Latin American Studies, the editors' co-written introduction suggests not only 1848 as a reference point but the notion of "We didn't cross the borders, the borders crossed us" as "paradigmatic in Chicana/o Studies." Indeed, most Chicana/o Studies scholarship has been constructed in a way that privileges 1848 as a starting point to Chicano history, with the CASA slogan of "Sin Fronteras" and the related "We didn't cross the border, the border crossed us" (in singular form) figuring prominently or implicitly in their accounts.[21] In contrast, its broadened equivalent and the attendant politics of "We didn't cross the borders, the borders crossed us" (in plural form) has long been present in Chicana feminist historiography, including Anzaldúa's *Borderlands*, with many arguing for a framework whereby colonization as an embodied socio-historical process is traced back to its proper place and its proper time: the initial encounter of westward-bound sailors with this hemisphere in 1492, and the consequent partitioning of the globe along nation-state lines.

Stolen at Gun Point

Tijuana NO is a ska, rock/punk Mexican band from Tijuana characterized by the piercing social critique of its lyrics, which openly express support for indigenous peoples. The band members often reference ongoing international conflicts and issues of race, colonialism, apartheid, and immigration. Frost, whom they partner with in "Stolen at Gunpoint," is a pioneer of Chicano rap made famous by his hit single "La Raza" (1990).[22] In "Stolen at Gunpoint," the collaborators begin with a direct reference to 1848, when the vocalist awakes "feeling suddenly in [his] throat un veneno" (a venom) upon "dreaming about Lopez de Santana," México's multi-term president in the mid and late 1800s, and realizing "this mother-fucker gave the gueros our terreno" (the light-skinned our territories). Indicating "we wouldn't mind to share it with Los Gabachos," Tijuana NO's lyricist scorns Santana's handing over of the Southwest with a stroke of a pen, a moment Mexicans credit for ending the US-México War. "Asking myself where is Pancho Villa?" the singer alludes to "a full scale invasion" and a fight with "the Ku Klux Klan y el pinche Gobierno." The first series of verses ends with a reminder in resoundingly deep voice, "Nosotros llegamos primero" (We got here first!), before a chorus and shift to Frost.

Whereas the chorus sounds off the various states that changed hands in 1848—"California, Stolen at Gunpoint! Arizona, Stolen at Gunpoint!"—Frost includes other lines, "El Alamo, Stolen at Gunpoint! Aztlán, Stolen at Gunpoint!" Here, El Alamo, a rallying cry for US nationalism, functions to dislodge the now memorialized historical museum from the American imaginary. Notably, in "The Aural Border," Kun cites Tijuana NO's "duet with LA Chicano rapper Frost on 'Stolen at Gunpoint,' [as] an urgent demand for the mexicano reconquest of what became the US southwest" (19). Where Kun fails, apart from the problematic invocation of an imagined "mexicano reconquest," is that the chorus continues, "Puerto Rico, Stolen at Gunpoint! America, Stolen at Gunpoint!" to the fading sound of "We're gonna get it back . . . We gonna get it back." Does this refer to the Southwest or to the unmapping of hemispheric-wide borders?

The re-inscription of an 1848 frame positing a Chicano de-colonial imaginary as grounded in a "reconquest" of the Southwest obfuscates a different cartography and calendar of resistance. Rather than boxing the anti-border anthem into a constricting lens suggestive of 1960s nation-statisms, such as those of CASA, the inclusion of Puerto Rico (occupied in 1898) points to a broader anti-imperialist impulse. The line "America, Stolen at Gunpoint!" articulates the stakes for Tijuana NO and Frost as not simply a matter of return to an earlier geopolitical arrangement (a pre-1848 border); rather, it appeals to an un-mapping of nation-state juridical boundaries altogether. In other words, they point to colonization and the imposition of borders, rooted not in 1848 but 1492, more broadly. While Frost soon returns the listener to 1994 California with a challenge to then governor Pete Wilson, he speaks of the border in plural form, "You say we crossed the border, shit, the borders crossed us!" Frost's sonic geography elucidates the scale jumping from Aztlán to Puerto Rico to America, California, and back again, emphasizing various borders that have crossed many peoples in the Américas. So what we see is a longer historical sensibility, expressing concerns with colonization of the Américas pre-1848 and for how indigenous peoples have been crossed by multiple nation-state borders.[23]

Somos Mas Americanos

Los Tigres del Norte is often regarded as the "voice of the immigrant." Many of their songs hold immigrants in high esteem and afford them with dignity as they sing terrifying tales of border crossing, Border Patrol abuse, and other hardships of immigrant life.[24] In "Somos Mas Americanos," the band continues this trajectory of defending immigrants but exceeds its previous enunciations. Surpassing its 1980s hit "America" (the continent), which proudly proclaimed "De América, soy yo" (Of America, I am), in "Somos Mas Americanos" we have a defiant Tigres del Norte, whose lyrical precision offers a poignant history lesson.

The lyrics begin: "Ya me gritaron mil veces / que me regrese a mi tierra / por que yo no quepo aquí / Pero quiero recordarle al gringo / que yo no cruce la frontera / la frontera me cruzo a mi" (They have already screamed at me thousands of times / For me to return to my land / Because here there is no space for me / But I want to remind the gringo / I did not cross the border / The border crossed me). Los Tigres continue, "America nacio libre / fue el hombre que la dividió / Ellos pintaron la raya / Pa' que yo la brincará / Y ahora me llaman invador" (America was born free / It was man that divided her / They painted the line / So that I could jump it / And now they call me invader). At this point, the historical becomes explicit, "Es un eror bien marcado / nos robaron ocho estados / quien es aquí el invador?" (It is a well-marked error / they stole from us eight states / Now, who here is the invader?). Proclaiming that the issue is not one of reconquest but of work and livelihood, Los Tigres make clear their stance on the history of the U-S///México border. While it could be argued their claim to "eight states" is indicative of a preoccupation with 1848 (yet again), Los Tigres quickly expand their cartography and calendar of resistance in their unapologetic chorus.

Spoken in a serious, slow voice and tone, the interlude qua history lesson follows, "Y si la historia no miente / . . . / Y si a los siglos nos vamos / Somos mas Americanos / Somos mas Americanos / Que el hijo del Anglo-Sajón" (And if history doesn't lie / . . . / And if to the centuries we go / We are more American / We are more American / Than the son of the Anglo Saxon). A reference to "Indian of two continents," and the calling upon centuries of history, like Frost/Tijuana NO, points to Los Tigres' keen awareness of a longer historical experience of colonization informing the U-S///México border. In their final analysis, Los Tigres' invoking of a long line of indigenous descent is contrasted to the shorter spatiotemporal frame the children of the Anglo-Saxon have spent in the Américas. Despite the name-by-name listing of southwestern states, the border is figured in their sonic geography, not only as the U-S///México border but also as the systemic ones that have crisscrossed two continents and its inhabitants.

In the final lines, Los Tigres del Norte reiterate, "Soy la sangre de Indio / Soy Latino / Soy Mestizo" (I am the blood of the Indian / I am Latino / I am Mestizo) and conclude, "Y si contamos los siglos / aunque le duela al vecino / Somos mas Americanos / que toditos los gringos" (And if we count the centuries / Even though it may hurt the neighbor / We are more American / Than each and every last one of the gringos). Increasingly brazen and pointed, Los Tigres' critique in "Somos Mas Americanos" stands as a key track in which the group explodes the limits of the 1848 narrative and recounts a longer historical trajectory questioning all borders in the Américas. In doing so, Los Tigres del Norte express their long-held hemispheric sensibilities, which are reminiscent of José Martí's "Nuestra América" and racially inflected in terms of an indigenous and mestizo presence; the song thus conveys an anti-border analysis and politics that challenges the nation-state proper.

Decolonize

Aztlán Underground's (AUG) 1998 "Decolonize" has the most direct usage of the shared phrase, "We didn't cross the borders, the borders crossed us!" As the longest track, over seven minutes long, "Decolonize" includes a complex interweaving of lyrics, sounds, instruments, languages, and tempos, and it is AUG's premier anti-border anthem. Based out of Los Angeles, the band has long captured an anti-colonial psyche and transcended listening groups with a rhythm and message of self-determination and decolonization.[25] Although the lyrics point explicitly to 1848 early in the song, we see a quick jump to colonization more broadly, "Stranger in your own land under exploitation / this is the state of the indigena today / under the oppression of the settlers way." Aztlán Underground's naming of *settler* colonialism is important, as it stands in contradistinction to most Chicano/1848 understandings of colonization. Instead, it speaks to an understanding within Native discourse of colonization as primarily a settler enterprise. Originally espousing a more nationalist politic, they developed an indigenist and hemispheric consciousness over the years. Shortly after repeating, "this is the state of the indigena today / under the oppression of the settlers way," we get a shift to a thunderous use of the line "We didn't cross the borders, the borders crossed us," as a chorus repeated in sequence three times. This ends with: "Yet the settler nation lives in disgust"—AUG's condemnation of ongoing colonialism, which is cheered by jumping and moshing throngs of fans. This sequence is repeated three more times, with cheering fans sounding back in unison the anti-border sonic geography, "We didn't cross the borders, the borders crossed us!" "We didn't cross the borders, the borders crossed us!" "We didn't cross the borders, the borders crossed us!" "Yet the settler nation lives in disgust!"

Much like "Somos Mas Americanos," AUG analyzes the workings of race in the United States and, thus, reconfigures the cartography and calendar of Chicana/o cultural resistance. "You try to be white and its very respectable / But be Xicano and its highly unacceptable / Then we're termed Hispanic as if we were from Spain / Trying to insert us in the American game / and we're called wetbacks like we've never been here / When our existence on this continent is thousands of years." In these lines, like Tijuana NO, Frost, and Los Tigres del Norte before them, Aztlán Underground forces us to expand our spatiotemporal frame and reminds us (twice), "this is the state of the indigena today / under the oppression of the settlers way." These lyrics make it clear that AUG's understanding of decolonization entails a critique of colonialism and nation-state borders. Writing of the emotional effect of rancheras on its audiences, Broyles-Gonzalez states there exists a "consonance of bioenergies across generations and geographies" (198) of listeners. Such release of energies and moments of collective consciousness and rehumanization are evident amidst AUG's audiences: ad hoc moshes at their performances intensify with the lyrics' changing tempos, and as the dance floor settles, we hear yet another shift to a slower, melodic indigenous floor drum and the sounds of a conch being blown in the background.

This multifaceted shift is at once disorienting and calming, which perhaps seems unusual to audiences not previously familiar with AUG seeking a hard punk sound but is soothing nonetheless. "To the Earth . . . / To the Air . . . / To the Fire . . . / To the Water" the audience hears, as a Lakota Honor Song gets louder and louder and the drumbeat deeper and deeper. The group then declares, "The Eagle and Condor have met" in reference to the Peace and Dignity Journeys, a spiritual and continental run started in 1992 and completed every four years, aimed at bringing together indigenous communities throughout the Américas.[26] The Honor Song and drumbeat are now the only sounds we hear, then "We must realize / our connection to this land / From Xicano to Lakota we're all sisters and brothers / . . . / from the top of Alaska to the tip of South America / Abya Yala, Anahuak, Turtle Island." The various names for these continents are recited as a different sonic geography expanding over "506 years of indigenous resistance" (at the time) is mapped and chronicled.

The Honor Song continues amidst a proclamation of *cihuatl* (women) reclaiming their place in a balanced set of social relations, then, one more time, "We didn't cross the borders, the borders crossed us!" "We didn't cross the borders, the borders crossed us!" "We didn't cross the borders, the borders crossed us!" "Yet the settler nation lives in disgust!" This time followed by an unambiguous, "GET THE F*CK OUT, GET THE F*CK OUT, Get the f*ck, Get the f*ck, Get the f*ck, Get the f*ck OUT! This sequence is repeated four times before a final "GET THE F******CK OUT!" While the "hardcore" lyrics are indicative of the genre and subculture of Aztlán Underground and their fans, the concluding lines and post-track remarks, "Y que Viva el Ejército Zapatista de Liberación Nacional," leave no doubt as to whether the group adheres to an 1848 reading of colonization and the arguably formative Chicana/o Studies discourse. Aztlán Underground's sonic geography highlights what I have attempted to elucidate as anti-border musics that not only transcend geopolitical boundaries but also challenge simplistic nationalist frames that retain allegiances to nation-state borders.

CONCLUSION

Although all three songs discussed here refer to the U-S///México War of 1845–1848 and the Treaty of Guadalupe Hidalgo, it is my contention these musical ofrendas must be considered anti-border music, for we otherwise risk compartmentalizing them to national narratives and particular temporal and spatial schemas. Instead, these sonic texts shift the cartography and calendar of de-colonial cultural production, knowledge, and resistance. The tendency to place the origin of "We didn't cross the borders, the borders crossed us!" in the immigrant marches, protests against Proposition 187, or the Chicano Movement by collapsing it with CASA's "Sin Fronteras" motto misses the different sonic geography and articulation that are at play. Although Proposition 187 coincided with the start of NAFTA and the Zapatista uprising in Chiapas, these did not occur in a vacuum. The year 1992 saw mobilizations in California and throughout the Américas against quincentennial celebrations of Columbus's voyage. In pointing to the colonization of the Américas and the emergence of nation-state boundaries as a modality of population management and social relations, the presence of the slogan in the three songs—and the slogan's popular currency more broadly—can be traced to lead-up activities to the quincentennial protests and as a critique of colonization dating back to1492 in particular.

To ground "We didn't cross the borders, the borders crossed us!" in a narrative that only replaces one colonial nation (the United States) with another (México) or simply blends the two into a new hybrid and unproblematized aural border, as does the Borderlands academic complex, is to underestimate the slogan's political trajectory and implications. A position that considers 1848 paradigmatic does not interrogate México's own erasure of indigenous peoples within its juridical boundaries. The Treaty of Guadalupe Hidalgo frame further limits the possibilities for a de-colonial feminist analysis like that of Anzaldúa by reducing colonization to a contest between two nation-states rather than treating colonization as an embodied, lived condition, as many Chicana feminists have long argued it should be viewed. Instead, I locate the sonic geography of the phrase as a critique to the European modern/colonial political project resulting in contemporary geopolitical alignments of nation-states today. De-coloniality, in this regard, entails not a re-drawing of national borders but an active stance against all borders and the interstate system they enforce, which is rooted in an episteme that manages bodies through racial/sexual technologies for the purpose of (ongoing) primitive and capitalist accumulation.

How might we continue to map anti-systemic sonic geographies? While this essay focused on three songs sharing the specific line "We didn't cross the borders, the borders crossed us!" other Chicana/o cultural productions also maintain and advance similar political and ethical stances against the U-S///México border and nation-state boundaries more broadly. Here, I have sketched an interpretive spatiotemporal frame I hope can be useful for analyzing contemporary and future border musics that speak to the materiality of the border as they sing their own sonic geographies into being. El Gran Silencio's recent Rock en Español reinterpretation of Los Tigres' "America," Ricardo Arjona's collaboration with Intocable on "Mojado," and Lila Downs's various songs are examples of such alternative sonic geographies. Oakland-based BRWN BFLO's "Corazón" (2009) and LA-based Cihuatl Tonalli's "Soy" (2007) similarly reflect an epistemic shifting of the cartography and calendar of resistance and of knowledge about the U-S///México border, the Américas, and the ongoing work of decolonization.

NOTES

1. My translation. Slashes signal when one of two migrants stops speaking and the other begins.

2. This inscription for the US-México border is an intervention in the discursive hegemony of US-México Border Studies discourse. It is meant to disrupt the "hidden transcript" that silences dissent and implies a timeless permanence and unity vis-à-vis the term "United States" and its abbreviation while visually voicing (protest of) the current "triple fence strategy" in San Ysidro.

3. Before Operation Gatekeeper (1994), families gathered in this park on the southwestern-most tip of the country with Mexican relatives unable to cross the border, sharing bread and stories through wire-mesh fences. After metal walls were erected, it was renamed Border Field State Park.

4. The scene is included in the documentary *New World Border* (Dir. Casey Peek, 2001).

5. Examples of such use abound. A review of various fields—film studies, anthropology, queer theory, literary criticism, and history, to name a few—will yield resonances of Anzaldúa.

6. See Josh Kun, "The Aural Border" *Theatre Journal* 52 (2000): 1–21.

7. Tim Dunn, *The Militarization of the US Mexico Border, 1978–1996: Low Intensity Doctrine Comes Home* (Austin, TX: CMAS, 1996) and Joseph Nevins, *Operation Gatekeeper: The Rise of the "Illegal Alien" and the Making of the US-Mexico Boundary* (New York: Routledge, 2002).

8. The corrido is a popular folk ballad along the US-México border with variations throughout México. See Vicente T. Mendoza, *El romance español y el corrido mexicano* (1939) and Celedonio Serrano Martínez, *El corrido mexicano no deriva del romance español* (1973), who argues it derives from la itotolca nahuatl (Aztec poetry). See also Américo Paredes, *"With His Pistol in His Hand"* (1958); José David Saldívar, *Border Matters* (1997); José E. Limón, *Mexican Ballads, Chicano Poems* (1992); and Alfred Arteaga, "The Chicano-Mexican Corrido" (1985).

9. Elsewhere, I interrogate three incidents marred by violence and the corridos narrating the events to illustrate how they are not simply "cultural" production but articulations of subaltern knowledge. See Roberto Hernández, "Violence Subalternity and *El Corrido* Along the US-Mexico Border," *The Berkeley McNair Research Journal* 8 (Winter 2000): 137–152.

10. Yolanda Broyles-González, "Ranchera Music(s) and the Legendary Lydia Mendoza: Performing Social Location and Relations" in *Chicana Traditions: Continuity and Change,* ed. Norma E. Cantú and Olga Nájera-Ramírez (Urbana: University of Illinois Press, 2002), 183–206.

11. Herrera-Sobek, *The Mexican Corrido: A Feminist Analysis* (1991); Emma Perez, *The Decolonial Imaginary* (Bloomington: Indiana University Press, 1999); and Maria Lugones, "Heterosexualism and the Colonial/Modern Gender System," *Hypatia* 22.1 (Winter 2007): 186–209.

12. My usage of this phrase refers to Africana philosopher Lewis Gordon and the Caribbean Philosophical Association's call for a "shift in the geography of reason" as a de-colonial project rooted in epistemic interventions and to Subcomandante Marcos's sketch of a "cartography and calendar" of theory, difference, resistance, land, fear, memory, and war in a seven-part series of talks, "Neither center, nor periphery," at the Coloquio Internacional Andres Aubry in 2007.

13. Exceptions include Saldívar's work on Santana and other early Chicano rock music, Héctor Calderón, Josh Kun, and Eric Zolov on Rock en Español, Broyles-Gonzalez and Deborah Vargas on Tejana/o music and rancheras, Michelle Habell-Pallán on Chicana/o punk, Pancho McFarland on Chicano rap, and Victor Viesca on the Chicano music scene in East Los Angeles.

14. In an African American context, see Angela Davis, *Blues Legacies and Black Feminism* (New York: Pantheon, 1998); Tricia Rose, *Black Noise: Rap Music and Black Culture in Contemporary America* (Middletown, CT: Wesleyan University Press, 1994); and Clyde Woods, *Development Arrested: Race, Power, and the Blues in the Mississippi Delta* (London: Verso, 1998).

15. Lugones, "Heterosexualism and the Colonial/Modern Gender System."

16. Héctor Calderón, "The Mexico City–Los Angeles Cultural Mosh Pits: Maldita Vecindad, a Chilanga-Chicana Rock Banda de Pueblo" *Aztlán* 31:1 (Spring 2006): 95–137.

17. Linda S. Bosniak, "Opposing Prop. 187: Undocumented Immigrants And The National Imagination," *Connecticut Law Review* 28 (Spring 1996): 555–619.

18. While Chicana/Mexicana musicians/artists such as Cihualt-Ce, Cihualt Tonalli, In Lak Ech, Lila Downs, and Mujerez de Maiz engage in the shifting of the cartography and calendar of knowledge/resistance, my choice of the three songs is based strictly on this shared phrase.

19. The recent work of Myrna Garcia, *Identity, Community, and Mexican Immigration: Creating and Contesting Mexicanidad in Chicago, 1968–1986* (unpublished dissertation, University of California, San Diego, 2010) is very instructive in this regard.

20. Vicki Ruiz and Viginia Sanchez Korrol, eds., *Latinas in the United States: A Historical Encyclopedia* (Bloomington: Indiana University Press, 2006).

21. CASA "won" a political battle against rival organization, the August Twenty-Ninth Movement (ATM), who argued the Southwest was a distinct Chicano Nation (with its own border separating it from México), whereas CASA argued for socialist "reunification" of Old and Stolen México, retaining its pre-1848 border. In both cases, national borders remained but were simply relocated.

22. Richard Rodriguez writes a piercing critique of Frost's heteronormative masculinity in his construction of nation/family. I concur with Rodriguez, yet his presence in "Stolen at Gunpoint" points to the contradictory subjectivity of colonized Chicano subjects struggling against their emasculation and dehumanization and should be examined in this multi-faceted way in light of such complexity. See Richard T. Rodriguez, "The Verse of the Godfather: Signifying Family and Nationalism in Chicano Rap and Hip-Hop Culture" in *Velvet Barrios: Popular Culture and Chicana/o Sexualities,* ed. Alicia Gaspar de Alba (New York: Palgrave, 2003), 107–122.

23. Steve Crum, "Border Crossings/Crossing Border: Native Americans and the Issue of Border Crossings" in *Indigenous Peoples and the Modern State,* ed. Duane Champagne (Walnut Creek, CA: Altamira, 2005), 24–32; Eileen M. Firebaugh-Luna, "The Border Crossed Us: Border Crossing Issues of the Indigenous Peoples of the Americas," *Wicazo Sa Review* 17.1 (2002) 159–182.

24. For a study of their most famous song, La Jaula de Oro, see Saldívar, *Border Matters* (1997).

25. Victor Viesca, "The Battle of Los Angeles: The Cultural Politics of Chicana/o Music in the Greater Eastside," *American Quarterly* 56.3 (2004): 719–739.

26. Roberto Hernández, "Running for Peace and Dignity: From Traditionally Radical Chicanos/as to Radically Traditional Xicanas/os" in *Latin@s in the World System: Decolonization Struggles in the 21st Century US Empire,* ed. Ramón Grosfoguel, Nelson Maldonado-Torres, and José David Saldívar (Herndon, VA: Paradigm Publishers, 2005), 123–138.

WORKS CITED

Acuña, Rodolfo. *Anything but Mexican: Chicanos in Contemporary Los Angeles.* London: Verso Books, 1996.

Alarcón, Norma, "Anzaldúa's Frontera: Inscribing Gynetics" in *Chicana Feminisms: A Critical Reader,* ed. Gabriela F Arredondo, Aída Hurtado, Norma

Klahn, Olga Nájera-Ramírez, and Patricia Zavella. Durham, NC: Duke University Press, 2003. 354–369.

Anzaldúa, Gloria. *Borderlands/La Frontera: The New Mestiza.* San Francisco, CA: Aunt Lute Books, 1987.

Arteaga, Alfred. "The Chicano-Mexican Corrido," *Journal of Ethnic Studies* 13.2 (1985): 75–105.

Aztlán Underground. "Decolonize," *Sub-Verses.* Xican@ Records, 1998.

Bosniak, Linda S. "Opposing Prop. 187: Undocumented Immigrants And The National Imagination," *Connecticut Law Review* 28 (Spring 1996): 555–619.

Broyles-González, Yolanda. "Ranchera Music(s) and the Legendary Lydia Mendoza: Performing Social Location and Relations," in *Chicana Traditions: Continuity and Change,* ed. Norma E. Cantú and Olga Nájera-Ramírez. Urbana: University of Illinois Press, 2002. 183–206.

Calderón, Héctor. "The Mexico City–Los Angeles Cultural Mosh Pits: Maldita Vecindad, a Chilanga-Chicana Rock Banda de Pueblo," *Aztlán: A Journal of Chicano Studies* 31.1 (Spring 2006): 95–118.

Crum, Steve. "Border Crossings/Crossing Border: Native Americans and the Issue of Border Crossings," in *Indigenous Peoples and the Modern State,* ed. Duane Champagne, Karen Jo Torenson, and Susan Steiner. Walnut Creek, CA: Altamira Press, 2005. 24–32.

Davis, Angela. *Blues Legacies and Black Feminism: Gertrude "Ma" Rainey, Bessie Smith, and Billie Holiday.* New York: Pantheon, 1998.

Davis, Mike, and Alessandra Moctezuma. "Policing the Third Border," *ColorLines* 2:3 (Fall 1999): 7–12.

Dunn, Timothy. *The Militarization of the US Mexico Border, 1978–1996: Low Intensity Doctrine Comes Home.* Austin: CMAS/University of Texas Press, 1996.

Fanon, Frantz. *Black Skin, White Masks.* New York: Grove Press, 1967.

Firebaugh-Luna, Eileen M. "The Border Crossed Us: Border Crossing Issues of the Indigenous Peoples of the Americas," *Wicazo Sa Review* 17.1 (2002): 159–181.

Garcia, Myrna. "Identity, Community, and Mexican Immigration: Creating and Contesting Mexicanidad in Chicago, 1968–1986." Ph.D. dissertation. University of California, San Diego, 2011.

Hernández, Roberto D. "Running for Peace and Dignity: From Traditionally Radical Chicanos/as to Radically Traditional Xicanas/os," in *Latin@s in the World System: Decolonization Struggles in the 21st Century US Empire,* ed. Ramón Grosfoguel, Nelson Maldonado-Torres, and José David Saldívar. Herndon, VA: Paradigm Publishers, 2005. 123–138.

———. "Violence Subalternity and El Corrido Along the US-Mexico Border," *The Berkeley McNair Research Journal* 8 (Winter 2000): 137–152.

Herrera-Sobek, Maria. *The Mexican Corrido: A Feminist Analysis.* Bloomington: Indiana University Press, 1991.

Kun, Josh. "The Aural Border," *Theatre Journal* 52 (2000): 1–21.

Limón, José E. *Mexican Ballads, Chicano Poems: History and Influence in Mexican-American Social Poetry.* Berkeley: University of California Press, 1992.

Los Tigres del Norte. "El Corrido," *Corridos Prohibidos.* Fonovisa Inc., 1989.

———. "Somos Mas Americanos," *Uniendo Fronteras.* Fonovisa Records, 2001.

Lugones, Maria. "Heterosexualism and the Colonial/Modern Gender System," *Hypatia* 22.1 (Winter 2007): 186–209.

Martinez, Ruben. "Prop 187: Birth of a Movement?" in *The Late Great Mexican Border: Reports from a Disappearing Line,* ed. Bobby Byrd and Susannah Mississippi Byrd. El Paso, TX: Cinco Puntos Press, 1996. 146–155.

Mendoza, Vicente T. *El corrido mexicano.* Mexico City: Fondo de Cultura Economica, 1954.

———. *El romance español y el corrido mexicano: Estudio comparativo.* México, DF: Imprenta Universitaria, 1939.

———. *Lírica narrativa de México: El corrido, Estudios de Folklore, no. 2.* Mexico City: Instituto de Investigaciones Estéticas, Universidad Nacional Autónoma de México, 1964.

Nevins, Joseph. *Operation Gatekeeper: The Rise of the 'Illegal Alien' and the Making of the US-Mexico Boundary.* New York: Routledge, 2002.

New World Border. Directed by Casey Peek. Peek Media, 2001.

Paredes, Américo. *Folklore and Culture on the Texas-Mexico Border.* Ed. Richard Bauman. Austin: CMAS/University of Texas Press, 1993.

———. *'With His Pistol in His Hand': A Border Ballad and Its Hero.* Austin: University of Texas Press, 1958.

Pérez, Emma. *The Decolonial Imaginary: Writing Chicanas Into History.* Bloomington: Indiana University Press, 1999.

Rodriguez, Richard T. "The Verse of the Godfather: Signifying Family and Nationalism in Chicano Rap and Hip-Hop Culture," in *Velvet Barrios: Popular Culture and Chicana/o Sexualities,* ed. Alicia Gaspar de Alba. New York: Palgrave, 2003. 107–122.

Rose, Tricia. *Black Noise: Rap Music and Black Culture in Contemporary America.* Middletown, CT: Wesleyan University Press, 1994.

Ruiz, Vicki, and Viginia Sanchez Korrol, eds. *Latinas in the United States: A Historical Encyclopedia.* Bloomington: Indiana University Press, 2006.

Saldívar, José David. *Border Matters: Remapping American Cultural Studies.* Berkeley: University of California Press, 1997.

———. "Towards a Chicano Poetics: The Making of the Chicano Subject, 1969–1982," *Confluencia* 1.2 (Spring 1986): 10–17.

Saldívar, Ramón. *Chicano Narrative: The Dialectics of Difference.* Madison: University of Wisconsin Press, 1990.

Serrano Martínez, Celedonio. *El corrido mexicano no deriva del romance español.* México: Centro Cultural Guerrerense, 1973.

Simmons, Merle E. *The Mexican Corrido as a Source for Intepretive Study of Modern Mexico (1870–1950).* Bloomington: Indiana University Press, 1957.

Stephen, Lynn, Patricia Zavella, Matthew C. Guttman, and Felix V. Matos Rodriguez. "Introduction: Understanding the Américas: Insights from Latina/o and Latin American Studies," in *Perspectives on Las Américas: A Reader in Culture, History, and Representation,* ed. Matthew C. Gutmann, Felix V. Matos Rodriguez, Lynn Stephen Lynn, and Patricia Zavella. London: Wiley-Blackwell Publishers, 2003.

Tijuana NO. "La Migra," *Contra-Revolución Avenue.* BMG Music, 1998.

Tijuana NO, featuring Kid Frost. "Stolen at Gunpoint," *Contra-Revolución Avenue*. BMG Music, 1998.

Viesca, Victor. "The Battle of Los Angeles: The Cultural Politics of Chicana/o Music in the Greater Eastside," *American Quarterly* 56.3 (2004): 719–739.

Woods, Clyde. *Development Arrested: Race, Power, and the Blues in the Mississippi Delta*. London: Verso, 1998.

THIRTEEN

Lila Downs's Borderless Performance: Transculturation and Musical Communication

BRENDA M. ROMERO

Suddenly, everyone is interested in Lila Downs! Her musical performances appeal to multiethnic, multilingual, and transnational audiences across hemispheres, gender boundaries, and musical cultures. These audiences include progressive academics, political activists, and radical artists with political consciences. Who *is* this remarkable new vocalist/composer? Lila Downs made her debut into the mainstream with four song credits in the acclaimed film *Frida*,[1] where she appears singing in the tango and bedside scenes. Certainly her proximity to the Frida cult via the movie has led her to capitalize on the pop cultural Frida image, as her critics are quick to notice, but Lila also claims indigenous ancestry, holds a bachelor's degree in anthropology on Oaxacan textiles, and is a musical activist. Lila Downs is the daughter of a Caucasian father and a Mixtec[2] mother; she straddles the middle of a divided world. This essay celebrates Lila Downs's artistic contributions and proposes that she offers a truly new brand of musical performance that not only represents her own journey of personal discovery but also integrates diverse musical ideas and fuses deeply layered indigenous ideas and beliefs about music with sounds and lyrical imagery. The result is truly engaging for listeners on both sides of the US–México border.

This work focuses largely on the ways that Lila uses sound quality, or timbre, as a multi-dimensional expressive device. Timbre in music has not been much considered for its contributions to music in the West, although it is central to musical expression in many world cultures. Indigenous people rely on timbre as an expressive device in many instances

(Navajo Yeibichai, Plains Grass Dance, Yurok Women's Brush Dance, and on and on). Tonal languages depend on pitch deviation for meaningful information, and other sounds might connect us with the natural world or rituals—sounds like rhythmic whoops and yells. Lila Downs explores this territory and creates stories within stories. She moves from one voice to another, from one sound icon to another. She stylizes wails and screams, sings "beautifully"; she weaves a tapestry of sound, like a pattern on a Mixtec textile made audible. No doubt she is aware that she is criticized for "playing Indian" at times, but then she *is indigenous.* What can life be when one is still young, vibrant, and a creative genius, a mix of (neocolonized) peoples decades from understanding each other! How do we represent ourselves meaningfully across the chasm of misunderstanding? How can I not be who I am?

I first met Lila Downs, a member of a community of musicians and artists living in Mexico City, in the spring of 2001 at a yearly Oaxacan arts and crafts festival.[3] I subsequently interviewed Lila at her Mexico City studio and have summarized the interview for encyclopedia entries.[4] The background information I share in this work is also based on that interview, but here I am focused specifically on tracking the works and ideas of someone who performs the US Latin@ borderlands in "borderless" performance, informed by her mixed race, bicultural, bilingual, and bi-musical experiences. The New Mestiza,[5] she personifies something new and complicated, as heralded by the great literary activist Gloria Anzaldúa:

> My Chicana identity is grounded in the Indian woman's history of resistance. The Aztec female rites of mourning were rites of defiance protesting the cultural changes which disrupted the equality and balance between female and male, and protesting their demotion to a lesser status, their denigration.[6]

HYBRID MUSIC CONSCIOUSNESS: SINGER, COMPOSER, ANTHROPOLOGIST, COLLABORATOR

Lila began singing at the age of five and began formal (Western classical) voice studies at fourteen at Bellas Artes in Oaxaca. She studied later in Los Angeles and at the University of Minnesota. She admires African American music in general, and Black female singers and jazz in particular, for showing her the many ways that the voice can be used as an instrument to articulate a wide palette of expressiveness. Other musicians who influenced her music making include the Grateful Dead, Woody Guthrie, Bob Dylan, Meredith Monk (her vocal techniques), Thelonious Monk, and John Coltrane (see also Campbell 2003). This list of musicians sums up important trends in pursuing the spiritual side of popular US music.[7] Consequently, Lila's group strives to make improvisation an integral part of performance.

Revealing her early political consciousness and activism, Lila completed a bachelor's degree in anthropology at the University of Minnesota, focusing on highland Oaxacan textiles. As she was studying about Oaxacan mountain Mixtecan textiles, Lila became conscious of the ways that women "could create a language of their own through the textiles as historical documents." The following testifies to the strength of this tradition:

> The Indian women weavers are the source of the handmade textiles in Oaxaca, sold to shops but mostly for their own use. In many Indian towns, a common sight is the weaver working on a backstrap loom, . . . sitting on a mat on the ground in front of her doorway. She moves back to extend more warp on her loom with the opposite end tied to a post. This simple loom has been used in Mexico for over 4,000 years . . . Native costumes achieve their effect mainly by the texture and decoration of the cloth itself, not the tailoring as with the clothing of North America and Europe. Oaxaca is [one of] the most important regions for handmade textiles, because the Indian traditions have endured more than elsewhere.[8]

Lila has also founded a weaver's cooperative for young indigenous women in Oaxaca, and she often wears special outfits by renowned weaver Tito Mendoza of Teotitlan del Valle, Oaxaca.[9] Lila transferred these ideas to her singing and compositional styles, becoming rather adept at interweaving a myriad of musical and cultural influences and always drawing on the many regions of Mexican music, and especially Oaxaca, for her repertoire. Lila's works also arise out of collaborations with husband, composer, and multi-instrumentalist Paul Cohen:

> We do things together—usually I'll come up with a poem that I'll be working on, for example in *The Tree of Life* we did some poems based on the images of the language. In the Mixtec language, for example, the term for *pulque,* which is the sacred drink from the *maguey* plant, from the cactus plant, it's called *duchaquihi,* in *Sasawi,* in *Mixteco,* and it refers to

> the dead mother, but it also refers to the white water, or the green water and these different expressions seem very beautiful to me, in the fact that they're also in the codices, in the pre-Hispanic documents that we have, the few that survive the Inquisition. . . . I would [work] with Paul and we would start doing some harmony and then I'd tell him I'd like something a little more simple, and he says why don't we try this, and sometimes it gets a little more sophisticated, thanks to his harmonic knowledge and his, I think, very spiritual approach to music as well.[10]

Originally from New Jersey, Cohen came to México as a circus clown and later decided to study music in Oaxaca, so "Paul's perspective is to keep things light," Lila says. In concert he juggles in time at least once to songs like the lighthearted *cumbia Maya* (Mayan *cumbia*) called "Hanal Weech" (from her 2001 CD *La Linea, The Border*), which Lila sings in Maya with a decidedly nasal timbre that is common to outdoor singing among mountain peoples the world over. The juggling calls attention to the carnivalesque textual elements and the precision required for a successful juggling act (like that of criticizing one's beloved). As Lila herself translates,

> You are a beautiful woman,
> even though you are attractive,
> the day will come when I will leave you
> because you smell like an armadillo.
> But if you put on some perfume
> I'll love you again!

Although this may sound to activist scholars like a critique of a neocolonial heteronormative relationship, it is typical of indigenous ways of poking fun at each other and their impoverished conditions, in which (cheap) perfume is more accessible than running water.

MULTI-RACIAL ACTIVISM

Lila's activism is steeped in a recuperation of indigenous heritage through languages: Mixtec, Maya, and Zapotec.[11] I asked Lila to comment on her use of indigenous languages and timbre in her songs:

> I really like to explore the different dimensions of the voice in the styles that predominate in the rural areas of México. In México we're a very classist society, as in many other places in the world, and I

> think that sometimes we tend to discriminate [against] those things and I think they're quite beautiful. To me they're just as legitimate, and they have this force, that I think has always created this communication between the urban and the rural people and the art that goes on is constantly going back and forth and feeding on one another. I really enjoy doing that locally.
>
> I speak English and Spanish. I don't speak too much Mixtec. I'm learning now as an adult. It's part of the story that many of us have where our parents are embarrassed and ashamed of teaching us the Indian language, because it always meant going backwards, and not progressing, not looking towards the future.
>
> I sing in these languages [Mixtec, Zapotec, Maya] because I feel that it's important for us to be feel proud of our roots . . . For a long time . . . when I was growing up I identified strongly with my father's side, which was the Anglo-American side, and I was very ashamed of my Indian roots, and I . . . I tried to even forget that part of my family, that my mother and my grandmother spoke the Indian language. So, somehow I think when I dropped out of college for a while, when . . . I followed around the Grateful Dead for a little while, and that made me come back to myself, and look at myself, and question myself. Why was I being somebody who I really wasn't? And I think that's why it's been kind of a journey for me to find myself. And this is what I do in songs, I think that especially here in México, we need to get in touch with this part of us and feel *proud* about it, because it helps us compare ourselves with the rest of the world.
>
> My mother helps me with the Mixtec language. In the Zapotec language I have a teacher and linguist that helps me with the pronunciation and also with the transcriptions. I'm always working with people that are specialists in each area, to make sure that it's done correctly.

Lila makes reference to the code switching that she has learned to use in negotiating a landscape of inequality. Living with her biracial identity has not always been easy, and it is evident that as an adult she has searched to find herself and recover her Mexican indigenous roots.[12] That does not mean that she is not privileged as half Caucasian who is married to a Caucasian and is a celebrity with a general appeal to the left. But privilege alone has not prevented her from thinking deeply about her role as a contemporary and responsible indigenous musician.

When her father died, in the mid-1980s, Lila's mother opened a car parts business in Oaxaca, and it was there that Lila first came into direct contact with the stories of the many who had crossed the border to work in the United States. Her bicultural experience has since shaped a social consciousness that is reflected in culturally sensitive performances of Afro-Latin and pan-Mexican music in general, much it original, rendered in flawless Spanish, English, and Mexican indigenous languages, sometimes mixing and code switching. Additionally, her innovative rock music, in English, is replete with social commentary on behalf of the Mexican immigrant:

> California and Arizona, I make all your crops.
> And it's north up to Oregon to gather your hops.
> Dig the beets from your ground, cut the grapes from your vines.
> To set on your table your light sparkling wine.[13]

Lila's songs often address social injustice and the crisis of identity in contemporary life, and she manipulates the dynamics of urban, rural, and class interactions and their effects on musical styles. Her use of timbre (sound quality)[14] in these instances is not merely symbolic; it is also a show of her ability to communicate with her songs in the musical language the community understands. By never leaving the "heart" of her music, Lila reveals her own indigenous/mestiza identities. By singing like an Afro-mestiza from the coast of Veracruz, she is paying tribute to the Black roots of Mexican culture. When she becomes the back-country mestizo wetback who crosses the border on his own, only to be deported as soon as he gets to the Great North, Lila identifies his struggle with a humor that will make insiders laugh at the social injustice that pervades their daily lives. "[S]elf-deprecating humor—whether in depictions of the Mexican peasant up against the US border patrol or of the undocumented immigrant in search of a green card—remains a distinctive element of the modern *norteña* song repertoire."[15] "El Bracero Fracasado" ("The Failed Wetback"), from *La Linea,* is dedicated to the Mexican immigrants who die crossing the border into the United States every day:

When I left the ranch, I didn't even wear underwear, but I made it to Tijuana hitchhiking.
Since I had no money, I would stand on the corners to see who would let me eat their chicken necks. Then you see what happened—I got to Santa Ana with scratched-out feet.
The sandals I was wearing got used up right away, the hat and shirt I lost when they chased me, these "white ones" when they almost caught me.
I got on the road dying of hunger and tired. I got on a cargo train comin' from Colorado going to San Francisco on a wagon I sneaked on but with such bad luck that they caught me in Salinas. Then you see what happened—The "migra" showed up, grabbed me by the hand, telling me I don't know what, they scolded me in English the "gabachos."
They told me you got to go back to your farm, but I felt really bad, having to go back to my country, as a failed bracero, with no money and no nothing. (English translation by Lila Downs)

The use of the violin, reminiscent of old time (US) fiddle music, is one way that this song merges north and south backwoods identities, subliminally likening the failed *bracero* to a poor white farmer. When the *bracero* is arrested in Salinas (California), the music changes to the melody of the first line of "The Star Spangled Banner" ("Oh, say, can you see?"), connoting the Northern Establishment. Lila nasalizes the account, bringing a freshness that reveals a stereotyped agrarian identity but is nonetheless effective in the momentum it generates in the story, whose vivid telling is capable of creating equally vivid mental images in the listener. It is as if we have added another layer of signification to the storyline typical of the *corrido,* the legendary borderlands song form on which "El Bracero Fracasado" is based.[16]

IDENTITIES THROUGH THE VOICE AS AN INSTRUMENT: TIMBRE AND "REHUMANIZATION"

As an emerging singer/composer, Lila Downs was already using music as a sophisticated symbolic language. From the beginning, she used vocal and instrumental timbres, texts, and other musical gestures to heighten the music's abilities to communicate feelings and ideas. Her idea that the musical sounds of the people are powerful forces is perhaps best proven by some of the reactions her work receives in México, where the uninitiated think she shallowly mocks and diminishes indigenous and disenfranchised Mexicans by singing their sounds. Perhaps they cannot imagine a different feminism and border consciousness working here, so they immediately assume that Downs is *distorting* local folk traditions by imitating them. Others imagine her to be an insensitive *gringa* or mestiza and her music to be a burlesque or parody, as in older Mexican genres. Once she is better known, some of the prejudices against her in México might give way to admiration—or perhaps not. She throws a wrench in the stereotype production line when she exhibits border consciousness as Alicia Gaspar de Alba defined "cultural schizophrenia":

> That state of cognitive disorientation—a psychological side effect of 150 years of Anglo colonization . . . Cultural schizophrenia is the presence of mutually contradictory or antagonistic beliefs, social forms, and material traits in any group whose racial, religious, or social components are a hybrid of two or more cultures (also known as *mestizaje*) . . . the moment of differentiation in which border consciousness becomes aware of itself as not only separate from, but more importantly resistant to, the hegemonic constructs of race and class and by the politics of assimilation and immigration.[17]

Broyles-González speaks to the power of music in transforming such deep-seated anxieties:

> Among the existential realms touched and transformed by the vibrational field of music is the untold suffering and indignities experienced at the workplaces of physical wage labor. Music is a physically and spiritually transformative process. Seen in this way, we can only fathom the survivalist importance of musical rehumanization by examining it in the context of dehumanizing working-class jobs and chronically violent raza histories.[18]

I mentioned to Lila that what most calls my attention to her singing is the variety of timbres she uses. When she sings something from the Costa, it sounds African:

> LD: It's a thicker sound . . . using the voice, or the mouth as this box of resonance.
>
> BR: Yeah, and then for the more Zapotec it's more nasal . . . that's quite amazing. Are you familiar with Meredith Monk's work? I wondered how much that might have influenced you.

> LD: Yes, I am. Mostly, I would say the jazz singers. I have taken a great deal . . . I have *learned* a great deal from African American music. I think that we owe much to this genre, if we can call it that . . . it's so filled with all these different varieties of expression. I really believe in using the voice as an instrument, as I think we can learn through this view . . . and it's not analytical at all.
>
> BR: It's not, it's experience, isn't it?
>
> LD: . . . it's just what comes out . . . yeah, it's this amazing thing. So jazz has been instrumental in my looking at it that way.

A good example of this is from the CD *One Blood Una Sangre* (2004), by "*Viborita*" ("Little Snake") "from the Afro-mixed coast of Oaxaca." The instrumental accompaniment sets up a very contemporary, urban, syncopated, Afro-Latin repetitive pattern, an ostinato, over which Lila sings the upbeat Afro-mestizo song. Harp riffs between the repetition of lines in the call and response refrain resemble the sound of the West African *kora* (a kind of harp-lute) at the same time they evoke Veracruz *son jarocho* harp traditions. Jazzy brass sections add another dimension to the sound; notably, Lila's vocal timbre changes to evoke a Black singer during the call and response.

A la orilla de la playa allá en la madrugada	
Bajo la enramada dentro el chachacual	
Hay un Diablo Viejo que te va a agarrar.	
Viborita de la mar no me vayas a picar	Call and response
Que me tire a la ruina porque me han pagado mal[19]	Vocal timbre alters

This is reminiscent of indigenous beliefs that sound itself has power, that sound itself is sacred because it has power—and the people say you can't really talk about it, you can only experience it. When she sings in the nasal sound of indigenous mountain Mixtec women, Lila legitimizes the struggles of the marginalized and forgotten peoples with ancient roots, Lila's roots. And although theirs is not the life she lives, she brings awareness to others as she finds connections for herself. Mixtec codices inspired the composition "*Yunu Yucu Ninu*" from her 1999 CD *Tata Arbol de la Vida / Tree of Life*. Lila sets to music a poem by Juan de Diós Ortiz, a professor and Mixtec poet from San Miguel el Grande, México, whose "work has been crucial in the research and recovery of the wealth of Mixtec literary tradition" (liner notes).

> Tree, Black Mountain
> Mountain of Yucuninu
> my appreciation is for you
> you feed so many animals
> when you burn
> how sad it is, how sad it is. (liner notes)

Lila explained the meaning of the tree of life: the Mixtecos believed that people were originally born from trees, as in the inscription on the CD: "From a tree is born the fruit of humanity, the fruits of her fertility will become the mother earth." This signals a common theme in Downs's ouvre. She often celebrates women and the female strength of the earth. She sings a *pirekua,* a Purhepecha woman's song, using a light vocal timbre, with unadorned elegance that is typical of Purhepecha female vocalists of Michoacán. As it is easy to hear, Lila is skillful at duplicating vocal timbres that resonate with ethnicities, and she likes to explore the different dimensions of the voice and styles that predominate in particular areas of México. As a highly expressive creative artist, however, she does not limit herself to México. At the end of her rendition of the Mexican *huapango* "*Cielo rojo*" ("Red Sky"),[20] also from *Una Sangre,* she incorporates flamenco vocal gestures, including timbres associated with flamenco singers.

Or consider *Ojo de Culebra* (*Eye of the Snake*), in which she collaborates, typically by alternating and overlapping sections with other singers, often women. Notable examples, among others on this CD, are the title cut, "*Ojo de Culebra,*" with La Mari de Chambao, and the fourth track, "*Tierra de Luz,*" with the famous *nueva canción* Argentinian singer, the late Mercedes Sosa.[21] Downs's liner notes preceding the Spanish text read, "Caminé como el polvo debajo de las nubes que flotaban sobre nuestros pasos." ("I walked like the dust beneath these clouds that floated over our footsteps.") This alludes in part to the name of the Mixtecs, which means "Place/People of the Clouds." The Oaxacan ensemble Grupo Pasatono, friends of Lila Downs, articulate this element, calling attention to music inspired by the landscape:

> Las nubes tienen muchos tonos, cuando son nubes que traen el agua, la tempestad o hasta culebras de lluvia. La nube es muy importante, "de ahí venimos," dice la palabra de los abuelos, de ahí bajaron los

> primeros mixtecos para habitar nuestra tierra que hoy la llamamos *ñuu savi* o pueblo de las nubes o de la lluvia.[22]

It is unclear whether communities in México benefit from Lila's use of the local sounds and musical ideas that are making her famous, but the general impression from interviewing Lila is that she is very much invested in being Mexican, and she performs often throughout México. Lila's dedication to "*Tierra de Luz*" continues, but without the English translations provided in the previous *La Cantina* CD liner notes. "Dedicado a los acordionistas Mixtecos que andan flotando por las ciudades, de mi Oaxaca, de mi México. Tierra de mi corazón aqui te traigo con fuerzas y orgullo" ("Dedicated to the Mixtec accordionists floating through the cities, of my Oaxaca, of my México. Land of my heart I keep you with me with strength and pride" Translation mine.) She then honors the great Mercedes Sosa essentially for her *indigenismo,* and pays tribute to Margarita Dalton, a prominent Mexican anthropologist from Oaxaca:[23]

> En honor a la hermosisima doña Mercedes Sosa por entregarnos tanto, por enseñarnos a ser concientes, por ser una cantante que busca la justicia y por cantarle a la pacha mama con mente cuerpo y alma. Al componer estos versos te recordaba, nuestra querida Margarita Dalton, ejemplo de mujer sabia.[24]

Too, her *One Blood Una Sangre* CD is dedicated "To women, who inhabit past and present times, the ones who have given birth to their ideals: one blood" (CD cover). And *Ojo de Culebra* is "To the sacred healer Doña Queta and to all the Shamans and sacred Medicine Women and Medicine Men who with pride have helped the traditional healing ways of our grandmother earth survive" (inside cover). Lila's sultry tones also speak of a vibrant connection with the earth; as a musical element, she explores the low range in the songs with La Mari and Mercedes. Sometimes Lila's upper tones pierce the sonic flow, as in "Skeleton" in *Ojo de Culebra* (Track 7), where she frames the spoken words below with a tone as incisive as a wolf's howl. The musical and textual allusion to a drowning, crying woman is the cultural icon of *la llorona,* the legendary colonial indigenous woman who drowns herself and her children after losing her husband to his Iberian wife, new to the "New World."

"Listen to the woman
at the bottom of the sea
floatin' in her hair
there is a reflection o' me." (liner notes)

When singing a popular *ranchera* lyrical song, she is sophisticated, urban, and eclectic in ways that can cross over to the blues. The *ranchera* itself is iconic of "rehumanization":

> The *canción ranchera* is far and away the most powerfully emotional of all Mexican song types. For those singing, listening to, or dancing a *canción ranchera,* the music and lyrics work together as a cultural channel of human flow and desire. There is a powerful release of deep happiness or deep sorrow, or just plain unmitigated enjoyment—often linked to other contexts in which that song was experienced or to the loved ones who cherish the song. These songs serve as a momentarily and autonomous space of rehumanization.[25]

Lila Downs is considered "part of an invigorating new wave of cross-border Latino music"[26] that includes others like Los Lobos, Los Abandoned, Los Villains, Maria Fatal, and Aztec Underground.[27] Joe Pepe Galarza, bass player for Aztlán Underground, voices a common philosophical undercurrent: "Music is art. All these different mediums that can be as a vehicle to really work toward social change in their communities."[28] Los Villains, a Chicano rock band, also from Los Angeles, comment on genocide of indigenous peoples in "Trail of Tears." Crossing the border to San Antonio, Texas, Lila collaborates with famous Tex-Mex musicians Flaco Jimenez and Max Baca in her 2006 CD *La Cantina,* "Entre copa y copa se acaba mi vida . . ." (*The Cantina, "From one drink to the next my life is near the end . . ."*).

The multiple ways in which Lila Downs uses musical means to relate particular socio-cultural messages are particularly interesting: we have noted nasality to evoke indigeneity or a backwoods character and using humor to poke fun at ourselves in a region that does just that. We have also noted a timbral and melodic gesture that reminds us of the *gitana* or flamenco singer and dancer and, still again, an Afro-mestiza or Black woman from the coast in conjunction with call and response, a prominent Afro-latin feature. Again from *La Linea,* her "Medley: Pastures of Plenty" grabs the listener with a beautifully innocent narrative in ballad style that is quickly juxtaposed with an admonishment in rap-style singing, a stylistic feature that has continued to appear in some of her songs over time. Much in the style of Lakota spoken-word artist John Trudell of the American Indian Movement, she demands:

> Say you're American but what does it mean?
> You are the particle the dust in the scheme
> Now that you have all the things that you want
> did you ever look around to see who you forgot?[29]

Then, as a refrain, Lila switches to a musical and textual variant of Woody Guthrie's "This Land is Your Land" ("and my land and your land"), and the 1960s social movements are suddenly brought to mind. Ethnomusicologist Mark Slobin explains:

> The spread of the protest song, from its roots in American union/left-wing/civil rights soil through its flowering in Latin American *nueva canción,* implies a third type of interculture, a global political, highly musical network that has not been comprehensively studied. It is somewhat allied with the post-peasant "folk" music movement, which drew inspiration from the American "folk revival" and grew to dominate a certain segment of youth music across Europe.[30]

There is no doubt that Downs represents a dynamic, experimental approach to musical performance, one that allows the complicated feelings of her very being to come into play. With that has appeared some visual emphasis on her sexuality, with contemporary clothing that reveals some skin (as in the cover to *Ojo de Culebra*). *Ojo de Culebra* is an intense collaboration of musical genius evident in many aspects; it never fails to be deeply and intensely dynamic, with a strong emphasis on the aesthetic dimensions of a vivid and varied musical palette. Moving away from providing all of the different characters by herself, Downs features duets with various artists. "*Ojo de la Culebra*" plays at *cumbia,* with an echo of La Mari de Chambao juxtaposing an improvisatory flamenco character. Track 2, "*Perro Negro*" / "Black Dog," is a collaboration with Ixaya Mazatzin Tleytól of Café Tacuba. Of special sweetness and remembrance now that Mercedes Sosa has left us is Track 4, "Tierra de Luz,"

"Land of Light," featuring both Mercedes and Lila alternating their low vocal ranges to wondrous effect. Track 5, "Justicia," includes Enrique Bunbury, Spanish rock singer-songwriter, and Track 6, "Black Magic Woman," features blind singer-songwriter Raul Midón, a guitarist born in New Mexico of Argentine and African American descent. Track 12, "Los Pollos" / "The Chicks" includes Gilberto Gutiérrez of the Veracruz *jarocho* ensemble Grupo Mono Blanco.

The remaining songs are collaborations between Downs and Cohen, with many creative details that evidence musical engagement at many levels of interaction. In "*Taco de Palabras*" ("Word Taco") in addition to the message of being betrayed by talk and lies, there are clever alliterations and rhythmic play between text and music that capture the way we feel when we realize how gullible we have been, repeating endlessly the self-reproach.

> Por mi raza, por mi casa, por mi pueblo te pedí tortillas
> y me diste chile picoso.
> Aye machete, ya no me castigues tanto, de todos modos yo Juan te llamo
> yo me entrego a ti en este canto
> Tomalá, tomalá, tomalá-tomalá-tomalá,
> Comía y comía y comía taco de palabras, comía
> Bebía, y bebía, y bebía aguas de mentira, bebía
> Comía y comía y comía taco de palabras y de mentiras
> Palabras, palabras, palabras que me engañarían.[31]

In addition to the musical resources at Lila's disposal—her voice, the güiro,[32] drums, and acoustic guitar, among others—are two professional groups, one in New York City and the other in Mexico City.[33] The *Ojo de Culebra* CD cover names the New York City band "La Misteriosa." They include Paul Cohen (New Jersey; this time playing tenor sax in addition to clarinet); Celso Duarte (México/Paraguay; harp, violin, guitar, *jarana, leona jarocha, vihuela, charango, kenacho, and zampoña*); Rob Curto (New York; accordion); Juancho Herrera (Venezuela; acoustic and electric guitars); Booker King (Brooklyn; bass); Yayo Serka (Chile; drums, percussion), and Samuel Torres (Colombia; percussion). Invited musicians include Brian Lynch (New York; trumpet, *sarcheta*); Clark Gayton (New York; trombone, tuba); Anat Cohen (Israel/New York; clarinet); Ken Basman (México/Canada; acoustic and electric guitar); Raul Midón (Argentina/African America; acoustic and electric guitar); and Gilberto

Gutiérrez (México; tamborine, *quijada* jawbone). The official Lila Downs website features photographs of these musicians (and others not listed above) as links that take us into their own musical worlds as well. As of this writing, her most recent CD is *Lila Downs y La Misteriosa Live Paris,* "recorded in May 2009 at the Radio France Studio 105 in Paris." Notably, the CD was released by Harmonia Mundi / World Village Music in May 2010.[34] That she has become a hot icon of transculturation is reflected in Lila's recent appearances singing "La Iguana" (which opens the album) and "El Relámpago" on the Chieftains/Ry Cooder CD *San Patricio* (2010).[35]

A layer of symbolism attaches to the musical sounds of the instruments or their manner of being played. The harp might play in Veracruzano style, for instance, or the *cajón peruano* might add an Afro-Latin (Afro-Peruvian) element, the wind instruments a jazz feel. All of these elements and the vocal ones described above combine to create an expressive music that is meant to "do something," much as indigenous music is considered to be an active force or a catalyst to set the forces of nature into action. It is not surprising, then, that Lila's first important concert was at the 1999 Festival of Sacred Music at the Hollywood Bowl in Los Angeles, where the Dalai Lama called upon the people of the Américas for peace. After that, Downs signed a contract with Narada, a subsidiary of Virgin Recordings.[36]

I have discussed a few of Lila's songs to demonstrate the degree to which sound itself is a central feature of expressive musical performance marked with cultural attributes that add significant meaning to the performance for people on both sides of the border, while embracing the multiplicity of identities that one can claim as *Latin@.* A decidedly indigenous *idea about music* predominates in Lila's work, a focus on the force of sound itself, "voices of the earth."[37]

CLOSING COMMENTS

Lila Downs amazes us with her musical communications and her artistic contributions to a growing multi-racial discourse that recognizes multiplicities of identities as the rule in contemporary societies. Her explorations into the musical world of timbre open up new avenues for a meta-expressiveness of spiritual characters expressed in musical sound.

Lila has performed to enthusiastic audiences at world music festivals throughout Europe, including in Spain, France, Germany, and England. Her website indicates that she has been well received in all of Latina América, and her group is, as of this writing, touring for the *Lila Downs y La Misteriosa* CD in Chile, Colombia, Uruguay, Bolivia, and Costa Rica in August and early September 2010. Upon returning to North America, her group is scheduled to perform in Mexico City, Chihuahua, Puebla, Querétaro, Chicago, Nashville, Atlanta, San Francisco, Seattle, Vancouver, Los Angeles, San Diego, Dallas, and Oaxaca. Earlier this same summer, she was featured as "World Music Singer-Songwriter" in a benefit concert for the Dolores Huerta Foundation, said to "unite several social movements and help raise funds for the Dolores Huerta Foundation."[38] In that same concert, she performed "Black Magic Woman" with Carlos Santana (a song she included on her CD *Ojo de Culebra*) and received a standing ovation from the sold-out concert at the Greek Theater in Los Angeles, California. We learn, too, that a little boy named Benito Xilonen[39] came into their lives as of July 2010,[40] which may signal new songs and messages in the foreseeable future.

ACKNOWLEDGMENTS

I wish to thank Lila Downs for granting me an interview on May 8, 2001, in Mexico City, and for being so candid. I am grateful also to Jorge Martinez Gil's attention and assistance to my work by introducing me to Lila Downs, and El Grupo Pasatono (Patricia García López, Rubén Luengas Pérez, and Edgar Serralde Meyer) for introducing me to Jorge. I am most grateful to the co-editors Chela Sandoval, Arturo J. Aldama, and especially Peter J. García, my kind and attentive colleague, whose suggestions greatly enhanced this contribution.

NOTES

Previous versions of this chapter were presented at the Annual Meeting of the American Folklore Society in Salt Lake City, Utah, October 2004; the National Association of Chicana Chicano Studies in Miami, Florida, April 2005; the College Music Society International Conference in Alcalá, Spain, in June 2005; and at the University of Colorado, Boulder College of Music, Musicology / Theory Colloquium on November 15, 2004.

1. The film score to *Frida* was awarded the Golden Globe award in January 2003.

2. The Mixtec (also Mixteca) are an important indigenous people who populate a large area called the Mixteca, which overlaps the Mexican states of Oaxaca, Guerrero, and Puebla. There are a variety of Mixtecan languages.

3. Because I identify with her community because of friends who share it, it seems awkward at times to refer to her impersonally by her last name alone, so I will refer to her simply as Lila (pronounced LEE-la).

4. See *The Encyclopedia of Latina and Latino Popular Culture in the United States,* edited by Cordelia Chavez Candelaria, Arturo J. Aldama, Peter J. Garcia, and Alma Garcia. Westport, CT: Greenwood Publishing Group, Inc., 2004. See also the *Grove Dictionary of American Music,* second edition. Alejandro Madrid, Latin American editor; Charles Garrett, editor-in-chief. New York: Oxtord University Press, forthcoming.

5. The New Mestiza is a reference to the work of the late Gloria Anzaldúa, *Borderlands / La Frontera* (San Francisco: Aunt Lute Books, 1987, 1999, 2007), in which the prominent activist, lesbian ("by choice"), and literary theorist Anzaldúa meditates on the experience of straddling cultural, psychological, sexual, and spiritual boundaries.

6. Gloria Anzaldúa, *Borderlands,* 43.

7. The Grateful Dead, led by the late Jerry Garcia (1942–1995), performed in San Francisco, their hometown, in the late 1960s and eventually became internationally known for their improvised and participatory, communal-like sets. They motivated other groups, like the renowned Phish. The Dead continue to perform without Garcia, and the surviving musicians known as part of the Dead (as listed on their website) continue to enjoy a strong fan base (see http://www.gratefuldead.com/). Bob Dylan (b. 1941) became known as the singing poet of the charged times surrounding popular protests of the Vietnam War in the 1960s. His youthful image has become iconic, as evidenced by his home page (see http://www.bobdylan.com/). I last heard by him a Christmas album in December 2009. At heart he has always been a backwoods boy and the real folk. I learned about Meredith Monk (b. 1942) through her vocalized improvised singing, but she is also known as a composer, choreographer, filmmaker, and director. Her 2008 CD *Impermanence* was nominated for a Grammy (see http://www.meredithmonk.org/). Thelonious Monk (1917–1982) was a US-born jazz pianist and composer whose famous style was marked by improvisation and Monk's character. In 1957, Thelonious Monk collaborated with John Coltrane (1926–1967), a US-born jazz saxophonist and composer particularly famous for his spiritual, avant-garde works in the 1960s (see http://www.johncoltrane.com/). His *Love Supreme* swept the world by storm when it appeared in 1964. He died at age forty.

8. http://www.oaxacaoaxaca.com/textiles.htm, accessed March 25, 2010.

9. http://elnahualfolkart.blogspot.com, accessed March 25, 2010.

10. Lila Downs. Interview with the author, Mexico City, May 8, 2001.

11. See also Elisa Diana Huerta's 2009 essay, "Embodied Recuperations: Performance, Indigeneity, and Danza Azteca" in *Dancing across Borders: Danzas y bailes mexicanos,* 3–18.

12. Lila's father, Allen Downs, a Scottish American former professor of cinematography at the University of Minnesota, was born in Colorado. Lila's mother,

Anita Sánchez, who sang Oaxacan traditional music professionally as a teenager in Mexico City, is indigenous, of Mixtec origins, from the Mexican state of Oaxaca. Lila was born on September 9, 1967, in the Oaxacan Mixtec mountain town of Tlaxiaco, but she has lived all her life equally on both sides of the border.

13. Lila Downs, "Medley: Pastures of Plenty and This Land is Your Land," Track 7, *La Linea / The Border,* Narada Productions, Inc., 2001. Lyrics reprinted courtesy of Cloud People Music and EMI CMG Publishing.

14. Timbre (TAM-ber) is the quality of a sound that differentiates it from another; for instance, the sound of a trumpet differs in quality from that of the guitar, and so on, due to differences in the combinations of resonating overtones.

15. Cathy Ragland, *Música Norteña: Mexican Migrants Creating a Nation between Nations,* Studies in Latin American and Caribbean Music series, edited by Peter Manual (Philadelphia, PA: Temple University Press, 2009), 44.

16. I am jolted to remembering a mojado hitchhiker I picked up in Albuquerque on my way back to Denver once. His feet were so torn and swollen that I stopped at a Walgreens and bought some spray disinfectant and pain reliever. I took an alternative route out of Walsenburg to I-25, and we drove past a state trooper's car. The hitchhiker was mistrustful after that; he gave in to terror when we were close to Denver, and I necessarily dropped him off at an exit, wondering how far he would get before being sent back.

17. Alicia Gaspar de Alba, editor, *Velvet Barrios: Popular Culture and Chicana/o Sexualities* (Basingstoke and New York: Palgrave Macmillian, 2003), 199–200.

18. Yolanda Broyles-González, "Ranchera Music(s) and Lydia Mendoza: Performing Social Location and Relations" in *Chicana Traditions: Continuity and Change,* edited by Olga Nájera-Ramírez and Norma E. Cantú (Chicago, IL: University of Illinois Press, 2002), 196.

19. "Down at the edge of the beach, around dawn
under a palm roof, inside the bar
there's an old Devil's gonna catch you.
Little snake from the sea don't you bite me
Now I'm down and out someone done me wrong." (liner notes)

20. Composed by the Hermanos Zaizar and arranged by Celso Duarte, Ernesto Anaya, and Lila Downs.

21. Mercedes Sosa (1935–2009) was one of the most beloved singers of the recent past. She became known as an activist and protest singer, and she was an important part of the *Nueva Canción* movement in Argentina. She served as an ambassador for the United Nations' Children's Fund (UNICEF).

22. "The clouds have many tones, when they bring the rain, or the tempest, or even rain snakes. The cloud is very important, 'from there we come,' say the grandfathers, from there descended the first mixtecs to inhabit our land that today we call *ñuu savi* or place/people of the clouds or of the rain" (translation mine).

23. Margarita Dalton was born in Mexico City but has lived in Oaxaca for more than thirty years. She has known Lila Downs for much of that time. She reveals that she and Lila have an excellent friendship, coinciding in a vision of a world with more justice for all (e-mail communication with author, March 28, 2010).

24. "In honor of the most beautiful Doña Mercedes Sosa for giving us so much, for showing us how to be conscious/conscientious, for being a singer who searches for justice, and for singing to the *pacha mama* mother earth with mind body and

soul. In composing these verses I remembered our beloved Margarita Dalton, exemplar of the wise woman" (translation mine).

25. Yolanda Broyles-González, *Lydia Mendoza's Life in Music/La Historia de Lydia Mendoza: Norteño Tejano Legacies* (New York: Oxford University Press, 2001), 197.

26. Duncan Campbell, "Mex Factor. Woody Guthrie to a Salsa Beat? Duncan Campbell Meets the Woman Changing the Rules of Latin Music," *The Guardian*, February 10, 2003. http://www.guardian.co.uk/music/2003/feb/10/artsfeatures.popandrock

27. Los Lobos have been a well-known Los Angeles–based Chicano rock band since the 1970s. They draw heavily on their multiple musical roots (rock, *son jarocho*, R&B, and so on) and sing both in Spanish and in English. Los Abandoned formed an alternative Chicano rock band in Los Angeles for a few years before their dissolution in 2007. Los Villains played briefly in the late 1990s and early 2000s (http://new.music.yahoo.com/videos/villains/trail-of-tears—2151627;_ylt=Agxdd4mc8sPkKItbRBMLXuDHxCUv). María Fatal became known for *rock en español* in Los Angeles in the 1990s (http://www.answers.com/topic/maria-fatal).

28. http://www.youtube.com/watch?v=4BkZFTFMwUM, accessed March 25, 2010.

29. Downs, "Medley," *La Linea / The Border*. Lyrics reprinted courtesy of Cloud People Music and EMI CMG Publishing.

30. Mark Slobin, *Subcultural Sounds: Micromusics of the West* (Hanover, NH: Wesleyan University Press; University Press of New England, 1993), 68.

31. For my people, for my home, for my village I asked you for tortillas, and you gave me *chile picoso*. Oh, machete, don't punish me so much; in any case I call you Juan, I give myself to you in this song. Take it, take it, take it–take it–take it. Eat, eat, eat word taco, I ate it. I drank, drank, drank water of lies, I drank it. Eat, eat, eat word and lie taco, words, words, words that would deceive me (translation mine).

32. "Güiro" (WUI-ro) is said to be a Taino word from the Caribbean meaning "gourd rasp." It is in essence a scraper with many incarnations throughout the Américas. Also "güira" and "güasa."

33. As listed on her *La Cantina* CD cover, the New York City musicians for this recording include Paul Cohen (clarinet, music programming); Guilherme Monteiro (electric bass); Yayo Serka (drums, percussion); Booker King (bass); Rob Curto (accordion); and Edmar Cantañeda (harp). The Mexico City group includes Celso Duarte (harp, violin, *coros*); Patricia Piñón (percussion); Ernesto Anaya (acoustic guitars, vihuela, violin, guitarrón, voice, and *coros*); Rodrigo Duarte (cello); Felipe Sousa (electric guitar); Moisés Garcia (trumpet); and Aneiro Taño (music programming, loops, vocals). Guilherme Monteiro was born in Brazil. One of the group's musicians in 2004 was Yunior Terry Cabrera, on acoustic bass, born into a legendary family of Cuban musicians, the Familia Terry.

34. http://liladowns.com/news/, accessed March 24, 2010. This CD was available in Spain on February 15, 2010, and in the rest of Europe and the United States in April, 2010.

35. No doubt *San Patricio* cements the Irish-Mexican connection represented by the St. Patrick Brigade, who fought in México against the United States in the Mexican-American War (1846–1848).

36. As of the first writing of this essay, she was touring internationally and dividing the rest of her time primarily between Mexico City and New York City. Her songs have been featured in various television programs and in the John Sayles film *La Casa de los babys* (*The House of the Babys*) (Betto Arcos 2003), where she sings "Naila" (composed by Jesús Rasgado), a crowd favorite. She also sings "Quizas, Perhaps, Quizas" in *Tortilla Soup* (2001) and "La Niña" in the film *Real Women Have Curves* (2002), and she performs in the acclaimed Spanish filmmaker Carlos Saura's *Fados* (2007) (Betto Arcos 2010).

37. http://liladowns.com, blog accessed March 31, 2009.

> It is to you people that I sing, to those who have inspired my songs:
>
> The Migrant workers, and those who have died crossing the border, those who have sought out more hard work and found the means to rise up from a humble beginnings.
>
> To those women who dance and sing, Zapotec, Mixtec, Huave, Mazatec, they give comfort in a troubled time, they give love and listen to the troubles of others, soulful to the body and the heart, alleviate the tortures of the mind.
>
> To the introspective or irreverent she-man or man/woman. He/she can hold the faith in humanity with the tenderness found [in] no other human. To the joy of life for the nature it has given us, and the wisdom to take it as such and not repress it.
>
> To the mountains and the shadows, the black dogs and iguanas, because I am you and you are me—we are all God and parts of the living movement, cascading buildings of earth, each compartment one story that connects to all.
>
> To celebrate the survival of our Native Indian nations, very much alive and well today, speaking hundreds of languages people thought to be extinct. Voices of the Earth, ¡Viva! ~ Lila

38. Dolores Huerta was co-founder of the United Farm Workers of America and is president of the Dolores Huerta Foundation. She is a legendary human rights activist.

39. Xilonen is misspelled on the website (Betto Arcos 2010).

40. See http://liladowns.com/news/

REFERENCES

Anzaldúa, Gloria. *Borderlands / La Frontera*. San Francisco: Aunt Lute Books, 1987, 1999.

Arcos, Betto. Former Special Assistant to Lila Downs. Telephone communications with the author, Los Angeles, California, 2003; e-mail correspondence August, 2010.

Broyles-González, Yolanda. *Lydia Mendoza's Life in Music / La Historia de Lydia Mendoza: Norteño Tejano Legacies*. New York: Oxford University Press, 2001.

———. "Ranchera Music(s) and Lydia Mendoza: Performing Social Location and Relations" in *Chicana Traditions: Continuity and Change*, edited by Olga Nájera-Ramírez and Norma E. Cantú. Chicago: University of Illinois Press, 2002.

Campbell, Duncan. "Mex Factor. Woody Guthrie to a Salsa Beat? Duncan Campbell Meets the Woman Changing the Rules of Latin Music." *The Guardian*,

February 10, 2003. http://www.guardian.co.uk/music/2003/feb/10/artsfeatures.popandrock
Downs, Lila. Interview with the author, Mexico City, May 8, 2001.
Frida, directed by Julie Taymor. Featuring Salma Hayek as Frida Kahlo and Alfred Molina as Diego Rivera. Based on a book by Hayden Herrera and screenplay by Clancy Sigal. Miramax Films, 2002.
Gaspar de Alba, Alicia, editor. *Velvet Barrios: Popular Culture and Chicana/o Sexualities.* Basingstoke and New York: Palgrave Macmillian, 2003.
Huerta, Elisa. "Embodied Recuperations: Performance, Indigeneity, and Danza Azteca" in *Dancing across Borders: Danzas y bailes mexicanos,* 2009: 3–18.
Nájera-Ramírez, Olga, Norma E. Cantú, and Brenda M. Romero, editors. *Dancing across Borders: Danzas y Bailes Mexicanos.* Chicago: University of Illinois Press, 2009.
Ragland, Cathy. *Música Norteña: Mexican Migrants Creating a Nation between Nations.* Studies in Latin American and Caribbean Music series, edited by Peter Manual. Philadelphia, PA: Temple University Press, 2009.
Slobin, Mark. *Subcultural Sounds: Micromusics of the West.* Hanover, NH: Wesleyan University Press; University Press of New England, 1993.

WEBSITES

http://www.bobdylan.com/ (accessed March 25, 2010).
http://elnahualfolkart.blogspot.com/ (accessed March 25, 2010).
http://www.imdb.com/title/tt0303830/soundtrack (accessed March 24, 2010).
http://elnahualfolkart.blogspot.com/ (accessed March 25, 2010).
http://www.gratefuldead.com/ (accessed March 25, 2010).
http://www.johncoltrane.com/ (accessed March 25, 2010).
http://www.liladowns.com (accessed March 31, 2009; March 25, 2010).
http//www.liladowns.com/news (accessed August 26, 2010).
http://www.meredithmonk.org/ (accessed March 25, 2010).
(http://new.music.yahoo.com/videos/villains/trail-of-tears—2151627;_ylt=Agxdd4mc8sPkKItbRBMLXuDHxCUv) (accessed March 25, 2010).
http://www.oaxacaoaxaca.com/textiles.htm (accessed March 25, 2010).
http://www.youtube.com/watch?v=4BkZFTFMwUM (accessed March 25, 2010).

DISCOGRAPHY

Downs, Lila. *Lila Downs y La Misteriosa Live Paris,* recorded in May 2009 at the Radio France.
Studio 105 in Paris. Harmonia Mundi / World Village Music, April 2010.
———. *Ojo de Culebra (Shake Away),* Narada Productions, Inc. 2008.
———. *La Cantina, "Entre Copa y Copa . . ."* Narada Productions, Inc. 2006.
———. *Una Sangre (One Blood),* Narada Productions, Inc. 2004.
———. *La Sandunga (The Allurer),* Narada Productions, Inc. 2003.
———. *La Linea / The Border,* Narada Productions, Inc. 2001.

———. *Tata Arbol de la Vida / Tree of Life,* Narada Productions, Inc. 1999.
———. *Trazos,* Narada Productions, Inc. 1999, 2000.
Pasatono, Tonos de nube, featuring Patricia García López, Rubén Luengas Pérez, Edgar Serralde-Mayer, and Julio García Sánchez. Oaxaca, México: Asociación Cultural Xquenda, A.C., 2005.

ACTO THREE

Nepantla Aesthetics in the Trans/Nacional

FOURTEEN

El Macho: How the Women of Teatro Luna Became Men

PALOMA MARTÍNEZ-CRUZ & LIZA ANN ACOSTA

ma·cho *adj*
having or showing characteristics conventionally regarded as typically male, especially physical strength and courage, aggressiveness, and lack of emotional response

n
a male who displays conventionally typical masculine characteristics[1]

If we accept Schechner's claim that performance is "twice behaved behavior," we must then ask, what is the force of that repetition?[2]

PEGGY PHELAN, *THE ENDS OF PERFORMANCE*

The play *Machos,* created and performed by Teatro Luna, Chicago's all-Latina theatre company, illuminates the project of el macho. Accepting performance as "twice behaved behavior," *Machos* interrogates the echoes of patriarchal conventions by dramatizing the boundaries of normative masculinity. The force compelling repetition of el macho's gestures, vocabulary, and drives is immediate and all-encompassing: minutes into the play, the cast, donning contemporary urban Latino drag, tells us, "I learned it from my dad." Socialization of the macho begins at birth and is reinforced at every juncture with pressures from peer groups, by mass communication, and by intimate relations and strangers alike. To relinquish any aspect of the performance of machismo is to be deemed less than a man. Our paper on Teatro Luna's staged iteration of this high-stakes repertoire submits that the company's performance of gender is a political act that ultimately awakens audience members to their own complicity in the construal of machismo: the revelation that gender is a ritual, rather than a biological imperative, implies that we are each an officiant laying down the liturgy of el macho. As an anti-oppression theater project, the ultimate aim of *Machos* is to denaturalize the binary construct of woman/man that habilitates patriarchal hegemony and to activate new social engagement with gender and sexuality as a dynamic continuum, a process of becoming, rather than a state of being.

TEATRO LUNA

Teatro Luna was founded in January, 2000, when Tanya Saracho (born in Los Mochis, México) met Coya Paz (born in Perú, raised in Ecuador, and of Russian-Peruvian-US parentage) and convinced her to form an exclusively female and collaborative theater ensemble. With such an ensemble, they hoped to establish a safe space in which Latina women could transmit their stories, express problems unique to their heritage, and actively respond to discrimination. Saracho explains that she was weary of the roles offered to her as an actress—inevitably, those of maids and prostitutes—while Paz was disillusioned by the lack of opportunities for Latinas in Chicago's commercial theater. Since then, Teatro Luna has dedicated itself to expressing the challenges, triumphs, and prospects of an international Latina community as well as to providing opportunities for Latina artists to write, perform, direct, and market their own work.

The same year of the formation of Teatro Luna in 2000, Maria Teresa Marrero, in her article titled "Out of the Fringe? Out of the Closet: Latina/Latino Theater and Performance in the 1990's" expressed a kindred sentiment: a felt need to create a space for the representation of complex identities beyond the limited categories imposed by male- and white-centered national paradigms. Marrero points out that Latino theater in the United States evolved from a medium focused primarily on the problems of political and national inclusion to one in which issues of sexuality and gender come out of the closet.[3] In his edited volume *José Can You See? Latinos On and Off Broadway,* Alberto Sandoval Sánchez submits that Latino theater at the turn of the century held inclusivity and cultural resistance as maximum production values, rather than the entertainment impact of aesthetic principles. He adds that, "Consequently, US Latinas have had before them a double task: to deconstruct the Anglo and Latin American representations of gender and to create a space for self-representation and US Latina experience."[4]

Saracho and Paz define their theater as feminist, collective, communal, autobiographical, and testimonial. The works of Teatro Luna frequently employ a collage form or, as Saracho puts it, "un proceso Frankenstein," that succeeds in integrating the diverse personal histories of ensemble members. To date, they have premiered six ensemble built shows: *Generic Latina* (2001), *Déjame Contarte* (2001), *The Maria Chronicles* (2003), *S-E-X-Oh!* (2006), *Lunáticas* (2007), and *Machos* (2007). Additionally, Teatro Luna has produced two shows of solo plays by various Chicago writers, *Sólo Latinas* (2005) and *Solo Tú* (2008), as well as the single authored plays *Kita y Fernanda* (2002), *Quitamitos* (2006), and *Jarred* (2008).

When *Machos* was still in the early stages of development, Paz explained in an interview for *Meridians: Feminism, Race and Transnationalisms* that with this show they wanted to critique gender but "we also don't want to demonize Latino men."[5] Paz explains that, as an artist with a background in Latina drag performance, she had long been considering the idea for *Machos*, which was originally conceived as a way to peer into men's intimate and honest thoughts and emotions about Latina women. The idea was pitched to the National Association of Performing Arts Presenters Ensemble Creation in 2005, which then awarded them a supporting grant to create the show in collaboration with the Guadalupe Cultural Arts Center in San Antonio. In 2006, Teatro Luna visited San Antonio to conduct interviews and workshops with a group of eighteen men. By January of 2007, they had developed a series of monologues based on the interviews, and they traveled back to San Antonio to present their staging of these edited interviews. It was at the conclusion of this trip that Teatro Luna arrived at the idea of developing a full piece for production as an ensemble, adding more interviews and workshops with men to ask questions and engage in candid conversation. The topics Teatro Luna members discussed with their male respondents included views on relationships, masculinity, gay and straight sexuality and their feelings about their mothers, sports, penis size, and how to use a urinal.

Intensive development workshops began in June 2007, and the show finally premiered in November 2007.

The ensemble members have been lauded for their ability to adopt masculine speech, body language, and vocal mannerisms. To perform *Machos,* they did not stop at clothing and facial hair but also wore strap-ons in order to more fully inhabit the stage as men. The show was met with enthusiastic reviews and impassioned responses from both audiences and critics. In an interview about the trajectory of her company, Saracho says that *Machos* has "been our mega hit," with performances selling out at Chicago Dramatists and again when the show moved to the suburb of Berwyn.[6] In June of 2008, *Machos* took home two Non-Equity Jeff Awards for Best Ensemble and for Best New Work.

An anti-oppression project, Teatro Luna most frequently develops plays as an ensemble, integrating the voices of community members and interviews at various stages in their writing process to bring untold or undervalued stories to the fore. With *Machos,* the pastiche of monologues and short scenes constitutes a theatrical experience in which the performers articulate confessions about the ossification of maleness in the real lives of their respondents. This process effectively transforms the audience into the men's confessors. However, the specific desires and fears of men are not judged on stage by antagonists of the male world order. As with Agusto Boal's "Theatre of the Oppressed," the activity of imagining the outcome is placed squarely in the hands of the audience.[7] The monologue form increases the weight of audience responsibility, as the viewer becomes the unseen interlocutor, the social force that considers the acts of the confessants and decides how to respond. Absolution? Condemnation? Indifference? Penance? Now that the actions of the menfolk are weighed in the balance, how do we find them? Teatro Luna exposes the project's perceivers (repertoire company, audience, readers) to a spectrum of choices.

WHY BECOMING A MACHO IS A LATINA'S JOB

The word macho comes from the Latin word *mas* (male). Its derivative *masculus* was shortened to *mâle* by the French and was borrowed as "male" by the English in the fourteenth century. On the Iberian Peninsula, *masculus* gradually became "macho," which then entered English language in the 1920s through Mexican Spanish. In the United States, it was primarily reserved to describe maleness in Latin American or Hispanic contexts, such as the bullfighter's arena. Eventually, it was picked up to describe the film heroes and football stars who demonstrated the most celebrated masculine characteristics of strength, endurance, and the pairing of aggression and stoicism. The contemporary US macho exploded onto the mainstream in the 1970s from the lips of both gay men and feminists. The Village People's boisterous 1978 party hit "Macho Man" celebrated the erotic ideal of disco's gay fan base: *Macho, macho man / I've got to be, a macho man / Macho, macho man / I've got to be a macho!* In the women's movement, the word became synonymous with male chauvinism. A quote from G. Gordon Liddy, a conservative voice in American media, laments the macho's semantic evolution in a 1980 interview with *Playboy.*

> Macho was originally a perfectly respectable Spanish term for a manly man, a designation I'd feel personally comfortable with, but in recent years it's been expropriated as a code word by the women's liberation movement and twisted into a pejorative Archie Bunkerish caricature of the loutish, leering male who believes that the only natural position for women in this world is horizontal.[8]

This nostalgia for the bygone neutrality of the term "macho" is fitting in *Playboy,* a publication that was created to provide men symbolic control over the images of supine and submissive women. Even so, Liddy's statement allows us to historicize the transformation of the word into a message about heterosexual maleness as an oppressive force. In sum, mainstream US usage of "macho" began early in the last century with its application as a Latino descriptor. Its implication then broadened to cover anything that was exceptionally and/or exclusively male. Finally, it came to be used to depict a general—if not lumpen—version of a male chauvinist.

For Latinas, mainstream handling of "macho" is mucho más complex. The idea that US English needs to borrow from Latin culture to describe its misogyny with aplomb is one that reminds Chicana and Latina feminists that historically, US women's movements have often colluded with the mythos of race. With the dominant US culture being so famously and vehemently anti-immigrant and anti-bilingual, few words borrowed from Spanish are welcomed to the national table, and the Romance language mainstays almost always have something to do with ranching in the Southwest or food. Naturally, as women of color feminists, we ask ourselves why Latino men are singled out to bear a cross for the crimes for which men of all known cultures are culpable. As in Ana Castillo's "Ancient Roots of Machismo," we are inclined to seek materialist explanations for patriarchal traditions that predate Christianity and Islam, traditions that extended widely as women became property to be bartered. In contemporary US society, oppressions based on race and class weigh profoundly on the realities of men of color, a group about which Castillo remarks, "It is understandable, even inevitable, that a people that has been subordinated by white supremacy would seek at some point retribution."[9] With compounded forms of discrimination contributing to the expression of Latino masculinity, Latina feminism in the United States is skeptical of "cultural deficit" explanations for gendered behaviors.

Fittingly, it is not with Archie Bunker–ish strokes that the ensemble members of Teatro Luna color themselves in order to portray the macho but with a compassion and curiosity that comes from deep and unapologetic love for the subjects of their inquiry: their fathers, brothers, sons, lovers, and friends. The macho represented by Teatro Luna is not a code word or an ethnic emblem or a scapegoat used by those wanting to conflate sexism and the "other" but rather the personification of its root designation: *mal*—*masculus*—macho—male.

Performance studies as a discipline deals with the repertoires of embodied activities that challenge or transgress socially prescribed roles. By studying a play, we are investigating an art form with both embodied and discursive points of impact. But it is not on the discursive plane that Teatro Luna's *Machos* so effectively challenges gender norms; it is through the live articulation of sexual transformation that the performance exposes gender as contingency. Interpreted by women who *become* men on stage, the dialogue in *Machos* takes on an entirely new dimension, as with Ricky's longing for the largest imaginable phallus.

> We keep repeating them, can't get over them. It's like atoms bouncing off a wall. It's like the molecule broke. Bam bam bam. Be a man. Be a man. I hate the phrase be a man. [mockingly] Be like me. Do what I do. But still . . . I mean, I know that I think. I know that I am considerate of other people and of women and of things like that and I think that regardless of

> what I think, I want a fourteen-inch penis I could swing around. It's true. [Calls, jokingly, as if to G-d] C'mon, give me another ten inches damn it! [back to audience] I'm just messing with you. I only need another five. Okay six . . . okay maybe seven. But why do I even care. But I do. I want a big old dick. I want the biggest dick in the room!

In the same instant, Ricky both rejects the force of repetition ("Be a man; be a man") and subscribes to its imperative ("I want a fourteen-inch penis"). He draws on the notions of thought production, self-awareness, and consideration ("I know that I think; I know that I am considerate") to demonstrate that he understands male-coded gender behavior as an outside imposition and strives to respond to gendered situations according to a set of personal criteria. This is followed by his self-deprecating call for an extra ten inches as he laughs at his own conformity to Patriarchy 101: The Largest Phallus Wins. As a real, anonymously recorded testimony, on the textual plane this reads as a poignant lament on the omnipresent pressures of male hegemony. However, elucidation is the precursor to emancipation, not its end. Performed by a woman, these lines go beyond the exposition of compulsory gender norms to achieve the destabilization of the gender binary. As Judith Butler argues, "In imitating gender, drag implicitly reveals the imitative structure of gender itself—as well as its contingency."[10] Men's testimonies about gender norms as severely policed imitations, when articulated by an all-Latina feminist ensemble, upset the notion that gender is what one *is* and introduces the message that gender is what one *does*. A man who confesses his dismay at the imitative structure of gender is imitated by a woman, thus exposing, and eroding, the imitative structure of both genders. The imitative ordinance of both femaleness and maleness is plainly bared.

Might a male-designated person perform *Machos* and cogently bring to life the problems of learning how to pee in a urinal, cheat on a woman, and long for a career in professional sports? Yes! Male actors? Certainly—why not? Men can move across the stage and perform the transcripts of men's lives with humor and pathos—and bring out into the open their common rituals, desires and fears.

> Emory: I wish I had a natural smile. My smile looks fake.
>
> Nick: My wife says that she loves me just the way I am but for some reason I still get bothered. A huge fat ass.
>
> Emory: My fingers are so long.

Noam: So now I use Rogaine. But, frankly, I don't think it's working.

Nick: You know I feel like a total choad when I stand in front of the mirror and look at my gut and realize that I once had a flat stomach and a six pack coming in. You know, who does that!!! What guy stands in front of the mirror and looks at his gut!! It's the most non-hetero thing to do.

Noam: $500 a year and for what?

Emory: What does she see in me?

Nick: Can't tell anyone what I do.

Noam: At least I'm not short.

Nick: I might lose my man card.

In the above segment of the Men's Health sequence, each character is acutely aware that he is the member of a restricted club, with rights and privileges that may at any time be revoked should he prove to be an inadequate representation of the group's mettle. But coming from a male-designated actor, the words run the risk of subscribing to, rather than inverting, the notion of essential masculinity: with the right hair, the right muscle tone in the stomach region, the right finger length, true man-ness can be attained! You too can be man-tastic! However, the representation of this longing for the elusive macho ideal is realized by a group of Latina feminists, thereby creating an oppositional—rather than corroborating—performance of the frontiers of machismo. At no point do audience members overlook this extra dimension of artifice, and it is this oppositional tension that creates the affectionate humor that makes *Machos* so powerful to experience. It is easy to laugh at women-as-men longing to be better at man-ness in the mirror, because it is ridiculous! And so the drift is quickly caught: gender ideals are arbitrary and incoherent. Latinas-as-machos create an oppositional immediacy that most convincingly denaturalizes the sedimentation of normative sexuality.

The transmission of *Machos* by a Latina feminist theater group heralds a victory over the patriarchal imagination by legitimizing the unstable moments of human sexual experience. The fear of losing one's man card culminates when the group performs "Girl I'm Not Gay." Recreating a "boy band" song and dance number, the situation operates as an interstitial zone on several levels. Boy bands in popular culture are a distinctly non-macho entertainment phenomena consisting of harmonious, bubble-gum vocals, high-school-cheerleader choreography, and a barely pubescent cluster of pretty faces. In between boys and men, lady-killers and lady impersonators, the sexual ambiguity of boy bands is employed by Teatro Luna to underscore the macho fears of homosocial behavior and its consequences.

> I like women, girls, and chicks
> Not interested in dicks
> Except that tranny prostitute
> [She was pretty cute]
> Didn't know till we were in the car
> By then it had gone way too far
> Already paid a ton of cash
> Closed my eyes, got it done real fast
>
> And yeah, okay
> I went back twice, but hey
> What can I say, girl I'm not gay
>
> (Chorus)
> Girl, I'm into you
> Girl, I swear to you
> Girl, I promise to
> Stay by your side
> You're my heart and soul
> My perfect angel
> Tell me you'll always be mine

With highly stylized choreography, the *Machos* cast appropriates the boy band phenomenon to explore the "I'm not gay" defense mechanism that protects the borders of "legitimate" masculinity. The lyrics of the song range from negations of homoerotic behavior (as in the above quote) to qualified acceptance of homosexuals—as long as they know their place and leave other people's heterosexual reputations intact. The double androgyny of this performance—women dressed as men who are warding off accusations of queer or effeminate behaviors—creates a liminal zone in which gender and sexuality are represented as a continuum, rather than a binary. Patriarchal imagination disallows this fluid conceptualization of gender, but Teatro Luna steers straight into the maelstrom—so to speak—in order to celebrate the continuum as legitimate human sexuality.

When women become "men," they also are forced to examine how they became "women." To represent the opposite gender is to chart the most basic ways by which we inhabit the body. At the cast talk-back after the North Central College performance in Naperville, Illinois, Maritza Cervantes, a Teatro Luna artistic ensemble member, shared that returning to her "female" economy of behaviors was eye-opening. In her "Mario" character, she felt grounded, in charge, and expansive. As Mario, she was strong and confident. Inhabiting "feminine" space again meant just the opposite. To behave as a woman, one must cede the ground to others, abnegate authority, contract. Working artistically to occupy male-designated behaviors, the ensemble came away from *Machos* with new ideas about the political ramifications of the body's vocabulary. Although Cervantes had already held a feminist perspective, when she performed the role of a man she was thrust into an exploration of the countless ways, both subtle and overt, in which gender codes are internalized, disciplined and ossified.

For ensemble member Yadira Correa, becoming a man was not as comfortable as it was for Cervantes, and she was ambivalent about the "luxury" of occupying more space. On her role as a macho, Yadira remarks,

> Well, it's kind of uncomfortable to be a man. Men have to carry themselves in a way that is more rigid than women. Actions are bigger. Basically I felt like I could take as much space as I wanted, which is a good, empowering feeling. My movements felt strong and definite (no limp wrist, etc.). "Being a man" feels safe. I felt tougher, rougher. The physical aspect of binding is certainly not comfortable, but it's a constant reminder of how tense men must be physically, at least the ones that were more my type. I'm sure some of the more feminine characters in the play may feel differently, but for me there was a lot of tension in my body. I also felt more quiet as a man, more reserved. I also felt like I had more control over my body and over what others thought of me, not to mention there was a cockiness that also kind of came through which was easier to play as a man.

For Correa—and there is no way to say this *sin albur*—the stiffness of masculinity is not spacious, but constricting. To be rigid and reserved contradicted her graceful poise and extroverted personality. After the North Central College performance, she shared that she had gained a

FIG. 14.1. Teatro Luna, "Boy Band."
Photo credit: Johnny Knight Photography, Teatro Luna: Machos.

greater sympathy for males who are taught to abnegate physical and emotional fluidity of expression in order to conform to the bylaws of the macho club.

Teatro Luna's performance shows how the category of "man" is a series of social dramas. Latinas who perform the drama of machismo in drag are not simply feigning one compulsory norm instead of the other but rather subverting both. The performers we have discussed experiment with and also experience gender expression as a continuum of being. Again, Butler's interpretation of the performativity of gender is helpful.

> That gender reality is created through sustained social performances means that the very notions of an essential sex and a true or abiding masculinity or femininity are also constituted as part of the strategy that conceals gender's performative character and the performative possibilities for proliferating gender configurations outside the restricting frames of masculinist domination and compulsory heterosexuality. (141)

An all-Latina cast must be called upon to denaturalize the dichotomy of gender and expose machismo as the imitation of political, rather than anatomical, volition. To be all-Latina and yet to surrender the "woman card" that is the theater group's premise is to renounce gender as a source of cohesion and identity. In relinquishing the tenets of their own formulation, in becoming machos by performing *Machos,* Teatro Luna endorses gender instability as a liberatory project.

NOTES

1. *Encarta World English Dictionary,* 1999 Microsoft Corporation, Bloomsbury Publishing.
2. Peggy Phelan and Jill Lane, eds., *The Ends of Performance* (New York: New York UP, 1998) 9.
3. Maria Teresa Marrero, "Out of the Fringe? Out of the Closet: Latina/Latino Theater and Performance in the 1990's," *TDR: The Drama Review* 44.3 (2000): 131–154.
4. Alberto Sandoval Sánchez, *José Can You See? Latinos On and Off Broadway* (Madison: U of Wisconsin P, 1999) 152.
5. Sobeira Latorre and Joanna L. Mitchell, "Performing the 'Generic Latina': A Conversation with Teatro Luna," *Meridians: Feminisms, Race, and Transnationalism* 7.1 (2006): 27.
6. Nina Metz, "Teatro Luna playwright Tanya Saracho is drawn to 'people's darkness'," *Chicago Tribune* 12 Oct. 2008.
7. See Augusto Boal *Theatre of the Oppressed* (London: Pluto Press, 1979).
8. "Macho," *The Merriam-Webster New Book of Word Histories,* 1991 ed.
9. Ana Castillo, *Massacre of the Dreamers: Essays on Xicanisma* (New York: Plume Books, 1995) 82.
10. Judith Butler, *Gender Trouble: Feminism and the Subversion of Identity* (New York and London: Routledge, 1990) 137.

WORKS CITED

Butler, Judith. *Gender Trouble: Feminism and the Subversion of Identity.* New York and London: Routledge, 1990.

Latorre, Sobeira, and Joanna L. Mitchell, ed. "Performing the 'Generic Latina': A Conversation with Teatro Luna," *Meridians: Feminisms, Race, and Transnationalism* 7:1 (2006).

The Merriam-Webster New Book of Word Histories, Merriam-Webster, Inc., 1991.

Marrero, Maria Teresa. "Out of the Fringe? Out of the Closet: Latina/Latino Theater and Performance in the 1990's," *TDR: The Drama Review* 44.3 (2000): 131–154.

Metz, Nina. "Teatro Luna playwright Tanya Saracho is drawn to 'people's darkness'," *Chicago Tribune* 12 Oct. 2008.

Phelan, Peggy, and Jill Lane, eds. *The Ends of Performance.* New York: New York UP, 1998.

Sánchez, Alberto Sandoval. *José Can You See? Latinos On and Off Broadway.* Madison: U of Wisconsin P, 1999.

FIFTEEN

Suturing Las Ramblas to East LA: Transnational Performances of Josefina López's *Real Women Have Curves*

TIFFANY ANA LÓPEZ

In the lexicon of media and visual culture, the term "suturing" describes the process by which a director or artist strategically connects various scenes by positioning them as mutually informative parts of a larger whole. The author makes full understanding of separate scenes contingent on reading them in conversation with one another; to ignore this crafted signaling is to refuse the lens of reading cast by the director or artist and, subsequently, to read narrowly and miss the full mark of the text.

Suturing is especially relevant to Josefina López's *Real Women Have Curves*, a play about women working in a garment factory sewing dresses they themselves cannot wear because the dresses are both priced and sized out of their range. Sewing carries much artistic and critical force as a consistently deployed action, metaphor, and theme. It emphasizes how the play's characters share their aspirations and struggles. Furthermore, López uses it to signify how several issues of violence, most especially economic and representational violence, are basted together via the mythos of the American dream.

In this essay, I discuss comparatively a Spanish and a US production of Josefina López's signature play, *Real Women Have Curves*, and focus attention on their engagement with a spectrum of violence associated with the borderlands, specifically the nodal points of immigration, labor, and body politics. My reading explores the ways that placing these two productions in dialogue with one another spotlights several structural forms of violence that suture Las Ramblas, Barcelona, to East Los Angeles, California, and, significantly, illuminates the limitations as well as the possibilities of locating Chicana feminist work in a transnational context. What happens when a work such as *Real Women Have Curves,* which is so emblematic of Chicana feminist theory and practice, gets translated into the transnational sphere?[1] What imprints of Chicana feminism remain fully legible? What remains mistranslated or willfully rejected or cast aside, and why? What does a focus on these performances ultimately bring to an understanding of Chicana feminist discourse in performance?

Teatro Poliorama is a large mainstream theater located on Las Ramblas, the arterial promenade of Barcelona, Spain. Under the direction of Garbi Losada, the play, whose title was translated as *Las Mujeres en Verdad Tienen Curvas,* began touring in 2003. My readings in this essay draw on two productions I viewed during the May–June, 2005, tour in Barcelona. However, my readings necessarily begin out of sequence with what I consider to be a paradigmatic Los Angeles staging of *Real Women Have Curves* (Feburary–April, 2006) directed by Anette Jeltsje Jacobs at CASA 0101, the theater space López created and built in the East Los Angeles community where she grew up. The production was primarily cast not with professional actors but rather with members of the local community, many of whose lives mirror those of the characters in the play. In post-play discussion, actresses spoke about joining the play to share their experiences and engage audiences in thinking about issues of invisible labor and criminalized immigration and to celebrate the too often denigrated or unacknowledged presence of women on the many stages of their lives.

The physical elements of the theatrical space also proved significant to the production. López's theater is located in the heart of the neighborhood Boyle Heights, one of the poorest in Los Angeles. Visiting this playhouse requires acknowledging the neighborhood. Because López's theater is an organic part of the community in which it is located, there is no sharp demarcation between the end of the sidewalk and the beginning of CASA 0101. Its translation from Spanish (*casa* meaning "home") invokes the image of the theater as a pedagogical space; read within the context of Chicana discourse, it resonates with fellow playwright and feminist theorist Cherríe Moraga's assertion that home provides the model for how we build community on multiple fronts, from intimate partnerships to artistic projects and political affiliations.

The theatrical location of CASA 0101 gave audiences a special opportunity to experience the cultural and political milieu described within *Real Women Have Curves.* The audience was seated hip to hip on folding chairs, with the actors' stage defined by a slightly elevated space not tremendously far from the last row of the cozy fifty-seat theater. Police sirens, loud cars, and outside conversations effectively became part of the production, further placing the audience directly into the play's atmosphere. One keenly had the sense that the performance could be fully disrupted at any moment, adding to the pervasive feelings of fear expressed by the characters on stage about being raided by the Immigration and Naturalization Service.

The spatial intimacy of the theater thus brilliantly underscored the tensions of the play. For example, it was a warm spring, and with the lack of air conditioning in the theater, the audience sweated alongside the cast. We physically perceived the "heated" environment that that charged the play's setting in a garment factory. Importantly, these elements also tangibly charged the humor that drives this play. We found ourselves laughing not so much at but rather with the women; like them, we would have felt so much better if, in the character Carmen's words, we could have disrobed and "let it all hang out."

Throughout the play, López consistently, creatively, and effectively draws structural connections between the individual and the communal, beginning with her introductory notes. She recalls growing up undocumented and being counseled by her parents to "be careful walking the streets."[2] Subsequently she feared the streets, going so far as to hide when she once mistook the "L.A. Police Meter Maid" for la migra. She describes some of the other autobiographical experiences that provided the inspiration for *Real Women Have Curves:* "I got my residence card soon after I graduated from high school and was then able to apply to college. I had been accepted to New York University, but I had to wait a year to be eligible for financial aid."[3] In desperation, she took a job working at her sister's "tiny sewing factory." López's comments about these foundational experiences clarify why the practice of sewing carries such tremendous metaphorical force throughout the play. Her playwright's notes are especially important for the ways they illustrate how she insistently positions as critically generative her personal experiences as an immigrant and garment industry laborer. "At the factory there were a few Latina women, all older than me. . . . We spent so much time together working, sweating and laughing, that we bonded. . . . We had something special and I wanted to show the world."[4]

López's stage play thus focuses on Ana receiving mentoring at the hands of a female collective, finding empowerment within her family and community to pursue her goals, and then returning to the community to actively participate in the tradition of mentoring. It shares a strong feminist message with audiences and makes clear that if women work together as factory garment workers, they also work together in other ways to bolster the very social fabric of our lives. In this way, the play acknowledges, celebrates, and makes visible both the physical and the emotional labor of women. In the film, the relationship between women is mediated and interrupted by the presence of male characters. The screenplay focuses on Ana's individual coming of age and her pursuit of the American dream by attending college. Her male high school teacher mentors her throughout the application process and helps to land her a scholarship. However, Ana must resign herself to her mother's expectations that her daughter follows a path similar to the one she tread. This entails Ana remaining in close physical proximity to her family and working full-time in her sister's factory. Because of a combined lack of financial and emotional support, Ana does not envision her dreams coming into fruition. While we see Ana working alongside the women in the factory, we also see her turning to men for support. In striking contrast to the play, it is the men in Ana's life (her male teacher, her father, her grandfather, and her boyfriend) who most help her to fulfill her dreams. The lessons she learns over the summer working alongside women supplement, rather than direct, her advancement.[5] Given López's authorship of both the play script and the screenplay (co-written with George Lavoo), the differences between stage and film are important to note, most especially because it is the film that circulates in the transnational sphere and that, for new audiences, thereby serves as the principal text for reading and, as I will soon show, performing *Real Woman Have Curves.*

Because main-stage productions of Chicana/o plays are rare even in the United States, López's film carries the most possibility for transnational cultural flow and political exchange, and it is by having viewed the film that director Garbi Losada came to *Real Women Have Curves* and began staging it for Spanish audiences. López co-authored the screen play, but the film and the play read as two distinct projects even though they share several characters, plot lines, and scenes (most notably, the disrobing scene).[6] López's play features an all-female ensemble and uses the setting of a garment sweatshop to suture together issues of body politics, immigration, labor, with the complex web of violence (state, domestic, and representational) that the play critically engages.[7] By contrast, the film molds itself to the Hollywood film genre by centering on the struggle of an individual person (as opposed to a collective body). Although in the play the mother participates in the paradigmatic disrobing scene, in the film she refuses to participate. Mother and daughter do not display any political common ground, either in spoken ideology or performed action. There is no generational sharing of feminist consciousness or cultural politics, effectively eroding the power of collective struggle and the female relationships—and, consequently, the feminist politics—that are absolutely central to the play.

What, then, was the import of Losada coming to the play via the film? What was imagined as most suturing Barcelona to East Los Angeles? What was the presumed shared transnational feminist experience? What about the play *Real Women Have Curves*—whose bilingual characters and politics López makes highly specific to the location of East Los Angeles and the context of US capitalism with her attention to the myth of the American dream, the politics of mainstream American ideals of beauty, and the dynamics of immigrant labor in the US borderlands—inspired the creation of a Spanish-language performance for audiences in Spain? What was captured and what was missed in the act of translation into the transnational sphere? Ultimately, what is most critically instructive about comparing and contrasting these two particular productions?

The play's disrobing scene (faithfully performed in both plays according to López's published script) is an important pivot point at which to begin this analysis, because it is meant to signal Ana's growing feminist consciousness. In this scene, Ana enacts a public declaration of her affirmation of self-love by boldly displaying her disrobed body, a gesture which then serves as an invitation to her coworkers, including Ana's mother, Carmen, to join her celebration of the female body and, by extension, the female self. The play's disrobing scene is powerful because it boldly visually counters the representational violence of the beauty myth. Furthermore, it shows the profound resonance of politics and social change through interpersonal relationships, from a younger to an older generation—specifically, from a daughter to her mother. The body that has been a source of cultural wounding (Carmen constantly picks on Ana's weight) can also become the source of healing: Ana re-presents her body to her mother so that her mother might revise her thinking by seeing the female body in a different light occupied by collective female display and viewership.

For film audiences, the phrase "Real Women Have Curves" signals a break with hegemonic ideals of beauty and body image. However, for theater audiences, the title of the play signals attention to body politics while it also speaks of the kind of political action needed to change the conditions that uphold the beauty myth and its violence. At the end of the play, the women have emotionally and physically revealed themselves by sharing life stories while working together. Their disrobing is about inspiration as much as perspiration. They recognize that just because they make clothing in model-thin sizes doesn't mean they have to accept these sizes as the norm. They realize that their labor should feed more than the economy of the American dream and its attendant exclusive beauty ideals. Following this revelation, they redefine their labor as more than economic necessity, as a talent that might fuel a greater sense of community. "Real Women Have Curves" becomes the name of their affordable clothing label and the fashions they make for women who share both their economic status and body type.

Significantly, López invested her various earnings—from her success with the film version of the play and other work she has done—to create CASA 0101 as a space designed to give back to the very community that provided the subject matter for so much of her work. This results in a theater that invites what I term "critical witnessing." More than a focused act of looking or bearing witness, critical witnessing entails working from a story's impact as much as from its intention to spotlight the very conditions that brought the story into being, actively insisting that an event is pivotal and in need of expanded context and critical address. "Critical" is the operative word, for it signals this work as engaged in a pedagogy of social justice whereby the story instructs in order to reconstruct. The CASA 0101 space is intentionally designed to augment the politics that drives the kind of work López stages in this space. The dynamics of critical witnessing position the audience in relationship to social change, with the work designed to provoke questions about agency and subjectivity in a way that causes audience members to leave with a sense of responsibility for either participating in the problem or creating a path for changing it.

In the play, we witness the female characters on stage move into a higher level of consciousness after watching one another disrobe—as a community and collective, they have become a mirror for one another that prompts a fresh way of seeing beyond the distorted body image each character individually harbors; they actively resist the violence of representation. The actions on stage serve doubly as a mirror for the audience. As Maria Figueroa observes in her reading of the play, "As viewers and readers, we are forced to face our own prejudices and negative internalizations of 'fat' bodies when we laugh at what we are most uncomfortable with—fatness."[8] Audience responses at the productions I attended ranged from horrified gasps when the women disrobe to powerful words of encouragement and admiration. Students whom I brought to the production spoke of this moment as one that demanded they confront their own anxieties and fears about body image, prompting them to think about the ways the beauty myth resonates into the practice of their daily lives. How might they, like the women on stage, shift the social scripts that structure their own senses of identity?

In an interview, director Losada reported being excited by the strong humor in the writing, the focus on an all-Latina cast, and the political message about body image that she saw represented in the disrobing scene. However, the overall content of the play was not seen as political. In an interview with Marta Saez, Losada stated, "No creo que sea un texto político. Creo que es más bien un texto 'humano.' Es precisamente lo que me interesa." [I don't believe that this is a political text. I believe it is more so a "human" text. That's precisely what interests me.][9]

Ironically, the refusal to read the play through a feminist lens actually diminishes the humanity of the work, when the staging of humanity is defined as the presentation of relationships in all their complexities and contradictions. Working counter to the play's central image of suturing, Losada dismembered parts of López's original text. The issues of body politics, immigration, and labor were not understood as symbiotic but rather as separate points that could be easily pried apart and separated from one another. For example, Losada reassigned lines to ensure that all five comic actresses had near-equal stage time to showcase their talents. The five original characters remained in name; however, this reassignment changed their function within the artistic and political trajectory of the original play.

That López originally assigned Rosali the least number of lines is significant, as it underscores her battles with body image, which are physically manifested in her extreme dieting practices. Rosali's sparse dialogue reflects the emotional life of her character; she fasts on V-8 juice and diet pills in a desperate attempt to fit into a size seven, the model sample size of the dresses she sews, which she believes will bring her happiness and grant her access to the American dream: "I've felt fat ever since I can remember and I didn't want anybody to touch me until I got thin."[10] Rosali gives up the pleasures of food and sex, but the play asks, to what effect? Additionally, Rosali is the only character with an American Express credit card; in part, she does not eat so that she can pay her bill on time. Rosali's severe acts of disciplining her body are directly connected to the social pressures of consumer culture in the United States, which create advertising designed to make women feel that they must spend and starve their way into perfection.

The most lines in the play are assigned to Ana not because she is the main character (López herself envisions Estella as the main character) but because she goes to great lengths to school the women in the factory in her brand of book-knowledge feminism: "I wanted to show them how much smarter and liberated I was. I was going to teach them about the women's liberation movement, about sexual liberation and all the things a so-called educated American woman knows."[11] In her mission to grow as a person, Ana literally works to inhabit more space in the play. Through partaking in shared storytelling and learning to engage in active listening, Ana eventually comes into a position of enlightenment: "I was not proud to be working there at the beginning. I was only glad to know that because I was educated, I wasn't going to be like them. . . . I was going to teach them. . . . But in their subtle ways they taught me about resistance."[12] López invites critical witnessing with this closing scene that concentrates on the performative force of lived experience in the making of social change.

In Losada's production, Ana's central position in the play is diminished by the abbreviation of her dialogue. Omitted are Ana's moments of self-examination and cultural critique. Additionally elided are Ana's references to what she learns through reading, the lessons she tries to impart to the women in the factory, and the various ways that the women, in the end, teach Ana about resistance, power, womanhood, and feminism. Other changes shifted the interwoven politics of feminism, immigration, and Chicana/o identity that drive López's original script. In the Barcelona production, Rosali—the thinnest actress—is the one with the boyfriend. It is significant in the original production that Estela, who is among the largest in the group, has a boyfriend. In López's original script, Rosali asks Estela if her boyfriend, "El Tormento," has a friend because she does not want to die a virgin. Omitted from the Losada production were references to abortion, the contemplated plans for bringing Estela back in the event of her deportation, Estela's description of her unfortunate sexually charged meeting with El Tormento ("I don't care if you're fat. I like you even better; more to grab"[13]), and the women offering their salaries to Estela so that she can fulfill her dream of launching her own clothing line.

Ultimately, Losada's production did not take into account the Chicana feminist consciousness that informs López's original script. Like the film, Losada's version privileged the staging of individual bodies in conflict rather than collective bodies in struggle. This contributed to significant limitations in reading and staging the text that neither communicated nor reflected the Chicana feminist politics that serve as the foundation for the play *Real Women Have Curves*. (Why were the forms of oppression and struggle that define the characters and drive the play not viewed as speaking to "universal" human experience?) Losada appeared to not discern any obligation to represent the politics that drive Lopez's text or translate them into a comparable context. (Can we imagine the same occurring with, say, Authur Miller's *All My Sons* or *Death of a Salesman*?) Rather, translations for Spanish audiences were limited to surface-level issues. Substitutions included: "NIE/NIF" (Número de Identificación Fiscal) for "Green Card," "mayonesa" for "mole," "talla thirty-six" for "size seven," "policia" for "INS," and "tarjeta de la Caixa" for "American Express." All served as ways to make the play more culturally specific for Spanish audiences. However, I want to ask, does this make for a full translation of the text that includes not only cultural specificity of people but also of politics? Despite the changes made to speak to Spanish audiences, the translated performance effectively deflated Chicana/o experience and aesthetics from the play rather than conveying them within a Spanish context.

Also problematic was how the Spanish production read the politics of the play as reducible to the single moment of disrobing. I do not want to disregard how this scene performs an important political gesture. Like my American students, my female students in Barcelona were extremely moved by this scene. However, the Spanish production unhinged this political gesture from the other related and pressing political issues that drive the original play. I most want to critique this moment because it so profoundly marks a missed opportunity to suture Barcelona to Los Angeles. Both are major cities known for their cosmopolitanism, fashion, and flair. However, they are also connected in other, more powerful ways concerning issues of immigration and labor that in a global economy resonate into the transnational sphere. As my students in Spain pointed out, Losada would have offered a richer point for comparison about immigrant groups if she had focused not on Cubans but on Moroccans, especially in Barcelona, who according to reports in *El País,* are linguistically and racially stigmatized, forced to live in poor housing conditions and to consider participation in alternative economies. Their multiple forms of oppression suggest comparative reading with the structural violence historically experienced by Mexican immigrants in the United States. Moroccans selling goods on the street act in ways that convey a state of hyper-vigilance about la policia that resonates with López's childhood memories of having as a youth to dodge la migra.

To enter Barcelona's grand Teatro Poliorama on Las Ramblas to see Losada's performance, one had to literally step over the "top manta" street sellers, the undocumented, predominantly Moroccan, immigrant vendors who unfurl across the sidewalks canvases covered with a wide variety of goods for sale. Las Ramblas is a long arterial avenue that spans across the city, but the naming commonly designates a mostly upscale commercial district. Near the Teatro Poliorama, Las Ramblas marks a particularly glaring contact zone where issues of class and immigration intersect and often clash. When the policia approach the vicinity, vendors grab the corner of their blankets, roll up their wares, and flee with their goods firmly cradled under their arms. Although not sweatshop labor, it appears a close cousin of what has been termed by too many politicians in the United States as "illegal immigrants" and what Chicanos and activists refer to as "undocumented laborers," who also work in fear of being caught by the INS, Border Patrol, or vigilante minutemen. Yet none of these possible connections were signaled by Losada's production. The play remained void of constructed references to the current political debates taking place in Spain about immigrants and labor. *Las Mujeres en Verdad Tienen Curvas* translated mole to mayonesa, but it did not realize the possibilities of shared political debates or histories of oppression so clearly offered by the script of *Real Women Have Curves.* The audience was not invited to make connections among the world we left to enter the theater and the worlds we might enter in witnessing the play.

One left the Barcelona production happily entertained, perhaps even with one's own sense of body image heightened. But leaving the Teatro Poliorama, streaming on to Las Ramblas, no one appeared compelled to give much thought to crossing back over those top mantas, nor to the haphazard suturing of Barcelona to East Los Angeles.

ACKNOWLEDGMENTS

I would like to give special thanks to Karen Mary Davalos for her insightful reading and commentary on an early draft of this essay. I would also like to thank Joelle Guzman and Sonia Valencia for their feedback on earlier incarnations of this work. Special acknowledgment and appreciation go to Lisette Ordorica Lasater for her keen editorial assistance with the final draft of this work.

NOTES

1. The landmark volume *Living Chicana Theory* begins with an excerpt from the closing monologue to *Real Women Have Curves,* in which Ana affirms the lessons about resistance, unity, and social change that she learned from working alongside the women at the factory, concluding with the lines, "Perhaps the greatest thing I learned from them is that women are powerful, especially when working together."

2. Josefina López, *Real Women Have Curves* (Woodstock, IL: Dramatic Publishing, 1996), 5.

3. López, *Real Women Have Curves,* 5.

4. López, *Real Women Have Curves,* 5–6.

5. The back of the HBO DVD box for *Real Women Have Curves* describes the story thus: "Should she [Ana] leave home, go to college and experience life? Or stay home, get married, and keep working in her sister's struggling garment factory? It may seem like an easy decision, but for 18-year-old Ana, every choice she makes this summer will change her life. At home, she is bound to a mother who wants her to become someone she's not. But at school, she's encouraged by a teacher who sees her potential, and adored by a boyfriend who loves her for who she is."

6. The Dramatic Publishing Company playscript of *Real Women Have Curves* provides the following synopsis: "Set in a tiny sewing factory in East LA, this is the outrageously funny story of five full-figured Mexican-American women who are racing to meet nearly impossible production deadlines in order to keep their tiny factory from going under. And while they work, hiding from the INS (Immigration and Naturalization Service), they talk . . . about their husbands and lovers, their children and their dreams for the future. The story is told from the point of view of Ana, the youngest among them. Just graduated from high school, Ana dreams of getting out of the barrio and going off to college and becoming a famous writer. Although she needs money, Ana doesn't like working at the factory, and has little respect for the co-workers, who make fun of her ambitions, and what they consider her idealistic feminist philosophies. However, Ana keeps coming to her job and chronicling her experiences in a journal. As the summer unfolds, she slowly gains an understanding and appreciation of the work and the women, eventually writing an essay that wins her a journalism fellowship which will take her to New York City. This play, a microcosm of the Latina immigrant experience, celebrates women's bodies, the power of women, and the incredible bond that happens when women work together."

7. At her website, López explains the artistic rationale that inform the differences between the two scripts, emphasizing, "What works on stage doesn't always work on film." She remarks that while Estela is the play's protagonist, Ana is the protagonist in the film because "she had the most to learn and was the better person to take us into the world of the sewing factory." She also explains that issues of immigration are absent from the film script because "they require venturing outside the factory." Of the harshness of the mother as depicted in the film, she offers, "Mother became the antagonist and symbol of tradition and culture." López sees the stronger portraits of men in the screenplay as "a step forward for Latino men and their representation. The greatest tragedy is that machismo is passed down by the mothers and we wanted to show that."

8. Maria P. Figueroa, "Resisting 'Beauty' and Real Women Have Curves," Alicia Gaspar de Alba, ed., *Velvet Barrios: Popular Culture and Chicana/o Sexualities* (New York: Palgrave Macmillan, 2003), 274–275.

9. Marta Saez, unpublished interview with director Garbi Losada on the staging of the Barcelona, Spain, Spanish-language production of *Real Women Have Curves,* Teatro Poliorama, May–June, 2005.

10. López, *Real Women Have Curves,* 59.

11. López, *Real Women Have Curves,* 69

12. López, *Real Women Have Curves,* 69
13. López, *Real Women Have Curves,* 59.

REFERENCES

Brady, Mary Pat. *Extinct Lands, Temporal Geographies: Chicana Literature and the Urgency of Space.* Durham, NC: Duke University Press, 2002.

Figueroa, Maria P. "Resisting 'Beauty' and Real Women Have Curves." Alicia Gaspar de Alba, ed., *Velvet Barrios: Popular Culture and Chicana/o Sexualities.* New York: Palgrave Macmillan, 2003.

Fregoso, Rosa Linda. *MeXicana Encounters: The Making of Social Identities on the Borderlands.* Berkeley: University of California Press, 2003.

Garcia, Laura, Sandra Gutierrez, and Felicitas Nuñez. *Teatro Chicana: A Collective Memoir and Selected Plays.* Austin: University of Texas Press, 2008.

López, Josefina. *Real Women Have Curves.* Woodstock, IL: Dramatic Publishing, 1996.

———. Yes! You Too Can Be A CHINGONA. Author's self-published chapbook, 1997.

———. "On Being a Playwright." *Ollantay Theater Magazine,* volume 1, number 2, July 1993.

———. www.josefinaLópez.com. The playwright's website offers detailed interviews about her writing for both the stage and screen, her theater company, and her life as an immigrant and Chicana; additionally, she provides links on issues of art and activism.

Marrero, Teresa. "*Real Women Have Curves:* The Articulation of Fat as a Cultural/Feminist Issue." *Ollantay Theater Magazine,* volume 1, number 1, January 1993.

Moraga, Cherríe. *Loving in the War Years / lo que nunca pasó por sus labios.* Cambridge, MA: South End Press, 1983.

Saez, Marta. Unpublished interview with Director Garbi Losada on the staging of the Barcelona, Spain, Spanish-language production of *Real Women Have Curves,* Teatro Poliorama. May–June 2005.

Taylor, Diana. *The Archive and the Repertoire: Performing Cultural Memory in the Americas.* Durham, NC: Duke University Press, 2003.

Torres, Edén. *Chicana Without Apology: The New Chicana Cultural Studies.* New York: Routledge, 2003.

Trujillo, Carla, editor. *Living Chicana Theory.* Berkeley, CA: Third Woman Press, 1998.

SIXTEEN

Loving Revolution: Same-Sex Marriage and Queer Resistance in Monica Palacios's *Amor y Revolución*

MARIVEL T. DANIELSON

The brilliant campaigning and historic outcome of the 2008 United States presidential election resonated on local and global levels, shattering—in the views of many—the glass ceilings hovering just above the heads of people of color in the United States. Yet amidst the echoes of celebration, a multitude of voters watched in disbelief as the passing of California Proposition 8 stripped away the rights of same-sex couples to legally marry—a right recognized by the state Supreme Court in May 2008. For nearly six months, queer couples across the state had enjoyed equal access to the rite and rights of marriage before this proposition reversed the historic court ruling.[1] Los Angeles–based Chicana writer and performer Monica Palacios staged her dissenting voice in the form of protest performance. Palacios's treatment of same-sex marriage and Proposition 8 first appeared in an updated version of her one-woman show *Greetings from a Queer Señorita* that ran for four weeks in Santa Ana, CA, in summer 2008.[2] In October 2008 at Highways Performance Space in Santa Monica, CA, Palacios merged the new pieces on same-sex marriage from *Greetings* to create *Amor y Revolución,* a silly, sex-laced, and politically charged romp through this defining political milieu for queer Californians.[3] From political propaganda to popular reception, Palacios's performances confront the issue of lesbian, gay, bisexual, transgender, and queer[4] rights through the reinscribed metaphor of revolution—a war and a fight for the right to love. Transcending the language of violence and combat, Palacios's works seize a productive theatrical space of revolutionary love in the face of hateful media representation, legislation, and political campaigning. Invoking Augusto Boal and Gloria Anzaldúa's living discourse on theater and theory, I will discuss how Palacios's performances fashion an interstitial space of queer reinscription, coalition, and inspiration for queer and Latina/o communities.

CREATION AND COLLABORATION

Tejana scholar and poet Gloria Anzaldúa posits theoretical discourse as a resource for revolutionary movement. In her landmark *Borderlands: The New Mestiza,* Anzaldúa's narratives—in the form of poetry, myth, testimonio, critical essay, and historical discourse—bleed into one another and into the readers' own memories, struggles, and stories, moving beyond the limits of discourse and into collaborative performances of coalition. Anzaldúa's hybrid theories open up spaces for readers' own lives to fill the gaps, authorizing countless additional intellectual revolutions to emerge each time someone slips inside the pages of her text. She speaks of her writings not as static artifacts but living forces, stressing the collaboration necessary to fully engage her discourse, "My 'stories' are acts encapsulated in time, 'enacted' every time they are spoken aloud or read silently. I like to think of them as performances and not as inert and 'dead' objects . . . Instead, the work has an identity . . . The work manifests the same needs as a person, it needs to be 'fed,' *la tengo que bañar y vestir.*"[5] Anzaldúa imbues her text with a life and human needs; she must bathe and dress her work.[6] Yet her notion of enacting necessitates action from the author as well as her readers in order to breathe life into the work. By including her readers, Anzaldúa envisions a process of symbiotic textual engagement that interrupts the primacy of authorial intention and fashions a view of discourse that transforms fact (written word on a page) into act (performative collaboration between author and reader). As such, *Borderlands* is not simply a manifesto but the movement itself. Her words do not simply call for action but demand a coalitional relationship between author and reader. She speaks directly with the individuals and communities who can and must interact to engage a state of collaboration. Anzaldúa's theory presents not a static narrative but one that lives, breathes, and transforms along with her readers.

Much like Gloria Anzaldúa's vision of an enacted text, Brazilian theater director and scholar Augusto Boal sees theater as a collaborative creative form, a transformative representational space capable of shifting worlds and inspiring revolutions. Boal's notion of a theater of the oppressed and in particular his conceptualization of rehearsal-theater afford performers and audiences the space to create worlds that stretch beyond public ignorance and oppressive legislation. He speaks of the potential for theater to function as a "rehearsal for revolution" as oppressed communities transform themselves from detached spectators to active collaborators through the creative act of dramatic production.[7] In contrast to spectacle theater, where playwrights, directors, and actors predetermine outcomes, Boal posits that rehearsal theater offers an experience where "one knows how these experiments will begin but not how they will end, because the spectator is freed from his chains, finally acts, and becomes a protagonist."[8] In his estimation, the primary determinant in truly vital and relevant creative production is not what takes place on the stage but rather what the audiences are moved to do during the show and after it. For a spectator to become a protagonist suggests a shift from passive to active, from marginalized to central, and from silent to speaking. Theater offers a safe space to rehearse these roles of action, voice, and visibility among a community of like-minded and similarly oppressed individuals.[9] Through their audiences, then, theatrical works may continue to live, move, and act long after the curtains close.

By staging the body, live performance also straddles the divide between language and act, giving birth to the written word in motion. Writer becomes performer; readers morph into audience. The immediate negotiation between public and performer presents yet another medium for collaborative ritual, especially when the performance aligns itself with the dialogic methodologies of Boal's rehearsal theater and Anzaldúa's enacted discourse. According to Boal, transmitting the means of theatrical production to oppressed communities allows them to employ drama to explore local problems and potential solutions.[10] As writers, actors, directors, and audience, oppressed subjects may interrupt their own pre-scripted marginalization and thus claim a central role in their own liberation. Monica Palacios's performances intervene into prevailing narratives of homophobia and hysteria regarding queer unions, human rights, and the institution of marriage. Palacios utilizes

Boal's notion of theatrical production as well as Anzaldúa's enacted text as means to mobilize an oppressed community to imagine and engage within a more egalitarian reality and to rehearse the action necessary to move toward change.

HERE COME THE BRIDES

Speaking through the medium of popular iconography, Palacios's performing persona, Monica,[11] opens *Amor y Revolución* with several verses of "Get Me to the Church on Time" from the Broadway musical and 1964 Warner Brothers feature film *My Fair Lady.*[12] Queering the spirited heteronormative tune, Monica proudly sings, "I'm gettin' married in the mornin'. Ding dong the bells are gonna chime."[13] Ironically, she does not assume the female lead role of diamond-in-the-rough female protagonist Eliza Doolittle but that of her father, Alfred, who prepares for his impending vows by drinking himself into a stupor while relying on his cronies to make sure he arrives at his own ceremony the next morning. Alfred's dread takes center stage in the musical number. When referencing the marital euphemism "tying the knot," he places a hand over his throat to signal a hanging or strangulation. Alfred's exit is morose; the rowdy pub crowd delivers the intoxicated groom to his nuptials, raising him in a prone position over their heads. In a final nod to matrimonial doom, the groom removes his top hat and places it over his chest, completing the makeshift funeral procession.

In contrast to the exaggeratedly morbid imagery in the film, Palacios employs the song to signal the hope, life, and possibilities presented to queer couples by the California Supreme Court's 2008 ruling. From her perspective, marriage is a privilege, not a sentence, and her use of the familiar song flips both the negative connotations of marriage as well as the heteronormativity of the institution itself, since according to Yvonne Yarbro-Bejarano, "centering the Chicana lesbian subject also means decentering the traditionally privileged spectator."[14] Beaming with joy, Monica's face evidences the excitement and anticipation of legalized marriage as a queer reality. Raising her palms toward the audience on either side of her face, the performer assumes the stance of a jazz dancer. With a wide grin and campy expression, Monica bounces from stage left to right, quite literally dancing for joy at the prospect of her own wedding. Contrasted with Monica's hopeful and positive portrait of the institution of marriage, the song's original context normalizes the queer version of marriage while portraying the heterosexual version as joyless and oppressive.

Both the Santa Ana and Santa Monica productions of Palacios's newer same-sex marriage material preceded California voters' November 4, 2008, passing of Proposition 8, and as such maintained a cautious but hopeful outlook on the status of LGBTQ rights in her home state. Both productions provided a space for the artist and her audiences to celebrate the California Supreme Court's historic ruling to recognize same-sex marriages just a few months earlier. Palacios's performance persona gleefully relinquishes her previous state of queer disenfranchisement, placing herself instead at the center of matrimonial rites and possibilities: "I was in the garment district in downtown LA, checking out the bridal shops. I was looking at dresses because now, *I,* can get married . . ."[15] Her delivery stresses the personal "I," that stands in defiance of the state's previous and the nation's continued denial of marriage rights for queer couples.

The declaration that she "can" take part in this long-denied ritual evokes the familiar "Sí se puede" refrain that defines the United Farm Workers' continued movement to secure human rights for farm laborers.[16] The popular affirmation, translating roughly to "Yes we can" or "It can be done," serves to unite a collective under the framework of possibility. By including the phrase, here and later in the performances, Palacios inextricably links the struggle for human rights across divisions of ethnicity, class, and sexuality. She extends the metaphor of universal possibility, moving from "I can get married," to "Lesbians can get married," and ultimately "Tom can marry Jerry." Monica speaks of the relevance and impact of the historic ruling first for herself as an individual ("I can"), then for a broader community ("Lesbians can"), and finally, in hyperbolic comedic form, for the inter-species union of a famously adversarial cartoon cat and mouse ("Tom can"). A projected image of the pair as tuxedo-clad grooms visually completes the sequence of matrimonial inclusivity. The inclusion of the fictional characters—icons of childhood innocence—also serves to reinscribe a familiar narrative with a queer subtext. By imposing the presence of same-sex marriage in unexpected sites of popular discourse, Palacios's performance moves

FIG. 16.1. "Here Comes the Bride." *Courtesy of Patricia Lugo Varela.*

toward a normalization of the institution of marriage as a queer construction and reality.

After a few bars of the song in the Santa Ana production, Monica introduces a bridal couple, played by two actresses listed in the program as "Lesbian Bride Dancers."[17] As physical manifestations of her earlier declaration that "Lesbians can get married," the blushing brides—in their matching gauzy white veils and vests—skip, arm in arm, across the stage to the classic melody of "The Wedding March." The spectacle immediately offers a partial adherence to the most familiar visual and aural traditions of marriage. Yet like the previous queer restaging of a Hollywood film classic, elements of non-conventionality—from the sneaker-clad feet to sporadic verbal outbursts of defiance—mark the brides both as participants in and as rewriters of the traditional rites of marriage.

In both productions, the initial formality of a traditional, heteronormative wedding quickly gives way to a funkier queer reality. In the Santa Ana production of *Greetings from a Queer Señorita,* Monica assumes the role of officiator, first leading an enthusiastic line dance performance of Van McCoy's "The Hustle" and then walking the brides through their vows on a dimly lit stage while spinning multi-colored party lights and the familiar disco anthem float through the theater. At the close of the ceremony, Monica signals for the brides to kiss and watches as they dance briefly and pose for a quick photo before happily skipping off stage. The creation of a disco club space to house a lesbian wedding undoubtedly queers the traditional church venue, substituting instead a space of 1970s liberalism and sexual freedom.[18] The disco wedding affords Palacios's audience the opportunity to rehearse an integral part of revolution, the affirmation of collectivity. When fearful families, ignorant lawmakers, and hateful community groups refuse to acknowledge the dignity of LGBTQ individuals or the validity of same-sex unions, Palacios's nightclub ceremony stands as a counter space of safety and positive affirmation. The audiences' gleeful support for the bridal couple stands as a revolutionary act of love in the face of hate and serves as a rehearsal for many future battles against homophobia and legalized and voter-sanctioned disenfranchisement of queer communities. Uniting performer and public, the medium of live performance provides the vehicle from which audiences and artist alike may celebrate newly granted rights and dare to collectively envision their possibilities within a more egalitarian future.

THE VIEW FROM BELOW

Just beyond the utopian vision of equality, Palacios's performative persona cites sources in popular media and political organizations as evidence of the marginalization of same-sex couples in California and the rest of the United States. Monica reluctantly admits, "Despite the celebrations, there have been truly hateful comments from people, in the news, online, on the radio—to my face." Climbing to the top of homophobic heap, Monica recounts comments made by one particularly outspoken conservative and co-host of a popular daytime television show: "The 'Ignorance at its Best' Award goes to that blond white chick on the TV show *The View*.[19] She said: 'If gays are allowed to marry, then what's going to stop them from marrying their pets.'"

Monica does not refer to the speaker by name, instead referring to her as only an amalgamation of physical characteristics. Although several of the show's co-hosts share this same race, gender, and hair color, audiences in Santa Ana and Santa Monica released a similar exasperated groan upon hearing Monica's description of "that blond white chick." Repeatedly, audience members chose this particular moment in the performance to release themselves from their spectatorial silence in order to vocally express their disdain for this individual. Yet the audience in this moment exceeds Aristotelian empathy[20] for Monica, rising up as fellow complainants alongside her. Utterances of "Oh, God!" and "Oh, no!" allow the public to verbally link themselves to Monica's experience, acknowledging the familiarity of offense and alienation via homophobic media commentaries.

After a brief ad lib with outspoken and outraged audience members, Monica proceeds to narrate an on-camera discussion about same-sex marriage and California's Proposition 8 wherein she quotes the television host as saying: "If gays are allowed to marry, then what's going to stop them from marrying their pets?"[21] In this single utterance, Palacios illustrates a narrowing of the gap between reality and ridiculousness. Palacios's imagery frequently employs the hyperbolic brushstrokes of ethnic and queer self-tropicalization, such as her earlier inclusion of cartoon characters Tom and Jerry in the collective of individuals positively impacted by the state's legal recognition of their same-sex relationships,[22] yet the suggestion of weddings between cartoon cats and dogs seems tame compared to the frequently cited argument that legalizing same-sex marriage will somehow open the floodgates for actual interspecies unions. Thinking aloud, Monica contemplates the bestial hypothesis, "Hmmm . . . let's deconstruct this. What's going to stop me from marrying my pet? Logic? Common sense?" Pitting her own clear reasoning against the television host's irrationality, Monica again marginalizes the heteronormative perspective, leaving homophobic fears of the breakdown of the sacred institution of marriage outside the periphery of reasonable and logical thought.

THE GREATEST SHOW ON EARTH

Palacios responds to such statements of ignorance and fear by staging a literal three-ring circus to echo the figurative media circus surrounding the issue of same-sex marriage in the spring and summer of 2008. Monica notes, "On June 17, same sex marriage become legal and of course the media overreacted . . ." As the performer exits the stage, the iconic circus theme "Thunder and Blazes" fills the theater with energy and anticipation for the great spectacle to follow. The Bride Dancers frenetically bounce pink hula hoops around their hips at either side of the stage as Monica reemerges dressed in a red velvet tailcoat and black top hat. Confronted with the media's grotesque representations of her community, Monica employs her performative space to claim the central role of ringmaster in the chaotic political milieu. No longer a spectacle, she seizes the reins as master of ceremonies.

Palacios's ringmaster serves as newscaster and commentator, providing play-by-play accounts of the first hours after the Supreme Court's ruling took effect on June 17th, 2008, allowing same-sex couples to marry legally. Stationed at the courthouse in the historically queer-friendly city of West Hollywood, Palacios's ringmaster persona—who refers to herself as "Janet Jaundice"—presents her report on same-sex marriage, including an interview with a groom from the crowd. Throughout the scene, Palacios occupies a single tight spot in the left downstage corner. Janet is hysteria personified, from her wide-eyed expression to her anxious mannerisms. Every inch of her body anticipates a truly shocking response to the question she poses to the groom: "What does this marriage license mean to you?"

Shifting from news reporter to interviewed groom, Palacios angles her body to reflect a dialogic exchange and removes her ringmaster top hat. Compared to Janet's wide frantic gestures, the groom's body language is calm, deliberate, and close to the body.

Immediately following Janet's question, the Bride Dancers freeze in anxious anticipation, and an extended drum roll sets the aural scene.

All clearly expect a freak show spectacle of queer monstrosity. The drum roll also calls up the image of a trapeze artist attempting a daring trick high above the fascinated audience below. The sound cue transforms a typical local news broadcast interview into a public spectacle with a gay couple—whom she addresses as "Sir & Sir"—as the feature act of extreme alterity. In staging the media coverage of these first same-sex couples' experiences legalizing their unions, Palacios extends the perception of excess (extreme allegations of immorality, hedonism, and danger)—as epitomized by her previous reference to marrying one's pet—with the reporter's frenzied delivery and the drum roll sound cue. Palacios's performance again counters popular narratives of hysterical excess and otherness with the sane and sedate realities of gay and lesbian couples.

The groom responds to Janet's question with anxious perplexity. He is visibly startled by the drum roll and nervously looks around for the source of the puzzling sound. Finally, hesitantly, he mutters, "Ah . . . we're affirming our love and our relationship."

A long pause follows the groom's response as the Bride Dancers look to each other and out toward the audience, bewildered by the groom's disappointingly conventional response. After a few seconds, a sound cue of the theme song from the 1976 film *Rocky* reanimates the stunned performers, including Janet, who resumes her role as news reporter. At this point, the Bride Dancers drop their hula hoops and begin throw punches and stretch as though preparing for a fight. The audience might interpret this battle for lesbian brides as both legal and psychological, since they rally against laws, voters, and media representation that all stand in the way of socially and legally legitimized queer unions. Janet attempts to maintain the hysteria, deeming the groom's mundane response "Extreme!" Palacios repeatedly pits the monstrous caricature of LGBTQ couples promoted by conservative media sources against the mundane reality—since, according to this respondent, his motivation for and understanding of marriage mirrors that of millions of couples, including those opposed to same-sex marriage. This radical notion, that queer couples marry for the same reason heterosexual couples do, calls into question the reasoning and propaganda behind legislation such as Proposition 8 and moves toward establishing a collectivity of heterosexual and queer communities unified by a common belief in committed, loving relationships and in marriage as a sacred and honorable institution.

Finally, Janet sends the broadcast back to an anchor in the news studio, who wraps up coverage of what she calls "SAME-SEX MARRIAGE 2008," approximating the panic of an impending hurricane, tsunami, or other catastrophic natural disaster. Like these types of environmental hazards, the final days before and the first days after the 2008 legalization of same-sex marriage were frequently sensationalized by the media as excessive and out of control. Echoing Otto Santa Ana's discussion of immigration metaphors, Monica also identifies media characterization of queer unions as both invasion and infection.[23] Through the voice of the news anchor, she warns the viewers of the approaching danger: "The county clerks are expecting an onslaught of same sex couples . . . overloading the system! The system is going to be overloaded with same sex couples . . . Do you know what this means, America . . . oh my god! What about the children . . . the children?!"

Prior to June 17, opponents of the Supreme Court ruling warned that California courthouses would be overwhelmed by masses of same-sex couples applying for marriage licenses. In anticipation of this horror—an expected collapse of the system—news crews eagerly awaited the impending chaos. Instead, turnout was manageable, and the process of obtaining marriage licenses continued without incident. From a legal perspective, same-sex couples joyously embraced a new sense of equality. On the level of discourse, however, popular media outlets continued to marginalize queer communities through the promulgation of antagonizing metaphors. Janet's prior statement, only a slight exaggeration of actual media reports, characterizes queer Californians as excessive in numbers, a mob-like force whose "onslaught" threatens to "overload the system." For the news anchor and her heterosexual viewers, there is additionally a sense of entitlement and ownership of "the system," whereas she represents same-sex couples as outsiders invading a system never meant to serve their needs. Palacios's staging of the media's language of queer excess additionally invites the audience to intervene into such discourses of sensationalized representation. Laughter emerges as a way of diffusing the authority of a conservative and heterosexist narrative. Palacios's performance mocks local and national news media's perspectives as ignorant and absurd, flipping the script from scrutinized sideshow freak to gleefully sardonic ringmaster. Set free from the spectacle of popular media's hysterical representations, Palacios and her audience indeed wield theater as a weapon for change.

THEATRICAL TRANSFORMATIONS

The transformational power of art underlines Gloria Anzaldúa's theorization of reading and writing discourse. She speaks of creative expression as an enacted text—as a spiritual rite—containing the power to dramatically alter both author and audience: "The ability of story to transform the storyteller and the listener into something or someone else is shamanistic. The writer, as shape-changer, is a *nahual,* a shaman."[24] Although Anzaldúa charges writers with the power of shamanistic transformation, the genre of solo performance is also a uniquely apposite form for practicing spiritual transcendence and social change. The constraints of solo performance (with limited participation from supporting actors) necessitate that Palacios play both oppressor and oppressed, enemy and adversary, problem and solution. From within this format, Palacios also encourages her audience to assume diverse roles throughout the performance. They are eager and ignorant consumers of sensationalist media, wedding officiators, and friends and family of the bridal couple. Both artist and audience constantly shape-shift, rehearsing situations of potential conflict and liberation for queer and allied communities.

Palacios uses dramatic techniques to inspire and inform while simultaneously engendering the collaborative participation of her audiences. Far more than static spectacle, Palacios's performative work—like Anzaldúa's enacted texts and Boal's theatrical methodology—necessitates immediate and ongoing action from her viewing public. At times, the performance necessarily shifts the relationship of audience and performer, and the viewers assume the roles of the unconverted or homophobic oppressors. Such inverted subject assignments allow the performance to approximate what Boal refers to as "train[ing] [one]self for real action."[25] Releasing themselves from silent observation, Palacios's audience members hold the potential to transform from spectators to subjects as they translate the coalitional forces fostered during the performance into "real action" both in and outside the theater space. From the theater to the voting booth, Palacios stages same-sex marriage and the ensuing legal battle as spectacles open to revolution via collaborative transformation of both performer and audience.

The call-and-response format reappears in the final scene of the Santa Ana run as Monica transforms into a presidential candidate for change. Echoing the familiar refrain of Martin Luther King, Jr.'s historic 1963 speech at the Lincoln Memorial in Washington, DC, Palacios's Queer Señorita Mariachi—introduced to her public here as Monica Palacios—delivers an impassioned campaign speech beginning with the declaration: "I have a dream . . . and I have a headache." Laced with both hope and heartache, Monica's speech details a general sense of dissatisfaction with her social and political environment that includes but is not limited to the issue of same-sex marriage. She decries failing healthcare and educational systems, rejects unwarranted attacks on immigrant communities, and condemns a faulty economy that inflates fuel and food prices to astronomical levels. In the face of difficult challenges, however, Palacios's Queer Señorita Mariachi holds fast to her dream of a brighter future for all.

Santa Ana's production includes the presentation of a campaign flag, "The United States Tortilla Flag of Peace," which, Monica explains, "Represent[s] the United States that I love; honor[s] the land that once belonged to Mexico; and [represents] The Peace—The Hope that we strive for."[26] A red, white, and blue circular peace sign purportedly made entirely of corn masa, the flag maintains the Queer Señorita Mariachi's earlier tortilla theme, as much a reference to Mexican cultural tradition as it is a nod to a queer subjectivity given the Spanish slang term for lesbian, tortillera.[27] The multifaceted iconography of the tortilla lends itself to a definition of Palacios's performative revolution as uniquely, but not exclusively, Chicana, Mexican, lesbian, queer, and female.

Although Boal admits that not all theater is revolutionary, he suggests that the tools of theatrical production ought to "evoke in [the spectator] a desire to practice in reality the act he has rehearsed in the theater. The practice of theatrical forms creates a sort of uneasy sense of incompleteness that seeks fulfillment through real action."[28] For Palacios's audiences, the dramatic uneasiness emerges in feelings of outrage and indignation at the notion of human rights as temporary or fleeting privileges. In her October 2008 production of *Amor y Revolución* in Santa Monica, Palacios brought the campaign against California Proposition 8 to center stage. As an alternative presidential candidate, Monica balks at the suggestion that same-sex marriage threatens the sanctity of the state constitution and urges audience members to "Vote NO ON PROPOSITION 8," since "Equal protection under the law is the foundation of American society."[29] Throughout the campaign speech, in both venues, audiences erupted with alternating boos and cheers, eagerly repeating catch phrases without prompting. Workers from the "No on 8" campaign spoke with audience members before and after Palacios's performance in Santa Monica, offering information and resources to potential voters and volunteers. This collaboration between artist and activists in the theatrical space served to harness the revolutionary power of Palacios's politicized audience. Boal's notion of incompleteness—in this case, the fear of losing the legal right to marry—may be managed through the "real action" of political participation, both in the "No on 8" campaign and in the state and national elections. Recognizing the power of the theatrical genre, Palacios sought out a means to bridge the physical and psychological divide between theater space and the external, or real-world, spaces where audience members could carry the impact of her performance beyond that evening's event.

LEADERS WHO LOVE

In addition to political engagement, Palacios's performance created a space for the expression of the queer community as loving. The fight against same-sex marriage presents an ironic dichotomy, the hateful resistance of loving and legally recognized unions of LGBTQ individuals. Stressing the importance of love as an defining rubric, Monica implores, "We need leaders who love us. We need leaders who let us love who we want to love. We need love activists, like Del Martin, Dolores Huerta[30] . . . the Pussy Cat Dolls—."[31] The suggestion of "love activists," plucked from both queer and Chicano civil rights movements, echoes Chela Sandoval's conceptualization of "an interrelated hermeneutics of 'love,' a methodology *for* the oppressed and *of* emancipation."[32] Palacios's liberatory revolution of love utilizes elements of Boal's rehearsal theater to channel performance as an emancipatory tool. Beginning within the theater space itself, Monica elucidates the praises of love, "Love is patriotic! Love is Coming Out Day! Love is hugging your neighbor!" Then, stepping off her literal soapbox—a black wooden cube—the performer weaves throughout the audience, instructing individuals to "Hug your neighbor! Kiss your neighbor! Tongue your neighbor!"[33] increasingly escalating the sexual nature of her requests. With little hesitation, guests turned to their neighbors—some familiar and others complete strangers—and began to greet and embrace one another. Though not necessarily queer in nature, the shrinking of physical space between audience members and the presence of more intimate contact performs a sort of shamanistic transformation along the lines of Anzaldúa's nahual. Strangers become neighbors, partners in the performative collaboration.

Ultimately, Palacios asserts that "Love and revolution—is the solution," and the final scene closes with the audience's enthusiastic chants of this defining slogan.[34] Her final pose in both productions is unmistakably revolutionary, from her wide stance to her defiant raised fist. In *Greetings from a Queer Señorita,* three large green, white, and red panels line the back wall of the space, suggesting the Mexican flag. In the final pose, Palacios and her Bride Dancers each stand in front of a single panel; one bride is now draped with Adelita-esque bullets across her chest, and the other, having just played the role of Palacios's campaign manager, wears slacks and a conservative black blazer. At once signifying the past and the future, the brides flank Palacios, whose black and white mariachi jacket and sombrero combined with sneakers and denim jeans place her somewhere in the middle of modern and traditional. Each a reinscription of archetypal Chicana femininity and sexuality, the three women position themselves upstage in front of their respective panels. Each panel is painted and backlit in the same saturated colors of green, white, and red while all other lights go black. This lighting intensifies the visual impact of the Mexican flag, with each woman's silhouette—fist raised—cast across one of the panels. The performance's living flag stands as a testament to Palacios's resolve to redefine Mexican, Chicano, lesbian, queer, woman, and citizen as interdependent categories of being. Just as Anzaldúa noted the power of story to transform both teller and listener, Palacios illustrates a revolution wherein she both defines and is defined by México, where her queer identity shapes her Chicana perspective and vice versa. Transformational artistic production represents both the struggle and the solution to survival in between categories, communities, or nations, as Anzaldúa defines living in the borderlands as "always a path/state to something else."[35] Both Anzaldúa's "something else" and Boal's "uneasy sense of incompleteness" suggest the power of art to push readers, listeners, and viewers—all collaborators in the creative process—to enact their own stories and to challenge the limits of what is acceptable, attainable, reasonable, or possible.

Palacios's performances stage the possibilities of an egalitarian world. As audience members step into and help explore this fantastical worldview, they begin to establish invaluable coalitions of empowered and engaged community mobilized around particular problems and goals. In this sense, art not only precedes revolutionary change but also initiates and continuously propels the revolution. Boal clearly delineates the gap between real action and theatrical rehearsal. Yet the discursive distance between the two concepts almost completely disappears under Anzaldúa's assertion that "Nothing happens in the 'real world' unless it first happens in the images in our heads."[36] Monica Palacios's performances target bastions of patriarchy and heteronormativity, saturating the sacred institutions of marriage and political office (the presidency in particular) with an infusion of queer desire—largely female—that intervenes in narratives of alienation and marginalization for lesbian and gay communities and creates an imaginary world of access to institutions that have historically been denied to queers and/or people of color. Althout participation in these queer worlds[37] may always not constitute "real action" in terms of Boal's theorization, these dramatic rehearsals certainly give birth to the images Anzaldúa posits as precursors to real change. If, indeed, visualization is the first step toward significant personal and social change, then performances like Palacios's provide a unique medium for expanding the public imaginary, pushing at the limits of possibility, forging and expanding politicized communities, and creating ample space for loving revolution.

NOTES

1. As of April 2010, the following states recognize marriage equality: Connecticut, Massachusetts, Iowa, New Hampshire, Vermont, and the District of Columbia. Forty states ban same-sex marriage by state constitution or statute. Several lawsuits challenging the constitutionality of California's Proposition 8 were heard by the state supreme court in 2009. Although the proposition and ban on same-sex marriage were upheld, all marriages performed before November 5, 2008, were ruled valid (National Center for Lesbian Rights publication, 2010).

2. Monica Palacios, *Greetings from a Queer Señorita.* Directed by Marivel Danielson. (Santa Ana, CA: Breath of Fire Latina Theater Ensemble, July 11 to August 3, 2008).

3. Monica Palacios. *Amor y Revolución.* Directed by Marivel Danielson. (Santa Monica, CA: Latino New Works Festival. Highways Performance Space, October 4, 2008).

4. Subsequent references will abbreviate as LGBTQ. My usage of this acronym accounts for the addition of the label "Queer" to Palacios's earlier reference.

5. Gloria Anzaldúa, *Borderlands: The New Mestiza*. 2nd Edition. (San Fransisco, CA: Aunt Lute Books, 1999), 89.

6. Anzaldúa uses the gender-specific feminine direct object pronoun to express the concept of her work. While this could relate to the Spanish translation of "la obra," it is more likely an expression of the feminine energy she associates with her writing. Her choice also evokes an intimate scene of one woman bathing, feeding, and nurturing another woman.

7. Augusto Boal, *Theater of the Oppressed*. Translation by Charles A. & Maria-Odilia Leal McBride. (New York: Theatre Communications Group, 1985), 141.

8. Boal, 142.

9. For more recent scholarship on queer and Latina/o theater as a space of intervention, resistance, and opposition, see Lawrence la Fountain-Stokes's *Queer Ricans: Cultures and Sexualities in the Diaspora*. (Minneapolis: The University of Minnesota Press, 2009) and Laura Gutiérrez's *Performing Mexicanidad: Vendidas y Cabareteras on the Transnational Stage*. (Austin: University of Texas Press, 2010).

10. Boal, 125.

11. In both performances, Palacios represents a character who shares her first and last names. To avoid confusion, and to honor the performances as creative manifestations rather than autobiographical facsimile, I will use "Palacios" to denote the actual artist and "Monica" to designate the fictional character created within the performances.

12. "Get Me to the Church on Time" from the Broadway production of *My Fair Lady*. Directed by Moss Hart. Composed by Frederick Loewe. Lyrics by Alan Jay Lerner (1956). Film version directed by George Cukor (Warner Brothers Pictures, 1964).

13. This song is present in both productions, but its placement in the script varies. The verses immediately open *Amor y Revolución* but appear about fifteen minutes into *Greetings from a Queer Señorita*.

14. Yvonne Yarbro-Bejarano, "The Lesbian Body in Latina Cultural Production" in *Entiendes?* ed. Emilie L. Bergmann and Paul Julian Smith. (Durham, NC: Duke University Press, 1995), 192.

15. *Amor y Revolución*. Written and performed by Monica Palacios. All subsequent references to unpublished script and Santa Monica, CA, performance on October 4, 2008 will be noted as (AR). Santa Ana performances of related material in Palacios's one-woman show *Greetings From a Queer Señorita* (unpublished script and Santa Ana production) will be designated with (GQS). Unless noted, quoted passages appear in both productions.

16. Dolores Huerta and César Chávez coined the phrase "Sí se puede" during their work with UFW in the early 1970s. The slogan, and especially its English translation of "Yes we can," has most recently been appropriated by the 2008 Barack Obama presidential campaign and the fight against Proposition 8 in the 2008 general election in California.

17. Diana Alvarez and Jackie Bustamante performed the roles of Lesbian Bride Dancers in the Santa Ana productions, and Bustamante was the sole Bride in the Santa Monica performance.

18. A character in Frances Negrón-Muntaner's 1994 film *Brincando el charco* expresses the comforts and conflicts presented by queer disco clubs in Puerto Rico and New York (New York: Hispanic Productions, 1994). Distributed by Women Make Films.

19. *The View* debuted in 1997 on the American Broadcasting Company.

20. Boal, 34.

21. While I was unable to locate a similar citation from *The View,* the "blond white chick" is emblematic of the ignorance and homophobic panic unleashed following the California Supreme Court ruling. The collapsing of gay marriage and bestiality emerges in political and popular discussions as early as 2004, when defense of marriage bills appeared on numerous state ballots. From ducks to goats, same-sex marriage opponents called up a diverse menagerie to proclaim the purported dangers of legalizing queer unions. See direct quotes from Texas Senator John Cornyn Lois Romano's "In Oklahoma, GOP Race Not a Given," in *The Washington Post,* July 12, 2004, Page A04, and Representative Bob Letourneau's statement about pet marriage in Elizabeth Mehren's *Los Angeles Times* article "Same-Sex Union Controversy Moves Into New Hampshire." February 18, 2004.

22. Frances Aparicio and Susana Chávez-Silverman discuss the strategic deployment of "tropicalization" as both a First-World and Third-World mode of representation. To tropicalize from above suggests a representation akin to Edward W. Said's notion of orientalism, while tropicalizing from below implies a subversive self-representation of Latinidad as critical excess. Frances Aparicio and Susana Chávez-Silverman, eds., *Tropicalizations: Transcultural Represenations of Latinidad.* (Hanover, MA: University Press of New England, 1997), 2–8.

23. Otto Santa Ana, *Brown Tide Rising: Metaphors of Latinos in Contemporary American Public Discourse.* (Austin: University of Texas Press, 2002), 69.

24. Anzaldúa, 88.

25. Boal, 142.

26. GQS only.

27. See Alicia Gaspar de Alba's iconic poem "Making Tortillas" in Alicia Gaspar de Alba, María Herrera Sobek, and Demetria Martínez, *Three Times a Woman: Chicana Poetry.* (Tempe, AZ: Bilingual Press, 1989), 44–45.

28. Boal, 142.

29. AR only.

30. Del Martin and Dolores Huerta are foundational figures in lesbian, labor, and Chicano civil rights struggles. See Jennifer Harper, "California Weds First Same-Sex Couple; Ceremony Sets Off Cultural Wave," in *The Washington Times,* June 17, 2008, Page 1, A01, and Mario T. García, *A Dolores Huerta Reader.* (Albuquerque: University of New Mexico Press, 2008).

31. AR only.

32. Chela Sandoval, "Dissident Globalizations, Emancipatory Methods, Social-Erotics" in *Queer Globalizations: Citizenship and the Afterlife of Colonialism,* eds. Arnaldo Cruz-Malavé and Martin F. Manalansan IV. (New York: New York University Press, 2002), 27.

33. AR only.

34. AR only.

35. Anzaldúa, 95.

36. Anzaldúa, 109.

37. José Esteban Muñoz. *Disidentifications.* (Minneapolis: University of Minnesota, 1999), 196.

WORKS CITED

Anzaldúa, Gloria. *Borderlands: The New Mestiza.* 2nd edition. San Francisco, CA: Aunt Lute Books, 1999.

Aparicio, Frances, and Susana Chávez-Silverman, eds. *Tropicalizations: Transcultural Representations of Latinidad.* Hanover, MA: University Press of New England, 1997.

Arrizón, Alicia. *Latina Performance: Traversing the Stage.* Bloomington: Indiana University Press, 1999.

Boal, Augusto. *Theatre of the Oppressed.* Translated by Charles A. and Maria-Odilia Leal McBride. New York: Theatre Communications Group, 1985.

Muñoz, José Esteban. *Disidentifications: Queers of Color and the Performance of Politics.* Minneapolis: University of Minnesota Press, 1999.

Negrón-Muntaner, Frances. *Brincando el Charco.* New York: Hispanic Productions. Distributed by Women Make Movies, 1994.

Palacios, Monica. *Amor y Revolución.* Directed by Marivel Danielson. Latino New Works Festival. Highways Performance Space. Santa Monica, CA. October 4, 2008.

———. *Greetings from a Queer Señorita.* Directed by Marivel Danielson. Breath of Fire Latina Theater Ensemble. Santa Ana, CA. July 11 to August 3, 2008.

———. "Greetings from a Queer Señorita." *Out of the Fringe: Contemporary Latina/Latino Theater and Performance.* Caridad Svich and María Teresa Marrero, eds. New York: Theatre Communications Group, 2000. 369–390.

Sandoval, Chela. "Dissident Globalizations, Emancipatory Methods, Social-Erotics." *Queer Globalizations: Citizenship and the Afterlife of Colonialism.* Arnaldo Cruz-Malavé and Martin F. Manalansan IV, eds. New York City: New York University Press, 2002. 20–32.

Santa Ana, Otto. *Brown Tide Rising: Metaphors of Latinos in Contemporary American Public Discourse.* Austin: University of Texas Press, 2002.

Sinfield, Alan. *Out on Stage: Lesbian and Gay Theatre in the Twentieth Century.* New Haven, CT: Yale University Press, 1999.

Yarbro-Bejarano, Yvonne. "The Lesbian Body in Latina Cultural Production." *Entiendes? Queer Readings, Hispanic Writings.* Emilie L. Bergmann and Paul Julian Smith, eds. Durham, NC: Duke University Press, 1995. 181–198.

SEVENTEEN

Is Ugly Betty a Real Woman? Representations of Chicana Femininity Inscribed as a Site of (Transformative) Difference

JENNIFER ESPOSITO

Popular culture texts inform us about our social world. They teach us about ourselves and also about "Others." We learn who is valued in the larger society as well as who is marginalized. Although popular culture reflects our society, as an institution it also helps construct ideologies that we live out and perform in our daily lives. People may turn to texts for information on what it means to be a particular race/ethnicity, gender, social class, and/or sexual orientation. Visual images thus become textual lessons that become inscribed on lived bodies and incorporated into ideological structures of society. For bodies already marginalized in the larger society, the power of representations becomes much more pronounced. In fact, a "burden of representation" exists whenever a marginalized group is represented in popular culture.[1] This is especially true for the Latina body, as Mary Beltrán argues: "media representations of the Latina body thus form a symbolic battleground upon which the ambivalent place of Latinos and Latinas in US society is acted out."[2]

Ugly Betty, originally a telenovela in Colombia that became a popular sitcom produced by Salma Hayek and Silvio Horta airing on ABC, is such a symbolic battleground. The series has been nominated for 128 awards and won fifty-five of them, including eight ALMA Awards, five NAACP Awards, three Emmy Awards, and two Golden Globes. It is the only prime-time television series that centers on a Chicana as the main character.[3] Betty Suarez (played by America Ferrera) works at a high fashion magazine as an assistant to the editor. As the title suggests, Betty performs a femininity that is coded as "ugly" by the people within the fashion world with whom she works. The "norm" at *Mode Magazine,* Betty's place of employment, is disciplined bodies, such as the slender body, which is represented as a sign of self-control. These disciplined bodies inhabit *Mode* literally and symbolically, as the magazine represents the high fashion world, with its narrow version of femininity.

This manuscript critiques the first and second seasons of *Ugly Betty* (focusing primarily on one episode) and examines the ways the Chicana body, in particular, exists as a site of conflict. *Ugly Betty* explodes some stereotypes about Latinas/Chicanas but reinforces others. As such, it operates in what Bhabha has called a third space[4] and Anzaldúa has named nepantla.[5] It is a hybrid space, a place that allows for complex and, sometimes, transgressive representations instead of only reifying stereotypes. This space allows identities to resist stable categories and, instead, recognizes them as contradictory, unstable, and historically shifting. While *Ugly Betty,* for example, may contribute to a homogeneous understanding of Latinidad (the dominant culture's understanding of United States Latino/as and Latin America) and erase some cultural specificity of Chicana/os, it also informs society's overall understandings of immigration, language, nation, and identity. The show contributes to and helps create cultural anxieties about the Latino/a place in United States culture.

THE LATINA BODY IN POPULAR CULTURE

The Latina body is not a stranger to popular culture representation. Unfortunately, however, our bodies have been stereotyped and represented in less than desirable ways. In this section, I will examine "tropicalization" the ways in which pan-ethnic difference is erased and subsumed under the umbrella "Latina," as well as other common stereotypical representations of the Latina body. The representation of the Latina body has been influenced by racial discourse which is often framed by the binary of Black/White. Such a binary erases difference between races and creates a Latina body that is ethnically undifferentiated.[6] As cultural theorists point out, this undifferentiated Latina body made it easy for a Puerto Rican woman (Jennifer Lopez) to be cast in the role of Mexican performer Selena.[7] The general public did not care about ethnic specificity, only that a Brown body played the role. The ethnically undifferentiated Latina body is a product of "tropicalism," defined by Frances R. Aparicio and Susana Chavez-Silverman as "the system of ideological fictions with which the dominant (Anglo European) cultures trope Latin American and US Latina/o identities and cultures."[8] Tropicalism erases ethnic specificity and instead helps construct homogeneous stereotypes such as bright colors, rhythmic music, and brown skin that are represented in visual texts.[9] Although *Ugly Betty,* as an overall text, represents Chicana/o identity, these representations are often either stereotypical or used to get laughs from the audience.

Tropicalization helps position the Latina body as oversexed[10] as well as sexually available.[11] This common stereotypical representation asserts that Latinas are also sexually desirable,[12] though not so desirable as to raise miscegenation fears.[13] Even though the Latina is often represented as attractive and sexually desirable, she is still Othered to the extent that her body will always be a source of curiosity and fascination as an exotic object. According to Isabel Molina Guzman and Angharad Valdivia, it is precisely the Latina's Othered status that marks her body as desirable.[14] Latinas have been subject to other stereotypes as well. Charles Ramirez Berg, in his examination of the history of Latino/a images in US cinema, outlined six basic stereotypes: el bandido, harlot, male buffoon, female clown, Latin lover, and dark lady.[15] The three stereotypes pertaining to Latinas all involve sexuality to some degree. For example, the harlot is lustful, and the female clown is sexually promiscuous. While the dark lady is initially virginal and aloof, according to Charles Ramirez Berg, by the end of the film she has often transformed into the harlot. Thus, "according to Hollywood, then, . . . at heart every Latina is a Jezebel."[16] Guzman and Valdivia argue that contemporary representations of Latinas are not only sexualized but also racialized, gendered, and shaped by the discourse of Latinidad:

> While these contemporary representations may provide the opportunity for individual Latinas to open spaces for vocality and action, they nevertheless build on a tradition of exoticization, racialization and sexualization, a tradition that serves to position Latinas as continual foreigners and

> a cultural threat. As such Latinas occupy a liminal space in US popular culture, that is, we can be both marginal and desired.[17]

We know that representations within popular culture help create culture and meaning. They do not merely reflect culture; rather, they exist in relationship with their audiences and are productive of culture, meaning, and signification. In fact, Ana Lopez theorized that Hollywood creates minorities and provides audiences with an experience of us.[18] Marginalized bodies are at more risk of being mis-represented and created based on racist, sexist, or homophobic notions. It is, therefore, tremendously important for us to examine the discursive production of the Latina/Chicana body. Latino/a critical race theory can be utilized as a backdrop to construct the argument that the popular culture industry is inherently ideological and, as such, that racist and sexist representations have material consequences on marginalized bodies.[19]

Textual racialization, sexualization, and genderization practices discursively construct the Latina/Chicana body, and that construction has implications for Latinas' place within United States society. In other words, what we learn from *Ugly Betty* and other popular culture texts becomes lived out on bodies—performed in everyday lives. These contradictory representations of the Latina body act as a site where fears about race, difference, and nation are played out.[20] Coco Fusco asserts that contradictory representations of cultural difference exist to represent anxieties about identity as society experiences a shift in borders.[21] As media and popular discourse troubles the notion of US "borders," the Latina/Chicana body becomes that much more hypervisible and contradictory as fears about "illegal" border crossing are discursively enacted. The Latina/Chicana body, then, becomes in need of discipline and regulation.

Ugly Betty exists as a site where we witness the regulation of racialized femininities. Those bodies not performing within the confines of narrow definitions of femininity, such as the main character Betty Suarez, are either disciplined with outright dismissal or, worse, made to be material for humor and degradation. According to Jillian Baez, commodified texts often offer women a "combined message of 'love your body' with subtexts that only certain types of bodies are acceptable and have to be disciplined through consumption."[22] *Ugly Betty* exists as a text that teaches us about Chicana femininity and its relationship to Eurocentric norms and ideals of beauty, but it also offers some contradictions and possibilities for transgression.

CONTEXTUALIZING UGLY BETTY: YO SOY BETTY LA FEA

Yo Soy Betty La Fea, a telenovela from Colombia, was produced between 1999 and 2001 by RCN Television. Writers included Fernando Gaitán and Liliana Hernández; Mario Ribero served as director. The show starred Ana María Orozco as Beatriz Pinzón (Betty). Betty was in her late twenties, from a middle-class Colombian family, and very well educated, with a bachelor's degree in economics and a master's in finance. Betty could only find employment as a secretary at a fashion company, Eco Moda. Betty fell in love with her boss Don Armando and decided to be the best secretary he had ever had. Although she was routinely humiliated because of her "ugliness," Betty formed a support network of other less than desirable female workers. In addition, her intelligence and diligence saved Armando and his company from impending disaster.

Betty La Fea was a huge hit in Colombia. It was widely received in many other countries and spawned a variety of versions including, in the United States, *Ugly Betty* on ABC and the Televisa show *La Fea Mas Bella*. The popularity of the show has been attributed to the fact that traditional telenovelas are escapist and full of fantasy and drama. *Betty La Fea* was more realistic and, in class-conscious Latin America, included some examination of important issues regarding social, economic, racial, and gender oppression. *Betty La Fea* illustrated that the poor could get ahead with hard work; this is an ideology similar to the United States' concept of meritocracy, which is promoted by the ABC version of *Ugly Betty.*

According to Yeidy Rivero, the "beautiful" body in Latin America is informed by both skin color and class status, with upper-class codes of conduct helping to construct desirable ideologies of beauty.[23] She continues, "Thus, one might say that the dichotomy between 'beautiful' and 'ugly' female bodies in Latin America is broadly informed by intertwined Eurocentric, patriarchal, racial, Western/Christianized ideologies of primitivism/civilization and class."[24] In Rivero's examination of the *Betty La Fea* text, she argues that Betty, through the hard work of electrolysis (hair removal) and bodily adornments (like contact lenses instead of glasses), demonstrated that any woman could become more sexually desirable for men but that true beauty remained something attainable only by those in the upper class. And yet the lesson of *Betty La Fea* is that lower-class women cannot become beautiful until they emulate the styles, mannerisms, and "tastes"[25] of the upper class. Although, as argued by Rivero, *Betty La Fea* problematized class, the text never examined multiple axes of domination (race, gender, and class) even though the viewers in Rivero's study all recognized class as the main source of beauty.

CAST OF CHARACTERS ON *UGLY BETTY*

Betty Suarez (played by America Ferrera), the fashion-challenged heroine of ABC's sitcom *Ugly Betty,* spends her days negotiating the high fashion world and her nights trying to perfect personal and familial relationships. While Betty might seem like just another character in a television series, she contributes in many ways to the cultural scripts of femininity available to women. As such, the construction of her character is in need of critical analysis, especially because the series explores complicated issues of race, class, gender, and sexuality in not-so-complicated ways. Betty is a young, working-class Chicana from Queens. *Mode,* a high fashion magazine, exists as the context for which battles of raced and classed femininity are waged. Betty was hired by the publishing mogul, Mr. Meade, to work as the assistant for his son Daniel, a White man from privileged background. When we are first introduced to Daniel (Eric Mabius), his current assistant, Alison (a blond white woman with a "disciplined" body played by Becki Newton), kneels under his desk performing oral sex on him. As viewers, we are led to assume that Daniel sleeps with his assistants—an act of which his father disapproves.

Betty is surrounded by White characters, with the exception of Wilhelmina Slater, an attractive African American woman afraid of aging who is played by Vanessa Williams. She is represented as a "bitch," a common stereotype reserved for representations of successful Black women. Wilhelmina is the magazine's creative director. Her assistant is Marc (Michael Urie) who is White, gay, and knowledgeable about high fashion. At home, Betty has a sister, Hilda (Ana Ortiz), who fits the Latina "vamp" stereotype[26]—that is, she dresses in colorful, tight clothes, over-accessorizes, and gets ahead by utilizing an aggressive sexuality. Unlike her sister, Betty wears loose-fitting clothes that do not match. Her hair is often disheveled, and she wears thick red glasses and a mouth full of metal braces. Although she does have romantic interests (two White men), Betty is portrayed as child-like, naive, and hard-working. Her sexuality is downplayed in contrast to that of her sister Hilda. Betty's family also includes her father Ignacio (Tony Plana), who is represented as having "illegally immigrated" to the United States, and her nephew, Justin (Mark Indelicato), a teenage boy who loves fashion and drama.

UGLY, BEAUTY, FEMININITY, BETTY

Ugly Betty, and in particular *Mode Magazine,* showcases a narrow version of the feminine "ideal." This version of femininity is raced as White and classed as upper-class Manhattan. Popular culture representations of the White upper-class body inform how Brown working-class bodies like Betty's are read. As Mary Beltran argues,

> Social constructions of the body and beauty that are perpetuated by the contemporary US media industries as universal ideals also play a role in non-white celebrity construction. Despite the existence of non-white stars and fashion models that are described as beautiful, they exist in tandem with fashion and entertainment industries that continue to uphold white standards of beauty as universal.[27]

Betty's style (or lack thereof) exists in tandem with the styles of the high fashion magazine and its long-legged models, who dress mostly in black instead of the vibrant colors Betty chooses to wear.

From Betty's beginnings at *Mode,* she is ostracized as different. She is hired by her boss's father because Mr. Meade believes Betty would be the one assistant his sex-addicted son would not try to sleep with. Betty is, in fact, hired because of her "ugliness," which is constantly contrasted to the thin, White, blond assistants Daniel Meade usually hired. After being hired by Mr. Meade as the assistant to the editor-in-chief of *Mode,* Betty returns home to announce the news. She has no idea what kind of magazine *Mode* is. Her fashionista nephew tells her that it is a fashion magazine and, thus, that she should wear something "fashionable." Betty's choice ends up being a multicolored poncho emblazoned with

"Guadalajara" (where her father is from in México). Upon her arrival to *Mode*'s offices, Amanda, the White receptionist, says to Betty, "Are you de-liv-er-ing something?" assuming that a Brown-skinned girl would not speak English and could only be some sort of messenger.

Betty's "ugliness" and lack of style are highlighted immediately. Wilhelmina, while being injected with Botox by her gay male assistant (Marc), announces to him, "[Daniel] is well on his way to falling fast on his face. Can you believe that assistant?" Marc responds, " This is *Mode,* not *Dog Fancy.*" Betty gets called "Fugly" behind her back, and Daniel is encouraged to "beat [Betty] down to a pulp" since, as editor of a high-fashion magazine, he should not have someone ugly representing him. Daniel is initially represented as determined to make Betty's life miserable and get her to quit. He spitefully asks her to model in a photo shoot. Betty's difference, when standing beside the other models, is striking. She is much shorter and heavier than the tall and thin bodies beside her. The other models know how to move and position their bodies for the photographer. Betty does not. It is excruciatingly painful to watch. Daniel eventually tells the photographer to stop. As viewers, we sense that he just maybe has a heart.

In only the second episode of the show, Betty decides that she needs a makeover in order to fit in at *Mode*. Part of Betty's assignment requires that she get in to a launch party. She is told by the bouncer at the door, "Come back when we let anyone in." Alison, who attended the launch party, makes fun of Betty the following day: "We missed you at the party. What happened? Sale at the ninety-nine-cent store?" Betty tells her she could not get into the party (which Alison knew, as she had walked by Betty on her own way inside, ignoring Betty's calls for her help). Alison retorts, "Oh you poor thing. Those jerks at the door. All they seem to care about is appearance." She tilts her head and swishes past Betty.

Betty's early time at *Mode* continues to encourage her to change her appearance because her particular femininity is not congruent with that of the magazine's. Daniel asks her to "dress up" for an important lunch with Bianci (a famous photographer Daniel wants to hire). Betty turns to Christina (a White, blond woman who works in the "Closet"—a room of the latest fashions provided at photo shoots). Betty tells Christina, "I can't walk in there looking like me. He's expecting to see one of those twenty-eighth-floor [*Mode* is located on the twenty-eighth floor of the building] girls." Christina responds, "Since when do you want to look like them? They're not even real. Real women snort when they laugh. They've got fat asses, wobbly upper arms, and they get PMS. I thought you wanted to run a magazine someday, not spend twelve hours wondering what your hair is doing." Here is a rare moment in the show when Christina, someone employed by the magazine, openly acknowledges the work involved in creating the type of disciplined body that does not appear "real" or "natural" anymore. She views Betty as having a real body that makes noise, carries excess weight, and does not need the type of hyper-diligent care and work a disciplined body requires. Betty is (somewhat naively) upset, however, because she recognizes that Daniel and others involved in *Mode* are caught up in appearances. Betty believes she has no future at *Mode* unless she works to discipline her body. Thus, she turns to her traditionally feminine sister Hilda for help. Hilda tells her, "You have to look it to be it."

Although the script does not explicitly mention how femininity is classed, it is clear that an upper-class (and perhaps White) version (Wilhelmina's) of femininity is starkly contrasted with Betty's and Hilda's performances of working-class Latina femininity. As salsa music plays in the background, Betty and Hilda, dressed in colorful clothing, run into a salon. Hilda pushes a woman out of the way and announces that Betty has a two o'clock appointment with Jolie. The salon located in Queens is classed through style signifiers. It is colorful and decorated in a way that is supposed to be read as gaudy or garish. Plastic pink flamingos line the dark blue walls. A woman teases the hair on a wig at the front of the store. There is noise and hustle and bustle. This is contrasted to the next scene, in which Wilhelmina, dressed in neutral toned clothes, sashays into an upper-class salon. She quietly purrs that she has a two o'clock appointment with Jean Luc. The salon is quiet, and people move slowly. The walls are painted chocolate brown with neutral accents. A client has her head wrapped in a towel, and she is wearing a robe. These images convey a sense of entitlement, relaxation, and pampering.

The contrasts continue. Jolie is a big-boned Black woman with a nose piercing, a black weave with long blond pieces attached, and colorful beads around her neck. She is dressed in an animal print. Jean Luc is a White man with perfectly coiffed hair. He speaks quietly, and, based on his name and his speech pattern, it appears that he is French. He holds Wilhelmina's shoulders as they both look at her reflection in the mirror. Betty holds a magazine picture of a White woman and asks Jolie, "Do you really think you can make me look like this?" Jolie assures her, "Honey, you sit back and let Jolie do her thing." In contrast, Wilhelmina has her hair wrapped in a towel. She wears a spa gown. As she gets her eyebrows threaded, she smiles like she enjoys it. She is represented as a willing participant in the quiet discipline of her body. She embraces it. In contrast, Betty gets her eyebrows waxed and screams out in pain. While Wilhelmina gets a slow massage and is handed a glass of champagne, Betty laughs as Hilda holds her down. In fast and frenzied movements, Jolie does Betty's hair while someone else gives her a pedicure. Betty looks pained, and when Jolie sprays her hair with hairspray, she coughs and chokes. This is contrasted with Hilda spraying hairspray and looking calm while at the same time Wilhelmina gazes demurely at the finished product of her salon stay. While Hilda and Wilhelmina are represented as embracing the work and sacrifice involved in cultivating femininity, Betty is represented as actively resisting it.

When Wilhelmina arrives at work the next day, she is dressed all in white, wearing a stylish but conservative dress. Her hair is pulled back in a chignon. Wilhelmina has on makeup, but it is the kind that represents Maybelline's famous campaign slogan, "Maybe she's born with it; maybe it's Maybelline." Her makeup looks "natural," as if she is not even wearing any. She has achieved a "classic" femininity—the kind that codes her as upper-middle class.

In contrast, Betty has teased hair that is piled on top of her head with possible extensions. She also has long acrylic nails painted red with designs. Her makeup is thick. It is obvious that the red on her cheeks is blush and not natural coloring. Her eyeliner is heavy and her mascara thick, and noticeable eye shadow coats her eyelids. At the salon, Betty again holds up the picture and asks everyone, "Are you sure I look like this?" Jolie tells her she looks "Better." Everyone in the salon claps. Betty believes, as do the women in the salon, that she has achieved the "classic" (and White) femininity represented in the magazine picture. Instead, viewers are to notice the classed aspect of her femininity and the differences between the magazine picture and herself.

As Betty walks the streets of Queens to the subway, Shakira and Wyclef Jean sing, "She make a man wanna speak Spanish." Her Latinaness is hypervisible at this moment. The working-class men of Queens

(Latino, Black, and White) notice her as she walks by, tripping in her red stilettos. She wears a multicolored flowered blouse, a green miniskirt, and a black leather jacket with gold chains and beads hanging from it. When she walks by a construction site where the workers have previously ignored her, the men whistle. Betty stops and asks "Me?" They nod. She smiles big and thanks them for their admiration. Clearly, her hypersexual femininity is accepted and appreciated in Queens. Betty, however, crosses a literal border from Queens into Manhattan. Her femininity in Manhattan and, especially on the twenty-eighth floor at *Mode,* is viewed as humorous. Betty, still confident from her Queens experience, struts into *Mode.* She passes by two very tall and thin women (presumably models). Betty only comes up to their chests, even in her stilettos. Even without her clumsiness, *Mode* women (and men) see her and snicker. Betty trips in front of the models and loses her shoe. Marc, Wilhelmina's assistant, takes a surprise picture of her on his camera phone to use as his screen-saver. Betty's attempt at disciplining her body is something of a joke.

Betty appears oblivious to the snickers. Daniel tells her to get a table in the back of the restaurant for their lunch with Bianci. He does not tell her that he is embarrassed to be seen with her. Wilhelmina tells Marc, "It looks as if Queens threw up." She utilizes Betty as a way of making a point about change for the magazine. While looking and pointing to Betty, she says "Sometimes change is a positive thing" and touches her own hair. She continues, "Sometimes things can spin out of control. Bold new colors, a daring new look." She points at Betty, "But the truth is you haven't improved on a thing." People laugh while Betty, who has realized Wilhelmina's true intent, fights back tears. By the end of the episode, Betty has removed most of her new femininity, realizing that she cannot get ahead at *Mode* through the alteration of her appearance. In a convoluted move, Betty tells Daniel to take Alison with him to the lunch with Bianci, since appearance matters. Alison is White, blond, thin, and privileged; she is the daughter of a wealthy investment banker. She has to pretend she is Betty Suarez from Queens. The differences between them are obvious; when Bianci offers her bread, she says strongly, "No carbs." Daniel suggests with a knowing look that women from Queens (or at least Betty) do not worry about carbs. Thus, Alison takes some bread and says, "Who cares about carbs when you're from Queens. Right?"

Then she winks. The façade does not last long. It is clear that Alison has no idea what it means to be from Queens; she says inappropriate things and makes whatever references to Spanish ("the barrio") she can. Daniel confesses the lie just as the real Betty Suarez walks in. She ends up sitting down with Bianci and, though viewers are not privy to what occurs, we see that she seals the deal for *Mode.* In the end, Betty, with her braces, facial hair, and unmatched clothes, is coded as ugly but competent and fiercely loyal to her White boss.

BETTY'S CHICANA BODY IS NOT REALLY TRANSGRESSIVE: A DISCUSSION

Betty's body represents both the necessity of the work required to achieve femininity and also the irony involved in attempting to discipline a real woman into a magazine image. As such, her body exists as a contradiction. It is a site where we can see how patriarchy and Eurocentric ideologies convene to compel a Chicana to want to achieve Whiteness and traditional femininity.

Ultimately, as hard as Betty tried to achieve it, the traditional White femininity represented in the magazine and symbolically in *Mode* was unattainable to her. Her body was marked as different. She represented excess in all its forms (weight, hair, colors, gaudiness) and that excess could not be tamed nor disciplined, regardless of her intentions or actions. Her race and class positioned her differently from the *Mode* girls, and she was not allowed to pass as such. Although Betty tried to pass as a *Mode* girl, her attempt was policed because she could not erase the markers of race and class. At *Mode,* Whiteness and privilege were the norm. Others were not welcomed and would not be accepted. In fact, in an episode when Hilda visited Betty at *Mode,* Wilhelmina looked at her and said, "It's Cesar Chavez in a push-up bra." Although Hilda is represented as prettier than Betty, and she does discipline her body, her version of femininity still does not measure up to *Mode* femininity because of differences in race/ethnicity and class. Her body is also represented as excessive—she over-accessorizes, shows a lot of cleavage, and wears tight, colorful clothes.

Betty's body, in contrast to those of Wilhelmina and other *Mode* women, exists as a site of social struggle. She is represented as someone who successfully crosses a literal border every day, and yet she still struggles with the mundane. Her struggles are constructed as part of the humor of the show. When issues of "ugliness" are laughed about, viewers can take things less seriously. We do not have to examine how we define beauty. We do not have to examine why Betty is a perpetual outsider; we are led to believe through the laugh track that she is an outsider due to her clumsiness, naivety, and refusal to become a twenty-eighth-floor girl. The reality that is overshadowed, however, is that Betty can never be a *Mode* girl because she is Chicana and from Queens. She will not be allowed to pass. This argument is proven in several few episodes, especially when a White woman (played by Lindsey Lohan) whom Betty went to school with in Queens is hired. She also dresses in a working-class femininity. However, what marks her differently than Betty is that when she starts her transformation to become a *Mode* girl, people accept her. She is even promoted to a position higher than Betty's. Her Whiteness allows the transformation to be accepted in ways that Betty's is not.

The issues raised by the *Ugly Betty* text have larger ramifications for Chicanas/os and Latinas/os. By continually representing Betty as a site of difference, the text inscribes Betty as someone who crosses borders every day but ultimately does not belong. Given the discussions in this country about "illegal immigration" and border protection, Betty's failed attempts at assimilating in Manhattan help reify incorrect notions about who belongs in the United States and who does not. Given that many non-Chicana/o viewers might watch *Ugly Betty* as an informational text, the construction of Betty's body as a site of ultimate difference is dangerous. It informs viewers not knowledgeable about Chicana femininity that there is no common ground between Betty and themselves. It teaches viewers that issues that have material consequences on the lives of Latinas/Chicanas are unimportant and, worse, humorous. It may teach Latinas/Chicanas that we are not beautiful enough as is. Or that we should aspire to be like White women in our performances of femininity. Even then, by watching *Ugly Betty* we learn that we will never be able to achieve a coveted version of femininity because we will be recognized as wrongly trying to "pass"; perhaps, like Betty, we will be laughed at or ousted.

Betty Suarez, like many other non-White characters, exists as a discursive contradiction. Although Betty remains ostracized and laughed at, she completes her job in ways that keep her sometimes incompetent Anglo boss, Daniel, afloat. Of course, there is no discussion of Betty following patriarchal roles. Often, it is her ideas and hard work that enable Daniel to remain employed as editor. Although she plays an integral role in many issues at *Mode,* her skills are set in the background; Daniel is the one who benefits from Betty's tireless loyalty and uncompromising intelligence. With the exception of the one day Betty acquiesces and disciplines her body in an attempt at White upper-class femininity, she remains "ugly," which is defined by the text as undisciplined and natural. She teaches us that a real woman can remain real and still be professionally successful—even in a world where image is everything. Is this message transgressive enough? Perhaps not. *Ugly Betty* does not examine issues of racism, sexism, classism, or homophobia in complicated ways. Instead, like many sitcoms, it utilizes humor to erase the power inherent in ideological constructions. Betty Suarez might be a contradictory site. The *Ugly Betty* text, however, does what Chon Noriega argues films representing Mexican Americans typically do: "they must still resolve these social contradictions and situate the Mexican-American within normative gender roles, sexual relations, social spaces, and institutional parameters."[28] *Ugly Betty* does precisely this.

NOTES

1. Ella Shohat and Robert Stam, *Unthinking Eurocentrism: Multiculturalism and the Media* (London: Routledge, 1994), 182.

2. Mary C. Beltrán, "The Hollywood Latina Body as Site of Social Struggle: Media Constructions of Stardom and Jennifer Lopez's 'Cross-Over' Butt," *Quarterly Review of Film & Video* 19 (2002): 82.

3. The ABC network, in response to criticism for its lack of Latino/a representation, aired a situation comedy *The George Lopez Show* from March 2002 to May 2007. Other shows with Latino/a characters include the PBS series *American Family,* airing since 2002, the WB's *Greetings from Tucson,* airing from 2002 to 2003, and *Good Morning, Miami,* airing on NBC from 2002 to 2004.

4. Homi Bhabha, "Cultural Diversity and Cultural Differences." In *The Post-Colonial Studies Reader,* ed. Bill Ashcroft, Gareth Griffiths, and Helen Tiffen (New York: Routledge, 1995), 206–209.

5. Gloria Anzaldúa, *Borderlands / La Frontera: The New Mestiza* (San Francisco, CA: Aunt Lute Books, 1987).

6. Angharad N. Valdivia, "Stereotype or Transgression? Rosie Perez in Hollywood Film," *Sociological Quarterly* 39, no. 3 (1998): 393–408.

7. Frances R. Aparicio, "Jennifer as Selena: Rethinking Latinidad in Media and Popular Culture," *Latino Studies* 1 (2003): 99.

8. Frances R. Aparicio and Susana Chavez-Silverman, *Tropicalizations: Transcultural Representations of Latinidad* (Hanover, NH: Dartmouth Press, 1997).

9. Isabel Molina Guzman and Angharad N. Valdivia, "Brain, Brow, and Booty: Latina Iconicity in US Popular Culture," *The Communication Review* 7 (2004): 211.

10. Baez, 2007.

11. Angharad N. Valdivia, *A Latina in the Land of Hollywood* (Tucson: University of Arizona Press, 2000).

12. Ibid.

13. Ana M. Lopez, "Are all Latins from Manhattan? Hollywood, Ethnography, and Cultural Colonialism." In *Unspeakable Images: Ethnicity & the American Cinema*, ed. Lester Friedman (Urbana & Chicago: University of Illinois Press, 1991), 404–424.

14. Guzman and Valdivia, "Brain, Brow, and Booty," 213.

15. Charles Ramírez Berg, *Latino Images in Film: Stereotypes, Subversion, Resistance* (Austin, TX: The University of Texas Press, 2002).

16. Ibid.

17. Guzman and Valdivia, "Brain, Brow, and Booty," 217.

18. Lopez, "Are all Latins from Manhattan?" 405.

19. Tara Yosso, "Critical Race Theory: Challenging Deficit Discourse about Chicanas/os," *Journal of Popular Film and Television* 30, no.1 (2002): 52–62.

20. Viviana Rojas, "The Gender of Latinidad: Latinas Speak About Hispanic Television," *The Communication Review* 7 (2004): 125–153.

21. Coco Fusco, *English is Broken Here: Notes on Cultural Fusion in the Americas* (New York: New Press, 1995).

22. Jillian M. Baez, "Towards a Latinidad Feminista: The Multiplicities of Latinidad and Feminism in Contemporary Cinema," *Popular Communication* 5, no. 2 (2007): 109–128.

23. Yeidy M. Rivero, "The Performance and Reception of Televisual 'Ugliness' in *Yo Soy Betty La Fea*," *Feminist Media Studies* 3, no. 1 (2003): 68.

24. Ibid.

25. See Pierre Bourdieu, *Distinctions: A Social Critique of the Judgement of Taste*, trans. Richard Nice (New York: Routledge, [1974] 1984), for a discussion of the classifications of taste.

26. Gary D. Keller, *Hispanics and United States Film: An Overview and Handbook* (Tempe, AZ: Bilingual Review Press, 1994).

27. Beltrán, "The Hollywood Latina Body as Site of Social Struggle," 82.

28. Chon Noriega, "Internal 'Others': Hollywood Narratives 'About' Mexican-Americans." In *Mediating Two Worlds: Cinematic Encounters in the Americas*, ed. John King, Ana M. Lopez, and Manual Alvarado (London: BFI, 1993), 51.

WORKS CITED

Anzaldúa, Gloria. *Borderlands / La Frontera: The New Mestiza*. San Francisco: Aunt Lute Books, 1987.

Baez, Jillian M. "Towards a Latinidad Feminista: The Multiplicities of Latinidad and Feminism in Contemporary Cinema." *Popular Communication* 5, no. 2 (2007): 109–128.

Beltran, Mary C. "The Hollywood Latina Body as Site of Social Struggle: Media Constructions of Stardom and Jennifer Lopez's 'Cross-Over Butt'." *Quarterly Review of Film & Video* 19 (2002): 71–86.

Berg, Charles Ramírez. *Latino Images in Film: Stereotypes, Subversion, Resistance*. Austin: The University of Texas Press, 2002.

Bhabha, Homi. *The Location of Culture*. New York: Routledge, 1994.

Fusco, Coco. *English is Broken Here: Notes on Cultural Fusion in the Americas*. New York: New Press, 1995.

Guzman, Isabel Molina, and Angharad N. Valdivia. "Brain, Brow, and Booty: Latina Iconicity in US Popular Culture." *The Communication Review* 7 (2004): 205–221.

Keller, Gary D. *Hispanics and United States Film: An Overview and Handbook*. Tempe, AZ: Bilingual Review Press, 1994.

Lopez, Ana M. "Are all Latins from Manhattan? Hollywood, Ethnography, and Cultural Colonialism." In *Unspeakable Images: Ethnicity & the American Cinema*, edited by Lester Friedman, 404–424. Urbana & Chicago: University of Illinois Press, 1991.

Noriega, Chon. "Internal 'Others': Hollywood Narratives 'About' Mexican-Americans." In *Mediating Two Worlds: Cinematic Encounters in the Americas*, edited by John King, Ana M. Lopez, and Manual Alvarado. London: BFI, 1993.

Rivero, Yeidy M. "The Performance and Reception of Televisual 'Ugliness' in *Yo Soy Betty La Fea*." *Feminist Media Studies* 3, no. 1 (2003): 65–81.

Rojas, Viviana. "The Gender of Latinidad: Latinas Speak about Hispanic Television." *The Communication Review* 7, no. 2 (2004): 125–153.

Shohat, Ella, and Robert Stam. *Unthinking Eurocentrism: Multiculturalism and the Media*. London: Routledge, 1994.

Stutzman, Ronald. "El Mestizaje: An All-Inclusive Ideology of Exclusion." In *Cultural Transformations and Ethnicity in Modern Ecuador*, edited by N. E. Whitten Jr., 45–94. Urbana: University of Illinois Press, 1981.

Valdivia, Angharad N. *A Latina in the Land of Hollywood and Other Essays on Media Culture*. Tucson: University of Arizona Press, 2000.

———. "Stereotype or Transgression? Rosie Perez in Hollywood Film." *Sociological Quarterly* 39, no. 3 (1998): 393–408.

Yosso, Tara. "Critical Race Theory: Challenging Deficit Discourse About Chicanas/os." *Journal of Popular Film and Television* 30, no. 1 (2002): 52–62.

EIGHTEEN

Indian Icon, Gay Macho: Felipe Rose of Village People

GABRIEL S. ESTRADA

As a backup singer in the multi-gold-album-winning disco group Village People, Felipe Rose performed "The Indian" that both marketed and masked his Lakota, Puerto Rican, and gay identities. "What do you see / When you look at me?" Felipe "Swift Arrow" Rose slowly sings with a harmonized chorus accompanied by a guitar and synthesizer as his website opens. Answers to this question are complicated because of Rose's history of ambiguous representations as a mixed-race, unenrolled urban Indian. The online text identifies Rose as both Lakota and Puerto Rican. On the website, Rose also describes his three-decade role in Village People and his fifteen-year experience with Native American music production. The musical comedy *Can't Stop the Music* (1980) gave an official, racialized, and straight version of the subversively multicultural gay story of Village People's original rise to fame. Rose more popularly identified as gay and Indian after Village People's appeal quieted down in the anti-disco 1980s and sexual and identity politics changed. Contemporary Native American, Two-Spirit, and queer Latino critical perspectives articulate how Rose plays Indian in *Can't Stop the Music* in order to partially resist racial and sexual oppressions as a gay performer of American Indian and Puerto Rican ancestry.

Phillip J. Deloria (Standing Rock Sioux) outlines a racialized history, in which many Natives and non-Natives were "playing Indian" for white and multicultural audiences, that forms a background for Rose's contemporary performance.[1] Patterson notes that Yavapai physician and pan-Native political spokesperson Carlos Montezuma joined the

Society of American Indian (SAI) pan-Native intellectual debates from 1911–1924 regarding the manner in which SAI would "carefully tread a line between pandering to white images of 'the Indian' and advancing their own model of the acculturated Indian American."[2] Deloria also recounts how a Dakota writer of Boy Scout books, Charles Eastman, performed mimetic Indian play by offering himself as a virtuous Indian model for mostly white Boy Scouts and camp girls in the early twentieth century. It was a time when "Indian people participated in the making of Indian Others as never before . . . miming Indianness back at Americans in order to redefine it."[3]

Deloria continues, "When Eastman donned an Indian headdress, he was connecting himself to his Dakota roots . . . but also . . . imitating non-Indian imitations of Indians . . . through his material body."[4] Eastman achieved a sense of respect for idealized Indian practices for modern Americans, but he modified his own Dakota culture to do so by playing into antiquated images of Indians in that process. Deloria warns that while these performances are "easily dismissed" as a mere Indian-White hybridity, they represent an actual Native American desire for "cultural power that might be translated to achieve social gains."[5]

As Eastman and others played Indian to protect their tribal interests, so Rose played Indian as an un-enrolled Lakota in order to make subversive, queer statements about the survival of urban Indians. His efforts to achieve personal fame by playing Indian were often criticized—an example of how early Native American debates regarding playing Indian are sometimes echoed in contemporary popular culture. One *Rolling Stones* reporter glosses Rose's inauthentic Indian persona.[6] Almost two decades later, *The Washington Post* echoed American Indian activist views of Rose's Indian, proclaiming "Politically minded gays were turned off by the stereotyping and disavowals, to say nothing of what some Indian activists perceived of Rose's get-up."[7] Rose's feathered headdress seemed to replicate the stereotypical images of Plains Indians in popular Westerns, these stemming from Buffalo Bill's Wild West Show and photographic images of disappearing "real Indians" staged by white photographers into the late nineteenth and early twentieth centuries.[8] After Plains Indian warriors defeated US Lt. Colonel Custer at Greasy Grass (Little Big Horn) in 1876, the Lakota were catapulted into iconic status as "The Indian" whose "feathers and beads" images were often distorted for profit.[9] With his brown skin, Plains warrior clothing, and mascot-like warrior face paint, Rose played Indian by performing a gay disco version of the iconic "traditional" Plains Indian warrior image. In doing so, he raised questions of authenticity for popular audiences, who rarely guessed his mixed Lakota/Puerto Rican heritage and gay dance roots. At worst, American Indian activists might have found Rose's Indian disco chief look to approximate the kind of playing-Indian mascot costumes that Charlene Teeters and American Indian Movement supporters later protested in the eighties.[10]

As *The Post* indicated, gay activists also wanted Rose and Village People to simply come out of the closet instead of merely teasing audiences with gay intimations. Village People did not openly acknowledge its gay roots and members in 1980.[11] French gay composer Jacques Morali and producer Henri Belolo would only market Village People through erotic worship of gay butch aesthetics that were also palatable to popular heteropatriarchal and hypermasculine tastes.[12] The Indian was part of the macho vocal crew that included five other racialized, homoerotic icons: three white, the Construction Worker (David Hodo), the Cowboy (Randy Jones), and Leatherman Biker (Glenn Hughes); and two black, the G.I/Sailor (Alex Briley) and Cop/Admiral lead singer (Victor Willis). Through passing as straight, the members of Village People were able to race up the charts that may have been closed to them had they proclaimed their gay history early on. The movie *Can't Stop the Music* actually foregrounds a straight, white, male protagonist playing a role based upon the queer life of Jacques Morali who shaped the group's sound and rise to fame. The film masks Village People's foundations in gay disco of the East Village and the identities of Village People's gay performers, Felipe Rose, Randy Jones, and Joseph Briley. Decades later, Jones and Mark Bego simply project an uncomplicated gay pride in the film that renders whiteness and homophobia invisible when they state "If the movie . . . did nothing else, it . . . helped bring positive 'gay-friendly' images into more of a relaxed and mainstream fashion."[13] They conclude, "Village People became the ultimate symbol of the disco era and a positive symbol of gay social progress, not only in America, but also on a global scale."[14]

Tatonetti would challenge Bego's positive reading of Village People by noting how gay whiteness in film often reenacts anti-Native American colonialism through "creation of a raced sexual order in which Anglo queerness becomes the de facto norm."[15] Many gay Native Americans would question *Can't Stop the Music*'s representations, which never directly confront the racial and sexual divides in gay politics in the fairly closeted film. Gay American Indians (GAI) organized around issues of gay white "discrimination," AIDS, and the visibility of gay American Indians in San Francisco during the 1980s.[16] Gay American Indian identity partially evolved into Two-Spirit identity after 1990. Joseph Gilley outlines that Two-Spirit implies "a contemporary connection with the historic roles of Two-Spirit ancestors and participation in traditional Native culture." Participation in Two-Spirit Sun Dances, Stomp Dances, or Powwows could never be replicated in a white setting, thus further separating Two-Spirits from white gay cultures by spiritual traditions.[17] *Two-Spirited* (2007) and *Two Spirits, One Journey* (2007) are films that openly portray Two-Spirit Lakota and Stoney protagonists who confront homophobia on reservation spaces by fortifying themselves with Two-Spirit traditions passed down orally by their grandmothers.[18] *Little Big Man* (1970) features an unabashed Cheyenne Two-Spirit character, Little Horse, who cross-dresses and flirts with the straight male protagonist at will. The film is an historical reconstruction that culminates in Custer's defeat at the Battle of Little Big Horn in 1876. In contrast to these films' out Two-Spirit characters, Rose was always the lone urban Indian in Village People performances. He appeared to have no Native American community or Nation to affirm his identity and traditions, a representation that ran counter to the other American Indian and Two-Spirit urban activisms of the 1970s and beyond.[19]

In contrast to the racial bliss of *Can't Stop the Music*, Arthur Dong's "Out Rage '69" documentary emphasizes racialized gay, lesbian, and transgender conflicts during the 1960s and 1970s gay movements. Dong features Latina/o gay activists such as "Sylvia" Rivera, who defends "street transvestites" like her/himself from gay white, male, middle-class attacks. S/he is one of the many Latina/o street people youth who sparked the riots at East Village Stonewall bar in 1969 that radicalized the gay, lesbian, bisexual, and transgender (GLBT) movements in the following decades. *To Wong Foo, Thanks for Everything, Julie Newmar* (1995) also portrays racial tension between its White, Black, and Latin drag queen protagonists. Felipe is not nearly as out as the voguing, Latin transgendered sex worker Venus Xtravaganza of the documentary *Paris*

Is Burning (1990) or the transgendered, Latina/o, AIDS-stricken street performer, Angel, of the Broadway (1996) and film (2005) versions of *Rent.* Both Venus and Angel die tragically in their respective films set in New York City. Because Felipe remains minimally framed by masculine heterosexual privilege and white, middle-class friendships in *Can't Stop the Music,* he considerably increases his chances of surviving in a transphobic and racist US society. Rose's partial assimilation into white society also resolves the kinds of personal problems of alcoholism, poverty, and violence that surround the segregated, gay-friendly Native American bar in Los Angeles in *The Exiles* (1961).

On the surface, *Can't Stop the Music* reflected popular assumptions of racial purity that one cannot identify as Native American if one is also of mixed Latino or African heritages. The racist politics of slavery and one-drop black blood definitions of African-ness created sharp historical divisions for mixed African and Native peoples, who were often legally forced to claim pure Native American blood in order to be considered as true Native Americans. These racially divided politics motivated the 1930s suicide of the Lumbee / African American actor Chief Buffalo Child Long Lance after the "disgrace" of his African heritage publicly discredited his Hollywood claims to be purely Blackfoot Native American.[20] As a mixed Lakota Sioux / Puerto Rican, Felipe keeps his race simply ambiguous throughout the movie. For example, when the white female protagonist's white "square" boyfriend refers to Felipe and asks, "Is there any reason why he's dressed like an Indian?" she replies, "Maybe it's his . . . um . . . fantasy" and giggles, casting doubt on Felipe's racial and sexual background. Rose is ambiguously Native American, Puerto Rican, and gay in the film, presenting a potential of wholeness in racial and sexual identity that the film never realizes. In the same party scene, the blond bombshell Sam and her friend Lulu prepare dinner as Felipe passes by, dressed to dance and sing in a beaded buckskin loincloth, bone breastplate, and a blue, black, and white feather headdress. The vampish white Lulu reacts to his entrance by fanning herself, saying, "Ohhhhh, the Indian is *hot*! I *go* for exotic *types,* particularly when they're half-*naked*! . . . Hmmmm, you tell *him* I'll make up for all the *indignities* they suffered in *Roots*!" and laughing.

While Lulu passionately loosens the Hays Code condemnations of lustful female sexuality[21] and overrides anti-miscegenation concerns that date back to D.W. Griffith's California Indian cinematic tragedy *Ramona* (1910) and Klu Klux Klan–supportive *Birth of a Nation* (1915),[22] she also eroticizes Felipe in a racially questionable way. Her reference to *Roots* implies that Felipe is Black and mocks Alex Haley's fictionalization of the indomitable will of African Americans to free themselves from slavery. Lulu's comments reflect the fact that Felipe's medium-brown skin tone may reference both Lakota and African heritage. The former promises savage, unrestrained passion.[23] The latter hints at stereotypes regarding large African genital size and sexual appetites in "the most exoticized and eroticized terms." These stereotypes apply to even very light-complexioned Puerto Rican singers like Ricky Martin, who was also known for his ambiguous sexual orientation before coming out as homosexual in 2010.[24]

The film subjects Rose to both anti-Indian and anti-Black racism rather than an embracing of his Lakota and "African, indigenous (Taino), and European" Puerto Rican ancestries.[25] Part of the answer to being multiracial lies untapped in Rose's Taíno ancestry, which is not mentioned on his website. Barreiro notes how Taíno activists were charged with wanting to deny African heritage by claiming to be Taíno. In response to these charges, Taíno ceremonial leader Daniel Rivera explains a holistic way of approaching African and Native American ancestry not reflected in the film. Rivera states, "I recently ran a biracial support group. The focus was precisely on reaching acceptance of all parts of oneself. You are not half this, half that. That's our philosophy about our identity as mixed peoples."[26] Some vocal Taíno elders are now transmitting a healing of African and Native American differences that would hopefully inspire more inclusive representations of Puerto Rican ancestries in future popular films.

However, in the 1980 film, Lulu simply grabs Felipe and forces him into a backbend kiss, covertly referencing Felipe's queer sexuality as a submissive bottom and submissive Indian. Felipe responds with surprised passion. While Felipe's posturing may resonate with the general suppression of the "manhood" of Native American men who were often unable to defend their Nations against white encroachment,[27] one remembers that Native Americans of all genders fought against colonization, not just straight men. Given Craig Womack's argument that the male "queer Indian . . . defies the stereotype of the stoic warrior,"[28] one can argue that Rose's performance in Village People at least complicates images of Native American masculinities, even though it doesn't completely break out of a heterosexist playing-Indian mode. Rose at least hinted at the survival of urban Indians who participate in modern life and gay subculture, contrary to the myth of stoic straight Indian men who vanished long ago. Lulu kisses the doubly racialized object of her fetishized desire in order to thinly mask Felipe's queer prancing throughout the film and dutifully respond to the strict Production Code that governed Hollywood censorship of homosexuality from 1934 to 1961.[29] Even so, extreme close-up shots of Rose's athletic rear code him as a gay bottom throughout the film, conveying visual details that a queer audience would likely register.

Two-Spirit comedian Charlie Ballard (Sac and Fox/Anishinaabe) presents a series of jokes in 2007 that critique whiteness, fetishization, homophobia, and playing Indian in the "Gay Native American" sketch posted on his website.[30] When Charlie opens with self-identification as an "American Indian," he follows with "I know most of you can't tell since I'm not wearing my casino shirt." He is jokingly reconfiguring Indian identity as lucrative and contemporary, but he refuses to wear a shirt that would mark him iconically as such. To present a non-iconic image is a choice Rose is never allowed to make in the film, as he wears a headdress at almost all times.

"Most guys like to date me just because I'm American Indian," Ballard continues, "So what the hell does that make me, a fetish? What the hell am I supposed to say to that? 'Hey do you want a lap dance?'" Ballard puts two fingers up behind his head like feathers and makes a whooping sound with his other hand on his mouth while unenthusiastically wiggling his bottom. "Woo! Woo! Woo! Woo!" he screams in the Indian falsetto featured in classic westerns. Ballard makes fun of the very kind of gay kitschy fetishism that Rose displays as a gay Indian go-go dancer and bartender in one of the scenes of *Can't Stop the Music.* As a go-go dancer and as a Village People performer, Rose plays Indian to capitalize on gay white fetishization of Indian male sexuality.

"I'm the fashion consultant in my Indian tribe," he concludes, "You might hear me say something like 'Oh, girl, I know you didn't bring that outfit on the Trail of Tears.'" Again, he pokes fun at the idea that Native Americans of today should have to dress as they did during the

FIG. 18.1. Felipe Rose in *Can't Stop the Music* (1980) finale.

1830s, a racist belief that many non–Native Americans in the audience might believe or have been taught. Ballard is clearly identifying as gay and Native American in order to broadly criticize white stereotypes and fetishization of gay Native Americans. The critique of whiteness is what Ballard and other Native comedians like Charlie Hill bring to an audience that eludes Rose as the singer and dancer attempts to humorously play an Africanized version of The Indian.

The film's grand finale Village People concert highlights Rose's go-go boy dance moves, which ambiguously identify his body as queer bottom and top and of both African and Native American descent. After a ruby red rhinestone cowboy backs onto the dark stage, a second spotlight falls upon a tipi from which Rose emerges. He then performs a standing splits kick that clearly reveals his bikini underwear, which disappears into his muscular buttocks. His displays of flexibility and pointed toes mark his dance as the most flamboyant among the Village People's macho men lineup. Queer aesthetics were common in disco outfits, but his shocking pink and purple war bonnet that cascades to the floor, matching pink bone breastplate, and glittery ribbons mark him as absolutely flamboyant. As Village People sing and perform the movie's disco title track, *Can't Stop the Music,* the strong overhead lighting catches the pink glitter and faux war paint that mark Rose's face with a superstar glow. At the same time, Rose also thrusts his pelvis rhythmically to the African-influenced disco beats and reestablishes a persona of a hypermasculine African top. His final performance ambiguously resists the heterosexist message that his earlier kiss with Lulu was meant to impart. It also resists the ideas that one must be one race or another and that one must be either sexually passive or active.

Rose's gender-bending performance echoes a long line of feminine renderings of playing Indian with a male warrior's war bonnet. A daughter of a Penobscot chief, Molly Spotted Elk gained fame in the United States and Europe by playing Indian in various song and dance venues and films. Spotted Elk joined the lively 1920s Prohibition Era speakeasies once she met "Tex" Guinan, "who soon featured Molly draped in a head to toe eagle feather headdress—and little else."[31] A picture of a barefoot Spotted Elk in skimpy fringed buckskin and a huge trailing war bonnet resembles Rose's performance look.[32] She even points her toes like Rose does to indicate that she has a dance background in Western styles, which she combines with iconic Indian movements in sexually fetishized displays of Indianness.

Cher glitters up and racializes the basic idea of Spotted Elk's outfit in her 1973 video "Half-Breed Blues." In a video that was filmed from her *Sonny and Cher Comedy Hour*, a barefoot Cher wears a white trailing war bonnet with a revealing sequined white two-piece Bob Mackey dress as she straddles a pinto horse. Her bronze skin and straight black hair, which is likely inherited from her Armenian and purported Cherokee ancestry, defiantly glows against the normative whiteness that defined most models and singers prior to the seventies. Cher's ascendency marks a time when playing Indian and other ethnicities came into vogue. Displaying her athletic body, she belts out her number-one hit:

> My father married a full blood Cherokee.
> My mother's people were ashamed of me.
> The Indians said that I was white by the law.
> The white man always called me Indian Squaw.
> (Refrain) . . . Half-breed. How I learned to hate the word . . .
> Half-breed. Both sides were against me since the day I was born.[33]

The song's indictment of both Indian and white rejections of mixed-bloods is a testimony that opposed racist white and American Indian nationalisms. Cher's song and performance directly take up the conflicts of mixed-blooded identity politics in a way that Rose never articulates, even though he is clearly affected by them as a racially mixed, non-enrolled Lakota. Cher's defiant stance places her outside of the Cherokee Nation and the previous white norms of performing US American nationalism. Her criticism of racism through the lyrics written by Al Capps and Mary Dean takes her beyond the usual white modes of playing Indian popularized by hippies in the 1970s.

The second millennium continues to generate transgender performances in the iconic Indian war bonnet, but these performances are framed by Native American nationalism and Two-Spirit criticism. When a white Miss America, Shandi Finnessey, entered a 1995 Miss Universe contest sporting a revealing white feathered war bonnet "and little else" as emblems of her US American pride, she found criticism in *Indian Country Today.* Tex Hall, president of the National Congress of American Indians and chairman of the Three Affiliated Tribes, the Mandan, Hidatsa, and Arikara Nation of North Dakota, protested, "We only use the war bonnet for war or for a chieftain's duties or for spiritual ceremonies . . . It is never worn by a woman."[34] Not only does Hall note the inappropriateness of Miss America's playing Indian, he views her performance as a kind of male drag that further distorts the proper gender meaning of the war bonnet. In light of Hall's statement, one could read Rose's queering of the war bonnet as a similar statement of inappropriate cultural and cross-gender performance.

On the other hand, Kent Monkman took a queer performance art approach to wearing the war bonnet in high heels at the Montreal Museum of Fine Art in 2009. Inspired by Cher and assuming the iconic poses of Spotted Elk, Monkman donned the war bonnet in high heels and a short buckskin-fringed dress as a criticism of George Catlin's homophobic renderings of Two-Spirit dance. Catlin had called a Two-Spirit dance "unaccountable and disgusting" and even went so far as to "wish that it might be extinguished before it be more fully recorded," although his 1830s painting of the dance was innocuous enough. Monkman openly performs "Dance of the Berdache," using the historical term "berdache" that many Two-Spirit scholars find offensive, in order to highlight the lack of disappearance of queer Native roles that have adapted themselves to colonial and contemporary times.[35] He performs as a person of Swampy Cree and Irish/English ancestry and operates under the alter ego Miss Chief Eagle Testickle. Monkman might applaud Rose for challenging white heterosexist visions of history through his use of a pink and purple war bonnet. In fact, s/he might recommend donning a matching pair of high heels to really drive that point home with tongue-in-cheek "Misschief" and "egotesticle" flair. Critics of Monkman's work rightly note the lack of more serious community education about Two-Spirit traditions and roles. Zebrowski-Rubin comments, "Monkman fails to really educate his viewers . . . He does not mention the now politically correct term two-spirit or the privileged role of these male/female figures in Native communities."[36] The same criticism can be leveled against *Can't Stop the Music* and early Village People performance. Although Rose subversively performs as a gay urban Native American, he does not really educate his audience about Two-Spirit histories, communities, and traditions.

NativeOut.com's Native GLBT online videos exemplify a more community-minded, AIDS activist sense of Two-Spirit identity and performance than Rose provided in a pre-AIDS *Can't Stop the Music.* Village People's gay optimism and rise to fame at the film's conclusion defines the end of the pre-AIDS era of performance. Rose's character in *Can't Stop the Music* basically rises from being a go-go-dancing bartender in the East Village to a recording star. When AIDS took the life of Village People gay creator Jacques Morali in the early eighties, the group was already winding down its short-lived glory as anti-disco sentiment sunk both the film and their subsequent records.

A gay reading by Pet Shop Boys vocalist Neil Tennant, who covered Village People's 1979 hit "Go West" in the 1990s, notes "it was such a pre-AIDS song with all the gays moving to San Francisco and it had such innocence."[37] One chorus proclaims "(Go West) Life is peaceful there / (Go West) In the open air / (Go West) Baby you and me / (Go West) This is our destiny."[38] The last line condones a utopic vision of gay westward expansion from the East and eerily resounds with Manifest Destiny dispossession of Western Native American lands. Gay Indian post-AIDS movements emphasized an anti-colonial sense of the West. For example, Wil Roscoe recounts how Gay American Indians (GAI) co-founder Randy Burns (Northern Paiute) participated with over twenty GAI members in San Francisco's Gay Pride Parade of 1992 while "wearing a chief's headdress in rainbow feathers reaching down to his knees."[39] Carrie House (Navajo/Oneida) films Burns walking in a gay parade with a feathered headdress with other GAI members in her documentary *I Am,* now posted on the NativeOut multimedia site.[40] For Burns, wearing a feathered headdress may be a way of playing Indian for a multicultural audience, but, unlike the pre-AIDS Rose, Burns's action is also strongly linked to his Native community's AIDS activism. In *I Am,* House interviews Burns, who recounts "tribal government [is] very 'closety' around . . . AIDS . . . We're organizing as gay and lesbian Native peoples who are the health providers to our brothers and sisters infected with the virus . . . Our urban and tribal leadership . . . [has] to wake up eventually."

The Northeast Two-Spirit Society posts the Kevin VanWanseele's (Barona Band of Kumeyaay) video *AIDS to Native Eyes* (2005).[41] Documenting the first Native American AIDS Awareness Day activities in New York City on March 21, 2007, the video begins by honoring the memory of White Cloud (Lakota) who died from AIDS-related causes in 1993. As an HIV-positive activist, Kent Lobsock (Lakota) recalls the importance of having a community Native house in New York when he was first diagnosed. Lobsock felt lucky to have been able to say, "I have a place to go within my community at the American Indian Community House" for HIV services. The video ends with Louis Mofsie (Hopi/Winnebago) singing a Winnebago honoring song once reserved for warrior societies. He explains that the song would honor the Northeast Two Spirit Society. As he sings, men stand and perform an impromptu dance wearing just jeans and casual shirts, no dancing regalia. Feathers are not needed to express what is most important at heart: a willingness to incorporate Native traditions and organize as Two-Spirit peoples united against HIV/AIDS. While Rose does separately mention that Village People has contributed greatly to HIV charities and Native American causes on his website, he never puts both Native and gay together as a community or an identity. In a post-AIDS context, the Northeast Two Spirit Society shows why it is vital to put both identities together, especially in Rose's hometown of New York City, an epicenter of HIV mortality and activism.

Although Rose played Indian in his gay, urban, mixed-blooded Village People performance, Rose claims that he has always been an authentic, traditional Indian.[42] One interview notes that "an aunt encouraged him to honor his father's heritage by dressing in his tribal regalia; this led him to don the Indian attire."[43] Rose entered into Native American music as an artist who was reclaiming his identity and heritage in 1996 with the formation of his small Tomahawk Entertainment recording company. His Native American Music (NAMMY)-winning 2002 *Trail of Tears: The Rise and Fall of the Cherokee Nation: A Historical Tribal Dance Recording* marks his shift from disco to Native American music. Rose joins the NAMMY Hall of Fame along with Native-heritage artists such as Jimi Hendrix and Richie Valens who, like Wayne Newton, are known more for their popular culture glitz than they are known for singing for and identifying with their Nations.[44] Rose follows a long line of Native American performers who have diminished the difference of playing Indian for white, multicultural, and Native American audiences. As a Village People board member, Rose still tours with Village People in a modified version of the Indian, often playing for GLBT festivals in celebration of queer pride. He also plays and produces his solo music at Native American venues.

In hindsight, Rose is a complicated figure in popular music and performance in past decades, which often did not allow for much Native American, Puerto Rican, gay, or Two-Spirit sensitivity. His 1970s popularity pre-dates the Native American AIDS activisms that would catalyze stronger identification as gay and Native American, as subsequent Two-Spirit films would demonstrate. As Native American music, AIDS, GLBT, and Latino political movements matured, Rose took the opportunity to identify as a commercially successful Lakota musician, only partially defying the popular constraints of separate, fragmented identities since he did not readily identify a winkte, or gay Lakota. Since the 1980 film *Can't Stop the Music*, Native American, Two-Spirit, and queer Latino scholars and performers have developed criticisms of white heterosexism that complicate an understanding of the semi-closeted macho Indian figure that Rose portrayed. In his performance, Rose opens up the possibility of expressing multiple racial and sexual aspects of oneself despite the limiting narratives that the film supplies him. Rose's particular legacy prompts one to question the future of nationality, race, and sexuality in music and film performance. How easily will Native

American performers gain an iconic Native American status easily without playing Indian? Will they be able to achieve both commercial and Native community successes by claiming their Native American Nation or ancestry and also identifying as African, Taíno, Two-Spirit, GLBT, and/or Latina/o?

NOTES

1. Philip Deloria, *Playing Indian* (New Haven, CT: Yale University Press, 1998), 4.

2. Michelle Wick Patterson, "Real Indian Songs: The Society of American Indians and the Use of Native American Culture as a Means of Reform," *American Indian Quarterly* 25, no. 1 (Winter 2002), 45.

3. Deloria, *Playing Indian*, 125.

4. Deloria, *Playing Indian*, 123.

5. Deloria, *Playing Indian*, 189.

6. Abe Peck, "Village People," *Rolling Stone Magazine*, no. 289 (April 1979), 11.

7. Hank Steuver, "Celebrity Artifact: Felipe Rose, Village Person and Lakota, Donates 'Y.M.C.A.' Record to the Indian Museum," *The Washington Post* (January 13, 2005), C01.

8. Ray William Stedman, "Lingering Shadows (Movie Stereotypes)," in *Native American Voices: A Reader*,ed. Susan Lobo and Steve Talbot (New York: Longman, 1998), 196.

9. Pauline Tuttle, "Beyond Feathers and Beads: Interlocking Narratives in the Music and Dance of Tokeya Inajin (Kevin Locke)," in *Selling the Indian: Commercializing and Appropriating American Indian Culture*, ed. Carter Jones Meyer and Diana Royer (Tucson: University of Arizona Press, 2001), 118.

10. Beverly Singer and Robert Warrior, *Wiping the War-Paint Off the Lens* (Minneapolis: University of Minnesota Press, 2001), 5.

11. Peck, "Village People," 13.

12. Richard Dyer, "In Defense of Disco," in *Out in Culture: Gay, Lesbian, and Queer Essays on Popular Culture*, ed. Corey K. Creekmur and Alexander Doty (Durham, NC: Duke University Press, 1995), 412.

13. Randy Jones and Mark Bego, *Macho Man: The Disco Era and Gay America's Coming Out* (Westport, CT: Praeger, 2009), 101.

14. Jones and Bego, *Macho Man*, 105.

15. Lisa Tatonetti, "Visible Sexualities or Invisible Nations: Forced to Choose in big eden, Johnny Greyeyes, and the business of Fancydancing," *GLQ: A Journal of Lesbian and Gay Studies* 16, no. 1–2 (2010), 158.

16. Randy Burns, "Preface," in *Living the Spirit: A Gay American Indian Anthology*, ed. Will Roscoe (New York: St. Martin's Press, 1988), 2–4.

17. Brian Joseph Gilley, *Becoming Two-Spirit: Gay Identity and Social Acceptance in Indian Country* (Lincoln: University of Nebraska Press, 2006), 91.

18. Gabriel S. Estrada, "Two-Spirit Film Criticism: *Fancydancing* with Imitates Dog, Desjarlais and Alexie," in *Post Script: Essays in Film and the Humanities. Special Issue: Native American/Indigenous Film,* ed. Elise Marubbio, 24, no. 1 (Summer 2010), 106–118.

19. Terry Straus and Debra Valentino, "Retribalization in Urban Indian Communities," in *American Indians and the Urban Experience,* ed. Susan Lobo and Kurt Peters (Walnut Creek, CA: Alta Mira Press, 2001), 85.

20. Judy Kertész, "Charles Chessnut's *Mandy Oxendine,*" in *IndiVisible: African-Native American Lives in the Americas,* ed. Gabrielle Tayac (Washington, DC: Smithsonian National Museum of the American Indian, 2009), 154.

21. Stephan Tropiano, *Obscene, Indecent, Immoral, and Offensive: 100+ Years of Censored, Banned, and Controversial Films* (New York: Limelight Editions, 2009), 273.

22. Chon Noriega, "Ramona: Birth of the Southwest: Social Protest, Tourism, and D. W. Griffith's *Ramona,*" in *The Birth of Whiteness: Race and the Emergence of US Cinema,* ed. Daniel Bernardi (New Brunswick, NJ: Rutgers University, 1996), 214.

23. S. Elizabeth Bird, "Savage Desires: The Gendered Construction of the American Indian in Popular Media," in *Selling the Indian: Commercializing and Appropriating American Indian Cultures,* ed. Carter Jones Meyer and Diana Royer (Tucson: University of Arizona Press, 2001), 66.

24. Juana Maria Rodriquez, *Queer Latinidad: Identity Practices, Discursive Spaces* (New York: New York University Press, 2003), 20.

25. Alicia Arrizón, *Queering Mestizaje: Transculturation and Performance* (Ann Arbor: University of Michigan Press, 2006), 19.

26. José Barreiro, "Taino-African Intersections: Elite Constructs and Resurgent Identities," in *IndiVisible: African-Native American Lives in the Americas,* ed. Gabrielle Tayac (Washington, DC: Smithsonian National Museum of the American Indian, 2009), 41.

27. Bird, "Savage Desires," 65.

28. Craig Womack, *Red on Red: Native American Literary Separatism* (Minneapolis: University of Minnesota Press, 1999), 279.

29. Artists such as George Quaintance, Beefcake magazines, and soft-porn films of the mid-twentieth century masked the obvious homoerotic content of nearly nude or nude cowboys and male Indians as mere examples of artful historical reconstruction or masculine physique building. The *US v. Spinar and Germain* decision of 1967 upheld the right to publish complete male nudity. By the time the rise of disco occurred in the 1970s, the gay pornography magazine and film industries had celebrated a lifting of bans on male nudity that increasingly depicted muscled naked men playing cowboys and Indians. Auer traces how early "hypermasculine" nude cowboy and Indian images were directly reflected in Village People's look while Tropiano considers continuing impacts of anti-gay censorship in film into the 2000s. Jeff Auer, "Cowboys on the Cover of a Magazine," *The Gay and Lesbian Review Worldwide* 15, no. 6 (Nov/Dec 2008), 13–15. Also see Tropiano, "*Obscene, Indecent, Immoral, and Offensive,*" 221, 273.

30. Charlie Ballard, "Being Gay and Native American," *Charlie Ballard, Stand Up Comedian,* 2010. http://www.charlieballard.com (accessed May 1, 2010).

31. Bunny McBride, *Molly Spotted Elk: A Penobscot in Paris* (Norman: University of Oklahoma Press, 1995), 92.

32. McBride, *Molly Spotted Elk*, 93.

33. Cher, "Half-Breed," *The Sonny and Cher Comedy Hour*, 1973. http://www.youtube.com/watch?v=uxoWtoo9Oyg (accessed May 28, 2010).

34. Jim Adams, "Miss USA's costume offends Native Viewers," *Blue Corn Comics Stereotype of the Month* (June 9, 2004). http://www.bluecorncomics.com/stype464.htm (accessed January 10, 2012).

35. Stefan Zebrowski-Rubin, "Dance of Two Spirits—Kent Monkman at Montreal's Museum of Fine Arts," *The Art Blog* (August 18, 2009). http://theartblog.org/2009/08/dance-of-two-spirits-kent-monkman-at-montreals-museum-of-fine-arts (accessed May 20, 2010).

36. Zebrowski-Rubin, "Dance of Two Spirits," 2009.

37. Mark Butler, "Taking It Seriously: Intertextuality and Authenticity in Two Covers by the Pet Shop Boys," *Popular Music* 22, no. 1 (January 2003), 10.

38. Butler, "Taking It Seriously," 11.

39. Will Roscoe, *Changing Ones: Third and Fourth Genders in Native North America* (New York: St. Martin's Press, 1998), 100–101.

40. Carrie House, "Balancing Factors," *NativeOUT*, 1992. http://www.nativeout.com/multimedia/34-video/349-balancing-factors.html (accessed July 1, 2010).

41. "Archive for Videos," *Northeast Two-Spirit Society, New York City*, 2011. http://www.ne2ss.org/category/videos/ (accessed January 12, 2012).

42. Jones and Bego, *Macho Man*, 84–85.

43. Teja Anderson, "Felipe Rose Village People's Macho Man," *Living Media In Print and Online*, October 25, 2008. http://www.livinginmedia.com/article/felipe_rose_village_peoples_macho_man.html (accessed May 11, 2009).

44. Sandra Hale Schulman, *From Kokopellis to Electric Warriors: The Native American Culture of Music* (London: Lightning Source, 2002), 176.

REFERENCES

Adams, Jim. "Miss USA's costume offends Native Viewers." *Blue Corn Comics Stereotype of the Month*. June 9, 2004. http://www.bluecorncomics.com/stype464.htm (accessed January 10, 2012).

Anderson, Teja. "Felipe Rose Village People's Macho Man." *Living Media In Print and Online*. October 25, 2008. http://www.livinginmedia.com/article/felipe_rose_village_peoples_macho_man.html (accessed May 11, 2009).

Arrizón, Alicia. *Queering Mestizaje: Transculturation and Performance*. Ann Arbor: University of Michigan Press. 2006.

Auer, Jeff. "Cowboys on the Cover of a Magazine." *The Gay and Lesbian Review Worldwide* 15, no. 6 (November/December 2008): 13–15.

Ballard, Charlie. "Being Gay and Native American." *Charlie Ballard, Stand Up Comedian*. 2010. http://www.charlieballard.com (accessed May 1, 2010).

Barreiro, José. "Taino-African Intersections: Elite Constructs and Resurgent Identities." In *IndiVisible: African-Native American Lives in the Americas*. Ed. Gabrielle Tayac, 34–41. Washington, DC: Smithsonian National Museum of the American Indian. 2009.

Bird, S. Elizabeth. "Savage Desires: The Gendered Construction of the American Indian in Popular Media." In *Selling the Indian: Commercializing and Appropriating American Indian Cultures.* Ed. Carter Jones Meyer and Diana Royer, 62–98. Tucson: University of Arizona Press. 2001.

Burns, Randy. "Preface." In *Living the Spirit: A Gay American Indian Anthology.* Ed. Will Roscoe, 1–5. New York: St. Martin's Press. 1988.

Butler, Mark. "Taking It Seriously: Intertextuality and Authenticity in Two Covers by the Pet Shop Boys." *Popular Music* 22, no. 1 (January 2003): 1–19.

Cher. "Half-Breed." *The Sonny and Cher Comedy Hour.* 1973. http://www.youtube.com/watch?v=uxoWtoo9Oyg (accessed May 28, 2010).

Deloria, Philip. *Playing Indian.* New Haven, CT: Yale University Press. 1998.

Dyer, Richard. "In Defense of Disco." In *Out in Culture: Gay, Lesbian, and Queer Essays on Popular Culture.* Ed. Corey K. Creekmur and Alexander Doty, 407–415. Durham, NC: Duke University Press. 1995.

Estrada, Gabriel S. "Two-Spirit Film Criticism: *Fancydancing* with Imitates Dog, Desjarlais and Alexie." *Post Script: Essays in Film and the Humanities. Special Issue: Native American/Indigenous Film.* Ed. Elise Marubbio 24, no. 1 (Summer 2010): 106–118.

Gilley, Brian Joseph. *Becoming Two-Spirit: Gay Identity and Social Acceptance in Indian Country.* Lincoln: University of Nebraska Press. 2006.

Howard, James T. "Pan-Indianism in Native American Music and Dance." *Ethnomusicology.* 27, no. 1 (January 1983): 71–82.

House, Carrie, dir. *I Am.* Balancing Factors, NativeOUT. 1992. http://www.nativeout.com/multimedia/34-video/349-balancing-factors.html (accessed July 1, 2010).

Jones, Randy, and Mark Bego. *Macho Man: The Disco Era and Gay America's Coming Out.* Westport, CT: Praeger. 2009.

Kertész, Judy. "Charles Chessnut's *Mandy Oxendine.*" In *IndiVisible: African-Native American Lives in the Americas.* Ed. Gabrielle Tayac, 150–157. Washington, DC: Smithsonian National Museum of the American Indian. 2009.

Klopotek, Brian. "I Guess Your Warrior Look Doesn't Work Every Time: Challenging Indian Masculinity in the Cinema." In *Across the Great Divide: Cultures of Manhood in the American West.* Ed. Matthew Basso, Laura McCall, and Dee Garceau, 351–273. New York: Routledge. 2001.

McBride, Bunny. *Molly Spotted Elk: A Penobscot in Paris.* Norman: University of Oklahoma Press, 1995.

Noriega, Chon. "Ramona: Birth of the Southwest: Social Protest, Tourism, and D. W. Griffith's *Ramona.*" In *The Birth of Whiteness: Race and the Emergence of US Cinema.* Ed. Daniel Bernardi, 203–226. New Brunswick, NJ: Rutgers University Press. 1996.

Northeast Two-Spirit Society. Prod. *AIDS to Native Eyes.* 2007. http://www.nativeout.com/multimedia/video.html?task=videodirectlink&id=31 (accessed August 30, 2010).

Peck, Abe. "Village People." *Rolling Stone Magazine.* No. 289. (April 1979): 11–13.

Rodriguez, Juana Maria. *Queer Latinidad: Identity Practices, Discursive Spaces.* New York: New York University Press. 2003.

Roscoe, Wil. *Changing Ones: Third and Fourth Genders in Native North America.* New York: St. Martin's Press, 1998.

Rose, Felipe. "Felipe 'Swift Arrow' Rose." December 17, 2009. http://www.feliperose.com (accessed March 16, 2010).

Schulman, Sandra Hale. *From Kokopellis to Electric Warriors: The Native American Culture of Music.* London: Lightning Source. 2002.

Singer, Beverly, and Robert Warrior. *Wiping the War-Paint Off the Lens.* Minneapolis: University of Minnesota Press. 2001.

Stedman, Ray William. "Lingering Shadows (Movie Stereotypes)." In *Native American Voices: A Reader.* Eds. Susan Lobo and Steve Talbot, 195–203. New York: Longman. 1998.

Steuver, Hank. "Celebrity Artifact: Felipe Rose, Village Person and Lakota, Donates 'Y.M.C.A.' Record to the Indian Museum." *The Washington Post.* (January 13, 2005): C01.

Straus, Terry, and Debra Valentino. "Retribalization in Urban Indian Communities." In *American Indians and the Urban Experience.* Ed. Susan Lobo and Kurt Peters, 85–94. Walnut Creek, CA: Alta Mira Press. 2001.

Tatonetti, Lisa. "Visible Sexualities or Invisible Nations: Forced to Choose in big eden, Johnny Greyeyes, and the business of Fancydancing." *GLQ: A Journal of Lesbian and Gay Studies* 16, no. 1–2. (2010): 157–181.

Tropiano, Stephan. *Obscene, Indecent, Immoral, and Offensive: 100+ Years of Censored, Banned, and Controversial Films.* New York: Limelight Editions. 2009.

Tuttle, Pauline. "Beyond Feathers and Beads: Interlocking Narratives in the Music and Dance of Tokeya Inajin (Kevin Locke)." In *Selling the Indian: Commercializing and Appropriating American Indian Cultures.* Ed. Carter Jones Meyer and Diana Royer, 99–156. Tucson: University of Arizona Press. 2001.

VanWanseele, Kevin, prod. and dir. *AIDS to Native Eyes.* 2005. *Northeast Two-Spirit Society, New York City.* New York.

Walker, Nancy, dir. *Can't Stop the Music.* Screenplay by Allan Carr and Bronte Woodarad. Perf. Alex Briley, David Hodo, Glenn Hughes, Randy Jones, Felipe Rose, Ray Simpson, Steve Guttenberg, Valerie Perrine, Bruce Jenner, Paul Sand, and Tammy Grimes. Prod. Allan Carr, Henri Belolo, and Jacques Morali. Anchor Bay Entertainment. 1980.

Womack, Craig. *Red on Red: Native American Literary Separatism.* Minneapolis: University of Minnesota Press. 1999.

Zebrowski-Rubin, Stefan. "Dance of Two Spirits–Kent Monkman at Montreal's Museum of Fine Arts." *The Art Blog.* August 18, 2009. http://theartblog.org/2009/08/dance-of-two-spirits-kent-monkman-at-montreals-museum-of-fine-arts (accessed May 20, 2010).

ACTO FOUR

(De)Criminalizing Bodies: Ironies of Performance

NINETEEN

No Somos Criminales: Crossing Borders in Contemporary Latina and Latino Music

ARTURO J. ALDAMA

Anti-immigrant discourse in general and anti-Mexican hate speech and hate crimes in particular are a central piece of contemporary US political and public culture. The racist sense of entitlement by anti-immigrant xenophobes is echoed in a variety of formats including public radio, prime time news shows, and the blogosphere, and it is a central platform of many Republican senators, governors, and elected city officials such as mayors. Anti-immigrant games such as "Catch the Wetback" are the new form of political theatrics on many college campuses, and the Southern Poverty Law Center that does the Klan Watch has noted an incredible increase in hate-motivated violence toward those perceived as undocumented in the United States in the last several years.

The issues that concern me most are the arrogance of power and the absolute sense of racial entitlement that drive the supposedly fringe paramilitary nativist and neo-Nazi vigilante groups along the border and throughout the United States (which, in a loose chronology, include the Barnett Brothers, Ranch Rescue, the American Border Patrol, the Christian Identity Movement, the National Alliance, and the Minute Men) that have spread into the American mainstream. In fact, the political and public cultures of the United States carry an enormous weight of transversal racial hostility, evidenced most recently by Arizona Senate Bill 1070.[1]

In exploring the vigilante claims to the cultural, political, and legal ownership of lands that are indigenous to sovereign nations along the border and the lands that belong(ed) to Mexican Indian families (and these groups' paramilitary enforcement of their ownership claims), I am concerned at how their vigilantism is tied to racial xenophobia and to fears of how they perceive the re-conquest of the Southwest by México and Mexican immigrants. In considering how well these paramilitary groups are financially and "morally" supported by the political mainstream and by general public sentiment, I argue that these groups attempt to capitalize on a national desire for safety and security and enact pre–civil rights, pre–Chicano Movement discourses of racial threat, social containment, and bio-power by the dominant culture, and that they will attempt to re-map fears of 9/11 terrorism onto fears of immigrants of color in general and Mexicans in particular.[2]

State-sponsored oppressive discourses and practices rarely exist without resistance from aggrieved communities. Communities subjected to forms of denigration and violence because of their skin color, cultural practices, linguistic diversities, gender, or sexuality, among other markers of difference from hegemonic norms, create spaces of resistance on a variety of fronts. These strategies of resistance can take on many forms, such as active militant struggles, marches, protests, sit-ins, boycotts, picket lines, legal challenges, and the creation of coalitions with other communities for the common purpose of social justice. Resistance can also drive the cultural lives of oppressed peoples and those opposed to oppression. Music, visual arts, theater, humor, and literature can serve as spaces to talk back to oppression in direct and parodic terms, to humanize denigrated subjects, and to imagine and seek a transformation of power relations. The purpose of this chapter is to examine several resistance sites in US-México borderlands music that contest racial and sexual denigration and the normalization of a type of bio-power violence toward those constructed as inferior and sub-human because of their perceived immigrant status. In specific my chapter looks at several artists in the US-México borderlands of pop, conjunto, Tejano, Norteño, rock en español, and Latin Alternative collaborations to see how Latino musicians provide a centrifuge of heteroglossic counter-narratives to the racist, anti-immigrant hostilities of mainstream American culture. As Laurent Aubert's *The Music of the Other* reminds us, "If music has its own place in all reflections on culture, it does so in my opinion by the stakes it represents. Music is indeed never insignificant. It is simultaneously a strong and unifying means of communication and a revealer of identity."[3] In thinking about the stakes of music as a space of opposition and contestation, my essay will consider 2006 Latin Grammy–nominated song and music video "Mojado"[4] by Ricardo Arjona in collaboration with the Tejano/Norteño conjunto group *Intocable;* Molotov's bombastic and punctic (Barthes) "Frijolero" (2003); and the neocolonialism and autocolonialism and the tacit acceptance of sustained human and women's rights abuses in popular Mexican culture found in Lila Downs's "Sale Sobrando" from *Border / La Linea* (2001).[5] I will look at how these borderlands song texts (and visual narratives in the music videos of "Mojado" and "Frijolero") offer discourses that resist criminalization, abjection, and the stigma of South-to-North immigration in the geopolitics of American bio-power. They give voice, maintain dignity, and, in some cases, express disdain and outrage at the unbridled nativist racism toward immigrants whose labor fuels several inter-related industries and economies of the US nation-state.

I start with a recent and interesting collaboration of the poetic Guatemalan artist Ricardo Arjona and the Tejano/Norteño conjunto group called *Intocable* on the gripping video essay montage and song "Mojado," or "wet" (wetback). I then discuss my quibble with the subtitle of Mark Slobin's *Subcultural Sounds: Micromusics of the West,* which re-legitimates the Anglo-centric gaze that would label Latino music as micro-music. In the case of Latino communities, both within the Mexican nation-state and in the border regions that create a third space between United States and México, conjunto style and popular ballads are perhaps the macro-musics, possibly even the superculture of popular consumption, to use Slobin's term. In addition, as Alicia Gaspar de Alba posits regarding the status of Chicana and Chicano cultures in her introduction to *Velvet Barrios: Popular Cultures and Chicana/o Sexualities,* "Chicano/a culture is not a subculture rather an *alter-Native* culture, an Other American culture indigenous to the landbase now known as the West and the Southwest of the United States. Chicana/o culture, then, is not immigrant but native, not foreign but colonized, not alien but different from the overarching hegemony of white America."[6] Having made my critiques of Slobin's idea of the micro-musics, I do find his discussion of the diasporic intercultural, "which emerges from the linkages that subcultures set up across national boundaries,"[7] as a useful entry into discussing how the song text "Mojado" articulates a politics of borderlands anti-racist opposition in a music form that dominates Spanish-language commercial radio waves: the conjunto, corrido, and ballad in the US-México nation-state.

In the final chapter of *Conventional Wisdom: the Content of Musical Form,* Susan McClary argues, "[i]nstead of searching vainly for continuous 'authentic' traditions, we need to pay attention to the kinds of ferment located in boundaries, to fusions of unpredictable sorts that continually give rise to new genres and modes of expression."[8] In this song text, we see a collaboration between two very different genres, artists, and styles: Guatemalan pop idol Ricardo Arjona and Texas–Northern México, Tejano-Conjunto-based *Intocable.* This group won the 2005 Latin Grammy award for their album *Diez* and best regional song for "Aire." Ricardo Arjona is known as a successful pop and soft Latin rock balladeer who employs language games, irony, and hints of Nueva Canción[9] protest and humanist aesthetics in his lyrics. He straddles a line between the intensely commercial and intentionally apolitical romantic balladeers who offer escapist tunes and those musicians who deal with violence, poverty, racism, exploitation, and direct political protest of imperialism, predatory capitalism, or any issues relevant to subalternity in Latino and Latin American communities. As a collaborative move, the political and emotional message of "Mojado" has a much greater possibility of reaching the Mexican immigrant audience whose lives and dignity are honored in both the song and the video, given the large abundance of Mexican regional music airwaves on AM and FM dials and their huge popularity among the immigrant and working-class communities in the United States and in México.[10]

The video-song essay (nominated for the 2006 Latin Grammies for best musical video, produced and directed by Omar Catalan and Andrea de Moral) starts with testimonios of men, and one in particular, most possibly Chilango (a slang term from someone who comes from México City based on one's accent) who clarifies that his intention for crossing the frontera (border) is so that he can "work" and "not steal."

The video uses testimonios, montage, and photo stills of the dead, of the crosses on metal walls and wooden crosses in the soil next to walls commemorating the dead, and of the border patrol chasing people down. These images weave into the hybrid musicality of the song to provide a potent visual and audio semiotics of melancholy, dignity, tenuous hope, and muted rage. The crosses, the still shots of the dead, and the black and white visual tonality of the video essay speak to the real bio-power of the border crossing, where countless humans die unnecessarily due to heat and cold exposure and violence as they flee economic starvation caused, in large part, by US economic policy.[11] For example, the 1994 NAFTA accord and its current updated versions caused a wide swath of US corn subsidies to supplant Mexican-grown corn. This drove small farmers to cities in México, and from cities in México to el Norte, in search of work to support themselves, their families, and their pueblos. Arjona's lyrics call for the humanization of subjects seen as abjects/criminals in the funny yet poignant jab at the absurdity and irrationality of racist nomenclature: "El mojado tiene ganas de secarse" ("The wetback wants to dry off"). As Peter García points out, the song itself has a moderate polka in a minor key that conveys melancholia and grief.

David L. Eng's "Melancholia in the Late Twentieth Century" can help us understand how melancholia creates identity and defines historic and institutional oppression. Eng re-situates Freud's theory of melancholia, which he summarizes quite eloquently as a "premier theory of unspeakable loss and inexorable suffering, melancholia serves as a powerful tool for analyzing the psychic production, condition, and limits of marginalized subjectivities predicated on states of injury."[12] Eng asks: "What, then, would it mean if minoritarian group identities were defined not through a particular set of physiological distinctions or cultural bonds but through a collective group memory of historical loss and continued suffering?"[13] This question is provocative. Here we have a situation of folks crossing and being crossed by the US-México border, seeking work in el Norte and negotiating their own survival amid the grief of ghosts of the unnecessary dead in a deadly axiom of bio-power wielded by the US nation-state. Is it as Eng suggests? Suffering and the collective memory of historical loss and the constant pain of otherization are what define the identities of South to North border-crossers?

In addition to Eng's provocative theories on how melancholia can serve as a substrate of subaltern identity formation, perhaps we can also look at how Achille Mbembe theorizes Foucault's notion of bio-power to consider the US-México border zone. In particular, we can examine the South-to-North border crossing from and through México to the United States by working-class indigenous and mestiza/o peoples who do not have the economic and cultural capital to obtain a visa and whose livelihoods within their home communities have been severely curtailed by transnational market economies inscribed by a predictable necropolitics as the US nation-state attempts to execute its sovereignty and promote the health and safety of its citizen subjects. Even though Mbembe's essay "Necropolitics" does not consider the US-México borderlands directly, his lucid analysis of how necropolitics works to maintain political systems like apartheid South Africa, the Nazi elimination of the Other, colonial rule, and plantation slavery through the death of the Otherized body can be useful to consider what many human rights activists and scholars call the killing fields of the tortilla curtain along the US-México border. His discussion of colonized space at the frontiers of empire is a useful frame to consider how a colonial nation-state produces "boundaries and hierarchies, zones and enclaves" and a large "reservoir of cultural imaginaries" that give "differential rights to differing categories of people" within "the same space."[14] Space, then, as Mbembe argues, is the "raw material" of sovereignty and the violence to maintain that sovereignty by reinforcing the boundaries of subjects versus objects and entitled humans versus non-humans. In the case of the US-México border, the space of sovereignty becomes a space where racialized subjects are profiled and constructed as illegal or legal. As argued in my 2001 *Disrupting Savagism* book, the border is a line that is constructed through American imperialism and that marks the edge of the nation-state yet it is elastic, as is demonstrated by how subjects who live far away from this line contend with state-sponsored and vigilante necropolitical acts. Examples include forced roundups by the US Immigration and Customs Enforcement (ICE), such as the December 12, 2006, Swift Factory ICE raids that took parents away from their children and left children to hope that someone would take care of them, detention in inhumane prisons of subjects suspected of being "illegal" because of their skin color or accent, and the huge rise in hate crimes (ranging from assault to murder) for being perceived as a "wetback," as seen in the famous 2008 Shenandoah, Pennsylvania, case, where teenage athletes kicked Luis Ramirez to death to teach the "spic" a lesson, leaving behind his white fiancée and their three children. An all-white jury acquitted the teens of serious charges in May 2009, amid cheers from the courtroom audience. They now face federal hate crime charges, as do three former

Shenandoah policemen for obstructing the investigation and protecting the well-liked football players.

In his "Analytics of the Modern: An Introduction," Jonathan Inda, a Chicano anthropologist and immigration scholar, summarizes the "Necropolitical Projects" section of the volume *Anthropologies of Modernity: Foucault, Governmentality, and Life Politics* in a forthright manner that can help us understand the visual montage and the emotive feelings of melancholia and muted rage that the song and video "Mojado" expresses. Inda argues that the "death of the other—that is, of those deemed dangerous, unfit, or diseased—will make life in general more healthy and pure."[15] In thinking about the border: the United States enforces a line won through war with México to determine the legality and illegality of human beings. This line was drawn over the land of several indigenous nations, such as the Yoeme, Kickapoo, Pima Apache, Pai Pai, and Tohono O'odham in Arizona, to name a few. After the passage of the 1994 NAFTA, the rapid devaluation of the peso caused extreme economic crisis and forced migrations in México. Several operations attempted to seal off sections of the US-México border. In California, there was *Operation Gatekeeper* (1994); in Texas, *Operation Hold the Line* (1993); and in Arizona, *Operation Safeguard* (2003). All attempted to seal the border against "unauthorized" human passage (and not to mention the August 2010 authorization of six hundred million dollars by the federal government to provide "border security"—the necropolitical consequences on causing predictable death for South-to-North border crossers remain to be seen).[16] The consequence of these 1990s necropolicies of border security is to drive border crossers into what Luis Alberto Urrea poetically refers to as *The Devil's Highway*, the title of his eloquent ethnographic-literary re-construction of men who died from heat exhaustion as they crossed the Sonora borderlands to begin their contracted work in the Tyson Foods slaughterhouses. The devil's highway, or the "camino del diablo" in the Arizona-Sonora desertscape, is marked by heat and cold extremes. Its aridity causes rapid and debilitating dehydration; its surface is covered with ruts, holes, poisonous snakes, and cacti that can pierce shoes and skin. Even four-wheel-drive vehicles of the border patrol and Mexican army get stuck, lost, and overturned in this treacherous terrain. In addition to environmental and ecosystem factors, bandits—human predators—lie in wait to rob, rape, and assault border crossers (especially Central Americans).[17] As the border line gets close, the border patrol and paramilitary vigilante groups wait to apprehend, chase after, shoot at, and terrorize Mexicanos and other Latinos. Subjects fleeing economic persecution cross to be exploited in a bio-power of low-paid, uninsured jobs (gardening, cleaning, restaurant work, and farm work, to name a few) that maintain the health and service of subjects in power at direct cost to the workers' psychic and social well-being.

Unlike "Mojado," the Molotov song "Frijolero," a single from *Dance and Dense Denso* (2003), does not count on the emotional/psychic strategy of melancholia as a means to gain sympathy and empathy, articulate identity, and promote a response to the necropolitical consequences of crossing in the borderlands. Both in tone and in content, this song is the most overt in its expression of anger and outrage at the unchecked racism of language and discourse toward Mexicanos as "beaners" or frijoleros, framed against a macropolitics of neoliberalism, globalization, US-sponsored war, invasion, and transnational drug economies. I have very mixed feelings about Molotov,[18] a three-time Latin Grammy winner censored by the Mexican government for its bold and confrontational lyrics. On one hand, I am mesmerized by their willingness to engage in an amazing mix of musicality (hip hop, punk, metal, rap, norteño, cumbia), experimentation, linguistic code switching, and a caustic, boisterous spirit of rebellion and anti-establishment position. As summarized by Enrique Lavin in the April 22, 2003 *Village Voice* piece called "Cocktail Nation,"

> Purposeful irony doesn't escape them, either. Performing "Frijolero (Beaner)," a languid, Old West–inspired polka-cumbia off their recent third release, *Dance and Dense Denso,* Randy Ebright (the son of an ex-DEA agent) used his best American drawl to spit curses at "beaners on the wrong side of the goddamn river," while in Spanish, Tito Fuentes, Mickey Huidobro, and Paco Ayala responded in chorus, "Don't call me a frijolero, pinche gringo."[19]

However, as much as I appreciate the direct anti-racist and anti-bourgeois impulses of their musical texts—for example, "Gimme the Power"—some of their work is also homophobic and sexist, as seen in the 1998 song "Puto,"[20] which unfortunately garners a huge sing-along in Spanish-speaking crowds, especially in México, and the album *Donde Jugaran Las Niñas* (1998), with its super-suggestive cover of a Catholic schoolgirl in a sexually submissive pose that parodies Mana's *Donde Jugaran los Niños,* an eco-conscious, family-friendly rock album. So how do we reconcile celebrating Molotov's anti-racist, anti-classist, and anti-globalization impulses and condemning their overt homophobia and sexism and their reproductions of a working-class, macho, heteronormative masculinity?[21]

In this particular Molotov song, the Michigan-born Anglo drummer, Randy the "Gringo Loco" Ebright, a son of a DEA agent stationed in México City, features prominently. In terms of white privilege and power, it is refreshing to see a Latinized or Chilango-ized white man confronting anti-Mexican racism in the United States, declaring that "he wants to smack the mouth of these racists." Again, musically you have the accordion intro and the predictable conjunto rhythm with a cumbia tinge. After sparring back and forth between racial and racist discourse of gringo and beaners, with Paco Ayala singing in an intentionally Anglo-ized Mexican accent, the song moves into Randy doing a freestyle-like rap that makes the final political point: "Now why don't you look down / to where your feet is planted / That US soil that makes you take shit for granted / If not for Santa Ana, just to let you know / That where your feet are planted would be México. / Correcto!" Randy Ebright and Molotov seem to know some basic tenets of Chicano and Mexican history, as he refers to how México lost almost two-thirds of its northern territories after the signing of the 1848 Treaty of Guadalupe Hidalgo that officiated the end of the US-México war; many blame General Santa Ana's dispersed leadership style for such a devastating loss.[22]

Greg Schelonka"s "Mexican Rock and the Border Under Globalization"[23] points out in his study of border metaphors in Mexican rock that Molotov's song is a "no-holds-barred" characterization of racism in the "contact zone" of two cultures:

> Frijolero continues the band's assault on the culture of decency attributed to middle class values with its vulgar examination of stereotypes on both sides of the border.[24]

As the song became more successful and popular after its 2003 release (it won a 2005 Latin Grammy for best animated video), the group's members were accused of being anti-US racists in their own right (a sociological impossibility) and subject to censorship in both the United States and in México. However, the June 2003 article from *El Universal* in Madrid,

Spain that discusses how "Frijolero" has been censored and modified in México and the United States (to delete Spanish expletives) quotes Paco Ayala as saying, "No somos anti yankis, somos anti ideología del presidente George W. Bush." ["We are not anti-Yankee, we are anti the ideology of President George W. Bush"; my translation].

Visually, the video makes quite striking use of a rotoscope technique (animation traced over live action filming frame by frame) by well-known animators Jason Archer and Paul Beck, who are perhaps most well known for their rotoscope animation in Richard Linklater's *Waking Life* (2001) and *Scanner Darkly* (2006). Their rotoscope color palette emphasizes the red, green, and white of the Mexican flag in how its main figures are depicted. The block color motifs reify the Mexican flag contrast with the reds, yellows, and oranges of the desert borderlands areas and the military dark green of the INS border patrol suit. In addition to its heteroglossic critiques of racism in the border through its use of racial bantering with internal ironies (with the Mexican members singing in a purposefully Anglicized Mexican accent and Randy the crazy gringo singing with a very fluent Mexican accent), the animation also critiques the neoliberal and warmongering policies of former president George W. Bush and vice president Dick Cheney. They are both drawn in their underpants cuddling up to former Mexican president Fox while bombs with dollar signs and oil barrels with American flags float down on the animated landscape. Two large breasts also appear on the horizon, sexualizing the desert landscape. The animation also critiques the issue of drug consumption and the stereotypes of Mexicans as drug dealers: "Aunque nos hagan la fama / de que somos vendedores / de la droga que sembramos / ustedes son consumidores" ["Even though you see us as drug dealers and growers it is you all that are the consumers"]. It can also serve as an indirect critique of how the US-led War on Drugs focuses more on punishing growers, users, and dealers and less on providing sustainable treatment for those embattled with addictions.

The transversal intersections between the norteño sound in conjunto with corridos and rock en español are not new, and most rock en español artists honor the legacies and influences of the traditional Mexican musics of their parents and the popular culture. For example, there is the tribute to Tigres del Norte from such groups as Maldita Vecindad, Café Tacuba, Los Lobos, El Gran Silencio, Molotov, Ely Guerra, and

Botellita de Jerez.[25] Also, in the Monterrey working-class, barrio-based Latin Rock / Latin Alternative "El Gran Silencio," we see how the song and video of "Chuntaros Style" with a cumbia overlay again pays homage to the conjunto roots of northern Mexican music. Even Intocable has a tribute album by such artists as Kinky, Reggaeton Afro–Puerto Rican artist Tego Calderon, and Volovan, among others, that forms the second disc of their 2005 EMI Latin album *Diez*.

Lila Downs[26] (the subject of a chapter in this book by Brenda Romero), a transnational mestiza figure of white and Mixteca-Mexican origin, practices another type of musical mestizaje and intersected genres with her song "Sale Sobrando" (Good for Nothing). The third site of musical resistance that I will discuss does not present me with the contradictory positions that Molotov does, of celebrating their anti-racism and being dismayed by the sexism and homophobia that they claim are satirical. "Sale Sobrando" is a song that drives a multifold critique of racism, sexism, colonialism, and border violence. Of all the song texts this chapter considers, I think that this song text is the most politically and musically nuanced and aesthetically complex. Musically, there are a range of musical elements and styles: danzón, habanera (with its güiro intro), solo violin played in the pizzicato, grand piano with a cabaret-lounge 1940s feel, even a tango nuance and a cumbia tinge.[27] The song even has a micro-song within the large song text that serves as an homage to the classic Mexican ballad in the core repertoire of most Mariachi music ensembles, "Cielito Lindo" (1882), which Lila re-subverts by calling it "México Lindo."[28]

In "Sale Sobrando," Downs plays the well-known music of "Cielito Lindo" but replaces the lyric of "Cielito Lindo" with "México Lindo," making an intra-textual gesture toward an extremely well-known song made famous by Jorge Negrete, "México Lindo y Querido." The lyrics of "México lindo and querido" pay a romantic homage to México as the "the love of loves" of the singer and to its pastoral beauty of volcanoes, flowers, and fields. Perhaps the most famous part of the song asks México to bring its children back to its land if they die, "lejos de ti" (far away from you). Both songs reproduce a type of femininity: "Cielito Lindo" is arguably a deeply romanticized song that implores the feminized subject cielito (which means little heaven) to sing and not cry ("ay, ay, ay, ay, canta y no llores"), and in "México Lindo," the entire country of México seems to be seen as a trope of the motherland. The song itself could arguably serve as a tribute from the children of México back to their motherland, eliciting a significant emotional response for Mexicans who are immigrants and/or exiles away from their country.

This clever intertextuality capitalizes on the emotive feelings of nostalgia and patriotism that the song "México Lindo" garners among Mexican listeners and plays into the discourses and practices of nationalism. The romantic, feminized, and utopic pastoral ideas and emotive responses that these songs garner among its audiences juxtapose with how Downs's own lyrics and performance expose the bio-power or necropolitics of gender and ethnic violence that reflect the social realities of the Mexican nation-state. A possible comparison might be if someone were to sing a song that promotes intense patriotism and national identity, such as the "Star Spangled Banner," and change the lyrics to condemn the United States for causing genocide on indigenous peoples and enslaving African peoples. But I suspect, given the resurgence of intensive patriotism post 9/11, that people would be more outraged at a change to the lyrics of this iconic song than at the thought of the colonial legacies of the United States on communities of color, even though this song is overtly anti-colonialist toward Britain.

In one stanza of the song, Downs juxtaposes the ways in which the bearded invaders (most probably referring to the Spanish conquistadores, including Christopher Columbus and Hernán Cortés) were "welcomed" by indigenous peoples to Mesoamerica with how the mojados (wetbacks) who go north are not told "welcome hermanos" (brothers). In addition to reflecting the US-México border zone, where migrants face the violence of narcotraffickers and the hostility of the border patrol, the song brings attention to the violence directed at women and children in Chiapas, México, which borders Guatemala (most probably referring to the 1997 Acteal, Chiapas, massacre in which forty-five people, including Mayan women and children, were cut down by machetes and bullets at a prayer meeting).[29]

The politics of the song bring the tropes of the sixteenth-century conquest of México, the normalization of violence toward Indigenous peoples, the violence of the border patrol and the border crossing, and the normalization of violence against Indian women in Chiapas into a geo-political ethnoscape evoked by the lyrics and the multi-voiced musicalities of the piece. It juxtaposes the utopian ideas of México Lindo (Beautiful México) that is good for tourism with the nation-state's institutionalized disregard of the human rights of its own dispossessed citizenry. Curwen Best's *Cultures @ the Cutting Edge* provides an excellent way to understand the musical complexities in contemporary musics that might be applicable to the multi-voicing of Lila Downs, which creates a type of dialogic community that speaks to gender and ethnic relations in México. In reference to Anglophone Caribbean music, Best argues that multi-timbrality has "to do with the existence of two or more similar or contrasting voices and their ability to be sounded simultaneously."[30] Although Downs's voicing of characters does not occur simultaneously, her bringing of the disparate voices into a dialogue shows a social theater of gender and ethnic relations that defines the modern Mexican state: a state where mestizos glorify Eurocentric and patriarchal values and denigrate darker-skinned Indigenous peoples, especially women, even though they themselves have strong Indigenous ancestry, evincing a type of autocolonialism.[31]

To conclude: to study songs like these confirms what Frances Aparicio and Candida F. Jacquez argue in their outstanding volume *Musical Migrations*. That is, the study of Latino musics in a transnational context must transform "traditional methodologies" that define music "through discrete categories such as national identity and musical genre" and "illustrate" how social meanings of musical structures "are embedded in the problematic of cultural identity in (post)colonial contexts."[32] These three songs, which vary in strategies and styles, can offer cultural and music scholars rich and complex opportunities to engage directly with what was a landmark essay of postcolonial studies by Gayatri Chakravorty Spivak titled "Can the Subaltern Speak?" (1980). If we take time to listen, we can hear how borderlands musics can and do create radical, hybridized, anti-racist, twenty-first-century performative sites of social justice. In their defense of dignity and respect, these performances straddle the psychic politics of melancholy and outrage. These song texts challenge the symbolic logic that drives racial, nativist acts of entitlement and the racial privilege of subjects who criminalize and rally against immigrants. Yet, ironically, Anglo-Western nativists are themselves in many cases descendants of immigrants who have as a group benefited from the direct colonization, enslavement, dispossession, and genocide of Indian peoples in the United States, México, and the Southwest, including but not limited to the ancestors of many Mexicans as original citizens of the Southwest or Aztlán.

NOTES

1. Governor Jan Brewer signed Arizona Senate Bill 1070, sponsored by Russell Pearce, into law on April 23, 2010. A provision of the law requires that police officers (who are not immigration enforcement agents) check the immigration and citizenship status of suspected illegal immigrants. This passage of the law has provoked international outcry against the legalization of racial profiling. Federal judge Susan Bolton blocked certain provisions of the law on July 28, 2010, including the ones that can lead to racial profiling. Maricopa County sheriff Joe Arpaio has arrested many protesters against SB1070.

2. To see actual footage of the paramilitary groups along the United States and México border, especially in Arizona, please see *Walking the Line: Vigilantes on the US-México border* by Jeremy Levine and Landon Van Soest (2005). Two scholarly sources that look at the neo-Nazi impulses of the border paramilitary groups and leaders are Justin Akers Chacón and Mike Davis, *No One is Illegal: Fighting Racism and State Violence on the US-México Border,* Haymarket Books, 2006: 248–258, and Leo R. Chavez, *The Latino Threat: Constructing Immigrants, Citizens, and the Nation,* Stanford University Press, 2008: 132–152.

3. Laurent Aubert, 2007, *The Music of the Other,* Surrey, UK: Ashgate Publishing, 1.

4. The Sony BMG Latin music video was nominated for a 2006 Latin Grammy and was produced and directed by Omar Catalan and Andrea de Moral. Ricardo Arjona won best male vocal for the album *Adentro* that carries the song "Mojado."

5. It is highly recommended that you listen to these songs and watch the music videos that accompany "Mojado" and "Frijolero" as you read through this essay. They are widely available on YouTube and other sites that carry music videos and songs.

6. Alicia Gaspar de Alba, 2002, *Velvet Barrios: Popular Culture & Chicana/o Sexualities,* New York: Palgrave, xxi.

7. Mark Slobin, 1993, *Subcultural Sounds: Micromusics of the West (Music Culture),* Middleton, CT: Wesleyan University Press, 65.

8. Susan McClary, 2000, *Conventional Wisdom: The Content of Musical Form,* Berkeley, CA: University of California Press, 168.

9. For an overview of the humanist and anti-imperial and anti-global aesthetics of the Nueva Cancion movement in Latin America, see the often-cited article by Rina Benmayor, "La 'Nueva Trova': New Cuban Song," *Latin American Music Review / Revista de Música Latinoamericana,* Vol. 2, No. 1, 1981, 11–44. For a more comparative analysis of Nueva Canción aesthetics in Chilean, Cuban, and US Latino contexts, see Jane Tumas-Serna, "The 'Nueva Cancion.' Movement and its Mass Mediated Performance Context," *Latin American Music Review / Revista de Música Latinoamericana,* Vol. 13, No. 2, 1992, 139–157.

10. See http://music.aol.com/video/mojado/ricardo-arjona/sony:1130125273 (last accessed August 20, 2010). This video is also widely available on YouTube.

11. For a critical legal discussion of the relationship between NAFTA and immigration from México, see Kevin Johnson, "Essay on Immigration, Citizenship, and US/México Relations: The Tale of Two Treaties." *Southwestern Journal of Law and Trade in the Americas,* Vol. 5, 1998, 121–141. For a more detailed analysis of the impacts of US corn subsidies on local economies in México among other factors promoted by NAFTA, please see Andy Gutierrez, "Codifying the Past, Erasing the Future: NAFTA and the Zapatista Uprising of 1994 Part Two," *Hastings West-Northwest Journal of Environmental Law and Policy,* 2008, 883–920.

12. David L. Eng, "Melancholia in the Late Twentieth Century." *Signs,* Vol. 25, No. 4, 1275–1281, p. 1276.

13. David L. Eng, "Melancholia in the Late Twentieth Century," 1276.

14. Achille Mbembe, Winter 2003, trans. Libby Meintjes, "Necropolitics." *Public Culture,* Vol. 15, No. 1, 11–40, p. 26.

15. Jonathan Inda, 2005, *Anthropologies of Modernity: Foucault, Governmentality, and Life Politics,* Hoboken, NJ: Wiley-Blackwell, 16.

16. According to the the September 30, 2009, NBC San Diego article "Operation Gatekeeper, 15 Years Later" by Gene Cubbison, an estimated 5,600 deaths due to trying to cross the rugged borderlands have occurred since the 1994 establishment of Operation Gatekeeper. http://www.nbcsandiego.com/news/politics/Operation-Gatekeeper-at-15—62939412.html (last accessed September 1, 2010). To mark the fifteen-year anniversary of Operation Gatekeeper, the ACLU released a report titled *Humanitarian Crisis: Migrant Deaths at the US-Mexico Border* on October 1, 2009, that calls for more humanitarian action on the border given the government's lack of compliance with international human rights law and failures to prevent migrant deaths. http://www.aclu.org/immigrants-rights/humanitarian-crisis-migrant-deaths-us-mexico-border (last accessed Sept 1, 2010).

17. According to an August 26, 2010, Associate Press article titled "Drug Cartel Suspected in Massacre of 72 Migrants" and reprinted on MSNBC, the bodies of seventy-two migrants mainly from Central America, fifty-eight men and fourteen women, were found stacked on top of each other in an abandoned warehouse room a hundred miles from the border. There was one survivor from Ecuador who reported that the migrants were forced to turn over money or be killed by a drug cartel. http://www.msnbc.msn.com/id/38843735/ns/world_news-americas/ (last accessed August 27, 2010).

18. For an overview of the aesthetics, musical dynamics, use of humor, irony, and overview of the band Molotov formed in 1995 in México City, see Ernesto Lechner, 2006, *Rock en Espanol: The Latin Alternative Rock Explosion,* Chicago, IL: Chicago Review Press, 123–129.

19. Enrique Lavin, April 22, 2003, "Cocktail Nation," *Village Voice,* 1.

20. During the July 31, 2010, *Biennal of the Americas* panel presentation called "Between the Lines: Explorations of Borderlands culture," a discussion of the song "Puto" came up as a possible act of parody that challenges Latino macho identities. Molotov defends their use of "puto" as referring to someone who is a coward, and they caused a huge uproar of applause in a 2003 New York City concert when they referred to former president George H. W. Bush as a "puto." However, it is hard to

reconcile the song as possible humor given the prevalence of homophobic violence outside of certain neighborhoods in Mexico City that are considered safe spaces of GLBT couples. A panelist from Tijuana, México, commented that, interestingly, the electronic remix of the song "Puto" is very popular in gay dance clubs throughout México.

21. Another gritty anti-globalization, working-class-origin Mexican rock band, Tex Tex, has similar macro-critiques of power as Molotov, yet as Mark A. Hernández points out in his "Breaking the Mold of Contemporary Working-Class Mexican Masculinity: The Rock Urban Music of Tex Tex" (*Journal of Popular Music Studies,* Vol. 20, March 2008, Iss. 1, 3–25), Tex Tex is willing to interrogate and disrupt what he calls the hegemonic working-class masculinity that constructs itself in homophobic and sexist terms.

22. "Frijolero"—the uncensored version—is widely available on YouTube. Here is a YouTube link last visited Aug 19, 2010: http://www.youtube.com/watch?v=qcwaDYc1IWY

23. See *Peace Review: A Journal of Social Justice,* Vol. 18, 101–108.

24. Greg Schelonka, "Mexican Rock and the Border Under Globalization," *Peace Review,* Vol. 18, Iss. 1, Jan. 2006, 101–108, pp. 103–104.

25. For a brief discussion of the impact of Norteño music on Latin rock, see Ed Morales, *Latin Beat,* 2003, 268–271.

26. A recurrent theme in published interviews with Lila Downs is her mixed racial and bi-national heritage with a Mixtecan mother and a University of Minnesota–based cinematographer father. See the interview with famed Chicano author, journalist, and poet Luis Rodriguez in *Xispas: Chicano Art, Culture and Politics* where Downs discusses her birthplace in the home of the Mixteca in Oaxaca, México, and in St. Paul, Minnesota, and a more recent interview in the October 2009 *Guernica Magazine* with Joel Whitney, "Wise Latina." http://www.guernicamag.com/interviews/1317/wise_latina/ (last accessed August 27, 2010).

27. I thank Dr. Peter J. García and Dr. Brenda Romero for their scholarly expertise in Latin American and Chicana/o ethnomusicology. I am nervous writing about music since I am not a trained ethnomusicologist but more of a cultural, literary, and film studies scholar, so I am deeply indebted to them for pointing out some of the musical elements found in these songs. Additionally, Brenda Romero points out that it is the range of Lila's voice styles and her theatricality that recall different archetypal characters in the body politic of México: indigenous women, mestizas, and border crossers. (See her chapter in this volume.)

28. For a discussion of the song "Cielito Lindo," its origins, and its transborder appeal, see John Storm Roberts, 1979, *The Latin Tinge: The Impact of Latin American Music in the United States,* New York: Oxford University Press, 20.

29. I am indebted to Sarah Ramirez's "Aquí la Justicia Sale Sobrando: Lila Downs and Transfontera Music" for her analysis of gender and neocolonial violence in the song. http://bad.eserver.org/issues/2002/61/ramirez.html (last accessed September 1, 2010).

30. Curwen Best, 2005, *Cultures @ the Cutting Edge,* Kingston, Jamaica: University of West Indies Press, 8.

31. For a discussion of a state-defined mestizo hegemonic oppression of indigenous peoples, see Guillermo Bonfil Batalla, 1996, *México Profundo: Reclaiming a*

Civilization, Austin, TX: University of Texas Press, and Jack Forbes, 2008, *Columbus and Other Cannibals: The Wetiko Disease of Exploitation, Imperialism and Terrorism,* New York: Seven Stories Press.

32. Frances R. Aparicio and Candida Jaquez, eds., 2003, *Musical Migrations: Transnationalism and Cultural Hybridity in Latin/o America,* New York: Palgrave, 9.

REFERENCES

Aldama, Arturo. *Disrupting Savagism: Intersecting Chicana/o, Mexican Immigrant and Native American Struggles for Self Representation.* Durham, NC: Duke University Press, 2001.

Aparicio, Frances R., and Candida F. Jaquez (eds.). *Musical Migrations: Transnationalism and Cultural Hybridity in Latin/o America.* New York: Palgrave, 2003.

Aubert, Laurent. *The Music of the Other.* Surrey, UK: Ashgate Publishing, 2007.

Best, Curwen. *Cultures @ the Cutting Edge.* Kingston, Jamaica: University of West Indies Press, 2005.

Eng, David L. "Melancholia in the Late Twentieth Century." *Signs,* Vol. 25, No. 4, Summer 2000: 1275–1281.

Gaspar de Alba, Alicia. *Velvet Barrios: Popular Culture & Chicana/o Sexualities.* New York: Palgrave, 2002.

Inda, Jonathan. *Anthropologies of Modernity: Foucault, Governmentality, and Life Politics.* Hoboken, NJ: Wiley-Blackwell, 2005.

Lavin, Enrique. "Cocktail Nation." *Village Voice,* April 22, 2003.

Mbembe, Achille. Translated by Libby Meintjes. "Necropolitics." *Public Culture,* Vol. 15, No. 1 (Winter 2003): 11–40.

McClary, Susan. *Conventional Wisdom: The Content of Musical Form.* Berkeley, CA: University of California Press, 2000.

Schelonka, Greg. "Mexican Rock and the Border Under Globalization." *Peace Review,* Vol. 18, Iss. 1, January 2006: 101–108.

Slobin, Mark. *Subcultural Sounds: Micromusics of the West (Music Culture).* Middleton, CT: Wesleyan University Press, 1993.

Spivak, Gayatri Chakravorty. "Can the Subaltern Speak?" in *Marxism and the Interpretation of Culture,* edited by Cary Nelson and Lawrence Grossberg. Chicago: University of Illinois Press, 1988, 271–313.

DISCOGRAPHY

Arjona, Ricardo, *Adentro.* Sony US Latin, 2005.

Downs, Lila, *Border / La Linea.* Narada, 2001.

Intocable, *Diez.* Emi Latin, 2005.

Molotov, *Dance and Dense Denso.* Universal Latino, 2003.

———. *Donde Jugaran las Niñas.* Universal Latino, 1998.

TWENTY

"Pelones y Matones": Chicano Cholos Perform for a Punitive Audience

VICTOR M. RIOS & PATRICK LOPEZ-AGUADO

Riviera is a small city on the California coast well known as a tourist destination and idyllic beachside community.[1] Its beautiful coastal geography inflates real estate values, attracting the development of hidden mansions along hillsides that offer scenic ocean views as well as upscale boutiques along Beach Street, the main corridor of its downtown commercial district. Home to numerous theaters, museums, and celebrity vacation homes, the city sells itself as having the culture and sophistication of elite Los Angeles without the big-city problems of crime or poverty. It is a city that, through the prioritizing and policing of public space, works to maintain the popular perception that it is exclusively wealthy and White.

However, despite its tranquil image, it is not a city immune from race and class conflicts. A few blocks from Beach Street, Chavez Street cuts through East Riviera as a kind of second main street, one that caters to the city's overlooked Chicano/a population.[2] The Chicano/a community constitutes approximately 30 percent of the city's population, and most of these residents work in the low-wage service sector of the local economy. This is a community largely hidden from the projected image of this city, and its residents are rarely acknowledged as belonging in Riviera. People of color here are seen as the servants to the served of the city. The east side of Riviera houses many residents of color who struggle to get by in the face of an extravagant cost of living, one of the highest in the nation. Cristina, a thirty-one-year-old mother of a fourteen-year-old girl, explains:

> I would like them to have the basic resources they need. How do I help them, if I don't have the money? . . . Rosy doesn't get a good lunch. She comes home hungry and I don't have much. I want to be able to provide them with the basics; shoes, food. I want to be able to feed my kids, to clothe them. I think that has a lot to do with how she acts. She gets frustrated with our situation. Frustrated over not having anything and living the life we live. I think this lifestyle is what drives her to hang out with her friends in the street; drives her to stay on the streets with her sister rather than come home. They have food. She is probably tired of top ramens or cup-o-noodles, or canned vegetables or peas, but that is what I can afford and sometimes they are free from the church. We don't even have money for laundry detergent. We have been wearing dirty clothes for the last few days. We haven't washed in three weeks.

The youth in this community commonly find themselves publicly racialized as criminal others. Racial tensions are reinforced by a local division of labor that designates Latino/as as the low-end service workers who cater to wealthy residents and tourists. These status differences become most visible at school and in encounters with Whites, which function as reminders to youth of color that they are dangerous people to be feared. Their responses are varied, but many turn to gang culture and the gang life; Cristina's daughter, Rosa, has recently become involved in neighborhood gangs. Adopting gang-associated attire often brings negative attention to Chicano/a youths. Johny, a sixteen-year-old gang-involved Chicano male, explains:

> If you go with your homies, they stare at you, baggy clothes make you look suspicious . . . around here if you're walking in a little group, people are all scared of you . . . if güeros [whites] are coming toward you, they'll get off the sidewalk so you can pass by. They're scared as fuck!

Other encounters in which Chicano/a youth report being disciplined by white residents reinforce local economic hierarchies. Johny continues:

> I used to work at the farmers market with my father and there was white people that would give you attitude about the color skin that you are. 'Cuz I'm working behind this table selling these things to you don't mean you have to be rude to me 'cuz you don't have to buy them from me and feel like I need you.

Race and class become inextricably tangled: young Chicanos/as are expected to represent a working class that caters to rich White locals and tourists, but instead the youths become defiant against the secondary status that local institutions impose upon them. They are supposed to submit to class oppression and become "good workers" while being robbed of opportunities to obtain viable occupations. Chicano/a youth respond to this unfair expectation through the development of a sub-cultural cholo performance. Cholo performance is a style that many Chicano/a youth have created in the United States. While the style varies by region, some classic artifacts include baggy Ben Davis or Dickies pants, shaved heads (for males), and tattoos that represent neighborhoods.

In Rivera, the marginalization process begins in school. Sixteen-year-old Mary, a student who was expelled for fighting and now attends an alternative high school, shares her perspective:

> I think they feel that like white kids are like better . . . like Mexican kids are I guess like gang related and I think they think they're like bad influences and they think we're like not smart. They think that like white kids . . . smart and they're like good kids, they're like good influences . . . you could tell how the teachers are, like how they look at you before you even start dressing different.[3]

This criminal labeling becomes a self-fulfilling prophecy for many youth of color. Francisco, a gang-affiliated seventeen-year-old, experienced similar treatment and pinpoints an incident that would strongly influence his decision to perform a cholo style and drop out of school: "The teacher chose on me, and the white guy, he said, 'Oh, he won't know the answer, he's Mexican.' The teacher didn't say anything!" When asked about his attitude toward school, Francisco simply replied: "Just skip school. Go to a friend's house, do drugs, bang [represent the gang], fucking just go look for fights, go to Beach Street. Just anything rather than school. I hate school." For many of these youths, school becomes a place where they feel disrespected and reprimanded rather than educated, instilling an oppositional stance toward educational institutions and leading them to create alternative spaces for acceptance and affirmation.[4]

PERFORMING FOR A PUNITIVE AUDIENCE

In this paper, we argue that cholo style is one dominant response to racial stigmatization, class subordination, and criminalization. Specifically, we examine the function that bald heads, baggy clothes, and visible tattoos play in the lives of Chicano male youth.[5] We argue that through cholo style, gang-associated Chicano youth perform a resistance that defies race and class-based marginalization, in the process developing a perilous sense of masculinity. In this way, race, class, and gender intersect to determine the performance of resistance and pleasure-seeking that cholos embrace. Margaret L. Anderson and Patricia Hill Collins argue that race, class, and gender are interconnected in a continuum that she calls the matrix of domination: "race, class, and gender are fundamental axes in society and, as such, are critical to understanding people's lives, institutional systems, contemporary social issues, and the possibilities of social change."[6] In this chapter, we examine the role that race, class, and gender play in cholo style.

The quotes and experiences presented in this paper are collected from thirty-two individual interviews, twelve focus group sessions, and ethnographic observations conducted in the street, a continuation school, and a community center over a fourteen-month research period, from September 2007 to November 2008. We started our project by recruiting students from a continuation high school for interviews about their experiences in the school system. To supplement the interviews, we also conducted observations at the school to examine how the students interacted with the staff and each other in the classroom. Most of these students had been expelled from the city's school district and many of them were currently reporting to or had recently been required to report to probation officers. Some of the members of the predominately Chicano/a student body had varying levels of gang affiliation, and almost all of them embodied some degree of a cholo/a identity performance.

Some of the students we interviewed introduced us to the gang youth of Eastside Riviera. We used snowball sampling to recruit self-identified gang members for weekly focus group interviews about their experiences growing up in Riviera. We held these group interviews at a community center in their neighborhood where they would be welcomed and not subject to the stigmatization they expressed feeling in many public spaces. The research team also regularly met up with these youth throughout the week in the street or at local parks in their neighborhood. These more informal meetings were useful for collecting observations and personal narratives, and they also helped us build rapport with the youth and recruit them for the weekly focus groups.

THE FUNCTION OF CHOLO STYLE: INTRODUCING MARGINALIZED YOUTH

Cholo style is a partial enactment of a deep-rooted desire held by working-class urban Chicanos to transform their social conditions and resist the punitive treatment they receive. Because of this racialized inequality, many of the youth we interviewed dress in ways that mark them as different from other youth in the city. In assuming this style, youth have a way of taking ownership of their difference; it is no longer something ascribed to them but rather something they create. It gives them the opportunity to control how they are identified and resist the privileged class they are expected to aspire to but obstructed from joining. Flaco, a nineteen-year-old gang member, explains, "If I grow my hair out then I'm a conform. Why do I want to do something they want me to do? I want them to accept me for me."

As individuals marginalized in multiple aspects, youth in barrio gangs experience some of the most extreme results of the inequality in their community.[7] In Riviera, most criminalized youth tend to be US-born Latinos caught between two cultures without being incorporated into either, too far removed from one and not yet accepted by the other.[8] Struggling against this cultural abandonment and rebelling against the marginal economic futures likely awaiting them, youth join neighborhood cliques as a form of resistance to the racial and economic subordination that leaves their communities vulnerable to exploitation.[9] Street groups not only offer some form of support for youth surviving the barrio but also a kind of cultural empowerment by providing youth an opportunity to reject a society that has rejected them.

In the process of separating themselves, gang youth develop their own countercultural performance to emphasize this position and use unique stylistic appropriations to mark their difference. The youth we got to know through this project commonly wore oversized work pants and large white or blue T-shirts. A few regularly wore Dodgers or Cowboys jerseys, which correspond with the blue themes common among Sureño street cliques. Others wore black T-shirts or hoodies saying "Riviera" or "Eastside." None of them ever wore brand names or logos. Many wore white sneakers that they kept impeccably clean, and their hair was always either shaved or cut to about half an inch at most. Tito, one of the continuation school students we interviewed, is a good example of somebody implementing this style. When he showed up for his interview, he was wearing khaki-colored work pants that were several sizes too big, pulled up high around his belly and fastened with a black belt. He had a large, untucked white T-shirt that came down to mid-thigh layered over another shirt, making him look bulkier than he actually was. His head was shaved, and he had letters representing his neighborhood tattooed on his forearms. He maintained this look throughout the duration of the weekly focus group meetings.

All of the twenty-two gang-involved males who attended our weekly focus groups had tattoos. Their reasons for getting their tattoos consistently resonated with embodying a style that they liked to have. A few of them went beyond this stylistic explanation and referred to having a tattoo as a means of resisting mainstream expectations. For these young men, tattoos serve as a "symbolic challenge to the overt and indirect forms of domination."[10] Ben Olguin (1997) argues that the Chicano male body has become a central battlefield in the war on crime:

> The "adorned" body of the collective and individual "hispanic male subject" is read and also written on by a variety of narrators—police officers, prosecutors, and judges, as well as prison administrators, guards, and even prisoners themselves. These interventions help transform the body into a network of signifiers that at once affirm the "suspected" and/or "convicted criminal's" personal identity while simultaneously confirming his abject status in society.[11]

In this struggle, Chicano males reclaim their bodies by inscribing their own meanings, performance, and resistance onto themselves. The tattoo or "placa" for Olguin is "The Chicano (lumpenproletariat) practice of ritually marking a space for the purpose of laying a symbolic and even material claim on it."[12] This reclamation of the body from a punitive landscape consists of gang and barrio references as well as religious, cultural, and family images.

Young Chicanos are expected to adopt secondary social statuses, and youth unwilling to do this take on criminalized personas as a form of resistant empowerment, transforming themselves into something local elites see as dangerous as opposed to exploitable. Appropriating this identity marks them for persecution from authorities, and the youth demonstrated a clear understanding of why they are so heavily policed: "Those fools will tell us to get the fuck out of here cause they don't want the tourists to be or the, yeah the tourists and the white people to get scared." These youth recognize that incorporating this style to stand out in the public sphere makes them targets for the police because they contrast with the image the city works so hard to project. But they remain firm in their stylistic stance because this visible opposition is the entire point of adopting their style.

Cholo style is not inherently deviant, but it is intentionally oppositional to the mainstream.[13] Understandably, cholo/a subculture has an appeal much broader than gang-involved youth. This culture of resistance, and the styles and performance attached to it, resonate with many unaffiliated barrio youth, as it speaks to struggles that affect the entire community. For example, fifteen-year-old Ricardo is not in the gang and does not plan to join. However, he dresses in baggy pants and occasionally shaves his head. We asked him if he thought that doing this made others believe he was a gang member: "Yea, but this is what I like to wear. I don't care what they think. They still gotta respect me. Just 'cause I don't want to be in the gang doesn't mean I don't like being gangster."

Robin Kelley links the appeal of the gangster to a response to socioeconomic subjugation and a challenge to authority in general, one in which the marginalized is imagined as all-powerful.[14] Similarly, Stuart Cosgrove describes the importance of the zoot suit to the pachucos as a means to contest their social invisibility.[15] To those who wore them, the suits were "a spectacular reminder that the social order had failed to contain their energy and difference . . . a subcultural gesture that refused to concede to the manners of subservience."[16] Segregated from mainstream society and therefore alienated from the ambitions of their immigrant parents, the pachucos rebelled by flaunting their difference. In the process, they developed a culture that critiqued racism and the American class structure. Both pachuco and cholo fashions "became cultural productions signifying unique forms of resistance by youth of color against the dominant image of style and culture embraced by other young people of these eras."[17] In embracing difference, youth subcultures empower what was previously socially devalued, making their styles attractive to marginalized youth.

Sociologist Erving Goffman has argued that individuals construct the impressions they make on others in social settings to create perceptions they want others to have of them.[18] In his dramaturgical theory, Goffman compares social interactions to a theatrical play in which individuals wear masks to manage the impressions that they make on others. Goffman argues that people constantly use the resources around them to develop the most ideal impression that they can create of themselves. Social scientists have argued that aspects of social interactions are used to convey individual identities through specific forms of dress, language, and mannerisms.[19] Individuals use aspects of daily self presentation to place themselves within specific cultural contexts and categories, reflecting particularities of their identity such as class, sexuality, and race.[20] In the case of the youth in this study, their "impression management" is centered on eliciting attention, fear, and respect.

Gang membership has been found to be a performed identity that defies mainstream values and the criminalization of their community.[21] Cholo style is instrumental in performing this identity, and because it projects the image of a Chicano challenging the cultural values of mainstream society, it holds an importance far deeper than belonging to a specific neighborhood. Many of the youth expressed not feeling comfortable in clothes that they claimed were for White people and said that they could not imagine ever giving up their chosen style. When asked why he maintained his style if he knew it would make him a target for police harassment, Santos replied, "I'm not gonna change our style just for a stupid ass cop that thinks I'm gonna, you know, get into something."

It is also important to remember that apart from resisting mainstream values and marginalization, cholo style is simply a practical approach to poverty conditions. A pair of youth discussing street styles with us reminded us that most articles of clothing become popular cholo fashions because they are readily available for poor urban youth:

> Juan: "Why does it matter what we're wearing in the first place? The cops are always giving us shit, like we're wearing a uniform, they say that we're wearing a uniform cuz we're wearing Dickies?! Well they're cheap. What little we have, we're gonna go buy a fuckin . . ."
> Jason: ". . . go buy some Dockers and whatnot."

PERFORMANCE AS A SOURCE OF EMPOWERMENT IN A DISEMPOWERING ECONOMIC CONTEXT

Unlike the mainstream fashions that would presumably be more acceptable for the authority figures that condemn the appearances of these youth, white T-shirts and Dickies pants are inexpensive and durable. Furthermore, a shaved head only requires clippers and a razor, which can be reused several times, as opposed to a monthly $15–20 barbershop haircut. These styles are now criminalized in the public eye because they are popularly linked to poor Chicanos and the stereotypes that have historically been ascribed to them. However, their incorporation into cholo culture transformed cheap clothes into powerful symbols.

In a community where young Chicanos/as are criminalized for their age and race and exploited for their class status, cholos develop a specific style that performs to a punitive audience. Devalued in mainstream society along race and class hierarchies, Chicano youth create oppositional street cultures as means of recognizing their own self-worth.[22] In creating their own culture, these youth establish their own styles and identities in which they are valued instead of adopting cultural norms that constantly remind them they do not belong. Within this street-oriented working-class Chicano culture, they at are the center, not the margins. This culture rejects the subservient roles ascribed to Chicano youth in the social order, and the economic aspect of this resistance is the adoption of self-presentations incompatible with labor roles catering to more privileged classes.

Sanchez-Jankowski theorizes that teenagers join street gangs as a youthful, temporary rebellion against the marginal economic futures that await them in adulthood.[23] However, John Hagedorn has argued that in the postindustrial economy, this temporary rebellion finds more permanence because working-class youth have greater difficulty finding stable employment.[24] Within a local economic context, the adoption of highly visible cholo styles can be seen as a resistance against the expectation to serve privileged Whites. Conscious of the fact that few opportunities exist for them to find legitimate career paths, Chicano youth adopt appearances that they know will prevent them from attaining the low-level service positions that they are expected to fill. By tapping into racist fears of their inherent criminality, these youth create a public impression of themselves as threatening instead as those willing to humble themselves as servants.

The significance of this racialized fear becomes clear through the comments of Luis, a seventeen-year-old gang member who wears forty-eight-inch pants on his thirty-four-inch waist: "I feel like when I dress like this, and like the way I look and everything, it gives me like power. Like I feel like, more like in control and all that." When asked about this sense of empowerment, one of his friends suggested that it was based on the ability to scare people. Luis replied: "Yea, like I could! . . . I don't think like 'oh people look at me bad', I think of people like they're scared." By dressing in a style that is popularly associated with Chicano criminality, Luis marks himself as a person to be feared by the mainstream public. By doing this, he forces people to respect him as a threat, creating a sense of power for himself within a public sphere that otherwise marginalizes him.

Adopting a style that resonates with popular imaginaries of young Latino criminality becomes a way for youth of color to contest the social invisibility that marginal status creates. Cholo style, despite its relatively minimalist fashions, demands attention in the public sphere because it taps into persistent racialized assumptions of the inherent danger Chicanos pose to public safety. Discourses of violent Mexicans have been used to challenge their citizenship rights in American society, keeping Latino/a migrants deportable and thus economically exploitable.[25] Perceptions of Mexican illegality extend this vulnerability to the Latino/a community at large, although much of the vulnerability is complexly mediated with various forms of status and cultural capital.[26] The hype of the public threat posed by gangs has magnified public fears of youth of color and made street styles all the more noticeable. Facing daily reminders of their marginality and relative inability to combat the structures working against them, youth of color play on these racialized fears to assume some element of power in the public sphere.

However, this resistant performance is rarely absolute, as the adoption of cholo style occurs across a range of implementation. As police evaluate the intensity of one's performance of cholo style and equate it with a corresponding degree of criminality, neighborhood youth recognize that they will experience greater levels of criminalization and violence with more intense displays of cholo identity.[27] This realization leads some to adapt their cholo performances. Chuy, a seventeen-year-old gang member, explained why he stopped shaving his head: "[a bald head] causes too much attraction. So . . . let it grow out a little bit you know"? However, Chuy's "growing his hair out" meant he cut it in a fade style that was about a quarter of an inch in length, and he still wears baggy pants and plaid Pendleton shirts. He has not abandoned his performance, but he modified its intensity after his shaved head caused too many problems.

Some youth also recognize a need to balance this self-presentation with those more accepted by mainstream society. They know that drastic or permanent displays of cholo identity could bar them from the limited opportunities they may really need, despite their reluctance to take them. While all of the youth have tattoos, most are on their chests, stomachs, backs or upper arms, where they can be covered up if need be. Few had tattoos on their neck or face, which could be seen as a more extreme performance and a much more firm refusal to ever occupy exploitable service positions, as these will likely permanently bar them from these jobs. Even Luis, who values the fear he can instill in strangers, recognizes that he can only embody this performance when he is not working at his job as a busboy in a high-end restaurant, where he must defer to wealthy patrons. He can only perform this identity when he is off the clock, where it becomes an opportunity to regain the empowerment that he sacrifices on the job. The youth resist their positioning in the local labor market, but most cannot afford to reject it entirely.

Because they contrast with the dominant image of a carefree resort town that is profitable for city elites, these youth are harassed by police and kept away from any public events expected to draw large crowds and considerable commercial revenue. Many are picked up before any holiday or city celebrations and detained for the duration without charges; others report being arrested on sight should they try to attend such public events. But this constructed image of Riviera is dependent on a docile servant community (of color) available to cater to the whims of this privileged population. By adopting cholo styles that magnify their visibility in the public sphere, marginalized youth challenge this popular image, but they pay the consequences for doing so.

BLOWBACK: AMPLIFIED CRIMINALIZATION AND THE TRAGEDY OF "PERFORMANCE"

The drawback to youth of color appropriating the fashions of specific subcultures is that they often adopt the group's criminalized status as well. Identifying oneself with criminalized street culture brings condemnation from racial, class, and generational others, but perhaps it simply makes visible the alienation already experienced along these lines. This may help explain why scores of unaffiliated Chicano youth adopt cholo styles; perhaps being feared is better than being invisible.[28] But in performing cholo identites, youth frequently become indistinguishable from criminal gang members in the eyes of authority figures, who in turn falsely inflate the threat posed by street groups by associating youth of color in general with violent street crime. In the past, anti-gang sweeps police have detained teenagers for wearing red shoelaces or exchanging complex handshakes.[29] Doing as much now is still enough to have one monitored on California's gang database.[30]

In adopting their style, cholos fit into the public perception of gang members and are criminalized by police as such, becoming the subject of intense surveillance and harassment:

> One time I was in front of (a liquor store) and the cops would say like you don't have to hang around with those losers. They are nobody. This guy was drinking a beer and they like got the beer and poured it out and said this is for your dead homies. That is very disrespectful. The cops would usually get off the car or if not just park somewhere and just watch us. I got kind of used to it already. But it does get on

> my nerves because we are just outside and they have to be looking at us all the time.

Once incorporated into the justice system, these youth are then sent to continuation schools where they experience further criminalization.[31] Local youth of color come to see school as an institution more concerned with regulating their behavior than educating them:

> It's like a jail. You can't wear like regular clothes like at a high school we have to wear either a shirt or a sweater. They always search you and there are cameras in every room and in the hallway. You can't go to the bathroom by yourself, can't take a pencil, cell phones. You have to leave everything in the front. They check your shoes, your socks. This happens every day . . . But this school isn't nothing compared to La Villa. Like discipline-wise they drug test you every day.

This criminalization is adopted by much of the general public as well, who come to recognize youth of color as criminals before they ever commit any offense:

> There was this lady that lives down the street . . . me and two other homies were walking by and she's "gringa" then I walked past her and she just dogs us she's like "go inside" . . . one night the narcs [gang unit police officers] had went by and she told her husband, don't worry, the cops are here, they'll get him.

While playing on racialized fears can create a sense of empowerment for marginalized Chicano youth, it also intensifies the level of criminalization they experience from authorities. This results in increased police and public surveillance, and it further marginalizes them by removing them from educational and economic opportunities. Youth perceived as criminals by school authorities are quickly disciplined for defiant behavior and transferred to continuation schools that do little to prepare them for higher education or the working world. Intense police surveillance also increases their likelihood of incarceration, making it much more difficult for them to find and keep stable employment. While street styles allow urban youth of color to resist social hierarchies, they are systematically punished for expressing this opposition.

Masculinity

Another consequence of performing a cholo style is the development of a perilous masculinity. Many of the males in this study displayed negative attitudes toward the young women in their lives, regularly referring to them as "bitches" and using phrases like "slap a bitch." The development of a perilous masculinity goes hand in hand with resisting class and race marginalization. The performance that young Chicanos develop in resisting subordination is characterized by toughness, violence, and defiance.[32] This performance is projected onto young women as the adoption of patriarchal identities becomes one available avenue to empowerment.

For most of the males we interviewed, the main milestones in achieving manhood were having sex and being arrested. Youth who demonstrated having frequent sex or having been arrested multiple times were given more respect. Whether the young men were committing crimes to acquire money, gain respect from peers, or resist their criminalization, their personal vendettas always had an effect on the young women around them. When the young boys resisted marginalization, it was often at the cost of young women, since many of them resisted by claiming their manhood in a more assertive way. As the youth claimed a pride, dignity, and resistance that countered subservience, their identities became more masculinized. As their identities became less self-consciously performed and stabilized as "masculine," their treatment of young women became more demeaning and brutal. The more that cholos resist marginalization, the more any identity they can identify as "feminine," in the narrowest of terms, becomes vulnerable to their aggression. Resistance against one or two axes of domination, such as race and class, may sometimes lead to the perpetuation of oppression based on gender and sexuality. Although these young men don't see themselves as performing resistance, they try to become what they perform. In doing so, they come to hate any differences that threaten this performance of identity as stable, solid, and real. The criminalization, racialization, and class oppression of Chicano males has a detrimental effect on young women through the development of perilous masculinity. This masculinity is not developed in a vacuum within "Chicano/a culture" but produced through interactions with education, criminal justice, and community institutions that inculcate a defensive masculine performance that oppresses women.

ECONOMIC OPPORTUNITY

The youth interviewed understand how the racial stigma ascribed to them is made worse by cholo styles. Some modify their appearance after reporting too much negative attention, while others take the police harassment that it brings them as validation that they are right to rebel against unjust authority figures. None of them are willing to switch to the "White" clothes that authorities prefer simply out of some social assumption that they ought to. The only thing they would be willing to change their appearance for is the promise of well-paying employment:

> S: Set me up with an interview I'd be there, get a pair of tighter pants, shit homes.
>
> I: You would change the way you dress for $16–20 an hour?
>
> S: Hell yeah once they paid me I wear some more Levis some Dickies. I'll even wear some tight pants!

This willingness to alter their performed identity for economic opportunity makes a case that the street styles these youth are adopting are a form of resistance against the marginal economic roles they are offered in the local labor market. If they can access better opportunities, they are willing to "code switch," and learn a new set of interaction skills and performances in order to make a living. Performance is a response to deep-seated race, class, and gender dynamics, but it is pliable, and it shifts as cultural and material resources become available (or are denied). But because employment these youth see as dignified isn't available, they adopt appearances that they know will prevent them from being hired for the marginal positions they do not want: "You can't just show up all bald headed and be all 'homie where's my application'. I'm growing my hair out to try to get a job. I tried it once but it didn't work so I just shaved my shit again."

CONCLUSION

Expected to assume subservient roles within Riviera's social hierarchy and labor market, local Chicanos are stigmatized within the city's institutions from a young age. But by becoming cholos, these youth find a way to publicly resist this degrading marginality. Cholo performance serves as a way of rejecting the social systems that have rejected them. As they grow up being labeled as criminals, young Chicano males defy being marked by marking themselves. This self-imposed deviation from a "normal" aesthetic provides cholos with both an element of control over how they are identified and a sense of empowerment within a public sphere in which they are treated punitively. By appealing to mainstream fears of nonwhite criminality, young Chicanos can contest their social invisibility by dramatizing their difference.

While adopting this criminalized appearance grants youth some level of social visibility in public, it also marks them for assault from rival neighborhoods and suspicion from law enforcement. Youth adopting cholo styles are commonly registered in gang databases used to determine eligibility for gang enhancements and injunctions that mandate prison time. Repeated arrests and prolonged prison terms further limit already marginal employment opportunities and present detrimental challenges for inmates' families.[33] The chaos of life in the streets and correctional facilities also facilitates drug and alcohol abuse, as few treatment options are made available to these individuals. Many end up incarcerated, dead, or permanently injured, and almost all end up with a negative credential from the criminal justice system that permanently marks them as unemployable and irredeemable.[34] Additionally, this performance can have a dangerous impact on young women in the community, as young men resist punitive systems by developing a defiant masculinity that reinforces female domination.

This essay is about not only cholo performance but also the cultural dynamics that underlie the city of Riviera itself. The youth's presentations of defiance, and the resistance symbolized within cholo styles more broadly, can actually be seen as attempts to integrate into societal mores; they constitute more a desire to be seen and valued than a stubborn decision to choose outsider status. This desire to be recognized is what hegemonic forces use to construct outsider identities. The construction of outsiders in turn enables the construction of obedient citizens who will protect their own misshapen modes of colonized, insider status by reinforcing a hegemonic social order. These outsider identities are negotiated by individuals who navigate these exclusionary frameworks, as both dominant structure and resistant agency work simultaneously to shape how these identities are positioned in relation to the hegemonic order.

Marginalized young Chicanos in Riviera utilize the final resistance frontier, the body, to perform a deviant identity that both resists criminalization and urges respect and recognition of their humanity. Tattoos and hair styles used to perform as "pelones y matones" ("bald-headed killers") are really performances that plead for basic human affirmation. Moreover, this performance produces blowback consequences for young men and women. The young men are pipelined deeper into the justice system, and young women encounter misogyny that mirrors the oppression encountered in other spheres; structural systems of punishment become embodied and performed by marginalized populations. Efforts to reduce violence and delinquency in Chicano/a communities must provide youth alternative scripts they can choose to perform.

NOTES

1. Names of the city, youth, and streets have been changed to protect participants' identities.

2. We use "Chicano/a" as a broad label for members of Riviera's Mexican American community.

3. Criminologist Jody Miller (1995) has argued that police determine culpability based on the performance of gangster style. She contends that "style has become a vehicle through which social control agents interact with gang members" (214). The more "gangster" a young person looks or acts, the more likely police and probation officers are to punish them.

4. L. Janelle Dance, *Tough Fronts: The Impact of Street Culture on Schooling* (New York: Routledge, 2002).

5. Although we interviewed Chicanas for this study, in this paper we focus on Chicano males in order to identify the specific ways in which race, class, and gender operate for this particular group.

6. Margaret L. Anderson and Patricia Hill Collins, *Race, Class, and Gender: An Anthology* (Belmont, CA: Thomson Wadsworth, 1995), 3.

7. James Diego Vigil, *Barrio Gangs: Street Life and Identity in Southern California* (Austin: University of Texas Press, 1988).

8. See Rubén Martínez, *East Side Stories: Gang Life in East LA* (New York: PowerHouse Cultural Entertainment, 1998).

9. Martín Sánchez, Jankowski, *Islands in the Street: Gangs and American Urban Society* (Berkeley: University of California Press, 1991).

10. Ben Olguin, "Tattoos, Abjection, and the Political Unconscious: Towards a Semiotics of the *Pinto* Visual Vernacular," *Cultural Critique* 37 (1997), 159–213.

11. Ibid., 161.

12. Ibid., 162.

13. Vigil, *Barrio Gangs.*

14. Robin D. G. Kelley, *Race Rebels: Culture, Politics and the Black Working Class* (New York: Free Press, 1994).

15. Stuart Cosgrove, "The Zoot-Suit and Style Warfare," *History Workshop Journal* 18 (1984).

16. Ibid., 78.

17. Cynthia L. Bejarano, *¿Que Onda? Urban Youth Cultures and Border Identity* (Tucson: University of Arizona Press, 2005), 90.

18. Erving Goffman, *Strategic Interaction* (Philadelphia: University of Pennsylvania Press, 1969).

19. Robert Garot and Jack Katz, "Provocative Looks: The Enforcement of School Dress Codes and the Embodiment of Dress at an Inner-City Alternative School," *Ethnography* 4 (2003), 421–454; Joanne Entwistle, "The Dressed Body," in *Body Dressing,* ed. Joanne Entwistle and Elizabeth Wilson (Oxford and New York: Oxford University Press, 2001), 33–58; Sue Widdicombe and Robin Wooffitt, *The Language of Youth Subcultures* (Hertfordshire: Harvester Wheatsheaf Press, 1995); David Sudnow, *Ways of the Hand: The Organization of Improvised Conduct* (Cambridge, MA.: Harvard University Press, 1978).

20. Jay MacLeod, *Ain't No Makin' It: Aspirations and Attainment in a Low-Income Neighborhood* (Boulder, CO: Westview, 2008); Kenji Yoshino, *Covering: The Hidden Assault on Our Civil Rights.* (New York: Random House, 2006); D. Lawrence Wieder and Steven Pratt, "On Being a Recognizable Indian Among Indians," in *Cultural Communication and Intercultural Contact,* ed. Lawrence Carbaugh (Hillsdale, NJ: Erlbaum Associates, 1989).

21. Robert Garot, "Where You From! Gang Identity as Performance," *Journal of Contemporary Ethnography* 36 (2007), 50–84; Norma Mendoza-Denton, "Muy Macha: Gender and Ideology in Gang-Girls' Discourse about Makeup," *Ethnos* 61 (1996), 47–63; Conquergood and Siegel, 1990.

22. Luis Rodríguez, *Hearts and Hands: Creating Community in Violent Times* (New York: Seven Stories Press, 2001).

23. Jankowski, *Islands in the Street.*

24. John M. Hagedorn, "Gang Violence in the Postindustrial Era," *Crime and Justice: A Review of Research* 24 (1998), 317–364.

25. Mae M. Ngai, *Impossible Subjects: Illegal Aliens and the Making of Modern America* (Princeton: Princeton University Press, 2004).

26. Mario Barrera, *Race and Class in the Southwest: A Theory of Racial Inequality* (Notre Dame, IN: University of Notre Dame Press, 1979); Rodolfo Acuña, *Occupied America: A History of Chicanos* (New York: Pearson Longman, 2004); Ngai, *Impossible Subjects.*

27. Jody A. Miller, "Struggles Over the Symbolic: Gang Style and the Meanings of Social Control," in *Cultural Criminology,* ed. Jeff Ferrell and Clinton R. Sanders (Dexter, MI: Northeastern University Press, 1995).

28. Elijah Anderson, *Code of the Street: Decency, Violence, and the Moral Life of the Inner City* (New York: WW Norton, 1999); Dance, *Tough Fronts.*

29. Mike Davis, *City of Quartz: Excavating the Future in Los Angeles* (New York: Vintage Books, 1990).

30. Christian Parenti, *Lockdown America: Police and Prisons in the Age of Crisis* (New York: Verso, 2000).

31. Many of these youth also experience shame before their parents' chagrin. This creates a process by which the family can become another institution of criminalization (see Rios 2006).

32. See Elijah Anderson (1999) and Janelle Dance (2002).

33. Megan Comfort, *Doing Time Together: Love and Family in the Shadows of the Prison* (Chicago: University of Chicago Press, 2008).

34. See Pager (2009) for an excellent study on how a negative credential and race affect the life chances of ex-convicts.

REFERENCES

Acuña, Rodolfo. *Occupied America: A History of Chicanos.* New York: Pearson Longman, 2004.

Anderson, Elijah. *Code of the Street: Decency, Violence, and the Moral Life of the Inner City.* New York: WW Norton, 1999.

Anderson, Margaret L., and Patricia Hill Collins. *Race, Class, and Gender: An Anthology.* Belmont, CA: Thomson Wadsworth, 1995.

Barrera, Mario. *Race and Class in the Southwest: A Theory of Racial Inequality.* Notre Dame, IN: University of Notre Dame Press, 1979.

Bejarano, Cynthia L. *¿Que Onda? Urban Youth Cultures and Border Identity.* Tucson: University of Arizona Press, 2005.

Comfort, Megan. *Doing Time Together: Love and Family in the Shadows of the Prison.* Chicago: University of Chicago Press, 2008.

Conquergood, D., and T. Siegel. *Heart Broken in Half.* Evanston, IL: Siegel Productions, 1990.

Cosgrove, Stuart. "The Zoot-Suit and Style Warfare." In *History Workshop Journal,* Vol. 18 (Autumn 1984).

Dance, L. Janelle. *Tough Fronts: The Impact of Street Culture on Schooling.* New York: Routledge, 2002.

Davis, Mike. *City of Quartz: Excavating the Future in Los Angeles.* New York: Vintage Books, 1990.

Entwistle, Joanne. "The Dressed Body." In *Body Dressing,* 33–58. Ed. Joanne Entwistle and Elizabeth Wilson. Oxford and New York: Oxford University Press, 2001.

Garot, Robert. "Where you From! Gang Identity as Performance." In *Journal of Contemporary Ethnography,* Vol. 36, No. 1 (2007): 50–84.

Garot, Robert, and Jack Katz. "Provocative Looks: The Enforcement of School Dress Codes and the Embodiment of Dress at an Inner-City Alternative School." In *Ethnography,* Vol. 4, No. 3 (2003): 421–454.

Goffman, Erving. *Strategic Interaction.* Philadelphia: University of Pennsylvania Press, 1969.

Hagedorn, John M. "Gang Violence in the Postindustrial Era." In *Crime and Justice: A Review of Research*, Vol. 24 (1998): 317–364.
Jankowski, Martín Sánchez. *Islands in the Street: Gangs and American Urban Society.* Berkeley: University of California Press, 1991.
Kelley, Robin D. G. *Race Rebels: Culture, Politics and the Black Working Class.* New York: Free Press, 1994.
MacLeod, Jay. *Ain't No Makin' It: Aspirations and Attainment in a Low-Income Neighborhood.* Boulder, CO: Westview, 2008.
Martínez, Rubén. *East Side Stories: Gang Life in East LA.* New York: PowerHouse Cultural Entertainment, 1998.
Mendoza-Denton, Norma. "Muy Macha: Gender and Ideology in Gang-Girls' Discourse about Makeup." *Ethnos*, Vol. 61 (1996): 47–63.
Miller, Jody A. "Struggles Over the Symbolic: Gang Style and the Meanings of Social Control." In *Cultural Criminology.* Ed. Jeff Ferrell and Clinton R. Sanders. Dexter, MI: Northeastern University Press, 1995. 213–234.
Ngai, Mae M. *Impossible Subjects: Illegal Aliens and the Making of Modern America.* Princeton, NJ: Princeton University Press, 2004.
Olguin, Ben. "Tattoos, Abjection, and the Political Unconscious: Towards a Semiotics of the *Pinto* Visual Vernacular." In *Cultural Critique*, Vol. 37 (Fall 1997): 159–213.
Pager, Devah. *Marked: Race, Crime, and Finding Work in an Era of Mass Incarceration.* Chicago: University of Chicago Press, 2009.
Parenti, Christian, *Lockdown America: Police and Prisons in the Age of Crisis.* New York: Verso, 2000.
Rios, Victor. "The Hyper-Criminalization of Black and Chicano Youth in the Era of Mass Incarceration." In *Souls: A Critical Journal of Black Politics, Culture and Society*, Vol. 8, No. 2 (2006), 40–54.
Rodríguez, Luis. *Hearts and Hands: Creating Community in Violent Times.* New York: Seven Stories Press, 2001.
Sudnow, David. *Ways of the Hand: The Organization of Improvised Conduc*t. Cambridge, MA: Harvard University Press, 1978.
Vigil, James Diego. *Barrio Gangs: Street Life and Identity in Southern California.* Austin: University of Texas Press, 1988.
Widdicombe, Sue, and Robin Wooffitt. *The Language of Youth Subcultures.* Hertfordshire: Harvester Wheatsheaf Press, 1995.
Wieder, D. Lawrence, and Steven Pratt. "On Being a Recognizable Indian Among Indians." In *Cultural Communication and Intercultural Contact.* Ed. D. Carbaugh. Hillsdale: Lawrence Erlbaum Associates, 1989. 45–64.
Yoshino, Kenji. *Covering: The Hidden Assault on Our Civil Rights.* New York: Random House, 2006.

TWENTY-ONE

Mexica Hip Hop: Male Expressive Culture

PANCHO McFARLAND

On Los Nativos' album *Día de los Muertos* (2003), the well-orchestrated, multi-layered musical production of Chilam Balam (Speaker for the Jaguar People) is somehow both funky and indigenous. The opening track, "Ometeoht," is a "Mexica prayer." The prayer opens with blowing conch shells, shaken beads, and Mesoamerican drums. Los Nativos chant in Spanish. The second track, "Like the Indigenous," begins with a deep bass drum pounding out a standard syncopated hip-hop beat and a jazz-inspired, synthesized high hat. The emcees, Balam and Cuauhtli (The Eagle), trade verses in which they rap about the many things they do that are "like the indigenous." Throughout the album, Balam uses drum machines, beads, shells, pianos, synthesizers, live drums, and other instruments to create polyrhythmic beats and a musical background that signals the myriad cultural, political, and economic factors contributing to Los Nativos' lyrical and artistic neo-indigenism. Los Nativos' lyrics and flow (cadence and meter) speak to their neo-indigenist ways (identity, traditions, customs, language, values, and cosmology) and militant resistance to colonialism and European domination. At the same time, their aesthetics and politics are indebted to a patriarchal, male-centered lineage in Chicano culture. These men of Mexican descent critique white colonialism and domination but retain their male privilege. Neo-indigenist privileging of the patriarchal imperial civilization of the Aztec/Mexica over the numerous cultures and nations in the pre-Columbian Américas that were matrilineal and matriarchal means that men dominate the social, political, and economic structures of an envisioned neo-Mexica/indigenism.

Cuauhtli and Chilam Balam express their indigeneity through album artwork that evokes the ancient Mexican ritual celebration of dia de los muertos honoring our ancestors and affirming our understanding of the cycle of death and life. The liner notes to the CD explain that dia de los muertos is "a traditional Mexica holiday to celebrate, honor, and remember those who have gone before us." The inside back cover of the CD depicts three *calacas* (skeletons) playing music. Two hold microphones while either rapping or singing, suggesting their fealty to a hip-hop background. One emcee is at a mixer or synthesizer (another staple of hip-hop iconography). The other, who wears an enormous, feathered, Mexica-style headdress, plays congas. The third calaca strums a four-stringed guitar-like instrument. The illustration recalls the famous lithographs of José Guadalupe Posada. Like Posada's, these calacas are active and full of energy; they are full of rhythm and full of life. For many Mexicans, the calaca and dia de los muertos represent our belief that death is not a finite end but a significant point in the cycle of life and death. As such, the calacas are a potent symbol of ancient Mexica indigeneity and contemporary Mexican-ness. In addition, the outside back cover includes a Tara Gatewood photo of Los Nativos in their hometown of Minneapolis / St. Paul. This photo illustration of their urban, Midwestern indigenousness depicts the artists' roots in hip hop. Both artists stare defiantly into the camera. Cuauhtli wears that hip-hop fashion staple, a hoodie.

Many rap artists who identify as indigenous/Mexica[1] claim a spiritual and political identity first broadly developed in the late 1960s by militant Chicana/o youth. Los Nativos exemplifies the indigenous subject position in Chicano hip hop that places them at odds with the white, colonialist power structure while claiming an indigenous heritage linked closely to positive and superior nature-society relations[2] and Mesoamerican cosmology.

INDIGENOUS IDENTITY AND RADICAL CHICANO POLITICS/POETICS

From the beginning of the radical working-class nationalist movement known as the Chicano Movement, an indigenous identity was central to Chicano political and cultural analysis, political activity, and artistic/literary expression. Many politically active Chicana/os understood themselves to be indigenous people adopting indigenous names, learning Aztec dances, and writing poetry and other literature that utilized pre-Columbian, Mesoamerican aesthetic forms and themes. Dance troupes, theater groups, and poets and writers have made their indigenous roots explicit in their work.[3] Additionally, the idea that Chicana/os are an indigenous people is fundamental to Chicana/o Studies and Chicana/o political activism.

The belief that Chicana/os are indigenous allowed for an analysis of contemporary conditions in the United States as one of internal colonialism (Barrera, 1980) in which the original homeland of the Aztec/Mexica was today's US Southwest, or what they call "Aztlán." Connections to an indigenous spiritual past have been used to critique imperialism. For example, in *Nationchild Plumaroja,* an important early work of Chicano nationalist literature by Alurista, the author "tailored 'recovered' knowledge into a vehicle for anti-imperialist critique" (Contreras, 2008:95). Using Aztec religious ideas, he created a perspective that saw imperialists such as the United States as evil like the Aztec god Tezcatlipoca. Chicanos and other anti-imperialists were the forces of good, like Quetzalcoatl, who should resist war and racism. In additional works, Alurista uses Aztec gods and spiritual practices as metaphors for capitalism, imperialism, and militarism.

Anahuac-centric thought is a contemporary elaboration of these early Chicano nationalist ideas. Anahuac-centric thinkers, such as those in the Mexica Movement, reject European control over Anahuac (Nahuatl for "the Américas"), including the imposition of European languages, borders, and religions. The original inhabitants of Anahuac (or Nican Tlaca), including contemporary Chicanos, are a part of an ancient civilization and thus indigenous to these lands. Importantly, Anahuac-centrists seek to maintain their ancestral cultures, especially their spiritual traditions.

Although Chicano indigeneity presents a critique of racist colonialism in the Américas, it leaves out a number of important elements relative to power, gender, race, and territoriality. The Chicano indigenist perspective brings up a number of questions. What are Chicana/

os' relationships to tribal issues in the United States? Why the focus on the Aztec (Mexica) instead of the dozens of other Mesoamerican peoples throughout México, Central America, and the United States? How do Mexica/indigenist Chicano men understand their relationship to women? What role do women play in the Mexica social order? Additionally, what roles do notions of biological race and mestizaje play in the identities of Mexica indigenists? Examining Chicana/o literary production since the 1960s, Contreras (2008) shows how much of Chicana/o neo-indigenism has developed from a primitivist rhetoric first posed by white anthropologists and archaeologists. Chicano indigeneity results not from a direct indigenous experience in North America (what they call Anahuac) but through the academic interpretations of recovered Mesoamerican documents.

LOS NATIVOS AND MEXICA CONSCIOUSNESS

The St. Paul, Minnesota, rap musical group Los Nativos is an affiliate of RhymeSayers Entertainment. RhymeSayers, home to Brother Ali, Eyedea and Abilities, and Atmosphere, is an important force in Midwest and independent rap music. With Chicano, Black, white, and multiethnic artists, RhymeSayers is a racially diverse independent music group that works on the margins of the mass music industry. The artist affiliates of RhymeSayers claim authentic hip-hop roots. Their music is original but stays true to hip-hop traditions including layering of sound, mixing and sampling multiple pieces of recorded music, heavy drums and bass sounds, and emphasis on flow. The artist affiliates also claim a politics of rebellion that has run through hip hop since its genesis. They critique the state, race relations, oppression, and class inequality and present personal narratives of struggling in the postindustrial inner city. These artists, like many that come out of the hip-hop tradition, appropriate European and capitalist technology and fashion and use them to make their own statements (Hoch, 2006).

In this cultural environment, Los Nativos was established in 1996 as The Native Ones, one of the original groups of the Headshots Crew (later RhymeSayers). They have recorded two compact discs to date: *Día de los Muertos* (2003) and *Red Star Fist* (2004). They have collaborated with numerous Chicano rap artists and are ardent supporters of indigenous and Chicana/o social struggles. They describe themselves on their website in the following terms:

> Los Nativos have polished their craft by taking all the music they have experienced to develop a Hip Hop structure accented by a broken Spanish and English flavor. With a conscious message, the lyrical style adds a political motivation, community awareness and current events of the world to give the listener a sense of what's going on in their world. By integrating Hip Hop, Jazz, Funk, Rhythm and Blues, Tejano, Mariachi, Salsa and Cumbia, the groups delivers an original musical collage of their own. (Los Nativos, 2009)

They, like other neo-indigenist rappers, foreground their aboriginal nature in their identities, tracing their racial and cultural roots to Meso-American native groups, especially the Mexica/Aztec and Maya. Their chosen names illustrate this point. Identifying with indigeneity meant going through a renaming process. Groups and artists such as Aztlán Underground, Groundkeepers, Tolteka, Olmeca, Cihuatl Ce, and El Vuh name themselves after indigenous peoples and concepts. Through speaking their word, these artists/musicians rebirth themselves in the tradition of the Mayan sacred book, Popol Vuh. According to the Mayan creation story, the gods created the Earth when they spoke. "Then the earth was created by them. So it was, in truth, that they created the earth. 'Earth!' they said, and instantly it was made" (Popol Vuh).

The very act of naming is a source of power in many sacred traditions. Indigenous/mexica rappers rename themselves and empower themselves. Like Black Nationalists from The Nation of Islam, who often changed their last names to "X," Mexica rappers rid themselves of the names that the (Spanish) colonizer gave them. The Spanish surnames of most people of Mexican descent reflect the power relations between the conquistadores and the colonized natives of México. They were forced to accept Spanish-language names and to lose their ancestral names. In an attempt to decolonize their minds, Mexica/indigenous rappers speak their names and remake their minds, bodies, and souls. They develop a "Mexica consciousness" as described in their song "Urthawhut?" (2003). They turn the tables on the colonizers and reject the colonizers' authority to define an indigenous person. Instead, they recreate an indigenous cosmology, epistemology, worldview, and politics through acts of creative expression, especially the spoken word. Like the Mexica/Aztec saying adopted by the Chicano Movement "por mi raza, hablaré el espíritu" (for my people I will speak the spirit), Mexica/indigenist rappers use the spirit of their voices to empower their people to seek an indigenous path of justice, creativity, and spirituality.

SONIDO INDÍGENA

Los Nativos' indigenous sound (*sonido indígena*) and identity as expressed in the song "Sonido Indígena" and other works involves two interrelated elements: aboriginality and conflict with colonizing Europeans. Los Nativos redefines an indigenous identity for twenty-first-century Chicana/os by examining idealized understandings of the uniqueness of American indigenous life and culture. In particular, they refer to indigenous nature-society relations and Mayan cosmology. In an urban, postindustrial, twenty-first-century context, their redefinition of indigeneity requires an analysis of the dominant white society and the history of white-native relations, including the contemporary facts of racism, inequality, and the disenfranchisement of natives and Chicana/os. In addition, Los Nativos defines and lays claim to an indigenous identity through the use of strategically placed indigenous sounds such as drums, rattles, and flutes.

In contrast to much of contemporary US male culture, Los Nativos' identity as Mexican/indigenous men involves multiple aspects of their humanity and their culture. Another aspect of their resistance to colonization, racism, and injustice is to turn toward their indigenous culture for strength and a source of life. In call-and-response fashion, Los Nativos chant "like the indigenous" after each aspect of native culture they continue to practice. They include "still write words," "native rituals," "still practice my beliefs," "still making music," and "still speak the tongue" ("Like the Indigenous," 2003). Their male indigenous identity relies heavily on resistance to colonialism and domination. Yet this resistance is not always violent. They strive to maintain indigenous languages, belief systems, aesthetic practices, and religions. Central to the maintenance of indigenous cultural traditions is their relationship to the land.

Los Nativos use natural imagery and Mexica ontological beliefs related to nature and natural occurrences in much of their lyrics. Bodies of water such as ríos and oceans; animals including eagles, quetzales, and other birds and jaguars; flora; earthy substances such as copal, tobacco, rocks, and sage; and forces such as fire, stars, the sun and constellations, the wind and rain, and clouds all contribute to Los Nativos' understanding of themselves and their indigeneity.

In the second verse to the song "Sonido Indigena" (2003), Felipe Cuauhtli raps, "I'm so deep in the earth / I can't believe that you found me." Here, Cuauhtli begins to define his indigenousness through the way in which he relates to and interacts with his environment. By claiming that he is "so deep in the earth," he expresses his intimate relationship with nature. Like his Mayan, Aztec, Lakota, and other indigenous relations,[4] he has an understanding and relationship to nature developed by many American indigenous cultures. For Cuauhtli, as for the new Mexica activists and thinkers, a more harmonious and balanced nature-society relationship is part of what it means to be an indigenous American. His identity as indigenous requires a historical connection to the land. As such, he says in "Like the Indigenous," "This was Indian land, is Indian land and will always be Indian land." He then goes on to list several native nations.

Additionally, and more specifically, Mexican indigenous culture as redefined by Chicana/os involves a certain reverence for corn. Cuauhtli continues rapping in verse two of "Sonido Indigena" that "my lineage lives on / We represent the corn / From here to Californ." Cuauhtli chooses to connect himself to his indigenous Mexican ancestors ("my lineage") through corn imagery. Here corn stands in for his indigenousness, which has a deep historical connection to his ancestors. Corn is used as a metonym for the indigenous Mexicans whom he is representing in his poetic performance. He makes this more explicit by connecting his representation of indigenous and Mexican people with the indigenous diet in the song "All My Native Vatos." He raps "Representin mis antepasados [my ancestors] / past, present, future livin the life / I had to crush average mc's with my beans and rice."

Representin' is an important concept in hip hop. Much of what hip-hop fans and performers do is represent themselves. Given the way in which others have represented and continue to represent people of color, especially youth of color, in the media and popular culture,[5] self-representation or representin' is vital to redefining their denigrated identities. Through representin'—whether via graffiti, breakdancing, rapping, or personal style, language, and attitude—this generation lays claim to the subjectivity required to challenge dominant institutions and systems. Representin' allows those in the hip-hop nation to overcome simple, degrading, and destructive identities imposed by the broader, white-dominated society and its institutions including media, schools, and government. In these lines, Cuauhtli "represent[s] the corn" or the progeny of pre-Columbian Mexicans from the Midwest to California ("from here to Californ"). The rapper is defining himself and others of Mexican descent in the United States as indigenous people with an intimate relationship to nature. Additionally, through his association with corn, Cuauhtli challenges beliefs that Mexicans are immigrants or foreigners. Instead, he argues that Mexicans and their ancestors, who have been breeding corn for hundreds, even thousands, of years, are among the first "Americans." As such, they have as much or more claim to life in the United States as anyone else. Referencing this idea, Cuauhtli raps, "We've traveled this continent in uncountable numbers / it's funny when you want to call my people border jumpers / you crossed the ocean / we crossed the river / and we're the wetbacks / how the hell you figure?"

The links to an indigenous Mexican past is also made through expressing another aspect of pre-Columbian Mexican culture: cosmology. Throughout the song, Los Nativos make references to themselves as "Mayan scientist(s)" or "cosmic navigator(s)." They also rap that "Los Na [is] comin live from the third planet." These references are intended to suggest that their worldview is influenced by Mayan understandings of the cosmos. Mayan life and spirituality revolved, in part, around careful astronomical observation. Contemporary Mexica and Mexican indigenist thought has attempted to revive a lifestyle and spirituality using Mayan astronomy, especially Mayan notions of cyclical time.

Many Mexica rappers, artists, and activists adopt Mayan understandings of time through appealing to their ideas of sacred and secular calendars. In particular, much has been made over the last forty years of the ideas of the fifth and sixth suns. The suns represent unique eras in Mayan cosmology. Each sun signals a rebirth. Mayan astronomers calculated that every 520 years, Venus completed a cycle. The belief is that along with this alignment, a new age would come into being. The new age would begin with cataclysmic or revolutionary events. The current era, or sun, is the fifth. Thus, many during the Chicana/o Movement referred to Chicana/os as sons and daughters of the fifth sun. This era begins in 1492, the first year of European presence in the Américas. The series of events that take place between Columbus's arrival and the early years of the Spanish colonial period constituted a complete upheaval of indigenous American society. The prediction of revolutionary change came true. Additionally, with the arrival of Cortés in México in 1519, the Mexican and Chicana/o people were born. Thus, we are the people of the fifth sun.

Importantly for many Mexica activists and artists, the fifth sun is coming to a close. In December of 2012, 520 years after what some call the beginning of the European invasion, a new era will begin. The sixth sun promises a new age. The coming of the sixth sun has been predicted by some to be the end of the world, but others envision a more hopeful era. They predict a return of the indigenous to prominence in the Américas. If the fifth sun saw indigenous enslavement, genocide, and impoverishment, the sixth sun holds out promises for a renewed indigenous society in which our worldview, spirituality, forms of governance, and resources, especially the land, will develop or return.

For Los Nativos and other Xicano indigenous rappers, phenotype, especially skin color, is a central marker of indigeneity. They often refer to themselves as brown or red and to their oppressors as white or pale. In the Los Nativos song "All My Native Vatos," they have "dark skin" and "long hair." In other songs, they represent the "red nation" ("Like the Indigenous), come from the "brown jurisdiction" ("Sonido Indigena") or refer to themselves as "red warriors" ("Con Tivos"). These references to their skin color and other aspects of their phenotypes signal difference from their perceived enemy, "white" people, and locates their superiority in their genetic makeup. Race or phenotype is used as a primary marker of difference and their supposed superiority in much the same manner that European colonizers justified their domination of Africans, Indians, and other Asians and pre-Columbian Americans. Like in justifications of colonialism and violence by Europeans, Los Nativos and other Mexica/indigenous rappers use phenotype to wage symbolic warfare on their oppressors. This is not to suggest that the situations are equivalent but to point out the irony of using "the master's tools to dismantle the master's house" (Lorde, 1984). On the other hand, one might also see this type of rhetoric as an act of strategic essentialism. Mexica rappers essentialize Chicana/o/native identity at a strategic moment in order to unify

Chicana/os in the cause of struggling against oppression. The struggle against oppression is a key aspect of indigenous identity for many.

American aboriginality or indigenous identity today is closely tied to native/white relations both historically and in their contemporary form. For Chicanos, the warrior and social bandit images implied adopting an oppositional stance and attitude to the White colonizer (McFarland, 2008; Paredes, 1959; Rosenbaum, 1981). Los Nativos express this attitude in "Sonido Indigena" and other songs. Los Natives rap, "I'll take power from the gringo [white]." Here, in a reversal of roles common in a great deal of rap music and the music, stories, and literature of many people of color, they place themselves in the role of the dominant. The racial other, "whites," becomes the inferior and powerless.

Los Nativos' indigeneity results in part from their resistance to racist, colonial structures and their fight on behalf of their people. On "Sonido Indigena," they rap, "soy las voces de los muertos de mi nacion / mi cancion / de la revolucion / es mi pasion" [I'm the voices of the dead of my nation / my revolutionary song is my passion]. The resistance to domination uses violence as a primary tactic. The final verse of "Sonido Indígena" explains, "This is a war zone homes / are you ready to bust up in they homes / invade their space and take the things they own / like they do our sacred places / where we bury our bones?" Here Los Nativos speak to their "recruits." They explain that the situation they are in is akin to a war zone. They ask if the recruits are ready to attack and pay back the colonizer for disrespecting native sacred places such as burial sites and stealing native resources.

In the song "All My Native Vatos," Los Nativos tie indigenous identity, male identity, and violent resistance together. The song speaks to indigenous/Chicano men or native vatos (guys). They rap "all my native vatos wave your ax in the air / scalp a muthafucka like you just don't care." They describe the situation "as revolutionary warfare brothers and sisters / a patrol in the Los Nativos militia / resurrect Nahua ancient tongue / When It's all said and done / I'm still standing / Native Ones." They are fighting to bring back the dominance of the Aztec language, Nahuatl. They fight to rid their communities of harmful substances and people. They say, "media you're killin me / alcohol you're killin me / tobacco you're killin me / government / you're killin me / gangstas pimps / you're really killin me." To be a real vato or Mexican/indigenous man is to be a warrior; to be strong and potentially violent. Like most understandings of maleness in US society today, the man from Los Nativos' perspective is hypermasculine, with his identity closely linked to his dominance and ability to fight back against oppression.

GUERRILLERAS AND SUFFERING WOMEN: GENDER POLITICS IN MEXICA RAP

Mexica rap and hip hop is dominated by men. Like in other subgenres of rap and hip hop, the biggest names and most successful groups and artists are male. This male-dominated space reinforces male perspectives as men interact with men. Female perspectives are mostly absent. Although Mexica rappers are no more sexist than other rappers or the general male population of the United States, and in many cases are much more progressive relative to women than most, they view women in limited ways and have a gender ideology based on patriarchal notions of strict roles for women and men.

Mexica/indigenist rappers display their outlook on gender and women in the fact that women are rarely discussed in their lyrics. As José Limón (1992) finds in relation to the lyrics of *corridos* (the male-dominated Mexican and Mexican American ballad genre), women are mostly invisible as actors in Mexica rap. In only a very few songs are women highlighted as subjects and agents in their own right. Women play a secondary role of wife and mother to men. Women's value results from their ability to serve and otherwise benefit men (Herrera-Sobek, 1990; Zavella, 2003).

In Mexica rap, as in Chicano expressive culture, women are passive objects with little and limited agency. When not serving men, they are acted upon by active men. For example, on "All My Nativo Vatos," a song that is directed at aggressive warrior-type Chicano men, women are seen as "tribal honeys" when they are told to get a man. They rap, "all my tribal honeys in the house tonight / find a warrior and hold him down tight." Women at this performance/event should get a man, while men ("native vatos," "warriors") are encouraged to be much more active in determining their lives through struggle with oppressive forces. They are directed to "wave their axes in the air / scalp a muthafucka like you just don't care." Women are put in passive and subordinate positions as aesthetic objects to men's active "warrior" subjectivity.

While Los Nativos' gender politics mostly render women invisible, many other Mexica rappers illustrate a gender politics that invokes notions of strict gender roles. El Vuh's "Native Sisters," from their second compact disc, illustrates this politics. They urge listeners to "respect" their mothers and wives. How they might show respect is not discussed, but they do tell us why we should respect women. Men should respect women because they are the "backbone / the foundation of a strong home." El Vuh claims further that

> You represent the strength in our community / because of you we have this longevity. / 5–13 years of resistance / due to your love and persistence. / I want to thank you for your insistence continuing our existence. / Your endurance prevented a complete holocaust / and if not for you the culture would have been lost. / I know it's been at great personal cost / and because of that we see today.

As in much of male-centered expressive culture, women who are related to and serve men are given the most respect. "Mothers, sisters, daughters, wives" are named in the song. All other non-related women are not identified. They could have given thanks to lawyers, teachers, spiritual advisors, organizers, and other active women.

In patriarchal societies, women are respected for their assigned roles as creators and sustainers. Within this patriarchal, heteronormative paradigm, mothers are given particular prominence and are equated with creation and nature. In the third verse of "Native Sisters," El Vuh raps,

> Your lives and love kept us afloat / when all else fails you bring hope / and inspiration. / Raisin[g] a nation / you are the source of all creation. / That's why I believe that a woman's the Creator / just look at Mother Earth and Mother Nature. / Grandmother Moon it's through your womb / that our life's derived and continues to shine / and every guy in the place knows that it's true.

The good woman, the valued woman, is the mother. El Vuh, like much of male expressive culture, essentializes women to their biological functions and reifies notions of the womb and creation. Women are reduced to their reproductive functions. Their essence and the source of their value are in procreation and nurturing.

El Vuh essentializes women, but it also sees women as more than mere passive objects or mothers as in most patriarchal culture. It sees women as physically, mentally, and spiritually strong. El Vuh borrows another trope from Mexican/Chicano culture when describing strong women: the guerillera. The *soldadera* (female soldier during the Mexican Revolution) is one of the enduring icons of Mexican/Chicana/o resistance. *La Soldadera* shows up as a *guerrillera* in "Native Sisters."

In "Triumph" (2007), El Vuh collaborates with Chicana indigenous rapper Lady Binx (now Kiawitl) of the group Almas Intocables.[6] In this song about fighting and triumphing over colonialism and racism, Lady Binx presents indigenous womanhood as warrior at the same time that she promotes a spiritual relationship to the Creator. Binx calls for "opposition to oppression." She raps,

> Revolution comes in stones and forms of violence / on these oppressors. / Bullets turning screams into silence. / There can be no submission to Bush's evil opposition. / Just listen to your heartbeat / and hear the Creator's wisdom.

Here Binx sees revolution and struggle against governments as violent and spiritual. She expresses her opposition to the former presidency of George W. Bush. At the same time that the oppressor is defeated, it remains important to maintain contact with the Creator. Her active, even violent, perspective as an indigenous woman differs drastically from the image of the passive and nurturing woman found in much of male-dominated expressive culture.

Kiawitl / Lady Binx identifies indigenous women as warriors. The lyrics to her solo work and collaborations with other artists and with her group, Almas Intocables, show women as active subjects playing numerous roles in their communities. In contrast to the limited images men have of women as venerated mothers or sex objects, Kiawitl shows how within traditional Mexica culture, women can be warriors who struggle on behalf of their people. On her website, she explains her perspective:

> The philosophy behind the Ollin allowed the admission of women in the Warrior Order centuries before the first feminist consciousness and movements; their beliefs said that a host of women warriors accompanied the Sun in the second half of its journey through the sky, so it was only natural to accept women into the new Order. Women can achieve the same rank and the same power as any Jaguar or Eagle Knight. (Kiawitl's website, www.myspace.com/kiawitlxochil)

Kiawitl argues for seeing traditional indigenous/Mexica gender relations in more complex and egalitarian ways than do her male counterparts. While in the lyrics of Mexica rappers men are the agents of action, especially resistance to colonialism, Kiawitl and other female Mexica rappers such as Cihuatl Ce place women at the center of indigenous culture, history, and struggle.

CONCLUSION

Los Nativos' *sonido indígena* is informed by their urban hip-hop roots and experience. Chilam Balam's musical production fuses indigenous sounds and sensibilities with an urban hip-hop and Chicano understanding. Along with ideas about their indigenous ancestors, Los Nativos' lyrics show the importance of urban Chicanidad, including lowrider car culture, tattooing, and language use. On *Red Star Fist,* Los Nativos describe their love of lowriders and lowriding while giving the listener a sense of the lowrider lifestyle in Minnesota. The funk, bass-driven music is infused with the sounds of hydraulics and car engines. Amid the descriptions of cruising and details about their Chevy lowriders, Los Nativos shout out (recognize in their lyrics) Los Padrinos car club. Lowriding car clubs have been a feature of Chicano male culture since at least the 1960s. Lowrider vatos, as Felipe Cuauhtli calls them, have historically chosen one street to cruise in each city. Los Nativos inform us that in San Antonio, the chosen stretch of road is Military Drive; in St. Paul, it is University.

The funk-based musical production of Chilam Bilam alerts us that at the root of Xicano rap is African musical sensibilities. Bilam's multiple syncopated rhythms played on a wide variety of instruments is part of the West African musical aesthetic that has remained an important force in American music since the 1600s, when Africans were enslaved in the United States, the Caribbean, and Latin America. Los Nativos are also a hip-hop group. Their aesthetic, worldview, music, attitude, and lyrics reflect hip-hop culture as it has developed since the 1970s. For example, using a record player and record as an instrument, hip-hop DJs have been adding rhythm to their songs since the late 1970s, when Grand Master Theodore invented the art of scratching and Grandmaster Flash developed and popularized it. The third member of Los Nativos, Tecpatl, joined the group for their second release. He provides nearly all of the scratches on the EP.

Los Nativos' lyrics attempt to instill in urban, working-class Chicana/os an understanding of their heritage and themselves as neo-indigenist Mayan/Mexica. The band members resent representations of Mexicans rendered by dominant institutions. They are not the stereotypical lazy Mexican, the greaser, the ruthless urban gangbanger, the drug dealer or killer, or the foreigner to the United States. They are spiritual, honorable, intelligent, and respectful. They honor and respect "all our relations" and use an earth knowledge combined with an indigenous cosmology to develop nature-society relations that benefit both humans and nature.

Los Nativos and other indigenous/Mexica rappers use their hip-hop expressiveness to put forth a vision of urban Mexican indigeneity at odds with colonialism, racism, and capitalism. Their indigenous perspective and politics rely heavily on the indigenism of the Chicano Movement, which created a new mythology out of archaeological theory, but indigenous rappers, as diasporic and colonized people have always done, reinvent themselves with a mix of ancestral tradition and contemporary culture. Los Nativos' hip-hop *indígena* reflects the ongoing process of *mestizaje* that has characterized Mexican-based cultures since the arrival of the Spaniards in the sixteenth century. This new millennial *mestizaje* is multiracial and multiethnic and develops in working-class Mexican/Chicano communities of the postindustrial period in the United States (McFarland, 2008, 2006). The music and lyrics of indigenous/Mexica rappers illustrate an oppositional consciousness at the heart of contemporary Chicano indigenity. Although their rhetorics of resistance forcefully critique capitalism, colonialism, and racism, their claims to a developing a more equitable society with superior nature-society relations fall short when women and women's ideas are marginalized and made into passive spectators of male warrior action. The patriarchal, heteronormative understanding of the world and especially of gender severely limits the possibility of the neo-indigenist cultural and political movement leading to a more equitable, open, and just world. Fortunately, female voices such as Kiawitl and Cihuatl Ce are beginning to challenge the male dominance of indigenous/Mexica hip hop.

NOTES

1. See the following for information and music from indigenous/Mexica rappers. El Vuh, *ElVuhlution, Jaguar Prophecies,* and www.elvuh.com; Victor, www.myspace.com/hastavictore; Olmeca, www.myspace.com/olmeca; Tolteka, *Reflexiones en Yangna;* Kiawtl (formerly, Lady Binx), www.myspace.com/kiawitlxochitl. Others use the ideas, concepts, and beliefs of indigenous/Mexica people in their music but do not necessarily identify with indigenous/Mexica. These artists include 2Mex, Krazy Race, Thief Sicario, Kemo the Blaxican, and Psycho Realm.

2. L. Pulido, "Development of the 'People of Color' Identity in the Environmental Justice Movement of the Southwestern United States," *Socialist Review* 26 (2009): 145–180. Pulido writes that "Nature-society relations is a broad term which refers to how a particular groups of people interact with their environment."

3. Yolanda Broyles-Gonzalez, *El Teatro Campesino: Theater in the Chicano Movement* (Austin: University of Texas Press, 1994). A. Castillo, *Massacre of the Dreamers: Essays on Xicanisma* (New York: Plume Books, 1994).

4. I use the term "relations" keeping in mind the sentiment expressed by the Lakota greeting "mitakuye oyasin" or "all my relations." The Mayan "in lak ech" (you are my other me) reflects a similar sentiment. The sayings reflect an indigenous ontology that views all people, all beings and, in some cases, nonsentient beings, as related to each other in an intricate web of life.

5. Escalante, 2000; Keller, 1994; McFarland, 2008.

6. Almas Intocables consists of Lady Binx, Jehuniko, and Ikuestion. See McFarland, op. cit., p. 43, and see Almas Intocables' website.

REFERENCES

2Mex. *2Mex.* Image Entertainment B00016XNS4, 2004, compact disc.

———. *Sweat Lodge Infinite.* Mush B0000C3I47, 2003, compact disc.

———. *B-boys in Occupied Mexico.* Meanstreet B00005OAFX, 2001, compact disc.

Barrera, M. *Race and Class in the Southwest: A Theory of Racial Inequality.* South Bend, IN: University of Notre Dame Press, 1980.

Broyles-Gonzalez, Y. *El Teatro Campesino: Theater in the Chicano Movement.* Austin: University of Texas Press, 1994.

Castillo, A. *Massacre of the Dreamers:Essays on Xicanisma.* New York: Plume Books, 1994.

Contreras, S. *Bloodlines.* Austin: University of Texas Press, 2008.

El Vuh. *ElVuhlution.* Xicano Records and Film, 2007, compact disc.

———. *Jaguar Prophecies.* Xicano Records and Film, 2003, compact disc.

Escalante, V. "The Politics of Chicano Representation in the Media." In *Chicano Renaissance: Contemporary Cultural Trends,* edited by D. R. Maciel, I. D. Ortiz, and M. Herrera-Sobek, 131–168. Tucson: University of Arizona Press, 2000.

Fregoso, R.L. *The Bronze Screen.* Minneapolis: University of Minnesota Press, 1993.

Herrera-Sobek, M. *The Mexican Corrido: A Feminist Analysis.* Bloomington: Indiana University Press, 1990.

Hoch, D. "Toward a Hip Hop Aesthetic: A Manifesto for the Hip-Hop Arts Movement." In *Total Chaos: The Art and Aesthetics of Hip-Hop,* edited by J. Chang, 349–364. New York: Basic Civitas Books, 2006.

Keller, G. *Hispanics and United States Film: An Overview and Handbook.* Tempe, AZ: Bilingual Review, 1994.

Kemo the Blaxican. *Not So Rich and Famous.* Dead Silence Records B000X25GEK, 2007, compact disc.

———. *The Simple Plan.* Dead Silence Records B000644J3O, 2004, compact disc.

Kiawitl. www.myspace.com/kiawitlxochitl, accessed 2008.

Krazy Race. *The Movement: Strength in Numbers.* MCR Productions / Realizm Rekords 809546042426, 2006, compact disc.

———. *New World Games.* MCR Productions / Realizm Rekords 809546018421, 2004, compact disc.

Limón, J. *Mexican Ballads, Chicano Poems: History and Influence in Mexican-American Social Poetry.* Berkeley: University of California Press, 1992.

Los Nativos. www.losnativos.com. Accessed April 27, 2009.

———. *Red Star Fist.* Rhymesayers Entertainment, 2004, compact disc.

———. *Dia de los Muertos.* Rhymesayers Entertainment B000254YIC, 2003, compact disc.

Mexica Movement. www.mexica-movement.org. Accessed April 27, 2009.

McFarland, P. *Chicano Rap: Gender and Violence in the Postindustrial Barrio.* Austin: University of Texas Press, 2008.

———. "Chicano Rap Roots: Black-Brown Cultural Exchange and the Making of a Genre." *Callaloo* 29 (2006): 939–955.

Olmeca. www.myspace.com/olmeca, accessed 2009.

Paredes, A. *With His Bullet in His Hand: A Border Ballad and Its Hero.* Austin: University of Texas Press, 1959.

Psycho Realm. *A War Story, Book II.* Sick Symphonies Records B0001ARVVU, 2004, compact disc.

Pulido, L. "Development of the 'People of Color' Identity in the Environmental Justice Movement of the Southwestern United States." *Socialist Review* 26 (1996): 145–180.

Thief Sicario. *Education of a Felon.* Realizm Rekords B0014950SI, 2008, compact disc .

Tolteka. *Reflexiones en Yangna.* Abya Yala Ixachilan Music B0018CWT9Y, 2008, compact disc.

Victor E. www.myspace.com/hastavictore, accessed 2009.

———. *Knowledge and Wisdom.* Xicano Records and Film B000SQLBBS, 2004, compact disc.

———. *Black and Red Ink.* Xicano Records and Film B000QRHZUU, 2007.

Zavella, P. "Talkin' Sex: Chicanas and Mexicanas Theorize About Silence and Sexual Pleasures." In *Chicana Feminisms: A Critical Reader,* edited by G. F. Arredondo, 228–253. Durham, NC: Duke University Press, 2003.

TWENTY-TWO

The Latino Comedy Project and Border Humor in Performance

JENNIFER ALVAREZ DICKINSON

This is a nation of aliens, going back to the first one: Christopher Columbus.

GEORGE LOPEZ, *ALIEN NATION*, 1996

In a 2007 article for the *Huffington Post,* Roberto Lovato calls attention to the proliferation of anti-immigrant humor in mainstream entertainment, particularly anti-Latino immigrant humor, providing several recent examples of demeaning humor: at the 2007 Emmys, Conan O'Brien showed a clip depicting his writing team as day laborers; one of Bill Maher's August 2007 "New Rules" is a ban on fruit- and vegetable-scented shampoos, quipping, "Gee, your hair smells like a migrant worker"; and Jay Leno observes that illegal immigrants arrested for prostitution are "just doing guys American hookers will not do" (Lovato). While it may be tempting to dismiss these jokes as simply comedic gaffes, they are reflective of a larger anti-immigrant discourse that has resurfaced in recent years, what Otto Santa Ana calls an "explosion" of anti-immigrant representations in American popular culture (Santa Ana 2009). With the emergence of border vigilante groups, increased proposals for immigration legislation, the ongoing construction of a border wall, and cable news anchors regularly vilifying immigrants, it is clear that advocates for immigrant rights face significant challenges in shifting public opinion. Despite the long history and significant economic and cultural contributions of Latinos in the United States, fears of terrorism and an economic slowdown can easily reverse gains made in improving the popular images of Latinos and Latino immigrants. As Santa Ana points out in *Brown Tide Rising*, "human thinking, at base, is not mathematical code or logical expression. Human thought is constructed with images that represent reality" (Santa Ana 2002, xv).

For Latino performers, the construction of reality through public discourse is as much an opportunity as an obstacle. Largely pro-immigrant, Latino comedic performance offers compelling counternarratives to the current anti-immigrant strains in mainstream media. This chapter seeks to understand both the political activism and cultural anxieties expressed in border humor by Latino performers. As a salient example, I examine the work of the Latino Comedy Project, an Austin-based sketch-comedy group.[1] The Latino Comedy Project's work is multi-dimensional, combining popular culture and political humor on stage and online. Reflecting a well-trodden theme in Latino humor, the Latino Comedy Project engages in border humor that critiques immigration policy while exploring a perhaps even older Latino tradition, *agringamiento* humor, or humor targeting Latinos who, as José Limón puts it, have breached in-group social norms by "emulating perceived Anglo-American customs, language, and values and socio-economic status, while implicitly or explicitly denying their own culture and society" (Limón 1984, 35).

THEORIES OF HUMOR

Sociologist Christie Davies notes that "Ambiguity and incongruity are central to most jokes" (Davies, 7). Despite humor's ambiguity and range of critique, there is some agreement on the nature and uses of humor. Generally speaking, then, humor is both universal and highly context-dependent (everyone laughs, but we laugh for different reasons); humor often acts as an "escape valve" for social pressures, allowing us to laugh about taboo subjects such as death, our bodies, and ethnic or racial tensions; humor is of the moment, relying on immediate recognition and spontaneous laughter; and, most often, humor relies on the juxtaposition of incongruent elements.[2] Not surprisingly, then, border humor frequently mines the incongruities between English and Spanish or between perceived differences in Latinos and Anglos for laughs. Puns, misunderstandings, and sharply contrasting socioeconomic circumstances supply a wealth of comic materials (Reyes).

In general, humorists have a cultural license for deviant behavior and "inappropriate" expression, but that license balances precariously between socially acceptable entertainment and true offense (Mintz). For ethnic minorities and groups marginalized by dominant cultures, humor can serve as an aggressive response to derogatory language, frequently preemptively acknowledging the foibles of a community in order to retain control over that discourse. For instance, performers such as Carlos Mencia and John Leguizamo reclaim the derogatory terms "beaner" and "spic," respectively, toying with Latino stereotypes in order to critique dominant cultural representations. As Christine List notes in her analysis of Cheech Marin's *Cheech and Chong* films, sometimes the comic use of stereotypes by ethnic minorities can indicate an ironic distancing that subtly critiques ethnocentrism and "image policing" (List, 193).

Humor, particularly satire, can attempt to regulate in-group behavior. Latino comic performers frequently ridicule "inauthentic" Latinos, such as pochos (Anglicized Mexicans) and vendidos (sellouts). As Guillermo Hernández explains in *Chicano Satire* (1991), parody and satire ridicule or invalidate the normative principles of the victim. At the same time, "Satire is also present when rival groups appeal to the loyalty of members who must decide upon the validity of opposing value systems" (Hernández, 5). Consequently, it is important to consider what is deemed "normal" and who gets to make the determination. The study of laughter frequently reveals power dynamics between and within groups. For Latinos and other ethnic minorities, satire and parody are often used to remind members of shared in-group experiences and cultural symbols in order to foster greater solidarity and social cohesion. Being so close to the US-México border and frequently interacting with newly arrived immigrants, Latinos in the borderlands negotiate complex identities that intertwine American, Mexican, and distinct border cultures as well as the increasing influence of global media and consumer goods.

MULTICULTURALISM AND LATINO HUMOR

Comedy emerging out of the "multicultural moment" of the 1990s raises intriguing questions about representation and audience. Many contemporary Latino comic performers grew up with both Mexican and American popular cultural influences, watching "El Chavo del Ocho" and "The Muppets," Cantinflas movies and "Saturday Night Live," Freddie Prinze, Jr. and Richard Pryor. Unlike the early revistas and carpas of the twentieth century, contemporary Latino comic performance is frequently English-dominant and addresses non-Latino audience members. Latino humorists engage in complex performative negotiations, simultaneously encouraging Latino audience members to enjoy in-group references and inviting non-Latinos to share in the laughter. Comic routines can quickly shift from ethnic inclusion to exclusion, often in one breath, as when stand-up comic Alex Reymundo opens his "Hick-Spanic" show in Albuquerque by welcoming the audience in Spanish and declaring, "Yo soy de Acapulco, México! For those of you who don't speak Spanish, time to learn fuckers! You're in America, learn the language" (Reymundo 2007). However, with an American public increasingly aware of cultural diversity between self-identified ethnic groups as well as within them, we will most likely see more humor by Latino performers that challenges the Anglo vs. Latino conflict model and invites audiences to laugh at the fine distinctions among Latino identities.[3]

In exploring these distinctions, it is important to ask what, then, happens when audiences are aware that what they are witnessing is a critique of culture, not a celebration of traditional cultural practices. Do non-Latino audiences still expect cultural translation from Latino artists whose primary goal is to toy with cultural symbols? Humor is a signal against realism, and a parody does not purport to recreate a "slice of life." Rather, it is meant to distort life in order to comment on hypocrisy, corruption, and human folly. It is particularly important to explicitly note humor's conscious break with realism when discussing humor by ethnic minorities because so much of minority cultural production is read as explanatory. Often, the need for cultural explanation becomes the joke itself. For example, the Latino Comedy Project's Nick Walker explains that when performing for predominantly white audiences, "We actually added pieces before sketches where we explained what a chancla is . . . and that actually becomes a joke itself. 'A chancla is a flip flop. And is also used by Mexican mothers to beat the hell out of their kids.'"[4]

Within this framework of mock-explanation, Latino humorists attempt to shift public opinion under the guise of laughter. While artists can take a humorous approach to virtually any topic, there are four dominant themes in Latino humor: the misrepresentation (or absence) of Latinos in the mainstream entertainment media; immigration and related topics, such as the mistreatment of migrants and the militarization of the border; the growing US Latino population and its impact on American culture; and the Latino's loss of authentic identity, or agringamiento. These topics have been addressed in Latino humor for decades and are closely related, each resonating with the others. Immigration is perhaps the most sensitive topic for humorists to broach, as it raises questions about how we define the nation, both culturally and politically.

THE LATINO COMEDY PROJECT

As Arturo Aldama notes, Mexican and Chicano "jokelore" dealing with border crossing, deportation, and the label "wetback" has developed into a significant subgenre of Latino comedy (2004). In response to the grim realities of the militarization of the border, a rise in migrant deaths, nativist xenophobia, drug-related crime, environmental devastation, and economic disparity, the past decade has seen a wealth of border humor performance. Some films include Cheech Marin's *Born in East L.A.* (1987), Lalo López and Alex Rivera's 1997 short films "Why Cybraceros?" and "Día De La Independencia," and Sergio Arau's 2004 film *A Day Without a Mexican.* Onstage, Culture Clash explores the complexity of the Tijuana–San Diego border region in their play *Bordertown,* and buffoonish Border Patrol agents open both the Latino Comedy Project's sketch-comedy show "Alien Nation" (2007) and Rick Najera's *Latinologues* (1997–present). Approaching the topic of immigration in diverse ways, these performances constitute a satiric discourse critical of the mistreatment and invisibility of immigrants.

Based in Austin, the Latino Comedy Project has found receptive audiences well outside the Southwest, from Seattle to Vancouver (Acosta). Sponsored by TEATRO Humanidad, the Latino Comedy Project formed in 1998 and focuses on showcasing Latino talent, although not to the exclusion of non-Latino performers.[5] Their work remains oppositional in its challenge to dominant entertainment media, celebrating ethnic identity yet remaining untethered to a belief in Latino "authenticity." Group member Danu Uribe's comment on writing comedy sketches reflects the group's approach:

FIG. 22.1. "The Latino Comedy Project." Back, left to right: Omar Gallaga, Adrian Villegas, Nick Walker, Guillermo de Leon, Danu Uribe. Front: Sandy Avila. Not pictured: Karinna Pérez and Yesenia Garcia. *Photo by Kenneth Gall. Courtesy of The Latino Comedy Project.*

> I always like to try to get a little political thing in there whenever humanly possible . . . I hope certain things change, people's perspectives change, that they lose their apathy a little bit . . . I can hopefully incite people's interest in the topic, at least, under the guise of entertainment.[6]

"THE MEXICAN 300"

Commenting on the desiring/reviling relationship America has with immigrants, particularly undocumented immigrants, writer, performer, and artistic director of the Latino Comedy Project (LCP) Adrian Villegas observes, "'there's such a Kabuki dance going on in this country right now with the immigration "debate" . . . We want to act like Mexican immigrants are separate from this country, but they're part of the fabric of the nation'" (qtd. in Pineo). In order to address this "Kabuki dance," the LCP produced the mock film trailer "The Mexican 300" (2007) which parodies the film *300* (2006) by depicting undocumented immigrants as menacing warriors, a commentary on the exaggerated fears some US residents have of "invading" aliens (www.lcp.org).[7] Although the dominant theme of "The Mexican 300" is immigration, the group's parody of a major Hollywood film also brings to mind Hollywood's virtual evasion of immigration stories and the lack of heroic images of Latinos in mainstream film.

The parodied film, *300,* is a retelling of the battle of Thermopylae in which the small but determined army of Spartans fends off an invasion by Persian forces.[8] But the audience need not be familiar with the details of the actual battle of Thermopylae or of ancient Spartan culture in order to grasp the central claim of the film: there is honor in fearlessly fighting to the death for one's people. Evoking imagery from the graphic novel upon which it is based, *300* employs violence, explicit sexuality, and hyper-masculine soldiers. Their most popular Internet short film, Latino Comedy Project's "The Mexican 300" similarly incorporates high-energy rock music, sepia-toned images, and warrior-like immigrants. The undocumented immigrants in "The Mexican 300," although numerous and depicted as invaders, wield brooms, rakes, and bags of oranges instead of swords and spears. The immigrants are rallied by an unnamed leader (Villegas) who delivers the trailer's only line of dialogue, yelling, "Mexicans! Tonight we dine in San Diego!" The crowd roars its approval and begins running toward the border, a scene that echoes the final scene of *Born in East LA* in which Cheech Marin's character, a "border Moses," leads a crowd of cheering immigrants across the border and into the United States. As "The Mexican 300" closes, the number "300" appears and then quickly increases to "321,138,873." As might be expected in a movie trailer, the film ends with the words "Coming Soon." These words are meant to be satirically menacing, however, and are immediately followed by, "And Bringing Cousins."

While the film uses stereotypical images, such as a pregnant Latina waddling across the border, the film conveys the absurdity of comparing undocumented border crossers with threatening warriors. Several viewers, however, have taken the parody quite seriously. Viewers of "300" have posted strongly worded comments both criticizing and praising the Latino Comedy Project's parody. "The Mexican 300" has been viewed on YouTube over five and a half million times and has received over twenty-five thousand comments. Several responses digress from the film itself and convey general hostility toward undocumented Mexican immigrants; others question the productiveness of Latino Comedy Project's use of immigrant stereotypes. Some representative comments:

> Robertolatino2002: This video should only be funny to ignorant Mexicans and mild racists. Smart Mexicans and people who actually articulate a sentence find this highly offensive[9]
>
> Lonewolfboy: hell i am mexican and thts funny as hell [*sic*][10]
>
> Wildlillie: creo que si no entienden la satira, habria que preguntarse quien es realmente el pendejo . . . este video no fue filmado por un racista, al contrairo es para que los que lo son acepeten la relidad de que vamos a seguir viniendo. Lo se de buena fuente . . . SATIRA, entiendes???[11]
>
> naxa321: This video is funny because its true. lol. We get 20,000 of those welfare sucking people each year.[12]

Responding to YouTube comments, Adrian Villegas writes on the LCP blog:

> One of the most fascinating developments of the Latino Comedy Project's "300" video's far-flung international exposure . . . has been the intense response it's provoked in the comments section. Specifically, the video's ironic and exaggerated use of immigration "invasion" imagery seems to have provoked an endless stream of comments that can most charitably be categorized as "Vintage Retro-Racist Harangue Chic."[13]

Tongue-in-cheek, Villegas goes on to explain that racists have been unfairly stereotyped as a monolithic group, when in fact there are a several categories of racists: the "ironically challenged," who watches the video as if it is a documentary; the "military porn fanaticist," whose comments call for killing immigrants; and the "amateur ethnologist," who argues that the deficiency of Mexicans is due to "impure" ethnic mixing.

While the overtly racist comments elicited by "The Mexican 300" should remind viewers that deep-seated xenophobia and bigotry remain with us, the film encourages a more compelling conversation about the use of stereotypes in ethnic humor. The proliferation and maintenance of negative Latino stereotypes in mainstream television and film is well documented.[14] On stage, the Latino Comedy Project excavate decades of stereotypes and Latino iconography: la Virgen, cholos, abuelitas, activists, immigrants, upwardly mobile "Hispanics." The television and film industries' history of Latino stereotypes foregrounds many Latino humorists' attempts to revitalize or discard these types, but the humor itself reveals inter-Latino debates about political iconography and the performance of identity. Humor, particularly humorous performance, relies on the audience's ability to quickly recognize and respond to incongruities and narrative excess. Stereotypes, in their abbreviation of historical and cultural context, are ideal vehicles for humor. In general, stereotypes, when recognized as such, disrupt a text's claims to reality, much like an actor's direct address to the audience. An obviously stereotypical character is presumed to be less than fully human, a surface summation of a group. The danger of stereotypes, however, is that they are frequently taken as truth. As Charles Ramírez Berg points out, stereotypes create their own histories. Singularly, stereotypes may be dismissed as mere narrative license, but "*With repetition . . . narration becomes representation*" (Berg, 19). Latino stereotypes, appearing over and again in film and on television, become part of narrative convention and an expression of the "preferred power relation" (Berg. 21). Frequently offering their flippant motto, "Will stereotype for food," the Latino Comedy Project is well aware that their use of Latino stereotypes comes with the potential for the reinstitution of negative Latino imagery. Their audiences, then, must bring their own critical attention to the performance. Clearly, the group risks offending large segments of its audience simply by portraying Mexican immigrants as menacing invaders, particularly when they are invading to sell fruit and rake leaves.

Surprisingly, Adrian Villegas is puzzled by the strong audience reactions, saying of "300," "it's weird. People projected so many things. To me, the only commentary is that there are a lot of Mexicans coming over."[15] Fellow group members Danu Uribe and Karinna Pérez add that immigrants are coming to the United States through México whether you support increased immigration or not.[16] Their job as performers is simply to get audiences to pay attention to public policies and the people they impact. Or, as Villegas notes,

> I looked at ["300"] as positive . . . I was putting it in people's faces. There's not any real deep commentary . . . To me it was taking a joke out of a reality . . . the country kind of has a very schizophrenic feeling about immigration. A big part of our economy is based on it, we all live around

> immigrants. And the other side is making hay out of it constantly on political talk shows. ["300"] definitely comes down on the side of being positive, but it doesn't spell it out, so people were able to project.[17]

"MEX VS. BC"

In the mock-commercial series "Mex vs. BC," the Latino Comedy Project parodies the "PC vs. Mac" Apple Computer commercials (www.lcp.org). The original commercials are not the target of satire; rather, they function as an easily identifiable reference upon which the sketches are built. In the LCP sketches, the awkward and malfunctioning PC character becomes the "BC," or "Born Citizen," and the Mac becomes the "Mex," a recently arrived Mexican immigrant. In another manifestation of the pocho figure, the BC is Anglicized and, in contrast to the Mex, unused to discomfort or hard work. On the surface, Adrian Villegas plays the Mex in stereotypical terms. He has a thick accent, shuns modern medicine, and prays to la Virgen de Guadalupe for beer. Upon closer examination, however, one finds that the Mex expresses the more desirable characteristics of the two. Frequently complaining, BC seems overwhelmed by life's inconveniences, whereas Mex is hardworking and optimistic. And while the BC expresses a sense of self-entitlement, Mex reminds BC that the dominant culture does not always distinguish between newly arrived immigrants and "born citizens."

The Latino Comedy Project's use of an immigrant figure is part of a larger discourse that contrasts acculturated Mexican Americans softened by life in the United States and hard-working immigrants vigorously pursuing the American Dream. Comedians such as George Lopez frequently note the determination of undocumented immigrants. For example, on his 1996 *Alien Nation* album, Lopez challenges those in power to put even greater obstacles in the way of immigrants crossing the Río Grande, saying, "You know what, put alligators, motherfucker. In an hour, they're shoes and belts. See guys coming out of the ditch with a new jacket. 'How do you like it? Does it go? Does it go?'" (Lopez). Lopez concludes *Alien Nation* on a serious note, reminding his audience that the United States is a nation of immigrants and laughing at the thought of educated American citizens losing their jobs to immigrants, "Oh yeah! You can see it. 'Oh yes, I'm only working in computers until something in produce opens up'" (Lopez). The Latino Comedy Project shares in Lopez's desire to praise the drive and endurance of undocumented immigrants. In a 2007 interview with the *Austin Chronicle,* Villegas notes that the LCP deliberately plays with the image of the "almost superhuman tenacity of undocumented Mexican immigrants . . . Because whatever roadblock is put up, historically Mexican immigrants always find a way around it" (qtd. in Pineo).

In the "BC vs. Mex" skits, the Latino Comedy Project draws from the contrasting character types of the PC vs. Mac commercials to highlight the Mex's positive qualities. In the original commercials, the PC is awkward and lacks the cool of the Mac, and much of the humor is based on PC's failed attempts to perform as well as the Mac. The Mac does not ridicule the PC, as the PC's inadequacies are obvious and do not require additional mocking. In this way, the Mac character remains likeable. Villegas explains the similarly contrasting characters in their skit:

> That is a true dichotomy in our community. The whole idea came from one of our members observing that when he's dealing with these different types of people that the BC-type guys are very easily rattled, and they complain about a lot of things. And the immigrant people are like, nothing rattles them.[18]

The LCP commercials signal a popular culture reference in order to access a shorthand for character types. Audience members familiar with the original commercials will know immediately that the BC is on the losing end of the comparison. Like the commercial's PC, BC is the object of ridicule because he is a second-generation pocho (Anglicized Mexican) who cannot "perform" as well as Mex when faced with life's challenges. Villegas explains, "With 'Mex vs. BC,' it's very obvious what the subtext is, and that was what we all agreed on . . . the formula will be taking something and making a very clear contrast and the Mex will always come out on top."[19]

In the first "Mex vs. BC" video ("Travel"), the protagonists, BC (Mical Trejo) and Mex (Adrian Villegas), cheerfully introduce themselves:

> BC: Hello, I'm a BC, a *born* citizen.
>
> Mex: Y yo soy un Mex.[20]

Immediately, the scene moves to the BC who is obviously frustrated as he ends a cell phone call, exclaiming, "Damn it! I can't believe this!" Mex asks with concern, "¿Qué?" BC explains that the airline lost his luggage and asks Mex if he travels much. When Mex explains that he traveled to get to the United States, BC cuts him off, "Yeah, well, I'm sure it's nowhere near the problems I had." Mex follows with a quickly delivered and animated barrage of the difficulties he endured. A coyote (human smuggler) took money from him and the other immigrants traveling with him and locked everyone in a truck. Surviving near suffocation, Mex and the rest of the group had to then crawl through a "pinche sewer" full of rats and snakes. Mex provides BC with a reenactment, exclaiming, "Here come the ratones!" [*sic*] as he claws at his face and screams. Mex adds, "Y the snakes! They get into your pantalones y bite your bolas!" With a tight close-up of his face, Mex provides a montage of suffering, screaming, "La Migra! . . . I'll come back for you Maria! . . . Noooo!" The scene briefly cuts to BC's appalled face and back to the now calm Mex, who explains, shrugging, "Pero, I was still able to work the next day."

In the second "Mex vs. BC" video ("Jobs"), BC complains that he lost his job and his "severance package isn't all that great," and he might "have to file for unemployment." Holding up two bags of oranges, Mex responds, "Pero, America is full of jobs!" Then BC replies:

> BC: But those jobs are for Mexicans.
>
> Mex: It's pinche work. Y que es eso que, "they're only for los mexicanos?" Estos gringos, they don't know the difference between you and me.
>
> BC: What?! We are *nothing* alike. I'm a BC, a born citizen. A fully integrated part of American society, and it feels great.

As BC is talking, Mex puts a bag of oranges in his arms. A white man comes up to BC, puts a quarter in his hand, takes the bag of oranges, and walks away, saying, "Gracias, muchacho." Dejectedly, BC stares at the quarter as Mex adds, "I told you so." Despite his education and professional job experience, the BC's social position is precariously close to that of the recent immigrant. Relying on the old ethnic joke, "they all look alike to me," the Latino Comedy Project subtly reminds Latinos of shared experiences as people of color, regardless of one's citizenship status.

Finally, in the Mex vs. BC video "Money," BC is looking over his stock statement while Mex is examining his lottery ticket. BC sighs contentedly, "Ah, capitalism!" Mex is puzzled, so BC explains, "I'm just looking at my stocks. [Condescendingly] Do you know what stocks are, my friend?" He proceeds to explain rates of return and market fluctuations to Mex, who quickly loses interest and begins scratching his lottery ticket. As BC drones on about staffing levels and market turmoil, Mex declares that he has won "three thousand dolares Americanos!" As Mex jumps up and down excitedly, screaming "I won, a la madre!," BC wads up his stock statement. The gag continues in the video "Citizenship," as we see Mex enjoying his winnings. Instead of his western shirt, black cowboy hat, and tight black jeans, Mex is wearing an outfit similar to BC's: khaki pants, a blue button-down shirt, and a tie. Mex blends the look of an acculturated Chicano ("business casual") with that of a working-class immigrant who has come into "new money." Mex keeps his black cowboy hat, a signifier of his rural Mexican background, while he smokes a cigar, holds an American flag, and wears gaudy white-framed sunglasses. Although supposedly ignorant of sophisticated investment plans, the Mex realizes his American dream through luck and prayer to la Virgen de Guadalupe, becoming a "citizen" through his participation in consumer culture.

CONCLUSION

> You know what pisses me off? People say Mexicans are lazy. That's bullshit, right? My father came to this country with five children, four dollars, and three jobs. That ain't lazy. That's fucked.
>
> ALEX REYMUNDO, *THE ORIGINAL LATIN KINGS OF COMEDY*, 2002

In "Narratives of Undocumented Mexican Immigration," Alberto Ledesma urges Chicano artists and critics to acknowledge their social responsibility to sensitively depict and examine the experiences of undocumented immigrants and the interconnections among undocumented Mexican immigrants and Chicanos. Ledesma asks, "Is not undocumented immigration one of those constitutive elements that make up what is collectively referred to as the Chicana/o experience?" (331). Although Ledesma may not have been thinking about comic representations of immigrants as a means of constructing protagonists with agency and interior lives, I believe the frequent depiction of the undocumented immigrant as the undaunted underdog encourages Latinos who are US citizens—particularly educated, acculturated Latinos—to rethink their place of privilege. As with any repeated trope, however, there is a danger that even positive stereotypes of immigrants can become rigid and limiting. The "hard-working immigrant," while preferable to the "lazy Mexican," comes with his/her own baggage—the stereotype of the enduring, not fully human immigrant may be taken as naturally suited only for manual labor. Humor, however, has the potential to complicate overly earnest caricatures through ironic distancing and implicit critique. Through the juxtaposition of incongruous elements, humor acts as a catalyst that reveals a culture's underlying absurdities and previously unimagined possibilities. In this sense, political humor is a superficial but important layer over serious debates about social justice and structures of power. Humor, in its refraction of meaning, allows audiences to participate in a reconstruction of signification. The moment of understanding—of getting the joke—is simultaneously a moment of release and participation. As "cultural symbolic action" (Limón 1982, 155) or "culture-in-action" (Lincoln, 20), joking reveals how we read meaning into situations and symbols.

Based on its origins in ethnic studies and civil rights movements, it would be difficult to argue that Latino comic performance is "just kidding." Considering the large number of US Latinos who continue to be economically and socially disenfranchised, humor that points to the current conditions of immigrant labor or re-imagines Latinos as the dominant culture of the future is a humor that taps into Anglo-American anxieties over national identity and a changing American dream. The issue is not merely about legality; it touches on America's conceptualizations of nation, citizenship, and ethnic identity. As David Montejano points out, public outcries over immigration frequently lump Latinos together with recent immigrants, illustrating the "ambiguous status of Mexican Americans as a 'legitimate' citizenry in American society" (Montejano, 241). At the same time, jokes about the "browning of America" retain their edge because, despite a growing Latino population, Anglo-dominated power structures and ideological frameworks remain in place. Terms such as "majority minority" point to the continued inability of many Americans to imagine people of color as anything but peripheral.

In his survey of Latino humor, Israel Reyes notes that "Latino and Latina humorists have demonstrated a great capacity to hold up a mirror to their own communities. This unique combination of honor and self-reflection adds a new texture to the American cultural fabric" (Reyes, 387). In the traditions of both carpa and American sketch-comedy performance, the Latino Comedy Project—influenced by an eclectic mix of comic performance, including Buster Keaton, Monty Python, Cantinflas, Richard Pryor, *The Simpsons,* and *Saturday Night Live*—finds inspiration everywhere. Villegas explains that besides parodying popular culture, the group need only look around to find day-to-day situations that are frustratingly funny, explaining, "the cool thing is when you can nail this pop culture phenomenon, but then you use that as a vehicle for something that's bothering you or that you feel needs to be commented on."[21] The immigration debates of the last decade have clearly bothered Villegas and the rest of the Latino Comedy Project. And while "The Mexican 300" and "Mex vs. BC" rely on stereotypical images of immigrants, Villegas points out, "We're also making fun of the people who believe the stereotypes. Or giving a character, giving a personality to someone they find stereotypical."[22]

NOTES

1. The Latino Comedy Project is sponsored by TEATRO Humanidad. www.teatrohumanidad.com [accessed 1 May 2009]. See also James E. García's description of TEATRO Humanidad in "Theater," *Encyclopedia of Latino Popular Culture.* Edited by Cordelia Chávez Candelaria, Arturo Aldama, and Peter J. García. Westport, CT: Greenwood, 2004: 839.

2. For a concise overview of humor theories and definitions, see Israel Reyes's "Comedy and Humor" in the *Oxford Encyclopedia of Latinos and Latinas in the US.* New York: Oxford University Press, 2005: 381–388.

3. See Américo Paredes's "The Anglo-American in Mexican Folklore." *New Voices in American Studies* (1966): 113–128.

4. Nick Walker. Personal interview. Austin, TX, 21 February, 2009.

5. Current Latino Comedy Project members include Adrian Villegas (artistic director), Nick Walker, Danu Uribe, Vanessa González, Guillermo de Leon, Karinna Pérez, Sandy Avila, Omar Gallaga, Mical Trejo, Raul Garza, Tim Mellonig (lighting/audiovisual), and Jeanie De Leon (lighting/audiovisual).

6. Danu Uribe. Personal interview. Austin, Texas, 21 February, 2009.

7. See the Latino Comedy Project's homepage, www.lcp.org, or their YouTube page, http://www.youtube.com/user/LatinoComedyProject.

8. The film *300* was written and directed by Zack Snyder and based on the graphic novel by Frank Miller and Lynn Varley.

9. From commentary section, www.youtube.com, Latino Comedy Project's "300." January 16, 2009 http://www.youtube.com/watch?v=17qKD-Ph7ds.

10. Ibid.

11. Ibid.

12. From commentary section, www.youtube.com, Latino Comedy Project's "300." 11 March, 2010 http://www.youtube.com/watch?v=17qKD-Ph7ds.

13. Adrian Villegas, *Latino Comedy Project Blog.* 14 November 2008. 18 December, 2008 http://www.LCP.org/LCPblog/page/3/.

14. See Clara Rodríguez, ed., *Latin Looks: Images of Latinas and Latinos in the US Media.* Boulder, CO: Westview Press, 1997; Fernando Delgado, "Moving Beyond the Screen: Hollywood and Mexican American Stereotypes." In *Cultural Diversity and the US Media,* edited by Yahya R. Kamalipour and Theresa Carilli. New York: State University of New York Press, 1998: 169–179; Chon Noriega, *Shot in America: Television, the State and the Rise of Chicano Cinema.* Minneapolis: University of Minnesota Press, 2000; Charles Ramírez Berg, *Latino Images in Film: Stereotypes, Subversion, and Resistance.* Austin: University of Texas Press, 2002.

15. Adrian Villegas. Personal interview. Austin, Texas, 21 February, 2009.

16. Danu Uribe and Karinna Pérez. Personal interview. Austin, Texas, 21 February, 2009.

17. Adrian Villegas. Personal interview. Austin, Texas, 21 February, 2009.

18. Ibid.

19. Ibid.

20. "Mex vs. Bc—Travel." Latino Comedy Project website, 20 September, 2008 www.LCP.org.

21. Adrian Villegas. Personal interview. Austin, Texas, 21 February, 2009.

22. Ibid.

WORKS CITED

Acosta, Belinda. "A Nation Laughs." *Austin Chronicle,* August 22, 2003, Arts.

Aldama, Arturo. "Comedy." *Encyclopedia of Latino Popular Culture.* Vol. 1. Edited by Cordelia Chávez Candelaria, Arturo Aldama, and Peter J. García. Westport, CT: Greenwood, 2004: 179–181.

Berg, Charles Ramírez. *Latino Images in Film: Stereotypes, Subversion, and Resistance.* Austin: University of Texas Press, 2002.

Davies, Christie. *Ethnic Humor from Around the World: A Comparative Analysis.* Bloomington: Indiana University Press, 1990.

Delgado, Fernando. "Moving Beyond the Screen: Hollywood and Mexican American Stereotypes." *Cultural Diversity and the US Media.* Edited by Yahya R. Kamalipour and Theresa Carilli. New York: State University of New York Press, 1998: 169–179.

Fregoso, Rosa Linda. *The Bronze Screen: Chicana and Chicano Film Culture.* Minneapolis: University of Minnesota Press, 1993.

García, James E. "Theater." *Encyclopedia of Latino Popular Culture.* Edited by Cordelia Chávez Candelaria, Arturo Aldama, and Peter J. García. Westport, CT: Greenwood, 2004: 839.

Hernández, Guillermo E. *Chicano Satire: A Study in Literary Culture.* Austin: University of Texas Press, 1991.

Ledesma, Alberto. "Narratives of Undocumented Mexican Immigration as Chicana/o Acts of Intellectual and Political Responsibility." *Decolonial Voices: Chicana and Chicano Cultural Studies in the 21st Century.* Edited by Arturo J. Aldama and Naomi H. Quiñonez. Bloomington: Indiana University Press, 2002: 330–354.

Limón, José. "Agringado Joking in Texas Mexican Society: Folklore and Differential Identity." *New Directions in Chicano Scholarship.* Edited by Ricardo Romo and Raymund Paredes. Santa Barbara: Center for Chicano Studies, University of California, Santa Barbara, 1984: 33–50.

———. "History, Chicano Joking, and the Varieties of Higher Education: Tradition and Performance as Critical Symbolic Action." *Journal of the Folklore Institute* 19:2–3 (1982): 141–166.

Lincoln, Kenneth. *Indi'n Humor: Bicultural Play in Native America.* New York: Oxford University Press, 1993.

List, Christine. "Self-Directed Stereotyping in the Films of Cheech Marin." *Chicanos and Film: Representation and Resistance.* Edited by Chon Noriega. Minneapolis: University of Minnesota Press, 1992: 183–194.

Lopez, George. *Alien Nation.* Rec. 1996. Oglio Records, 2005. CD.

Lovato, Roberto. "No Laughing Matter: Anti-Latino Humor Has Entered the Mainstream." *The Huffington Post,* November 28, 2007. Web. 15 October 2008.

Montejano, David, ed. *Chicano Politics and Society in the Late Twentieth Century.* Austin: University of Texas Press, 1999.

Mintz, Lawrence E. "Standup Comedy as Social and Cultural Mediation." *American Quarterly* 31:1 (1985): 71–80.

Noriega, Chon A. *Shot in America: Television, the State and the Rise of Chicano Cinema.* Minneapolis: University of Minnesota Press, 2000.

Paredes, Américo. "The Anglo-American in Mexican Folklore." *New Voices in American Studies.* Edited by Ray B. Browne, Donald M. Winkelman, and Allen Hayman. West Lafayette, IN: Purdue University Press, 1966: 113–128.

Pineo, Barry. "'Alien Nation': Making Cabrito of Immigration Scapegoating." *Austin Chronicle,* August 3, 2007, Arts.

Reyes, Israel. "Comedy and Humor." *Oxford Encyclopedia of Latinos and Latinas in the US.* New York: Oxford University Press, 2005: 381–388.

Reymundo, Alex. *Hick-Spanic.* Produced by Payaso Entertainment. Vivendi Entertainment, 2007. DVD.

———. *The Original Latin Kings of Comedy.* With Paul Rodriguez, Cheech Marín, Joey Medina, and Alex Reymundo. Produced by Payaso Entertainment. Paramount, 2002. DVD.

Rodríguez, Clara E., ed. *Latin Looks: Images of Latinas and Latinos in the US Media.* Boulder, CO: Westview Press, 1997.

Santa Ana, Otto. *Brown Tide Rising: Metaphors of Latinos in Contemporary American Public Discourse.* Austin: University of Texas Press, 2002.

———. "Did You Call in Mexican? The Racial Politics of Jay Leno Immigration Jokes." *Language in Society* 38:1 (2009): 23–45. *Academic OneFile.* Web. February 27, 2011.

TWENTY-THREE

(Re)Examining the Latin Lover: Screening Chicano/Latino Sexualities

DANIEL ENRIQUE PÉREZ

Marriage? Not for me.

RAMÓN NOVARRO

Chicano/Latino males have been caricatured, stereotyped, and eroticized on the screen throughout the history of US cinema and television. In *Latino Images in Film,* Charles Ramírez Berg highlights the most common stereotypes for these men: bandido, gang member, buffoon, and Latin lover.[1] Although several Chicana/o and Latina/o artists have created images that challenge these stereotypes, they nonetheless persist. Here, I am interested in examining the Latin lover archetype in US popular culture to demonstrate how this image has evolved over the years and how the Latin lover has always had queer characteristics. I trace the trajectory of the Latin lover, beginning with Ramón Novarro and ending with Mario López, and highlight queer aspects of his identity while also underscoring the influence he has had on male aesthetics and on facilitating non-normative discourses on gender and sexuality.

First, I am using the term "queer" to include a wide range of non-heternormative social and sexual behaviors. As most queer theorists argue, "queer" can include all aspects of identity that digress from heteronormativity. According to Alexander Doty, "'Queer' can now point to things that destabilize existing categories, while it is itself becoming a category—but a category that resists easy definition. That is, you can't tell just from the label 'queer' exactly what someone is referring to, except that it is something non-straight or non-normatively straight."[2] Thus, "queer" is not a synonym for "gay," although some may choose to use it as such. For David William Foster, the term "gay" elicits "a set of sexual identities that refer to a preference for same-sex erotic relations and to whatever overall subjectivity and lifestyle is necessary to ensure the legitimation and realization of homoerotic acts," whereas "queer" can be used to "signify the critique of the heterosexist paradigm."[3] Eve Kosofsky Sedgwick points out that "queer is a continuing moment, movement, motive—recurrent, eddying, troublant."[4] Evident in these definitions is that "queer" is not a singular or static category and that it can be used to describe a multiplicity of subject positions with antithetical relationships to things that are considered "straight" or normal. As I make clear, the Latin lover is not and has never been heteronormative.

I am not interested in labeling the Latin lover as gay, bisexual, heterosexual, or any other fixed category related to sexuality; none of these adequately permits the wide spectrum of ambiguities and contradictions that the Latin lover actually embodies to coexist. "Queer" includes a vast range of gendered positions, sexualized subjects, and erotic permutations. For example, having multiple sex partners, assuming unconventional sexual positions, having fetishes, and being bisexual can all be considered queer subject positions. I argue that the Latin lover is queer because his identity and his sexuality are constantly fluctuating and digressing from heteronormativity. His continuous movements along a gender and sexual continuum prevent his identity from being categorized in any fixed way; "queer" is the term that best describes these varied positions.

The Latin lover archetype has been prevalent in US cultural production for almost a century. If anything, the representation of the Latin lover in cultural production has increased exponentially since the 1920s: Desi Arnaz, Ricardo Montalbán, Fernando Lamas, Anthony Quinn, Jimmy Smits, Andy García, Antonio Banderas, Javier Bardem, John Leguizamo, Mario López, and Víctor Manuel Resendiz Ruis (the Mexican "Latin lover" of world wrestling) are all examples. The majority of these actors have participated in mainstream film and television projects, and their identities off-screen are very much intertwined with the Latin lover stereotype they portray on-screen. These men often continue to perform as Latin lovers in other parts of the public sphere: in commercials, interviews, guest appearances, and tabloids. Although social and economic imperatives may require them to sustain this image on- and off-screen, I maintain that they do have some agency concerning the image they project and the Latin lover identity they perform. Therefore, I propose that performing the Latin lover archetype be seen in and of itself as a form of Chicano/Latino cultural production.

The Latin lover image and subsequent craze emerged in the early twentieth century with the presence of two larger-than-life actors in silent films: Rudolph Valentino and Ramón Novarro.[5] In *Dangerous Men: Pre-Code Hollywood and the Birth of the Modern Man,* Mick LaSalle claims that it was during this era that the mainstream in the United States began to see the "primitive-type lover" as fantasy.[6] These men were portrayed as sexy and dangerous, sometimes naive and innocent and at other times evil and savage. Charles Ramírez Berg suggests that this stereotype was constructed around the Latin lover "as the possessor of a primal sexuality that made him capable of making a sensuous but dangerous—and clearly non-WASP—brand of love" (76). In general, the Latin lover identity is constructed around the synthesis of eroticism, exoticism, and danger; he is attractive and irresistible, but not to be trusted.

Physically, the Latin lover possesses three basic attributes: good looks, masculine features/behavior, and ethnic markings (whatever may be construed as "Latin"—dark hair, olive skin, a foreign accent). Furthermore, his public persona is typically constructed around women and compulsory heterosexuality: his unyielding pursuit of women and the women who find themselves irrevocably attracted to him. In *Hollywood's Latin Lovers,* Victoria Thomas suggests that the Latin lover "was the man your mother warned you about. He was the man women yearned to touch. He was the man other men yearned to become" (9). Besides at times being portrayed as a tough guy or bandit, the Latin lover was dangerous because he could hypnotize women into doing things they presumably did not want to do and, unlike his repressed Anglo counterpart, his sexuality was insatiable and unrestrained. As Thomas explains, he was a "creature of the erotic imagination" designed to appeal to men as well "because he represented their most ungentlemanly urges, unbound" (10). Thus, the Latin lover is designed to have a universal appeal, much like the male models Susan Bordo describes in "Beauty (Re)Discovers the Male Body," a highly masculine and erotic aesthetic that is designed to appeal to a variety of consumers: female and male, gay and straight.[7]

According to LaSalle, it was in the early twentieth century that men began developing a consciousness of themselves as sexy (3). Examples of the eroticized male body abound throughout the twentieth century in popular culture. Although Bordo suggests that the display of such bodies in the media and popular culture is primarily linked to consumerism, there is no doubt that the male body has become objectified. In *Stiffed: The Betrayal of the American Man,* Susan Faludi explains that at the core of an "ornamental culture" like ours lies a voyeuristic lens where sex is the "gold standard."[8] In an interview with Sam Shahid, an advertising executive who was instrumental in shaping the Adonis-like images found in numerous ads for companies such as Abercrombie & Fitch and Versace, she quotes him as saying, "Pecs are the new breasts now" and "Men have become *bigger* sex objects than women! They are the sex gods now! They have replaced women!" (506). Although his claims might appear to be exaggerated and over-generalized, they do highlight the male body as an erotic object, which is a queer phenomenon in and of itself because it rejects the masculine and male imperative that men always remain in control of their environment. As Faludi contends, "The man controlling his environment is today the prevailing American image of masculinity. A man is expected to prove himself not by being part of society but by being untouched by it, soaring above it" (10). In essence, the display of the male body as erotic "feminizes" the subject. Besides men's pecs being seen as a substitute for women's breasts, the erotic male body on display is stripped of agency as viewers gaze freely, fantasize about it, and, ultimately, consume it. Men as sex objects are queer in the way they assume a passive role in the exchange between viewer and subject. Eroticized male subjects have little to no control over their environment or the display of their bodies. Whether their bodies are intended to be consumed by male or female viewers is ultimately irrelevant because both types disrupt the active/passive binary by placing a man in a submissive position and thereby destabilizing normative gender and sexual roles.

I also argue that the eroticism of the Latin lover extends well beyond merely women yearning to touch him and other men wanting to be like him. Victoria Thomas fails to recognize that some women may fantasize about being a Latin lover themselves and endlessly seducing other women while some men may fantasize about being seduced by Ramón Novarro or Mario López. Moreover, their on- and off-screen persona often include homoerotic acts and other forms of non-heteronormative sexualities that make these lovers what I call "queer machos": men who possess the courage to be who they are without bowing completely to the heteronormative or ethnocentric precepts of the dominant culture.[9]

If one looks beyond the heterosexual facade, queer cultural signifiers abound in the Latin lover archetype. The Latin lover is by default non-heteronormative. His foreignness, promiscuity, and body are all sites for mapping queer identities. Because the Latin lover has been portrayed as someone who has an insatiable sexual appetite, there has existed a certain amount of ambiguity with respect to his sexual object choices. Moreover, one cannot disregard differing aspects of identity development. The Latin lover is not a one-dimensional character, although some might portray or imagine him as such. What he does outside of the Latin lover box must also be taken into consideration when examining his identity.

In *Mambo Mouth* (1991), John Leguizamo portrays Agamemnon, the host of *Naked Personalities*—a fictitious talk radio show. Agamemnon is the quintessential Latin lover, satirically portrayed. Throughout the performance piece, he delineates Latin lover traits: passion, omnipotence, dominance, and egocentrism. He claims he never falls in love and would never marry a woman: "Let's get something straight, I don't get involved with my women. I'm a short term guy, I don't fall in love, and I certainly am not going to marry you. The only thing you can count on me for is satisfaction, gratification, ecstasy, passion, decadence, debauchery, and, maybe, kissing."[10] The Latin lover not only disrespects women but often abuses them verbally, sometimes physically. Agamemnon instructs one male caller who is trying to woo a woman by showering her with gifts that he must stop the gift-giving, mistreat her, and sleep around in order to tip the scale his way and get what he wants. When Agamemnon reenacts a movie scene in which he played a typical Latin lover, he demonstrates how he slapped the woman he was trying to seduce when she kissed him, punishing her for breaking a Latin lover code: always be in control of the situation, always be the chingón. Although Leguizamo's portrayal of the Latin lover is intended to be farcical, it does summarize what could be considered features of the Latin lover: good-looking, hypersexual, "Latin," masculine, dominant, self-centered, irresistible, dangerous, womanizing, and disrespectful of or violent with women. All these traits have repeatedly been used to construct a Latin lover identity in popular culture since the early twentieth century. Although the Latin lover image that remains in the box can be seen as queer in and of itself, when the Latin lover steps outside the box, his identity remains rooted in queerness.

Many actors have assumed roles in film and television that displace their Latin lover identities. For example, many of those who have played the Latin lover part have also played gay and transsexual roles: John Leguizamo as Manny the Fanny in *Mambo Mouth* and as Chi-Chi Rodríguez in *To Wong Foo, Thanks for Everything! Julie Newmar* (1995), Antonio Banderas as Miguel in *Philadelphia* (1993), Mario López as Greg Louganis in *Breaking the Surface* (1997), and Javier Bardem as Reinaldo Arenas in *Before Night Falls* (2000). Playing such roles simultaneously disrupts and reiterates the Latin lover archetype. It disrupts it by reconfiguring the erotic coupling of the Latin lover with a man as opposed to a woman or by imaging him as a woman instead of as a man; it reiterates the Latin lover stereotype by confirming a pansexual or unrestrained sexuality. Furthermore, the actor's private life has often been under a gender and sexual lens, where questions abound regarding his sexual and love interests, male and female alike: Ramón Novarro was known to have sexual relationships with other men, and Mario López continues to joke and play gay as a response to the rumors that he is gay. All these non-heteronormative discourses contribute to a queer Latin lover identity in which ambiguities with respect to gender and sexuality proliferate. The Latin lover does not adhere to heteronormative gender or sexual codes. Although his identity is constructed around his erotic relationship with women, it is equally constructed around his inability to maintain a relationship with one woman. Moreover, his perceived foreignness permits his sexuality to veer significantly from heteronormativity by, for instance, having multiple partners, having savage sex in indiscriminate places, using little or exotic clothing (sarongs and turbans), and having sex scenes with S&M overtones. I now look at a couple of key Latin lover figures to demonstrate specific ways in which their identities are queer.

RAVISHING RAMÓN NOVARRO

Ramón Novarro (1899–1968) is mostly known for the title role he assumed in the most expensive silent film ever made: *Ben-Hur* (1925). Also known as "Ravishing Ramón," he was considered one of the most beautiful of the Latin lovers of his time. Novarro was born José Ramón Gil Samaniego in Durango, México; he was a cousin of the legendary Mexican actress Dolores del Río. Although he attempted to begin his acting career using his birth name, he was advised to change his name in order to advance his career, which proved to make his identity more ambiguous and mysterious. The roles that Novarro assumed ran the gamut with respect to cultural mappings: Frenchman, sheik, pagan, Jew, Italian, German, Polynesian, and Native American. As Victoria Thomas explains, Latin lovers were often cast in a variety of roles that were deemed ethnic or Latin:

> The sad truth is that Hollywood knew little about Latin cultures, histories or traditions. Latin characters were conceived and scripted with only a tourist's postcard-understanding of *Latinismo;* the results are as laughable as a souvenir sombrero (or simply insulting, depending upon your point of view). In addition to seducers, most Latin leading men have played rollicking gypsy-boys, mustachioed banditos, gangsters and other all-purpose scoundrels, roles which reinforced the notion of ethnic people as morally inferior. In this sense, Hollywood's Latin Lover was truly a man without a country. (12)

The Latin lover's exoticization is thus rarely linked to a particular nationality. Instead, it is his body that becomes the site of a compendium of markings that signify his otherness and his immorality. By being stripped of national origin, the Latin lover remains countryless, and his body is appropriated and eventually consumed by mass culture in ways that relegate him to an abject status. In essence, it is used the way many male models have been used in place of women as sex objects; it is displayed freely, eroticized, exoticized, and used to create fantasy narratives where the Latin lover fulfills the hidden desires of unsuspecting victims or of the viewers themselves.

In *Ben-Hur,* Novarro captivates his audience by displaying his body in a variety of scenes. At times he is bare-chested and wears a small wrap around his waist. In other scenes, his chest, biceps and muscular

FIG. 23.1. Francis Xavier Bushman (left) and Ramón Novarro in the original *Ben-Hur* (1925).

legs protrude from his Roman uniform (Figure 23.1). These revealing costumes played an important role in establishing Novarro as an erotic Other. Besides accentuating and displaying the actor's body, they function as disguises that mask certain aspects of the character's identity. For example, in his Roman uniform, the leading man's Jewish identity is concealed. In this way, the audience receives the cautionary message that the Latin lover is a man of many disguises—thereby reinforcing xenophobia.

After *Ben-Hur,* Novarro went on to play a wide range of characters from various racial, ethnic, religious, and nonreligious backgrounds. In *The Pagan* (1929), he plays the title role of a native Polynesian who wanders throughout a tropical island in a skimpy sarong (Figure 23.2). His role in this film is emblematic of the Latin lover as primitive and erotic. According to Mick LaSalle, at the time Novarro was at his pinnacle with respect to his physical features: "It was his apotheosis, providing him with a role that capitalized on his physical beauty and sex appeal and made a virtue of his intrinsic air of innocence" (8). Besides his physical

FIG. 23.2. Ramón Novarro as a Polynesian in *The Pagan* (1929).

beauty, the film made use of Novarro's singing talent. As his last silent film, the title theme song, "Pagan Love Song," plays throughout. Nevertheless, as Thomas suggests, "it was the star's skimpy sarong, not sound, which caused the epidemic of front-row fainting" (27). Novarro's voice, taut body, and good looks fed the fantasies of many of his viewers. As he is one of the first men to replace the female body as an erotic site in US popular culture and, in essence, become a sex object, his body is "feminized" and queered.

Besides the objectification of Novarro's body, his off-screen identity is also queer. In his biography on Novarro, *Beyond Paradise: The Life of Ramón Novarro,* André Soares discloses intimate details of the handsome film star's sexuality. He documents some of the sexual relationships Novarro had with other men, his escapades to male bordellos, and his brutal murder at the hands of two male hustlers. Clearly, Novarro's private life was quite different from the Latin lover image he projected on the screen. Unlike some gay male actors who resorted to "lavender marriages" in order to protect their image,[11] Novarro never married and made remarks dismissing or disparaging the institution of marriage or a long-term commitment to any woman. Although this could be considered a way to maintain a Latin lover image, knowing what we know now about his private life, we see that his rejection of serious intimate relationships with women was related more to his homosexuality than to maintaining a Latin lover reputation. I see this refusal to adhere to conventional norms as a queer macho stance. Novarro risked tarnishing his Latin lover image by not succumbing to a lavender marriage or playing the compulsory heterosexuality card. Although he did not live an out and proud gay lifestyle, his public persona challenged heteronormative thinking by engaging the public in non-heteronormative discourses, with the actor's queer lifestyle at the center of the discussion.

Novarro was devoted to his family, had a reputation for being a devout Catholic, and at times projected conservative views with respect to cultural values. This presented a conflict with his unconventional lifestyle. Plenty of rumors and evidence surfaced of his sexual encounters with other men; moreover, there were unsubstantiated rumors that he and Rudolph Valentino were lovers. Nevertheless, he did not marry and did not resort to projecting a heteronormative lifestyle off-screen. I must emphasize that Novarro did not handle these conflicts very well. Soares suggests that the internal conflicts plaguing Novarro contributed to his problems with alcohol, his risky sexual encounters, and, ultimately, his demise. All these issues tarnished his image, and his brutal murder at the hands of two male hustlers would become one of the events most difficult for the public to separate from his legacy.

Nevertheless, Novarro can be seen as a queer macho. He refused to allow heteronormativity to completely dictate parameters on his life. At a time when not succumbing to the projection of a heterosexual and heteronormative image in the public sphere was tantamount to committing career suicide, Novarro did not participate in a lavender marriage. What is more, the fact that so many rumors existed around his sexuality and his relationship with Rudolph Valentino—his fellow epitome of ideal male ethnic beauty in the United States—gives rise to a compendium of issues related to sexual identity politics. It also opens the door—or closet—to the ways in which Latin lovers can be queer and queer men can be Latin lovers.

MARIO LÓPEZ: ON BEING A SEX OBJECT AND THE RECONQUISTA OF BEAUTY

Although there are a number of celebrities I could use for a contemporary analysis of the Latin lover, I believe a look at Mario López (b. 1973) will suffice to show how the Latin lover image has remained virtually static in almost a hundred years and how he retains queer characteristics. Besides the fact that today the majority of images of the Latin lover are projected in color as opposed to black and white, not much has changed with respect to this archetype in the last century; privately and publicly, he continues to live in and outside of the Latin lover box, constantly challenging gender and sexual codes of behavior by his varied performances.

Mario López became a teen heartthrob while portraying A. C. Slater in *Saved by the Bell* (1989–1993). He has since gone on to participate in a number of film and television projects. There are a number of ways in which he and his body are queer. On a couple of occasions, he has played overt gay roles in films and on television: *Breaking the Surface: The Greg Louganis Story* and *Wetback Mountain*. The latter is a *Brokeback Mountain* parody that aired on *Mind of Mencia* in 2006 in which he and Carlos Mencía pretend to be gay in order to prevent others from suspecting they are Mexican immigrants (the video is available online). López continues to toy with the rumors that he is gay by playing the role in a farcical manner. In 2007, he appeared on *Mind of Mencia* to address rumors that he was gay. He takes part in what Carlos Mencía labels a "Carlos Slam," where celebrities do spoken poetry performance pieces. When Mencía introduces López, he claims that he wanted to give his friend the opportunity to address the rumors "because way too many people be talking shit about him."[12] As expected, the appearance is a ruse to continue to perplex and entertain the public. Nevertheless, López's performance piece is a poem titled "I Am Not Gay," which highlights the politics surrounding his identity:

> I'm not gay.
> What? You think I'm gay
> because I'm all in good shape
> because I can dance

and I got dimples?
Maybe you think I'm pretty.
Would you be willing to bet your wife on it?
Come on.
Just give me 5 minutes.
I'll do all sorts of gay stuff to her.
With my big gay tool.[13]

After his reading, López steps off the stage and approaches a male-female married couple who are obviously actors planted in the audience. He asks the man if the woman next to him is his wife; he then grabs her, stands her up, and kisses her passionately—demonstrating his virility and his ability to seduce unsuspecting women. After the lengthy, deep kissing, he throws her back in her seat, where she remains dazed by the incident. He then turns to the husband and says, "You're next, homes." The entire routine is designed to be comedic, but the politics at play have serious implications and are designed to maintain the ambiguity of his identity. López feels compelled to address the rumors that he is gay. To both dispel and confirm the rumors, he capitalizes on his Latin lover identity by daring men to leave their women with him for five minutes so that he can do "all sorts of gay stuff" to them, publicly demonstrating an erotic act with a woman, and threatening/teasing that the husbands are next. The performance is a way to maintain López's appeal to a wide range of erotic interests; the Latin lover remains pansexual and omnipotent, dangerous and irresistible. Regardless of whether the rumors are true, the fact that López plays gay roles both disrupts and reiterates his image as a Latin lover.

Another queer cultural reading one can do of López is around the homosocial relationship between his *Saved by the Bell* character, A. C. Slater, and Zack Morris (played by Mark-Paul Gosselaar). The two characters have an intimate relationship that has obvious homoerotic overtones. There is an excellent *Brokeback Mountain* parody of this relationship available online that summarizes their relationship in less than four minutes: *Brokeback by the Bell* (also known as *Saved by the Bell: Brokeback Style*).

Although the abovementioned roles are fruitful sites for conducting a queer analysis, I am interested in focusing on two areas with respect to the display of López's body in popular culture: (1) the way it is consumed by mass culture in a manner that relegates it to a submissive position and (2) the way his body and his looks have conquered the United States and white male beauty—what I am calling a *reconquista* of male beauty.

López's sculpted body and good looks have become icons of male beauty. He proudly displays his body and his muscles in various forms: from his naked Burt Reynolds–like pose in *People* (2008) to his shapely butt in *Nip/Tuck* (Season 4, 2006). He even has his own exercise book, *Mario Lopez's Knockout Fitness* (2008), where fans can gaze at him shirtless or in skimpy exercise attire under the guise of being interested in his diet and exercise program. Photos abound of Mario López's body in the media and on the Internet. At a young age, López began displaying his muscled body for the viewing public. It has been consumed by mass culture for almost twenty years and continues to entertain and intrigue viewers and his fans. Although López is an actor, dancer, musician, and exercise guru, the primary way he entertains is through the erotic display of his body. Both the media and the entertainer himself have long recognized that his beautiful body is a commodity to be exchanged for money, pleasure, and erotic interests.[14] Little commentary focuses on his acting ability, his talent as a musician, his ethnicity, or his intellect. Instead, his abs, chest, arms, and buttocks dominate the media attention he receives. Although one might imagine that López would like to be taken seriously as an actor and entertainer, he has been reduced to a sexual object, and his body has become the property of voyeurs—male and female alike. What is clear is that López has little control over the public and erotic display of his body. Although some might argue that he has some agency when it comes to such displays or underscore the actor's narcissistic traits, I believe there exists a socioeconomic imperative that obligates him to remove his clothing and display his body. In *People* (online, September 15, 2008) he was quoted as saying, "My shirtless photo-shoot days are behind me."[15] Nevertheless, he is repeatedly asked to do roles that require him to remove his shirt and other articles of clothing even though he may not feel comfortable having his body used in this way.[16] For example, in his photo shoot for *People* magazine he imitates Christopher Atkins's pose in *The Blue Lagoon* (1980) by wearing a primitive bikini that looks like a cross between Tarzan's underwear and a diaper. In the magazine he is quoted as saying, "This was the most embarrassing and uncomfortable picture to shoot . . . I felt like Mowgli

FIG. 23.3. Mario López as Mike Hamoui (left) and Julian McMahon as Christian Troy in *Nip/Tuck* (2006).

from *The Jungle Book*."[17] Thus, although at times he may not be comfortable displaying his body in highly provocative ways, he is compelled to do so in order to maintain his identity as a sex object, obtain roles, and continue to capitalize on his body. López's identity as a Latin lover has always been ambiguous. He has established a reputation as a man who can seduce others with his good looks, but he is also accused of being too pretty (his dimples often provoking special mention) and appearing gay. López has a body and a look now often associated with the gay macho clone.[18]

Undoubtedly, López's body is something to be admired and consumed. In *Nip/Tuck* (Season 4, 2006), López plays a fit and striking plastic surgeon named Mike Hamoui.[19] In a now famous scene, he is showering at the gym when Christian Troy (played by Julian McMahon)—another plastic surgeon and one of the leading characters of the series—walks into the room. Troy is immediately captivated by Hamoui and, through Troy's eyes, the viewer gets to ogle López's body—he soaps, poses, and caresses his naked body while the camera traces his muscles, abs, and buttocks. The background music is seductive, like that used in strip clubs or bathhouses. After Hamoui seduces Troy—not to mention us—with his naked dance, Troy takes the shower area right next to

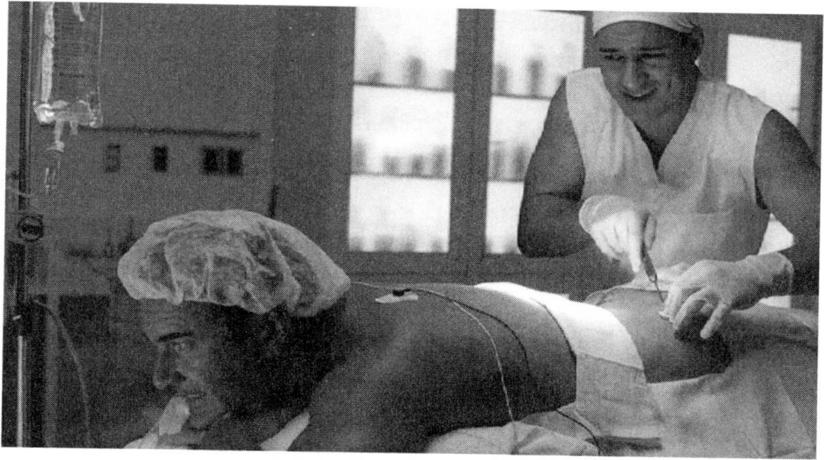

FIG. 23.4. Mario López (top) and Julian McMahon in *Nip/Tuck* (2006).

him even though they are the only two men in this part of the locker room and there are several other showers from which to choose. This brief scene is highly homoerotic. The two men engage in a conversation that centers on Hamoui's body while they stand naked in the shower and size one another up (Figure 23.3). The conversation begins when Hamoui catches Troy peering at his body and asks, "Are you staring at my dick?" To which Troy responds, "No, I'm checking out your ass." After a short dialogue related to their work, they return to the issue of Hamoui's body: his abs, his workout routine, his eating habits, and his sex life. Throughout the homoerotic exchange, Hamoui clearly comes out on top—so to speak. One of the last scenes of this episode is of Troy visiting Hamoui for plastic surgery. With all of its phallic imagery and implications of sodomy, the scene is of Troy lying facedown in Hamoui's procedure room, naked, with his buttocks exposed. Hamoui moves a suction tube in and out of Troy's love handles and buttocks, penetrating him while removing fat deposits (Figure 23.4). This erotic exchange between Hamoui and Troy is symbolic of the way López conquers other white males and male beauty in general. Although Julian McMahon is good-looking and a former soap opera star and model himself, López's good looks clearly trump McMahon's and, in effect, López colonizes his body. This reversal of roles between Chicano/Latino and Anglo men is even more evident in the *People* magazine photo shoot for which López posed in 2008.

In the June 30, 2008, issue of *People,* Mario López was named the Summer's Hottest Bachelor—beating out a number of primarily white men. Besides the fact that López was named the hottest bachelor out of a number of current heartthrobs, what I find most intriguing about the photo shoot is that López displaces a handful of historical white male heartthrobs. The theme of the photo shoot is that of restaging famous poses by sexy men. In all, he does five "sexy poses" that are labeled as such: "Sexy Pose 1," "Sexy Pose 2," and so on. Three of the poses are full-page pictures and two of them are centerfolds (images available online). The famous poses López restages are as follow: Burt Reynolds in *Cosmopolitan* (1972), Richard Gere in *American Gigolo* (1980), Marky Mark in the famous Calvin Klein ad (1992), Brad Pitt in *Thelma and Louise* (1991), and Christopher Atkins in *The Blue Lagoon.* The title of the "article" is somewhat misleading: "Mario Lopez Bares All!" Even though he is completely naked in the first pose, where he imitates Burt Reynolds's famous picture, his arm is placed between his legs, and his pubic hair is airbrushed away. The pictures are all obviously digitally altered. Nevertheless, López's beauty emanates from each one. For each photo, there is a small box with a picture of the original pose with bibliographic information. Mario's presence dominates each page while the original men—all Anglo—are reduced to a small corner and basically stripped of their respective titles as sex objects. In one fell swoop, López conquers a whole generation of sex objects (ranging from 1972 to 2008, if one includes the images of the current contenders for the title) and replaces their Anglo bodies with his prized Latino one.[20]

The *People* layout and the interview itself have several queer signifiers. In addition to the erotic display of his body, each photo is accompanied by a quote from López. With respect to the Marky Mark pose ("Sexy Pose 3"), he remarks, "My buddies tease me because I'm always running around my house in my underwear. I'm a boxer-briefs kind of guy. That's my deal."[21] If the vague "that's my deal" and being a "boxer-briefs kind of guy" identification is not evidence enough that López is queer, one should certainly question why he runs around in boxer-briefs when his "buddies" are "visiting." Moreover, with respect to his Brad

Pitt pose, "Sexy Pose 4," he says, "I loved *Thelma and Louise*, and Brad Pitt's role was iconic. Messing around with the blow dryer was fun."[22] It is impossible not to notice the resemblance to a gay macho clone in this image: shirtless, jeans unbuckled, and with long strands of hair protruding from his cowboy hat while holding a phallic symbol in his hand. As a phallic symbol, the rather large hair dryer can be considered a means of displaying that mysterious part of López's anatomy that remains behind the zipper that his unbuckled jeans invite the viewer to search for and fantasize about, but it can also represent Brad Pitt's phallus, or anyone else's. The use of the hair dryer in both the original Pitt scene and in López's photo replaces a potentially destructive phallic symbol—a gun—with something that is not as dangerous and is typically associated with female beauty.

Overall, López's body has been used to set a new standard of male beauty where the Chicano/Latino male body replaces the white male body as the paragon of male beauty. This aesthetic is now more mainstream than not. Whereas the original Latin lover identity was constructed around him as the ethnic other, López's body relocates the Latin lover to the center of popular culture; as a paragon of male beauty, it is presented to be consumed by mass culture. It is not so much the exotic other as the erotic ideal to which all men are compared and measured. López's body and looks are to be showcased and admired; he exudes an unrestrained and ambiguous sexuality. As such, the Latin lover remains within the parameters of a Latin lover identity while simultaneously possessing queer characteristics that shape a queer identity.

CONCLUSION: LATIN LOVERS ARE QUEER

The Latin lover has a long trajectory in popular culture in the United States. His identity has been shaped by his exotic and erotic markings and his limitless capacity to seduce others. He has been used to fulfill hidden fantasies, to establish male aesthetics, and to model illicit and unrestrained sexuality. To some degree, the Latin lover has not changed at all. As I have shown, he has always possessed queer characteristics; his gender and his sexuality have consistently fluctuated along a gender and sexual continuum in a way that prohibits his identity from being categorized in any fixed way. The Latin lover is not Latin or a lover but rather a product of the hidden desires of the people who have consumed him for almost a century.

ACKNOWLEDGMENT

The epigraph is from Victoria Thomas, *Hollywood's Latin Lovers: Latino, Italian and French Men Who Make the Screen Smolder* (Santa Monica, CA: Angel City Press, 1998), 34.

NOTES

1. Charles Ramírez Berg, *Latino Images in Film: Stereotypes, Subversion, Resistance* (Austin: University of Texas Press, 2002), 68–76.
2. Alexander Doty, *Flaming Classics: Queering the Film Canon* (New York: Routledge, 2000), 8.
3. David William Foster, *El Ambiente Nuestro: Chicano/Latino Homoerotic Writing* (Tempe, AZ: Bilingual Press/Editorial Bilingüe, 2006), 7.
4. Eve Kosofsky Sedgwick, *Tendencies* (Durham, NC: Duke University Press, 1993), xii.
5. Although Valentino and Novarro are often considered the first Latin lovers in film, Antonio Moreno made his debut in 1912, thereby predating the two. See Thomas, *Hollywood's Latin Lovers,* 37. I must also note that the Latin lover has roots in the infamous Don Juan character, which can be traced all the way back to seventeenth-century Spain; his Italian counterparts are Romeo and Casanova.
6. Mick LaSalle, *Dangerous Men: Pre-Code Hollywood and the Birth of the Modern Man* (New York: St. Martin's Press, 2002), 7.
7. Susan Bordo, "Beauty (Re)Discovers the Male Body," in *Beauty Matters,* ed. Peg Zeglin Brand (Bloomington: Indiana University Press, 2000), 122.
8. Susan Faludi, *Stiffed: The Betrayal of the American Man* (New York: Morrow, 1999), 505.
9. For more on queer machos, see Daniel Enrique Pérez, "Queer Machos: Gender, Sexuality, Beauty, and Chicano/Latino Men," in *Rethinking Chicana/o and Latina/o Popular Culture* (New York: Palgrave Macmillan, 2009).
10. John Leguizamo, *Mambo Mouth,* directed by Thomas Schlamme (New York: Island Visual Arts, 1992).
11. The expression "lavender marriage" came into use during the 1920s when Hollywood began imposing morality contracts. It refers to marriages of convenience orchestrated to protect an actor's reputation and career. The legendary William Hames is largely associated with the proliferation of lavender marriages after his career was destroyed for trying to live openly as a gay man; Rock Hudson is perhaps one of the most cited examples of a gay male actor who participated in a lavender marriage.
12. "Carlos Slam," *Mind of Mencia,* Comedy Central, season 3, episode no. 304. First aired April 15, 2007.

13. Ibid.

14. The Latin lover's body and looks have been used in this way for almost a century in US popular culture. López's identity as a sex object is not much different from that of Ramón Novarro, with the exception that López's look has become more mainstream than ethnic. He is not viewed as being exotic but as the purveyor of a beauty standard for all men.

15. Bryan Alexander, "Mario Lopez: No More Going Shirtless," *People* online (September 15, 2008), http://www.people.com/people/article/0,,20225738,00.html. This statement created a mini scandal that was called Chesthairgate. Pictures surfaced of him with chest hair. Why was this a scandal? Well, just a few weeks earlier when asked in *People* if he manscaped (shaved parts of his body), he responded, "Not at all. That's the Latin Indian blood in me. My dad has a hairy chest, but I don't" (Antoinette Coulton and Monica Rizzo, "Mario Lopez Bares All!" *People* 69, no. 25 [June 30, 2008], 62).

16. In a reprisal role as Dr. Mike Hamoui in *Nip/Tuck,* he appears as a dominatrix, in a corset, panties, and garter (Season 6, Episode 3, first aired October 28, 2009). In 2009, López appeared on the *Ellen DeGeneres Show* to promote his children's book (*Mud Tacos!*). Within a few minutes, he was shirtless and being dunked in a water tank, presumably to raise money for cancer (Season 7, Episode 32, first aired October 21, 2009).

17. Coulton and Rizzo, "Mario Lopez Bares All!" 60.

18. For an analysis of the gay macho clone, see Michael P. Levine, *Gay Macho: The Life and Death of the Homosexual Clone* (New York: New York University Press, 1998); Michelangelo Signorile, *Life Outside: The Signorile Report on Gay Men: Sex, Drugs, Muscles, and the Passages of Life* (New York: Harper Perennial, 1997).

19. Notice the erasure of his Latino identity. Once again, the Latin lover becomes countryless. My best guess is that the producers assigned him Middle Eastern markings in order to make his character more believable. Who ever heard of a Latino medical doctor, right?

20. This role reversal is especially interesting if one considers that Ramón Novarro's leading role in the original *Ben-Hur* (1925) was taken over by Charlton Heston in 1959.

21. Coulton and Rizzo, "Mario Lopez Bares All!" 57.

22. Ibid., 68–69.

REFERENCES

Alexander, Bryan. "Mario Lopez: No More Going Shirtless." *People* online (September 15, 2008): http://www.people.com/people/article/0,,20225738,00.html.

Ben-Hur: A Tale of the Christ. Directed by Fred Niblo, written by Carey Wilson and Bess Meredyth, starring Ramón Novarro. MGM, 1925.

Berg, Charles Ramírez. *Latino Images in Film: Stereotypes, Subversion, Resistance.* Austin: University of Texas Press, 2002.

Bordo, Susan. "Beauty (Re)Discovers the Male Body." In *Beauty Matters,* edited by Peg Zeglin Brand, 112–154. Bloomington: Indiana University Press, 2000.

Breaking the Surface: The Greg Louganis Story. Directed by Steven Hilliard Stern, written by Alan Hines, Greg Louganis, and Eric Marcus, starring Mario López. Green/Epstein Productions, 1997.

Brokeback by the Bell. Created by Sean Connolly, Michael Hill, Chris Mongilia, and John Smith, 2006: http://www.youtube.com/watch?v=yHLr5AY15f4.

"Carlos Slam." *Mind of Mencia.* Season 3, episode no. 304. Comedy Central. First aired April 15, 2007.

Coulton, Antoinette, and Monica Rizzo. "Mario Lopez Bares All!" *People* 69, no. 25 (June 30, 2008): 54–63.

Doty, Alexander. *Flaming Classics: Queering the Film Canon.* New York: Routledge, 2000.

Faludi, Susan. *Stiffed: The Betrayal of the American Man.* New York: Morrow, 1999.

Foster, David William. *El Ambiente Nuestro: Chicano/Latino Homoerotic Writing.* Tempe, AZ: Bilingual Press/Editorial Bilingüe, 2006.

LaSalle, Mick. *Dangerous Men: Pre-Code Hollywood and the Birth of the Modern Man.* New York: St. Martin's Press, 2002.

Levine, Martin P. *Gay Macho: The Life and Death of the Homosexual Clone.* New York: New York University Press, 1998.

Lopez, Mario, and Jeff O'Connel. *Mario Lopez's Knockout Fitness.* New York: Rodale, 2008.

Mambo Mouth. Directed by Thomas Schlamme, performed and written by John Leguizamo. Island Visual Arts, 1992.

Nip/Tuck. Season 4, episode no. 403. FX Networks. First aired September 19, 2006.

The Pagan. Directed by W. S. Van Dyke, written by Dorothy Farnum, starring Ramón Novarro. MGM, 1929.

Sedgwick, Eve Kosofsky. *Tendencies.* Durham, NC: Duke University Press, 1993.

Signorile, Michelangelo. *Life Outside: The Signorile Report on Gay Men: Sex, Drugs, Muscles, and the Passages of Life.* New York: Harper Perennial, 1997.

Soares, André. *Beyond Paradise: The Life of Ramon Novarro.* New York: St. Martin's Press, 2002.

Thomas, Victoria. *Hollywood's Latin Lovers: Latino, Italian and French Men Who Make the Screen Smolder.* Santa Monica, CA: Angel City Press, 1998.

Wetback Mountain. Mind of Mencia. Season 2, episode no. 201. Comedy Central. First aired March 22, 2006.

TWENTY-FOUR

Rumba's Democratic Circle in the Age of Legal Simulacra

BERTA JOTTAR-PALENZUELA

The procession to the rumba in Central Park starts at West Seventy-second Street, and the first spiritual stop is John Lennon's memorial, "Imagine." Each Sunday, fans adorn the shrine with flowers, candles, and idiosyncratic offerings as devotees play acoustic guitars, flutes, and, occasionally, drums. The rumba procession continues past Asian masseuses promising full relaxation in twenty minutes and Daniel Webster's bronze statue reminding us: "Liberty and union, now and forever, one and inseparable." At this point, you can hear the rumba drums; on your right, a jazz band plays along West Drive. As you walk toward Cherry Hill fountain, the rumba pulse fuses with the sounds of the pan-African djembe circle at Bethesda Terrace. Continue toward the lake, where the Colombian opera singer navigates his gondola through the Victorian landscape and the tourist economy surrounding it. Down the hill, near the bow bridge, is where you'll find the rumba circle.

The rumba community has contributed to this idyllic landscape since the early 1970s, when a group of mostly Puerto Rican aficionados began gathering by the lake to perform rumba music with a *bomba* and *salsa* tinge. Since then, Central Park rumba has been the public and cultural epicenter of New York City's pan-Latina/o and Afro-Latina/o communities.[1] However, with the inauguration of the Giuliani administration in 1994, the increased presence of police officers (the Plainclothes Anti-Crime Unit and undercover agents), particularly at the rumba, disturbed this eclectic environment. The authorities' reasons for patrolling the rumba varied and developed over time, from their requirement of a Special Events permit to the confiscation of the rumberos' drums on the basis of "unreasonable noise" charges.[2] However, Giuliani's Zero Tolerance regime also galvanized a series of responses by the rumba community in Central Park. Two particular gestures highlight the significance of this conflict: Jesús Guerra's unwillingness to stop playing his drum in spite of the police's demands, resulting in his "fake" arrest, and León Felipe Larrea's symbolic action of wearing of a gas mask while holding up a handwritten sign stating, "I Love rumba, and Columbia please!" In the pages that follow, I will employ a post-structuralist theoretical analysis of Zero Tolerance to illuminate the links between performance, the "Quality of Life" politics of deterrence, and how the predominantly Afro-Latino/a rumberos in Central Park creatively resisted the repressive measures employed to silence them.[3]

ORIGINS AND CONTEMPORARY MANIFESTATIONS

Rumba is a Cuban expressive culture based on singing, dancing, and a polyrhythmic music structure executed with *tumbadoras* (cylindrical membranophone drums) or *cajones* (wooden boxes of different dimensions). Rumba is one of the earliest, if not the first, native popular music genres in Cuba. Rumba manifests organically as a drum circle and has three variants: *yambú, guaguancó,* and *columbia*. Drumming and singing are predominantly male practices; women mostly participate by dancing and singing.

Rumba columbia, the form I discuss here, is a style mostly performed by men. It originated in the Cuban countryside, in the rural areas located in Matanzas and the surrounding provinces like Unión de Reyes, Jovellanos, and Colón. According to the most important living columbia singer in Havana, Miguel Angel Mesa "Aspirina," rumba columbia was first sung in the Port of Matanzas. In his version of the story, the first four slaves brought to Cuba were of Congolese, Mandinga, Lucumí, and Calabar origin. One day, the tide was very low in Havana's port, so the ship had to be redirected to the Port of Matanzas. At that time, the Port of Matanzas was called Columbia's Port, a name that was kept until 1956. Miguel Angel told me that, of the four slaves, the

Congolese was the one who began singing the columbia at lunchtime in the *portales* (Spanish and Moorish style arches surrounding an enclosed outdoor market). During colonial times, columbia lyrics became a way for slaves to depict their labor conditions. Different from the guaguancó, a rumba that developed in the early 1900s from the *Coros de Clave* (choral ensembles) within Havana's urban areas, rumba columbia signals a particular labor force and environment—the countryside, the sugar mill industry, and the ports where stevedores continued to entertain themselves playing rumba during their recess.[4]

The rumba is a circle that produces difference as part of its internal sovereignty. Like other African drum circles, the rumba circle is perceived as a space of continuity, infinity, and spirituality. All participants must promote and maintain a call-and-response dialectic within rumba musical and kinesthetic codes. The circle's creative tension also promotes a competitive energy among dancers, singers, and percussionists. In rumba columbia, men challenge one another via the singing of *puya,* a game of provocation in which the rumbero manipulates verbal symbols against his opponent without losing his cool, or the dancer proves the uniqueness of his choreography by creatively incorporating everything from acrobatics to the use of props like handkerchiefs, glass bottles, chairs, and knives. This elaboration is based on skillful improvisation and profound knowledge of rumba's ethics, aesthetics, and spiritual roots. Indeed, difference is constituted by individual dexterity based on improvisation; mastering improvisation is what makes one free and independent. Rumba's competitive circle sustains a democratic longing based on equal participation, skillful improvisation, and the continuity of difference. In Central Park, however, difference functions not only within the circle's sonic space but also as a racialized space/practice to the outside viewer.

In New York, the present-day rumba community includes a predominantly male group of Afrocubans who migrated to the United States in the 1980s Mariel exodus and the 1994 balsero exodus. However, the combination of other Afro-descendant and mestizo-origin Dominicans, Puerto Ricans, Nuyoricans, and Colombians with African Americans, Jews, and even Japanese rumberos or aficionados outnumbers Central Park's Cuban community.[5] Thus, as Miguel Angel's story recounts, just as rumba columbia became a concrete secular contact zone for different African territories in colonial Cuba, Central Park rumba also functions as a contemporary contact zone for a larger multi-ethnic Afro-Latin diaspora. Indeed, during the Giuliani administration, the rumba circle in Central Park became a paradigm in the creation of Latino alliance based on difference.

THE GIULIANI ERA: QUALITY OF LIFE AND POLICING DIFFERENCE

Major Rudolph Giuliani's "Quality of Life" initiative established an intense drive to privatize public life in the name of public order; its goal was to eradicate any sign of "visual disorder" that might contribute to New York City's "urban decay." By focusing on the control of public space, Giuliani sought to protect the interests of affluent taxpayers and corporations.[6] Therefore, it became paramount to erase any public signs of "visual disorder" (such as "deviant" subjects) to sustain New York City's property value for landowners. The maintenance of a visible public order and, hence, a "safer city" would also attract tourism and external revenues. The city implemented its Zero Tolerance policing regime via the display of visual signs, from the New York Transit Authority's massive poster campaign to the visible increase of police presence in public spaces such as parks, neighborhoods, and beaches. The initiative reimplemented Prohibition-era legislation (like the 1926 cabaret laws) and zoning regulations, and it increased the punishments for minor offenses such as "unreasonable noise," "disorderly behavior on park department property," and "littering."[7]

The immediate precedent for the Quality of Life initiative is the "broken windows theory," which proposes a causal link "between physical disorder and actual crime." Therefore, the argument is that "policing lower-level public disorders—loitering, drug use, gang activity, and public drinking—best diminished the fear and social disorder that allowed more serious crimes to flourish."[8] The broken windows theory merges "crime" with "disorder problems" on a neighborhood level, and the most visible subjects affected by the Quality of Life initiative have been the homeless, squatters, panhandlers, and squeegee-ers—"persons who approach vehicles in traffic."[9] The Quality of Life policies of public cleaning and embellishment also resulted in the criminalization of public African American aesthetic practices like graffiti-writing and rapping and in the eviction of rumba from Central Park for two consecutive years. Thus, for the city, reclaiming public space (the streets, parks, and the subway) came down to controlling and policing particular subjects whose public performance and presence threatened the administration's definition of order. Most of the charges against these minorities were "disorderly conduct" misdemeanors such as "unreasonable noise."

However, the Quality of Life interpretation of the broken windows theory deviates from the concept's original intent. Rosen argues that the broken windows theory was not designed to serve as a tool of intolerance but rather the opposite. James Wilson and George Kelling, the authors of the broken windows theory, "urged cities to use quality-of-life offenses to increase police discretion, not to eliminate it."[10] Contrary to Giuliani's Zero Tolerance, the original conception of the broken windows theory considers arrest a last resort. However, once applied under the Zero Tolerance regime, the theory was used to create criminals out of turnstile jumpers, marijuana smokers, and minorities. Indeed, these subjects' public arrest and frisking became a public spectacle that functioned discursively and theatrically as proof and promise of Zero Tolerance's efficacy.

Baudrillard's theory of simulation situates simulacrum in a relationship to power (and the law), reproduction (via industrialization), and multiplication (at the genetic or atomic level). Here I argue that these former modes were mastered by Giuliani's Quality of Life initiative via both the reproduction of visual signs of authority (from posters to police presence) and the multiplication of low-level offenses fines and summons as symptoms of "real crime." In other words, the power of the law and Zero Tolerance is constituted through simulation, a series of policing models based on reproduction, multiplication, and serialization that constitute criminality as sign and symptom. Thus, there is no real criminal or real crime behind the "scene of the crime," only a simulation with real symptoms: summons, detentions, and the confiscation of drums. Under the Quality of Life regime, reproduction also functions at the discursive level of consensus-making as, in fact, public opinion sustained the need for Zero Tolerance. Thus, Zero Tolerance builds momentum with the multiplication of simulated signs and symptoms of "crime."

THE ARREST OF THE DRUMMER IN THE AGE OF LEGAL SIMULACRUM

The day Jesús was arrested was like any other Sunday of rumba in the Park, except that some regulars were already expecting the police. Indeed, the police arrived before sunset. Two officers approached the rumberos and told them they had to stop the music if they did not have a special event permit.[11] Jesús, a Marielito who was playing the quinto solo drum, decided not to stop. He argued that on several occasions, other individuals had applied for the permit but were unsuccessful at obtaining it because the rumba's cultural specificity and practice did not qualify as a "Special Event." The musicians did not utilize any amplification device, the rumba circle was not an organized event, nobody was responsible for its performance, and the participants did not comprise a non-profit organization. Jesús further argued that, in reality, the police were trying to eradicate the rumba community because the American Museum of Natural History needed the area to promote their own exhibits—ironically, their ongoing show "Spirits in Steel" dedicated to Kalabari Masquerade.[12] Jesús decided to continue playing, and the police called for reinforcements. Jesús (together with his instruments) ended up handcuffed inside a patrol car. The rumba stopped abruptly. Everyone present was angry, indignant, shocked, and worried about Jesús's future. Why did we have to ask for permission to play a drum? I called Jesús later that night to make sure he had been freed. In our conversation, he stated that at the precinct, all they did was confiscate his drums and fine him for "disorderly conduct." Jesús even claimed he sold the officers some original Cuban cigars.

This scenario and its traces (the summons given to Jesús that Sunday) show how the Quality of Life initiative had legally defined the rumba social gathering as a low-level offense (disorderly conduct) on the basis of rumba's content: drumming.[13] Through this incident, Jesús became part of a broader history of persecution against African expressive culture and drums. In Cuba, drums have historically signaled the presence and therefore unlawful congregation and practices of African people.[14] Ironically, those criminalized drums became part of Havana's contemporary display of Cuban instruments in the "captive drums" section of the Museum of Music in Havana.[15]

For the Dutch, English, and French colonies settled in the United States and the Caribbean, the use of African drums also signaled delinquency, if not insurgency.[16] The drums' spiritual and communicative force became evident; burials and dances were prohibited or highly surveilled because of their "dangerous consequence."[17] Accounts such as the 1739 Stono Rebellion in South Carolina that described slaves marching triumphantly with "drums beating and colors flying" also increased the fear of slave congregations.[18] In New York City, beginning in the late 1600s, various laws were passed to regulate slaves,[19] or to "prevent insurrection," mandating that no more than three slaves could assemble or meet in public areas without their masters' consent.[20] On June 29, 1812, a series of regulations for "Preventing & Suppressing Riots" and to "preserve the peace of the City" stated that "it shall not be lawful for any person or persons to beat a Drum or play a Fife within any of the Streets of this City at any time between eight OClock in the Evening and four OClock in the Morning throughout the Year . . . And be it further ordained that every person contravening this ordinance shall be considered a disorderly person."[21] Hazzard-Gordon argues that the prohibition of drums in the United States eventually affected and altered the expressive culture of black people.[22]

The rumberos' persecution on the basis of playing (Afro-descendant) drums in Central Park illustrates the ongoing perceived threat of unregulated gatherings of people of African descent. Furthermore, Jesús's "fake" arrest demonstrates how Zero Tolerance and Quality of Life policies simulate crime in order to create a social consensus that justifies Zero Tolerance policing as symptomatic of crime. Indeed, Baudrillard argues that simulation threatens the difference between "true" and "false," between "real" and "imaginary"; he defines simulacrum as that which produces symptoms that appear to be real.[23] For instance, he analyzes the difference between a man who is sick versus one who simulates being sick. Baudrillard questions whether the simulator is "ill or not" if he produces "true" symptoms.[24]

In an example that is related, yet almost inverse to Jesús's experience, Baudrillard invokes a person who simulates being a thief in a department store. Baudrillard proposes that the "simulator" will be sanctioned and repressed as though he were a real thief. Again, if simulation becomes "real" through its production of symptoms, the police will react to the simulator as if he were a thief. Thus the "fake" thief will find himself in the realm of the real, because the real "devour[s] every attempt at simulation, [in order] to reduce everything to some reality—that's exactly how the established order is, well before institutions and justice come into play."[25] However, in Jesús's case, it is the police officer's performance of institutionalized simulation that establishes "real order" and justifies Zero Tolerance. Still, Jesús's ersatz arrest illustrates Baudrillard's assertion that simulation "is infinitely more dangerous . . . since it always suggests, over and above its object, that law and order themselves might really be nothing more than a simulation."[26]

This "fake" arrest could be seen as a warning meant to make an example out of Jesús and to show other rumberos what could happen if they also disobeyed police orders. This brings up the question of what the relationship between the warning and the simulation actually is. The idea of performing an example of what would happen relates to Augusto Boal's theorization of rehearsal. In his "poetics of the oppressed," theater production functions as the means for people to mobilize and act consciously. Rehearsal becomes a space of action, a place through which the relationship between spectator and actor collapses and the audience members become the performers.[27] Indeed, the difference between action and rehearsal also collapses, preparing the people/actors for future action. If the phony arrest was a rehearsal of possible outcomes, indeed acting out what would happen in the real future, there remains the assumption that this action is training for the real, for what "would happen" next.

But Baudrillard complicates this future, arguing that simulation is non-referential to any origin; in other words, the real is only resurrected as a system of signs that act to substitute the real. Simulation is not a representation of the present or the future real because, on the contrary, there is no real or original behind it, as "simulation . . . is the generation by models of a real without origin or reality: a hyperreal."[28] Following this logic, Jesús's "fake" arrest is the hyperreal, a model that assumes no original, no real crime—unless the above-mentioned colonial laws are still effective. In other words, the reality of Jesús's criminality only manifests with the continuity of symptoms, the ongoing criminalization of the rumberos/as' community at large, and the subsequent eradication of the rumba performance from Central Park for the following two years.

However, contrary to Baudrillard's understanding of simulation as that which challenges the reality of the law and power, Zero Tolerance policing techniques demonstrate that simulation is already an operational function of New York City's legal regime, which has indeed mastered its condition as simulacrum.

Indeed, this fake scenario of arrest is the *expressive* mode of legal simulacra. Harcourt (via Foucault) has similarly argued that these policing strategies constitute the disorderly and therefore criminal subject: there is no reality behind this subject's categorization. The category of the disorderly is itself a reality produced through the methods of policing. It is a reality shaped by the policy of aggressive misdemeanor arrest, the product of a technique of punishment that combines several different historical modalities, including classical strategies of excessive force and modern disciplinary mechanisms like surveillance and spatial control.[29] Thus, Jesús's fake arrest is part of the city's operations. His "detention" is the simulation of the law in action. Thus Jesús (as a sign) becomes the cause and effect of Zero Tolerance. Jesús becomes the "ends and means," and visual authority also becomes the "ends and means" for the Quality of Life initiative to become real and necessary. Jesús's categorization as "criminal" constitutes a statistical presence and has material consequences.

However, Tanya Erzen argues that no "statistic[s] have proven that arresting people for drinking beer in public, for instance, reduces murders."[30] Michael Tonry's investigation agrees and states that despite its popularity, it is "almost certainly wrong" that tougher crime sentencing and hard policing (such as the three-strikes and zero tolerance rules) have resulted in the decline of crime rates.[31] But Jesús's fake arrest did play into the detention of "people accused of even minor misdemeanor offenses for the purpose of verifying their identities and whether any outstanding warrants exist."[32]

Consequently, Zero Tolerance produces consensus and functions as the hyper model of security. The over-determined argument that "more police in the street equals more security" justifies both the need for Zero Tolerance and a further increase in summonses.[33] Indeed, the success of Zero Tolerance is based on its generative multiplication of summonses, suspects, criminals, and disorderly rumberos. They all become the meaning rather than the product of the initiative.[34] They become expressive proof of the reality that simulation produces. This generative multiplication becomes a mode within the serial production of legitimate order.[35]

But Jesús's hyperreal arrest in this system of Zero Tolerance deterrence complicates Baudrillard's argument that "we no longer live in a society of spectacle," as he situates spectacle only in relation to mass media, and for him, TV was no longer spectacular. However, Guy Debord (1967) argues that "spectacle is not a collection of images, but a social relation among people, mediated by images."[36] Thus, I am arguing that Zero Tolerance policing techniques are both spectacular and expressive once the rumba enters the broken window theory logic of "visual disorder" as actual crime. Rumba's "criminality" is the result of police spectacle (their public use of space, force, and high-tech surveillance machinery). Spectacle in this case is performative; it constitutes the real through the repetition of the same normative relations as symptoms: constant police presence, visual order, and spectacular detentions.

Rumba's "criminality" is also the result of an expressive manifestation of the law. Thus, the law, as a simulation or a space constituted via its generative and constitutive modes of repetition, functions as a matrix between police spectacle and rumba's hyper-real criminality. Baudrillard's theory of simulation is useful in thinking through the law's simulation only if understood in relationship to simulation's performativity, the standardized actions that simulation requires. Thus, the law is a performative apparatus because in its repetitive constitution of the "legal real," it produces material symptoms (the numerical increment of summonses, suspects, criminals, and prisons) and real objects of the law—real criminals, economic punishment, and the confiscation of more drums.[37] Thus, Jesús's willingness to enter the Zero Tolerance spectacle evidences the performative aspect of the Law as simulation. Simulation acts upon and constitutes the criminals—their identity, history, containment, and their punishment and possible future. Simulation, as a performative legal space, constitutes the real as a regulatory system in which symptoms have material and discursive consequences. While Jesús made evident the simulations of the legal apparatus by performing within it as a sign and a symptom, other rumba participants appropriated other signs and symptoms, rerouting them into a performance of difference and sovereignty.

SECOND RESPONSE: RESIGNIFYING THE SIGNS OF SIMULATION

The Sunday after Jesús's "arrest," the politicized gestures of protest continued. León Felipe showed up at the rumba wearing a gas mask and carrying a handwritten sign stating, "I Love rumba, and Columbia please!" León Felipe's gas mask reminds us how toxic and dangerous the policy really was. Like masks in general, the gas mask had its own potential for humor, though in this case it was quite dark. Certainly, given the statistical increase of police brutality during Giuliani's administration, it was not meant as a joke.[38] The brutal sexual assault of Abner Louima, the police repression of the first NYC Million Man March participants, and the murders of both Amadou Diallo and the mentally impaired Gidone Busch at the hands of police death squads provided the backdrop for León Felipe's grim gesture. In 1999, an annual survey by Latino New Yorkers concluded, "for the first time since 1993, crime is not the number one problem for all Latinos . . . Now the number one problem is police brutality."[39] The city's atmosphere was indeed toxic, particularly for men of color, because the police's racial profiling tactics systematically targeted them.[40] As León Felipe told me, "that's why we were already expecting this situation because we aren't the ones who commit the offense. It's them. We know their brutality; they always use tear gas, clubs, nightsticks. . . ."[41]

León Felipe's gas mask was not a poetic prop but a material defense mechanism highlighting the presence of police brutality in New York City's Quality of Life campaign. Furthermore, his written utterance, "I Love rumba, and Columbia please" functioned in two registers: the visual (as image), and the verbal (as speech act). As an image, León Felipe's sign both mimicked and contested the Quality of Life "anti-crime" signs and posters placed in subways, train stations, and public areas. Rhetorically, while the gas mask he was wearing functioned as the literalization of Zero Tolerance, the "I Love rumba" sign served as a performative utterance. It was neither a recitation nor a description but an action, a speech act in which "I Love" meant "I do" as the reaffirmation of the existence of the self, as an assertion against legal, discursive, and social restrictions.[42] The performative value of this utterance remained, even when transcribed in its written form. León Felipe's sign occupied a space somewhere between political poster, commercial slogan, and portable graffiti.

The performative sign, "I Love rumba, and Columbia please!" also co-opted the serial element of simulation via the art of sampling, an interventionist gesture of recycling and appropriating of the ubiquitous, commercialized slogan "I Love NY," which is replicated endlessly on tourist souvenirs. León Felipe's sign called attention to the way the Zero Tolerance campaign opened spaces for some (paying tourists and "lawful" citizens of New York) while closing them off for others (immigrants and minorities perceived as "disturbing the peace"). Furthermore, this portable graffiti illustrated the poetics of rumba columbia's resistance: To love New York is to love rumba, and to love rumba is to love NY in its performance of difference.

Through appropriation, León Felipe's sign unsettled the multiplicative force of the Zero Tolerance signs and their production of fear against difference. His sign subverted the rhetoric of the ideal and the logic behind Quality of Life: that New York City is the capital of the world and the economy, and that Zero Tolerance's pro-active policing was necessary in the fight against New York City's urban "decay." Moreover, the appropriation of "I Love NY" disrupted the law's seriality of the "same" as "order" and "difference" as "visual disorder." León Felipe's sign was not only a response to previous and future encounters with the police but an internal call and *puya* to the present rumberos/as to uphold columbia's ethics of skillful competition and integrity. Thus, within Central Park's rumba, León Felipe's poetic gesture and written statement ("Columbia please!") conveyed a collective call for the unification of rumberos in a struggle between rumberos and policemen and against a patriarchal rule that has historically vilified the African drum's secular and religious power.

León Felipe's call was not a nationalist mourning but an appeal for the unification of New York City rumberos in an Afro-Latino alliance of those who belong to the various nationalities facing US neo-colonial politics (Puerto Rico, the Dominican Republic, and Cuba). "I Love rumba" was a call for post-national, diasporic subjectivities of the Américas to resist the Quality of Life campaign, itself an ideological model based on the marriage of corporate and public interests via the privatization of the "public good." León Felipe's call for a post-national space must be understood historically. Given his experience with labor unions in Colombia, his poetic call invoked a multinational *cabildo* politics that called upon and retrieved the historical force that oppressed colonies had wielded in their demand for independence during Spanish colonialism.[43] León Felipe's poetic call for cabildo politics opposed the subjugation of rumba's diasporic performance by Afro descendants and mestizos.

His poetic gesture also reminds us that rumba continues to be an example of transculturation, the cultural and racial intermingling of various ethnic groups from West Africa and Spain in Cuba, now replaying itself in New York as a multinational, interethnic space based on the interaction and negotiation of peoples from several post- and neocolonial locations. Rumba functions as a matrix in which conflict and resistance intersect here and there, now and then. The spirits of the four slaves performing columbia during their lunch break were being channeled in the here and now. They were present. Under the Giuliani regime, to state "I love rumba" was also to proclaim "I Love NY." León Felipe's sign takes the poetics of rumba into a performative place where the written redefines "NY" as "rumba," a circle of differences right in Central Park, the heart of New York City. Thus, while Zero Tolerance tried to eradicate rumba's cultural practice with its own spectacles, Jesús's and León Felipe's interventions articulated not an "I" but a "we," an intercultural sphere in which rumba becomes a post-national poetic praxis and a utopic project articulated through the performance of difference and sovereignty. Thus the Central Park rumba continues to this day in spite of the City's legal simulations.

NOTES

1. To read more about Central Park rumba's pan-Latino formation, see my Ph.D. advisor Diana Taylor's article "Hemispheric Performances" in *The Archive and the Repertoire: Performing Cultural Memory in the Americas* (Durham, NC: Duke University Press, 2003): 266–278.

2. Unreasonable noise is defined as "any excessive or unusually loud sound that disturbs the peace, comfort or repose of a reasonable person of normal sensitivity or injures or endangers the health or safety of a reasonable person of normal sensitivity . . ." Regulated Uses. Noise; Musical Instruments; Sound Reproduction Devices New York City Department of Parks & Recreation Regulations, sec. 1–05(d) (1). www.nycgovparks.org.

3. Although migrants or exiles tend to identify themselves by their countries of origin, for the purpose of this chapter I use the Afro-Latina/o conceptual framework to categorize the existing difference yet common history of Afro-descendants from the former Spanish colonies. However, for other definitions of Latinidad

based on a common heritage of colonialism, mestizaje, and transculturation, see Raquel Z. Rivera, "Hip Hop, Puerto Ricans and Ethno-Racial Identities in New York," in *Mambo Montage,* ed. Agustín Lao-Montes, Arlene Dávila (New York: Colombia University Press, 2001); Mérida M. Rúa, "Latinidades," in *Oxford Encyclopedia of Latinos and Latinas in the United States,* ed. Deena J. González and Suzanne Oboler (New York: Oxford University Press, 2005); Taylor Diana and Constantino Roselyn, "Introduction," in *Holy Terrors Latin American Women Perform,* ed. Taylor Diana and Constantino Roselyn (Durham, NC: Duke University Press, 2003). Afro-Latinos/as in Central Park acknowledge their African heritage as central in their discussion of culture and resistance.

4. By 1917, during the sugar harvest season, famous rumberos traveled the island in search of seasonal farm work. They were known as the "rumbero invasion." After their arduous labor, they competed among themselves, offering complicated performances that demonstrated their proficiency as columbia dancers.

5. However, a consistent group of females has participated over the years: the Jewish-American singer and producer Paula Ballán; the Nuyorican *tumbadora* drummer Beatriz Gómez; Gloria, the Marielita who sings and knows how to *virar* the *montunos;* and Merceditas "la zorra" and Akua, both skillful guaguancó dancers.

6. Former mayor Rudy Giuliani's administration lasted from 1994 to 2001. For more about Central Park rumba in relationship to the Quality of Life policing campaign, see my "Zero Tolerance and Central Park Rumba Cabildo Politics," *Liminalities: A Journal of Performance Studies* 5, no. 4 (2009). Also see Lisa Maya Knauer, "Racialized Culture and Translocal Counter-Publics: Rumba and Social Disorder in New York and Havana," in *Caribbean Migration to Western Europe and the United States: Essays on Incorporation, Identity, and Citizenship,* ed. Ramón Grosfoguel, Margarita Cervantes-Rodriguez, and Eric Mielants (Philadelphia, PA: Temple University Press, 2009) and Lisa Maya Knauer, "The Politics of Afrocuban Cultural Expression in New York City," *Journal of Ethnic and Migration Studies* 34, no. 8 (2008). This current essay is a chapter from my Ph.D. dissertation, which analyzes the community responses to Zero Tolerance policing techniques in Central Park rumba: Berta Jottar, "Rumba in Exile: Irrational Noise, Zero Tolerance and the Poetics of Resistance in Central Park Rumba" (New York University, 2005).

7. Tanya Erzen, "Turnstile Jumpers and Broken Windows: Policing Disorder in New York City," in *Zero Tolerance: Quality of Life and the New Police Brutality in New York,* ed. Andrea McArdle and Tanya Erzen (New York and London: New York University Press, 2001), 27.

8. Jeffrey Rosen, *The Naked Crowd: Reclaiming Security and Freedom in an Anxious Age* (New York: Random House, 2004), 24.

9. Erzen, "Turnstile Jumpers and Broken Windows," 35.

10. Rosen, *The Naked Crowd,* 25.

11. A Special Event is defined as "a group activity including, but not limited to, a performance, meeting, assembly, context, exhibit, ceremony, parade, athletic competition, reading, or picnic involving more than 20 people or a group activity involving less than 20 people for which specific space is requested to be reserved. Special Event shall not include casual park use by visitors or tourists." Definitions,

New York City Department of Parks & Recreation Regulations, sec. 1–02. www.nycgovparks.org.

12. Many of the Cuban rumberos participating in Central Park belong to the Abakuá brotherhood; ironically, this religion comes from the same culture that the museum was exhibiting.

13. Berta Jottar, "Zero Tolerance and Central Park Rumba Cabildo Politics," *Liminalities: A Journal of Performance Studies* 5, no. 4 (2009).

14. Fernando Ortíz, *El Hampa Afrocubana Los Negros Brujos (Apuntes Para Un Estudio De Etnología Criminal)* (Miami, FL: Ediciones Universal, 1973 [1906]); Robin D. Moore, *Nationalizing Blackness. Afrocubanismo and Artistic Revolution in Havana, 1920–1940* (Pittsburgh: University of Pittsburgh Press, 1997); Ned Sublette, *Cuba and Its Music from the First Drums to the Mambo* (Chicago: Chicago Review Press Incorporated, 2004).

15. Osmany Ibarra Ortiz, "Orígenes De Una Colección," in *Sala Fernando Ortiz Instrumentos Musicales Afrocubanos* (La Habana: Museo Nacional de la Música, 2001).

16. Leonard E. Barrett, *Soul Force: African Heritage in Afro-American Religion,* 1st ed. (Garden City, NY: Anchor Press, 1974); Eileen Southern, *The Music of Black Americans: A History,* 3rd ed. (New York, London: W. W. Norton, 1997); A. J. Williams-Myers, "Pinkster Carnival: Africanisms in the Hudson River Valley," *Afro-Americans in New York Life and History* 9, no. 1 (1985); Dena J. Epstein, *Sinful Tunes and Spirituals: Black Folk Music to the Civil War* (Urbana: University of Illinois Press, 1977); John Codman Hurd, *The Law of Freedom and Bondage in the United States,* 4 vols., vol. 1 (New York: Negro Universities Press, 1858); Anand Prahlad, "Musical Instruments," in *The Greenwood Encyclopedia of African American Folklore,* ed. Anand Prahlad (Westport, CT: Greenwood Press, 2006).

17. Codman Hurd, *The Law of Freedom and Bondage in the United States,* 234.

18. Katrina Hazzard-Gordon, *Jookin' the Rise of Social Dance Formations in African-American Culture* (Philadelphia, PA: Temple University Press, 1990), 34.

19. *An Act for Regulating of Slaves* (November 27, 1702), Colonial Laws of New York, vol 1, 1664–1719, pp. 519–521.

20. *An Act for the More Effectual Preventing and Punishing the Conspiracy and Insurrection of Negro and Other Slaves* (October 29, 1730), Colonial Laws of New York, vol 2, pp. 679–682.

21. *Minutes of the Common Council of the City of New York,* June 29, 1812. Vol. 6, p. 189.

22. Hazzard-Gordon, *Jookin' the Rise of Social Dance Formations in African-American Culture.* Notice that, other than the jazz ensemble, all the Afro-diasporic circles in Central Park are organized around drums foreign to the United States: the West African *djembe,* the Brazilian *atabaque,* and the Cuban *tumbadora* (conga) drum. Interestingly, Central Park Conservancy officers used city regulations that differentiated drums from musical instruments: "No person shall play or operate any musical instrument or drum, radio, tape recorder or other device for producing sound in any park between the hours of 10:00 PM and 8:00 AM except under the express terms of a permit . . ." Regulated Uses. Noise; Musical Instruments; Sound Reproduction Devices sec. 1–05(d)(3). www.nycgovparks.org.

23. Jean Baudrillard, *Simulations*, ed. Jim Fleming and Sylvére Lotringer, trans. Paul Foss and Philip Beitchman, *Foreign Agents Series* (New York: Semiotext(e) Inc., 1983).

24. Ibid., 5.

25. Ibid., 39.

26. Ibid., 38.

27. Augusto Boal, *Theatre of the Oppressed*, trans. Charles and Maria-Odilia McBride, Leal McBride (New York: Theatre Communications Group, 1965), 122.

28. Baudrillard, *Simulations*, 2–10.

29. Michael Tonry, *Thinking About Crime: Sense and Sensibility in American Penal Culture* (New York: Oxford University Press, 2004). 297.

30. Erzen, "Turnstile Jumpers and Broken Windows," 23.

31. Tonry's research shows that nationwide, crime in general, and homicide rates in particular, began falling in 1990. Tonry, *Thinking About Crime*, 122.

32. Erzen, "Turnstile Jumpers and Broken Windows," 23.

33. From its inception in 1994, the pilot program of the Quality of Life initiative took place in the West Village, a highly populated tourist area with an "inordinate number of bars." This context served as the perfect model for demonstrating the impact of targeting Quality of Life offenses. As a result, the district precinct issued "more Quality of Life summonses than the whole Borough of Manhattan combined." The initiative became effective citywide in July 1995. In 1997 alone, there were 7,400 Quality of Life–related summonses falling under three main categories: public urination, drinking in public, and noise. Ibid.

34. "Product" here would be the national decrease rate.

35. In fact, the discursive collapse of this national ongoing decline with this harsh anti-crime policing approach only favored former California governor Pete Wilson and former New York City mayor Rudolph Giuliani. Both of their political identities were shaped precisely by these anti-crime politics of fear.

36. Guy Debord, *Comments on the Society of the Spectacle*, trans. Malcolm Imrie, Verso Classics 18 (New York: Verso, 1998).

37. This is similar to Butler's idea of gender performativity as related to constitutive acts that are not self-referential to any individual subjectivity. For Butler, there is no essential or natural gender but a normative series of acts and discourses that constitute gender realness through repetition. Judith Butler, "Performative Acts and Gender Constitution, an Essay in Phenomenology and Feminist-Theory," in *Performing Feminisms: Feminist Critical Theory and Theatre*, ed. Sue-Ellen Case (Baltimore, MD: Johns Hopkins University Press, 1990). However, theories of embodiment, such as Amelia Jones, *Body Art: Performing the Subject* (Minneapolis: University of Minnesota Press, 1998), have questioned the lack of agency embedded in Butler's theorization. Jesús's willingness to get arrested exemplifies this agency, regardless of its effectiveness.

38. The number of New Yorkers arrested for low-level offenses, such as Quality of Life infractions, increased 69 percent between 1992 and 1997, and civil rights claims against abusive police behavior grew 75 percent between 1994 and 1998. R. Jennifer Wynn, "Can Zero Tolerance Last? Voices from inside the Precinct," in *Zero Tolerance: Quality of Life and the New Police Brutality in New York*, ed. Andrea McArdle and Tanya Erzen (New York and London: New York University Press, 2001), 115.

39. Kevin A. Santiago-Valles and Gladys M. Jimenez-Muñoz, "Social Polarization and Colonized Labor: Puerto Ricans in the United States, 1945–2000," in *The Columbia History of Latinos in the United States since 1960*, ed. David Gutiérrez (New York: Columbia University Press, 2004), 111.

40. In his analysis of Giuliani's community policing policy and the relationship between the militarization of police tactics and the rise of police violence, Andy Alexis-Baker reports that "from 1994 to 1996, the city paid about $70 million as settlements or judgments in claims alleging improper police actions, compared with about $48 million in the three previous years." Andy Alexis-Baker, "Community, Policing, and Violence," *The Conrad Grebel Review* 26, no. 2 (2008): 104.

41. León Felipe Larrea. Personal communication with the author.

42. For a discussion of performative utterances, see J. L. Austin, *How to Do Things with Words*, 2nd ed. (Cambridge, MA: Harvard University Press, 1975).

43. Before and after Cuban independence, cabildos were mutual aid associations formed by different African ethnic groups composed of free and enslaved men. They sustained, perpetuated, and promoted African culture through secular and religious manifestations. They negotiated with slaveholders for the freedom of individual slaves. Cabildos were fundamental to gaining independence from Spain because of their alliances with the pro-independence Criollos (Creoles). See Barrett, *Soul Force;* David H. Brown, *The Light Inside: Abakuá Society Arts and Cuban Cultural History* (Washington, DC: Smithsonian Books, 2003); and Ivor Miller, *Voice of the Leopard: African Secret Societies and Cuba* (Jackson: University Press of Mississippi, 2009).

WORKS CITED

Alexis-Baker, Andy. "Community, Policing, and Violence." *The Conrad Grebel Review* 26, no. 2 (2008): 102–116.

"An Act for Regulating of Slaves" (November 27, 1702), *Colonial Laws of New York*, vol. 1, 1664–1719, pp. 519–521.

"An Act for the More Effectual Preventing and Punishing the Conspiracy and Insurrection of Negro and Other Slaves" (October 29, 1730), *Colonial Laws of New York*, vol. 2, pp. 679–682.

Austin, J. L. *How to Do Things with Words*. 2nd ed. Cambridge, MA: Harvard University Press, 1975.

Barrett, Leonard E. *Soul Force: African Heritage in Afro-American Religion*. 1st ed. Garden City, NY: Anchor Press, 1974.

Baudrillard, Jean. *Simulations*. Translated by Paul Foss and Philip Beitchman. Edited by Jim Fleming and Sylvére Lotringer, *Foreign Agents Series*. New York: Semiotext(e) Inc., 1983.

Boal, Augusto. *Theatre of the Oppressed*. Translated by Charles and Maria-Odilia McBride, Leal McBride. New York: Theatre Communications Group, 1965.

Brown, David H. *The Light Inside: Abakuá Society Arts and Cuban Cultural History*. Washington, DC: Smithsonian Books, 2003.

Butler, Judith. "Performative Acts and Gender Constitution, an Essay in Phenomenology and Feminist Theory," edited by Sue-Ellen Case, 270–282. Baltimore, MD: Johns Hopkins University Press, 1990.

Codman Hurd, John. *The Law of Freedom and Bondage in the United States.* 4 vols. Vol. 1. New York: Negro Universities Press, 1858.

Debord, Guy. *Comments on the Society of the Spectacle.* Translated by Malcolm Imrie. Verso Classics 18. New York: Verso, 1998.

"Definitions." *New York City Department of Parks & Recreation Regulations,* sec. 1–02. www.nycgovparks.org.

Epstein, Dena J. *Sinful Tunes and Spirituals: Black Folk Music to the Civil War.* Urbana: University of Illinois Press, 1977.

Erzen, Tanya. "Turnstile Jumpers and Broken Windows: Policing Disorder in New York City." In *Zero Tolerance: Quality of Life and the New Police Brutality in New York,* edited by Andrea McArdle and Tanya Erzen, 19–49. New York and London: New York University Press, 2001.

Hazzard-Gordon, Katrina. *Jookin' the Rise of Social Dance Formations in African-American Culture.* Philadelphia, PA: Temple University Press, 1990.

Ibarra Ortiz, Osmany. "Orígenes De Una Colección." In *Sala Fernando Ortiz Instrumentos Musicales Afrocubanos.* La Habana, Cuba: Museo Nacional de la Música, 2001.

Jones, Amelia. *Body Art: Performing the Subject.* Minneapolis: University of Minnesota Press, 1998.

Jottar, Berta. "Rumba in Exile: Irrational Noise, Zero Tolerance and the Poetics of Resistance in Central Park Rumba." PhD dissertation, New York University, 2005.

———. "Zero Tolerance and Central Park Rumba Cabildo Politics." *Liminalities: A Journal of Performance Studies* 5, no. 4 (2009).

Knauer, Lisa Maya. "Racialized Culture and Translocal Counter-Publics: Rumba and Social Disorder in New York and Havana." In *Caribbean Migration to Western Europe and the United States: Essays on Incorporation, Identity, and Citizenship,* edited by Ramón Grosfoguel, Margarita Cervantes-Rodriguez, and Eric Mielants, 131–168. Philadelphia, PA: Temple University Press, 2009.

———. "The Politics of Afrocuban Cultural Expression in New York City." *Journal of Ethnic and Migration Studies* 34, no. 8 (2008): 1257–1281.

Miller, Ivor. *Voice of the Leopard: African Secret Societies and Cuba.* Jackson: University Press of Mississippi, 2009.

Minutes of the Common Council of the City of New York, June 29, 1812. Vol. 6, p. 189.

Moore, Robin D. *Nationalizing Blackness. Afrocubanismo and Artistic Revolution in Havana, 1920–1940.* Pittsburgh: University of Pittsburgh Press, 1997.

Ortíz, Fernando. *El Hampa Afrocubana Los Negros Brujos (Apuntes Para Un Estudio De Etnología Criminal).* Miami, FL: Ediciones Universal, 1973 [1906].

Prahlad, Anand. "Musical Instruments." In *The Greenwood Encyclopedia of African American Folklore,* edited by Anand Prahlad, 507. Westport, CT.: Greenwood Press, 2006.

"Regulated Uses. Noise; Musical Instruments; Sound Reproduction Devices." *New York City Department of Parks & Recreation Regulations,* sec. 1–05(d)(1). www.nycgovparks.org.

Rivera, Raquel Z. "Hip Hop, Puerto Ricans and Ethno-Racial Identities in New York." In *Mambo Montage,* edited by Agustín Lao-Montes and Arlene Dávila, 235–261. New York: Columbia University Press, 2001.

Rosen, Jeffrey. *The Naked Crowd: Reclaiming Security and Freedom in an Anxious Age.* New York: Random House, 2004.

Rúa, Mérida M. "Latinidades." In *Oxford Encyclopedia of Latinos and Latinas in the United States,* edited by Deena J. González and Suzanne Oboler, 505–507. New York: Oxford University Press, 2005.

Santiago-Valles, Kevin A., and Gladys M. Jimenez-Muñoz. "Social Polarization and Colonized Labor: Puerto Ricans in the United States, 1945–2000." In *The Columbia History of Latinos in the United States since 1960,* edited by David Gutiérrez, 87–145. New York: Columbia University Press, 2004.

Southern, Eileen. *The Music of Black Americans: A History.* 3rd ed. New York, London: W. W. Norton, 1997.

Sublette, Ned. *Cuba and Its Music from the First Drums to the Mambo.* Chicago: Chicago Review Press Incorporated, 2004.

Taylor, Diana. "Hemispheric Performances." In *The Archive and the Repertoire: Performing Cultural Memory in the Americas.* Durham, NC: Duke University Press, 2003.

Taylor, Diana, and Roselyn Constantino. "Introduction." In *Holy Terrors: Latin American Women Perform,* edited by Diana Taylor and Roselyn Constantino, 401–416. Durham, NC: Duke University Press, 2003.

Tonry, Michael. *Thinking About Crime: Sense and Sensibility in American Penal Culture.* New York: Oxford University Press, 2004.

Williams-Myers, A. J. "Pinkster Carnival: Africanisms in the Hudson River Valley." *Afro-Americans in New York Life and History* 9, no. 1 (1985): 7–18.

Wynn, R. Jennifer. "Can Zero Tolerance Last? Voices from inside the Precinct." In *Zero Tolerance: Quality of Life and the New Police Brutality in New York,* edited by Andrea McArdle and Tanya Erzen, 107–126. New York and London: New York University Press, 2001.

CONTRIBUTORS

LIZA ANN ACOSTA is Professor of English and Comparative Literature at North Park University and serves as director of Teatro Luna, an all-Latina theatre company.

ARTURO J. ALDAMA serves as Associate Professor and Associate Chair of the Department of Ethnic Studies at CU Boulder and recently served as Director of CSERA (Center for Studies in Ethnicity and Race in the Americas). His books include *Disrupting Savagism: Intersecting Chicana/o, Mexican Immigrant and Native American Struggles for Representation* (Duke University Press); ed., *Decolonial Voices: Chicana and Chicano Cultural Studies in the 21st Century* (Indiana University Press, 2003); and *Violence and the Body: Race, Gender and the State* (Indiana University Press, 2003). *Enduring Legacies: Colorado Ethnic Histories and Cultures* (University Press Colorado), ed., appeared in print in March 2011.

JENNIFER ALVAREZ DICKINSON teaches at St. Edward's University. Her research interests include Chicano literature and popular culture, humor studies, life writing, and Latinos in the media. She is currently working on an examination of contemporary Chicano humor and its role as sociopolitical critique.

YOLANDA BROYLES-GONZÁLEZ, an elder in Tucson's 39th Street Yaqui ceremonial community, serves as Professor in the

Mexican American Studies & Research Center at the University of Arizona. Her books include *Lydia Mendoza's Life in Music* (Oxford), *El Teatro Campesino: Theater in the Chicano Movement, Re-Emerging Native Women of the Americas,* and *Earth Wisdom: A California Chumash Woman* (University of Arizona Press, 2011).

NORMA E. CANTÚ currently serves as Professor of English and U.S. Latina/o Literatures at the University of Texas at San Antonio. She is author of the award-winning *Canícula Snapshots of a Girlhood en la Frontera,* and co-editor of *Chicana Traditions: Continuity and Change, Telling to Live: Latina Feminist Testimonios* and *Dancing across Borders: Danzas y Bailes Mexicanos.* She has just finished a novel, *Cabañuelas,* and is currently working on another novel tentatively titled *Champú, or Hair Matters,* and an ethnography of the Matachines de la Santa Cruz, a religious dance drama from Laredo, Texas.

ANGIE CHABRAM-DERNERSESIAN is Professor of Chicana Studies at the University of California, Davis. She is the editor of *The Chicana/o Studies Forum* and *The Chicana/o Studies Reader.* She is the coeditor of *Speaking from the Body: Latinas on Health and Culture.*

MARIVEL T. DANIELSON serves as Associate Professor of Transborder/Chicana/o Studies at Arizona State University. She is author of *Homecoming Queers: Desire and Difference in Chicana Latina Cultural Production* (Rutgers University Press, 2009). Her research interests include Chicana/Latina literature, sexuality, gender, performance, and race/border/diaspora theory.

KAREN MARY DAVALOS, Chair and Associate Professor of Chicana/o Studies at Loyola Marymount University, is currently writing *Chicana/o Art: Improbable Subjects and Political Gestures,* which is informed by seventeen life histories of Los Angeles artists and a decade of ethnography in the arts scene.

MICAELA DÍAZ-SÁNCHEZ served as the Mellon Postdoctoral Fellow in Latina/o Studies at Northwestern University. Her current projects focus on gender and sexuality in the contemporary practices of Bomba, an Afro–Puerto Rican musical tradition, and Son Jarocho, an Afro-Mexican musical tradition. She is also working on an article about Chicana/o cultural producers as part of the African Diaspora through what she conceptualizes as "Afro-Chicana/o Diasporic Aesthetics." In the fall of 2011 she joined the faculty in the Department of Spanish, Latina/o Studies, and Latin American Studies at Mount Holyoke College.

JENNIFER ESPOSITO serves as Associate Professor in the College of Education at Georgia State University. Her research interests include Research Measurement and Statistics (Qualitative Methodology; Negotiating Race, Class, Gender Identities; Urban Education).

GABRIEL S. ESTRADA is Associate Professor in American Indian Studies at California State University, Long Beach. He is author of "Two-Spirit Film Criticism: Fancydancing with Imitates Dog, Desjarlais and Alexie" in *Post Script;* "Star Wars Episodes I–VI: Coyote and The Force of White Narrative" in *The Persistence of Whiteness: Race and Contemporary Hollywood Cinema;* and "The 'Macho' Body as Social Malinche" in *Velvet Barrios: Popular Culture & Chicana/o Sexualities.* Dr. Estrada honors his Raramuri, Caxcan, and Chicana/o ancestries as he teaches and researches American Indian / indigenous genders, histories, and cultures.

PETER J. GARCÍA serves as Associate Professor of Chicana/o Studies and Musics at California State University, Northridge. His book *Decolonizing Enchantment: Lyricism, Ritual, and Echoes of Nuevo Mexicano Popular Music* was published in 2010 (University of New Mexico Press). His publications engage decolonial theory, third-world feminism, ritual studies, borderlands, "new mestiza/o" and musical consciousness, gender/sexuality, semiotics, music (auto)–ethnography, the political economy of music, and global perspectives of music.

CARL GUTIÉRREZ-JONES is Professor in the English Department at the University of California, Santa Barbara, where he has taught since 1990. He is the author of *Critical Race Narratives: A Study of*

Race, Rhetoric, and Injury (2001), *Rethinking the Borderlands: Between Chicano Narrative and Legal Discourse* (1995), as well as numerous articles on literature, film, legal studies, and cultural studies.

ROBERTO D. HERNÁNDEZ grew up along the San Ysidro–Tijuana border. He received his PhD from the Department of Ethnic Studies at UC Berkeley and is Assistant Professor of Chicana/o Studies at San Diego State University. His research, teaching, and publication interests include border violence, comparative social movements, decolonial feminisms, and radical political thought.

BERTA JOTTAR-PALENZUELA is a video artist scholar with a Ph.D. in Performance Studies from NYU. Her research interests are in music and dance in the Afro-Latin Diaspora, border art, and Latina/o and Latin American Theater and Performance.

TIFFANY ANA LÓPEZ is Associate Professor of Theatre at the University of California, Riverside, and dramaturge and community outreach scholar for Breath of Fire Latina Theatre Ensemble. Her research and publication activity focuses on issues of violence and trauma in Latina/o literary, performance, and visual culture and the role of creative responses in fostering personal and cultural healing. She is currently finishing a book, *The Alchemy of Blood: Violence, Trauma, and Critical Witnessing in U.S. Latina/o Drama and Expressive Culture* (Duke University Press).

PATRICK LOPEZ-AGUADO is a doctoral candidate in Sociology at UC Santa Barbara. He is currently researching how mass incarceration shapes the social environments of criminalized youth.

MARIA LUGONES is a philosopher and popular educator. She serves as Associate Professor at Binghamton University in the Philosophy, Interpretation, and Culture Program, and at The Escuela Popular Norteña. She is the author of *Pilgrimages/Peregrinajes: Theorizing Coalition Against Multiple Oppressions* (Rowman and Littlefield, 2003). She translated, with J. Price, Rodolfo Kusch's *Indigenous and Popular Thinking in América.*

She is finishing two books, *Intimate Interdependencies: Theorizing Collectivism;* and *Radical Multiculturalism.*

PALOMA MARTÍNEZ-CRUZ, PH.D., is Assistant Professor of Spanish and Latino Studies at North Central College and coordinator of the Gender and Women's Studies Program in Naperville, Illinois. Martínez-Cruz's book titled *Women and Knowledge in Mesoamerica: From East L.A. to Anahuac* (University of Arizona Press, 2011) argues that medicine traditions among Mesoamerican women constitute a hemispheric intellectual lineage that thrives despite the legacy of colonization. She is the translator of Conçeicão Evaristo's Brazilian novel *Poncia Vicencio.*

PANCHO McFARLAND is Associate Professor of Sociology at Chicago State University. He is author of numerous articles on hip-hop and Latin@ culture and history, and the book *Chicano Rap: Gender and Violence in the Postindustrial Barrio* (University of Texas Press, 2008). He is active in the food and environmental justice movements.

WILLIAM ANTHONY NERICCIO directs the Master of Arts in Liberal Arts and Sciences program (M.A.L.A.S) at San Diego State University where he also teaches comparative literature and Latin American Studies. Trained at the University of Texas at Austin and Cornell University, Nericcio works with and between literature, film, comics, critical theory, and the digital humanities. He is the author of *Tex[t]-Mex: Seductive Hallucinations of the "Mexican" in America* (2007) and *Eyegiene: Permutations of Subjectivity in the Televisual Age of Sex and Race* (2012), both with the University of Texas Press; his latest works are archived at http://textmex.blogspot.com.

DANIEL ENRIQUE PÉREZ is Associate Professor of Chicana/o and Latina/o Studies and chair of the Ethnic Studies Program at the University of Nevada, Reno. He holds a Ph.D. from Arizona State University and has published several articles related to Jotería Studies. His monograph *Rethinking Chicana/o and Latina/o Popular Culture* (2009) is part of Palgrave Macmillan's Future of Minority Studies series.

EMMA PÉREZ, Chair and Professor of Ethnic Studies at the University of Colorado, Boulder, is author of *The Decolonial Imaginary: Writing Chicanas into History* (Indiana University Press, 1999). Her current novel, *Forgetting the Alamo, Or, Blood Memory* (University of Texas Press, 2009), a "Chicana lesbian western" that challenges white-male-centered westerns, was awarded the Christopher Isherwood Writing Grant in December 2009, won second place in Historical Fiction from International Latino Books, and was a finalist in Fiction from the Lambda Literary Fiction Awards as well as a finalist in Historical Fiction from the Golden Crown Literary Awards. She is currently conducting research on a speculative novel that uses Antonio Gaudí's architecture in Barcelona as the backdrop and landscape of the novel.

VICTOR M. RIOS is Associate Professor of Sociology at the University of California, Santa Barbara. He is the author of *Punished: Policing the Lives of Black and Latino Boys* (NYU Press, 2011).

BRENDA M. ROMERO is Associate Professor and Coordinator of Ethnomusicology at the University of Colorado in Boulder, where she has been on the faculty since 1988, serving as Chair of Musicology from 2004 to 2007. She is co-editor with Olga Nájera-Ramírez and Norma Cantú of *Dancing across Borders: Danzas y Bailes Mexicanos* (University of Illinois Press, 2010). Dr. Romero is best known among her friends for providing English translations and research notes for the 1987 Elektra recording *Canciones de Mi Padre* by Linda Ronstadt. In 2000 she was awarded a Fulbright Research Scholarship to conduct field research on the Matachines music and dance in Mexico. She received the 2005 Society for American Music's "Sight and Sound" award, a subvention toward the production of her 2008 CD, *Canciones de mis patrias: Songs of My Homelands, Early New Mexican Folk Songs.*

CHELA SANDOVAL is chair emerita of the Department of Chicana/o Studies at the University of California, Santa Barbara. Her award-winning book *Methodology of the Oppressed* (University of Minnesota Press, 2000) is one of the most influential contemporary theoretical texts worldwide. Sandoval is co-editor of *The Chican@ Studies Reader: An Anthology of Aztlán* (2001). Her recent work on social movement, third-space feminism, and critical media theory includes "Chican@ Digital Artivism" (2008), "Global Homo-Erotics" (2004), and "Liberation Philosophy" (2012). At UCSB Sandoval teaches courses on spiritual activism, de-colonial feminism, power and truth, liberation philosophy, and radical semiotics. She received her PhD in the History of Consciousness at the University of California, Santa Cruz. Sandoval's current book project is on story-wor(l)d-art-performance as activism (SWAPA) and the shaman-Nahuatl/witness ceremony.

DAPHNE V. TAYLOR-GARCÍA was a UC President's Postdoctoral Fellow in Chicana/o Studies at UC Santa Barbara and is now Assistant Professor in the Department of Ethnic Studies at UC San Diego. Her current research and book project deals with colonialism, sexuality, and visuality in the construction of racial schemas in the Americas.

INDEX

Page numbers in italics indicate illustrations.